JOHN G. CARLISLE
FINANCIAL STATESMAN

AMERICAN POLITICAL LEADERS
EDITED BY ALLAN NEVINS

RUTHERFORD B. HAYES
By H. J. Eckenrode

THOMAS B. REED
By William A. Robinson

JAMES A. GARFIELD
By Robert Granville Caldwell

JOHN G. CARLISLE
By James A. Barnes

In preparation

GROVER CLEVELAND
By Allan Nevins

CARL SCHURZ
By Claude M. Fuess

ANDREW JOHNSON
By St. George L. Sioussat

JOSEPH G. CANNON
By William Allen White

CHESTER A. ARTHUR
By George F. Howe

THEODORE ROOSEVELT
By Charles R. Lingley

JAMES G. BLAINE
By David S. Muzzey

ROBERT M. LaFOLLETTE
By Frederick C. Howe

SAMUEL J. TILDEN
By Alexander C. Flick

JOHN HAY
By Tyler Dennett

WILLIAM McKINLEY
By Geoffrey Parsons

GEORGE FRISBIE HOAR
By Frederick H. Gillett

WILLIAM JENNINGS BRYAN
By Henry Steele Commager

ULYSSES S. GRANT
By William B. Hesseltine

J. G. Carlisle

JOHN G. CARLISLE

Financial Statesman

By

JAMES A. BARNES

Illustrated

GLOUCESTER, MASS.

PETER SMITH

1967

Copyright, 1931
By Dodd, Mead and Company, Inc.
Reprinted, 1967 by Permission of
Dodd, Mead and Company, Inc.

To

ELINOR SHAFER BARNES

*Loyal companion and devoted coworker
without whose assistance this book
could never have emerged from
an awkward adolescence*

PREFACE

The story of John Griffin Carlisle might well be told in broad and flowing generalities. A log cabin, youthful indiscretions, brilliance and honor, and at last sacrifice on the altar of intellectual conviction and burial in poverty—all set in an economic and political society of "fools," "thieves," "robbers," "goldbugs," "bloated aristocrats," and "heartless money holders"—invite the facile pen to stray afar from the paths of historic righteousness. Such a course is made more enticing by the fact that Carlisle never saved one letter or preserved a single document which might aid—or hamper—his biographer. The author has, however, chosen to tell the story, if possible, in the simple language of his subject's life and to wrap the whole in the deadening coils of many manuscripts.

The published material on the life of Carlisle could easily be reproduced in a dozen average-sized pages, and the Library of Congress contains in its card catalog only three references to him. The man who is here presented is a figure reconstructed from an infinite number of bits of information and, what has been more difficult, of necessity synthesized in reverse order: from the setting to the man. The author has examined several hundred thousand pieces of manuscript; he has read more or less thoroughly a large number of books which touch directly or indirectly upon the questions involved in Carlisle's life; and he has wandered in more than twenty States of the Union (roughly, those included in whole or part in a triangle whose corners lie in Massachusetts, South Dakota, and Georgia) in search of local papers, documents, pamphlets, manuscripts, and the tales of those who knew the Kentuckian.

The writer has endeavored to present in their proper environment the burdens and vexations which came to Carlisle as one of the leading statesmen in the administration of national affairs, political and financial. He could experience no greater gratification than to know that he had accomplished this object with the

PREFACE

same freedom from invective and recrimination which characterized the subject of this work, and he would deeply regret to feel that he had lacked sympathy with those who opposed the man whose life he has endeavored to portray. To depict Carlisle and his services as a gold advocate is not to condemn in any way the unfortunate farmers of the South and the West whose drab lives led them into a great crusade. Their story, too, needs to be told, but there is not space here. Already, in order to keep this book within the bounds of tolerance, the bibliography has been reduced to simply an illustrative one, and the footnotes have been limited to the barest necessity.

The author cannot, however, forgo the opportunity to express his appreciation to Miss Elizabeth Curtis for valuable and sympathetic assistance and to acknowledge his debt of gratitude to Mr. Allan Nevins, editor of the series. He is indebted, too, to the Brookings Institution of Washington for fourteen months of uninterrupted research and to the members of that Institution for helpful consultations on the monetary question. The staff of the Library of Congress in general and Dr. J. Franklin Jameson, Dr. T. P. Martin, and Dr. C. W. Garrison of the Manuscript Division in particular have given valuable aid. Many University, State, and private libraries, as well as State archives and the records of local historical societies, have been generously opened for unlimited use. Professors Carl Russell Fish, Frederic L. Paxson, James L. Sellers, R. C. Buley, Robert McElroy, and Charles R. Lingley have given valued counsel and advice, and Dr. M. A. DeWolfe Howe, Judge George G. Perkins, Mr. H. A. Mackoy, Miss Elizabeth Straw, Miss Sophia Breckinridge, Mrs. W. J. Bryan, Mr. Carlisle B. Morrison, Mr. W. D. Bynum, Mrs. Henry Watterson, Major Simon Bolivar Buckner, Jr., the Honorable Benton McMillin, the Honorable Charles S. Hamlin, and the Honorable and Mrs. John C. Schafer have contributed freely of their assistance. The author must, too, express here general heartfelt appreciation to those whose names are not included; and to those whose identity he does not know, but whose aid has been equally real, he tenders his thanks.

JAMES A. BARNES

CONTENTS

CHAPTER		PAGE
I	THE LAND OF HIS BIRTH	1

Kentucky a land of conflict and tradition—Carlisle's humble parentage—Political events of his youth—Schooling—The long journey to Covington—School teacher—Marriage—A student of law—Practicing attorney—Characteristics.

| II | CIVIL WAR AND RECONSTRUCTION IN KENTUCKY . . . . | 11 |

The lawyer turned politician—Election to the Kentucky House of Representatives—Frankfort, the State capital in 1859—John Brown's raid and the Lincoln-Douglas debates—Kentucky and the election of Lincoln—Special session of the Legislature, 1860—Attitude of the State toward Civil War—Carlisle's vote for neutrality—Defeat in the fall elections—Kentucky in the Civil War—The rise of the Peace Party—Kentucky and Reconstruction—Military interference in elections of 1866—Carlisle's election to State Senate in contested election—Lieutenant governor and a student of parliamentary law.

| III | FIRST YEARS IN THE NATIONAL GOVERNMENT, 1877–1881 . | 28 |

The Forty-fifth Congress—The new members—National politics in 1877—Monetary conflicts and resumption—The beginning of the free-silver movement—Carlisle on silver—His fight to repeal the election laws—His views on the South and the Civil War.

| IV | EARLY EFFORTS AT TARIFF REFORM, 1881–1883 . . . . | 44 |

Carlisle not a "Bourbon"—Inclination to tariff reform because of economic destitution and political impositions in the South—Intellectual advocate of a "New South"—The tariff-reform movement since the Civil War—Division in the Democratic party—Randall of Pennsylvania—The Treasury surplus, the tariff, and silver—Carlisle's opposition to the Tariff Commission—Republican defeat—Carlisle as leader of the reform forces.

| V | THE FIRST SPEAKERSHIP, 1883–1885 . . . . | 64 |

Degradation of politics—Confusion in national life—Congress an incompetent and impotent instrument of government—James A. McKinzie's characterization of the committees as a burial ground—The tariff question and the Forty-eighth Congress—Carlisle, Randall, and Cox the Speakership candidates—Carlisle's success in the Democratic caucus—Election as Speaker—Filibustering by the protectionist minority—Randall's defeat of the Morrison bill—Presidential election of 1884—Carlisle and Cleveland in conference on the tariff hopes of the party—The inauguration—Jacksonian Washington.

CONTENTS

CHAPTER		PAGE
VI	THE FORTY-NINTH CONGRESS AND THE TARIFF, 1885–1887	93

Carlisle's election as Speaker—Revision of the rules of the House—Scattering of appropriations to the winds—Objections from Randall—The second Morrison tariff bill—Randall's second defeat of tariff reform—Dissatisfaction among laborers and the Haymarket affair—Cleveland's conversion to tariff reform.

VII	THE LAST SPEAKERSHIP: CLEVELAND'S DEFEAT	114

The surplus and the Democratic tariff action—Preparation during the summer of 1877 for the great battle in December—Opening of the Fiftieth Congress—The Speaker's plea for reform—The President's message limited to tariff—The Speaker's contest for his seat in Congress—"The Great Tariff Debate of 1888"—The presidential campaign and Democratic defeat—Carlisle's relinquishment of the gavel after six years as Speaker with nothing accomplished toward reform—The rising West.

VIII	PERSONAL AND POLITICAL CHARACTERISTICS	151

Carlisle's principles as Speaker—Use of the cudgel of recognition to forge legislation—His views on the question of the quorum—Clarity of his rulings—A great parliamentary athlete—Carlisle at home—Amusements—A persistent student—Not a typical Southerner.

IX	MINORITY LEADER IN THE HARRISON ADMINISTRATION	163

Democratic caucus nominee for Speakership—Defeat by Thomas B. Reed—The political dangers confronting the Republicans—Reed's counting of a quorum—Excitement in the House and Carlisle's arguments against the Speaker's drastic action—The "Reed rules"—Randall and Carlisle—The McKinley bill—The minority report—Carlisle's election to the Senate—Appointment to Committee on Finance—His opposition to Republican measures—Republican defeat in the Congressional elections of 1890—The presidential campaign of 1892—Democratic success and its threats to the party.

X	CLEVELAND'S SECRETARY OF THE TREASURY	201

The political and economic heritage—Reasons for Carlisle's selection—Cleveland's Cabinet—The Cabinet wives—The Treasury and politics.

XI	THE FINANCIAL HERITAGE AND THE PANIC OF 1893	216

The Treasury problems—Dissipation of the surplus by the Harrison administration—Politics in the West—Evils of the Sherman law—Bare escape from calamity by the Republicans—The banks and their assistance to the Treasury—Suspension of gold certificates—Carlisle's interview on redeeming the Treasury notes—The encroachment on the gold reserve—The breaking of the panic—Carlisle's issuance of National Bank notes to relieve the currency shortage—Arrival of gold from Europe.

XII	MIDSUMMER MADNESS: THE REPEAL OF THE SHERMAN ACT	250

Inaugural day—The Democrats' obligation to reform the tariff—Carlisle's Cabinet paper on buying silver with gold—

CONTENTS

CHAPTER		PAGE
	The necessity of repealing the Sherman law—The demands for a special session of Congress—Objections of the West—"The Great Conspiracy"—Opening of the great "battle of the standards" with Cleveland's message to Congress—Passage of repeal in the House—Filibuster in the Senate—The valedictories of the silver Senators—Passage of repeal in the Senate—The beginning of the break in the Democracy.	
XIII	THE FIRST BOND ISSUE UNDER CLEVELAND	287
	The demand for a bond issue—The dangers to the party program of such a course—Carlisle's doubts as to authority to sell bonds—Attorney-General Olney's ruling—The Secretary's New York sound-money address—His request for authority from Congress to issue bonds bearing a low rate of interest—Refusal of Congress to aid—Assistant-Secretary Curtis' conference with New York financiers—The announcement of the first sale—The Knights of Labor—No offers within forty-eight hours of the time for closing bids—Carlisle's appeal to the New York bankers.	
XIV	THE YEAR OF CALAMITIES AND THE SECOND BOND ISSUE	320
	Financial and political troubles—The Wilson tariff—Democratic division—The income tax—The demand of the silverites for the coinage of the seigniorage—Coxey's army—The strikes—Federal troops in Chicago—The dangers threatening the Treasury branches—The tariff scandals—"Party perfidy and party dishonor"—The Wilson-Gorman tariff—Failure of tariff to bring relief to the Treasury—Democratic defeat in the Congressional elections—Rumors of a rupture between the President and Carlisle—The second bond sale—Carlisle's proposed currency plan.	
XV	THE MORGAN-BELMONT SYNDICATE BOND ISSUE	363
	The inefficacy of the first two sales in stopping gold demands—The Secretary's second request for relief from Congress—Response of Congress with a free-silver bill—Cleveland's special message on the state of the finances on January 28—The gold reserve at $45,000,000 on January 31—Assistant-Secretary Curtis' conference with Belmont—Belmont in Washington—Gold in Treasury less than outstanding certificates—The Springer bill—The gold reserve $41,000, on February 7—Carlisle's decision to try the dangerous experiment of a public issue—Morgan's trip to Washington—The conference on February 8—The bond sale—Criticism by the country and further loss of party members.	
XVI	PULITZER'S ATTACK AND THE LAST BONDS	399
	Guardianship of the reserve until September by the syndicate—The reserve below $100,000,000 again on September 30—Recurrence of hoarding and export—The Venezuela message—Current rumors that Cleveland and Carlisle contemplate another syndicate sale—Pulitzer's appeal to the country—The public sale—Oversubscription—Contraction of the currency and the run on the Treasury for gold—Jordan's need for aid in chasing the money changers from the sub-treasury at New York—Political consequences of bond sales in time of peace.	

CONTENTS

CHAPTER	PAGE
XVII	THE SILVER HERESY AND THE DEMOCRATIC SCHISM, 1893–97 . . 425

Severest criticism of Secretary Carlisle from members of his own party—Two Democratic parties in 1896 not an accident—William Jennings Bryan—The beginning in April, 1895, of the open battle for the control of the Democratic convention in 1896—Carlisle's endeavor to hold the South to the gold standard—The Nashville Sound Money Convention—The silver movement in the South and West—The great crusade in progress by the spring of 1896—Carlisle's sound-money address at Chicago—A presidential possibility—The Democratic convention—Its results not accidental.

XVIII BRYAN'S CRUSADE AND DEFEAT, 1896 461

Bryan and his silver army—Division in the two established parties and parting of personal friends in bitterness—the Gold Democrats—Bryan's appeal to the people—Union of the Gold Democrats and the Republicans—The desperate situation of the Treasury—Practical assumption of the finances of the nation by the bankers in an effort to avoid a bond sale and its consequent effects—The weakening of the silver movement and the resort of the silverites to violence—Insult to Carlisle in his home city—The results—Bryan's defeat—Grief of the midlands at the failure of their cause—"It may be Fo(u)r Years and it may be Forever."

XIX CARLISLE'S LAST YEARS 495

Bitter hatred of Cleveland and Carlisle—Carlisle as a Supreme Court lawyer—Death of his two (and only) sons—His opposition to imperialism—His plea for party harmony—His support of Parker in 1904—Death of Mrs. Carlisle—Carlisle's last unhappy days—Death without honor and in poverty in 1910.

XX THE MAN AND HIS WORK 513

Universal admiration for Carlisle both in his own party and among the opposition—A great intellect—One of the few great Speakers—Consistent advocate of the gold standard—His record as a statesman buried under an avalanche of bitterness incident to the silver controversy.

ILLUSTRATIONS

J. G. Carlisle . . . . *Frontispiece*

FACING PAGE

Log cabin in which Carlisle is supposed to have taught his first school, now a tourist-camp attraction 8
The Kentucky Statehouse in 1860 8
Captain Carlisle waking the Democratic shaughraun 72
The Democratic Benedict Arnold 96
The old hose won't work 96
"The tribute to the Minotaur" 144
Mr. Cleveland's cabinet 204
The ladies of Cleveland's cabinet 208
The political safe-breakers foiled 224
Kentucky's tariff-reform leaders 240
The golden calf 256
John Bull grinds out his tunes to his American monkeys 256
William E. Curtis 368
The lone worshiper of the silver god 384
To the pawnshop at last 384
Conrad N. Jordan 416
Richard Olney 416
Richard P. Bland 432
William Jennings Bryan 432
Thanksgiving, 1896 464
The grand revival meeting in 1900 464
The Republican national convention in 1896—a Western view . . 480
Bryan and his cabinet—an Eastern view 480

JOHN G. CARLISLE

FINANCIAL STATESMAN

CHAPTER I THE LAND OF HIS BIRTH

THE nation has mothered many of her greatest sons in obscure cradles, and time has rendered it difficult to discover even the simplest facts regarding their childhood. Little is known of the early life of John Griffin Carlisle save that he was born in Kentucky. This fact must not be forgotten. Contending forces and warring opinions in the commonwealth leave an indelible impress upon her citizens. Kentucky has always been a land of strife; before the white man made his way over the Alleghenies into her rich Blue Grass section, the Indians made war upon one another in this territory immediately south of the silvery Ohio. Founded on the eve of the Revolution and reaching statehood shortly after the adoption of the Constitution, Kentucky has known a constant political conflict. Hers is a land of contrasts; her sons, though brothers, have grown up in controversy. The topography of her soil, coupled with her geographic position in the Union, has nurtured this characteristic. Rich and poor, radical and conservative, Whig and Jacksonian, Unionist and Confederate, Democrat and Republican, have all been numerous in this border State. The five geographical divisions—the mountains, the Blue Grass, the knobs, the dark-tobacco section, and the "Purchase"—are still sources of political jealousy. More than any other commonwealth, perhaps, Kentucky is adored by her children, but less than any other does she demand a uniform theory of politics.

But Kentucky is nothing if not traditional, and her traditions wrap themselves about the rivers, the Blue Grass farmlands, and the stately homes of her aristocrats. The Clays, the Breckinridges, the Todds, the Helms, and a host of other families scarcely less notable brought the State in the twenty years preceding 1850 to her golden age. Beautiful ladies and fast horses, loves and duels, mint juleps and Bourbon, dignified colonels and devoted slaves, were the materials from which was woven a colorful fabric of life in the commonwealth. From his home under the pines at Ashland, Henry Clay ruled a devoted legion of followers, and near at hand John C. Breckinridge, who was to be Vice-President under Buchanan, charmed his hearers with his golden eloquence. From Pennsylvania came a wanderer to the Blue Grass—"Stephen Collins Foster buried himself in Kentucky associations, drank deep its spirit, opened wide his heart, and put into imperishable poetry and song, from across thresholds, out of blooming fields, that which warmed the world with love of negro and master. 'My Old Kentucky Home'—'the tenderest of legendary folk songs of any land'—written at Bardstown, Kentucky, touches the tender chord of home-love with a master hand." The roads of blue limestone resounded to the tread of the noblest breeds of racing horses ever reared in America. Transylvania University was one of the proudest and best seats of learning in the country. There were many in the State who would have agreed with the backwoods preacher in his description of heaven: "Heaven, my brethren, is a Kentucky of a place!"

This was the State of Carlisle's birth. If the record written in the family Bible is correct, John Griffin Carlisle was born "September Friday the 5th, 1834." The place was the extreme northern part of the Blue Grass section of Kentucky, near where the placid Licking flows into the Ohio at Cincinnati. This western metropolis, already calling itself "the queen city of the West" and boasting of numerous brick and limestone buildings scattered among its wooden houses, had 30,000 people. Cholera sometimes raged in the city, and Mrs. Trollope thought it a raw, uncouth place; yet it had pretensions to fashion, and Charles Fenno Hoffman tells us that a wanderer along its streets would be surprised to see so many "pretty faces and stylish figures." Just across the river on the Kentucky side stood Covington, with fewer brick buildings, but according to Kentucky tradition just as many pretty faces and trim figures.

Carlisle, born on a farm in the rolling country back of Covington, was reared in poverty and knew little of the aristocratic glories of the State. No devoted slave, no "Aunt Sarah," fanned his bed or broke open hot biscuits for the hungry boy and "steeped their halves in the rich leavings of the skillet from which fried chicken and cream gravy had gone to the dining room." He ate the simple fare of the Kentucky farmer: bacon, beans, and corn pone. Even in his young manhood he could seldom have heard the jingle of cracked ice in perspiring glasses, or have caught the fragrance of the bruised mint as it mingled with the aroma of the Colonel's cigar and the perfume of his exquisite daughter. He knew instead the toil of Kentucky corn and tobacco fields. The farm had to sustain a large family, for he had twelve younger brothers and sisters.

Family name was the golden key which turned the locks on the doors of Kentucky's great, and Carlisle labored long before he achieved the recognition which his birth had denied him. He belonged to that great Southern class, the "plain people," which U. B. Phillips describes in his delightful volume on "Life and Labor in the Old South." The records yield no connected history of the family from which he sprang. Doubtless somewhere in the misty past the family was connected with the Carlisles or Carlyles of England and Scotland, who have given literature one of its most illustrious names, but there are no genealogical tables which definitely establish the fact. His mother, who was Mary Reynolds, came from Rhode Island, and his father's ancestors were Virginians. There was always, says Judge George G. Perkins, a Carlisle among the justices of the peace in Kenton County, but a "squire" was only a local figure. Carlisle's greatness must be sought in himself, and not in his forbears. His State has produced many intellectual giants who had little more than her rugged soil from which to grow. Sometimes the poorest outstripped those better favored by fortune; the child of a pathetic Kentucky cabin named Lincoln was destined to leave far behind the neighboring lad of means named Jefferson Davis.

The years immediately succeeding 1834 held much that was

interesting to any boy in Kentucky, regardless of his origin. John Griffin unquestionably heard much of both politics and horse-racing early in life. Certainly many years did not pass before he was familiar with the names and deeds of the magnetic Henry Clay, the sage Crittenden, and the dashing Richard Malcolm Johnson. He must also have heard much of old General Jackson of the Hermitage at Nashville, sworn enemy of "the Money King, Nicholas the Great," and all that the latter represented to many Kentuckians. Carlisle's father, Lilbon Hardin Carlisle, endeavoring to make a living from a hilly farm, probably preferred Jackson, the friend of the people, to Mr. Clay of Ashland and his "blustering coalition."

As John Griffin grew older, his boyish interest in life sometimes carried him over to the Lexington-Cincinnati turnpike to see the four-in-hand stagecoach dash by; he was perhaps awed, by the august coachman high on the box, "his whip perpendicular in his right hand and the reins in his left hand just opposite the third button from the top of his great-coat," and thrilled by the guard on the rear top seat, whose bugle-notes reverberated among the wooded hills. The coaches brought the little towns that lined the post-roads not only bags of mail, but all the political gossip of the day as well. In the middle 'forties, like De Quincey's mail-coach with its reports of the Peninsular victories, they brought news of the exploits of Kentucky heroes on the distant plains of Mexico, while a little later they carried word of the Great Compromise, "Uncle Tom's Cabin," and the Kansas-Nebraska bill. Young Carlisle was an eager student of all that came his way.

His opportunities for formal schooling were unfortunately meager. Attending the common school of the neighborhood, he received a scanty education in the three R's, and little else. The school was held in a one-room log cabin, the session beginning in the fall after the corn had been gathered and ending the next spring before time to begin burning the beds for the tobacco plants. During the cropping season young Carlisle was kept hard at work on the farm, but in the winter he spent much of his time in study. "I have known him," said a Covington lawyer in later years, "since he was a boy. The first time I met him he was a country boy on a farm just back of Covington. He was a pale, studious lad, working hard all day on the farm, and studying and reading by night. I visited his family several times, and I always found John sitting off in a corner with a big book in his hand. He was a quiet kind of a fellow, speaking only when spoken to." Joe Avot, a wandering Frenchman, taught him French in return for instruction in English.

Being thus naturally studious, Carlisle before he was sixteen was teaching in a one-room log cabin similar to that in which he had spent his own brief schooldays. Though he still labored on the farm in summer, he did not devote himself assiduously to his work. He had, in fact, a reputation for indolence. Tradition tells us that the horses which he drove to the field were fortunate indeed, and that his serious-minded mother often disturbed his thoughtful reveries in the shade of some wide-spreading tree, and at times brought his extempore stump-speeches to an abrupt end. Throughout life he remained averse to physical exertion, and loved to lie on his back and mull over the problems of government. Yet if he sometimes seemed an idler, he was all the while cultivating the brilliant mind which eventually made him a worthy successor of the great Kentucky leaders—Clay, Breckinridge, and Crittenden. Years later, when a few devoted friends were paying their last homage to him, the editor of the *Nation* wrote: "The late John G. Carlisle offered as clear a case as perhaps even this country ever exhibited of a man's rise by sheer mentality."

By 1854 Carlisle's ambitious mind had begun to chafe under the restrictions of his rural surroundings. He longed to see the world of which news had been brought by the stagecoach, now replaced by the trains of the Southern Railway. His father had died about two years before, and the farm was certainly not large enough to require the services of six young boys, who had also the intermittent aid of seven sisters. Which way should he go? Eighty-five miles to the southwest was Lexington and the great Transylvania University; here roses bloomed on the grave of the "Great Compromiser." To the north, under the shadow of Cincinnati, lay Covington, fifteen miles distant. Even that seemed a long journey into a foreign land.

The hot summer days of 1855 decided the matter, and the young teacher set out northward to conquer new fields. Covington was reached at last. Thirty-one years later Carlisle, then Speaker of the House of Representatives, told his fellow-citizens: "I came to this city an awkward, inexperienced country boy to seek a situation as teacher in your public schools. I was not then twenty-one years old, and had comparatively little education, and that had been acquired partially in the common schools of the country, but principally by solitary reading and study during evenings, and at other times when not engaged in labor on the farm. You will readily see that under these circumstances my aspirations for that place among a strange people were not very reasonable nor my prospects very encouraging, but the time had come when it was necessary for me to seek some occupation in which I could at least support myself. I determined, notwithstanding many misgivings and many apprehensions of failure, to come down to your city and try to secure a place. Very well do I remember, my friends, how often my courage almost failed me as I came down that hot and dusty road, and how strong the temptation was to abandon an enterprise which seemed almost hopeless and go back to my mother's farm in the country! The great obstacle which constantly presented itself to my mind was the examination which every applicant was obliged to undergo before a Board appointed at that time, I believe, by the City Council. This was an ordeal which I dreaded very much. In time, however, I appeared before that tribunal and was examined. . . . After a most indulgent examination, in which my knowledge of various subjects was kindly taken for granted, they gave me a certificate of examination, and removed the first obstacle from my path."

Carlisle was soon teaching the eighth-grade class in a school a stone's throw from the shop of Jesse Grant, "a tall figure with slightly bent shoulders, a long staff his unfailing stay, and a stop at the tavern a customary habit,"[1] whose son was soon to lead the armies of the North. One day Major Goodson, staunch old Jackson Democrat, invited the young teacher to come to his house to live with him; when he arrived, Mary Jane, the vivacious daughter, laughed at the ugly, awkward boy—and a few years later married him. For nearly half a century she was a watchful though at times a none too gentle helpmate. In his early manhood Carlisle did not grasp the importance of the temperance movement. Strong drink occasionally claimed him as a victim, and at these times his young wife vigorously pulled him into the path of righteousness.

Even before his marriage in 1857 the schoolroom had lost its charm for Carlisle, and he turned to the study of law. He entered the office of John W. Stevenson, after a short novitiate was granted a license, and in 1858 formed a partnership with Judge Kinkead.[2] His work at the bar was an immediate success. Of his first effort a Covington attorney has said: "The case was of a dry, hard, knotty character, full of legal subtlety, . . . I can see Carlisle now as he stood up in the courtroom with a copy of the Revised Statutes in his hand. . . . You could see that he had mastered every detail. . . . Without telling an anecdote or cracking a joke there was something so winning in his voice and in his manners that the interest never flagged." He soon took rank as one of the most analytical and clearest thinkers among the young attorneys of Kentucky. Possessing a memory of unfailing accuracy and an ability to use unerringly and rapidly the records before him, he made himself a leader of the Kentucky bar. "I never knew a more purely intellectual man," wrote one of his colleagues. "His opponents said of him that he was all intellect—but

---

[1] Perkins, *A Kentucky Judge*, p. 133.
[2] See Thomas P. Carothers, "Some Great Lawyers of Kentucky," in *Proceedings of the Kentucky Bar Association*, 1923, p. 125.

lacked in feeling, which, by the way, was not at all true. I think he won his case by his *initial statement* of the point at issue, and the principles involved in the particular case, so clear, concise, and lucid was his presentation." [1]

Carlisle was an eminently skilful pleader. In making an argument he was never known to indulge in sarcasm or wander from his subject into trivial things. He possessed neither the personal magnetism of Henry Clay nor the silver-tongued oratory of John C. Breckinridge, but he excelled both in breadth of grasp and force of logic. He had a lucidity of statement unequaled by any other Kentucky lawyer, and had he not turned to politics he might have been at middle age a great legal advocate and a wealthy man. As it was, he was called to all parts of the State, and participated in almost every outstanding case that occurred in the commonwealth during his active legal career. Many have called him the greatest lawyer Kentucky has ever produced.

It is said that in the early 'seventies an official of Covington defaulted and fled to Canada. He was returned on an extraditable offence, but tried on a different charge because it was known that he could not be convicted upon the first one. Carlisle defended the culprit and won the case; moreover, he was the first to contend successfully that when the Federal government entered into an extradition treaty and a fugitive was brought back under that agreement, the delinquent was exempt from prosecution for any offence other than that named in the extradition papers. The contention was sustained by the Kentucky Court of Appeals and later by the United States Supreme Court.[2]

Carlisle was not by nature genial. Many say that he never had any intimates, but those who knew him best deny the assertion. While he lacked the smooth tongue of many of his associates, he was easy of approach, quick in appreciation of wit, and

---

[1] Letter of C. U. McElroy, of the Kentucky bar, to the writer, October 22, 1925.

[2] Carothers makes the statement that William M. Evarts sent to Carlisle for the

LOG CABIN IN WHICH CARLISLE IS SUPPOSED TO HAVE TAUGHT HIS FIRST SCHOOL, NOW A TOURIST-CAMP ATTRACTION

THE KENTUCKY STATEHOUSE IN 1860. (FROM COLLINS' "HISTORY OF KENTUCKY.")

THE LAND OF HIS BIRTH

good at repartee. He had the ability to meet every caller, listen to his question, and in a moment send him away in a good humor. In spite of his cold mien his personality was very attractive. One of his associates said, "He has a remarkably sweet voice, and . . . there is something about the man that is inexpressibly winning." That he had the ability to adjust himself to others is attested by a fellow-attorney: "He had the capacity for enjoyment in every environment, and no matter whether the party, gathering, or crowd were rich or poor, high or low, intellectual or uneducated he became one and sank the lawyer and statesman." [1] "He liked good short stories and frequently told them," says George G. Perkins. "Our law offices, when I was practicing, were next door to each other on the ground floor. He welcomed visits from neighboring attorneys when not engaged, and often on warm days gathered with them in chairs at the shaded east front doors of the offices for neighborly talks." [2] But his laugh was never heard; it was only seen.

Many of the traits which marked Carlisle's later years appeared early in his life. He was always frail of body but vigorous of mind. He was generous and kind. Religion did not interest him and he regarded death as an eternal sleep, although in his last years he turned to the Church. Reticence and serenity were two characteristics which endured through his long life. "His manner before court and jury was gentle and refined," said an associate. "Never captious, never brusque, he never spoke very long and quoted but seldom. His citation of authorities was masterly. . . . He stated his case, his facts and argument from them, and it needed but little imagination in any who heard him to supply in his own mind and heart all the rest." [3] A Democrat from early life, he grew more Jacksonian as the years brought their difficulties and trials. According to his

---

argument and authorities and used them in an international case; see Louisville *Courier-Journal*, August 3, 1910.

[1] Carothers, "Some Great Lawyers of Kentucky," p. 133.
[2] George G. Perkins to the writer, February 28, 1931.
[3] Carothers, "Some Great Lawyers of Kentucky," pp. 130–131.

own statement, he began his labors for the party in his youth. "Here in this county, when less than twenty years old, I first addressed the people in public, in opposition to a new and dangerous political party secretly organized to proscribe a large and meritorious class of our fellow-citizens on account of their nativity and their religion"—the Know-Nothing party.[1]

Coming upon the political stage just as the long-gathering storm of war broke over Kentucky, Carlisle joined the group which was to take up the post-war problems. As a member of his State legislature he labored for political reconstruction, and as a leader in Congress he devoted his services to the economic reconstruction of his section—a task which was scarcely completed at his death a half-century later.[2] His first political experience was in the Civil War legislature of his State.

[1] Speech at Covington, Kentucky, October 22, 1896.

[2] See James L. Sellers, "Economic Incidence of the Civil War," *Mississippi Valley Historical Review* 14:183; Hallie Farmer, "The Economic Background of Southern Populism," *South Atlantic Quarterly* 29:77-91.

CHAPTER II CIVIL WAR AND RECONSTRUCTION IN KENTUCKY

LOCAL history has left no delightful stories with which the biographer may tell of Carlisle's progress in his young manhood. No furtive pages of an intimate diary reveal his youthful philosophy of life. His intellectual opportunities were abundant, for only the Ohio separated Covington from Cincinnati, the great metropolis of the West. The records which are left do not reveal his attitude toward the momentous political questions of the day; they do not tell his opinion of the Dred Scott decision, nor do they say how he regarded the darkening war clouds as slaves, guided by unseen hands, crossed the bordering river to freedom. He may, although evidence is lacking, have taken the ferry across the Ohio to hear the eloquent George E. Pugh plead in Smith and Nixon's Hall for peace between the sections, or he may have joined the throng which heard William L. Yancey, famous orator of the South, extol the flag and the Union of States while recalling that many of the men who wrote the Constitution were slaveholders. If he ever visited the old National Theatre on Sycamore Street, where he might have seen the elder Booth, the great Forrest, or Charlotte Cushman in classic drama, or have watched Lola Montez in her spider-dance, no note is left of the occurrence. Tradition reports that he was likely to be found in more convivial places.

It is certain that he had been practising law little more than a year when a political career began to attract him. He had before him the example of his teacher in the law, John W. Stevenson, whose father had been Speaker of the national House and Senator, and who was himself elected to Congress in 1856. The Kentucky *Yeoman* of May, 1859, reported that "John G. Carlisle, Esq., being nominated as a candidate for the legislature from the Covington portion of the county, was declared the unanimous nominee of the convention." He stood upon a platform which demanded reform of the burdensome court system of Kenton County. With this demand he outstripped his opponent nearly two to one.

When Carlisle arrived in Frankfort early in December, he found his party overwhelmingly in control of State affairs. It faced perplexing problems. Little knots of excited men talked of John Brown's raid at Harper's Ferry and condemned the North for inciting it. Far into the night legislators argued over their glasses upon the chief questions involved in the Lincoln-Douglas debates. Doubtless some were there who had known Lincoln's father, but few indeed could approve of "Abe's" contention that the Union could not remain part slave and part free. By day the halls of the statehouse resounded with defenses of the right to carry bondsmen into the territories. A resolution calling upon Congress to pass a law protecting this right was defeated by nine votes, but in a milder form it passed with only two noes. There was already evident a tendency to criticize both the North and the South for their hasty words. The Kentucky *Yeoman* expressed the rising sentiment when it declared at the close of the session that the duty of the State was "on the one hand to rebuke the fanaticism of the North . . . yet not to throw her moral weight into the dangerous arms of the secessionists and extremists of the South"; she was under an obligation "to observe a just and patriotic balance that the voice of Kentucky should come like an Evangel over the seething waters."

When the legislature adjourned, Carlisle returned to Covington to practise law, but he was preoccupied with the great national questions which grew more acute during the summer of 1860. Events moved rapidly. When the Democrats failed to agree upon a presidential candidate, the party in Kentucky found itself bitterly divided. Breckinridge, a Kentuckian, was unacceptable to many because he represented the demands of the extreme slaveholders; Douglas seemed to even more voters to be shifty and double-faced; and Bell, the Constitutional

Unionist, did not satisfy those who called for aggressive measures, for he stood for little but the vague sentiment of Union. The young Republican party had not yet won many followers in the State. The "black Republican" delegates went to Chicago with the intention of supporting William H. Seward, but they returned with the news that Lincoln, unalterably opposed to the extension of slavery into the territories, was the party nominee. Kentucky felt no inclination to support this unclaimed son. Her citizens cared little about taking their slaves to the territories—they had few to take—but the constitutional right to that liberty was a question upon which they could not compromise.

The campaign was exciting. On election day Breckinridge swept the lower South and Lincoln the North. Kentucky, having cast her electoral votes for Bell and the Union, began an aggressive movement for reconciliation.

Over Kentucky rang the question, "Does the election of Lincoln mean war?" It does not, said Beriah Magoffin, the little-known and underrated governor. He pointed out that thirteen of the Northern States had set aside the Constitution by passing personal liberty laws, and reminded them that Kentucky, because of the seven hundred miles of border-line across which abolitionists drew her slaves, suffered more than all the other slave States together. If war must come, he said, Kentucky should unsheathe the first sword. "We say to you [the South] and to the Republicans [the North], we stand here as pacificators, as arbitrators," he declared. "We entreat you of the South not to take this rash step; and to you of the North we say calmly, but firmly, without threats, you must not encroach upon our Constitutional rights as expounded by the highest tribunal of our land. You must stay your arm of fanaticism, of passion, of vengeance, of violence, and of power, for we are resolved to resist unto death any violation of our rights under the Constitution. We will resist aggressions; we will defend the Union under the flag of our fathers . . . no matter what the odds may be against us." To South Carolina's invitation to follow her into peaceful secession he replied that "the mouth and the sources of the Mississippi river cannot be separated without the horrors of civil war. . . . We cannot sustain you in this movement merely on account of the election of Lincoln."

The governor, however, expressed the beliefs of but one group of partisans in his State, and he could not act upon his own initiative. Seven days after the secession of South Carolina he issued a proclamation calling the Kentucky legislature in special session. As they read it, some Southern sympathizers must have hummed the derisive "Lincoln Ode":

> All around the American Flag
> All around the eagle
> That's the way the Country goes
> Pop! goes the Union.

The legislators who had been summoned to meet at Frankfort on January 17, 1861, were as divided on the question of what course Kentucky should take as their constituents. Opening day offered typical winter weather; rain, marked with flurries of snow, had been falling intermittently for several days, and underfoot all was mud and slush. The rivers were rising rapidly, and the Kentucky flats were covered with backwater. On the sixteenth a Louisville paper said in its "River Notes": "Yesterday . . . we had rain all day. The streets are almost impassable. There is slush and garbage on the slippery pavements, and miles of mud and water on the streets. It was enough to make one secede." When the roll was called, few members were absent. John G. Carlisle, a conservative although sympathetic with the South, was there to represent his Covington district.

The legislature heard the message of the governor. "We, the people of the United States are no longer one people, united and friendly," were among the first startling words. "The ties of fraternal love and concord, which once bound us together, are sundered. . . . The confederacy is rapidly resolving into its original integral parts. . . . Reluctant as we may be to realize the dread calamity, the great FACT OF REVOLUTION stares us in the face, *demands recognition,* and will not be theorized away. . . . We are not yet encouraged to hope that this revolution will be bloodless. . . . It is under these circumstances of peculiar gloom that you have been summoned." The gloom was deepened by the fact that six States had already seceded from the Union. "To your trust must now be committed, in great measure, the destinies of our beloved State," declared the executive, "and upon you devolves the solemn responsibility of so wielding the accorded influence of Kentucky in this momentous crisis, as shall conserve the honor and happiness of our people and promote the good of all." [1]

It is doubtful whether members of any other legislature met so perplexing a problem as these of Kentucky on that January morning. Their constituents had given them no definite instructions, and it is improbable, moreover, that they could have agreed on any course. Kentucky felt that *the Union* was composed of herself and the remaining part of the nation which was neither North nor South—neither slavocracy nor abolitionist. That Union did not desire war, but it was now in danger, attacked by a radical South which expected Kentucky to be a bulwark against the foe and beleaguered on the north by a group of "black Republicans" and abolitionists who would use her fair blue-grass fields as a theater for war.

"Demagogues at the North and demagogues at the South have divided the country," said one orator, "[but] I will not be driven to desert my country and my country's flag." "We would do nothing to excite commotion," wrote the editor of the Lexington *Statesman,* "but when the first Lincoln soldier sets foot on our soil, our cry shall be resistance, let come what may. We would rather see the State drenched in blood than have her submit to such degradation and dishonor. If this be treason, we are guilty." Kentucky was determined to keep her

[1] See House *Journal,* Called Session, pp. 4-11.

soil sacred from the hostile tread of either army. Few believed the assurance of Joseph Holt that "If called to press her soil, they [Northern army] will not ruffle a flower of her gardens, nor a blade of grass of her fields in unkindness. No excess will mark the footsteps of the army of the Republic."

On May 20 the governor issued a proclamation "notifying and warning all other States, whether separate or united, and especially the 'United States' and the 'Confederate States,' that I solemnly forbid any movement upon the soil of Kentucky or the occupation of any port, post, or place . . . for any purpose . . . until authorized by invitation or permission of the Legislative and Executive authorities."[1] The delegates to the Border States Convention declared of Kentucky: "In all things she is as loyal as ever to the constitutional administration of the Government. She will follow the Stars and Stripes to the utmost regions of the earth, and defend it from foreign insult. She refuses alliances with any who would destroy the Union. All she asks is permission to keep out of this unnatural strife." The question of slavery had little to do with the situation in Kentucky; to her citizens the war was for the preservation of the Union. If war came, she desired no greater glory than to stand "in armed neutrality beneath the white flag of peace— an asylum for the victims of Civil War, and a sublime example to our erring countrymen." Indeed, during these perplexing months the people of the State held to three dominating principles: Kentucky should be the defender of the Union, she should act as mediator between the sections, and she should furnish an asylum for the oppressed.[2]

It was these sentiments that distracted the members of Kentucky's Civil War legislature. Carlisle was not a great leader in these trying days. He was merely a young legislator, as

---

[1] Quoted in the *Tri-Weekly Commonwealth*, May 20, 1861.

[2] Ellis Merton Coulter, *Civil War and Readjustment in Kentucky*, gives a thorough treatment of Kentucky throughout this period. See also *Rebellion Record*, edited by Frank Moore; A. C. Quinsenbery, "Kentucky's Neutrality in 1861," in Kentucky Historical Society *Register*, January, 1917.

confused as his associates. He was greatly respected, however, and most of the bills and resolutions introduced by him were passed. He protested against forcible retention of the States of the South. On January 19 he voted with three-fourths of the members to hoist the stars and stripes over the Capitol building; two days later he joined a greater majority in declaring that Kentucky had learned with sorrow of the vote of Northern States tendering men and money to the President for the purpose of coercing a State, and that "whenever the authorities of these states shall send armed forces to the South for the purpose indicated in said resolution the people of Kentucky, uniting with their brethren of the South, will, as one man, resist such invasion of the soil of the South at all hazards and to the last extremity." On January 23 the legislature magnanimously offered—except to "emancipationist or abolitionist"—the floor of the House to any visitor who wished to discuss the important subjects agitating the country. The following day Carlisle introduced a resolution asking for continued efforts at conciliation and urging the furtherance of the Crittenden Compromise. Two days later the members voted to accept the suggestion of "our old mother, Virginia," and named five commissioners to attend the National Peace Convention in Washington.

The legislature adjourned until March 20, when it met again to hear the report of the peace delegates. The Committee on Federal Relations, of which Carlisle was a member, took up the report for consideration. The majority favored the Thirteenth Amendment as suggested by Congress, but the minority accepted the amendment with the understanding that it should not be considered as a final decision but—in the words of Carlisle—as an evidence "of our sincere desire to provide, by constitutional enactment, against all pretext for agitation of the distracting and dangerous question of African slavery, in any of its forms."

After declaring its allegiance to the Kentucky Resolutions of 1798 the special session came to an end in late March; but a shell from a Confederate battery which arched over the waters of Charleston Harbor in the gray dawn of the morning of April 12, 1861, and fell within the walls of Fort Sumter, called the legislators together again. For the second time Carlisle listened to an executive message on the state of the Union. "You are now called upon," declared the governor, "standing in the presence of a violated Constitution, a subverted Government, and a broken Union, to adopt such measures as, in your wisdom, may be demanded for the honor of the Commonwealth and the safety of the people."

The outbreak of the war brought definite alignments in the legislature. With the purpose of deciding the official attitude Kentucky was to take toward the contending forces, the divergent groups appointed a conference committee, of which Carlisle was a member. The majority report declared that Kentucky would occupy a position of "strict neutrality." The commonwealth would "take no part except as a mediator and friend of the belligerent parties." By a vote of sixty-nine to twenty-six the legislature officially sanctioned this peculiar stand, which most of the citizens of the State undoubtedly demanded.[1] The policy was thoroughly compatible with that which had been thus far pursued and seemed logical to a Kentuckian, but it was one which could not be maintained.

The avowal of neutrality helped the legislature but little. The State had little less than a civil war of its own. Stories of raped arsenals and rumors of "Lincoln guns," complicated by the fact that the commonwealth possessed in reality two armies, kept the population in constant turmoil. Soldiers of the contending forces rarely came to blows, but boats on the inland waters of Kentucky were in some instances brought to by shots across the bows—and at least once by bullets through the engineer's hat—and searched as though on the high seas.

Carlisle sought to reduce the expenditures for arms, and he resisted as unconstitutional the efforts made to take from the governor his title and authority as commander-in-chief of the

---

[1] Passed May 16, 1861; see House *Journal* of that date.

armed forces of the State. He upheld the investigation of the alleged "Lincoln guns," and urged an equal division of equipment between the "Home Guards" and the "State Guards." He demanded, however, that every man receiving weapons of any kind swear allegiance to the Constitution.

When the session adjourned on May 24, Carlisle returned to Covington to find that his constituents did not thoroughly approve of the stand which he had taken. He belonged to that large group of Kentuckians whose sympathies were with the South though their reason held them to the Union, and his constituents, dominated by Cincinnati influences, demanded a more aggressive Unionism than he had manifested. Accordingly, he was defeated in the September elections; indeed, only eleven men who had voted on the question of Kentucky's neutrality were returned to office. This did not mean that the State condemned those who had made a praiseworthy effort to avoid the inevitable bitter division of neighbor and neighbor. It meant only that the events of the summer had carried the conflict beyond the ability of any State to stay it, and that many former members had joined one of the opposing armies. In September, when Confederate troops invaded the little town of Columbus on the Mississippi, Kentucky joined what to her most nearly represented the Union—the "black Republicans" of the North.

Throughout the war Carlisle continued to follow his convictions. The position of neutrality which he had supported in the legislature fitted his own personal belief, and his name is listed on the rolls of neither the Northern nor the Southern army. A native of the borderland, he could with equal honor choose any one of three courses of action: fight for the Union, join the forces of the Confederacy, or remain entirely outside the conflict. He chose the last, but spent much time in political efforts for peace. Many years later he said at Washington in the presence of a distinguished assemblage: "I never made a speech or gave a vote that was not in favor of the Union of the States, and in support of the flag, but I confess to you, gentlemen, that when I heard of a Confederate victory, I could not help feeling a sympathy for it. Now gentlemen, if you can reconcile my record as a Union man to that of having an inner exultation at a big rebel victory, in sympathy with relatives and friends, I stand before you for just what I am."

Indeed, a majority of the people in Kentucky felt no bitterness toward the South, and they were never able to comprehend the sin in kindly feeling toward a neighbor. Neither did they see why they should not lend the hand of mercy to a fleeing wounded Southern soldier. Fathers and mothers had watched their sons part to join opposing armies; they saw no reason why they should be compelled to obliterate every memory of days that were peaceful and friends who were dear. Moreover, the Union troops aroused resentment by their severe economic restrictions. Trading privileges were given only to those "of known loyalty," and then for a maximum period of four months. If the Boards of Trade suspected the patriotism of an applicant, they might compel him to take oath that he had never given "the slightest aid" to the enemy. The governor declared the practice "a most shameful and corrupt system of partisan political corruption and oppression." "It is certainly better," he wrote Lincoln, "to risk the chances of even a disloyal man trading, than cut off hundreds of loyal men by such regulations, and exasperate them and diminish the sources of revenue. A hearty support of the Government by loyal men, though differing in views of policy from you, is better than a hollow quasi loyalty purchased of a semi-rebel by a trade permit."[1]

Even more obnoxious than the trade regulations was the "hog swindle." Farmers were prohibited from selling their hogs without a permit, and they could not dispose of them across the Ohio River on any condition, Cincinnati, one of the chief markets, being thus interdicted. Louisville buyers were forbidden to solicit trade. Agents of the military went about the country telling the farmers that they must sell their hogs

[1] See Senate *Journal*, 1865, pp. 42–43 for correspondence.

CIVIL WAR AND RECONSTRUCTION

to the government, but the price offered was far less than that quoted on the market. Lincoln eventually ended these restrictions, but not until much dissatisfaction had been created.

Kentucky suffered more than any other State from suppression of the press and arbitrary arrests for political reasons. Arrests and censorship were of necessity greater on the borderland than elsewhere, and yet the State never forgot the independent position which she had held in theory during the first months of the war. Indeed, every act of the national government which concerned her, whether necessary or not, offended some of the group who had held the State to the Union. Lincoln's declaration of martial law in Kentucky on July 5, 1864, displeased many. The "Peace party" gained daily in numbers, and John G. Carlisle was among its members.

The presidential election of 1864 showed decidedly that Kentucky was tired of oppression and disappointed because the main issue of the war was no longer the preservation of the Union. The enormous number of military arrests on the eve of the balloting was galling and brought from the governor a scathing criticism when the legislature met on January 6, 1865. "Wanton oppression of citizens, fraud, corruption and imbecility have too frequently characterized the military career of some officers in Kentucky during the time since your adjournment," he told the members of that body. "Shameful criminality," he added, had marked the course of many officials of the United States government. "The greatest matter of military outrage has been, and yet is the arrest, imprisonment, and banishment of loyal citizens without a hearing and without even a knowledge of the charges against them." The arrests on the eve of the election had been, he asserted, "merely for partisan political vengeance, and to force them to pay heavy sums to purchase their liberation. How the spoils so infamously extorted, are divided, has not transpired to the public information."

Many other questions were pressing; the members of the legislature argued vehemently in these days and talked long and earnestly at night in the Frankfort taverns. The surrender of the Confederate forces brought little happiness to Kentucky, for after having put aside her sympathies to join the North, she found herself treated as a rebelling State at the end of the struggle. Military law took the place of her courts; soldiers of the Union which she had fought to preserve stood at her polls and prevented the free expression of her wishes; and the government laid a protecting hand upon the wandering negroes whose bare feet stirred up eddies of dust along the Kentucky roads in the summer of 1865.

A majority of the citizens saw no reason for interference by the national government in what they regarded as the internal affairs of their commonwealth.[1] The first question that presented itself to the voters was whether they would submit to the arbitrary dictation of Congress. Carlisle, in announcing his candidacy as a Peace Democrat for the State Senate in the fall elections of 1865, declared that the reconstruction which was being inflicted upon the South was unjust and unconstitutional. He strenuously objected to the presence of United States troops in his State when the nation was no longer at war, saying that their only purpose could be the preservation of an undesirable political system. Proof of his assertions was soon at hand, for scarcely had the nominations of his party been announced when the military began active work. Thousands of copies of Major-General Palmer's *General Orders No. 51*, which called attention to the odious fact that "Martial law prevails in the Department of Kentucky, and certain classes of persons are especially under military surveillance and control,"[2] were spread over the State. A few weeks later com-

---

[1] The Thirteenth Amendment was particularly irksome to them, for they felt that the problem of the negro was for the State to settle. Members of the legislature objected to submitting the question to the newly erected governments in the South. "That the acts of States in rebellion, having no recognized rights under the government, shall be made to destroy the rights to property of citizens in a loyal and adhering State, is anomalous in the history of governments," declared Senator Helm. See Senate *Journal*, 1865–1866, pp. 240–241.

[2] Kentucky Documents, 1865–66, II, Doc. 20, p. 11.

panies of soldiers began to arrive, particularly in Covington, for the purpose of voting. The fact that each man was shouting for the Unionist, or Republican, party was not explained until investigation revealed that only Republicans had been invited to participate.

Election day was exciting throughout the State. The military guarded the polls. In some districts of Covington the voters were compelled to file through a double column numbering as many as fifteen soldiers. Democratic judges were in a few instances driven from the booths. Such statements as "There comes a damned rebel," "Here is a Southern sympathizer," "This man has given money to the rebellion," and "He has been in Camp Chase" frequently sufficed to bar voters. One judge asked each individual, "Have you ever sympathized with the rebellion, ever rejoiced over a Union defeat, or mourned over a Union victory or felt like doing either?" A man was prevented from voting because another swore that two years before he had said that "it was better to let the South go than have a war." Most of the disqualified voters were not even allowed to see the judges, but were prohibited from casting a ballot or sent under a negro guard to the military prison on the outskirts of the city, where they were kept until the next day. A few were tied to trees until the election was over. No affidavit was required of those voting the Union ticket, and soldiers were allowed to vote regardless of whether or not they were citizens.

Although the Conservatives, or Democrats, swept the State, M. M. Benton of Covington, Unionist, was declared elected senator from the twenty-fourth district. Carlisle returned to his law office feeling that the election had been illegal, and when the legislature met the following month the Committee on Elections found—along with many other petitions—a protest from him. Investigation proved that his charges were correct, and the Conservatives declared a number of seats vacant and announced new elections. At one of these Carlisle was duly chosen to the upper chamber.

The elections in the years immediately succeeding the war were little less bitter. The question of slavery was settled, but the rights of the negro were burning issues. Should he be allowed to give testimony before the courts? Should he be permitted to sit on a jury? Was he to be given the vote? And, still more important, must the schools open their doors to the pickaninnies? Many Kentuckians believed that the radical members of Congress at Washington were determined to force upon them the same indignities which were being imposed on the South. The "sensible-looking farmer" whom a correspondent of the Cincinnati *Commercial* chanced to meet expressed the sentiment of many when he answered the query as to how he would vote with the emphatic statement, "I'll vote agin the niggers, by God!"

Throughout these years the Kentucky legislature remained hostile to Congressional Reconstruction. In spite of the governor's plea in 1867 for forbearance with the government and his admonition, "We must be tolerant to the caprices of folly and prejudice," [1] the Senate passed a resolution calling for a national Democratic convention to meet in Louisville to take into consideration such measures as would maintain "inviolate the Constitution of our fathers." Carlisle supported the resolution and voted to commend Andrew Johnson in his efforts to restore the Union, "now dissevered by the unconstitutional revolutionary acts of Congress." Through the period of readjustment he stood firmly by constitutional rights as he saw them, opposing every appearance of their violation.

Carlisle's popularity in the Senate steadily increased. Because of his training as a lawyer and his clearness of mind he was early placed on the Judiciary Committee, where he rendered efficient service. In each of the three years 1866–68 he was nominated for President *pro tempore* of the Senate, but always failed of election by a few votes. In 1869 he was reelected to the Senate, but did not complete his term of office; the State was to select a governor and a lieutenant governor

[1] Senate *Journal,* December 7, 1867, p. 32 ff.

CIVIL WAR AND RECONSTRUCTION

in 1871, and Carlisle became a candidate for the latter position.

The Democrats were excited over the campaign. Great crowds began to throng the capital on May 3, 1871. Every train and road disgorged passengers until the accommodations of the little town on the Kentucky River were filled to overflowing. In the hotels even the halls were brought into use, but not all the delegates and visitors found themselves at nightfall with a bed on which to sleep. It was truly a Kentucky Democratic convention! There was a multiplicity of candidates, and the delegates agreed on nothing except hostility to the policy of the national government. At eleven o'clock on May 4 the meeting was called to order by Colonel Craddock, chairman of the Central Committee. A dull rain fell as the huge crowd endeavored to force its way into the Hall of Representatives. The meeting adjourned to the front of the Capitol in order to have more room. A reporter for the Cincinnati *Commercial* wrote that "The poor darkies throughout the State can sleep peacefully for a few nights at least, for the Ku-Klux Democracy from Dan to Beersheba are here in force."

The temper of the convention was forcefully expressed by the nomination and election of Lucius Desha, a previous Confederate sympathizer and war-worker, to be the permanent chairman of the meeting. At the close of a session which lasted far into the night Preston H. Leslie was nominated for governor. The next day the listless delegates met to nominate a lieutenant governor. Six candidates were named, one of whom was John G. Carlisle. Balloting began, and before the end of the first vote it was evident that Carlisle had polled a majority. "Counties began to change for Carlisle, amid the wildest enthusiasm"; a motion that the nomination be made unanimous was promptly passed. "Amid an enthusiasm not hitherto displayed in the convention," the young nominee appeared and thanked the body.

The platform, a declaration of the individuality of Kentucky, clearly revealed her hostility to coercion and usurpation. Statesmanship and patriotism required universal amnesty, declared the first plank. An equitable system of taxation was demanded, the preservation of liberty throughout the State was called for, the concentration of power into a despotism was condemned, and the suspension of the habeas corpus and other guarantees of liberty was declared unconstitutional. Leslie and Carlisle had not been nominated solely on this platform, however, for the influence of the railroads had been a factor. The Louisville & Nashville supported the former, while the Kentucky Central lent its strength to Carlisle. The Democrats won the election, Carlisle receiving 125,000 votes to 86,000 for his opponent.

As lieutenant governor in the years 1872-75 Carlisle presided over the State Senate, and there prepared himself for the great parliamentary career that lay before him. His work was chiefly as a presiding officer. In a few instances he cast the deciding vote in a tie. Because of one such act the Kentucky Central Railroad owes its existence to him. After a long and bitter fight the bill incorporating the road came to a vote, and the result was 19 to 19; victory was assured, for Carlisle, coming from central Kentucky, cast an affirmative ballot. He took all his duties seriously, and received a thorough training in parliamentary practice. "When lieutenant governor of Kentucky he made a profound study of parliamentary law and sounded its philosophy as no other man had," asserts O. O. Stealey.

At the expiration of his term Carlisle felt prepared to enter national politics. He announced himself a candidate for a seat in Congress in the elections of 1876. The time was propitious. The nation wanted peace and reform, it was tired of the misgovernment and corruption under Grant, and new blood was badly needed in Washington. The hour had come for turning the people's energies to economic and social reconstruction. The closeness of the presidential vote demonstrated the decadent state of political ideals; indeed, the Democrats were never convinced that Hayes was actually elected. But in Kentucky the Democratic majority was quite overwhelming. Not a single district in the State returned a Republican Congressman, and Carlisle was among the new members sent to the national capital.

By this time Carlisle was thoroughly fitted for effective service in the national House. Nearly forty years old, he possessed a mature judgment and a ripened mind. He was an expert lawyer. He was thoroughly acquainted with legislative procedure and amply experienced as a presiding officer. In many directions he was well read, and he possessed a special knowledge of the sectional problems which he had studied from the vantage point of his own war-torn State. He was unprejudiced, earnest, and conservative, and his intellect was admirable in its lucidity and precision. As in the fall of 1877 Carlisle made preparations to join the older Democratic leaders in the House —Randall, Mills, Morrison, Hewitt, Springer, and others—a close observer might have predicted that he would soon surpass them all.

CHAPTER III   FIRST YEARS IN THE NATIONAL
                          GOVERNMENT, 1877–1881

JOHN G. CARLISLE, arriving in the national capital at the beginning of the Forty-fifth Congress and taking his seat with the other Representatives, carried with him certain characteristics and habits of thinking developed in his previous political career. Being a well-grounded lawyer, he was an upholder of old-fashioned constitutional views. A Democrat in theory as well as in politics, he held to the libertarian and egalitarian ideas of Harrington, Locke, Rousseau, and Montesquieu, and, more recently, of Jefferson and Jackson. Having witnessed a reconstruction which his State felt to be needless and unjust, he was thoroughly opposed to any further coercion of the South. Above all, having been born and reared among people who received little of the surplus wealth of the world, he was determined to fight against the grant of special privileges to the rich at the expense of the poor.

The Forty-fifth Congress convened in special session on October 15, 1877. Directly in front of the Speaker's chair sat the venerable Alexander H. Stephens, his frail body weighing only ninety pounds. Near him, on the Republican side, was Benjamin F. Butler, once the fiery associate of Thaddeus Stevens and other radicals, but now a politician of doubtful party loyalty. Half-way down the hall on the Democratic side, confident that he would be elected Speaker, sat Samuel J. Randall; across the aisle was William D. Kelley, at this time a sympathizer with the greenbackers and silverites, but soon to become engrossed in his fight for protection. Among the Democrats sat William R. Morrison, who since the war had been unsuccessfully trying to reform the tariff rates. Fernando Wood, Morrison's successor as chairman of the Committee on Ways and Means, was singled out by his bristling white mustache and his gold-rimmed spectacles, dangling aristocratically from his delicate

FIRST YEARS IN THE GOVERNMENT

finger tips. There were other important figures among the older Congressmen, but as a group they were less interesting than the new generation.

Carlisle was among this new membership. He had probably never been in the city of Washington before, though he had visited New York City in 1868 as a delegate at large to the Democratic National Convention. His reputation, limited entirely to his own State, was not sufficient to win him a place on any committee of importance, and with many another new member he served an apprenticeship on such obscure committees as that on ventilation of the House. He was, however, appointed on the committee to revise the rules concerning the counting of the votes for President and Vice-President. His desk, number 140, was located on the outer circle near the east door. In the seat to his left sat Thomas Turner, who had been a member of the Kentucky legislature in 1861. J. Proctor Knott, genial Kentucky wit and former Confederate soldier, sat directly in front of him. A few seats away was Hilary A. Herbert, a former Confederate captain and newly elected member from Montgomery, Alabama, with whom Carlisle was to be associated in Cleveland's second Cabinet. On the opposite side of the House, in seat 135, was William McKinley, fresh from his first successes in Ohio politics; he and Carlisle were to know years of conflict over the tariff question before the silver crusade forced them into a fleeting alliance. Thomas B. Reed of Maine was also present for the first time.

Carlisle's expertness in parliamentary law soon won recognition, causing him to be called frequently to the Chair in Committee of the Whole. His judicial attitude and freedom from personal rancor made him respected by the opposition. He was shortly honored by election as Speaker *pro tempore*. He was always open to conviction and ready to admit an error. Early in his Congressional life he said on the floor: "Now, if I decided in that Chair, or elsewhere, anything contrary to that opinion, my present opinion is that I decided erroneously. I am not one of those who regard consistency as the most precious of all jewels. I think that truth and right are more precious than the mere consistency of any individual. I would rather be right to-day than to be wrong all my life, even though I have to change my previously expressed opinions."

Carlisle entered Congress at the opening of a new and dynamic era. Fresh forces, long obscured and hindered by the problems left by the war, were beginning to make their appearance. The political reconstruction of the South was apparently completed, and Rutherford B. Hayes was giving actuality to General Grant's unfulfilled wish, "Let us have peace." The nation could now turn to problems of an economic and financial character. Tariff, greenbacks, free coinage of silver, and the monetary standard were among the questions which were to be argued at wearisome length during the next twenty-five years. Labor was another urgent problem, for in this summer of '77 the country had witnessed a long series of destructive strikes; the laborers were endeavoring to stay the falling wages.

The most serious question facing Congress was that of the national finances. The roots of the monetary difficulties lay far back in the Civil War, for during that conflict some $431,000,000 of greenbacks had been issued with nothing more than the promise of the government to make them good. They had immediately depreciated and prices had risen accordingly. The premium on gold had stood at one hundred and fifty when Lee surrendered. The creators of this paper money had meant to retire it along with the soldiers of the war, but they had found this impossible. The efforts of Secretary McCulloch to call in the United States notes had met with immediate opposition because the contraction increased the fall of prices which had begun when Appomattox had pricked the bubble of inflation.

The monetary situation was made worse by the fact that the financial machinery of the nation was thoroughly inadequate to the needs of the country. Each spring and fall funds were urgently needed in the interior to plant, harvest, and market the crops. The demand had to be met by withdrawing the money from the channels of commerce in the Eastern financial centers.[1] This money did not always reach the interior in time to render the most efficient service, and its absence in the East often brought financial stringency. In the periods of stress the bankers, looking about for assistance, struck upon the plan of asking the Treasury to buy bonds with the surplus money which the high tariff had poured into its coffers. The tariff thus enabled the Treasury to give the currency a certain amount of elasticity, though at excessive cost to the country in general. As the years went on, the government's possession of an ever-increasing amount of the money medium of the nation led to greater demands upon the Treasury Department for assistance.

The decade of the 'seventies brought many changes in the finances. The processes of national growth were hard hit by the panic of 1873, and the inflationists rejoiced over the issue of twenty-six more millions of greenbacks. The panic had enhanced the value of this paper money, however, and many believed that the country "with little strain and no serious damage, . . . might pass . . . into the safe and tranquil haven of specie payments." But the five years of grinding depression which followed made the establishment of gold payments appear impossible. As conditions grew worse, farmers, laborers, and debtors in general found it increasingly difficult to meet their obligations; year after year the amount of money which they were able to obtain for themselves decreased. The farmer found that he received far less money for his products than formerly and that it took many more bushels of farm products

[1] Edwin Walter Kemmerer discusses this movement in his "Seasonal Variations in the Relative Demand for Money and Capital in the United States," Senate Doc. 588, 61st Cong. 2d Sess., in *National Monetary Commission* publications. The flow of money into and out of New York can be clearly seen in the tables presented by the *Commercial and Financial Chronicle*. The bankers paid interest on the deposits from Western banks; this forced them to put it to work, but it had to be in such a position as to be subject to recall when wanted. Each succeeding Secretary of the Treasury severely criticised this practice of interest-paying by the banks.

to cancel his debt than in previous years. As for labor, the *Commercial and Financial Chronicle* graphically described the situation which it confronted: "In many places the whir of the spindle, the quick flight of the shuttle, the ponderous blow of the triphammer, the click of the sewing machine, and other usual sounds of happy and profitable industry are heard no more, or are heard only at intervals, as 'short time' compels joyless holidays; and the lights of the furnace, the kiln, the forge, and other places where fire and steam are men's obedient and untiring servants, have gone out."

The debtor class explained these painful facts by the theory that the wealthy were contracting the money medium in order to profit at the expense of the poor. They were even convinced that the government shared in the conspiracy. But Benjamin H. Bristow, Grant's Secretary of the Treasury, laid down the true facts in his annual messages. "No nation," he wrote in 1874, "can long neglect the wholesome maxims, founded upon universal experience, that uphold public credit without suffering financial disturbances and bringing serious consequences upon its people." He pointed out that "the history of irredeemable paper currency repeats itself whenever and wherever it is used. It increases present prices, deludes the laborer with the idea that he is getting higher wages, and brings a fictitious prosperity from which follow inflation of business and credit and excess of enterprise in ever-increasing ratio, until it is discovered that trade and commerce have become fatally diseased, when confidence is destroyed, and then comes the shock to credit, followed by disaster and depression, and a demand for relief by further issues. . . . The universal use of, and reliance on, such a currency tends to blunt the moral sense and impair the natural self-dependence of the people, and trains them to the belief that the Government must directly assist their individual fortunes and business, help them in their personal affairs, and enable them to discharge their debts by partial payment. This inconvertible paper currency begets the delusion that the remedy for private pecuniary distress is in legislative measures,

FIRST YEARS IN THE GOVERNMENT 33

and makes the people unmindful of the fact that the true remedy is in greater production and less spending, and that real prosperity comes only from individual effort and thrift."

The passage in 1875 of the Resumption Act, to take effect on January 1, 1879, brought immediate resistance from all who opposed contraction. Those who favored specie resumption sincerely believed that they were being compelled to undergo heavy losses because of the financial ignorance of a minority. On the other hand, those who favored paper money honestly felt that resumption would be a robbery because it would enhance the debt of the man who was least able to pay his obligations. This belief led to a constant demand for the repeal of the resumption law from the time of its enactment until it actually became effective. Western and Southern legislators discovered that if they wished to keep their seats in Congress, they had to exert themselves to secure more instead of less of the "rag babies" of the Civil War. In 1878 they were able to stop the retirement of the greenbacks at $346,681,000, but they could not prevent their appreciation to the value of gold. The men who had forced through resumption had hoped to reduce the amount of this paper currency to $300,000,000 or less.

Carlisle was among those who vigorously opposed resumption. He objected to any measure which contracted the amount of money in circulation, and he saw no justice in adding to the debt of the farmer and laborer while the government voted away millions of acres of land to railroads and in addition aided them with bond loans. As he argued in a speech in Congress, referring to the lavish Pacific Railway land grants, "The Government has donated to private corporations a magnificent empire embracing almost every type of soil and climate, and capable of producing almost everything that can contribute to the wealth and happiness of the human race. . . . The sixty-five million of bonds issued to these companies are still outstanding, having many years yet to run before maturity, and the interest is falling due regularly every six months;

... If we cannot retrace our steps, if we cannot restore to the public the lands and money of which the people have already been despoiled, I hope at least that we will not multiply these corporations or increase their power." [1]

The attempt to repeal the resumption law was followed by a demand for the free coinage of silver, which grew rapidly as the hopes of the repeal bills waned. If resumption was attained, greenbacks would no longer be a cheap money, but would be worth one hundred cents in gold. Those who had borrowed when money was cheap would now have to repay in dear money. For this reason the forces which had opposed resumption joined the movement for the free coinage of silver. The movement was stimulated also by the discovery of rich deposits of silver in the Western States and territories. Increased production caused Western mine owners to discover that "the dollar of our daddies" had been deliberately dropped by Congress in 1873 after having been out of circulation for almost forty years. Congressmen from the silver-producing States proclaimed that a "crime" had been committed. Carlisle believed that silver should hold an equal place beside gold in our currency. He did not, however, approve the Western plan of free coinage. The holders of silver bullion, he declared, should not profit at the expense of those who possessed other forms of property; if there was a seigniorage, the government and not the owner of the bullion should receive it. He opposed the idea of forcing the "overloaded taxpayers of this country, already staggering and sinking under the burdens imposed upon them by unwise legislation," to bear the cost of coining "the bullion of capitalists at home and abroad." To do so would "engender a spirit of discontent which sooner or later must disturb the harmony if not the peace of society."

Carlisle supported the Bland free-silver bill, which passed the House in November, 1877, but he hoped that the Senate would amend it. On February 21, 1878, he championed Senator Allison's amendment to strike out the free-coinage silver

---

[1] *Congressional Record*, vol. 8, pt. 3, 45 Cong., 3d Sess., Apx., pp. 122–23.

clause and substitute a provision for the purchase of from two to four million dollars' worth of silver per month. He told his silver associates that "while this amendment is objectionable to me in some respects, I am constrained to say that it is not on account of its repudiation of the free-coinage provisions of the original bill." His chief regret was that the execution of the bill could not be entrusted to "a public officer whose opinions on the subject were in accord with those of the great majority of the American people, and whose sympathies were with the struggling masses who produce the wealth and pay the taxes of the country, rather than with the idle holders of idle capital." A more sympathetic Secretary of the Treasury than John Sherman would coin the maximum instead of the minimum amount allowed by the amendment. "Situated as we are, we all know, or at least we all have reason to believe, that not a dollar beyond the minimum amount will be coined and consequently the process of getting this money into circulation will be too slow to afford the full measure of relief which the people now demand and need. But it will certainly afford some relief. It will reverse the grinding process that has been going on for the last few years. Instead of constant and relentless contraction—instead of constant appreciation of money and depreciation of property—we will have expansion to the extent of at least $2,000,000 per month, and under its influence the exchangeable values of commodities, including labor, will soon begin to rise, thus inviting investments, infusing life into the dead industries of the country, and quickening the pulsation of trade in all its departments."

Carlisle at this early date urged international agreement in regard to the use of silver and gold, despite the fact that even then a reference to "the money of the world" was a red flag in the face of the silver advocates. Some of this hostility was expressed in the query of Stanley Matthews in the Senate, "What have we got to do with abroad?" The idea that there was a conspiracy of the moneyed classes of the whole world to subjugate the poor man was apparently fixed in Carlisle's mind, and he was emphatic in his demand that it be thwarted. "The struggle now going on cannot cease, and ought not to cease," he stated, "until all the industrial interests of the country are fully and finally emancipated from the heartless domination of the syndicates, stock exchanges, and other great combinations of money-grabbers in this country and in Europe. Let us if we can do no better, pass bill after bill, embodying in each some one substantial provision for relief, and send them to the Executive for his approval. If he withholds his signature, and we are unable to secure the necessary vote, here or elsewhere, to enact them into laws notwithstanding his veto, let us as a last resort suspend the rules and put them into the general appropriation bills, with the distinct understanding that if the people can get no relief the Government can get no money." He asserted that the effort of the wealthy to destroy half the money of the world was one of the greatest crimes ever perpetrated.

Carlisle at this time labored under a strange combination of ideas in regard to the silver question. Like many of his associates, he understood the grievance better than the proposed remedy. The greenback opposition to contraction of the currency appealed to him, and he approved the demand of the silver advocates for more money; on the other hand, he thoroughly opposed free coinage, and he was convinced that the word "coin" in the United States bonds meant gold coin. He voted against the proposal that silver be made a full legal tender. He never commended the selfish mine-owner phase of the silver demands, and within ten years was to become one of its most strenuous opponents. However, when he became Secretary of the Treasury he was not allowed to forget these early utterances. It was especially unfortunate that he should say that Congress must "faithfully hold" the advantages of the Bland-Allison Act.

The attacks of the silverites and greenbackers were not strong enough to prevent resumption. On January 2, 1879, United States notes became worth one hundred cents in gold.

FIRST YEARS IN THE GOVERNMENT

The day passed without any run on the Treasury Department. Only New York, in fact, appeared to be conscious of the event, and even there only one man was present when the doors of the sub-treasury were opened. He took $210 in gold and left an equal amount of legal-tenders. The New York *Herald* recorded that the city was hung with bunting and flags; the *Tribune* predicted that the closing of the "Gold Room" would go down as one of the great events in American history. The "financial rebellion" had been conquered, said the editor. But he was wrong. The financial rebellion had just begun.

Congress had given the Secretary of the Treasury power to sell bonds in order to establish in the Treasury a reserve fund of gold for redeeming the greenbacks when presented. Although no definite amount was set aside, the people came to regard $100,000,000 as a safe minimum; but there was no way to prevent the reserve from dropping below that point. The amount of gold came to be, in fact, an ever-fluctuating barometer, the movements of which were keenly watched by all financial men for nearly two decades, while the silver advocates continued their increasingly successful fight against the gold standard of value. Had John G. Carlisle been able to foresee the bitter fight which was to be waged in the future against him as guardian of that fund, he would have been less outspoken in his disapproval of resumption.

Failure to prevent resumption did not stop Carlisle's opposition to the "moneyed aristocracy." He disapproved of the payment of war-time interest rates to the holders of Civil War bonds and objected to the power of the National Banks to contract the circulating medium. He demanded the funding of the national debt into bonds bearing a lower rate of interest, and in 1881 sought to force the banks to give up their old bonds by making the new three per cents the only security for National Bank notes. Because they had found Congressional action unsatisfactory, he said, the banks had contracted the circulating medium eighteen million dollars in thirteen days. "This experience warns us that we cannot safely permit this great power to remain in the hands of these institutions unchecked by legal restrictions. It is an engine of destruction standing in the very narrowest part of the way to permanent industrial and commercial prosperity in this country; for there can be no such prosperity anywhere in the midst of sudden and enormous contractions of the currency; nor will prudent and experienced business men embark in large and expensive enterprises when the power to make such contractions is held by private and interested parties who acknowledge no restraints except public sentiment and their own views of the public welfare."[1] He did not understand, as he did in later years, the disturbances which Congressional financiering bring to the business of the nation.

Carlisle did not limit his interests to financial questions. Urged by Henry Watterson, he labored for a change in the postal rates on manuscripts. Much more important, he strenuously objected to the encroachment of the national government upon the police power of the States. In 1865 the Democrats had been a weak factor in the government of the nation. With their Senators and Representatives powerless in Congress, their only hope had seemed to lie in the executive branch. In that year, seeking to limit in some manner the excessive power of the radical Congress, the Democrats had introduced a bill prohibiting civil, military, and naval officers from stationing troops at any place of election. Powell, a Republican, had added, "unless it shall be necessary to repel the armed enemies of the United States," and Senator Pomeroy, recalling the bloody clashes in the early Kansas elections, had added the eight words, "or to keep the peace at the polls." Now, in 1878–79, the Democrats threatened to tie up all appropriations unless the Federal Election laws and the requirement of a test oath were repealed.

Carlisle had long been familiar with the use of troops at elections. In 1866 he had lost a State election because of their activities, and only the favorable attitude of his State legisla-

[1] *Congressional Record,* 46 Cong., 3d Sess., pt. 3, Vol. 11, pp. 245–251.

ture had enabled him to return to his political career. Together with Springer, Chalmers, and others, he led his party with vigor. The Republican leader, James A. Garfield, now chief lieutenant of the President, was ably backed by Frye of Maine. Partisan hostility was increased by the fact that the Democrats were sure that one of their own number ought to be occupying the White House, while many Republicans felt that the Democrats were still rebels from whom the country had been saved in 1876 only by a bold stroke of statesmanship. The approaching election of 1880 was not forgotten.

Carlisle, Springer, and Reagan were assigned the task of drawing up a bill concerning the use of troops at the polls, and that which they presented closely followed the British law prohibiting any soldier stationed within two miles of a voting place from leaving quarters on election day except to relieve guard or to go to the polls to vote, in which case he was to return immediately. Other committees were set to work on measures for the repeal of the juror's test oath and other political disabilities in the South.

When Congress met in special session in March, 1879, the Democrats were ready. They attached their measure for repeal of the Federal Election laws to the army appropriation bill, and the Republicans immediately challenged its legality. Speaker Randall overruled the point of order that the bill was not germane, and the debate began.

Carlisle at once turned to the constitutional issue. He asserted that the President had no power to arm and equip soldiers or sailors and send them where he wished. "I undertake to affirm, and I do it deliberately, that under the Constitution of the United States the President has no right to use the Army or Navy, or any part of the Army or Navy to protect the States against domestic violence or to enforce State laws unless he is authorized so to do by Act of Congress." He argued that the government could not anticipate trouble. The President, he asserted, might, by the Act of February 27, 1795, as amended in 1807, call out a force sufficient to put down an insurrection in any State, but he could not use this power "to send soldiers into the States of [the] Union to stand around the polls on election day for the purpose of keeping the peace." [1] Garfield, greatly alarmed by the assertion, declared that the efforts of the Democrats were little less than a "revolution" against the Constitution and the government. "You turned down a leaf of the history that recorded your last act of power in 1861," he told his Democratic opponents, "and you have now signalized your return to power by beginning a second chapter at the same page." In the Senate Blaine used similar terms. "We found you poor and suffering; we found you ragged and we clothed you," he said. "We put upon you the robe of American citizenship which you had forfeited, and we killed for you the fatted calf and invited you to the feast, supposing that, after being clothed, you were in your right mind; and when we have invited you to the feast you say, 'We always owned that calf, and you have no interest in it.'" Both speeches made unblushing use of "the bloody shirt." The New York *Herald* commented that "General Garfield's effort was not an argument, but a harangue. If facts, logic, candor, and personal consistency are of any value in parliamentary eloquence Mr. Garfield's speech lacks them all." [2]

Carlisle drew an exaggerated picture of the danger of Executive domination. He complained of the President's power to send thousands of officers to interfere with elections to the House; he harped upon the determination of the Hayes administration to retain this power. "If Congress is a mere machine to be set in motion by the hand of the Executive to grind out such appropriations as may be recommended, then we

---

[1] "The United States shall guarantee to every State in this Union a republican form of government, and shall protect each of them against invasion; and on application of the legislature, or of the executive (when the legislature cannot be convened) against domestic violence," did not mean to the young lawyer that the President could send out troops, for he was not *the United States*.

[2] April 1, 1879; see *Congressional Record*, 46 Cong., Sess. 1, Vol. 9, pt. 1, p. 115 ff.; *Life and Letters of James A. Garfield* by Theodore Clark Smith, II, p. 674 ff.

are wrong," he declared. "He may not come into this hall and dictate the measures we shall pass, or shall not pass; he may not, without the grossest indecency, even send his emissaries here to influence our deliberations either by threats of disapproval or by expressions of approbation; and yet it is contended that he ought to have the power to dictate our policy in advance by choosing the men who are to constitute our membership."

He pointed out that in 1878, although eleven thousand special deputy marshals had been appointed to watch the elections in New York City and nine or ten thousand men had been prevented from voting, yet not a single case had been prosecuted to a final hearing. "My doctrine is," he asserted, "and always has been that every man in this country who is entitled by the Constitution and the laws of his State to the right of suffrage, no matter what may be his race, or his color, or his politics, or his religion, or his standing in the community, ought to be offered a free and unobstructed pathway to the polls. . . . These odious and oppressive statutes must be repealed, and this dangerous power of the Executive to control the election of the people's representatives must be taken away."

The Democrats were able to pass their repeal bills, but they were immediately vetoed by the President. Indeed, Hayes stubbornly exercised that privilege no fewer than five times before the Democrats decided to try separate measures. The Army Appropriations bill was eventually passed and became a law. One clause provided that none of the money should be used in furnishing "subsistence, equipment, transportation, or compensation of any part of the army of the United States to be used as a police force to keep the peace at the polls at any election held within a State." The victory was a hollow one, good for only two years at most.

The country in general remained entirely unmoved by the proceedings in Congress. On May 1 the *Nation* spoke of the supposed crisis which was approaching: "A gloomy picture!

The worst of it is that we care so little about it. Not a man turns from his accustomed avocation to prepare himself for the fray. Not a man takes down the old family Bible at eventide and reads to his assembled household words reminding them of their duty in the hour of peril." New York, which had never before failed, he added, had not even called a mass meeting "irrespective of party." Furthermore, the banker was going on with his banking, the merchant with his buying and selling, and the lawyer with his arguing; railroad securities were continuing to increase in value—and the government "sells a hundred millions of four per cents at par!" Out of respect to the hot summer sun which was beginning to beat down upon Washington, Congress, with only the proverbial mouse to show for its labor, adjourned on July 1. The tempest in the teacup was over.

Representative Carlisle, upholding the Constitution as though a great danger threatened it, had been an important figure in that little storm. Perhaps the entire effort of Garfield had not been, as one correspondent said, to answer Carlisle, but nevertheless the young Kentucky lawyer was forging toward the leadership of his party. He was already accepted by the South as one of its ablest spokesmen, and in a notable speech at Tammany Hall on May 15, 1879, he gave felicitous expression to the attitude of that section:

For four years past the people of the South have believed that there was no longer any desire to awaken sectional strife and a conflict of races; but this security has been broken by those who care more for party success than for National peace. It is not sufficient to say that the South accepts the results of the war, unless we state what these results are as we understand them. The question of the right of a State to withdraw from the Union was settled, and the South will never again raise it. In the entire South there is not a single man of influence who desires to reopen it. The institution of African slavery was destroyed, and left not many mourners in the South. The war did that but it destroyed no other institution in the country. The Constitutional amendments declare the terms of the settlement that followed the war, and upon these the States of the South were readmitted without any reservation. These terms the South to-day accepts and will abide by. . . .

There is perfect harmony between the two races, and if politicians will only let us alone there will be peace on all our borders, and the two races will work side by side in harmony. Peace is already restored; let us restore the Constitution. I have an abiding faith in the determination of the Democratic party to preserve the interests of the country. Let us see to it that its strength is not wasted by dissensions and diversions; that the common enemy does not march to victory through gaps left open in our lines.

CHAPTER IV   EARLY EFFORTS AT TARIFF REFORM, 1881–1883

JOHN G. CARLISLE came to Washington with the "Bourbon Democracy" of the post-war South, but he was not a "Bourbon"; he had been born in the borderland, and his ancestry was that of the small farmer. The largest single group in the motley Democratic party of his day was made up of persons of similar heritage. The war had been disastrous to the Southern agriculturist. "No other class had been so completely ruined; nor did any other find the task of rehabilitation so difficult. Their labor disorganized, their farms run down, their land a drug on the market, their products constantly falling in value, their interests sacrificed to those of industry by a protective tariff, the farmers found themselves in the toils of ever-mounting debts, while returning prosperity reserved its smiles for merchants and manufacturers, bankers and railroad promoters." [1]

Carlisle had not been sufficiently interested in the war to join either side, but he had sympathized with the Confederacy. He had not seen his old homestead overrun by "Damyankees" or by "Damrebels," but he had seen his State go through a period of reconstruction which, if not as severe, was as distasteful to its inhabitants as the stricter coercion of the "old South." He had seen his farm neighbors of boyhood days grow restive under economic oppression in the post-war years, and he had often aided his mother in meeting the deficit of his own home farm.

As a witness of reconstruction in his own State, Carlisle was fully conscious of the unfortunate condition of the South; he knew the utter desolation of the section and resented the efforts of Northern radicals to impoverish it further. Like other

[1] R. D. W. Connor, "The Rehabilitation of a Rural Commonwealth," *American Historical Review*, October, 1930, pp. 44–62.

young men of the border States, he felt outraged when he saw political justice withheld from half the nation—outraged when he saw hostile Congressmen denying the South a right to begin its life again and at the same time giving to wealthy individuals and corporations millions of acres of land from the national storehouse. He had no desire to restore the "old South," but, like Walter Hines Page, he wanted to build out of the wreckage a new South. Unlike Page, he had never attended a university, he had never been to Europe, and he knew none of the devices of the journalist and few of those of the orator; but he did understand clearly what he knew. As a member of his State legislature he had been chiefly interested in the cause of the farmer and laborer. Entering national politics when the wreckage of Reconstruction was at last being cleared away, it was natural for him to turn to the economic burdens which pressed so severely upon the farmers of the South and West. Within a short time he had become known as a militant advocate of tariff reform. He was well fitted for the task to which he set himself, for he was of but not quite in the South, and, while his heritage was that of the "common man," he possessed an aristocracy of mind which gave him a balance not common in his class. This explains why, although not of the Gordons, the Hamptons, and the Vances of the old order, he did not join the Watsons, the Tillmans, and the Danielses of the new.

When Carlisle entered the House in 1877, the movement for tariff reform was already well advanced. A short time after he took his oath of office as Congressman, David A. Wells wrote to William R. Morrison of Illinois: "Happening in town, Moore showed me your letter. I think the plan of tariff action you propose eminently wise—that is, to embody in a bill a few of the monstrosities and absurdities. If the Republicans oppose, all the better. They will take on themselves a load of reproach, that cannot well be got rid of . . . I do not think I shall be in Washington this winter. I am tired of serving the public, and getting nothing but kicks for pay. I am taking a little time to myself, as the longtime church member said when reproached for an exceptional drunk."[1] But the workers for the cause were still few; Morrison was the foremost among the Congressmen who were advocating revision, while Wells shared with Edward Atkinson, William Graham Sumner, J. S. Moore, E. L. Godkin, and Horace White the leadership of a small school of economists who were trying to teach the evils of protection. Carlisle, with the "enlightened Bourbons" of the South behind him, at once joined this band, and his progress was remarkable; he was appointed to the Committee on Ways and Means at the beginning of the Forty-sixth Congress, and four years later was Speaker of the House and unquestioned leader of the reform forces.

The political complexities of the situation in Congress, coupled with the desire of powerful interests to retain the tariff which had resulted from war-time efforts to produce a revenue, tended to make revision difficult during Carlisle's early days in the House. Many had forgotten that the tariff rates had not existed forever, and the question had been practically removed from politics, for the attacks by a few Congressmen in the early seventies had produced little impression. But as the strength of the Democratic party grew, the effort for revision began in earnest. A surplus of revenues and the agricultural discontent added force to the movement.

The Democrats at this time were divided into the Northern protectionists and the Southern and Western tariff reformers. Samuel J. Randall, about whom was gathered a body of like-minded Democrats from Pennsylvania, New York, New Jersey, Connecticut, Louisiana, and Ohio, was the leader of the former group. In so far as the tariff was concerned he and his followers were Republicans, but they could not agree with the Republican party on other questions. Randall himself had originally been a Whig, had turned at the demise of that party to the Republicans, and in 1865 had deserted to the Democrats. He was neither a great thinker nor a great leader—he was a

[1] Wells to Morrison, December 10, 1877. Morrison MSS.

EFFORTS AT TARIFF REFORM 47

politician; but he was a man of iron will, and his associates clung to him with extraordinary devotion. His statement that "the devil can't beat me in my own district" shows something of his self-confidence.[1] Actually there was no desire on the part of the Republicans in Pennsylvania to defeat him, for he was one of their greatest assets. His ability to thwart the reform element in his own party was recognized, and the Pennsylvania protectionists vetoed every effort to gerrymander his district.

The Southern Democracy was not harmonious even within itself. There were at least two dividing issues—tobacco and sugar. Mr. Connor says that when Washington Duke and his three sons loaded the little store of tobacco which Sherman's "bummers" had left him—pulverized and packed into bags and labeled "Pro Bono Publico"—into "an old patched-up wagon, drawn by two blind mules," and began peddling it in eastern North Carolina, the American Tobacco Company, the Southern Power Company, and the Duke Foundation rode in the decrepit vehicle. There was also in that wagon a new industrial interest which was to cause much trouble to tariff reformers. The Louisiana sugar growers were to be no less bothersome.

During the year 1880 the low-tariff men were busily exchanging advice. They were particularly interested in the presidential nomination. Moore was doing his best to prevent the selection of "Sammy" Tilden, while David A. Wells continued his efforts to "put the Republicans in a hole." On January 12, 1880, Moore wrote Morrison: "I shall be in Washington I hope on Monday the 19th. I come specially to see you. I shall bring my *tools* with me and we will consider what is best to be done. I have a very simple plan which will require not more than 10 lines, and I feel sure will be a beginning of real tariff reform." He remarked that Tilden "is not only dead, but stinks like a rotten corpse. He is not working for himself I hear, but wants to throw his mantle over Sam Randall."[2] Two days later Wells wrote: "Of one thing we ought to be convinced, and that is that

[1] Black MSS.
[2] Morrison MSS.

there is little use in trying to launch a complicated and long tariff bill. Then, if we can't attack the iniquity as a whole, let's go at it piecemeal. This has been my conviction for some time. The greatest victory, because it weakened and frightened the enemy, we have won for years, was the repeal of the duty on quinine. . . . Now let's be wise politically. Take the most indispensable things in the tariff, not more than one or two, or three at a time. Set the Republicans to vote against repeal or amendment, and you have them in a tight place for the Presidential campaign. . . . One or two more duties on highly protected articles repealed, and the protectionists will begin to fight among themselves, one fox having got his tail cut off will go for cur-tailing all the other foxes. . . . If you can't agree with Wood, go it independently. If you make up your mind the exact line of attack, and will send me word, I will see what I can do in the way of providing you with ammunition. But force the fighting. Set the Republicans to vote in favor of retaining all the damned odious things, and Moore and I will give you all the powder and shot you need for the campaign." [1]

But nothing was accomplished, and General Hancock, the party candidate of that year, expressed his views on the tariff question by saying that it was "a local issue."

Political and economic developments were aiding the Southern Democracy in getting its reform campaign under way. The end of the 'seventies had brought resumption, prosperity, the silver question, and the beginning of an enormous revenue to the government. The surplus for the fiscal year 1881 amounted to over $100,000,000. It was indeed "a matter of gratulation" that the business of the country could flourish after paying such heavy taxes as were still assessed. It is not the business of the government, however, to gather into its own coffers the money which it supplies its citizens, and the problem of returning this immense surplus to circulation became acute.

There were at least three possible courses: taxes might be

[1] Morrison MSS.

EFFORTS AT TARIFF REFORM

reduced through tariff reform, expenditures might be increased, or the government might buy bonds. The Republicans were apparently fixed in their belief in protection, and so long as they were in control there could be no hope of tariff reform. The "billion dollar Congress" was still in the future. The policy of buying bonds was adopted, but this proved more and more expensive as competition forced the prices upward. The government had been, in fact, redeeming its bonds through a large part of the preceding decade, and in most years had encroached upon the cash balance in order to do so. This practice, which took money from the pockets of the whole people and poured it into the coffers of a few, was bound to bring criticism whenever a pinch for money began to be felt. Just now, however, the United States was enjoying a great wave of prosperity. In 1880 Secretary Sherman reported that nothing had occurred to "embarrass the easy maintenance of specie payments," and he added that United States notes, the "favorite money of the people," were taken at par in every part of the country.[1] In June of that year our imports exceeded our exports as the people began again to consume liberally. The stock market rose under a flood of buying orders. In 1879 and again in 1880 calls for money from the interior took from the New York banks $100,000,000, which did not return as usual when the crop season was over; apparently the people were increasing the amount of money which they carried in their purses.[2] The West was becoming a favorite field of investment.

There was one factor, however, which threatened the continuation of this prosperity, and that was the silver question. Scarcely two years after the passage of the Bland-Allison Act the Secretary of the Treasury, who had countenanced the new law if he had not supported it, said in his annual report to Congress: "The coinage of gold at Philadelphia had to be made subordinate to that of silver, in order to comply with the re-

[1] *Report of the Finances,* 1880, p. xiv.
[2] Ibid., p. 116.

quirements of the law directing the purchase and coinage of $2,000,000 bullion each month."[1] Sherman's few words tell the beginning of the story of how silver, like the camel that pushed his master out of the tent, crowded gold slowly but surely out of the government coffers; they were the first of the warnings which were to be repeated by each succeeding Secretary of the Treasury until near the end of the century. The law had provided for the coinage of the silver dollars, but it could not force them into circulation. Regardless of executive rulings which required their use in the payment of government obligations wherever possible, they never wandered far from their place of creation. "The dollar of our daddies" promised to become a greater problem to the Treasury Department than the "rag babies" of the Civil War.

Moreover, world events and the caprices of nature seemed to conspire against this period of prosperity. The British expedition into Egypt and a sudden demand for gold on the part of Italy took much of the "money of the world" which the Atlantic seaboard possessed at this time; and the alarm which this created was intensified by the cry of discontent set up by many "shorn lambs" who had gambled too heavily on the stock market. In July, 1881, the East was thrown into a near panic by the assassination of Garfield, whose lingering prostration brought stagnation to the stock market. In the West the crops of this year were poor, and the railroad wars further complicated the situation. Each section of the country blamed the other for the evils that were appearing. The East, afraid of the financial policies of the West, was alarmed whenever Congress was in session. The *Commercial and Financial Chronicle* expressed the attitude of the business and commercial men when it declared that "Congress always acts on the mercantile community something like a fly-blister." Financiers suffered until the session was over, and then rushed to the Secretary of the Treasury, urging him to purchase bonds in order to give them relief. On the other hand,

[1] Ibid., p. xvi.

the farmers were demanding that Congress do something to relieve the economic pressure which they were suffering because of crop failures. These two groups, one having the ear of the Treasury and the other of Congress, could agree on only one fact—that the government should not call into its vaults so much of the currency. Under their pressure the Treasury at times made overzealous efforts to get the money back into the hands of the people.

By the close of 1881 it was evident that something must be done for the general financial situation. The silver forces in the West were getting their crusade for more money under way; the new South was in a position to exert political pressure; corruption was eating into the vitals of the Republican party; and protection was being questioned even in the industrial East. The people of the West may not have understood the principles of the low tariff, but they were fully aware that the government had a great surplus which it was handing to the wealthy in an ever-increasing premium on the bonds which Eastern moneyholders had purchased during the war. They were ready to join any movement which promised to reduce these gifts to the rich.

The Democrats, with Carlisle now a leading member of the party, chose this apt moment to push forward their theory of tariff reform.

But the Republicans were conscious of the danger, and made strenuous efforts to save themselves. In his first message to Congress in December, 1881, Chester A. Arthur recommended that a commission be appointed to deal with the tariff. The Republicans had been discussing this method of procedure for some time. A bill in conformity with the recommendations of the President was introduced early in 1882, but Carlisle vigorously opposed it. He had seen the need of the people neglected too many years to believe that a commission would regard their interests. He severely condemned the practice in Congress of encouraging the industrialists and discouraging the common man:

The unskilled and unpretending laborer who guides the plow and gathers the harvest is as much entitled to the protection of the law and to the encouragement of the government as the scientific artisan who has mastered all the mysteries of the craft. Each one of the busy millions who helps to create and distribute the varied products of this wonderful land of ours has an undoubted right to demand an equal participation in all the advantages conferred by the laws of his country; and I repudiate every definition of American industry or American labor which excludes a single honest and useful occupation. Whoever challenges the right of the humblest citizen, whatever may be his trade or occupation, to an equal participation in the benefits conferred by the Government so long as he bears an equal share of its burdens, denies the equality of man; whoever asserts that one class of men or one species of industry has a right to exact tribute from another for its own benefit, or has superior claims upon the consideration of the Government, asserts a doctrine utterly at war with the first principles of our political system. To call such a doctrine the "American doctrine," and to announce it in high-sounding and patriotic phrase, is simply an attempt to hide its deformity beneath a rhetorical and sentimental garb, and will deceive no one who looks beyond the surface.

While there is no party here that would injure labor or impair the security of capital, there always will be and in my opinion there always ought to be, a party in this country pledged to the establishment and maintenance of a constitutional and equal system of taxation.

To provide such a commission, declared Carlisle, would be tantamount to saying that the people were not capable of dealing with the subject of government. The tariff question, he argued, could be finally settled only in Congress, and therefore a commission was neither necessary nor desirable; it would cost the taxpayers $200 a day, and there would be no compensation for the delay which it would cause. He wished the tariff lowered on all commodities which the laborer and farmer used, and he felt that the need for such reduction would be better recognized by the representatives of the people than by a commission.

But in spite of Carlisle's demand for immediate action on the tariff question by Congress, and his plea to the House not to neglect the opportunity to enter upon a course which would "develop every industry in the country, do justice to all its people and demonstrate to the world the wisdom and beneficence of the free institutions under which we live," the Republicans pushed their measure forward. On May 6, 1882, Roger Q. Mills endeavored to recommit the bill and substitute a declaration for tariff reform, but failed; on the same day the commission bill passed the House and two days later the Senate. The President signed it on the fifteenth.

Carlisle's fears were confirmed when the appointments to the commission were announced, for all the appointees were protectionists, and John L. Hayes, secretary of the Wool Manufacturers' Association, was named chairman.

Throughout the summer of 1882, while Walter Hines Page was traveling over the country with the Tariff Commission, Carlisle and his Democratic associates were attacking the Republican policy of protection at every opportunity. Speaking on the existing tariff, Carlisle maintained that it would be difficult to create one more unequal and unjust. "It would be a high compliment to the ingenuity of its authors to say that they had purposely made it as bad as it is." Its evils, he said, were the results of changes which had come since its enactment and which had all tended to make it burdensome to the average consumer. Since the lowest grades and cheapest class of goods bore the highest rates, the heaviest burdens were placed "upon those who are least able to bear them." He demanded a freedom of trade which would "open the channels of commerce in all parts of the world and invite the producer and the consumer to meet on equal terms in a free market for the exchange of their commodities. . . . Prohibitions and embargoes . . . are inconsistent . . . with the spirit of the age in which we live."

July came, and Congressmen were still beating the old straw which Hamilton and Jefferson had long before threshed. On

July 3 William D. Kelley of Pennsylvania introduced a resolution to suspend the rules and correct an error in section 2504, Revised Statutes of the United States, dealing with woolen goods. If this passed, it would increase the tax on cheap woolen goods, miners' lamps, and other articles used largely by the poorer classes. At once the Democrats objected. Edward S. Bragg, brigadier general of Wisconsin volunteers in the Civil War, took up the fight. "This House," he declared, "after deliberate discussion, decided that it did not know enough to revise the tariff so as to reduce it; and in accordance with that judgment rendered against ourselves I make the point that the House is not competent to increase duties if it is not competent to reduce them." [1] He was vigorously supported by Morrison and others.

Carlisle was particularly incensed by the proposed changes in the schedule which covered woolens and knitted goods. He skilfully laid bare its weaknesses:

> Stripped of its artificial surroundings, this is a simple proposition to more than double the tariff tax upon a large class of necessary articles worn by the men, women, and children in all parts of the country, and the only way to treat it fairly is to consider it as a measure to increase the profits of protected capital and diminish the rewards of unprotected labor. Within a week this House, by a very considerable majority, has passed a bill to relieve banks and bankers from an annual tax of more than $9,500,000 upon their capital and deposits and to relieve depositors in banks from a tax of $2,500,000 on checks. This was done upon the plea that we were collecting too much money from the people, and yet every attempt to extend the measure of relief by reducing or repealing other taxes which really affected the great body of the people was promptly voted down by the advocates of that bill. Having relieved the banks and bankers, who are neither more nor less meritorious than those engaged in other pursuits upon the avowed ground that they were being taxed too much, the advocates of the pres-

---

[1] *Congressional Record,* 47 Cong., 1st Sess., Vol. 13, pt. 6, p. 5601.

ent bill, in order to be logical and consistent, ought to urge its passage upon the ground that the people are not being taxed enough. But whatever may be the real motive of gentlemen on the other side, the important fact to be borne in mind is that the legislation repealing taxes on capital is now to be supplemented by legislation increasing taxes on labor. The bill passed last week repealed taxes and reduced the revenue; this one will increase taxes without adding a dollar to the receipts of the Government, and consequently the people will bear a heavier burden, while the Treasury will receive no corresponding benefit.

But Carlisle was not through. Goaded on by Tom Reed's irritating "Precisely," he began a scathing denunciation of the efforts of the Republicans to increase the tariff before the commission which they had created could make its report:

During the present session of Congress a law has been enacted creating a tariff commission to make certain investigations with a view "to the establishment of a judicious tariff, or a revision of the existing tariff, upon a scale of justice to all interests;" and now, sir, before that extraordinary body has even commenced its labors we are asked to suspend all the rules of the House and pass, without opportunity to offer amendments, a bill changing the tariff laws in a most important particular. When we protested against the delegation of our powers to a commission to be appointed by the President, we were invariably told that Congress was not competent to deal with so great and complicated a subject as the tariff; that the representatives of the people could not be safely trusted to legislate on a matter of such vital importance without advice and assistance from an executive commission, . . . the tariff-commission bill was passed, and those of us who did not endorse either the character or purpose of the measure had no alternative but to submit and wait with such patience as we could command the vindication of our position. That vindication has come earlier than we expected. Before the commission had been appointed, almost before the two-hundred applicants for places on it could transmit their names to the President, appeals began to reach Congress for relief from the inequalities and hardships of the tariff, . . . [coming] . . . in every instance . . . from the very interests which had denied the competency of Congress and demanded the commission. The millions of consumers, who at last pay all the duties, with interests and profits added, knew very well that the creation of the commission was fatal to all their hopes for early relief.

The demand for immediate legislation comes . . . from the protected classes, . . . who want higher duties and larger profits at the expense of the people, who are compelled by law to pay whatever they choose to ask or do without the necessaries and comforts of life. . . . Why this hot haste to comply with the demands of the manufacturers of hosiery and knit goods? If the people at large can wait, . . . for justice at the hands of the commission, why cannot the manufacturers and advocates of the commission wait also? If this Congress is the representative of all the people . . . it will treat them all alike. . . .

This legislation is all on one side. When the consumer asks for a reduction of duties upon his clothing and the tools and implements of his trade the doors of the committee-rooms and the House are slammed in his face, and he is told to carry his complaint to the commission, but when the man to whom he pays tribute demands the privilege of increasing his exactions, all the rules which govern ordinary legislation and afford opportunity for ample debate, amendments, and deliberation in the enactment of laws must be summarily suspended upon a mere motion, and nothing can be done, not even a second motion to adjourn can be made, until the demand is fully complied with.

The arguments continued until Congress adjourned in August. Three months later came the fall elections, and a Democratic majority was returned to the House. To explain their defeat the Republicans pointed to the Chinese issue in the Far West, the Stalwart-Half-Breed schism in New York, and the prohibition craze in the midlands. But the Democrats loudly proclaimed that the administration party had been beaten because of its failure to reduce the tariff. Carlisle was assured that his July predictions had come true. A few days after the election he wired a friend in New York that in response to the demand of the people for tariff reform he would become a candidate for the Speakership.

The Republicans were faced with the absolute necessity of passing a tariff measure of some kind before surrendering their power the following March. When Congress assembled on December 4, the President's message and the report of the Tariff Commission were ready. Both recommended a reduction in the tariff rates. The fight began. The House Committee on Ways and Means began the preparation of a bill, and the Senate Republicans, forbidden by the Constitution to initiate any financial legislation, took from the table an old bill for reducing the internal revenue which they had talked to death the session before, blew it into life again, struck out all but the enacting clause, and began grafting a tariff measure upon it. During the few months which were left, the Republicans in both houses of Congress worked valiantly.

The House bill, clearly protectionist, was reported on January 16 by William D. Kelley, chairman of the Committee on Ways and Means. On account of illness Kelley could not guide the measure on the floor, and Dudley C. Haskell of Kansas did service in his stead. Under threat of an extra session of Congress the Republicans drove forward with all the force they could muster, but the Democrats made their existence miserable. When they endeavored to increase the rate on castor oil, "Sunset" Cox of New York chided them for trying to destroy this "infant industry" and told them that they were "thoroughly dumb." Roger Q. Mills called for "the Western man who will have the temerity to vote to increase the duty on fencing-wire and then return to his home on the prairies that stretch toward the setting sun and tell the people whose only dependence for fencing their farms is wire that he bowed the knee to the Pennsylvania Baal." Carlisle declared that their announced intention to maintain all interests meant "all interests except the interest of the consumer, who at last pays all the duties, whether they be imposed upon the machinery, or the raw material, or only upon the finished product." The manufacturer, he said, merely advocated the taxes in the first instance and "then adds them to the price of his goods." Carlisle did not expect to make any immediate gains, but his attacks were demoralizing to the enemy; as each succeeding item of the tariff bill was read in the Committee of the Whole, he made a stand and forced a vote. On January 28 he discussed the subject at length. As the debate continued, it grew less parliamentary, and physical encounters often seemed imminent. The Republicans longed for the return of "Pig-iron" Kelley.

The situation was indeed discouraging for both the Republicans and the protectionist Democrats. The President was insistent that the former do something immediately; while Randall, as opposition leader, wished for nothing more than to get the question out of the way, because a divided party would do much toward defeating him in the contest for the Speakership in 1883. Lobbyists rushed into the breach. From Ohio came the "wool trinity"—Columbus Delano, William Lawrence, and David Harpster—while many another industry sent its best men. In New York the protectionists held a great mass meeting for the purpose of rallying the workingman to their cause. "The speeches at the Cooper Union meeting were fairly overflowing with tender solicitude for the comfort of the working classes," declared the *Nation*. They have pretended, it said sarcastically, that "It is not for the purpose of making any manufacturer rich that we impose high duties upon imports. It is not for the purpose of putting dollars into the pockets of the stockholders in woolen mills or in Bessemer-steel works and a multitude of other establishments, that we make the whole people pay taxes to them by obliging them to pay higher prices for the articles they have to buy. It is not the benefit of the capitalists that we have in mind at all. It is only of the poor laboring man that we think, and it is in his behalf that we tax the American people.

If we did not tax them, the industries in which the laboring man is employed would go to the bottom; the laboring man would have nothing to do, and would perish in misery." [1]

The Republicans saw only one method of relief—to close the debate—but the opposition was immediately up in arms. "Such a proposition," said Carlisle, "has never been heard of in the parliamentary history of this country, a proposition to destroy the freedom of debate on a bill to raise revenue." To Haskell's demand that they stop their filibustering he replied, "Never under gag rule." There was only one hope of escaping defeat, and that was to accept the Senate bill; it was clear that the Democrats would never agree to the House measure.

The Senate bill, based on the recommendations of the Tariff Commission, was passed on February 20 and immediately sent to the other end of the Capitol. The reform Democrats were perfectly willing to accept it, but Kelley, who was again leading the Republicans, saw no protection in the measure and began vigorous efforts to prevent it from coming before the House. He advocated higher rates, but it was obvious that the opposition would never allow him to revise the bill in conformity with his desires; the only apparent solution was to force the measure into a conference committee of the two houses. But a conference committee cannot be appointed unless there is first a disagreement, and there had been no disagreement, for the Senate bill had only reached the Speaker's table. Of the 110 pages of the bill, said Representative Blackburn, not one line, word, or syllable had ever been in the House.

The ingenious Thomas B. Reed of the Committee on Rules solved the perplexing problem. On February 24 he reported to the House a proposed rule which provided that the tariff bill might be taken from the Speaker's table at any time during the remainder of the session for the purpose of disagreeing and sending it to a conference, but not for the purpose of adopting it. Lest a political accident should occur, the provision was added that "If such motion shall fail, the bill shall remain on the

[1] Feb. 8, 1883.

Speaker's table unaffected by the decision of the House on said motion." A majority could declare a disagreement, but not an agreement—it could non-concur, but not concur! "The 'protected interests' are evidently at their wit's end," said the *Nation*, and a New York *Herald* correspondent characterized the rule as a fulfillment of the Irishman's dream of a gun "which would fire so as to hit an object if it were a deer and miss it if it were a cow."

The Democrats offered strenuous opposition, making many appeals from the decision of the Chair, but the Republicans held together even though they were compelled to record their votes for future Democratic use. The rule which the protectionists were endeavoring to pass was a "monstrous proposition," said Carlisle, while Cox denounced it as "revolutionary." Reed himself admitted that the proceedings, though necessary, were unusual and arbitrary in character. But he had his way, and the Conference Committee was created on February 27. Carlisle was among the five Representatives appointed from the lower House. Several refused to serve, and as the committee was eventually composed, he was the only tariff reformer included. Again he fought the protectionists' proposals paragraph by paragraph, but with no greater success than before, for the rates in many instances were raised above those asked by the Senate or the House individually. The report of the Conference Committee reached the Senate on March 2, and the House on the following day.

Belligerent Democrats, hopeful of defeating the Republican tariff within the next twenty-four hours, gathered on Capitol Hill early on the last day of the Forty-seventh Congress. Speaker Keifer rapped for order at the regular hour; the chaplain thanked God "for all the wise and useful legislation that Thou hast permitted them [the Congressmen] to do"; and anxious Republicans began a determined effort to push their tariff bill through the House before noon of the coming Sunday brought the end of the session. William D. Kelley hurriedly presented the conference report, but Carlisle requested a full explanation

EFFORTS AT TARIFF REFORM

of the work of the committee, and Springer of Illinois demanded a reading of the bill. Two dull but precious hours were wasted by the clerks in reading many pages of tariff technicalities to which nobody listened. The protectionists forced an abandonment of the regular five-thirty recess and attempted to limit the debate, but their opponents were determined to talk.

Carlisle, "the chief opponent of the Committee's work," led the Democrats. The hour of debate found him a little paler than usual. Never robust, he was probably not in good physical condition on that day; he took frequent sips from a cup of black coffee at his elbow. Before him lay a pile of statistics which he had collected the previous session while serving as a member of the Ways and Means Committee, and which he had been revising since December of the preceding year. His speech, pure Democratic doctrine, made his party feel that he was the high priest who was to light afresh the fires before the altar of tariff reform. Business safety and public interest demanded a reduction, he declared, and added that he would willingly support any proposal which made even as much as a twenty per cent reduction, if "justly and equitably distributed." In clear, simple sentences he recited, instance by instance, the cases in which the conference committee had placed the rates higher than either house of Congress had asked. He had other objections. Common earthenware, the dishes of universal use among the poor, had formerly paid forty per cent, he explained—now they paid sixty, an increase of one-half; steel of the finest grade paid less than that used in the ordinary business of the farmer and the laborer. But time was pressing, and other Democrats were eager to say a word. Carlisle concluded:

> I will have to cease my remarks, Mr. Speaker, in order that a little time may be left for other gentlemen on this side; but I desire to say again that I have been anxious to see this Congress pass some measure of actual relief to the people. I have been willing and am willing now to make what I consider large concessions in order to secure a just and equitable revision of

the tariff. I cannot expect to see incorporated in a single measure all that in my opinion ought to be done; and if the absolute power to dispose of this great question were in my own hands to-day I would not make radical changes at once, but would be disposed to proceed by cautious and conservative methods to relieve the people from taxation and to reduce the revenues of the Government without injuring or alarming the industrial interests of the country. We must all recognize the fact that large interests have grown up under the existing system; that they have been fostered and encouraged by it, and that they have so adjusted themselves to it as to become in a large measure dependent upon the assurance that it will not be suddenly swept away.

Under these circumstances, while I would strenuously insist upon actual and substantial reductions, I would be willing to accept very reasonable and moderate measures as satisfactory indications of a fixed purpose to relieve the people at large without embarrassing special interests. The business of the country will soon adjust itself to any reasonable change that may be made but it must be more or less injured by the agitation which inevitably results from persistent refusals to settle our revenue system upon a just and permanent basis. The people demand justice and stability in tariff legislation, and when these essentials shall be secured the manufacturing interests of the country will no longer require the interposition of the Government to force prices up and give them the control of the home market, but will become self-reliant and self-sustaining. Then, sir, all our great industrial interests will grow and prosper together, and we will go on developing our wonderful resources and augmenting the wealth and power of the country through all time.[1]

By five-thirty in the morning the debate was ended, and the Republicans passed their tariff measure by a vote of 152 to 116. Before the news reached New York, the *Tribune* went to press carrying the hopeful comment: "It is very close shaving; but the faith of those who have clung to the hope that this Congress

[1] *Congressional Record,* 47 Cong., 2d Sess., Vol. 14, pt. 4, pp. 3724–3727.

might yet give us a readjustment and reduction of the tariff in accordance with protectionist principles, and an abolition of all war taxes save those on whiskey and tobacco, seem, at the last moment, likely to be vindicated." Yet the tariff which was passed was an inharmonious affair which nobody liked. "That the Tariff Bill was a game of grab played on a large scale, is made apparent by the cries of those participants who lost more than they gained by it," said the *Nation* on March 8. Because he failed to secure favors for the wool growers of his State, Senator Sherman later expressed regret that he had helped defeat the mild proposals of the commission. Several years later William D. Kelley wrote in the *Forum* that a public disavowal of the responsibility for tariff legislation in the Forty-seventh Congress was "a privilege for which I have long wished." [1]

But though the Democrats were defeated, the debates had brought one member of the party to the front. Carlisle's speeches were recognized as masterful, were reprinted in pamphlet form, and were distributed over the country for campaign purposes. The Democratic reformers had found a leader. In the small hours of the morning of March 4 (the legislative day of March 3) Abram S. Hewitt and Samuel J. Randall engaged in a lively clash in one of the cloak rooms of the House. "I shall not be dictated to," cried Randall, and Hewitt thundered, "You will find your days numbered next December in the Democratic caucus." The split in the party was perfectly apparent.

[1] Vol. 4, p. 147.

CHAPTER V   THE FIRST SPEAKERSHIP, 1883-1885

ON October 9, 1882, T. Dewitt Talmadge of Brooklyn delivered a sermon on "The Degradation of Modern Politics" for which he chose the Biblical text, "This place shall no more be called Tophet, nor the Valley of the Son of Hinnom, but the Valley of Slaughter." The minister was not directing his remarks at the party in power, but the text applied to the Republican defeat which came that year. On November 9 Henry Watterson, editor of the *Courier-Journal,* told his readers in flaring headlines that "The Rickety Republican Craft [is] Run Down and Scuttled from Fore to Aft." Indeed, the people East and West had given a stinging rebuke to the Republican party. The opposition won in both State and National elections, and the new House was overwhelmingly Democratic.

It was a disturbed and fretful period. Suspicion of corruption in the White House; malfeasance in the Federal departments; dishonesty in Congress; crookedness in city governments; strikes in Eastern factories; agrarian discontent in the midlands; silver demands in the West—all these revealed the ferment of the time. The exclamation, "There is nothing definite in American society for the dramatist to get hold of," characterized the confused social order. The great concourse of Missourians who gathered to view the remains of Jesse James in April, 1882, was evidence to the East that moral standards were low; and the applause which Samuel L. Clemens won with his rude tales proved to them that the literature which New England had so carefully nurtured had fallen upon evil days. Never before had Congressmen depended so slavishly upon the caprices of their constituencies; and never before had constituents seemed so changeable in temper. Because of this fact the tenure of either party in Congress was often precarious, and the general result was that Congressmen, in their efforts to gain favor for themselves, became proficient in petty trickery. Statesmen were not lacking, but statesmanship was practically impossible. The business of Congress was no longer conducted on the floor, but in the committee rooms, and the recommendations of the committees had to run a painful gauntlet before they became law.

The variety of national interests resulted in a flood of proposed legislation, and each bill, good or bad, was regarded as of major importance by its author. The House was so cluttered with miscellaneous measures that its machinery became clogged and was regarded by the members as only a delaying instrument, the intricacies of which nobody apparently understood. Senator Bayard declared: "I know nothing really of the rules of the House, I confess. There is a veil of mystery surrounding those rules which I have never been able to penetrate." All Congressmen understood, however, that the committees had come to be a dominating factor. James A. McKinzie of Kentucky, a tariff reformer, gave in the Forty-sixth Congress a clever description of the situation:

There are two places of interment in this House in which all legislation looking to reform in our revenue or custom duties is buried. One is the gorgeous mausoleum of the Ways and Means Committee, a tomb as magnificent as that which Artemisia built at Halicarnassus to the memory of Mausolus, and the other is the Calendar of this House. A member introducing a bill here can decide whether he prefers to have it buried with that sort of splendid interment which the Ways and Means affords, or that it should go to the Calendar, which is the potter's field of legislation. . . .

In preferring the Calendar as a place of interment for relief measures, I do not wish to be understood as invidiously discriminating against the Ways and Means Committee, for I desire here and now to say that as a place of permanent and reliable sepulture it is the equal if not the superior of any grave-yard that has existed since the ancient and unknown artificer conceived the idea of the Catacombs of Egypt. But it is too pretentious in the matter of architectural embellishment to suit the simple taste of the average tariff reformer. The chief mausoleums besides the one at Halicarnassus are the mausoleum of Augustus; that of Hadrian, now called the castle of Saint Angelo at Rome; that erected in France by Catherine de Medici to Henry II; that of Saint Peter, the martyr in the church of Saint Eustatius, and that erected to the memory of Louis XVI. But none of these compare in architectural splendor, in uniqueness of design, in gorgeousness of execution, nor are any of them so suggestive of death without benefit of clergy or hope of resurrection, as the Ways and Means Committee of this House.

When an ambitious member drafts a measure looking to revenue reform and presents it to the House in the morning hour of Monday, it is no stretch of the imagination to say that he can detect the dolorous notes of the "Dead March in Saul" as the Clerk sings out, "Ways and Means, and printed." I can recollect but one instance of verification where the cadaver had either lain or was about to be deposited in the tomb of the Ways and Means, and that was the case of Mr. Townshend, of Illinois, who was discovered trying to galvanize the corpse in the Committee on Revision of Laws, was tried on a charge of burking or body-snatching, and the somewhat mutilated remains were restored by the solemn vote of this House to its family vault.[1]

Woodrow Wilson, in writing his *Congressional Government* a few years later, said on this subject: "The fate of bills committed is generally not uncertain. As a rule, a bill committed is a bill doomed. When it goes from the clerk's desk to a committee-room it crosses a parliamentary bridge of sighs to dim dungeons of silence whence it will never return. The means and time of its death are unknown, but its friends never see it again."[2]

Congress could accomplish nothing. The old issues which had been predominant had become stale, and no one appeared to be able to lead a new cause. Parliamentary affairs were slowly moving toward a crisis. Few could ignore the fact that the House was becoming an intolerably creaky, slow, unsatisfactory in-

---

[1] *Congressional Record,* 46 Congress, 2d Sess., Appendix, p. 139.
[2] P. 69.

strument of government, which Henry Watterson a few years later called a "Gulliver-snail of politics." Reform could not be expected, however, until some issue of overshadowing interest could be brought forward, and even then it would be fraught with danger.

The interest in the question of the Democratic Speakership grew apace through the summer of 1883. The question was, said the editor of the *Nation*, "Shall the tariff question be discussed or dodged?" The fiscal situation, coupled with the determination on the part of the reform Democrats to be heard, made it impossible to avoid the issue, but the protectionists in the party were powerful. Despite the statement in the New York *Times* that a "drove of dark horses will stamp about in the Democratic stables," there was little doubt as to who the candidates for the Speakership would be: Samuel J. Randall of Pennsylvania would lead the protectionists; Samuel S. Cox of New York would gather to his banner the "middle-of-the-road" group; and Carlisle of Kentucky, if J. C. S. Blackburn of the same State relinquished his claims, would represent the Southern and Western advocates of a "tariff for revenue only." William M. Springer of Illinois might poll a few votes, but not enough to influence the decision. Carlisle and Randall were the chief aspirants, and the result would indicate the future tariff stand of the party.

On November 20 Henry Watterson wrote: "If the utterances of the Democratic press for two or three years mean anything; if the vote of the last Congressional election means anything; if the views expressed by leading Democrats of the country mean anything, then the Democratic party has decided that there shall be no cessation of intelligent tariff reform." Eight days later Carlisle declared in a letter to Professor A. L. Perry of Williams College: "In my opinion a retreat from our present position on tariff reform would be disastrous. If we shall find ourselves unable to go forward we can at least stand still and hold the ground already won, which is far safer and more honorable than to go backward. The election of Mr. Randall or any other gentleman entertaining his views would be very properly regarded by the country as an abandonment of the contest, and, as you say, it would drive away from us thousands of earnest men who care more for principles than spoils. My own position on this subject has been deliberately taken and will be consistently maintained. I do not wish to succeed in this or any other contest by concealing any real sentiments or purposes concerning any public question."

Early November found a host of politicians crowding the hotel lobbies in Washington. Northerners and Southerners, industrialists and agriculturists, rubbed elbows with one another and discussed the subject of the tariff. "Ward-rounders and strikers from Philadelphia and Harrisburg are very conspicuous in all public places," said the Baltimore *Sun*. The candidates themselves, much to the disgust of *Harper's Weekly*, soon appeared to set up their headquarters. Accompanied by his wife, Carlisle arrived on November 11 and registered at the Riggs Hotel. Cox arrived a few days later, but Randall, suffering from the gout, did not make his appearance for a week. Carlisle opened his headquarters on November 19 in parlors 162 and 164 of the Metropolitan Hotel. Blackburn and Thompson of Kentucky were the official hosts, but one could usually find there the gaunt six-foot figure of Carlisle as well. He felt a little handicapped in a contest for himself; "I never asked a man to vote for me in my life for anything," he told a reporter of the *Evening Star*.

Randall, backed by powerful influences and assisted by important newspapers, conducted his campaign from the Ebbitt House. "Around Mr. Randall, the great Tilden candidate, the man who was held up as a sort of Moses, who was to lead the Democrats into the promised land under the banner of Tilden and Hendricks and reform, but not tariff reform," said the New York *Times* on December 2, "were gathered the members of the Pennsylvanian delegation in Congress, a great throng of Philadelphia politicians clothed in silk hats and the Randallian air of mystery, and 'bet-yer-five-hundred-dollar' confidence." Randall was lulled into unwarranted assurance by his asso-

THE FIRST SPEAKERSHIP 69

ciates; he obviously misjudged the qualities of the statesman who was opposing him. The Pennsylvanian might well have studied more seriously Carlisle's statement of November 12:

> I think it is entirely safe to say that while there is a very general feeling of dissatisfaction with the existing system of unequal and unjust tariff taxation, there is no disposition to strike a radical, much less a fatal, blow at any of the great mechanical or manufacturing interests of the country. Nor is it necessary, in my judgment, to strike such a blow in order to afford a reasonable degree of relief to the people. We cannot close our eyes to the fact that under this system, whether it was originally wise or unwise, large and valuable interests have grown up, and great masses of capital have been withdrawn from other pursuits and embarked in manufacturing enterprises, and that labor, following as it always does where capital leads, has been to a great extent diverted from its previous channels, and has permanently identified itself with these various interests. In any revision of the tariff that may be made, proper regard should be had for the welfare of these great interests, and they should be carefully considered—not alone, not as something separate and distinct from the other industries of the country, not as special favorites of the Government having peculiar claims on its bounty, but in connection with every other legitimate interest in the country, all being recognized and treated as equally entitled to favorable consideration.[1]

While the Democratic candidates were laying their plans in Washington, the press—Republican as well as Democratic—was carrying on a Speakership campaign of its own. Many Northern papers asserted that the Carlisle men were reviving the sectional issue, and saw in the forces which were supporting him a dream of the South to dominate again the national government. The financial stringency which was then temporarily gripping the country afforded the protectionists a potent argument. "I see that they are charging that the closing of mills and factories

[1] New York *Sun*, November 12, 1883.

is due to my probable election," said Carlisle on November 20. Six days later the Cincinnati *Enquirer* observed that "If Mr. Carlisle had been content with the leadership of the floor, Mr. Cox with the Foreign Affairs Committee, Mr. Springer with modesty, and Mr. Morrison with magnanimity, there would not now be such ridiculous huckstering at Washington for the office of Moderator. The undercurrent here is strongly in favor of Randall without regard to party, on the ground that he is not a naked coffin making a raid on somebody's business." The Philadelphia *Times* reminded its readers of the "Carlisle panic" which he was supposed to have caused some time before by his three per cent funding bill. But the cry of "Wolf, wolf!" had been used too many times by the protectionists.

As the opening of Congress approached, it was obvious that Randall's lead was weakening. His followers pinned their faith on his ability to extricate himself from a tight place. They depended a great deal upon their plan for a secret ballot, for by this method there might be lured into his fold some undecided Southerners. A keen observer might have noticed in Washington the presence of William Henry Barnum of Connecticut, and had he been versed in the ways of politics he would have understood the explanation which was offered—"buying mules" for Randall. Little evidence is available, but it is certain that the protectionists were active in Randall's cause, and that the railroads and the Standard Oil leaders were particularly anxious to prevent the threatened regulation of interstate commerce.

All was astir on the eve of the Democratic caucus. The Carlisle forces, "walking on air," were jubilant. A member of Congress from Arkansas expressed the sentiment of his associates when he wrote: "I am for Carlisle against the world, the flesh and the devil." The Randall men were quieter, but no less enthusiastic. Betting at the Willard was $500 to $350 that Randall would win, but an Avenue saloon-keeper announced a $10 reward for anyone betting $10,000 that Carlisle would not be elected. In Cincinnati politicians were scraping up all available assets to cover the money of the Carlisle enthusiasts from across the river

THE FIRST SPEAKERSHIP 71

in Covington and Newport. A member of the staff of the Cincinnati *Enquirer* is said to have placed $100,000 on the contest in favor of Randall. At Louisville the *Courier-Journal* had in its office $1,000 to be wagered on Carlisle.

The Democratic caucus met on the evening of December 1. A real principle was at stake, and eager party members began to arrive in the House of Representatives long before the meeting was to open. At seven-thirty General Rosecrans called the caucus to order. George W. Geddes of Ohio was elected chairman, and the roll began. One hundred and eighty-eight were present, but the candidates were not among them. Carlisle sat in the room of the Committee on Appropriations talking to Senator Morgan of Alabama, Senator Williams of Kentucky, and a few Washington and Kentucky friends; in the next room, that of the Committee of Ways and Means, was Randall, surrounded by a group of Philadelphia business men, who, according to the New York *Times*, "looked much like a crowd of New York's City Hall politicians." Cox held forth in the room of the Committee on Foreign Affairs. On the floor of the House Morrison of Illinois, Curtin of Pennsylvania, and Slocum of New York placed the three candidates in nomination.

The effort of Randall's supporters to force a secret ballot was defeated, and their failure was ominous. Before the voting had passed New York, it was evident that Randall had lost. The tall figure of Morrison emerged from the hall and started rapidly toward the room of the Appropriations Committee, shouting, "Carlisle has won!" Carlisle turned to a friend with the request, "Go telegraph my boys."

Before the cheering in the halls was over, the shiny hats of the Philadelphia business men had disappeared from the corridors, their wearers declaring that the Democrats had thrown away the chance of victory in 1884. Randall was bitterly disappointed, but joined Curtin and Cox in escorting the nominee before the caucus. "This contest closes," said Carlisle, "as far as I am concerned, without the slightest change in the friendly personal relations that have heretofore existed between us."

Randall promised the candidate his "firm, fixed, [and] honorable support." For the first time since the Civil War the protectionists had been unable to elect one of their members Speaker.

"[It] is in no sense a personal triumph, not even for the distinguished and brilliant Kentuckian who won it," wrote Henry Watterson. "He stood for a principle and that principle has prevailed. . . . The South and West elected Carlisle to-night on a principle. . . . It is the tariff, and how it shall be revised." The time was fitting, said the editor, for those who could not agree with the action of the caucus to slip out of the party—"Drive on the revenue coach!" The press of New York rejoiced that the "political trimmers" and "dead wood" of the party had been eliminated—that the young men had come to the front. "The party stands for something of its own, for the reform of abuses, and for the rights of the people against monopolists of all kinds," said the *Herald*, while the *Tribune* commented: "We are glad of it. His nomination which means his election, is an approach toward a frank expression of feeling on the part of the Democrats. . . . Mr. Carlisle's nomination places his party on a platform on which we shall be glad to fight it." "The chances of Democratic success next year are not increased by the election of Mr. Carlisle," admitted *Harper's Weekly*, but asserted that "the Democratic party now professes to represent something besides evasion and trickery, which is a great improvement in the political situation." In Philadelphia, which the *Nation* pictured as "a sort of blue grotto, where there is no diversity of color, but everything wears the cerulean hue," the *Press* described Carlisle as "the ablest champion among all the democratic Representatives of the opposition to protection."

On the Monday following Carlisle's selection by the Democratic caucus the Forty-eighth Congress opened. The day dawned bright and beautiful, with just coolness enough to remind all that winter had come. By ten in the morning crowds were thronging Pennsylvania Avenue on their way to the Capitol. The hallways of the House were crowded long before the doors to the

CAPTAIN CARLISLE WAKING THE DEMOCRATIC SHAUGHRAUN

(*Puck*, 1883)

gallery were opened; those waiting, wrote one correspondent, were mostly well-dressed ladies, "but this did not seem to keep them from doing as much pushing as the common herd." Carlisle, dressed in "neat black cloth, well laundered linen, . . . and black tie," sat in his old seat. A few steps away was Randall in a spick-and-span suit of black. On the Republican side, well to the front, was Keifer, large and loose-jointed, with "trifle of look that he had lost a scepter which he gave to the Kentuckian with reluctance." Beside him sat the unkempt Judge Kelley, sage of the House and arch-champion of protection. A few Senators wandered here and there among the Congressmen.

At twelve o'clock, noon, Clerk McPherson called the House to order. The floor was almost a bed of roses. To J. Warren Keifer, the unpopular Speaker of the preceding Congress, had come a miniature rose chair, which the Congressional reporters probably hoped would be thorny; the desks of Randall and Cox were covered with roses; while in front of Carlisle was a floral tribute from a group of Kentucky women representing a hatchet resting on the mossy stump of a tree. On the attached card were the instructions:

> For noise use hammer end as gavel
> And blade when knots you can't unravel.

There was no chaplain present, and nominations were made immediately. George W. Geddes, chairman of the Democratic caucus, presented Carlisle, while Joseph G. Cannon of Illinois named J. Warren Keifer. The balloting resulted in 191 votes for Carlisle, 112 for Keifer, and 2 for George D. Robinson of Massachusetts.[1] Carlisle was escorted to the Chair by Randall and Keifer. Thus the Democracy, after an interval of two years,

---

[1] At Covington, Kentucky, home town of the Speaker, all was joy; Republicans united with Democrats in the general celebration. Fire bells vied with those of St. Mary's Cathedral in announcing the good news; blue lights were burned, and "Squire" John G. Ewan displayed a "large and elegant" portrait of the honored son. At midnight a cannon was dragged forth and fired in salute; the telegraph office was crowded by men sending their congratulations to Washington. *Daily Commonwealth* and *Courier-Journal,* Dec. 3, 1883.

again took control of the lower House. But it was a changed Democracy, for the few strides which carried Carlisle to the Speaker's dais brought the revenue-tariff element of the party once more into a position of undisputed dominance. So far as the lower House is concerned, the steps have never been retraced.

To many observers Carlisle's elevation seemed to threaten danger to the industrial interests. *Harper's Weekly* declared that the event "shows the probability of an active and vigorous policy of tariff revision in what is called the free-trade direction. It tends, therefore, to alarm that great manufacturing and industrial interest which a large part of the Democratic party wished to propitiate by silence and evasion." The *Nation* offered some reassuring words. "We do not look for any immediate radical changes to follow Mr. Carlisle's elevation to the Speaker's chair," wrote Godkin. "His election signifies the direction in which the thought of the country has turned in respect of its tariff policy, rather than any determination or desire to knock away at once the crutches upon which so many of our crippled industries are hobbling."

But those who feared that a rash agitation of tariff reform might endanger American prosperity were greatly relieved by Speaker Carlisle's opening address. "Sudden and radical changes in the laws and regulations affecting the commercial and industrial interests of the people ought never to be made unless imperatively demanded by some great public emergency," he asserted, "and in my opinion, under existing circumstances, such changes would not be favorably received by any considerable number of those who have given serious attention to the subject." The House, he said, would decide just how far reform should go, but "If there are any who fear that your action upon this or any other subject will be actually injurious to any interest, or even afford reasonable cause for alarm, I am quite sure that they will be agreeably disappointed. . . . What the country has the right to expect is strict economy in the administration of every department of the Government, just and equal taxation for public purposes, a faithful observ-

THE FIRST SPEAKERSHIP

ance of the limitations of the Constitution, and a scrupulous regard for the rights and interests of the great body of the people, in order that they may be protected, so far as Congress has the power to protect them, against encroachment from every direction." When the address was completed, Kelley administered the "iron-clad oath," a grim vestige of reconstruction days.

The new Speaker was forty-nine years old. His face was clean-shaven. As he picked up his gavel and looked over what Woodrow Wilson ironically called "the vast spaces of . . . the hall of the House of Representatives," he may have wondered if he would be able to prevent such turbulent scenes as had often occurred in the past. His fellow-Congressmen, many of them new, could not fail to note the natural dignity of the man. From the farthest reaches of the hall his broad forehead, long straight nose, and handsome chin were apparent; a closer look revealed bushy eyebrows, gray-blue eyes, and brown hair parted on the right side. Resolute in bearing, he appeared thoroughly capable of carrying through the party program.

When Speaker Carlisle looked over the membership of the Forty-eighth Congress, he saw many familiar figures. On the Democratic side was the gigantic William Dorsheimer, whom nobody could miss, and near him S. S. Cox, late candidate for the Speakership. William R. Morrison, old warrior in the tariff cause, was prominent, and near by were Charles S. Crisp of Georgia, Roger Q. Mills of Texas, J. C. S. Blackburn of Kentucky, William S. Holman, "the great objector" from Indiana, John R. Tucker of Virginia, and many others, all surrounded by the "youngsters" who were yet to take the painful journey of apprenticeship in the House. There were so many Democrats, in fact, that they overflowed into the Republican side; and along with Thomas B. Reed of Maine, William McKinley of Ohio, John A. Kasson of Iowa, J. Warren Keifer of Ohio, and "Pig-iron" Kelley of Pennsylvania sat William M. Springer of Illinois, Frank Hurd of Ohio, and Perry Belmont, Abram S. Hewitt, and Henry W. Slocum of New

York. Carlisle made a gesture toward party harmony when, disregarding the demands of his friends, he appointed Randall as chairman of the Appropriations Committee.

It was evident to everyone that the Congress was opening under unfavorable auspices. The coming presidential campaign hung like a pall over the members, deadening any initiative which they might have shown; the impending contest, moreover, revived the sectional question. Shortly before Christmas, 1883, Henry Watterson wrote that "there appears little room to doubt that the Republican party will mount the old sectional war-horse, and, hoisting the worn out bloody shirt for an ensign, ride forth in the coming Presidential campaign to fire anew the Northern heart." S. S. Cox introduced a resolution to abolish the "iron-clad oath," appealing to his hearers to "bridge over the abyss of civil strife as the Romans did, with a bridge of gold." The Republicans had passed a similar resolution in a previous Congress, but now on second thought they discovered that those who cheered Cox were mainly representatives from the solid South and that his speech "was really an appeal for the payment of 'hundreds of millions of Rebel claims.'"[1] John Sherman, with his eye on the possibilities of 1884, urged the Senate to investigate the Canville and Copiah riots in the South. Randall discussed the evils of a low tariff.

The subjects to which the first session of this Congress gave its attention were numerous, but few things were accomplished. No bill of importance made any progress until its essential provisions were removed, after which it was, as Breckinridge of Arkansas remarked, allowed to march through the House in "mucilaginous majesty." In February the Mexican War pension bill was called up, and a member of the House asked to have it made the order of the day on February 21 and thereafter until disposed of. Immediately there began one of those blockades so common in Congress and so much at variance with responsible government. The minority wing of the Demo-

[1] *Nation*, Vol. 31, Jan. 31, 1884, p. 90.

crats joined with the Republicans in a filibuster which showed Congress at its worst. A minor provision in the bill provided for pensions to Indian fighters, and the sectional issue immediately appeared because many still believed that these wars had been fought only with the object of securing runaway slaves among the Indians.

The filibuster began at an evening meeting when a member questioned the presence of a quorum. His demand brought on an all-night session of monotonous roll calls. Speaker Carlisle struck hard at the anarchy: "This is a matter of business and not of jest," he told his associates, but, although the Washington *Evening Star* said that the Speaker's emphatic statement prevented "much of the hilarity which frequently attends the call of the House," the proceedings continued to be a farce. The doors of the House were closed, and the Sergeant-at-Arms and his assistants combed the city for absent members, who were brought before the House only to be excused after a bit of fun at their expense. One member suggested that "Sunset" Cox be excused on condition that he present each member with a copy of his book, "Why We Laugh"; another proposed that a case be referred to the new Civil Service Commission. Difficult as it was to assemble the members, little was gained by the process, for they sat dumb in their seats when rolls were called. Carlisle was helpless, for his convictions concerning the powers of the Speaker forced him to say, "The Chair knows of no process by which a member of the House can be compelled to vote."

Over and over such ridiculous performances as the following occurred:

Speaker. Mr. Henley, you have been absent from the sitting of the House without its leave. What excuse have you to offer?

Mr. Henley. Mr. Speaker, I have to say in entire sincerity that when I left my house this morning a member of my family was taken ill with an attack of the measles. [Laughter] That is the first time in my experience that I ever knew that statement to elicit amusement; but I suppose it is all right in Washington. [Renewed laughter] And this afternoon at about 5 o'clock, having some solicitude in respect to the matter I repaired home. . . . I knew nothing about these proceedings until I was advised by the myrmidons . . . of the Sergeant-at-Arms [Laughter] that my presence was required. . . .

A Member. How about that dress suit?

Mr. Henley. Some gentleman desires to know something in respect to the matter of my habiliments. I have nothing to say about that at all. . . .

Mr. Gibson. If the gentleman will only divide his bouquet with us I will move he be excused.

All through the night the light in the dome of the Capitol told of the waste of time. At two in the morning the Sergeant-at-Arms ceased his man-hunt for a moment in order to quell an outburst of turbulence on the floor; by daybreak the clerks could scarcely speak above a whisper, and sympathetic members were sparing them from the task of calling the roll wherever possible. Shortly before seven o'clock a quorum was obtained, and the pension bill was made a special order by a vote of 176 to 35, with 109 not voting. At 8:55 the House adjourned to meet "next Wednesday." The Democratic majority had won, but the victory was futile.[1]

Shortly afterward William R. Morrison introduced the "bill to reduce import duties and war-tariff taxes" which the election of Speaker Carlisle had made certain. There was nothing drastic in Morrison's proposals. He asked only a general reduction of twenty per cent to be applied horizontally to all duties on manufactured articles. Moreover, in order to forestall the objection that the reduction might bring certain duties back to the detested rates of 1857, he put in the proviso that no duty should be lower than that provided by the Morrill tariff of 1861. The Morrison bill, however, soon brought into action all the forces of the "third house," whose demands were

---

[1] See *Congressional Record,* Feb. 18, 1884; Washington *Evening Star,* Feb. 19, 1884.

ably taken up by Samuel J. Randall and his followers.[1] The sugar, iron, and wool interests proved their power before the bill had long been in the House.

The industrial situation also conspired to hinder the Democratic efforts at tariff reform. Depression was widespread, and in nearly every trade there were wage reductions, lockouts, and strikes—a situation which was naturally used as a potent argument against tariff tinkering. The reformers were often perplexed. David A. Wells wrote Morrison on February 29:

> I received your letter of the 24, almost immediately after mailing one to you, asking for a report of the situation. . . . I know we are gaining ground, but there is some discouragement and some dissatisfaction at the apparently chaotic condition of things growing out of this hostility of the Republicans generally to tariff reform, and the division of the democrats on the same subject. But keep one thing ever before you and make it the burden of your talks to politicians.—That this thing has come to stay from the necessities of the country and is getting stronger every day. . . . For the party to shuffle and dodge on this question, is to make defeat certain. If you want to strengthen your soul, and harden your nerves for the fight, read a pamphlet by S. M. Turnbull published by the *Iowa State Leader*, "History of the Free Trade Struggle in Great Britain" . . . It gives the history of the counterpart of our experience and shows that in England they had the same

---

[1] On May 6 James M. Swank, Secretary of the American Iron and Steel Association, wrote from Philadelphia to Senator Justin S. Morrill:

Dear Sir: I have received your letter of the 3d inst. I have also received a copy of your speech on the tariff. This Association can not *directly* engage in the distribution of your speech, as we have many Democratic members, but we occasionally "whip the devil around the stump." On Saturday last I gave Mr. McPherson $2,000, which our Democratic members will know nothing about. This money is to be used for the distribution of just such speeches as yours. . . . If we had not placed the sum above mentioned in the hands of Mr. McPherson last Friday we would have been glad to make a liberal subscription towards the distribution of your speech; but we now presume that General Hawley and Mr. McPherson will see that this is attended to. I will this evening write to Mr. McPherson, calling his attention to your speech. . . .

rot to meet and the same discouragement. You may be sure, that if the party does not do something, there will be a convention of independents called, who will fight against the Randall-Barnum influence right through, and make lots of mischief.

Now as to future, if you can't carry your 20 per cent. reduction, I would abandon the effort and make a simple free list. I would keep in view the point which has always seemed to me most important, *i. e.*, to break the protectionist chain of mutual interests. Put lumber on the free list, and Conger and Sawyer will go smashing everything. Salt will sicken Hiscock and lots of others. So will coal. Old Blair in the Senate voted for free coal last winter. Quinine gives no money now to the cause, or writes any pamphlets favoring protection. Dwell in your speech first on the certainty that reductions have got to be made in the tariff, and that it will profit nothing to put off the day of action. . . .

I should charge the present distress and stagnation to the limitation of our markets for our manufactured products to this country, and that it is a mighty poor exchange to take the small advantage this gives us, in place of the great markets of the world,—for it is a fact that neither Kelley or any one can question—that 90 per cent., certainly 80 per cent., of all our manufactures would exist and flourish under complete free trade and be retained by us, and that all the system of protection is kept up for the benefit of the other 10 or 20.[1]

The greatest difficulty which the Democrats faced was not the Republican opposition, but the protectionist minority in their own party. To force the tariff issue might endanger the united effort which was being planned in the national campaign of 1884. However, Speaker Carlisle gave notice in a public address on March 15 that the fight for tariff reform would continue regardless of the consequences, and the *Nation* declared: "If the Democratic party is to split upon it [the tariff issue], let it split." Indeed, for the next few weeks Carlisle and Morrison drove forward their tariff program with a vigor which did justice to their determination—but Randall quietly

[1] **Morrison MSS.**

waited for an opportune time to strike. On April 15 Morrison proposed that the House resolve itself into a Committee of the Whole for the consideration of his bill. Randall was not prepared. He had been ill for a week in his Philadelphia home, and his army had wilted under the lash of the tariff reformers. The motion prevailed by two votes—a narrow margin, but sufficient to enable the advocates of reduction to rejoice over another victory. On May 1 the author of the bill before the House brought up a motion to close debate on May 6. McKinley immediately notified the House that an effort would be made at that time to strike out the enacting clause of the measure.

Carlisle and Morrison prepared for the announced Republican attack. The day for the vote came. Randall was ready; in an address which must have pleased the Republicans greatly he attacked the tariff measure which his party had introduced. When he had finished, Morrison closed the debate. The Democrats waited for McKinley's motion, but the Ohioan sat silent while from the Democratic side rose George L. Converse of his State, who, to the chagrin of the tariff reformers, introduced it. If it carried, the tariff bill was dead. The roll began. One after another the Randallites joined the Republicans, and the dreams of Carlisle and Morrison tottered; these two leaders had misjudged the power of the Pennsylvanian. The vote ended 156 to 151 in favor of the Converse resolution. The reformers vented their feelings without restraint upon "Randall and his forty thieves," who had blasted their hopes.

For many weeks Congress listlessly plodded on, arguing over the appropriation bills, the redemption of the trade dollars, government-owned telegraph lines, the bankruptcy bill, and educational projects of various kinds. At last, on July 5, 1884, amidst the applause of the House, a resolution "that the thanks of this House are due and are hereby tendered to Hon. John G. Carlisle . . . for the ability, efficiency, and strict impartiality with which he has discharged the arduous and responsible duties of his office during the present session of Congress" was unanimously adopted. Congress adjourned two days later with little accomplished. There can be no doubt that Carlisle should have used his gavel with more determination and less impartiality.

The defeat of the Morrison bill did not lessen the zeal of the tariff reformers; they at once prepared to carry their fight to the Democratic National Convention which met that summer. Henry Watterson, belligerent tariff reformer and friend of the Speaker, arrived early at Chicago with his "tariff-for-revenue-only" plank, but he was beset by "the widow" Butler,[1] Abram S. Hewitt, George L. Converse, and others who demanded a compromise because they were not yet convinced that the Southern demand for tariff reform was a wise issue upon which to face the country in the fall elections. Randall and his friends insisted that the taxes on whiskey and tobacco be repealed, but loudly protested the removal of a similar levy, indirectly collected, upon the necessities of life. The three groups—the Randall faction, which was interested only in protection and determined to have it at any price; the Carlisle forces, ready to defend against all comers their theory of a tariff for revenue only; and the politic school which believed that Democratic victory was better than a determined principle—were all represented on the platform committee, with the result that the Democracy again made no specific declaration of principles in regard to the tariff.

The compromise platform at the Democratic convention was definite assurance that neither protection nor free trade would be a major issue in the presidential campaign. There were too many other interests, and too few people understood the tariff question to make it profitable campaign material. Since the Civil War the nation had attained through the completion of its great transcontinental railway system a physical unity, but intellectually it was disorganized. Countless groups

[1] Benjamin F. Butler was so known to the cartoonists because of his declaration that the way to seek office was not as a maiden coyly and reluctantly, but as a widow who knew her own mind.

put forward their particular claims to being heard, and together their strength was such as to demand a hearing by any party which desired to control the government of the country or by any individual who aspired to the Presidency. In addition, the nomination of James G. Blaine by the Republicans had offended many independents and reformers whose support the Democrats—if they were not too Democratic—might temporarily win.

It was evident that the Democracy could succeed only through a wise choice of presidential nominee. But who could select a man who would promise something to everyone and offend no one? Certainly the low-tariff men would not support a protectionist advocate, and therefore Samuel J. Randall could not lead the party. Most assuredly the Southern Democracy could not win on tariff reform alone, and for this reason neither Carlisle nor Morrison was available. As early as April Henry B. Payne wrote James R. Doolittle of Wisconsin: "But for the insanity at Washington we could and would have carried the State [Ohio] in October by 25 or 30,000. Then with the prestige of such a victory the states you named would have all followed suit and secured the national victory in November. But Devils and fools would have it otherwise. Carlisle was made Speaker. Hurd the fanatic free-trader was, against the united protest of all our members and the known wishes of the entire party in the state placed on the Ways & Means Co., and under the lead of Watterson and the Kentucky Statesman a crusade was commenced for 'revenue only' and against the 'Ohio Platform.' All that was wanted to secure success on our part was that the tariff for this Congress should be let alone. . . . But demented, conceited, desperate schemers would not have it so. They proclaimed 'free trade or defeat'! Hence the 'Morrison Bill,' with its senseless illogical and ridiculous *horizontal* strike. . . . Now how can we expect that the wool growers can be induced to vote with us in Oct. or Nov.? Unless the democratic members by some bold step rebuke the free trade madness and with the coming convention pronounce distinctly for the Ohio platform it will in my opinion be utterly useless to enter upon a canvass to carry Ohio in October [or November]."[1]

There were many objections to the "old line" party members in the East, the most important of whom was Samuel J. Tilden. Thomas F. Bayard was capable, but not otherwise qualified. The Western candidates—Allen G. Thurman, Thomas A. Hendricks, and Joseph E. McDonald—were not suitable. Of all the leaders who were being mentioned in Chicago in these July days, Grover Cleveland alone possessed the qualities needed in fighting the forces of monopoly and greed. The presence of six hundred Tammany "Tigers" whom all knew to be after the scalp of this reform governor merely made his appeal to the supporters of good government stronger.

When nominations were called for, Cleveland's was the first name presented to the convention. The third was that of John G. Carlisle, of whom James McKinzie said in his nominating speech: "In all the essential characteristics of manliness, courage, ability, integrity, and patriotism, he is the peer of any that has been or will be mentioned in this great presence. Since ill-health compelled the retirement of the Sage of Greystone from the arena of active politics, no name carries with it more of talismanic charm and the respect of the American people than that of John G. Carlisle." Cleveland won on the second ballot. Carlisle drew but twenty-seven votes, and it was well, for he was ill-fitted for the Presidency. He could render the party greater service in the Speaker's Chair.

One month after the triumphant election of Cleveland the second session of the Forty-eighth Congress convened. The tariff reformers were still smarting under the defeat which the members of their own party had inflicted in the previous session, but they were heartened by the knowledge that a Democratic President was soon to occupy the Executive Mansion.

Carlisle and Morrison, realizing the futility of any imme-

[1] Payne to Doolittle, April 10, 1884, Cleveland, Ohio. Doolittle MSS.

diate attempt, decided that no further action should be taken in regard to the tariff until the new Executive had been installed. Randall, however, did not relent; he introduced a resolution reducing the duty on whiskey and tobacco, but the reform group refused to consider it so long as the laboring man found the necessities of life taxed. The Interstate Commerce measure passed, but the Blair Education bill and others of its kind failed to get a hearing. The House was scarcely less chaotic than it had been in the preceding session. The editor of the Washington *Evening Star* aptly described the legislative situation when he wrote early in the year, "It takes a two-to-one vote to pass anything in the House to-day and it is more than two-to-one that no bill can pass under such circumstances."

While party leaders floundered at Washington, the Democratic press of the country bewailed the fact that the President-elect did not reveal his views in order that Congress might have some basis of action. But Cleveland remained quietly at Albany and allowed Congress to take care of itself. Though he did not advertise the fact, he was slowly and methodically planning his course of action. As yet he knew few of the national party leaders, but he was not averse to accepting advice from them. As early as December 2 George Ticknor Curtis had urged him to come to Washington for conferences with prominent public men—even suggesting that he talk to Arthur concerning the Presidency. Cleveland decided to call the party chiefs to him, and on January 24 wrote Carlisle:

> I should be very glad to confer with you in relation to matters connected with the incoming administration.
> Cannot you come and see me next Saturday January 30th?
> I shall possibly spend a large part of the week succeeding this in New York and I should like to talk with you before going there.
> If you can comply with my request, and will inform me as nearly as possible of the time of your arrival, I will arrange my engagements with reference to your visit.[1]

[1] Cleveland-Carlisle MSS.

On January 31 Speaker Carlisle arrived in the snow-covered capital of the Empire State, the electoral vote of which had given the Democracy its first national success since the Civil War. In the evening he hailed a passing sleigh and rode to the peculiar little building called "The Towers" in which the President-elect was then living. The two men talked over the policy of the incoming administration, and at Cleveland's request the Speaker commented on the leaders of the party. After midnight Carlisle departed, and at two in the morning Vice-President-elect Thomas A. Hendricks arrived. Immediately after breakfast the Speaker, accompanied by Mrs. Carlisle, was back at "The Towers." A week later Cleveland went to New York for consultation with other members of the party. Never since Lincoln had a man who knew so few of the national figures of his party been elected to the Presidency, but he was working valiantly to correct the omission.

While the Speaker was in Albany, the situation in Congress became more complicated; filibustering began on the bankruptcy bill, and difficulties appeared in amending the rules to provide an extra hour to succeed the regular morning hour. The silver question, too, arose to vex the political leaders.

The financial situation was indeed discouraging. The period of prosperity which had come in with a rush during 1879 was over by 1883. In that year business was dull and stagnant, money was offered without takers at extraordinarily low rates, the number of failures increased, and prices shrank. Financial men were sure that silver had brought the change, and they anxiously regarded the declining gold balance in the Treasury. The *Commercial and Financial Chronicle* facetiously said of the silver dollars that it was a "comforting assurance, that not the least danger exists of our people getting short of these precious coins for nearly two generations."[1] The Secretary of the Treasury wrote in his December report that "to keep up an aimless purchase of silver bullion, at the rate of over twenty-

[1] On the basis of the previous yearly demand. January 6, 1883, vol. 36, p. 3.

four millions of dollars each year, is a needless loss of the interest on the sum thus expended." [1]

The year 1884 was no less disheartening. The tariff fight itself was partly responsible for the continued economic depression, but it could not explain the rapid decline in bank deposits and the sharp curtailment of consumption. Thirty-three and one-half millions of dollars of deposits disappeared from the banks betwen the last day of February and the tenth day of May, and yet the mints continued to turn out 2,000,000 silver dollars monthly. Railway rate wars in the West added their burdens. On April 15 the *Commercial and Financial Chronicle* said that "gold is flowing out like a river, and about the only straws the street has had to tickle its fancies with, have been the hourly settlement and re-settlement of the Union Pacific difficulty with the Chicago Burlington & Quincy, and the reorganization of the trunk line pool showing a similar perversity." The crisis came to a climax in May with the tragic failure of Grant and Ward. The attending panic was primarily limited to Wall Street, but it added fuel to the discontent which was slowly kindling in the midlands.

Congress was severely criticized for not relieving the situation by stopping the coinage of silver, but its sound-money members lacked the ability to take that action. Moreover, the tariff-reform Democrats were convinced, perhaps correctly, that the difficulty was fundamentally due to the exactions of protection. And so the depression continued. "Capitalists and business men know that we have entered upon a course which sooner or later must end in disaster," wrote a financial editor. "They are therefore in a listless mood, waiting, watching, unwilling to engage in any enterprise, or to trade except with the utmost caution. It is not because gold has left us, or continues to leave us, but because of the unknown power of the volcano that is working underneath and producing the outflow, which disturbs our people and industries. In the meantime the two

[1] *Report of the Finances,* 1883, p. xvii.

parties in Congress, instead of doing anything to relieve the situation, are just keeping up that ceaseless, wearying, face to face, steady stare at one another, like two dogs over a presidential bone, apparently thinking that the one displaying the most humbug and the least principle will hold the winning cards for November." [1]

Throughout the year the gold balance in the Treasury continued to decline; from September, 1881, to July, 1884, it had fallen $50,000,000, while the silver coinage had increased some $68,000,000 during the same period. Secretary McCulloch's final report was pessimistic. He frankly expressed the opinion that a panic or an adverse current of exchange "might compel the use in ordinary payments by the Treasury of the gold held for the redemption of its gold obligations." In regard to the large amount of money which the government held, he wrote that "there is no plethora of any kind except of silver dollars, for which there is no demand." There was imminent if not immediate danger, he added, that silver and not gold might become the standard of value.[2]

It was this fear of a suspension of gold payments, with the consequent calamity to the party, which stirred the Democrats to action in the early days of 1885. Tariff animosities were forgotten, but new enmities were born. Samuel J. Randall —"the traitor," "the renegade," "the Ali Baba with his forty thieves"—joined his erstwhile opponents in trying to meet the situation, and was ready to act with Hewitt and Morrison. On the other hand, Roger Q. Mills, L. H. Davis, Robert B. Vance, and others of the party deserted their late tariff-reform associates and signed a petition demanding that nothing be done to lessen the amount of silver coinage. In spite of the need for affirmative action, Carlisle again found himself totally unable to harmonize the warring factions.

[1] *C.F.C.*, Vol. 38, p. 492.
[2] *Report of the Finances*, 1884, pp. xxxi–xxxii. The Comptroller of the Currency said in his report that "statistics have been worn threadbare, and the number of articles and essays . . . written on the subject are of almost interminable extent." Ibid., p. 135.

The President-elect was no less perplexed than Congress, and he was almost as undecided as to what course to pursue. He believed that silver coinage was an evil, but he was not yet prepared to make it an issue of battle. On February 24 Samuel J. Randall wrote him: "I am not sure what will come out of my silver coinage amendment but in any event I do not think it desirable for your own sake that you cover the issue at this time in your inaugural. It will be in time for legislation for you to speak on this subject in your message in December. Your letter I shall keep until I see you and hand the same to you in person." [1] But on the same day there appeared in the press a letter (written by Manton Marble and reluctantly signed by Cleveland) "To the Hon. A. J. Warner and others, Members of the Forty-eighth Congress," in which the President-elect condemned silver and recommended a suspension of coinage.[2]

But Congress took no action on the silver question. The appropriations bills were demanding the attention of every member. The Rivers and Harbor appropriation bill, especially, excited a great deal of opposition. On February 25 began a call of the House which rapidly degenerated into a farce. One man was called who was no longer a member of the House, and Browne of Indiana suggested that "as we need a quorum we might as well send for him." The Speaker struck hard against the prevailing confusion, but it availed him little. Every member had some pet project which he desired to have adopted before the session ended. White of Kentucky was vainly endeavoring to get a prohibition bill through the House, while another member was championing a measure to pension the last surviving granddaughter of Thomas Jefferson. Out of the mêlée came one constructive action—the announcement that U. S. Grant had been appointed to the position of General of the Armies which Congress had just created. In the Senate the cheering was so unrestrained that the President of that body threatened to clear the galleries.

[1] Cleveland MSS.
[2] See McElroy, I, pp. 107-109.

The legislative day of March 3 lasted until nearly noon the next day. The struggles of the past twenty-four hours had demonstrated the inability of Congress to attend to the multiplicity of obligations which were being thrust upon the representatives of the American people; the complex demands of the new America were threatening to overwhelm completely the old machinery of the government. The retiring Speaker compared the tasks of the first Congresses to those of the Forty-eighth and expressed the belief that "unless some constitutional or legislative provision can be adopted which will relieve Congress from the consideration of all, or at least a large part, of the local and private measures which now occupy the time of the committees and fill the Calendars of the two Houses, the percentage of business left undisposed of at each adjournment must continue to increase from year to year." He saw little hope of relief unless the Executive and Judicial Departments could be used for the disposal of minor affairs.

March 4 was a glorious day for the Democrats. Everybody was good-natured. "Our political feelings were at their highest point of gratification and we went around shaking hands and crowing with delight," wrote one individual. "The enthusiasm of everyone over everything was intense." Dignitaries in high silk hats posed for tintypes. Many of those present had never before seen a member of their faith installed in the Executive Office; the shouting Democracy had been mute for nearly a quarter of a century. Pennsylvania Avenue was crowded. "About once in five minutes an organization would come marching along with a good, or, more frequently, a *bad* band, the men all in black or white hats and overcoats alike wearing enormous silk badges and carrying canes." Tammany turned out a thousand men, and lesser societies sent whom they could. Pennsylvania was represented by nine hundred of her militia, who performed their evolutions on Capitol Hill. The ward heelers and patronage hunters—sure signs of a democracy—were there in force.

THE FIRST SPEAKERSHIP

The inaugural ceremonies in the Senate were simple and impressive. "The Diplomatic Corps in full court dress sat behind the justices of the Supreme Court in their black silk gowns, and the House members behind them. On the other side the retiring cabinet were in front, then the General of the Army and Admiral of the Navy with their staffs in full uniform, then Senators, Governors, officers, who had received the thanks of Congress, and others. . . . Then appeared the Army and Navy officers. Then the Diplomats, the justices, the cabinet, the Vice President elect, House members and then President Arthur, who took a seat in one of two large arm chairs facing the Senate in front of the Speaker's desk [President's desk]. He was greeted with applause. Then Mr. Cleveland came in and was seated on Arthur's left. There was a perfect roar of cheers which the Vice President vainly tried to control, and some *ass* in the reporter's gallery shouted for '3 cheers for Cleveland.' They were not given and he was put out."

After the ceremonies at the Capitol came the procession to the White House grounds and, at night, "superb" fireworks. At nine-thirty the President's ball began in the new Pensions Building. Cleveland and Arthur were present; diplomats, statesmen, politicians, generals, admirals, and mere Democrats were there in great number. There was a slight odor of the Jackson inaugural of 1829, for, despite rules to the contrary, many were not in evening attire. "You would see a magnificently dressed lady on the arm of a foreign minister, in court dress, followed by three or four coarse fellows from some country village, dressed in rough jackets and colored shirts, not over clean." [1] The last were wondering, perhaps, why William C. Whitney, New York millionaire, had been appointed to the Cabinet of a Democrat.

"The tumult and the shouting" died, and the bachelor President was left alone in the White House. Two days later

[1] William E. Curtis to his mother, March 8, 1885. Curtis was Assistant Secretary of the Treasury in the second Cleveland administration. Curtis MSS.

he sent for Carlisle to come see him before his five o'clock drive. It is not known whether they talked about silver coinage, the tariff, or the patronage, but it is evident that the friendship which was to mean much to both of them was coming into existence.

CHAPTER VI   THE FORTY-NINTH CONGRESS AND
THE TARIFF, 1885–1887

THE months immediately preceding the opening of the Forty-ninth Congress in December, 1885, were exciting ones to the Democrats. A new generation of voters had come to manhood since a President of their faith had perspired over a message to Congress. There was only one cloud to mar the party horizon, and that was the fact that the Senate was Republican. The unfortunate death of Vice-President Hendricks on November 25, 1885, made it certain also that a Republican would preside over that body. The Democrats were full of ambitious political plans, and the problems which they had to attack were legion. When Carlisle, whose ability as a presiding officer had silenced all opposition, was nominated by acclamation in the Democratic party caucus for the Speakership, he reminded his political associates that victories had brought to the party "responsibilities which have heretofore rested on our opponents." He expressed the hope that the party under its new responsibilities and with its new power might reduce the expenditures, reform abuses in the Civil Service, restore good feeling in all sections of the country, and guarantee a long line of Democratic administrations—as ambitious a program as ever the brilliant Clay had dared to dream!

To Carlisle's tariff-reform associates the first Monday in December had seemed to approach slowly. Henry Watterson, whose editorials entitled "Down with the Tariff" had stirred his party throughout the summer months, grew restless; he could not view his cause with equanimity from afar. The opening day found him in Washington as special editorial correspondent for his paper, the Louisville *Courier-Journal*. No ordinary reporter could be trusted to explain satisfactorily to the country the beginning of the first real fight for tariff reform since the Civil War; only the "great scribe" whose "copy" nobody but Mrs. Watterson ever blue-penciled could do justice to the occasion. Congress convened on December 7, 1885. It was a beautiful day, and great crowds thronged the Capitol. In the House pages hurried down the aisles with flowers for favored members. At three minutes to twelve, noon, the clock behind the Speaker's desk stopped; but the clerk did not notice the fact until seven minutes later, and so the Forty-ninth Congress, with an urgent program, a Democratic Speaker, and a Democratic President at the other end of the Avenue for the first time in a quarter-century, was launched four minutes late with "every prospect of never catching up." Clerk John B. Clark, awkward and slow of tongue, stumblingly read the list of members, many of whose names he had known for two years.

When the nominations for Speaker were called for, Tucker of Virginia arose to name John G. Carlisle, while Joseph G. Cannon of Illinois presented Thomas B. Reed in the name of the Republicans. The formality of the election over, Carlisle thanked the House for its second honor to him, but he did not outline any policy for his party to pursue. The President would perform that duty. The Speaker did, however, remind his hearers that they were entering upon an important session, "more important perhaps than any that has preceded it for many years," and he spoke of the changes in administration which a new régime always requires. He sensed the coming conflict. "It is probable," he said, "that many subjects not heretofore prominent in our deliberations will engage a large share of your attention during the present Congress. It may reasonably be anticipated also that wide differences of opinion will exist upon many of these questions, resulting in long and perhaps exciting contests upon the floor; and it may be that these differences will not always be defined by recognized party lines."

Again Judge Kelley, "father of the House," administered the oath of office—done, says Henry Watterson, in a tragic tone of voice learned from Edwin Forrest. For the first time since the Civil War the "iron-clad oath" was omitted from the ceremony, an evidence that the nation was slowly exorcising the political ghosts of the conflict. The tariff reformers were pleased. The new administration, wrote Henry Watterson, had sailed like an old fashioned ship of the line out into the wide ocean of Congressional legislation "with a wet sheet and a flowing sea, and a wind that follows fast. . . . The Irish gentleman, who wanted somebody to tread on the tail of his coat, would pronounce the situation here disgustingly quiet." The peace, however, was short-lived.

The question of the rules at once came up for consideration, and it was evident that many of the members elected to the Forty-ninth Congress desired a change. The tariff-reform Democrats had a special reason for regarding the existing system with ill will. They could do little while Samuel J. Randall headed the Appropriations Committee; he had, said a news writer, "like a Jupiter Tonans . . . sat in his committee room, holding the thunder-bolts of legislation, frightening and driving his party like sheep whither he would." Congressmen had learned that without the approval of this man they could obtain none of those financial appropriations which so please constituents, and they paid politically for that approval. His power was so great, contemporary opinion believed, that "not a dollar of appropriation was possible in any direction without Mr. Randall's sweet approving will."

Many people had been waiting for an opportunity to demote Randall, and none had expected to enjoy it more than Morrison of Illinois, who for more than a month had been working on a scheme which would take from the chairman of the Appropriations Committee a part of his power. He presented his proposed changes on December 14, and pushed them with a vigor inspired by his ten years of conflict with Randall. The three main amendments which he advocated were that the former morning hour be restored in such a way that bills reported might have immediate consideration; that the unanimous consent ruling be abolished; and that the power to appropriate money, which had rested solely in the Appropriations Committee, be distributed among several committees. In the process of rearrangement seventeen general committees and eight minor ones were to be abolished. Only four new committees were proposed. The reduction was heartily approved by public-sentiment.

This attack on the situation which had grown up in Congress was a typical Democratic effort to achieve decentralization, but unfortunately it promised grave disadvantages as well as gains. Many criticized the Committee on Rules for not recommending the old procedure by which the Committee on Ways and Means had framed all tax bills and made all appropriations, but that would have offered no improvement so far as the removal of the dictatorial rule of this all-powerful committee was concerned. Decentralization was the only way by which the growing autocracy in the management of the House could be abolished; but the greater the amount of decentralization, the greater the possibility of extravagance. No committee would ask for a modest sum when its neighbor might request a handsome appropriation.

There was one man, however, who did not propose to have the legitimate rights of the Appropriations Committee scattered to the four winds of the Capitol; Samuel J. Randall could not watch the curtailment of his powers without making an effort to prevent it. Before he made his minority report to the House opposing the changes, he gave an interview to the press in which he said that the proposed action of the Democrats would, along with many other evils, open the floodgates of expenditure. It was intensely annoying to the party to have every move it made questioned by this "half-Democrat." The interview stirred the belligerent editor of the *Courier-Journal*. "Mr. Carlisle has loaded Mr. Randall with favors," wrote Watterson, "yet Mr. Randall goes about posing alternately as a hero and a martyr at Mr. Carlisle's cost." The editor did not approve of the one committee on appropriations because of the necessary slowness with which, under that system, all measures

THE DEMOCRATIC BENEDICT ARNOLD
(*Puck*, 1884)

THE OLD HOSE WON'T WORK
(*Puck*, 1884)

must move; he saw no good reason why anyone should defend the inefficiency and tardiness of Congress. "Mr. Sam Randall has something to say in the defense of the patent steam brake, which the lower House of Congress, for some inscrutable reason invented to keep itself from going too fast," read one of his editorials. "Of all the slow going old carryalls in the world, that this great lumbering Gulliver-snail of politics should conceive of a necessity to slow itself down is unmistakably a wonder of wonders; and that of all men in the world that it should be willing to trust the brakes to Sam Randall!"

Four days after their introduction into the House the new rules were adopted by an overwhelming majority, only 70 votes being cast in opposition.

This decision of the House in regard to the rules immediately presented to the Speaker the task of selecting the members of the new committees. The responsibility was heavy. "The task devolved upon Mr. Carlisle in the arrangement of the House committees was perhaps the most laborious and embarrassing that has fallen to the lot of any Speaker in this generation," said the *Nation*. "The Democratic party has for the first time in years found itself charged with the full responsibilities of government. It comes to this task not as a united body, having a clear programme and a settled platform of principles on the leading questions of the day, but with very marked divisions in its ranks on all the leading issues. This division is so marked that the leaders of the party are not even agreed on the question what is the leading issue."[1] Committee arrangement would have been far easier had not each member of the party been so sure of his especial fitness for a leading position. Carlisle had always allowed every member to express in writing his first and second choices, but he had never contemplated a demand for positions. The Speaker struggled through the entire Christmas recess on the composition of the committees and had not completed them when Congress reassembled on January 5. Shortly afterward some strange

[1] Jan. 14, 1886.

grapevine telegraph diffused the news of the various assignments, and immediately the Speaker's room was the scene of many a furtive visit by Congressmen who felt that the country could better be served if they were placed on more important committees. When the list was announced, the Eastern press accused Carlisle of having made up the committees without consulting the President. The *Courier-Journal* had early foreseen the appointment of Bland to the Committee on Coinage, and had predicted that Carlisle would be accused of slapping the President in the face. The Speaker had slapped no one; he had simply formed the committees in conformity with his ideas of Democracy. A great majority of the chairmanships went to representatives from the South and the West, nineteen to the former and twenty to the latter, while the Middle Atlantic States received eight and New England only one. This was not strange, for these first two sections represented to Carlisle the majority sentiment of the party. Moreover, their ideals more nearly fitted his conception of Democracy. Cleveland was a reformer whose election had not been due to the tariff issue; but Carlisle felt that he was under an especial obligation to lead Congress in reducing the tariff.

While the Speaker was appointing the members of the committees, Congressman Morrison, who would be chairman of Ways and Means, was preparing a conservative tariff bill. The party had never adopted radical ideas on the question, and had it been inclined to a drastic revision, the message of the President would have held it to a moderate course. Early in February Speaker Carlisle called on Cleveland to talk over the tariff question and the policies of the administration. The Speaker promised a tariff bill shortly, but in the meantime Congress was not idle. The pension bill for veterans of the Mexican War and the Bland Education bill were again debated at great length.

The controversy between the protectionists and the moderate revisionists grew more intense as the session progressed. When a petition was presented from Mrs. Sarah A. Kelly of Honesdale, Pennsylvania, asking that she be made Poet

Laureate of the United States, Henry Watterson did not disregard the opportunity for some sarcasm at the expense of her State. It was only natural that she as a Pennsylvanian, said the editor, should call upon the government; "She sees no reason why poetry should not be subsidized as well as pig-iron, particularly as poetry is an infant industry to which many American women may devote themselves." The fact that the Pennsylvania Democrats held the balance of power angered the tariff reformers. On April 13 A. K. McClure of Philadelphia wrote President Cleveland that Morrison's new tariff bill would be defeated by fifteen to twenty votes. Carlisle and Morrison were anxious to pass the tariff measure, said McClure, but they would also be glad of an opportunity to kick Randall out of the party. He expressed the opinion that conferences with the Randall group, sponsored by the President, would bring out a better tariff measure than the one which Morrison was about to present. When Cleveland first became President, he had consulted with Randall, but as he became more inclined toward tariff reform he became less willing to accept advice from the protectionist wing of his party.[1]

On April 14 Morrison reported his tariff bill, which avoided the horizontal provisions that had caused so much opposition to his proposals in the previous Congress. A great deal of time had been spent in its preparation. David A. Wells and J. S. Moore, the "Parsee Merchant," who figured so prominently in the tariff arguments of the day, had come down to Washington to aid in writing the measure. Speaker Carlisle and President Cleveland had been consulted. The bill was one for which both Democrats and Republicans might have voted without violating any real party principles, but there was no hope of its becoming a law. The manufacturing interests which had long supported protection by fair means and foul were unalterably opposed to any reduction in the tariff. Friction rapidly developed, and the apparent harmony which had been present in the opening days of the session was soon entirely

[1] Cleveland MSS. McClure to Cleveland, April 13, 1886.

gone. Morrison was particularly vindictive toward Randall.

The crisis demanded action, and influential Democrats who favored tariff reform began a determined effort to undermine the strength of the protectionist members. On May 29 Abram S. Hewitt, although denying any intention of criticizing Randall, characterized Carlisle before an anti-Randall free-trade meeting in Philadelphia as the clearest-headed and most honest-hearted statesman in public life. A few weeks later the Americus Club of the same city passed a resolution that "members of Congress representing a Democratic constituency who fail to support the Ways and Means Committee bill are false to the Democratic party and no longer worthy of the confidence of the Democrats." The resolution failed, but there could be no doubt as to who was the target of the shaft, for Randall was the only Democrat in Congress from Philadelphia. The press of the country said much about the obligations of party members. "Every man has a right to his own opinion," wrote the editor of the New York *Herald*, "but when on the faith of such action, his party places him in a position of trust and influence, it has usually been held that he is bound in honor to carry out by his votes and acts the policy of the party that has trusted him." But representatives of Pennsylvania iron and steel, of Ohio wool, of West Virginia coal, of North and South Carolina tobacco, and of Louisiana sugar remained heedless of these criticisms.

The troubles of the party were brought into relief by the unhappy fate of the tariff bill. On June 17 Morrison moved that the House resolve itself into a Committee of the Whole for the consideration of the measure, but the motion was rejected by a vote of 140 to 157. Speaker Carlisle recorded his vote in favor of consideration, and the tariff reformers gave him a hearty cheer. Thirty-five Democrats—"renegades and violators of their pledges"—voted against the motion. Randall had lost much of his power in the House, but he was still able to block Democratic legislation on the tariff question. Congressmen barely kept their words within the bounds of parliamentary license.

But it was futile for opposing Congressmen to berate one another over the tariff, for all unperceived the scene of conflict was shifting to the nation at large. However unpalatable it might be, the grim fact was that American democracy was beginning to be divided into class groups on the basis of wealth. Economic pressure had brought a consciousness of injustice to the laborer and farmer, and had given them courage to speak. They began in their own way to demand relief. The ever-increasing army the members of which were the human machines in the economic system and "the purchasables" in the political scheme at last threatened action. The Southwestern railway strike and the other labor troubles of 1885–86, with the rapid growth of the Farmers' Alliance, were portents of an approaching storm. The two old parties sensed the coming danger, and some of the leaders vaguely understood that the change meant an attack on Republican protectionism and a reshaping of the lines of Bourbon Democracy.

The gradual closing of the American frontier had done much toward bringing about this upheaval in the social order. Under the leadership of those who might otherwise have found an easy existence on the open fringe of civilization, the workers began to rebel at the inexorable laws which limited their future to factory walls and tenement rooms. Moreover, the discontent became more acute with the heavy influx of European immigrants who had left their homes largely because of their dislike for their own governments.

The dissatisfaction among laboring America had been growing for several years. In 1885 Terence V. Powderly, Grand Master Workman of the Knights of Labor, wrote an article on "the army of the discontented" for the *North American Review*, but it appealed to few. The demand of labor for a share in the rich harvest which the manufacturers were reaping found little response, and the threats of radical European anarchists could not convince conservative America that revolt and violence might take root in a democracy. No amount of writing could have persuaded the nation that the advice which

The Alarm had given its radical readers in February, 1885, could find a single individual to entertain it. No real American would stultify himself by reading such twaddle as some dunderhead had written for that paper! "Dynamite! Of all the good stuff, this is the stuff. Stuff several pounds of this sublime stuff into an inch pipe . . . plug up both ends, insert a cap with a fuse attached, place this in the immediate neighborhood of a lot of rich loafers . . . and light the fuse. A most cheerful and gratifying result will follow." [1]

The country was shocked out of its complacency, however, by the memorable Haymarket affair in Chicago in early May, 1886. Bomb-riddled policemen were mute evidence that the impossible had happened. The editor of the *Commercial and Financial Chronicle* declared that if the same punishment were meted out to the offenders, "their entire following will become convinced of the unsuitableness of America as a camping ground for Anarchists"; [2] Judge Joseph E. Gary voiced the unanimous sentiment of the people when he laid at the door of all radicals the responsibility for this outrage. But political leaders were not yet stirred to thought. In the House Speaker Carlisle was pushing forward tariff reform with all his powers, and in the Senate Nelson W. Aldrich was attacking an Interstate Commerce bill which sought to lessen the tyrannies of the railroads in the West. Both Carlisle and Aldrich were representative statesmen of the old order, the former holding the doctrine that free trade would bring peace and prosperity to all, and the latter maintaining that it was sacrilege for the Western voter to question the right of the capitalistic East to heap high its hoard regardless of the cost to the country at large.

Labor was not the only disturbing factor in this trying summer. The silver question, as has already been seen, was one of the perplexing questions which faced Cleveland and his party.

---

[1] Quoted by Charles R. Lingley, *Since the Civil War*, pp. 299–300.
[2] Vol. 42, p. 558.

The advance into the West was not yet ended, and an unwise speculation in lands which sooner or later must bring bitter disappointment continued apace. Moreover, the great Mississippi, Missouri, and Ohio valleys were being invaded by this monetary "heresy" of the unlimited coinage of silver. The tillers of the soil were becoming possessed of a hatred of the money powers of the East. On January 6, 1886, Judge J. Q. Ward, of Frankfort, Kentucky, wrote W. C. P. Breckinridge: "Nothing should be done which will affect the monetary or paying value of the silver in circulation, that which we now have and of the value we have should be kept good to pay all debts public and private as now provided by law. It is good money to the debtor class and with it the poor man can buy all the staples, corn, wheat, meat and clothes, cheaper than he has bought them for years. When you furnish a currency that will pay debts and buy necessaries at a low price it is sound. Nothing should be done to contract the amount of money in circulation, but it ought to gradually expand with population and wealth." [1]

A month later Silas Reed of Boston wrote John Sherman: "I came in from Salt Lake a few weeks ago, after being eight months at my mines there, and am astonished at the extent of the *Gold craze* in these cities. The West and South, as you see, sustain the Silver coinage and its true relation to gold—in defiance of Banks, and Capitalists, and the domination of England and Germany in regard to silver." [2] Every Congressman's mail bag was filled with letters demanding that something be done for silver.

Silver continued to fall in price despite the fact that Senator Beck was urging that the "bloated bond holders" of the East be paid in that metal. On February 27 Abram S. Hewitt presented a petition to the House deprecating the efforts of the silverites in Congress to make hundred-cent dollars worth

[1] Breckinridge MSS.
[2] Silas Reed to John Sherman, Boston, Feb. 13, 1886. Sherman MSS.

only eighty cents. The appeal was signed by the presidents and cashiers of all the savings banks of the State of New York, "representing 1,165,000 working men and women, whose combined savings amounted to $437,000,000." The financial East did not understand the extent to which the silver movement had already taken possession of the country. A free-coinage bill was defeated in the House in the early days of April by a vote of 163 to 126, and the editor of the *Commercial and Financial Chronicle* consoled himself with the remark that "it is a sad commentary upon the intelligence of our chief legislative body that 126 members should have been found inane enough to support with their votes such an extreme and foolish proposition, but this reflection is tempered by the confident feeling that the public is ahead of their representatives in this matter."[1]

The silver question was alarming not only to the financial interests of the East, but to the government officials as well. The declining gold reserve and the increasing surplus demanded immediate action of some kind, and both Congress and the President took a hand. Cleveland had refused, when he came to office, to continue the policy of bond redemptions, and the money had been allowed to accumulate in the vaults.

The Treasury was also able to make an agreement with the New York Clearing House by which that institution agreed to keep the Treasury gold fund undiminished, and this, coupled with the policy of paying out no money except on actual obligation, had enabled the government to build up its gold reserve from $126,000,000 to $151,000,000 in the first twelve months of the Cleveland administration. But this had been done at the expense of further enlarging the silver hoard in the vaults of the government. Some plan must be devised whereby the gold fund could be increased without adding to the general sum in the Treasury. In an effort to solve the problem the Department abandoned the old plan of offering a premium in order to get silver into circulation, and attempts

[1] Vol. 42, p. 446.

were begun to make that metal the only available money for a particular class.[1] It was a well-known fact that small bills did not return to the government vaults so readily as those of a larger denomination. They remained in the hands of those who made infrequent and small purchases. If silver certificates could be put into the purses of this class of people, then the new supply of money might become of permanent value. This could be done only by actually withdrawing from concurrent circulation the competing money. With this in view no new United States notes of the denominations of one and two dollars were issued from 1886 to 1890; in 1887 the first of the silver certificates of those denominations appeared.[2] In the years 1887, 1888, and 1889 slightly more than $36,000,000 of one-dollar silver certificates were issued. During the same period the one-dollar greenbacks fell from $17,000,000 to $3,000,000.[3] This creation of a vacuum into which silver certificates might be drawn succeeded in getting more silver into circulation, but it had no effect on the accumulating surplus.

The President was thoroughly convinced that it was not the business of the government to gather into its vaults an excessive sum of the people's money; but Speaker Carlisle had failed in his efforts to reduce the tariff, and the Treasury was forced to turn to the redemption of bonds in order to get the money back into the channels of trade. After 1886, however, it was necessary to secure the permission of Congress to buy

---

[1] Silver had been forced into circulation by compelling its use in the payment of government obligations wherever possible; institutions taking money from the Treasury were furnished silver free of transportation, but were compelled to pay the express charges on any other kind of money.

[2] The contraction of the National Bank notes which was going on at a rapid rate helped in this experiment. See Treasurer Jordan's report in the *Report of the Finances*, 1886, p. 44; in 1886 only $4,000,000 of silver certificates were issued. The $100, $500, and $1,000 were also discontinued from 1885 to 1890. Ibid., p. 71.

[3] The silver certificates in circulation in January, 1886, amounted to $89,000,000; on January 30, 1889, this amount had increased to $245,000,000; at the same time the United States notes in circulation increased from $298,000,000 to $303,000,000. The National Bank notes shrank from $272,000,000 to $164,000,000.

bonds in the open market, because all of those redeemable at the pleasure of the government were by that time called in. To enter the open market meant that the government must compete with all other purchasers of these securities—a decidedly costly procedure. Nevertheless, the frequent use of this expedient came to establish the Treasury in the position of an agency of relief whenever financial stringency appeared. The increasing tendency of business to call upon the Treasury to release money at every sign of such a stringency did not differ greatly from the rising demand of the people that Congress coin more money for their use. Secretary Manning said in his report for 1886 that "it is no defense of the condition of things which has grown up since the war, and which has gradually converted the Treasury into such an overshadowing fiscal power, invoked at every commercial crisis, to say that we are accustomed to it." [1] He felt that he could not enter the market as an individual buyer for the Treasury without promoting the pecuniary advantage of one group or involving the disadvantage of another. The Secretary further objected to bond redemptions on the ground that the saving in interest on the public debt was not more than $1\frac{1}{2}$ per cent.[2] The money which made up the large surplus in the government vaults came from the people of the United States, mostly through the customs and internal revenue. If the theory that the consumer pays the tariff tax is correct, then it came largely from the common people and was returned for the most part to wealthy individuals, bankers, corporation owners, and citizens of Europe. This was more than ample ground for condemnation by any Jacksonian Democrat!

Throughout the disturbing summer of 1886 Congress plodded on along its barren way. Labor disturbances, decreasing gold, increasing surplus, Western expansion into the arid

[1] P. xlii. This habit of the Treasury to come to the aid of business whenever a stringency appeared is clearly seen in reading the financial journals of the time. It is clearly proved in the tabulation of the monthly averages of public debt redemptions, as also in the calls by the Treasury.

[2] *Report of the Finances,* 1887.

plains—none of these alarming facts could divert the House from its tariff squabbles. Speaker Carlisle kept persistently at his task. Day after day he went his thoughtful course, with rarely a departure from his accustomed habits. He took the business of statesmanship seriously.

It is needless to ask what Carlisle thought of Congress, for there is no answer. He had no personal animosities, and he never imputed ulterior motives to his opponents. Throughout his Congressional career he remained a friend of everyone, and yet he must have been greatly annoyed at the opposition within his own party. He must have been tried too by the parade which passed daily before him in the Speaker's room: a withered old woman explaining in poor English that unless her son were given a job in the House as page, the family would starve; a broken soldier of the Mexican War hobbling in to seek a pension; a host of temperance advocates insistent as only ladies can be in presenting a cause; and, most persistent of all, Clara Morris, insisting that the Speaker sign his name on her curiosities made from macerated greenbacks.

The summer passed at last, and Congress adjourned on August 5. In the late autumn four "anarchists" who had been convicted of responsibility for the Haymarket affair were hanged while a mob of sympathetic onlookers sang the "Marseillaise." Terence V. Powderly's "army of the discontented" had become a reality which even Congressmen could not fail to see.

When Speaker Carlisle called the second session of the Forty-ninth Congress to order on December 6, 1886, he was not so hopeful as twelve months before. There were many lame ducks in the House, and the session must come to an end by March 4; the Speaker himself was not certain that he had been successful in the November elections, for he had already been served with notice of contest by the Knights of Labor candidate who had opposed him in his district. Morrison received Randall's outstretched hand when the two met in the hall of the House, but he turned immediately away without replying to the greeting of the Pennsylvanian. The President's communication brought some encouragement. In his first message Cleveland had called the attention of Congress to the fact that the revenues were in excess of the needs of the country, and he now stated that "in view of the pressing importance of the subject I deem it my duty to again urge its consideration." He reminded the legislators that there were no bonds of the government redeemable at the pleasure of the Treasury and that the continuation of the existing revenue system "would soon result in the receipt of an annual income much greater than necessary to meet Government expenses with no indebtedness upon which it could be applied. We should then be confronted with a vast quantity of money, the circulating medium of the people, hoarded in the Treasury when it should be in their hands. . . . Its worst phase is the exaction of such a surplus through a perversion of the relations between the people and their Government and the dangerous departure from the rules which limit the rights of Federal taxation. . . . When more of the people's sustenance is exacted through the form of taxation than is necessary . . . such exaction becomes ruthless extortion." The manner of exacting these taxes, said the President, tended to conceal their true character and extent. "The tariff tax adds to the price of things which supply their [the laborers'] daily wants, as certainly as if it was paid at fixed periods into the hands of the tax-gatherers." The amassing of huge fortunes by private individuals, he asserted, hindered "the natural growth of a steady, plain and industrious republic." But Cleveland did not favor radical changes. Reforms should be effected, he believed, in a manner thoroughly fair to the business interests.[1]

Speaker Carlisle and the other tariff reformers rejoiced over the President's message, for they felt assured that they had an ally in the Chief Executive. They decided to try again to bring a tariff measure before Congress; and they were encouraged by the report that the New York delegation in the House,

[1] *Congressional Record*, 49 Cong., 2d Sess., pp. 3-12.

which had been divided on the preceding vote for consideration, would now all vote in the affirmative. But the Republicans were not pleased, and Senator Morrill of Vermont introduced a resolution declaring that any further attempts at revisions were "inexpedient and detrimental to the revival of the trade and industry of the country." On December 14 Morrison announced that four days later he would renew the effort of the previous session to bring his tariff bill into the Committee of the Whole for discussion. There at once began a desperate attempt to force all members of the party into line. Morrison and Randall marshaled their respective forces. When the question came before the House, the tariff-reform group was again defeated. The vote was 148 to 154, twenty-eight Randallites voting in the negative. Morrison had failed in his last skirmish with his old enemy from Pennsylvania. Their days of battle were over, for Morrison, because of his failure to carry his own district, would retire from Congress on March 4, while Randall, stricken in health, was approaching the end of his long career.

Randall, having thus blocked the efforts of his party to revise the revenue system by a reduction of the custom rates began immediately to urge his own particular theory of a reduction of the internal revenue taxes. Carlisle, however, met him at every turn with a determined opposition. The Speaker believed that the people had demanded a reform in the protective system. No revenue-reduction measure which did not provide a tariff in conformity with his ideas could expect to get a hearing. Moreover, the Speaker would not recognize members who desired to introduce appropriation bills by which the surplus in the Treasury might be ruthlessly dissipated.

Speaker Carlisle agreed to meet Randall in the Democratic caucus or the Committee of the Whole with his tariff proposition, but the great Pennsylvanian knew that he had nothing to gain by such a procedure; his desire was to place before the House itself his measure for the abolition of the tax on tobacco and whiskey. He grew restive under the same treatment which he had so often administered to others. On February 5, "at the instance of many Democratic members of the House," he wrote to Carlisle earnestly requesting that he recognize some member who would "move to suspend the rules for the purpose of giving the House an opportunity of considering the question of the total repeal of the Internal Revenue taxes on tobacco." "We believe," he declared, "that the country is ready for the repeal of these taxes, and that a large majority of the House will so vote when the opportunity occurs. For a Republican to make the motion would give the Republican party all the credit accruing therefrom, and would almost certainly cause the loss of no less than two Southern States at the general election in the year 1888." The Pennsylvanian argued that "favorable action on this proposition will not interfere with other efforts that are being made to reduce the burdens of the people."

Reform editors supported the Speaker. "Cannot the wrangling, pig-headed Bourbons who are responsible for legislation in the House see that inaction and negligence may bring the country to a monetary crisis within twelve months?" asked the Chicago *Tribune*. "Tobacco and whiskey are cheap enough," declared Joseph Medill, the editor, and added, "Congress must reduce the tariff on the necessaries of life."

As the closing days of the Forty-ninth Congress approached, the appropriation bills again became a serious problem. Through his use of the power of recognition Speaker Carlisle did what he could to mold them according to his own conservative ideas, but the pressure for the consideration of local measures was insistent. ". . . It is fortunate for the Democratic party and for the country that the Speaker can be relied on to thwart all schemes for raiding the Treasury during the closing hours of the session," wrote Henry Watterson, "and it is equally fortunate that his rulings are so clear and consistent that no one questions them." It was only his determined hand which prevented the loosening of a flood of expenditures. The House deserved again the title of the "bear garden." A hundred men shrieked to the Speaker at the same moment, and confusion reigned everywhere as individual members struggled to get a hearing for their particular political measures. One Representative, on having the floor yielded to him, said to the Speaker, "I call the attention of the Chair to whom it is the gentleman from Pennsylvania has yielded, so that the speaker may recognize me when he sees me again, because I want recognition." Another, endeavoring vainly to secure recognition in order to introduce a bill for a public building in his district, "walked for two hours up and down in front of the desk, entreating, cajoling, and ejaculating, and in the end tore his bill into fragments, and deposited them as a protest at the Speaker's feet." [1]

It was at one of these turbulent sessions that Speaker Carlisle became excited and in pounding for order accidentally struck an ink bottle, which overturned on William Tyler Page, then a page in the House and now (1930) Clerk of the House. The Speaker gave him ten dollars with which to buy a new suit.

The Speaker was accused of holding up the appropriation bills for political purposes, but the charges were unjust; he was, in fact, somewhat alarmed by the situation. On February 28 he wrote the President: "We are in a very bad condition here about the appropriation bills. I am very uneasy as to the result." [2] Indeed, they were completed only by the most strenuous efforts; on the closing day, March 4, Carlisle twice turned back the minute hand of the clock.

The Forty-ninth Congress left no great record behind it. It had passed some good laws, including an act to regulate the order of presidential succession, the repeal of the Tenure-of-Office Act,[3] restrictions on the manufacture and sale of "bogus

[1] A. B. Hart, *Practical Essays on American Government*, p. 14.
[2] Cleveland MSS.
[3] Many Republicans had opposed these two measures. John Sherman wrote Senator George F. Hoar on December 16: "I fear very much that in the passage of this bill and still more in the passage of the bill to repeal the Tenure of Office Act, and also in the bill changing the order of succession, we are making dangerous concessions to our adversaries which weaken our position as a party

butter," as oleomargarine was known at the time, and the establishment of the Congressional Library on its present site; but it had failed to carry out the desires of the party in control. The course followed by many members had, indeed, been evidence of the growing looseness of party lines. According to political theory the Democrats should have opposed the Blair Education bill; yet Willis, a Kentucky Democrat, had been as warm a supporter of the measure as was its Republican sponsor from New Hampshire. On the tariff question 35 out of 170 Democrats in the House had voted against the Morrison bill, and the most strenuous efforts of the Republicans had not been able to prevent the Minnesota Representatives from supporting a low tariff. The St. Paul *Pioneer-Press,* the leading Republican paper in the State, had said that "there is now one State, reliably Republican which can be depended upon to work for the interest of the burdened consumer against the manufacturer who has grown great upon profits extorted by the power of Government."

Yet the Republicans were always able in critical situations to hold their forces as a unit. Carlisle, on the other hand, could never depend upon his party for harmonious action. He could never force his political associates to carry out what he believed to be the wishes of the people. A few days after the adjournment the *Nation* commented: "The Congress which expired at noon on Friday failed to discharge the chief duty imposed upon it. It found the revenues of the country far outrunning the reasonable requirements for the efficient support of the Government, and the public demanding a reduction of the surplus through a reform of the tariff."

The determination of the Democratic party to push tariff reform in the succeeding Congress is well illustrated in the protest which immediately greeted the rumor that Carlisle

---

and place a power in their hands that will be surely abused. I beg you to think of the fact that the Democratic party is solidly in favor of these measures, and that any division among us places us in their power. This is the subject of much earnest and almost prayful reflection among Republic Senators." Sherman MSS.

would be made Secretary of the Treasury to replace Daniel Manning, who had resigned. "What will become of our party with Morrison and Carlisle out of the next Congress?" wrote a friend to the President. "The country demands him as Speaker of the Fiftieth Congress, and as a friend to you and our party I would say Carlisle shouldn't be taken out of Congress."

CHAPTER VII   THE LAST SPEAKERSHIP: CLEVELAND'S DEFEAT

JOHN G. CARLISLE's belief that a high protective tariff was an evil which would sooner or later bring the nation to grief promised to be vindicated as the end of the 'eighties approached. Partly because an argument for or against the tariff has never greatly appealed to the mass of the American people, the protectionist Democrats had been able to defeat every effort of the majority of the party. Randall and his followers had won a ready response with their demand for a removal of the tax on tobacco, for the grower often ran afoul of the law in his effort to dispose of it; and the tax on whiskey had been the cause of one of the earliest uprisings against the revenue system. The government which levied these taxes appeared to the plodding laborer as an oppressor, but the government which made him pay more for the rough dishes from which he ate or increased the cost of his coarse woolen clothes did not offend him, for he could not understand an indirect tax; he did not comprehend the statement of President Cleveland that the tariff added to the price of the things which he bought as certainly "as if it was paid at fixed periods into the hands of the tax-gatherer." Nevertheless, Carlisle's predictions of disaster appeared to be on the verge of realization—not, it is true, because of the unseen workings of a protective system, but because of the accumulation of a huge surplus in the Treasury.

The President himself was influenced to attack protection more by the dangers and embarrassments of the surplus than by the "robbery" which had filled the great vaults of the national government. On taking office he had not been so certain of the benefits of a low tariff as the Speaker, but whether he realized it or not, his course in regard to the monetary question necessarily resulted in turning his energies toward tariff reform.

His decision to abandon bond redemptions in order to strengthen the weak gold reserve had increased the surplus to a dangerous amount, and the consequent contraction of the currency had produced a financial stringency. It was indeed a fact and not a theory which led Cleveland to join the attack on the protectionists.

The needless storage of money in the Treasury was a powerful force in giving tariff reform a semi-popular appeal. The presence of the ever-increasing surplus tended to drive into the ranks of the tariff reformers those people of the East who were not directly connected with manufacturing. The Westerners were likewise driven to support the policies of the major wing of the Democratic party, which had so long been trying to reduce the war taxes; but their support was due not so much to their opposition to a protective tariff as to their belief that the surplus was responsible for their shortage of currency.

For the Democrats the months preceding the opening of the Fiftieth Congress in December, 1887, were a period of preparation for the great battle. As early as June 2 W. C. P. Breckinridge had written Colonel Morrison urging a unified effort by the party. He advised that Carlisle make a Speakership race on the tariff issue and that Cleveland and Fairchild draw up a tariff plan before the meeting of Congress. He pointed out, "We can make nothing by giving Randall power and the sooner we know exactly what the President will really do and find out how many members we can depend upon the better." He urged that Carlisle present the matter to the President and secure his coöperation if possible. If no reform was accomplished in the field of taxation, he declared, "I personally feel like quitting." Yet before he ended the letter he added, "Of course I will never give up the fight, for if we can't win it some day we are gone." [1]

But the President had been fully converted to tariff reform, and he was now ready to lend all his energies to the movement. Although he had been compelled to begin bond redemptions again, he continued to express the belief that the excess money

[1] Morrison MSS.

gathered by the government would be of far greater value if left in the hands of the people. He fully approved his Secretary's objection to the dominating position which the Treasury had come to hold in the business world. Indeed, the President was so determined to correct the situation that he considered calling a special session of Congress in the summer of 1887. He did not do this, however, because of the fact that the economic situation improved; and he may have been influenced by Speaker Carlisle's objections to a special session.[1]

Democratic leaders were not alone in demanding tariff legislation; the reform press of the county was urging affirmative action. On November 16 the New York *Times* said: "The Democratic majority in the House of Representatives has an opportunity to shape the fortunes of its party for a long time to come. As Mr. Carlisle is the acknowledged leader of that majority, and as he has it within his discretion largely and probably decisively to influence its action, the opportunity may be justly said to be his, and the responsibility also." Little action in regard to tariff could be expected, however, until Randall was sheared of some of his power; on the twenty-second the editor of the *Times* called on Carlisle to remove the Pennsylvanian from the Appropriations Committee, but the great Kentuckian was not certain that he could safely displace his tariff opponent. "It ought to be clear to him that he cannot do anything else," wrote a reform editor. "It is as certain as sunrise that if Mr. Randall is left to himself he will defeat the tariff reform policy of the party. He may be able to do so if he is not put upon the Appropriations Committee."

Congressman Carlisle, conscious of the widespread demand for reform and assured of the fact that he would again be reelected Speaker, turned over his law practice at Covington to his partners in late November and hurried off to Washington. On the twenty-sixth he called at the Executive Mansion to discuss with the President the problem of the protectionist Democrats. The effectiveness of President Cleveland's con-

[1] Carlisle to Cleveland. Cleveland MSS.

templated message would certainly be lessened if Randall's power was not curbed in some way.

The President had some months before decided upon a novel experiment in American politics—he would focus the attention of the country upon the tariff question by presenting a message to Congress which would treat that one subject alone. He was conscious of the fact that such a procedure would do much toward retiring him to private life in the next presidential campaign, but he had honestly convinced himself that a tariff in excess of the needs of the government was an evil, and his stern Presbyterianism would allow no compromise. Throughout the summer he had kept at his message; Carlisle had been called for consultation and advice. The former Speaker heartily approved the proposed message; he suggested "substantially equal" for "equal" in one sentence, and Cleveland agreed, but substituted "at least approximately equal" instead, on his consistent theory that the longer a statement the better. Other leaders of the party came to discuss the subject with the President, but Randall never appeared at Oak View —he was not invited. The Pennsylvanian, however, was accustomed to such treatment; he had been called every name and given every slight that the more radical of the tariff reformers could think of, and yet he remained a power in the party. He was still determined to fight for the repeal of the internal revenue taxes. As early as June the *Nation* had said: "There are indications here and there that the high-tariff men of the North and the 'Moonshiners' of the South intend to make common cause to repeal the whiskey tax at the next session of Congress. Mr. Randall and Judge Kelley are at one on this point."[1] And indeed the upper South was inclined to join in such a movement. James Charn of Mount Sterling, Ky., expressed the sentiment of many Democrats in that section when he wrote Congressman Breckinridge on December 12: "I would repeal the tobacco tax entirely and if it could be done take the tax off of distilled fruits. Then touch tariff gently and in

[1] Vol. 44, p. 499.

such a manner as to interfere as little as possible with all manufacturing interests now in operation. Be sure, however, to adjust it in such a way as to stop the overflow of money into the Treasury. In short, so shape the bill as to get clear of the present surplus with as little interference with existing manufacturing institutions as can be done. Upon this depends the success of our party in the coming campaign." [1] But the Democracy was at last fighting in earnest for tariff reform, and Randall, poor in health and rich in political enemies, had come to his final battle ground.

The Democrats were hopeful, and indeed they were in a better position to push tariff reform at the end of the summer of 1887 than ever before since the Civil War. In June Carlisle had written Cleveland: "If you make a visit to St. Louis in September it might not be inconvenient for you to go out west before returning to Washington. It would be a pleasant trip in every way and . . . would certainly not injure us politically." [2] In October the President, accompanied by Mrs. Cleveland, began a "swing around the circle" which, it was hoped, would do much toward uniting the people in the Democratic cause. In Southern cities thousands of negroes who twelve months later were actually quaking for fear the reëlection of Cleveland would put them back into slavery were induced by Democratic politicians to march in the great parades; in Memphis 10,000 of them plodded through the dust while the cotton aristocracy shouted for the young mistress of the White House.

It was rumored that Carlisle would not accept the Speakership, but would take the chairmanship of Ways and Means instead and lead the tariff fight on the floor. Few, however, gave credence to the report. Carlisle could not be spared from the Chair—he had given his party the little cohesion and driving force that it had.

The efforts of the Democratic leaders to bring tariff reform to the front were not the only signs of activity preceding the

[1] Breckinridge MSS.
[2] Cleveland MSS.

opening of the Fiftieth Congress. In the cities the great industrial organizations were assiduously marshaling their defense against the attack which Cleveland and Carlisle were planning. Columbus Delano of the Wool Growers' Association and James W. Swank of the American Iron and Steel Association were pushing forward a publicity campaign in which less-known figures of other industries eagerly joined; in Virginia and West Virginia the coal miners were excited over the possibilities of free coal; on the hillsides of Virginia, Tennessee, and North and South Carolina farmers were threatening vengeance upon the only party they had ever supported if the tax on tobacco was not removed immediately; and students at the University of Pennsylvania were burning the midnight oil in laborious effort to win the $250 prize which the American Protective League of Philadelphia had offered for the best essay on the benefits of the protective system.

While Democratic politicians continued their arguments as to the best way to rid the party of Randall, the Republicans were concocting schemes for eliminating the surplus. The easiest solution would be to spend it, and members of the party were already dreaming of a great coast defense, of a shipping fleet which would be the envy of the world, and of rivers and harbors which would be a joy to the rapidly passing river captains. Public buildings were planned for every town in America. The G.A.R. was preparing a pension bill which promised to be in Washington even with the earliest Congressman. In Ohio John Sherman was urging a two-plank platform—protection and "a fair count of the vote in the Southern States" —while Knute Nelson, a Minnesota Republican who had won his election by a majority of 42,000 was preparing a defense of the Democratic tariff which Mills even now was having printed. Free traders were wielding vigorous pens in defense of their cause; Terence V. Powderly of the Knights of Labor was urging a government telegraph to the Pacific coast; silver advocates were demanding a greater use of the white metal; and sympathetic readers were moved by the newspaper serial,

Ione, the Pride of the Mill or the Daughter of the Knight of Labor.

December came at last, bringing to Washington a host of Congressmen, politicians, and parasites who settled down upon the city, some to seek favors and others to await the great tariff battle. The Democratic caucus heard Carlisle, for the second time the unopposed nominee of his party for the Speakership, plead for harmony in the impending conflict, and witnessed a fist fight over who should be doorkeeper between Clifton R. Breckinridge of Arkansas and James H. Blount of Georgia, in which the former emerged with "one drop of gore on his shirt front," while the latter suffered an abrasion under the left eye.

The early morning hours of December 5, the opening day of the Fiftieth Congress, found throngs pouring down Pennsylvania Avenue toward Capitol Hill. The weather was a bit too cold for loitering, but some no doubt stopped to look at the new Garfield statue before clambering up the unfinished west staircase to the Capitol. From every entrance eager individuals poured into the House and Senate until they had filled the galleries and the corridors, and others waited outside.

In the Senate the day was "dull and stupid." The only thing which promised excitement was the rumor that David Turpie, who for two months in 1863 had occupied the seat made vacant by the expulsion of Jesse D. Bright, would be rejected. Twenty-five newly-elected members, ten of whom had never before sat in the Senate, took the oath of office. Charles J. Faulkner of West Virginia was temporarily denied the oath, but no interesting row occurred, and no one questioned Turpie. The swearing in of the novices provided a temporary center of interest. William B. Bate of Tennessee, who had been a member of the convention which nominated Breckinridge and Lane, and a major general in the Civil War who had surrendered with the Army of the Tennessee in 1865, was sworn in along with William E. Chandler of New Hampshire, formerly Secretary of the Navy under "Chet" Arthur, and

THE LAST SPEAKERSHIP

Rufus Blodgett of New Jersey, banker and manufacturer. John W. Daniel of Virginia put away his crutch and leaned heavily upon the arm of Zebulon B. Vance of North Carolina as he hobbled down to the front of the Senate to take the oath. He had suffered many wounds in fighting for the "Lost Cause," and one received on May 6, 1864, in the battle of the Wilderness, had made him a cripple for life. By his side stood Cushman K. Davis, at one time first lieutenant in the Twenty-eighth Regiment Wisconsin Volunteer Infantry, but now leading Republican statesman of Minnesota. The two former antagonists were to feel scarcely less bitter enmity regarding the silver question than they had known during the war. Samuel Pasco of Florida, Englishman and Harvard graduate who had been wounded and captured by the Yankees at Missionary Ridge, took the oath with Matthew Stanley Quay, astute politician of Pennsylvania, who, in spite of the fact that his "stock laws" had offended his rural constituents, had become a dominating political figure in his State. In the last group to be sworn stood Francis B. Stockbridge, Michigan lumber king, and John H. Reagan of Texas, who had served as a member of the Provisional Congress of the Confederacy and as Postmaster-General in the Cabinet of Jefferson Davis. One section of the Senate gallery was enlivened by the delegation from Nebraska who had come to Washington to urge the selection of Omaha as the meeting-place of the National Republican Convention the following year.

The reorganization necessary in the House at the beginning of every Congress gave the Hall of Representatives an interesting and varied appearance. A new green carpet with flame-colored pattern furnished a lively background. Long before noon the members began to gather. The veteran of the House was still William D. Kelley, who had entered Congress in 1861, four years before the youngest member of this Congress was born. Many were graduates of Harvard; a goodly number had come from Amherst; Annapolis and West Point furnished one each; but nearly half had been educated in the school of experience. Hugh F. Finley of Kentucky, son-in-law of James Russell Lowell, had begun life for himself at the age of twenty-one, penniless and without education. Numerous members wrote in their biographical sketches that they possessed a "limited education." None, perhaps, had spent fewer days in the schoolroom than had the man who was about to be elected Speaker for the third time.

The buzz on the floor of the House increased as the hour of twelve approached. Flowers were not quite so plentiful as on the two preceding openings, but they arrived later. Outside in the corridors an old lady searched frantically for the gentleman for whom her basket of roses was intended; in the hall many Congressmen were craning their necks for a look at the long-haired gentleman from Texas who had blown out the gas in his room instead of turning it off.[1] Pages shuttled in and out among the desks on winged feet which would turn to lead as soon as their reappointments were sure. The exceptionally large number of new members wandered aimlessly about, "strangers in a new land"; many, perhaps, did not understand the connection between their presence there and the great question which was certain to be paramount in this Congress. Mrs. Carlisle, accompanied by several ladies, occupied the Speaker's row.

At twelve noon, as he had done two years before, John B. Clark called the House to order and began to read the names of the members. All was quiet until in the North gallery, directly opposite the Speaker's Chair, a somewhat battered-looking gentleman stood up, lifted his left hand, and asked that all join in singing the "Doxology." In a thin, plaintive voice he haltingly began, "Praise God from Whom All Blessings Flow." The galleries roared in laughter; the would-be religionist finished the entire four lines before the man dispatched by the Sergeant-at-Arms could reach him. As the singer was led away, he was seen to reach under his seat and

---

[1] William H. Martin, who had been elected to fill the vacancy created by the election of John H. Reagan to the Senate.

THE LAST SPEAKERSHIP 123

pull out a bundle; an immediate exodus began in that part of the gallery, for the recent labor disturbances had caused every unkempt package to be suspected as a deadly load of dynamite.

When the excitement was over, the Clerk called for nominations for the Speakership. John G. Carlisle was named by S. S. Cox of New York, while "Honest Old Joe" Cannon again gave the complimentary Republican nomination to Thomas B. Reed. The vote was 163 for Carlisle, 147 for Reed, and 2 for Brumm of Pennsylvania. A cheer went up as the new Speaker came down the aisle "with little Mr. Cox on one side and big Tom Reed on the other." W. D. Kelley, father of the House, again administered the oath of office.

The Speaker presented a masterly picture as he picked up the ivory-headed gavel on his desk. His slow-moving figure and the strong lines of his clear-cut face revealed a reserve of power sufficient for any conflict, and his dull gray-blue eyes told of a temperament not easily ruffled. Judicious, calm, courteous, he was a Southern gentleman without the effusiveness usually associated with the term. The dark hair on his head had grown a little thinner since his election two years before, and the cow-lick on the right side had moved farther back from his massive brow. The straight-lined lips were tightly closed. It is not strange that his associates said that he would have graced a Roman Forum.

When Carlisle looked out over the membership of the Fiftieth Congress, he beheld many familiar figures, but some who had been prominent in the previous session were absent. Kelley and Randall, who had grown gray in the service of Pennsylvania, were in their seats; but Morrison of Illinois was not present, and neither was the "gigantic Cobb." Jehu Baker, author of "An Annotated Edition of Montesquieu's 'Grandeur and Decadence of the Romans,' " had succeeded the former—thanks, perhaps, to the political connivance of Samuel J. Randall—while the latter had retired to till his Indiana farm. Roger Q. Mills of Texas, he of "a free poker and a taxed Bible" fame, occupied the seat which Morrison had used in the previous session and indicated his eagerness to assume the leadership of the majority by making a point of order against the confusion on the floor. William McKinley, as calm and smooth as the Speaker himself, was present, and "Tom" Reed stood in his usual place—half-way down to the pit—wondering, said the reporters, when he could stir "Sunset" Cox to wrath. General Spinola, New York Democrat, sat among the Republicans, bent and pale, leaning heavily upon the cane which the two wounds that he had received in the service of the Union made necessary. Amos J. Cummings of New York, once youthful member of Walker's filibustering expedition to Nicaragua, was beginning his first service in the House; near him stood Bourke Cockran of the same State, also a novice, dressed in a new suit, "trying to look unconcerned, and reading his newspaper upside down." Far back under the gallery sat Fitzhugh Lee, son of the great Civil War General. But one cannot name them all; there were 168 Democrats, 152 Republicans, 2 labor members, 2 independents, and one greenbacker.

If there had been any doubt concerning the policy of the Democratic party in the Fiftieth Congress, it could not have survived the address by Speaker Carlisle on taking the Chair; as the leader of his party in the House, he clearly announced the principles on which the Democrats of that Congress would act. He knew how vigorously the President intended to present the tariff question the following day. No length of service in "this trying position," he remarked, could ever enable an incumbent to begin a new term "without an oppressive feeling of embarrassment and apprehension." But his hesitancy disappeared when he approached the subject of the tariff and the justification of his arguments for its reduction which he had been preaching for a decade. "Gentlemen," said the Speaker, "there has scarcely been a time in our history when the continued prosperity of our country depended so largely upon legislation in Congress as now, for the reason that the dangers which at this time threaten the commercial and industrial interests of the people are the direct results of laws which Congress alone can modify or repeal. Neither the executive department of the General Government nor the local authorities of the several States can deal effectively with the situation which now confronts us. Whatever is done must be done here; and if nothing is done the responsibility must rest here."

Carlisle recognized, however, the fact that because of the risks to established business "hasty and inconsiderate legislation" must not be passed. "Investments made and labor employed in the numerous and valuable industries which have grown up under our present system of taxation ought not to be rudely disturbed by sudden and radical changes in the policies to which they have adjusted themselves, but the just demands of an overtaxed people and the obvious requirements of the financial situation cannot be entirely ignored without seriously imperiling much greater and more widely extended interests than any that could possibly be injuriously affected by a moderate and reasonable reduction of duties."

The Speaker thoroughly understood that a tariff revision which brought with it a financial depression would defeat the ends for which the party was laboring; he saw that a period of economic depression would strike severely at the class of people whom the Democratic party was laboring to relieve. "No part of our people," he said, "are more immediately and vitally interested in the continuance of financial prosperity than those who labor for wages; for upon them and their families must always fall the first and most disastrous consequences of a monetary crisis; and they, too, are always the last to realize the benefits resulting from a return to prosperous times. Their wages are the first to fall when a crisis comes, and the last to rise when it passes away." He laid down the doctrine that the efforts of the party "should be to afford the necessary relief to all without injury to the interest of any; . . . it seems to me that course of legislation should be pursued which will guarantee the laboring people of the country against the paralyzing effects of a general and prolonged financial depression, and at the same time not to interfere with their steady employment, or deprive them of any part of the just rewards of their toil."

This "lecture," as the Chicago *Tribune* termed it the next day, was unusual, and only the urgent demand that something be done by a party which for many years had been promising relief could have caused Carlisle to make the statements he did. He expressed the belief that his "perhaps not altogether pertinent" words would be excused "because they relate to subjects which, as we assemble here to-day, are uppermost in the minds of the people. Upon the correct solution of the questions which these subjects necessarily involve may depend not only the fate of political parties, but, what is far more important, the permanent welfare of the greatest and most intelligent constituency in the world." When he had finished, the House gave him hearty applause—but Randall sat silent in his chair.

If the course of the Speaker was "unusual," the action of the President the following day was unprecedented. The message to which Congress listened was devoted entirely to the question of tariff reform; his statement, "It is a *condition* which confronts us, not a theory," has gone down in the annals of tariff history. Congressmen who had retired to the smoking rooms had scarcely finished their cigars before the message was ended; the document was read in just twenty-six minutes, and yet it served to arouse America as few presidential declarations have. The metropolitan press sent out scores of reporters, who fell upon manufacturers, producers of raw materials, college presidents, and leading statesmen without mercy in an effort to extract from them their views on the question of the tariff. Democrats prepared to mail thousands of copies of the message as Christmas gifts to their constituents. In Chicago Joseph Medill's Republican *Tribune* began its fight for tariff reform.

Although President Cleveland's emphasis upon the fact that tariff was a tax aided in arousing public sentiment, it also concentrated the entire energies of the Republican party into an effort to divert the thoughts of the country from this point. The American Protective Tariff League began a vigorous drive to secure one thousand new members willing to become "Defenders of American Industry" at one hundred dollars each. James G. Blaine, then in Paris, gave out an interview in which he decried the reform efforts of the Democrats and recommended immediate repeal of the tax on tobacco, which he said was one of the necessities of the workingman. "Watch, if you please, the number of men at work on the farm, in the coal mine, along the railroad, in the iron foundry, or in any calling, and you will find 95 in 100 chewing while they work." [1] "Never has hurled spear been more deftly caught, or sent back with more startling swiftness and sure aim," wrote "A Republican" in the *North American Review*,[2] but the New York *Herald's* comparison between the relative values of Blaine's "free chaw of terbacker" and Cleveland's cheaper clothes was pregnant with thought for many.

The message of the President brought encouragement to those who had almost become hopeless of any action by Congress. On December 6 R. R. Bowker wrote Representative Breckinridge urging that the Democrats take some action "which means something instead of everything." A few hours later he added the postscript: "Since the above was dictated, comes the message. How it clears the air like a thunderstorm on a sultry day." [3] "Permit an absolute free trader to congratulate you upon the steps taken in your recent message to Congress," wrote Henry George, and Congressman Clifton R. Breckinridge of Arkansas declared that "it will be read in the hut as well as in the mansion." [4] "My gratification is intense," said Melvin W. Fuller, and the legislature of Maryland

[1] New York *Tribune*, December 8, 1887.
[2] January 1888, Vol. 146, 1–13.
[3] Breckinridge MSS.
[4] Cleveland MSS.

passed a joint resolution approving the message. "The most courageous document that has been sent from the Executive Mansion since the Civil War," commented the *Nation*.

In spite of the vigorous beginning, the cause of tariff reform was delayed for a time by the contest which Carlisle faced for his seat in the House. The fact that there was a question whether he was legally a member of Congress had not prevented his being elected Speaker, but the possibility of unseating him was eagerly seized by the protectionists. Carlisle had indeed come dangerously near being defeated in the fall elections of 1886, as much because of the inexcusable indifference of himself and his associates as on account of the efforts of the high-tariff advocates to defeat him. No Republican candidate had presented himself in the campaign, and few Democrats had taken any note of the appearance of a Knights of Labor nominee, George H. Thobe, who was commonly expected to receive but a handful of votes. In keeping with his lifelong policy of asking no one to vote for him, Carlisle had exerted little effort in the campaign, and the slender opposition which he had met in the ten years he had represented the Sixth Kentucky District had caused the party to grow careless. On counting the votes on November 3, it was found that the Knights of Labor candidate had polled a majority in the city of Covington and Kenton County. During the day hundreds of laborers had absented themselves from the factories and the shops of Cincinnati where they worked in order to vote for their candidate, and few others had taken the trouble to go to the polls. It looked for a time as though the unknown candidate of an unrecognized party had defeated a national statesman; when, however, the vote had been tabulated in the back counties and had shown a majority for Carlisle, the cry immediately went up that the returns had been delayed until enough ballots could be forged to elect him. Rumors that closed carriages occupied by Democratic politicians had been driven through the streets of Covington at midnight on election day filled the laborers with resentment. Many sympathized with Thobe because he was the under dog in the contest.

The Republicans had certainly been at work among the Covington voters who earned their living in the shops of Cincinnati, but there was no evidence of an organized effort to defeat Carlisle such as there had been to defeat Morrison in Illinois, where, under the direction of Randall, men had been paid "three dollars a day and expenses" for that purpose. This close call for the Democrats had been caused entirely by their own carelessness; the entire vote cast had not equaled that received by Carlisle's opponent two years before. Editors derived much fun from their Shakespearean parody: "Tho-be or not Tho-be."

Carlisle did not appoint the Committee on Elections. On December 12 he called Crisp of Georgia to the Chair and informed the House that "it is well known that there is a contest pending which makes it improper for me, as presiding officer of the House, to appoint, in the usual manner, the Committee on Elections. I have left the Chair, therefore, for the purpose of asking the House to excuse me from the performance of that duty, and to take such proceedings in reference to the matter as its judgment may dictate. I have no suggestion whatever to make except to say that the formation of the other committees of the House will be facilitated by having this subject disposed of at the earliest date that will suit the convenience of the members." The House thereupon refused to appoint a special committee to consider the case, and decided to elect the membership of the Elections Committee.

The report of the Committee on Elections was made on January 17, Speaker Carlisle being absent from the Chair, without having named anyone to preside in his place. There is no evidence for the statement that "a feeling existed that the methods of his friends would scarcely bear exposure to the gaze of a fastidious public, and to escape the charge of complicity he had absented himself from the Capitol on a plea of illness during the consideration and settlement of the case."[1] He was in fact ill and had been so for some time; in the evening his personal physician was called to the Riggs House, and it was believed that he was about to suffer an attack of pneumonia. In the House the Chaplain offered public prayer for his recovery. Samuel S. Cox of New York was elected Speaker *pro tempore*.

The majority report of the Committee recommended that Carlisle be declared elected from the Sixth Kentucky District; the minority report, while it agreed that the allegations of Thobe had been disproved, asked that the case be re-opened. A re-opening of the case, however, could scarcely be justified except on the grounds that the actual ballots from many of the districts in question were complete forgeries, and that the man who brought them was an impostor. Thobe was permitted a seat on the floor of the House during the discussion of the case; here he heard Henry Cabot Lodge argue that, although there was no definite evidence warranting such action, the case should be sifted again because of the "enormous disparity of political position between the contestant and the contestee." Such a course was justified, said Lodge, if only it might do something toward removing the feeling among workingmen that the trusts, rings, money, and position were against them. This solicitude for the worker was something new for the narrow New England aristocrat. When Lodge had finished, Crisp asked that the contestant be given unanimous consent to address the House. Thobe made a creditable speech, which, as printed in the *Congressional Record* the next morning, displayed a knowledge hardly to be expected of a mechanic; indeed, those who had been endeavoring to do justice to this workingman had, before the *Record* went to press, also done justice to his English and his logic!

When the resolution to declare Carlisle the elected member of Congress was put to a vote, 140 voices spoke in the affirmative and 3 in the opposition—181 either were absent or sat

[1] Alexander, *History and Procedure of the House of Representatives,* p. 46.

THE LAST SPEAKERSHIP

silent when the roll was called. A political party with a national program before it and an excess of the necessary votes had by inexcusable indifference brought itself into contempt by failing to provide a quorum at this critical moment—and Randall was not to blame. Republican orators were not wholly wrong in declaring that the Democratic party was incapable of consistent action. There was no objection to Carlisle as Speaker, but certainly the Republicans did not feel obliged to lend a helping hand to a party which expected to take a course opposite to what they desired. After three days of strenuous effort the Democratic leaders were able to secure the presence of enough of their members to constitute a quorum, and Carlisle was declared elected.

When his right to a seat in the Fiftieth Congress had been determined, Carlisle proceeded to the selection of the committees. The most important committee was that on Ways and Means, and it was one of the chances of politics that William R. Morrison of Illinois, who had so persistently led the reform forces, should now be absent from Congress. The Speaker selected Roger Q. Mills of Texas to head the committee, and with him a group of sympathetic members who included only one representative from a State which in any way indulged in manufacturing. Mills was a somewhat irascible but hardworking Congressman who had ably represented his district in Congress for the past fifteen years. A liberal whenever any question of justice was concerned, he was an uncompromising partisan in politics. To him free trade and free speech were the cardinal tenets of Democracy. He would not compromise his political ideas in any way; no representative of big business could ever have a word with him. The "Parsee Merchant" once sought to induce him to talk with W. O. Havemeyer, but when the representative of the sugar interests entered one door, Mills left by the other. It was to be expected that his tariff bill would reflect his uncompromising attitude.

The first announcement of Chairman Mills of the Ways and Means Committee was that no more testimony would be taken in regard to the tariff question. He explained that these "hearings" had been growing longer and more futile. Carlisle supported Mills, for he felt that the people whose opinions Congress should know never came to present their cause. The greasy mechanic, the soil-stained farmer, and the tired laborer never presented themselves.

Mills had brought with him to the Fiftieth Congress a tariff bill already drafted and printed; he had spent much time in preparing it, but his associates forced him to abandon many of its provisions. In spite of unlimited assistance from theoretical free-traders and from clerks of the Treasury Department, it took the Committee nearly four months to form a bill. As usual, the minority was not allowed access to the committee rooms while the majority was framing the tariff; but great was the gossip which spread concerning the origin of the measure. Congressman James Buchanan of New Jersey said on the floor in the course of the debate:

> The parentage of that bill is unknown. The authors of its being have not yet felt proud enough of their offspring to claim their own. Even its birth-place is uncertain. Whether it came into existence in some dark cellar of the Capitol, attended by free-trade theorists and interested importers, or in some out-of-the-way place in the Treasury building, by clerks hired and paid by the nation to do other work, or in some back room at some hotel, while members of this House pored over Adam Smith, Frank Hurd's speeches, and Cobden Club tracts, and Kentucky inspiration flowed free, it has not yet been vouchsafed for us to know.[1]

The President had sent his urgent message to Congress on December 6, and on April 2 following, the Democratic tariff bill was presented to the House. It was a partisan measure which tended to be sectional, as was stated by Tom Reed when the bill came up for debate. With cyclonic force the tariff-reform spirit hit the Canadian border, said the gentleman from

[1] *Congressional Record*, 50th Cong., 1st Sess., Apr. 26, 1888, p. 3410.

THE LAST SPEAKERSHIP 133

Maine, but the violent storm in that region became only a gentle breeze before it reached the South. Indeed, the tariff on sugar was reduced but little, while the tariff on wool was entirely removed. Yet one part of the South felt the proposals of the Mills bill keenly. Throughout January and February there was great excitement in the squalid villages which clung precariously about the black mouths of coal mines on the hillsides of Virginia and West Virginia; huge mass meetings were held for the purpose of protesting against the Democratic proposal to place coal and coke on the free list. The mine owners had convinced the workers that free coal meant unemployment and starvation, and, although ignorant of the reasons for their rapidly mounting debt at the company store, the laborers were bitter against "Mr. Carlisle, the distinguished Free Trade crank." The editor of the Pocahontas, Va., *Headlight* closed an editorial on the subject with the comment: "We very cordially regret that Mr. Thobe didn't run a little livelier race." [1]

The internal revenue tax on tobacco and spirits was another source of Democratic division. On December 8, 1887, the Virginia House of Delegates adopted a resolution "That the Senators from Virginia be instructed and our Representatives in the Congress of the United States be requested to use their best efforts to secure the repeal at an early day of the entire internal revenue system of taxation, and failing in that, to secure if possible the repeal of so much of said system as imposes a tax upon tobacco in any of its forms and upon spirits distilled from fruits." The Republicans were alert to this discontent in the section from which the reformers drew their strength. One member wrote John Sherman that when the proper time came some Republican should "make a proposition to reduce the revenue by taking the tax off sugar and tobacco except cigars that sell for 10 cents each, retail, and upwards—and a clear speech made that will show the workingman who uses tobacco to chew and smoke in pipes or 5 cent

[1] Jan. 26, 1888.

cigars, that the Republican party is anxious to lift all the tax possible from him."[1] North Carolina tobacco growers approved this principle.

On April 17, 1888, general debate on the Mills bill began in Congress, and the time devoted to it reveals the importance attached to the question. Springer, who presided over the 151 speeches, declared that they should always be known as "The Great Tariff Debate of 1888," but in a few years the discussion was forgotten; only three speeches—those of Reed, McKinley, and Carlisle—justify a reading at the present time.

Democratic opposition to a high tariff had one fundamental basis, and that was the contention that the protective policy took from the laboring man his sustenance and gave it to the wealthy. In this great effort of the party in 1888 victory would depend upon proof of the assertion. In order to achieve success the Democrats must first disprove the Republican statements that the protective tariffs added to the wages of the laborer, and then demonstrate that the tariff was indeed a tax paid as truly, as the President had suggested, as though given to the tax-gatherer at stated intervals. Science came to the aid of the Democrats, and three statisticians working independently of one another—Worthington C. Ford, E. B. Elliot, and Simon Newcomb—decided that only a small part of wages was affected by high-tariff rates. The highest estimate of the labor interest involved left 94 per cent of the wages of a community which was not benefited by protective rates.

The Republicans in their arguments turned far afield from the economic analysis which the Democrats were endeavoring to introduce. The pleasant practice of baiting the English was not overlooked; Cleveland and his cohorts were seeking, announced the protectionists, to lead the United States to the throne of Great Britain as an offering upon the altar of free trade. The membership of the Cobden Club served as evidence of this unholy alliance, although inconsiderate Democrats sometimes reminded the House that there were Republican names

[1] L. T. Hunt, Springfield, O., Dec. 13, 1887 to Sherman. Sherman MSS.

on this scroll of the unpatriotic. The issues of slavery and the Civil War were not forgotten, and along with those lists of members of the Cobden Club went the roll of those who had seen service in the Confederacy, and whose arguments for low tariff should therefore not be regarded with seriousness. Many Republicans had objected to the appointment of L. Q. C. Lamar, Civil War soldier and diplomat, to the Supreme Court bench.

The protectionists did not neglect to point out the inconsistencies in the Mills bill. Congressmen Guenther's query, "If 30 per cent is outrageous on Republican Epsom salts, why is 55 per cent any less so on Democratic castor-oil?" was difficult to answer. The arguments for the removal of the internal revenue levies were also telling. The tariff-reform assertion that an individual was taxed from babyhood to the grave through the customs dues found little response, but many were impressed by the words of the Republican Congressman who declaimed: "Hardly has the baby been ushered into this internal-tax ridden world and stands in need of a little paregoric or a few drops of essence of peppermint, or some other remedy to soothe the griping in its little bowels, up steps the internal-revenue collector, clothed with all the powers of the General Government, with the Army and Navy at his back, and inexorably extracts from the little yelling infant 315 per cent internal revenue on the paregoric, 425 per cent on the essence of peppermint. It is pay or yell. Being a bright American child, with an eye to business, it takes the paregoric, because that bears the lowest tax, saving thereby 90 cents on the dollar and giving an object lesson in Economy is wealth." "Farmer Goodman" figured quite prominently in the discussion. "The nice old gentlemen" unfortunately suffered from rheumatism and was compelled to pay $3.60 every year for alcohol in which to dissolve the gum of camphor with which he rubbed his aching limbs. This expenditure was necessary because the Democrats had refused to abolish the revenue taxes. Mrs. Goodman believed that the tariff tax on the shawl which she had bought the year before was an injustice, but the young son, generous enough to admit that there was a tax, pointed out that it was far more than compensated for by the extra price of the wool which they received from their sheep. The Democrats were in some instances at least keen enough to see that not all the Goodmans who bought shawls owned a flock of sheep.

The Republican argument of the necessity for a high tariff to furnish protection to "infant industries" had disappeared, but, said Wickham of Kentucky, ". . . we are told that the farmer and laborer ought to pay the present rate of taxation cheerfully because the manufacturer needs it and uses it to pay the farmer better prices for his produce, and the laborer better wages for his service."[1] The Democrats denied the fact that the tariff left the laborer with an advantage at the end of the year. The levy on the goods which he bought, according to their philosophy, was uncompensated. The party was aware that one great ambition of every farmer on the Western plains was to own a wooden house, and Mills pointed out that it was far more important that the Westerners should get out of their sod huts than that the Michigan lumber kings should receive millions of dollars through the tariff on lumber.

The climax of the protectionist argument came on May 18, when William McKinley displayed on the floor of the House a suit which, according to the bill held in his other hand, had cost him $10. To the unwary this suit was proof that the tariff did not add to the cost of clothes; but Mills was not convinced. He had not said that suits could not be bought for $10; he had said that the tariff tax increased the price which the wearer paid for his clothes. Upon investigation the author of the Mills bill found that the suit which McKinley had shown actually cost $4.98, and that the tariff had permitted it to be sold at $10.71, but that in order to fall just under the price at which the suit could have been imported, the merchant had left off the seventy-one cents. When this became known, Republican plans for distributing photographs of the suit for

[1] *Congressional Record,* 50th Cong., 1st Sess., May 16, 1888, p. 4293.

campaign purposes disappeared as quickly as did the argument that the tariff was not in any way a tax.

Speaker Carlisle was the driving force behind the tariff-reform efforts of the Democrats in the Fiftieth Congress. By his power of recognition, which at times he exercised in an almost autocratic way, he guarded the surplus in the Treasury so that it might not be disbursed in reckless spending. The Blair Education bill again failed to get consideration, and by various rulings measures which would needlessly have depleted the surplus were refused consideration. Carlisle believed that no greater danger threatened the States than the possibility that the surplus would be used for purposes which would take from them their right to determine their individual and local affairs. He realized that should the floodgates of expenditures be forced open, the hope of tariff reform would be greatly reduced; Congressmen who had once known the pleasures of a well-filled "pork-barrel" would scarce forego them in order to reduce the taxes of a class who could see no evidence of the evil which they suffered. The arguments which the Democrats were beginning to drive home had rested upon the visual evidence of the exactions of a protective tariff. Many Republicans saw that a large surplus and a high protective tariff were incompatible; some perceived the use to which the Democrats were putting the presence of the great fund in the vaults of the government. Cannon of Illinois, in speaking of the Cleveland message and the "foundling now called the Mills bill," said that they "both use the surplus as the fulcrum wherewith to apply the free trade lever to dislodge the protective system." [1]

The Speaker did not content himself with the powers which he could exercise as presiding officer, but also sought to direct the course of legislation through his work as floor leader in Committee of the Whole. With Springer presiding over this committee, Carlisle closed the debate on the Mills bill on May 19. Of the argument of "the gentleman from Maine" on the

[1] *Congressional Record,* 50th Cong., 1st Sess., May 2, 1888, pp. 2345-2346.

preceding day, he said that absolute freedom of trade was no more the logical point to which the free trader should go than total restriction was the ultimate goal of the protectionists. In his two hours of discourse, said Carlisle, Reed had not touched upon the actual situation which confronted the Congress—"a situation which makes it the imperative duty of the Representatives of the people to reduce the revenues before this Congress shall adjourn." The Speaker pointed out that the Treasury held at the close of April $136,000,000, every dollar of which "had been taken by law from the productive industries and commercial pursuits of the people at a time when it was sorely needed for the successful prosecution of their business, and under circumstances which afford no excuse whatever for the exaction." He regarded as one of the greatest dangers threatening the government "the growing disposition among those who represent particular classes and special interests to disregard the checks and break down the barriers of the Constitution in a promiscuous scramble for a division of the public treasury." As he declared:

When the Government has collected or is collecting, more money than its needs, the people, realizing the injustice of a policy which unnecessarily deprives them of a part of their earnings, are almost sure to demand its return in some form or other. If the Government may rightfully exercise the power of taxation for other than public purposes, it is difficult to convince those who pay the money that it cannot also exercise the power of appropriation for other than public purposes. It is safe to say, therefore, that so long as this policy shall be continued, not only will largesses and bounties for the promotion of purely private interests be demanded, but new fields for the exercise of legislative power and new objects for the appropriation of the public money will be discovered.

Before two years passed, the Harrison administration had made the wisdom of these words evident.

"The Communism of Business" was a much-used phrase in

THE LAST SPEAKERSHIP

the tariff-reform argument in these days; many feared that the government through tariff exactions might become the possessor of all money and, in consequence, the necessary supporter of all individuals and industries. Even New England was beginning to realize that there were two sides to the tariff controversy. As early as January 11, 1888, William F. Jones of Boston wrote concerning this new attitude: "As an illustration of the awakening in Boston in tariff matters, I mention that at the table at which I sat at the Tariff Reform dinner were about a dozen friends of whom not more than three or four would have attended such a dinner five years ago. Some of them have completely changed sides in that time and others have come part of the way."[1] In April, however, Arthur T. Lyman could still complain of New England persistence in refusing tariff reform: "The trouble with them is that they are playing for the Presidential trick and they think 'Protection' is trumps."[2] From Missouri, Frank P. Blair wrote for copies of the tariff-reform speeches of the leading Democrats: "I expect to have a word to say next fall from the stump. . . . I want these speeches to furnish me with modern powder and ball. Never fear. The 46 million farmers (when they understand this problem) will cease to pay tribute to the 10,000,000 mechanics' employers."[3] But at the same time James J. Wilson, Jr., of Hillsboro was writing John Sherman: "I shall do my best to re-capture the Government from the Rebels this fall. And if the Tariff question is properly handled Missouri will wheel into line."[4]

While Carlisle was endeavoring to push the Mills bill through Congress, the presidential campaign of 1888 was beginning to get under way. It was, in fact, the coming election, rather than the immediate tariff question, which had turned the discussion into the "great debate." Tom Reed appropriately

[1] Breckinridge MSS.
[2] Arthur T. Lyman to W. C. P. Breckinridge, Boston, April 23, 1888. Breckinridge MSS.
[3] Blair to Breckinridge, May 28, 1888. Breckinridge MSS.
[4] Sherman MSS.

remarked that the most insignificant thing in the arguments concerning the Mills bill was the Mills bill itself. Speaker Carlisle, however, was not willing that the campaign should swallow up the labor done; he drove Congress forward, and by caucus vote laid down the ruling that no Congressman should leave Washington for the Democratic convention without first obtaining a pair for his vote. He knew that regardless of the many facts which made the President unpopular, his party was bound to nominate Grover Cleveland or retract on the question of tariff reform. During these busy days the Speaker found time to call at the Executive Mansion for a conference regarding the platform of the party. A few days before the convention opened, Senator Gorman left for St. Louis with a set of resolutions tucked safely in his pocket; Cleveland and Carlisle had seen the paper, and it bore "interlineations, changes, and corrections in the handwriting of those two great tariff reformers." [1]

On May 31 the advance wave of the oncoming delegations —California, Oregon, and Nevada—arrived in St. Louis. The Californians, dressed in flame-colored suits and provided with a seemingly inexhaustible supply of twenty-dollar gold pieces, brought with them 100 cases of native wine for the purpose of showing "friends from the East what California can produce." Far-off Alaska was represented for the first time in a National Convention. The delegates from the Pennsylvania Democracy, all shouting for Cleveland, reserved thirty rooms at the Southern Hotel.

Early on the morning of June 3, while its godfather lay sick in bed, the Samuel J. Randall Club of Philadelphia, sixty-two men strong, with blue suits, high white hats, white gloves, and canes, marched to the convention quarters. Every hour new delegations poured into the Union Station, each one seemingly more bizarre than the last. Tin helmets, linen dusters, high hats, canvas suits, and red bandannas gave the city the appearance of a great circus ground with the actors on parade.

[1] Champ Clark, *My Quarter Century of American Politics,* Vol. II, 216–217.

THE LAST SPEAKERSHIP

As a vast throng panted in the great hall on the morning of June 5, the Democratic National Convention was called to order. The floor and the two tiers of galleries were crowded to suffocation. Numerous bands blared forth their lively tunes, and flags waved frantically. In all the crowd, though many had read the scurrilous pamphlet which pictured the President as "the Beast of Buffalo" who became drunk and beat his wife until she fled from the Executive Mansion, few doubted that Grover Cleveland would be nominated; but the presentation of a solid silver gavel by the Colorado delegation was significant of the fact that not everyone was wholly interested in the question of tariff.

The nomination of Cleveland by acclamation announced to the country that the Democrats expected to continue the reform fight. Seven days later, in a letter to the Reform Club of New York, the President clearly expressed his views on the question before his party: "The reform which of all others at the present time is most needful, is a reduction of the tribute exacted by the Government from our citizens. I do not believe our country can long survive the loss of confidence and the disappointment, which must result in the minds of the people, from a consciousness that their earnings and their incomes are uselessly and ruthlessly diminished, under the pretext of supporting the instrumentality which they have created for their safety and benefit. The Government is theirs. They have decided its purposes; and it is their indisputable right, to demand that its cost shall be limited by frugality, and that its burden of expenses shall be carefully measured by the actual needs of its maintenance..When it wilfully takes from the people, through the power they have entrusted to it, more than sufficient to meet their needs, the creature has rebelled against its creator, and the masters are robbed by their servants."

The Republican National Convention met on June 19 and nominated Benjamin Harrison, and the fierce political fight of 1888 began.

While the two great parties were selecting their nominees,

Speaker Carlisle and his tariff-reform associates continued their labors at Washington. The Mills bill reached a vote on July 21—nearly eight months after the President's urgent message. The measure was passed by a majority of 162 to 114. Four Democrats voted against it. The announcement in the House that Randall, too ill to vote, was paired against the bill, which he designated as "a patch-work on the existing law," brought groans and hisses from the Democrats. Although the Pennsylvanian's little army had at last melted away, the leader could not give up the fight—to do so would mean the end of his political career as a representative from the protectionist State of Pennsylvania.

The Mills bill went to the Senate; and while a new measure was being prepared there as a substitute for it,[1] the country was witnessing the presidential conflict. Matthew Stanley Quay, newly elected Senator of Pennsylvania, "whose career as a public official left much to be desired," directed the Republican campaign. Cheap coats, cheap labor, and cheap men were decried by the protectionists, and tons of literature were sent over

[1] Many members of Congress had early admitted that the Mills bill would be passed in the House by the Democrats, but the representatives of the industrial interests who were closely allied with the protectionists in Congress at this time fought the measure vigorously and urged its defeat in the Senate. James W. Swank, Secretary of the American Iron and Steel Association, wrote Senator Morrill on April 18: "I am sorry to have your opinion of the probability of the Mills bill passing the House. If such a calamity should occur would it not be possible for the Senate to substitute a financial measure of its own, providing, for instance, for the repeal of the tobacco taxes and for the 20-per-cent reduction in sugar embodied in the Mills bill in the Senate and afterwards send it to a Committee of Conference would certainly result in legislation unfriendly to many industries, and besides it would be a victory for the Democrats, who would make the most of it in the Presidential campaign. No matter how nearly perfect the Senate might make the Mills bill it would still be the Mills bill. Furthermore, the Senate amendments might be rejected, first by the House and afterwards by a Committee of Conference. An entire Senate substitute for the Mills bill would, on the other hand, have a standing of its own. It would embody a Republican policy. If it should become a law the credit would be with us; if rejected we could afford to go to the country on the merits of the legislation we had proposed." Morrill MSS.

America with the hope of convincing the laborer that high wages depended upon high tariffs.

A great deal has been written about the "blocks of five" which were voted and the "fat" which was fried out of the industrial leaders in this campaign, but much which history would like to know was reduced to ashes when the Republican records were burned. "Dead men tell no tales" was a part of the political philosophy of Quay and Wanamaker.

The mosquitoes came up in legions from the swamps by the river's banks, and "Potomac malaria" drove many a high official from Washington; but Congress plodded through the hot summer and on into the dog days of the fall before the Democrats would give up the tariff fight. Whoever could be spared was permitted a few days' leave for the purpose of preaching Democratic tariff gospel in the country; in September Carlisle relinquished his gavel for a time and went down to Kentucky to attend to his own campaign for reëlection. The Democracy of his hilly district gathered in convention at Covington on the nineteenth. They had come to nominate the man who had grown up a poor boy among them and who was now Speaker of the House, and they had come, too, to hear what he would say about the taxes which were burdening them and the trusts which were stealing their money.

Carlisle was received by his constituents of the Sixth Kentucky Congressional District with an enthusiasm which only honest tillers of the soil can give. When the last husky shout of applause had died away, he drove straight at the points which he wished to make, using a language which all those present could understand. "The great question before this country," he said, "is the question of federal taxation. It makes but little difference whether I am elected to Congress or not, but it is of overwhelming importance to the people that the next House of Representatives should be democratic, and that the next President should be a democrat also." Regarding the tariff and the proposal of the Republicans to reduce the revenues by increasing the taxes, he declared: "It might as well be said that a man can make himself rich by picking his own pocket. In addition to the fact that it [protective tariff] is imposing enormous and unnecessary burdens upon the people it is the parent of trust and combination and conspiracy to control products and prices of the necessary articles which the people are compelled to use." Carlisle certainly did not agree with James G. Blaine's statement that a trust was a private affair not to be noticed by the government. "Larceny is a private affair too. The highwayman who meets you on the public road and demands your money or your life is engaged in the transaction of a private enterprise, but still the law takes cognizance of his act and punishes it as a crime." Moreover, "the plumed knight" had not been in a favorable position from which to view the interests of the American workingman, farmer, or consumer. "The top of Mr. Carnegie's coach, as it bowls along with its liveried outriders over the hills of Scotland, is not a good place to look at the interests of America," said Speaker Carlisle. "Nor are the festal halls of Cluny Castle a very good point either. . . . Had he come here to his own country and mingled with the farmers, with the consumers, with the laboring men of the land, he would have a far better opportunity to know what they desired than he could possibly have dining and wining with the aristocracy of Europe." He also denied the Republican assertion that a high tariff brought higher wages.[1]

The Cleveland campaign continued apace, and the mail bags of the Executive Department told the President of the hostility of the G.A.R., of the fear which the negroes had that he would return them to slavery, and of the "Cleveland poles" which were being erected in the country. One erected at Haynes Junction was described by the postmaster there as "a solid Hickory measuring sixty eight feet; it is a beautiful pole."

Congress plodded along, and eventually adjourned on October 20 with the Mills bill still unpassed. Never before had Congress sat so long in one session, and the record was exceeded

[1] Baltimore *Sun*, September 19, 1888.

"THE TRIBUTE TO THE MINOTAUR"

The Interests of All Other States Sacrificed to the Protection Monster of Pennsylvania. (*Puck*, 1885)

THE LAST SPEAKERSHIP

only when the son of another Presbyterian minister occupied the White House and another Kentucky Democrat the Speaker's Chair.[1]

The Republicans won the election, but history has as yet rendered no verdict as to what part the tariff question played in the contest. Cleveland received only 168 electoral votes out of the 401, but his popular vote was almost a half-million larger than that of Harrison. Hope of tariff reform was gone for the present; Congress was now Republican in both branches; and John G. Carlisle, although reëlected to membership, was serving his last year as Speaker of the House of Representatives.

The short session of the Fiftieth Congress could hope to do nothing in regard to the tariff; the Senate would certainly block a reform measure, and the President would most assuredly veto a protective-tariff bill should it by any means be shoved through the House. That strange quirk in American politics which compels a Congress and a President to labor on after defeat had its demoralizing effect. The President faced tedious and difficult days. "The gloom of defeat was upon his followers; his enemies were little disposed to consider a discredited leader, as they chose to designate him; the people, a majority of whom had voted for him, had their faces turned toward the rising sun; and foreign nations approached him convinced that his day of power was gone forever."[2] In his difficulties Cleveland turned to Speaker Carlisle. On December 1 he wrote: "I have understood that you were to be in the city to-day. If this reaches you could you call and see me before half past four. If that is impossible cannot you come to Oak View to-morrow? There isn't a man in the United States I would give more to see than you just at this time."[3] On the sixteenth he again wrote, "I dont like to trouble you but I am not going

---

[1] Wilson administration—the 62nd and 65th Congresses; Champ Clark, a Kentuckian elected from Missouri, was Speaker.

[2] McElroy, *Grover Cleveland, The Man and the Statesman*, II, 302.

[3] Cleveland-Carlisle MSS.

to church to-day and should be very glad to see you at such time as you can make it convenient to come to me."[1]

The inability of the tariff reformers to accomplish anything in this session of Congress only whetted the appetites of the revenue reformers; the border States were even more urgent in their demands that the internal revenue taxes be removed. Harry Weissinger of Louisville wired W. C. P. Breckinridge on February 22, 1889: "Tariff reform, however desirable, is now impossible but it is possible to abolish the tobacco tax and thus conserve the tobacco planting and manufacturing interests of Kentucky. Tobacco growers favor the repeal to a man while only two or three larger manufacturers outside of the state oppose it. Are our people to be the victims of theory and etiquette when practical relief can be had for the taking? Show this to Mr. Carlisle."[2]

But Congress ended with nothing accomplished. It had not been a thoroughly creditable one; Carlisle's refusal to count a quorum if sufficient members did not make themselves known came dangerously near making the entire Congress a total failure. He was a determined taskmaster, and he freely used the policy of recognition to further the wishes of the majority of the people; but he could not bring himself to violate what he believed to be a constitutional privilege in the House. Few bills were passed except by unanimous consent.

In the closing days of the second session Thomas B. Reed again introduced a resolution of thanks to the Speaker; and the minority, as evidence of their affection, presented him with a silver service, toward the purchase of which the Democrats were asked not to contribute. As the legislative day of March 3 came to a close amid the confusion incident to such an event, John G. Carlisle took up the Speaker's gavel for the last time and rapped for order. "Looking back over the scenes of excitement and contention which necessarily occur, from time to time, in a body like this," he said in a low, even voice, "it is

[1] Ibid.
[2] Breckinridge MSS.

impossible not to remember with regret many hasty words and unpleasant incidents; but it is gratifying to know that no feeling of resentment survives to disturb our friendly personal relations in the future. And now, gentlemen, in declaring an adjournment which closes the first century of our legislative history under the constitution, may I be permitted to express the earnest hope that when another hundred years shall have rolled around the Union of these States, under which the capacity of the people for self-government has already been demonstrated, will still endure, and that the Representatives then assembled in this or in some other and greater Hall may have constituencies as intelligent, as patriotic, and as free as those who have sent us here."

Thus ended the Fiftieth Congress—the third that had come and gone since Carlisle the Speaker had begun his persistent efforts at tariff reform. All his attempts had brought only disappointments. Moreover, the petty political habits and practices which had grown up had come to be intolerable; the House was ready for a change which Carlisle was not quite ruthless enough to make. He had, however, by sheer intellectual force made perfectly obvious to even the most unseeing the faults of Congressional government. Through his failures he had accomplished half the battle of reform, and although Thomas B. Reed must not be deprived of any of the laurels which are his, he may justly share some of the honor with the man who for the past six years had occupied the Speaker's Chair.

The decade of the 'eighties had seen a great host of settlers, drawn on by the glowing promises of the railroads and encouraged by the stable East, pour into the arid regions of the West. George Bancroft, historian of the preceding generation, wrote Grover Cleveland in May, 1886: "Suffer one of your sincerest friends to express the hope that . . . you will enforce at an early day the duty of protecting the laborer in his right to purchase with his savings a bit of public land for actual settlement. This cannot be done except from effectually repressing the tendency to its monopoly by wholesale domestic forestallers and English capitalists, who are seeking to establish on the larger scale the British system of landlord and tenant. Our democratic doctrine is for the plough in the hands of the owner of the soil." [1]

Concurrently with this migration, which was to play such an important part in the politics of the next decade, had come the return of the Democrats to power in the national House of Representatives. The election to the Speakership in December, 1883, of John G. Carlisle, a Southerner, had marked the beginning of a persistent effort on the part of the Democracy to reduce the war-time taxes which had been levied on the people solely for the purpose of raising a revenue for the emergency purpose of carrying on a great war, but which the representatives of the industrial interests had been able to maintain in time of peace in spite of the recommendations of a Republican President and a Republican Tariff Commission. Slowly, however, the conflict between the North and the South was displaced by dissension between the East and the West; the Mississippi succeeded the Ohio as the dividing line between two radically different political sections. The West was rapidly becoming a political giant with unorthodox and dissenting doctrines; the established East itself was being disrupted as hitherto timorous laborers grew brazen enough to demand rights as well as duties, and, failing to win them, indulged in the unforgivable and un-American crime of resorting to violence. Even the muse of History had begun to take notice of these political undesirables. John Bach MacMaster, an instructor in mathematics in the University of Pennsylvania, turned historian and came very close to discovering the theme which in the next decade gave Frederick Jackson Turner's name to a new field in America's chronicles.

The decade of the 'eighties, despite its varied interests, was primarily concerned with economics. Regardless of the persistent arguments of the protectionists, the constantly increasing sur-

[1] Bancroft to Cleveland, May 4, 1886. Cleveland MSS.

THE LAST SPEAKERSHIP 149

plus in the Treasury showed the inequity of such excessive taxes as existed; the rise of great mansions in New York, erected largely by the *nouveaux riches,* and matched in Chicago by palatial homes like that of Mrs. Potter Palmer, added to the bitterness which was welling up in the hearts of the farmer and the small-town dweller in the midlands. Surely the beginning of the 'nineties held little promise for the political party in power. The great movement into the West had come to a standstill, and would soon begin its recession; the innumerable political cults which had arisen in the previous decade were slowly devouring the two old parties; with the passage of the Sherman silver law in 1890, the financial development reached its height and began its collapse; social visionaries and reformers, largely under the leadership of women, began to probe into the vitals of society, and Congress must hear the results. In 1889 Edward Bellamy wrote his *Looking Backward;* in September of the same year the College Settlement was opened in New York; a few days later Jane Addams and Ellen Gates Star founded Hull House in Chicago; and in 1890 Jacob Riis published his incredible *How the Other Half Lives.*

The best politicians were awake to the stirring new forces. William L. Wilson, recently president of the University of West Virginia, and now Congressman from that State, wrote W. C. P. Breckinridge:

> We must "stamp out"—to use the language of the Bureau of Animal Industry,—the renaissance of ultra Federalism, we are suffering under Harrison and the republican party, fostered by so much of the literature of the day, as the American Statesmen Series, McMaster's History etc.
>
> I want to see a grand revival of Democracy by an appeal to the manhood of the people as against the selfishness of the money power, and I don't know any body as able to lead such a revival with fire and enthusiasm as yourself, I will follow as best I can, *magno cum intervallo.* . . .[1]

[1] Wilson to Breckinridge, April 22, 1889. Breckinridge MSS.

But the Democrats were already weakening before the new forces which were arising. Thomas R. Moonlight's note to Grover Cleveland on November 17, 1890, saying that "the Democracy of Kansas is hopelessly gone" described the condition of the party in many States. The Republicans were no less embarrassed, and, in addition, their party was burdened with its self-imposed task of revising the tariff rates upward in these days of political anarchy when party programs could be prosecuted only at the cost of concessions.

CHAPTER VIII   POLITICAL AND PERSONAL CHAR-
ACTERISTICS

WHEN the Fiftieth Congress was over, John G. Carlisle stuck his gavel in his pocket and stepped for the last time from the Speaker's dais, leaving a worthy record behind him. He had created a great deal of dissension by his "personal rule" of the House, and even the members of his own party had excused themselves to their Southern constituents for not having repealed the tax on tobacco and spirits by saying that Speaker Carlisle would not allow such a measure to be presented to Congress; but nevertheless he was a notable Speaker. During his six years in the Chair only one of his decisions was ever questioned, and then but one vote was cast in opposition. No one ever accused him of doing an unfair thing, although his political associates often felt that he leaned backward in his desire to be impartial.

Carlisle had come to the Speakership with two fundamental principles: to carry out the will of his party as interpreted by himself in regard to tariff reform, and to protect the constitutional rights of the minority. He could not see that the two were in many ways incompatible. Before his years in the Speakership were over, the first had brought a new development in the history of the House, while the second had come dangerously near overshadowing his brilliant record. The power of recognition was his aggressive and defensive sword; for six years he used it to a far greater extent than had ever before been practiced in cutting his way through the maze of political complexities and in holding back the horde of Congressmen eager to beat down the doors of the Treasury that they might despoil the surplus for political gain. His views in regard to counting a quorum, however, made him an immobile fighter, capable of warding off the enemy but unable to carry his tariff-reform banner forward.

Carlisle did not exercise the powers of the Chair in the spirit of balancing favors to majority and minority; he used them for the purpose of forwarding the legislation demanded by a majority of the people, but the popular will he himself interpreted. At the beginning of the Forty-eighth Congress (December, 1883) he appointed to the membership of the Rules Committee the chairman of Ways and Means and the chairman of Appropriations. This gave him watchful floor leaders and a control of Congress not otherwise obtainable. In the Forty-ninth Congress the Rules Committee greatly extended its jurisdiction; at one time the order of business was fixed for sixteen legislative days by a mere majority vote.

In addition to constituting the Rules Committee to act as an aid in carrying through his political program, Speaker Carlisle composed the other committees with the same purpose in mind. Few Speakers have ever expended as much labor in selecting the membership of the committees as did Carlisle; certainly nobody tried harder to be fair, and yet he felt constrained by the will of the people to form them so as to promote Democratic legislation. The Speaker also kept in mind the fact that he must prevent any developments which would tend to make less obvious the need for tariff reform. A reduction in the surplus would certainly do this, and that fact may partially explain why Carlisle throughout his Speakership chose Randall to head the Appropriations Committee, even though that individual was his strongest opponent in the party. Carlisle was able to dominate his committees; Richard Parks Bland, "high priest of free silver," served as chairman of the Committee on Currency, and still no free-silver law ever reached the point where its backers could bargain with the tariff reformers.

Having the machinery of the House organized in conformity with his own political principles, Carlisle used the cudgel of recognition to beat legislation into the way he would have it go. For the entire six years of his Speakership the Blair Education bill was before the country, and although it passed the Senate in each successive Congress, it never once reached a vote in the House; the Speaker would recognize no one for the purpose of calling it up for consideration. The most interesting of the bills which were prevented from coming to vote was the one for repealing the internal revenue taxes, particularly those on tobacco and whiskey. A majority probably favored such repeal, and yet the measure was never introduced. Carlisle is said to have told a friend that "no man with that damned bill in his hand can ever secure recognition." In February, 1887, three prominent Democrats of the House— George D. Wise, John S. Henderson, and Samuel J. Randall —petitioned the Speaker for permission to introduce a bill for the repeal of the tobacco tax. Carlisle replied that he could not entertain a motion "against which the caucus of the party having a majority in the House has pronounced itself." In spite of the fact that this was an age of political trickery, no one ever attempted to introduce the measure through irregular means. The Speaker told one of his intimate friends that should a member attempt to present the bill after having secured the approval of the Speaker for some other purpose, he would immediately declare: "The Speaker has been deceived in the purpose for which recognition was obtained, and the recognition is withdrawn." [1]

John Sherman said before the Home Market Club in February of 1889: "I know that at any time in the last Congress taxation could have been reduced but for the desire of the Speaker of the House and the President to strike at home industries rather than to reduce taxation. A majority of the House, though Democratic, would have passed in an hour a bill reducing taxation if it had been permitted by the Speaker to vote upon a reduction of internal rather than external taxes." Replying to this statement in his tariff speech in the Senate on September 30, 1890, Carlisle declared: "This, Mr. President, was an entirely legitimate political criticism upon the action of the Speaker."

[1] Benton McMillin, whom he consistently appointed to preside at the night sessions. Conversation on September 6, 1930.

The many Congressmen who desired to secure special appropriations for their own districts were doomed to disappointment. Many a closing hour was marked by restless individuals pacing up and down before the Speaker's desk in vain efforts to secure recognition. There was nothing for the Congressman to do but give up in disgust when his patience had been exhausted, for there was no legal basis for an appeal. Carlisle later said in the Senate: "While the general parliamentary law and while the rules of most legislative assemblies make it the duty of the presiding officer to recognize the member who rises first and addresses the Chair, yet as a matter of fact, we all know that it is absolutely within the power of the presiding officer to determine at all times which member he will recognize, and from his decision in that matter I know of no appeal, for no one man can say with absolute certainty that the presiding officer saw or heard one member before or after he heard or saw another member."[1]

Speaker Carlisle, regardless of the autocratic powers which he exercised in regard to recognition, could never bring himself to violate certain rights of individuals. To him a visible presence seemed insufficient until that presence made itself known through some regularly constituted method of voting; and this, because of the lack of a quorum to do business, led to much embarrassment and humiliating delay. On one occasion a mere handful of men reduced the proceedings to roll calls for eight consecutive days, while Carlisle, an active fighter and scorner of petty things, was forced by his intellectual convictions to sit helpless as members of Congress performed their schoolboy antics. In spite of it all his was a great Speakership, and he was so eminently fair that his autocratic actions did not offend. His rulings read like the decisions of a learned judge —so clear and concise that they alone often served to defeat a proposed measure.

Regardless of the facts that the duties were heavy and that Congressional results were often disappointing, Carlisle en-

[1] Jan. 21, 1891, *Congressional Record,* 51st Cong., 2d Sess., p. 1605.

joyed the Speakership, which gave him an opportunity to match his wits with every man in the House. But the inability of that body to accomplish anything in these years undoubtedly vexed him, for he hated lost motion. He wrote under a news article on the rules for a successful life which Mrs. Carlisle had pasted in her scrapbook: "If all the men that waste their time in the repetition, parrot-like, of what is known to everybody would devote that time to some useful occupation, there would be much more success in the world." [1]

The period of the 'eighties witnessed in the House an unworthy development of petty political practices; and yet there were remarkable parliamentarians in the body. Reed and Carlisle stood head and shoulders above all the rest. Robert M. La Follette has said of them: "Both were as fine parliamentary athletes as were ever to be found. I remember vividly a characteristic passage between them. It was near the end of the session, and three o'clock in the morning. An appropriation bill was pending. Some one offered an amendment. If it passed, some advantage would accrue to the Democrats, if it failed some advantage to the Republicans. A point of order was raised against it and Carlisle overruled the point. Reed was on his feet—Reed, three hundred pounds, six feet tall . . . 'I contend,' he said, . . . 'that the Speaker is wrong.'

"Carlisle standing there in the Speaker's place answered, 'I shall be glad to hear the gentleman from Maine.'

"Reed retorted: 'The Speaker is wrong for this reason'—and put it in a nutshell.

"'Ah, but the gentleman from Maine is in error because'—and Carlisle stated his contention without a superfluous word.

"'Yes,' answered Reed, 'but Mr. Speaker,' and for ten or fifteen minutes it was parry and thrust, thrust and parry, Reed pressing Carlisle from position to position until finally the Speaker said:

"'The gentleman from Maine is clearly right. The Speaker

[1] Scrapbook in the collection of Mrs. William K. Carlisle.

is wrong and reverses his ruling.'"[1] But Carlisle was seldom wrong, and few were the times that he consulted Nat Crutchfield, the young legal adviser who sat by the Speaker's desk.

Carlisle was regarded as a commanding Speaker not only by his own party, but by the opposition as well. In the hundred years between March 4, 1789, when Frederick A. C. Muhlenberg of Pennsylvania called the first session of the House to order in New York, and March 4, 1889, twenty-nine individuals wielded the gavel in that body, but perhaps not more than six can be numbered among the truly great Speakers. The name of John G. Carlisle must go down in that short roll with Henry Clay, Robert C. Winthrop, Nathaniel P. Banks, Schuyler Colfax, and James G. Blaine. Alexander, in his *History of the House*, has said: "Carlisle believed in a tariff for revenue only, and for six years maintained the principle as masterfully as Sir Robert Peel engineered the abolition of the corn duties." But withal he enjoyed to a greater extent than any other man in Congress the universal respect of his associates.

The Speaker was no less charming at home than in Congress. The same simplicity of life and honesty of heart which rendered him a favorite among his Congressional associates also made him a thoroughly admired figure in Washington society. Until 1888 he lived in a modest apartment on the fifth floor of the Riggs Hotel; the one small reception room offered little opportunity for elaborate social entertainment, but many guests enjoyed the simple hospitality of this Kentucky statesman and his wife. Mrs. Carlisle, although "of vigorous mind and action that had assertion many times when gentleness would probably have served better,"[2] contributed much toward her husband's political success and added a great deal to the attractiveness of the Carlisle home. A majestic and intellectual woman without a trace of deception, she was a charming hostess. She gave money lavishly to the poor and needy and as

---
[1] Robert M. LaFollette, *Autobiography*, pp. 91–95.
[2] George G. Perkins, a lifelong friend of the family, in a letter to the writer.

freely curbed the ambitions of the "social climbers" of that day. "Mrs. Carlisle's most striking characteristics," wrote Mrs. Hoke Smith, "were a strong mind that scorned conventionalities and a heart that was full of kindness, especially toward the poor and unfortunate. She was sharp of wit, and always interested the distinguished circle of men who gathered about her in Washington. She knew politics. She knew politicians and their wire pulling. She loved genuineness and enjoyed piercing the bubble of show wherever she found it." The Chicago *Tribune* said of her: "In temperament she is vivacious, genial, and pleasant, with a charming open manner. During a recent conversation with Susan B. Anthony she expressed herself as delighted with the courage and energy displayed by the woman's-rights people, whereupon Miss Anthony suggested that Mrs. Carlisle ought to know more of the women suffragists personally. To this Mrs. Carlisle responded that it was doubtless because she did not know them nearer that she esteemed them so much." [1]

The Carlisle home was the center of all things Kentuckian and an open house to natives of that State in the capital city; the frequent arrival of Kentucky hams, preserves, jellies, blackberry jam—and, incidentally, Kentucky belles—added to its attractiveness. The Carlisles received on Wednesday afternoons, "Cabinet wives' day"—for during the Arthur administration and until the marriage of President Cleveland in June, 1886, Mrs. Carlisle was the "first lady" of the land. During their receptions the house was always crowded, and political opponents have frequently left pleasant records of these occasions. Sunday evening, too, always found a small group gathered for an informal dinner. "It was a pleasure to meet Mr. Carlisle in his own house," wrote an associate. "He could not do too much to make your visit enjoyable and the many famous people who for a number of years enjoyed the Sunday evening dinners given by Mrs. Carlisle will never forget them. They

[1] May 25, 1886.

were old-fashioned Kentucky dinners, in which fried chicken and corn bread predominated, to be followed with fish and cold buttermilk."

Teas were prominent in Washington in the 'eighties; sometimes as many as 750 invitations were sent out from the Carlisle home for a single tea. The social columns of the Washington papers noted that at one of these occasions at the Speaker's home a part of the Marine Band furnished the music, and said of Mrs. Carlisle that she "looked very stately in her Parisian toilet of electric blue brocaded velvet with a long-trained skirt. The front breadth of white satin had velvet tulips embossed upon it. The skirt was vandyked around the bottom, over which silk and lace were arranged in jabots down each side. The front lace also finished the neck and sleeves. Her ornaments were diamonds."

In 1888 the Carlisles bought a seventeen-room home at 1426 K Street, Northwest, then one of the most fashionable thoroughfares in the capital. On April 23 Carlisle wrote to George G. Perkins, a lifelong Kentucky friend, "We have got into our house and are much pleased with the change. We will now be able to entertain our friends when they come to Washington and will be glad to see them at any time."[1] To the Speaker "entertainment" meant the delightful old practice of "spending the night."

Bridge had not come into vogue, and an evening with the Carlisles was occupied chiefly with talking; they were both charming conversationalists, and the Speaker could tell a good story or enjoy one told by a friend. Contrary to what all the surviving newspapermen of that day would have one believe, no liquors were ever served in his home. In the winter occasional evenings found the Carlisles at the opera or at a good play, and in the summer they spent a few weeks at some resort —White Sulphur Springs, Bar Harbor, and Hot Springs, Ark., were the favorite places. The summer of 1889 was spent in

[1] Letter in possession of the writer through the kind donation of Mr. Perkins, now living in Washington, D. C.

Mexico. But the superficialities of formal Washington society irked the Speaker; Lent was always a great relief. He probably did not enjoy the vacation weeks as much as Mrs. Carlisle, for they took him away from his thoughts and his study.

The Speaker much preferred thinking to entertaining, and could usually be found in his study after six in the evening and before ten in the morning. Always physically lazy, he loved to stretch at full length on a lounge chair and mull over the problems of government. He read rapidly—apparently up and down the page rather than across; his favorite subject was constitutional law. Fiction attracted him occasionally, but he cared little for poetry. He did not, like the great political figures of the next generation, read detective stories, but he was a devoted slave to solitaire. "For hour after hour," wrote a correspondent, "he solemnly deals and lays down and picks up the cards as though the fate of empires depended upon the result. And all this time the cards and their combines are to him as though they did not exist. The game goes on, but it goes on purely mechanically. The player is plunged deep in some intricate question of law, or of the tariff, or is blocking out and putting into crisp logical sequence some report he is planning or some speech he is to make." He often "beat the devil," but he never could conceive of a plan clever enough to beat the Republicans at the tariff game. The few letters which he wrote —he usually allowed events to answer his correspondence— were often dictated while he played at his game of cards. Once a particularly difficult form of the game distracted his mind for three days before he mastered it to such an extent that he could play it without application.

The Speaker indulged in few amusements, but he did enjoy an occasional evening of poker or seven-up with intimate friends if the ante was small. He knew little of the game, asserts no less an authority on cards than Henry Watterson, but even poker was a serious matter to him. Although he would give his last penny to a friend, he insisted on exact settlement in these amicable games. Needless to say, his was not the poker which Henry Clay, the illustrious Kentucky Speaker before him, played; he never threw his winnings into the last pot, and the noise which he made in his enthusiasm would never have disturbed even staid old John Quincy Adams in the perusal of his Greek!

After the Democratic success of 1884 the Speaker often walked up Pennsylvania Avenue to number 1600 for a sociable game with the bachelor President and a few friends. The records do not say who of the little group answered the single telephone which the Executive Mansion boasted in those days if William, the one personal servant, was out. The coming of a mistress to the White House did not stop these friendly sessions, although she did wonder how the President could play cards with an odd number of players!

Carlisle took no exercise, for he felt that he could not spare the time. He drove to the House in his wide, low-hung, roomy brougham, drawn by one horse; and if his carriage was not waiting for him at the end of the day, he rode home on the horse-cars. Back again in his study, he began his thoughts and his solitaire; his world was purely intellectual, and his mind apparently never tired. His one great hope was to free trade and industry from the fetters of protective tariff and thus bring prosperity to the common man. Always he was busy filling his mind with neat and compact deductions, filed in such careful order as to be available whenever needed for the demolition of an opponent or for the assistance of a friend. He cared nothing about his physical self. "He went to bed when he got ready, and got up about 9 o'clock in the morning. He didn't care much when he ate or what was served him. His luncheon was usually a cracker and a glass of milk." He did learn to eat sea-food and to keep his black, square-toed shoes shined. His clothes were always, in these Speakership years, of the orthodox black; his circular collar cut in priestly fashion added to his clerical appearance. "Only the waistcoat is not rigidly theological," wrote a correspondent. "It is a Protestant waistcoat, and not even a Church of England garment. In Great Britain it would be a dissenting waistcoat, but always the waistcoat of the pulpit."

That Carlisle was charming will bear repetition, and yet one cannot justly omit saying that he also possessed the cold aloofness of the intellectual—a characteristic most evident to those who knew him least. He had few of the graces which men of his greatness possessed; William Allen White, then a budding young journalist, who later wrote that a handshake with Woodrow Wilson was much like shaking a cold mackerel, might have said the same of John G. Carlisle and have found many to agree. And yet the workingmen of Cincinnati and Covington called the Speaker "John," and there is truth in the statement made by an observer that "a child would climb upon his knee to caress him." One must wish that he had possessed a little of two qualities which he entirely lacked—egotism and temper; one could love him more had he made greater use of the overworked "I" of Theodore Roosevelt, or had he even once in a fit of anger torn his tall silk hat into pieces as passionately as did James G. Blaine. But Carlisle went on an even way. Although always on a high pitch intellectually, he had no enthusiasms.

"As he becomes more animated in conversation," wrote a friend, "he makes a swift, quick gesture with his right hand at intervals and fires the projectile sentences with a quick, sharp snap forward of the head." Another wrote: "His face does not warm up as he talks. The gray eyes open wider and become more piercing and keen. He speaks rapidly, shooting out his sentences like mathematically weighed and measured projectiles, of modern weapons of precision. They are perfect projectiles, and they fly straight to the core of the topic. Not a gleam of humor dances about his mouth or his eyes. If he laughs it is in a mirthless sort of way, and it reveals a rather grim mouth, with small and not white teeth. The general and habitual expression of his face is rather one of sadness—a sort of thoughtful, intent melancholy."

The Speaker was a scholar, sound and whole, and was acknowledged as such by all who knew him. Certainly his close friend, Henry Watterson, beloved Colonel and mint-julip mixer of the Blue Grass, must have recognized in Carlisle the exception to his generality concerning the Southerner: "The people of the South are nothing if not sentimental . . . The southern lad who has been educated at home knows a little Latin, less Greek, and a great deal of English; his repertory embraces a crude knowledge, sometimes familiar, sometimes useless, but always engaging, crowded in between Addison and Swift and Hallam and Macaulay. Of mathematics he is almost as ignorant as of Greek; and, with a store of what, for the want of a better term, the world agrees in calling *polite* learning, lacking not in readiness, he lacks accuracy, the source and resource of modern thought and action. He is thus, in the materialistic debates of a thoroughly materialized generation, an ill match for the cool and wary disputant, who throws rhetoric to the dogs and plies the heartless logic of statistics." [1]

[1] *North American Review,* March, 1879, pp. 51–52.

CHAPTER IX MINORITY LEADER IN THE HARRISON ADMINISTRATION

As the opening of the Fifty-first Congress approached in 1889, Washington became excited over a Speakership race for the first time in half a dozen years. Again rival headquarters were the meccas of countless visitors and the sources of "certain" information as to who would win. The Democracy, however, was not interested; it was now the minority party for the first time, with the exception of one Congress, in fourteen years. The pleasing gift which the Republicans had presented to Carlisle at the close of the previous Congress was evidence that they did not expect his party to return to power for some time to come.

On Carlisle's first election to the Speakership the great issues had been between the North and the South, but the sectional bitterness was at last being superseded by other interests, and the principal division came to be between the East and the West. The leader of the "Lost Cause" was even now desperately ill in New Orleans; and before Thomas B. Reed won his title of Czar, the body of Jefferson Davis lay in state in the heart of the South. The Civil War was being buried more deeply each day under the avalanche of new political doctrines which were coming out of the West—doctrines which threatened to submerge the unsuspecting Republicans.

In the Republican party caucus Thomas B. Reed was chosen as the candidate for the Speakership over Cannon of Illinois, Burroughs of Michigan, and McKinley of Ohio. His selection promised to usher in an exciting period in American party government. Reform in the procedure of the House was absolutely necessary, and many Democratic editors were already predicting a bitter controversy. On the whole, however, the country was well pleased, for, in spite of the fact that he always mixed his statesmanship with practical politics, Reed was a statesman.

During the days preceding the opening of Congress Capitol Hill was thronged; most of the newly elected members came up early in order to become acquainted with the place. They were disappointed, however, in not being able to enter the hall of the House, for the doors were always locked a few days before the opening of a session to prevent visitors from "knocking the desks and chairs about and spitting on the new carpets." The crowds were unable to get into the hall even on the morning preceding the opening of Congress, for the Democrats were holding a party caucus. Having succeeded in securing a quorum, they gave John G. Carlisle the complimentary nomination, and adopted a declaration of greeting to the Democracy of the country, with assurances that they would continue to work for tariff reform "as embraced in President Cleveland's message to the last Congress." The caucus had little time, however, to discuss the party program, for the huge crowd outside was pressing for admittance into the galleries.

Reed and Carlisle were nominated for the Speakership, and the former was chosen by a majority of twelve votes. The *Courier-Journal* said that "a presiding officer of the House who will prove arrogant and dictatorial" had been selected, and predicted that in less than two weeks he would so antagonize the minority members that they would always be found in front of the Speaker's desk fighting bitterly for their rights. Carlisle and McKinley were appointed to conduct the new Speaker to his desk. The tall, broad-shouldered man from Maine looked like a giant as he came down the aisle between his two escorts. Judge Kelley again administered the oath of office, but the dramatic effect of other years was missing. Reed's noticeably brief address was admirable in temper and elicited deserved applause from the Democrats, particularly when he promised to adhere to the elevated standard of the duties and obligations of the Speakership as set up by Carlisle "and strictly maintained by that gentleman for six years."

Though the Republicans were now in control of every branch of the government, they were faced with difficult problems.

MINORITY LEADER UNDER HARRISON 165

The party leaders had little more than victory over which to rejoice. The enchantress Protection lured them on, but thick in their path lay political dragons. Three of these—the "new" West, the Democrats, and the surplus—were indeed dangerous. The demands of the West could not be allayed except at a price; Democratic opposition, which Carlisle was now leading "by unanimous consent," could, according to the philosophy of Henry Cabot Lodge, be snuffed out only by encompassing the ballot box with bayonets; and the surplus could not be reduced without granting to individual Congressmen concessions which would surely endanger the fiscal situation. The party was burdened, moreover, with James G. Blaine—but the "Plumed Knight" could do little toward making the situation better or worse. Even Nelson W. Aldrich himself could convince only a handful of New Englanders that the corruption of the railroads in the West was a good thing for the country. It was not strange that the hot summer days of July found Congress dealing with the McKinley Tariff bill, the Sherman Silver bill, the Force bill, and numberless measures calling for unwise expenditures of money.

Regardless of the dangers in their way, the Republicans felt impelled to push on toward the enchanted isles of protection. The party regarded its conquest of the House as a mandate for a high tariff, and action was made more urgent by President Harrison's message upon the subject. "The existence of so large an actual and anticipated surplus should have the immediate attention of Congress, with a view of reducing the receipts of the Treasury to the needs of the Government as closely as may be," wrote the Chief Executive. "The collection of moneys not needed for public uses imposes an unnecessary burden upon our people, and the presence of so large a surplus in the public vaults is a disturbing element in the conduct of private business. It has called into use expedients for putting it into circulation of very questionable propriety. We should not collect revenue for the purpose of anticipating our bonds, beyond the requirements of the sinking fund." These words were not greatly different from those which Congress had been receiving from the Executive Mansion during Cleveland's four years; but the recommendation for increased expenditures in pensions, rivers and harbors appropriations, and other "extraordinary demands" was unprecedented. But neither Democrats nor Republicans appeared to be greatly interested in the message. While the monotonous reading was in progress, many Congressmen wandered about on the floor, and numerous stories were told. Ripples of laughter emanated from various points in the hall where well-known jokers, surrounded by admiring friends, were holding forth. Carlisle took the opportunity to go over to Randall's residence a few blocks away to discuss with the sick Pennsylvanian the policy of the party concerning tariff, the proposed federal election laws, and the impending contests for seats in the House.

Despite the President's message, Congress had its own ideas upon reducing the surplus, and the Republicans had a man in the Chair who was partisan enough to put into effect the wishes of his party and strong enough to overcome the objections of an excited and angered minority.

Throughout the 'eighties the ability of the majority in Congress to conduct business had been growing less and less. The Republicans knew that unless some drastic action was taken, their margin of only twelve votes would not enable them to carry out their tariff plans. Their chance of success depended solely upon the ability of the Speaker to destroy at a stroke the obnoxious practices which had been growing in strength for more than a decade. The point had been reached where if the party in power desired to accomplish any legislative action, theoretical arguments concerning the constitutional rights of a member must be disregarded. The situation had come to such a pass that one individual could often delay the whole House indefinitely; indeed, such obstruction had come dangerously near bringing complete failure to the Fiftieth Congress.

Two of the most effective methods of delaying legislation

were the disappearing quorum and dilatory motions. To overcome the former, some State legislatures had lately adopted the expedient of counting persons present who did not vote. Such a procedure in the national Congress would certainly bring hot objections from the Democrats, who were far from convinced that the country had declared for protection. The Republicans, however, knew that they must at all costs take some steps for reducing the revenues, which were every day becoming more of a threat to the protective system. Small as was the majority which the Republicans held in the House, the party leaders were sure that they would be able to whip their members into line if only they could prevent the minority from interfering. The method decided upon was to strip the individual of practically all of his power and thus put the majority in complete control, making the minority as a group or as individuals incapable of either affirmative or negative action. This not only enabled the party to dominate the Democrats, but it also gave it the opportunity to control its own recalcitrant members. On the opening day enough Republicans had bolted the agreement of the party caucus to defeat the nominee for the chaplaincy.

Reed, already determined as to the course he would pursue, began preparations for the battle. On December 5 he announced the membership of the Committee on Rules, which included Carlisle. Five days later the Ways and Means, with Carlisle again the principal Democrat, was made known. Headed by William McKinley, now the favorite of William D. Kelley since the death of Haskell of Nebraska, the membership of this committee was unusually strong. Burroughs, McKenna, and La Follette represented the West, which was to influence powerfully the course of politics before the Congress was over. The Committee on Ways and Means immediately began work on a protective-tariff bill.

Long before the bill reached the House, however, the question of Republican supremacy in that body was settled. While the Committee on Rules had been appointed early, the House continued under the personal guidance of the Speaker for two months before the committee even made its report. Open conflicts between the two parties began to appear as Speaker Reed drove forward the Republican program. Coming events were casting their shadows before them, and on December 16 the Speaker announced that he expected to look out for the interests of the Republican party and that the Democrats would have to take care of themselves.

Shortly after the Christmas recess a difficulty arose over a question of procedure as raised by Breckinridge of Kentucky. Debate was bitter. The great contest between the two parties did not actually begin, however, until January 29, 1890. Shortly after the House opened on that day, Crisp of Georgia made the point that no quorum had voted. The Speaker, unabashed, said in reply, "The Chair directs the Clerk to record the following names of members present and refusing to vote" —and immediately pandemonium broke loose in the House. Those members who had sat silent during roll call were immediately upon their feet in front of the Speaker's Chair vehemently denying their presence. Reed, however, began to call the names: "Mr. Blanchard, Mr. Bland, Mr. Blount, Mr. Breckinridge of Arkansas, Mr. Breckinridge of Kentucky." He was forced by the confusion and the threatening gestures of some of the Democrats to stop for a moment, but soon resumed: "Mr. Brookshire, Mr. Bullock, Mr. Bynum, Mr. Carlisle, Mr. Chapman, Mr. Clements, Mr. Clunie, Mr. Compton." And so the names continued until the Speaker had counted a sufficient number to constitute a quorum, albeit one man was named who was in the cloakroom. The vote was declared legal. Excitement was intense; the *Congressional Record* caught but a portion of the picture. The Speaker was defied, he was called all the parliamentary names that could be thought of, and he was accused of all the constitutional crimes which could be brought to mind. Crisp of Georgia quoted Shakespeare:

> Get thee glass eyes;
> And, like a scurvy politician, seem
> To see the things thou dost not,

while others furnished less classical quotations. Before the controversy ended, one Democrat was censured for his "disorderliness," but he regarded the reproof as only a "decoration of honor."

When the first excitement was over, discussion of the legality of the Speaker's action began. "Honest Old Joe" Cannon of Illinois admitted that formerly he would have said that the proceedings were illegal, "but after a careful and honest examination of the Constitution itself, and of the discussions which were had at the time it was made and at the time of its adoption, and construing it in the light of sound reason and parliamentary usage, I must confess that I find myself standing to-day upon the Constitution and saying that if I am present in this House of Representatives . . . I count, under the Constitution, one towards making a quorum, whether I vote or refuse to vote." Others had been as suddenly convinced. While Carlisle, the Democratic leader of the floor, did not participate in the demonstration made by his party colleagues, he felt constrained to defend calmly the points which they had made in the heat of passion. The case, he argued, was not one of parliamentary law, but "a question of constitutional law," and it seemed to him that the makers of the Constitution had expressly intended that a quorum should be present in order "to do business." He further argued that the courts of the various States and the Supreme Court of the United States had ruled many times that the record of the House was "the only and conclusive evidence of the facts." The only men who had "participated in the transaction of that business" over which the controversy had arisen were the 163 members whose votes were recorded in the *Journal;* the names set down at Reed's direction were not a record, but a memorandum of the dictates of the Speaker, who had no authority to make the *Journal*. If he possessed such a right, said Carlisle, then one man could pass a bill, and the same number could pass a measure over the veto of the President.

Carlisle could see nothing but ultimate harm from the practice which had just begun. "I am not here," he said, "to deal in epithets, but it is evident to every one that if this ruling stands it will work a complete revolution in the methods of transacting business in this House. For more than a hundred years the people of this country have rested secure in the conviction that no less than a majority of all the members elected here could pass laws binding upon them. During all that time the courts, whenever the question has come before them, have decided that they could look and would look to the Journals kept by the House as the final and the conclusive evidence upon which the question of fact as to whether or not there was a quorum present and participating must be determined. But now we are told for the first time that any number of men, however inconsiderable, may pass in this House upon the most important legislation that can come up for the consideration of the Representatives of the people, provided the Speaker, after looking over the House, determines that there are a certain number present besides those who vote and orders that fact to be entered upon the *Journal*."

The former Speaker could see no logical basis for Reed's action. "Suppose," he said, "the Speaker . . . counts and finds that this House is full, and that therefore there is a large majority of members actually sitting in the House who did not vote. Their refusal to vote, if it can be construed in any way, admits of but one reasonable construction, and that is, that it is a protest against the passage of the motion; yet the Speaker counts them to pass it! When gentlemen sit here and refuse to vote for or against a measure, I repeat, the only reasonable construction that can be put upon their action is that they are protesting against it; and yet the Speaker counts them to pass it— counts them, too, after the tellers, the only officials authorized by the House to make the count, have made their report."

Carlisle's speech closed the first day of the quorum controversy, but just before adjournment William McKinley announced that he would discuss the question on the morrow. Although he was somewhat embarrassed by continual interruptions, McKinley defended the Republican position in a logical and quiet argument. In a sharp reply Breckinridge characterized the course which he was upholding as "usurpatory, revolutionary, and corrupt." Efforts were made to expunge that part of the *Journal* which recorded the action of the Speaker, but they failed.

Throughout the succeeding days Speaker Reed continued, in calm good humor, to carry on the business of the House, and the Clerk continued to read the roll of votes; while at the same time Crisp, Springer, Bland, McMillin, Breckinridge, and others were making denunciatory speeches on the floor. On every question the minority refused to vote, and the Speaker accordingly named them present and not voting. The Democrats endeavored to delay legislation by obstructive motions, appeals, and other dilatory tactics. Reed simply refused to entertain them, and the "Czar" of the House was heaped with more unsavory epithets. During the entire proceedings, however, he retained his urbanity and sense of fun; and his rare gifts of humor, wit, and sarcasm probably saved the situation from an outbreak of violence.

While the Republicans were establishing themselves in the House, the formal revision of the rules of that body was postponed; Speaker Reed and William McKinley kept the committee in suspense for many weeks. On February 1 Carlisle reminded the House that "the gentleman from Ohio" (Mr. McKinley) had promised three weeks before that the rules would be reported soon, and yet the first committee meeting had not occurred until two weeks later (January 23). The Democrats unjustly blamed Carlisle for the delay, drawing from Randall a spirited defense of the Kentuckian. But the rules were about ready; on February 5 Carlisle wrote Benton McMillin:

I understand the program this morning is to adjourn as soon as possible after the *Journal* is read in order that the Reps. may have a caucus on the Rules. If they insist upon having the *Journal* approved before the adjournment, I think our friends had as well agree to have only *one vote;* that is let it be understood that McKinley need not call for the previous question but take the yeas and nays directly on the motion to approve the *Journal.*

We had another meeting on Rules yesterday evening, and the code is now complete, but they want to consult a caucus before reporting it. I do not see any objections to this, provided they will adjourn without attempting to do business.

I write this because I have to go to Mr. Randall's and may not get back before the House meets.

Yrs,
J. G. Carlisle.[1]

On the following day Cannon of Illinois reported the proposed rules to the House for its consideration, and Carlisle and Randall presented a minority report giving the views of the Democrats. The majority report embraced all the radical changes which Reed had brought into existence. It gave the Speaker the power to count a quorum and to refuse to entertain dilatory motions, and provided that in the Committee of the Whole one hundred members should constitute a quorum. The minority report declared that the new rules were so formulated as to destroy the right of the individual. "If the proposed rules are adopted," it said, "there will be one way only in which an individual member, not acting by direction of a committee, can secure consideration of a bill, and that is by a motion to suspend the rules." Even in that event the individual must win a two-thirds vote, while the same motion from a committee required only a majority to pass. The rules did, in fact, take little note of the individual, who was left scant opportunity to make a motion except "as the representative of a committee and by

---

[1] Breckinridge MSS. McMillin apparently passed the letter to Representative Breckinridge.

its directions." The two minority members believed that "the only reasonable explanation for this discrimination is that it is the policy of the proposed rules to suppress the individual member of the House as far as possible and increase the powers of the committees," and many Republicans, particularly those from the West, agreed.

The minority, while further objecting to the new powers proposed to be given to the majority, declared that the "most radical and in our opinion the most dangerous innovation proposed" was the modification of the old Rule XXIII by which the Speaker was empowered to count a quorum present where members refused to vote. As for the right to refuse to entertain any class of motions, the minority said: "To provide that members shall have the right to make certain motions, and at the same time to provide that the Speaker may refuse to entertain them, and may also refuse to entertain an appeal from his decision, is simply to place the whole law of the House, so far as parliamentary motions are concerned, in the hands of the presiding officer, and deprive the members of every right in this respect which the rules purport to confer upon them." [1]

The discussion of the majority report was vigorous and far from orderly. It was incomprehensible to the Democrats that most of the Republicans supported the party program, each apparently convinced that logic and wisdom had dictated the change. Well might they wonder, for the Democrats in Congress had never been able to accomplish anything as a party except under the lash of an outstanding Executive—and even a strong President had never been sure of his following.

In defending the Republicans McKinley said that "they [the framers of the Constitution] never fancied that sullen silence was a statesmanlike way of stopping public business. The later generation of statesmen have inaugurated it. We have done it —all of us. I am not saying that you gentlemen on the other side are doing differently from what we have done for fifteen or twenty years past. [Cheers on the Democratic side.] I have

[1] House Report #23, 51st Cong., 1st Sess.

sat here and filibustered day after day in silence, refusing to vote, but I can not now recall that I ever did it for a high or a noble or a worthy purpose. . . . There was never a time I did it that I now remember when I did not feel ashamed of myself. [Applause on the Republican side.] . . . We commenced our filibustering, sometimes on one side, sometimes on the other, because of a personal pique, or because we thought that some slight had been put upon one side or the other or upon some member of the majority." Congressman Enloe, a Democrat, remarked that this confession "would have been [more] beautiful and touching if it had been made when he was in the minority," and said of Speaker Reed, who had been a leader of the Republican filibusters, that "he too has seen the error of his way in the same 'childlike and bland' manner that he sees a quorum when he needs one." The rules were passed on February 14 by a vote of 161 to 144.

Though for a time the minority continued its objections, Carlisle announced on February 17, after a party conference, that the Democrats would no longer object to approval of the *Journal* so far as the new rules were concerned, but that if the opportunity presented itself they would test the constitutionality of the practice of "counting a quorum." The opportunity evidently never appeared, and the excitement subsided as the doubtful Republican bills of 1890 began to be reported out. The incident was the most exciting in American parliamentary history, and the days were among the most tumultuous ever witnessed in Congress. The Republicans drove all opposition before them with a harshness which was certain to react upon the party itself. The practice of a hundred years and the philosophy of democracy were both against the action of the Speaker; but the course of American politics since the Civil War had been such that political obstruction had superseded statesmanship, and the time had come when it must be checked.

It was a happy fact that Carlisle and Randall, for many years opponents upon the tariff question, were drawn together in opposition to the new Republican practices. The Pennsylvanian lay on his death-bed and fretted that he had not the strength to wield the political weapons which he knew so well how to use. It is evidence of Carlisle's entire freedom from personal animosity that, during the illness of the man who had been responsible for defeating his greatest political ambition in the past ten years, he called on him daily at his home. Randall died on Sunday morning, April 13, just as the bells were ringing five o'clock. Carlisle said of him: "Although we differed widely on some very important subjects, we never allowed those differences to interfere with our friendship. I have always regarded him as an honest man in public life, and he was undoubtedly a man who had strong convictions and the courage to stand by them. I think that his death is a great loss to his party and to the country." His death was indeed a loss, for the Democrats needed the aggressive spirit of which he possessed so much, and Carlisle so little.

Throughout the spring Carlisle continued to fight the arbitrary acts of the Speaker. He objected particularly to hurrying appropriation bills through the House without proper discussion. The rules, he declared, had been made for the purpose of speeding action, and yet proposed measures were taken from the regular schedule and rushed through with precipitate haste. On April 30 he said in regard to a pension bill which amounted to $76,000,000 that "after it was found that it was impossible to pass this bill by a two-thirds vote and with only forty minutes debate and no opportunity for amendment, it is now proposed to do the next worst thing that can be done [laughter and applause on the Democratic side]; that is, to take the bill out of the Committee of the Whole on the state of the Union and consider it in the House, where the previous question can be applied to every amendment, provided any gentleman can get the floor to offer one [laughter], and to take the final vote upon it at 4 o'clock this afternoon. Now, I ask gentlemen on the other side of this House, inasmuch as there is no necessity for this summary and harsh proceeding, what is the reason for it? Is it because gentlemen fear discussion? I imagine not, for if these are meritorious bills the more they are discussed the more plainly their merits will appear."

When the turbulent scenes in the House had ended and the Democrats had given up their fight, the Committee on Ways and Means under McKinley began the preparation of a tariff bill. The Republicans, anxious to convince the people that the party was not allied with the wealthy few against the masses, allowed every opportunity for discussion. Hearings were conducted and the gates thrown open to all, even the "cranks." The Democrats were allowed full privileges, not even being barred from the committee proceedings while the majority was framing the bill. The open forum, however, did not prevent the effective presence of lobbyists for the great manufacturing interests, and the party grew less liberal as political exigencies became more embarrassing.

As a counter measure, in the first days of April Carlisle, Mills, and Breckinridge began work on a minority bill. Many Democrats protested against this procedure because it might allow the Republicans a moment of relief; and on April 7 Grover Cleveland, now a lawyer in New York, wrote Carlisle from 45 William Street:

Is it true that our people in the House Ways and Means Committee propose to present a tariff bill to antagonize the McKinley Bill?

I do not wish to assume to obtrude any advice upon those who are on the spot and whose judgments are better than mine, but I cannot help feeling some apprehension on that subject. I have thought as I have seen the Republicans getting deeper and deeper into the mire that our policy should be to let them flounder.

I suppose the bill which would be presented by us would not be exactly the Mills bill. If it is not the cry will be raised that the passage and then the abandonment of that bill for something else shows that we do not know from one session to another what the Country needs.

A bill presented by us (the Mills bill or any other) will give the enemy what I should think they would want: an opportunity to attack some of this measure instead of defending their own. In this way they can shift ground and throw more dirt in the eyes of the people.

Is there any danger that it will be impossible to rally all our people in favor of a really good bill, with such promptness and unanimity as will make a good showing before the Country? Won't you get into all sorts of tangles among the private and local interests in our party and won't this rob us of the advantage we are now gaining from the alarming and disturbing selfish grabbing going on among our opponents? Of course I take it for granted that nothing really good coming from our side would go through—I mean something fully up to our line all the way through. If this can be done it should be for the Country's good and without counting policy for I do not think we would get any credit for it with the masses of the people or that it would add a bit to the advantage in our hold, in a pure partisan sense.

I have no doubt that you and the rest of our people on the Committee have thought of all these things, and perhaps this is foolish matter; but I shall send it; and I enclose a letter I received as I was writing the above, as a specimen of those of a like character, I receive every day.[1]

On April 16 the tariff bill was introduced in the House by Chairman McKinley of the Ways and Means Committee. On the same day the minority, under the direction of John G. Carlisle, presented the views of the Democrats on the Committee. This report was vigorous in condemnation of the bill, declaring that "we are now at the parting of the ways." The arguments offered were numerous, all resting upon the fundamental contention that the Republican majority had not followed the policy of "equal taxation upon all, according to their ability to bear the burden," but "had thoroughly committed itself to the policy of unjust and unequal taxation of the many for the benefit of the few." The Democrats further argued

[1] Cleveland-Carlisle MSS.

that "Any policy of taxation which under the pretense of protection imposes burdens upon the mass of the people and divides the representatives of different occupations into warring classes, each struggling to make use of the power of legislation to obtain an advantage over the other, is obviously unjust and unwise and ought not to be continued." To do so could lead only to a renewal of this conflict among the beneficiaries of the protective system.

The Democrats accused the Republicans of having deserted the principles for which protection had first been asked. "The original argument in favor of protective duties," said the minority, "was that they were necessary to foster infant industries by preventing ruinous competition from abroad until they could secure a hold on the home market and thus become self-sustaining, and it was again and again predicted by the earlier advocates of the system that a few years of public support would enable them to do this. But the present bill is based upon precisely the opposite view. It is framed upon the assumption that as our industries grow older they grow weaker and more dependent upon the bounty of the Government and the forced contributions of the people who purchase and consume their products; and accordingly we find that, as a general rule, the important increases in the rates of duty are made with a view of still further protecting the products of our oldest industries, such as manufactures of iron and steel, woolen goods, cotton goods, manufactures of flax, hemp, etc. . . . If it be true that these old industries need more protection now than they needed a hundred years ago, it must be because they have been existing under an unnatural and unhealthy system and have lost that spirit of self-reliance and independence which is essential to the permanent growth and prosperity of every business enterprise." The minority was certainly not entirely wrong in its statement that the bill disregarded the demands of the great mass of the people "so long as two or three firms or corporations insist that the tax will be beneficial to them."

The Republicans had asserted that their purpose was to

check the importation of articles which could profitably be produced at home, adding that the "general policy of the bill is to foster and promote American production and diversification of American industry." The minority members declared they could see no reason why there should be a tax on camel's hair, carpet wool, and other items which could not be produced in this country. Moreover, they did not understand why the people should pay a bounty of a dollar per pound for any silk which an experimenter might produce, or why wool, a commodity which even in Ohio amounted only to three per cent of the value of the farm products of that State, should be generously protected when that protection added to the wealth of so few and highly taxed so many. The value of the wool crop, said the Democrats, was not more than that of the egg crop, and far below that of hay, wheat, or corn; furthermore, it made the people of Ohio "pay high taxes on at least 10 pounds of wool contained in the woolen goods they buy in an attempt to raise the price of 5 pounds of wool they produce." [1]

The Republicans, however, were determined to move quickly, and McKinley gave notice that only four days would be allowed for general debate; the will of the people had been registered, said the Ohioan, and it must be carried out with dispatch. This statement was beyond the comprehension of the Democrats, who for a half-dozen years had possessed a greater popular support than the Republicans now held. The discussion was long enough to give the Democrats opportunity to say many uncomplimentary things about the bill, which the Republicans described as "national" and "non-sectional." The measure was, its sponsors believed, the consummation of the "American System," but Congressman McAdoo asserted that "Mr. Clay . . . would not recognize in this bill the offspring of which he is the reputed father."

Although the Democrats could accomplish little after their defeat upon the quorum and dilatory motions, Carlisle did what he could as minority leader to delay the McKinley bill.

[1] House Report 1466, April 16, 1890.

But at this juncture occurred his election to the United States Senate to take the place of James B. Beck, who died on May 3, 1890.

The rank and file of the citizens of Kentucky were undoubtedly in favor of Carlisle as Senator, although perhaps no man could expect to receive a unanimous decision from the State, the various sections of which are rarely free from political jealousies. The direct election of United States Senators was a Western idea still in its infancy, and the election of a Senator devolved, of course, upon the State legislature. There were several strong candidates, but Carlisle retained the lead from the beginning. The nominating speech of Senator Mulligan was an impressive piece of oratory which is still remembered in the commonwealth—and it throws some light upon the strange fact that a few years later Carlisle lost much of the love and admiration which the State held for him at this time.

"The times are strangely out of joint," said the orator. "The very excess of liberty seems to be on the verge of defeating her holiest ends; the very freedom of the franchise seems to make it an easy prey to combined greed; the camp-fires of Seventy-six emit but a pale and fitful gleam; the national air of the day is the jingle of dollars, the one topic of the hour is money, money—nothing but money. Capital piles on capital, in combination reaching alpine heights, crushing the masses in its avalanches, chilling and impoverishing the multitude beneath its dark and freezing shade; the shadow of the custom-house falls across every threshold, darkening every fireside; wealth accrues to but few, and then in unnatural proportion; the people, as in classic times, are amused by the inspiring prosperity of the few and the specious parade of progress, and, while they sullenly look on, are assured that all this gallant parade, decked out in so much bravery, is solely for their benefit.

"The fields are fruitful, but no riches come to the husbandman. . . . The rich grow richer, and the poor become poorer; the nation trembles under the tread of discontented thousands;

strikes are the order of the day, the combine, the trust, the enthroned vampire of protection, drawing through a hidden taxation drains the country and its virgin fruitfulness to a few centers."

Carlisle was characterized as the man "who was first to recognize and grapple the monstrous wrongs of legalized robbery, who in spite of the dismay and remonstrance of all mere politicians, became an apostle, who brought the American Democracy solidly to its support through the power of his intellect and the simple sincerity of his faith . . . a man who gave to Democracy a living issue . . . one who carries the myriad details of government at his fingers' ends; a statesman in its highest sense . . . the hope, the guiding star of the vast army of toilers; the champion of the people, as against the robber barons and monopolists . . . a man who unites with all these qualities the simplicity of a child . . .

". . . In the name of the Democracy of the Union, in the name of the millions who wearily follow the plow, in the name of the brawn and the sweat of the Republic, in the name of all who grow deaf amid the clatter of shuttles, the roar of the wheels and the crash of machinery, in the name of those who crisp at the door of furnaces, of those who in darkness tread the slippery roof of the train, of those who forge and those who saw, in the name of equal laws and fairness of justice and equal rights, in the sacred name of freedom and equality, I nominate for the position of Senator in Congress of the United States John G. Carlisle."[1]

Carlisle was elected to the Senate on May 17. On the following day came a letter of congratulation from 816 Madison Avenue, New York City, in the "copperplate" writing of Grover Cleveland, private citizen but earnest Democrat: "Need I say to you how delighted I am by your selection to succeed Senator Beck? This was a happy household when the news reached us and our congratulations are as sincere as they can possibly be. Somehow it seems to me that with much that

[1] *Courier-Journal,* May 14, 1890.

is bad, one good and wholesome thing has been done. Mrs. Cleveland joins me in all this and we both send love to the Senator's wife."[1]

But Carlisle did not take his seat immediately; he desired to remain a member of the House a few days longer in order to vote against the McKinley bill, which he termed an "outrageous measure." He wanted in particular to express his opinion of the "bold and revolutionary" actions of the majority party. On May 21 he began a persistent effort to force the Republicans to record their votes on item after item in their tariff bill. He came near carrying several reductions; tin plate rates were maintained by only one vote, and many others with little more than that margin. As the time for voting on the bill approached, he introduced a resolution asking "that the pending bill be recommitted to the Committee on Ways and Means, with instructions to report the same back to the House at the earliest possible day, so amended by substitute or otherwise as to reduce the revenues of the Government by reducing the burdens of taxation upon the people, instead of reducing the revenues by imposing prohibitory rates of taxation upon imported goods." The resolution was defeated, and a few minutes later the McKinley tariff bill passed the House by 164 to 142.

On May 26 Carlisle took his seat in the Senate, and two days later he was appointed, much to the chagrin of older men in that body, to the membership of the Committees on Finance, Territories, and Woman Suffrage. In other words, Carlisle served no apprenticeship in the Senate; he stepped immediately into a leading position among the solons of the nation. A correspondent has described him as a Senator as follows: "He goes to bed when he gets ready and gets up about 9 o'clock in the morning. He has his breakfast shortly after rising, and it doesn't make much difference to him what he eats. After eating he goes to the Capitol in his carriage and looks over his mail. He does this in a little committee room in which the sun never shines. It is located near the crypt and is practically

[1] Cleveland-Carlisle MSS.

in the basement of the Capitol, and is, I should say, one of the most unhealthy of the rooms belonging to the Senate. He works away here until about noon and then takes a lunch, eating when he gets hungry. His lunch is usually a cracker and a glass of milk, and he is especially fond of the latter. He spends his afternoon in the Senate and usually rides home again at about 5 o'clock. He is a very polite man and will never keep his seat while a lady is standing, and I saw him one day rise and give his place to a sickly-looking colored girl who had a bundle under her arm. He has his dinner about 6:30 o'clock, and after it spends his evening either at home or with his friends here and there about the city."

In the Senate Carlisle was interested chiefly in tariff reform, as he had been in the House, and his clear, concise arguments carried great weight. He was earnest, but never dogmatic. Toward the end of his career in that body Senator Hiscock said of him: "If in the course of this discussion I assign a wrong position to the Senator, I desire to be interrupted, because I say to him, I say in this Senate, in his presence, that he is one of the fairest men in discussion whom I ever knew. I speak from an association of ten years with him in the House of Representatives and of two years with him here." [1]

When the McKinley tariff bill went to the Senate, anyone who cared to look might have seen an alarming economic and political prospect. The international as well as the domestic situation was discouraging. The trade balance for the calendar year 1889 was some $56,000,000 in favor of the United States, but she had sent out $38,000,000 in gold in the same period. In the preceding year the trade balance had been $33,000,000 against her, and yet she had sent out only $13,000,000 in gold.[2] Every year the ledger showed a constantly increasing debt to Europe for freight charges, interest, and other items of an invisible nature; at the same time, the

---

[1] *Congressional Record*, 52d Cong., 1st Sess., p. 6991.

[2] Statistics for the United States, compiled by A. Piatt Andrew, Senate Doc. 570, 61st Cong., 2 Sess. In *National Monetary Commission* publications, pp. 10–11.

only money with which these charges could be paid was growing timid as silver rapidly mounted in volume. During the fiscal year 1889 the total stock of gold in the country decreased $25,000,000—the first reduction of the kind since resumption.[1] Business men daily watched the $100,000,000 gold reserve with growing misgivings; "it is the essential link in the chain of influences sustaining confidence," said the *Commercial and Financial Chronicle* in March. Secretary Windom of the Treasury Department refused to deposit government money in the banks, but depended wholly upon bond redemptions for returning the surplus to the channels of trade. As the finances became more stringent and failures began to appear, the demands upon the Secretary to call bonds increased.

Nor was that all; in domestic affairs the political situation was growing acute. Before the close of the first session of the Fifty-first Congress six new States took their places in the national government. The soil of these new commonwealths, as Senator Platt had declared concerning Wyoming, was not as fertile as the valley of the Nile, but the citizens were earnest supporters of Western politics; their representatives were all silver men, and they gave to the advocates of the white metal in the Senate the balance of power. This was very unfortunate, especially at a time when the country was doing its trading and its banking on silver certificates, which filled the channels of trade to such an extent that no deposit of cash had much else in it, and no check was paid in any other currency unless gold or legal-tenders were demanded.[2] There was little danger from silver or its representatives while it was in the hands of the people; but it had been for the most part forced into circulation, and any sudden alarm or even a too-plentiful appearance of silver certificates might immediately drive them back into the Treasury to displace all other forms of money there. Silver had continued to pile up in the vaults of the government in 1889, and the Secretary had closed his report to Con-

[1] *Report of the Finances*, 1889, p. 10.
[2] Ibid., p. 62.

gress in December of that year by saying that he concurred "in the opinion of all [his] predecessors since 1878, of both political parties, that there is a limit beyond which it is not safe to go in the coinage of full legal-tender dollars, the nominal value of which is far in excess of the bullion value." [1]

The Sherman silver law is discussed elsewhere, but its political complications may properly be noted at this point. Long before the Fifty-first Congress assembled, it was evident that the silver question would be important. In his first report the Secretary of the Treasury had urged that "something be done for silver," and President Harrison, while he had lacked time to study the proposals of his Secretary, had recommended that Congress give them careful consideration. The future success of the party depended largely upon the ability of the Republicans to soothe the discontent of party members from the West. The silverites did not themselves possess the power to write a free-silver law upon the statute books, but if they joined the Democrats, the combined strength might be sufficient to send a bill to the President. They could also block general legislation by the Republicans. Thus it was that the Republicans were forced to "tread gently" and at times, perhaps, along secret paths in this summer of 1890. The party was justified in expending every effort to prevent the political disasters which a veto would bring.

Although a silver measure had been introduced in the House on January 20, 1890, little notice was taken of it until the McKinley bill had gone to the Senate. Speaker Reed, aided by his Rules Committee, then began a vigorous attack upon the silver proposals; this brought immediate opposition from the silverites and a great deal of acrimonious discussion in the House. Reed was unable to control his party caucus, but he did secure a moderated silver bill, which passed the House on June 7. In the meantime the Senate had shelved the McKinley tariff bill until something should be done concerning silver. The Baltimore *Sun* said on June 6 that there seemed to be

[1] Page lxxi.

considerable truth in the statement attributed to Senator Stewart of Nevada that "there will be no tariff legislation this session unless a silver bill is passed." Indeed, the Democrats and "Silver Republicans" appeared to be in the ascendancy in the Senate.

On June 11 the Finance Committee reported the House silver bill to the Senate, and two days later it was substituted for the measure which had been before that body early in the year. The silverites, both Democrat and Republican, together with those Democrats who felt impelled to oppose the party in power, began a concerted rush to drown the House bill in a flood of amendments. The climax was reached on June 17, when a free-silver amendment was carried. Senator Carlisle voted for the proposal, but he did so reluctantly and at the final passage refused to record his vote. He particularly did not like the legal-tender clause. "I am too good a Democrat," he declared, "to vote to make a piece of printed paper such as this a legal-tender when gold and silver is the basis of our currency." A few days later he told the Baltimore *Sun* that he was aware that certain persons were inclined to censure him because he did not rush headlong into the arms of the mine owners who were anxious to dispose of their product. He declared that the Western Congressmen who were howling the loudest for free silver were in many instances personally interested, that they were not sincere in their demands for free coinage, and that they had no idea that Congress would go so far as to accede to their demands. "They don't expect to go beyond limited coinage," he said, "and at the proper time will be voting so." Personally, he remarked, he was not willing to sink his deep-seated convictions on the subject. He had, however, voted as a party member and not as the statesman that he was.

On June 18, while the House was discussing the Indian appropriation bill, the Clerk of the Senate appeared in the middle aisle carrying a small bundle of paper. A few minutes later, amid round after round of applause from the Democrats, he announced the silver bill as passed by the Senate. Republican leaders looked solemn. Having called Hatch of Missouri to the Chair, Speaker Reed was on the floor, and in a significant undertone he immediately began a conversation with his party lieutenants. He knew that he must get the bill into the House Coinage Committee. The next morning the *Journal* made no mention of the Senate bill, for Reed had quietly referred it to the Committee without reference to the House; Mills demanded an explanation, and the Speaker suffered his first defeat. The silverites were determined to have an open vote. The Republicans were not prepared for this, as many of their members were away. Efforts were begun to secure pairs for the absent Republicans, but word soon went around that "live" Democrats should not pair with "dead" Republicans. In the meantime the telegraph wires were carrying many an urgent message to absent Republicans to return immediately. They arrived in the House "with stains of travel on their faces and gripsacks in hand," but they were in time, and the free-silver bill was defeated.

The story of the conference committee and the passage of the Sherman silver law is well known, and it is needless to recite it here. The economic results will be seen presently.

The introduction of a Federal Election bill by Henry Cabot Lodge on June 14 was still another embarrassing political episode in this trying summer of 1890. It aroused a terrific storm and caused many Democrats who might otherwise have sustained Republican action on the silver question to vote with the silverites. The "Force bill" was drafted for the purpose of clearing all restrictions, whether wise or unwise, from the pathway of the Southern negro to the polls. Some undoubtedly supported the measure because they believed in full race equality, but it is obvious that the revival of this long-dormant principle was not unconnected with the growing threat of the representatives of the South to the policy of protection.

Senator Carlisle vigorously opposed the "Force bill"; he told the Republicans that if a "free and fair election and an honest count" were what they wanted, then the principles of the measure were wrong. He was supported in his contention by many fair-minded Republicans. On June 30 E. W. Sawyer of Lynnfield, Massachusetts, wrote W. C. P. Breckinridge: "I am so disgusted with Mr. Lodge's course in relation to the general election bill, which I presume you are also opposed to, that I cannot refrain from letting you know that his course is so disapproved of by the best people here that in spite of the almost universal custom of re-election of an Overseer for Harvard College for the second term, he was rejected at the election last week by a decisive vote." Two days later William E. Russell wrote from Boston: "You cannot condemn too strongly, to meet my views, the pending election bill. All of us here think it an iniquitous partisan scheme without precedent, in violation of the Constitution and state rights, and certain to be disastrous in its consequences to the harmony, peace, and prosperity of the people."[1]

The "Force bill" tended to strengthen the alliance between the Democrats and the Westerners; whether there was any actual union of forces cannot, perhaps, be told, but certainly the West believed that she was aiding the South in this hour of need, for in a few years she asked a return of the favor.[2] Senator Quay was probably responsible for squelching the bill until after the tariff question was settled.

Although he had been in the Senate only a few months, Carlisle was an important figure in the political controversies at this time. His greatest interest lay in the tariff question, because he believed that a proper settlement of that economic problem would do much toward relieving all other difficulties. He saw no reason why valuable time should be spent in discussing free silver. "In my opinion," he declared, "the continued agitation of the silver question in this Congress is not

[1] Breckinridge MSS.
[2] See Fred Wellborn, "The Influence of the Silver-Republican Senators, 1889-1891," in the *Mississippi Valley Historical Review*, xiv, pp. 462-480.

only useless, but very unwise. Everybody appears to admit that no free coinage bill can become a law, because if passed by both houses it would be vetoed by the President and there the matter would end. Practically, therefore, there is nothing whatever to be accomplished by the agitation, except to engender divisions and dissensions among those who are substantially united upon all other economic and political questions. Our true policy, it seems to me, is to secure as far as possible economy in public expenditures."

Throughout the summer Senator Carlisle fought the McKinley tariff bill paragraph by paragraph wherever possible, and his party was actually able to win a few victories. He demanded a cheaper rate on lumber because, he said, "our forests of pine, of white pine, at least, are being rapidly diminished, and . . . in the course of a . . . few years the supply in this country will be practically exhausted." He would not argue concerning the benefits of free lumber, but merely cited the Maine ultra-protectionist who some time before had introduced into the House a resolution to admit lumber duty-free to citizens of that State whose homes had been burned by a disastrous fire. He also urged a cheaper rate on binder twine and the sisals from which it was made, whereupon Senator Aldrich twitted him for having deserted the Kentucky hemp fields; but he did not believe in taxing the wheat growers on the Western plains for the benefit of the few farmers in Kentucky who grew hemp, and neither did he believe in taxing mica. All along the line he forced the Republicans to defend their proposals.

Meanwhile, in the House the Democrats were endeavoring to curb the autocratic actions of Speaker Reed. They had lost the fight to prevent the counting of a quorum; and as the Republicans continued to decide the contested election cases in favor of their party in order to provide a much-needed voting strength, the Democrats adopted the expedient of absenting themselves from the House when important votes were to be taken, leaving Representative O'Ferrall for the sole purpose of making the point of no quorum. The Speaker ordered the doors of the House locked, and trouble began. C. Buckley Kilgore of Texas presented himself at the exit at the Speaker's left. "Unlock that door," demanded the stalwart Texan of doorkeeper Hayes and, having no time to lose because the vote was already in progress, brought one of his enormous shoes into action. The frail baize structure flew open, and Kilgore strode out into the corridor with Congressman Craine in his wake. Cummings of New York and Coleman of Louisiana bore down upon another door with a look of determination on their faces, and a prudent doorkeeper unfastened the latch.

Several results followed this "foot" attack of the Democrats: the Republicans relented, Kilgore won the title of "Kicking Buck," and Dingley of Maine carried a sore nose for several days. The flying door which Kilgore had kicked loose struck him fair in the face, and for a time it was feared that his nose had been broken. There was humor in the whole episode, but locked doors and kicking Congressmen are sadly out of place in the council halls of a democracy.

The conference report on the tariff bill reached the Senate on the last day of September. Senator Carlisle was ready again to attack the measure on the floor. He seriously objected to the bounty provisions. They would bring no additional compensation to the producer of the raw materials, he said, and would in no way reduce the price of the finished article to the consumer, for the money expended would go entirely for the benefit of the manufacturer. He did not forget to call attention to the fact that the Republicans were primarily interested in the preservation of protection while they abolished the excessive revenues which were making the evils of the protective system apparent. "According to the statement submitted to the Committee on Finance from which I have read," said the Senator, "this is confessedly a bill to reduce the revenues by increasing taxation. . . . Then, Mr. President, this enormous increase in taxation is made mainly upon articles in common use among our people, and which they are compelled to buy."

As for the results of the McKinley bill, the Senator declared:

Mr. President, no man can predict what the effect of this enormous increase will be upon the taxation of the people, nor can any man predict what its effect will be upon the revenues of the Government. All we can certainly know is that the very purpose, in fact, the sole purpose and object of the imposition of these rates of duties upon these necessaries of life is to increase the price of the domestic product so as to enable in some cases, as it is claimed, new industries to be established here, and in other cases to enable old industries to realize larger profits. To compensate the farmers and mechanics for these great increases of taxation upon their tools and implements of trade, and upon their cotton and woolen and linen clothing, the bill proposes to repeal internal-revenue taxes to the amount of $5,897,380 on manufactured tobacco, snuff, and on dealers in these articles.

Heretofore we have been told by our Republican friends that the internal-revenue taxes upon tobacco ought to be repealed entirely, and during the last two or three years, while the Democratic party controlled the House, there was a great and persistent demand here and at the other end of the capitol to have them removed. The Senator from Ohio (Mr. Sherman), who spoke yesterday in advocacy of this bill which proposes to reduce the tax upon manufactured tobacco and snuff only 2 cents per pound, or from 8 to 6 cents, has heretofore been an ardent advocate of the whole tax. This proposition . . . will, in my judgment, afford no relief to any man in this country and be beneficial to nobody except the manufacturer and the retail dealer, who will divide the amount between them. No producer of tobacco and no consumer of tobacco will be benefited, in my judgment, to the extent of 1 mill, for the man who purchases in small quantities will pay hereafter exactly the same price as he paid heretofore.

He opposed Secretary Blaine's proposition of reciprocity:

I assert [he said] that there are no markets there [in South America] for our agricultural products and never will be. . . .

I am contending that the pretense, if Senators will excuse the expression, that the reciprocity now suggested is for the benefit of our farmers is a false pretense. . . .

"Commerce is not war; it is peace," declared Carlisle in answer to Senator Evarts of New York. "Commerce has, in my judgment, contributed more to the civilization of the world, more to establish fraternal relations between the peoples of different countries, than all other human agencies."

But the McKinley bill passed the Senate on September 30 by a vote of 33 to 27. On the following day it was signed by President Harrison and became the law of the land. The new tariff did not give the relief which its sponsors had prophesied. On the contrary, the dark predictions which opponents had made during its passage promised, as the time approached for the November elections, to be fulfilled. The tariff on agricultural products did not materially reduce the discontent of the West, and the evils of the new tax on tin plate were apparent to all who cared to look. It is true, perhaps, that hired peddlers hawked pots and pans over the country at exorbitant new prices "due to the McKinley bill," but it is true also that John Wanamaker, a member of the President's Cabinet, urged his customers to buy before prices went up. The purchases of every housewife were powerful arguments for the Democrats.

In the Congressional campaign the Republicans carried a heavy handicap. As the evil consequences of the Sherman silver law became apparent, a financial crisis appeared imminent. The party had endeavored to win the West by levying a tariff on agricultural products and giving the silver States a government market for their metal, but neither the tariff nor the Sherman Act really aided the party. Moreover, the conviction of the Republicans that the surplus must be reduced had led them into further difficulties. The statement, "God help the surplus," which Corporal Tanner made on assuming his position as pension commissioner, had expressed the feeling of all who controlled the finances of the government. The Secretary of the Treasury was perhaps the greatest offender in extravagant expenditures. The relation of these incidents to the financial disasters which came later must be left for another chapter. It will suffice to say here that the party suffered an overwhelming defeat in the Congressional elections of 1890, and the Democrats were returned to power in the House by a tidal wave; the Republican majority of 20 was changed into a Democratic majority of 138.

Senator Carlisle told a correspondent from Covington that he had anticipated popular disapproval of the party in power, but not such a sweeping condemnation. "It was," he said, "an indignant uprising of the people against the domineering methods of the republican leaders in Congress, against the continuance of war taxes in time of peace, against extravagant pension legislation and against the insolent trampling upon the rights of suffrage by ousting Congressmen from seats to which the people had selected them and putting in their places men whom the people had rejected, and the threat to still further subject the popular suffrage to partisan manipulation by the enactment of the federal election law, better known as the 'force bill.' Of course, the tariff was a prominent and in many places the principal issue, but the result of the election is a condemnation of Reedism and Lodgeism as well as McKinleyism."[1]

With the gloom of defeat hanging over the Republican party, the second session of the Fifty-first Congress accomplished little legislation. The "Force bill" was again postponed, but the silverites could not be quieted. They were vigorous in their condemnation of the Sherman silver law, and in the early months of 1891 persistently urged a free-coinage measure. The dangers which Senator Carlisle had foreseen in the summer of 1890 were being realized, for his party was rapidly dividing on the issue. On January 9 Edward Atkinson wrote from Boston: "The Republicans have now waived their right of objection to taking a vote [on the free-silver meas-

[1] Baltimore *Sun*, November 12, 1890.

ure], and have waived further debate, in order that having been sold themselves, they may give the Democrats in the Senate the opportunity to *sell out their own party;* deprive it of the support of Independent votes, and risk if not throw away every chance of carrying any Eastern State. The Democrats have the field on the platform which originated with you; reform and reduction of the tariff. That might have been kept the sole issue. It should be if it can be. If the Democratic party now commits itself to the free coinage of silver, the stigma and responsibility will be removed from the Republican party and they will lose the East without gaining the West. . . . I trust this question can be deferred, and that the Democratic party may not commit itself in the Senate to its own destruction."[1]

The movement gained such momentum that Grover Cleveland, private citizen and possible candidate for the Presidency, felt impelled as leader of his party to condemn the measure which a majority of Democratic Senators were supporting. In a letter to E. Ellery Anderson of the New York Reform Club he gave warning of the disaster which might follow "the dangerous and reckless experiment of free, unlimited, and independent silver coinage." "So say we all of us!" said President Eliot of Harvard when he saw the letter, and William F. Vilas wrote: "Let the fools have it direct. It may have been not unwise to engage the Silver State Senators against the Force Bill, dealing with Mammon in Mammon's way. Perhaps if I had been a Southern State representative, I might have tried to work with them to that end. We cannot tell how great anxiety will sway judgment. But to commit it to such a heresy or attempt to throw the Democratic party after the Sop to Cerberus is to cast everything to ruin as well as to abandon all principle."[2]

The country was temporarily relieved from the danger of being committed to the "false and fatal fantasy" of free silver

[1] Atkinson to Cleveland. Cleveland MSS.
[2] Vilas to Cleveland, Feb. 15, 1891. Cleveland MSS.

by the adjournment of Congress on March 3, 1891. The Democratic party began immediate preparations for a tariff campaign to be launched in the Fifty-second Congress. Senator Carlisle, leader of the tariff-reform movement, did all he could in the intervening months to organize the Democratic forces. Walter Hines Page was publishing in the columns of his New York *Evening Post* the letters of a young Westerner, William Jennings Bryan, who was soon to lay aside his tariff principles to lead a monetary crusade, but who was now requesting permission "to combat McKinleyism on its native heath"—if expenses were paid.[1]

The summer ended at last, and with the opening of the Fifty-second Congress in December the victorious Democrats appeared in Washington, determined to undo the work of the previous Congress. In the House they overflowed the Democratic side and took possession of many seats recently occupied by Republicans. Before they could proceed to business, they had to dispose of the problem of organization. There was no one who could really take Carlisle's place in the Chair. Crisp, Springer, and Mills were the most important candidates; Mills probably had the lead, but because he would make no promises in exchange for votes he was finally defeated by Crisp. The selection did not prove thoroughly satisfactory, but the party, nevertheless, urged on tariff reform. Springer, Democratic floor leader, began the introduction of a series of bills dealing with specific articles. This method was admirable for political purposes, for it compelled the opposition to place itself on record—and the record could often be made embarrassing. In the early 'seventies David A. Wells had suggested such a course to William R. Morrison. The Republicans dubbed Springer's measures "pop-gun bills." There was of course no hope of Democratic tariff reform so long as the Senate and Presidency were both controlled by the Republicans, but this did not prevent the Democrats from carrying on "a

[1] Bryan to Springer, June 26, 1891. Bryan MSS.

campaign of education." They were looking forward to 1892, when they hoped to win the Presidency again and to abolish the impositions of the Republican party.

In the Senate Carlisle began an attack on the McKinley bill. He believed that the report on wages and prices just made by the Senate Committee on Finance, of which he was a member, had been falsely turned by some into a support of the protective system. Prices on commodities had been falling, and the compensation of the wage-earner had been on the increase as the "necessary result of our improved methods of production, transportation, and exchange," said Senator Carlisle. When the cost of production was lessening and the product of labor increasing, he asserted, the capitalist could afford to pay higher wages and still make more profit. He thoroughly opposed needless taxes, and his arguments were not without point. "Whatever makes it easier for the people to live decently and comfortably; whatever makes the necessaries of life . . . cheaper and less expensive to the masses is a blessing to mankind. I have never been able to appreciate the wisdom of that policy which compels men to work longer and harder in order to procure food, raiment, and shelter for themselves and their families; I have never been able to appreciate either the economic truth or the humanity of the proposition that the people can be made happy and prosperous by taxation, whether the purpose of that taxation be to defray extravagant expenditures on the part of the Government, or to increase the prices which the people pay for what they eat, drink, and wear."

While Congressmen fought over the tariff question, the two parties prepared for the presidential campaign. The selection of a Democratic candidate was a perplexing problem. Grover Cleveland was the outstanding man in the organization, but he had already announced his unqualified condemnation of free coinage, and party success seemed to depend upon winning the vote of those Democrats who were locally allied with the Populists. John G. Carlisle, persistent advocate of tariff reform, had done little to offend the silverites, and his following was large—but he lived "on the wrong side of the Ohio river." David B. Hill, William E. Russell, Horace Boies, Arthur P. Gorman, William R. Morrison, and Adlai E. Stevenson were possibilities, but none possessed the popularity or the qualities of statesmanship which marked Cleveland and Carlisle.

Carlisle's support in the Middle West and South was very strong. He was, perhaps, the nearest approach to a universally admired statesman that the South had produced since the Civil War. Many had "dreamed for years of putting him in the White House," and no one desired this more ardently than his old friend Henry Watterson. Along with many other editors Watterson had begun early to urge the candidacy of the Kentucky statesman. He particularly opposed the choice of any candidate from the East. Speaking of Cleveland, he told the delegates to the Kentucky convention that "if we go there [New York] for a nominee we shall walk through a slaughterhouse into an open grave."

The State convention, however, eventually instructed for Cleveland. On May 30 Carlisle wrote the editor from Washington:

MY DEAR WATTERSON:

The *Courier-Journal* containing the proceedings of the Convention was not received until yesterday which accounts for my delay in writing. After looking over the whole ground and talking with Gov. Vest I am entirely satisfied that you and my other friends pursued the wisest course under the circumstances, and that the defeat of the opposition is just as apparent—and less irritating—as it would have been if positive instructions had been given for me. While I believe that such instructions could have been secured if insisted upon, I think the present gain would have been more than counterbalanced by the offence given to the friends of Mr. C. I notice that some of the papers are claiming that it was a Cleveland Convention, but I fail to see the evidence of it in the proceedings. Undoubtedly he is very strong in Kentucky and cannot be wisely fought except upon the ground of availability.

Accept my thanks and the thanks of Mrs. Carlisle for all you have done.[1]

Watterson was able to force a tariff-for-revenue-only plank into the Democratic platform, but he could not prevent Cleveland from becoming the nominee. Though not nominated, Carlisle received fourteen votes—six from Kentucky, five from Ohio, and three from Florida—throughout the balloting. Cleveland was the wiser selection, and Carlisle vigorously supported him throughout the campaign. The Senator and Mrs. Carlisle visited the Democratic leader at his home at Buzzard's Bay, where the two ardent fishermen talked over the tariff program which they expected to pursue if the party was successful in November.

In 1890 A. L. Taylor of Iola, Kansas, "Dealer in White Pine and Poplar Lumber," had written W. C. P. Breckinridge of Kentucky, "If the next Congress will give us free silver and a new tariff bill with free lumber you may put Kansas down for Cleveland in '92."[2] In the national campaign of 1892 the party threw a sop to the silverites by nominating Adlai E. Stevenson for Vice-President, and began a vigorous campaign for tariff reform. Party leaders made desperate efforts to convince the poor and dissatisfied that high tariffs were the cause of all their evils. Poets and song-writers plied their trade in the interest of tariff reform; the grief of the factory lord at the poverty of the workingman was sung all over America:

> In order that he might hoodwink
> All such as did not stop to think
> This Factory Lord with cheeks of brass,
> And voice as loud as any ass,
> Just on the eve of voting day
> Was often heard to shout and say,
> We MUST protect our laboring poor
> By putting up our tariffs more.

[1] Watterson MSS.
[2] Breckinridge MSS.

> Yes, tariffs are the poor man's boon,
> Put tariffs on each knife and spoon,
> Put tariffs on each pot and kettle,
> And tariffs on all kinds of metal;
> Put tariffs on the nails and shingles,
> And tariffs on each bell that tinkles;
> Put tariffs on the plows and hoes,
> And tariffs on the scythe that mows;
> 'Tis tariffs high that fill the purse,
> While tariffs low will bring a curse
> On those who toil for daily bread;
> And this it is that makes me shed
> Big tears of grief and bitter woe,
> Because I love the poor man so. . . .

The Democrats may have received a little assistance from German opposition to the McKinley tariff bill. In some German papers there appeared articles urging the German-Americans to help in the cause. "Personal influence and friendly relations ought to be used in order to cause all such American voters, who still cling to their fatherland and wish for its best, to stand shoulder to shoulder and vote against the law, which has brought such distress and trouble to us," wrote one editor. "Every German who has relatives, friends or acquaintances in the United States should write to them repeatedly and give an account in his letters of the deplorable effects of the McKinley bill in Germany." The German-Americans did vote the Democratic ticket, but the effect of the letters from Europe, if any were written, was slight.[1]

The Republicans, under the leadership of Benjamin Harrison, carried on an uninspiring campaign and were badly defeated in November. The Democracy was again ready to undertake tariff reform. Carlisle was early selected by Cleveland for a position in the Cabinet, and it was expected that he would write the tariff bill which the Democrats believed the country had demanded by its vote. Disappointments, however, were

---
[1] See Consular letters, Annaberg, vol. II—Department of State.

again in store; the financial situation which had been rapidly growing worse during the Harrison administration threatened to bring immediate calamity. John G. Carlisle, tariff reformer, was compelled to turn his attention to the financial situation, and the consequences to him were far from pleasant.

Indeed, the victors in the campaign of 1892 could be only losers; the political and economic situation was such that whichever party won was bound to find itself divided into bitter and hostile camps, for the day of compromise on the financial question was over. Whoever was invested with the dignity of the Presidency was certain to meet with vilification and ultimate rejection by the electorate. Senator Carlisle had undoubtedly enjoyed his years of service to the people, but as one of the leaders of the victorious group his days of happiness were over; soon his followers were to melt away and leave him the victim of a memorable political tragedy.

CHAPTER X CLEVELAND'S SECRETARY OF THE TREASURY

GROVER CLEVELAND set to work immediately after his election upon the problems which would face the administration. In the Mills Building in New York or in his retreat at Lakewood, N. J., he was already taking upon himself the cares which four years before he had passed to another. Political perplexities which had then been burdensome had now reached such a stage that a satisfactory solution was practically impossible. The Republicans, through the autocratic dictation of Thomas B. Reed and the unwise expedient of bargaining and compromise, had been able to pass the McKinley tariff and the Sherman silver bill. The former defeated the party, and the latter made the silver question far more dangerous than ever before.

Indeed, the situation was critical. The surplus which John G. Carlisle had so carefully guarded in his Speakership years was gone, and the government was a pauper; the East, long fearful that silver would eventually displace the gold in the Treasury, had apparently lost all faith in the nation's ability to maintain the gold standard; the West, dissatisfied with the provisions of the Sherman silver legislation, was united and determined to push forward its cause—the "great army of the discontented" awaited only a leader; and Europe, which for twenty years had been watching the monetary conflict in the United States, certain that it would end in disaster, was ready to return the remaining American securities held there.

The difficulties which faced the President-elect in 1893, while similar to those which had confronted him in 1885, were far more perilous. Cleveland, however, was prepared to assume heavier burdens, for he was a much greater statesman at his second inaugural than he had been at his first. Those characteristics which had reminded many of his associates of the county sheriff had disappeared, and he had emerged the outstanding leader of his party. One other man had made rapid growth in those intervening years; John G. Carlisle now stood second only to Cleveland. He may even have excelled him in knowledge of the science of government, but he lacked the courage which marked Grover Cleveland a statesman among statesmen. The President-elect expressed something of this complementary relation when he said, "We are just right for each other; he knows all I ought to know, and I can bear all we have to bear." Faced with overwhelming problems of government, he could not overlook the former Speaker in making up his official family.

Cleveland would certainly have need of competent and efficient associates during the next four years, and he showed his appreciation of this fact in the careful study which he gave to the selection of Cabinet members. The Treasury particularly required a well-balanced and judicious statesman, for its relation to the welfare of the nation had gradually brought it into especial prominence. Except in an international emergency few people were interested in the personal peculiarities or policies of the head of the State Department, but the nation at large had learned to watch the man who had charge of fiscal affairs. Business was always hesitant pending the appointment of a Secretary, and it continued so until that individual had given definite expression of his personal policy regarding the purchase of silver bullion and the distribution of the surplus.

The Secretary of the Treasury is responsible both to Congress and to the President, and during the 'eighties and 'nineties those two branches were rarely ever in harmony concerning the finances of the nation. Congress had passed legislation concerning the coinage of silver, and the Executive had done what it could to invalidate the laws. The Bland-Allison Act, passed in 1878, had directed that from two to four million ounces of silver be bought each month, and each succeeding Secretary of the Treasury had purchased only the minimum amount; the Sherman silver law had demanded that 4,500,000 ounces of silver be purchased each month, and had stipulated that the Treasury notes issued thereon should be redeemable "in coin," but the Secretary, using to support his action the clause in the Sherman law declaring that the metals should be maintained "at a parity" with each other, had clung to gold coin alone.

The Secretary of the Treasury personally influenced the financial life of the nation in other ways. He had come to be regarded as an ever-ready relief in all monetary difficulties. The reason for this was that the income of the government under its long-continued war taxes was far in excess of its needs. Throughout the 'eighties the money in the vaults of the Treasury had constantly increased until by 1888 it exceeded one-third of the entire circulating medium. At every sign of a financial crisis, as we have previously said, business men rushed to the Treasury demanding that the government purchase bonds in order to release some of the money which it held— but all purchases were made solely on the personal inclination of the Secretary.

The practices of the day were not consistent with the principles of sound finance, and, complicated by political developments, they made a crisis inevitable. The collapse came during the Harrison administration, when Congress, freed from Carlisle's staying hand, rushed upon the surplus with the determination to spend it immediately, and the Secretary of the Treasury, in a desperate effort to avoid a panic, poured out millions in the redemption of bonds at a high premium. When Cleveland was elected, the money in the Treasury was scarcely twenty-five million above the hundred-million reserve, free silver was threatening, and gold redemptions had begun in earnest. The fear for the standard of value had become acute. Whoever had a debt to pay carefully counted out his Treasury notes (silver), and passed them on, and their prominence in the circulating medium heightened the financial uneasiness. During the months of November and December, 1892, and January and February, 1893, the public expenditures had exceeded the receipts by more than $5,000,000, and there was no surplus in the Treasury on which to draw.

Foster, faced with an empty Treasury, appealed to the bankers for assistance. "The Secretary sent word to the banks through one of their number," wrote the *Commercial and Financial Chronicle* on February 11, "that unless they would replenish his stock his $100,000,000 reserve would speedily be encroached upon." The New York financiers gave what gold they could and received therefor Treasury notes of 1890. The Secretary was trying desperately to ward off the impending catastrophe until he could surrender his office to his successor. *Harper's Weekly* declared on February 25 that "this shift [borrowing from banks] to tide the administration over the remaining weeks of its term not only postpones the inevitable, but fosters and increases uncertainty, and encourages the opponents of repeal to persist in their hostile attitude to the business interests of the community." The editor regretted the fact that an effort to settle the difficulties by the repeal of the Sherman law was not attempted "instead of seeking temporary makeshifts that will enable it to cast its burdens upon the incoming President and his Secretary of the Treasury."[1] But political disaster was sure to come to the party that sponsored repeal.

Cleveland clearly realized that the situation in the Treasury Department demanded that a real statesman be placed at its head—a statesman who was learned in finance and whose reputation for judicious action and calm thinking was already well established. He wanted someone, too, who could prepare a tariff bill for presentation to Congress in December. The man in the party who fulfilled these qualifications was Carlisle. Henry Watterson tells a delightful story of Cleveland's first promise to Carlisle of a position in the Treasury Department. The editor was in Washington shortly after the marriage of the

[1] Vol. 37, p. 170; See Chapters 11 and 13 for a description of the actual situation in the Treasury.

MR. CLEVELAND'S CABINET

President in 1886 and was invited to a card game at Secretary Whitney's home. He later wrote:

> Mr. Carlisle, at the time Speaker of the House—who handled his cards like a child and, as we all knew, couldn't play a little—was seated on the opposite side of the table.
>
> After a while Mr. Cameron and I began "bluffing" the game—I recall that the limit was five dollars—that is, raising and back raising each other, and whoever else happened to be in, without much or any regard to the cards we held.
>
> It chanced on a deal that I picked up a pat flush, Mr. Cleveland a pat full. The Pennsylvania Senator (Don Cameron) and I went to the extreme, the President of course willing enough for us to play his hand for him. But the Speaker of the House persistently stayed with us and could not be driven out.
>
> When it came to a draw Senator Cameron drew one card. Mr. Cleveland and I stood pat. But Mr. Carlisle drew four cards. At length, after much banter and betting, it reached a show-down and *mirabile dictu*, the Speaker held four kings!
>
> "Take the money, Carlisle; take the money," exclaimed the President. "If ever I am President again you shall be Secretary of the Treasury. But don't make that four-card draw too often." [1]

The wheels of political fortune turned, bringing Cleveland again to the Presidency, and the first man he thought of for the Treasury was Carlisle!

It is not definitely known just when Carlisle was offered the post or when he accepted it. As early as January 3 he had been called to New York for consultation with the President-elect, but the purpose of the visit was to canvass the policies to be pursued. On January 9 Carlisle arrived at Frankfort, Kentucky, ostensibly to give some attention to the senatorial race in the State, but he returned to Washington three days later after having talked with the leading Democrats in regard to the distribution of the federal patronage in Kentucky under

[1] *Marse Henry, An Autobiography*, II, pp. 211-212.

the incoming administration. In Cincinnati he freely discussed his acceptance of the position as Secretary of the Treasury, and on January 18 he mailed to the governor of his State his letter of resignation as United States Senator from Kentucky. A few days later he wrote Henry Watterson:

MY DEAR WATTERSON: I have not written you before because I have understood that you were away from home, and also for the reason that there has been nothing of importance to write about. There is in fact nothing now, except to say that when you get an opportunity I hope you will come here so we can talk over the situation as to the tariff, currency, etc., etc.[1]

"It is the general opinion that an abler man for the chief of the United States Treasury could not have been selected by Mr. Cleveland," said the New York *Times*. *Harper's Weekly* commented: "The fitness of this selection was universally recognized. Mr. Carlisle has made his reputation as a public man on questions of public policy that relate to the department over which he is to preside. He was elected Speaker of the House in opposition to the candidacy of Mr. Randall on the issue of tariff reform. At the same time he was known to be expert in all questions of the currency and on all laws relating in any way to the fiscal policy of the government. It was natural for Mr. Cleveland to turn to him for an adviser on the tariff issue, on which, mainly, the late campaign was conducted. In the recent financial troubles of the country arising from the existing silver law, Mr. Carlisle's advice has proved to be singularly sound and useful. He really began his duties as a cabinet officer weeks before he assumed office. Besides his knowledge of the affairs of his department, he is a sound constitutional lawyer, and is a safe and conservative man. No public man within the present generation has a more enviable reputation." [2]

Woodrow Wilson, predicting that questions concerning the

[1] Carlisle to Watterson, Jan. 27, 1893. Watterson MSS.
[2] March 4, 1893, p. 198.

finances would be the most important which would face the administration, expressed the opinion that "Mr. Cleveland has shown real statesmanship in placing at the head of the Treasury Department a man who is not only a real leader of his party, but its leader first of all and most notably in the field of financial legislation." Of the duties which would fall to the new Secretary of the Treasury, Wilson further said: "The financial legislation of Congress is so dependent upon the Treasury for its wise effectuation, the policy of the department so intimately touches at every point the most sensitive business interests of the country, the Secretary of the Treasury has so often to determine questions which really fix a financial programme on the government, that it is always hazardous to put any man at the head of the Treasury who does not possess tested political judgment as well as approved business capacity. The appointment of Mr. Carlisle is a better appointment than that of Mr. Manning was, wise and efficient officer as Mr. Manning proved himself to be. Mr. Manning was no statesman, as Mr. Carlisle is. The two appointments illustrate in their contrast the development of Mr. Cleveland himself." [1]

There was some adverse criticism of Carlisle's appointment. It was pointed out that he was not a business man, that his fortune probably did not exceed twenty-five thousand dollars, and that he was a purely theoretical financier who had gleaned his knowledge from books and from discussions heard during his Congressional career. Carlisle did carry a great handicap— he was not familiar with big business and, in fact, had an abhorrence for it. He went into the office with a record of long years in the service of the people. His chief conception of legislation had always been that its purpose was to help the masses. This was a high conviction; but as Secretary of the Treasury in these particular years he would have to come into contact with financiers who held very different views and who were certain that successful business could not be carried on according to this doctrine. Carlisle was clearly in earnest when he

[1] "Mr. Cleveland's Cabinet," in the *Review of Reviews*, VIII, pp. 286 ff.

announced that he did not mean to allow Wall Street to influence the financial policy of the United States while he was Secretary. He did not fully realize that the Treasury Department must protect all interests alike.

The portfolio of the Treasury was not a promising one in 1893. "Probably no financial administration in our history has entered office under such disheartening conditions. . . . The Treasury was empty and the public credit shaken." On the day of the inauguration the *Commercial and Financial Chronicle* said: "The change in the head of our Government and in the administration of our Treasury finances which will occur to-day take place under very peculiar circumstances. Never since the war closed have the embarrassments bequeathed to succeeding officials been as great as now. . . . It seems to us that one can hardly overestimate the difficulties that the Secretary of the Treasury will have to contend against. That this should be understood at the start will be useful in moderating public expectations and is only fair to Mr. Carlisle, who has had no part in creating the environment of the Department of the Government he is about to assume." Few men in public life have ever taken over a more dangerous and uncertain public office than that which Carlisle assumed at this time.

His duties were made less onerous, however, by the appointment of capable assistants. William E. Curtis, a prominent New York lawyer and anti-Tammany man, was entrusted with the Public Debt, and he bore the brunt of the negotiations with the New York financiers during the bond sales. Charles S. Hamlin was placed in charge of Customs and the Bureau of Statistics, and Scott Wike of Illinois was assigned to Warrants, Estimates and Appropriations. Mr. Hamlin is the only surviving member of the group, and is today (1931) a member of the Federal Reserve Board.

"It is a rather remarkable group of young men which is gathered around Secretary Carlisle in the Treasury Department," wrote the correspondent of the Springfield *Republican*. "Mr. Bowler, the first Comptroller, is the oldest of the group

THE LADIES OF CLEVELAND'S CABINET

Mrs. Cleveland seated in center. Mrs. Carlisle standing second from right

and he is not yet thirty-eight. He is an able lawyer, however, very popular in Cincinnati, and a warm friend of Representative Harter of Mansfield. Assistant Secretary Curtis of New York is about the same age, and then comes a drop of four years to Comptroller Eckels. Mr. Eckels is not a striking looking man, but he is already infusing a deal of energy into the Comptroller's office and doing his best to secure the stockholders and creditors of the banks which have recently failed. This is true also of Assistant Secretary Hamlin, who is thirty-two years of age and the youngest of the group. . . . Mr. Hamlin and Mr. Quincy have given a surprise to the Kentuckians who have tried to limber them up with good Bourbon and cigars, for neither of them either smokes or drinks. The Kentuckians are probably more than ever convinced of the truth of the remark one sometimes hears here—that Massachusetts Democrats are only half Democrats anyway."

On March 6, 1893, the various members of Cleveland's Cabinet assumed the duties of their offices; all were interesting and important men, but only one was a statesman of the first rank. The Republicans departed, and Democratic Washington went to work. Walter Q. Gresham, a Republican whose views on the tariff question had turned him to the Democracy and who was cordially hated by those who hungered after patronage and had not been fed, was Secretary of State. Cleveland's "Come, Gresham, I need you," had brought coals of fire upon the President's head from those who supported Democratic favorites. In the Treasury Building was John G. Carlisle, tall and stately and dignified without effort. His dress—"In the fall, winter and early spring . . . a dark frock coat, and . . . black silk hat. In the summer . . . a frock coat of a drab or gray color with a white silk hat [made especially by Knox] with waistcoat and trousers to match"—had become so familiar in Washington that he was easily recognized the distance of a square. In his office, he sat at his desk making memoranda with the goose-quill pen which he himself had fashioned from a feather; on the street, he strode along with slow, unexpressive movements, but his long farmer's stride carried him rapidly; he often walked with his hands clasped behind his back, and always with his gaze bent downward and to the left, preoccupied with his thoughts. One day he stepped into a horse car on Pennsylvania Avenue and handed the conductor a lead quarter!

At the Attorney-General's desk was Richard Olney of Boston. "Mr. Olney looks like Randolph Churchill . . . ," wrote Arthur Brisbane at the time. "Lord Randolph Churchill looked like a terrier, and Mr. Olney, who is bigger than Lord Randolph, looks like a very big terrier." Like many politicians, he had no neck, and there was no color whatever in his face. "He looks like a man rather tired of things in general." Heading the War Department was Daniel S. Lamont. He had served as private secretary to the President in his first administration, and his importance at that time is reflected in the answer which a Congressman gave to the query as to whether he spoke for the President: "I do not even speak for Mr. Lamont!" Wilson S. Bissell, an old friend and law partner of the President's, watched over postal affairs. Hilary A. Herbert, a Confederate veteran carrying wounds received in the battle of the Wilderness and a member of Congress since 1877, was at the head of the Navy Department. At his appointment Carlisle had wired Cleveland: "Our real friends will be well pleased and you need not care what the enemy says. Alabama and the South will be delighted."[1] Hoke Smith of Georgia, "representative of the new and progressive South" and editor of the Atlanta *Journal*, which later defended the cause of William Jennings Bryan, then a member of Congress, was Secretary of the Interior. J. Sterling Morton, who, it was rumored, had not always supported Cleveland, directed the Department of Agriculture.

The social life of the Cabinet ladies, although by no means brilliant, was a bit more inspiring than the official life of their husbands. Mrs. Cleveland, charming and tactful, possessing

[1] Carlisle to Cleveland, February 22, 1893. Cleveland MSS.

the politician's gift of never forgetting a face, was a delightful hostess, particularly to older women. The Vice-President's wife, Mrs. Letitia Greene Stevenson, daughter of a Presbyterian minister, president of the Daughters of the American Revolution for two full terms, and devotee of literature and home and foreign missions, was handicapped because her husband was a free-silver advocate. Mrs. Gresham entertained in her elegant apartments in the Arlington, but her husband had little taste for dinners or soirées. Mrs. Carlisle, "painful but interesting and always blowing about Kentucky," drew to her home on K Street a numerous group. As has been previously said, she was a charming hostess, and her receptions had been noted for many years. Even during the first Cleveland administration they had been more largely attended than Mrs. Whitney's.

Mrs. Carlisle continued her Wednesday afternoon receptions and the informal Sunday night suppers which had made her home so popular during her husband's Speakership. Although she probably did not relish the New Englanders, she knew everybody in Washington worth knowing. In some years she made as many as fifteen hundred calls. She enjoyed having her friends "drop in" to gossip for a moment or to tell her of the success or failure of a tried recipe from "Mrs. Carlisle's Kentucky Cook Book," recently off the press. In their friendly chats they certainly did not overlook the expected event at the White House. Mrs. Carlisle felt intimately enough acquainted with the President to request that he name in her honor his little daughter born on September 9, 1893. The President took time from the repeal fight to write her a delightful letter:

My Dear Mrs Carlisle:

Jane is a very pretty name and there is no living person whose name I would rather our new baby should bear than yours.

The responsibility of selecting her name was put upon me long before her birth and I feel that responsibility very much indeed. It may be very disappointing to those still alive whose names are passed by but I have determined to ignore mother, grandmother and great grandmother and avoid all jealousy by going back to Biblical times.

I mean to call the little girl Esther. It is a favorite name with me and associated in a pleasant way with things I remember besides the hanging of Haman.

You are the first one in the world except her mother, to know the name of our second child.

I hope "Jane" can wait.

Yours very sincerely
GROVER CLEVELAND [1]

The Carlisle home was a three-story structure with bay windows, large halls, long parlors of the old-fashioned kind, and ceilings twelve feet high. Great fur rugs carpeted the hall floors, and the parlors were crowded with furniture—too crowded, perhaps, from an artistic point of view, but the general impression given was one of genial Kentucky hospitality. "The house looks as if somebody lived in it," wrote a reporter at the time, and, indeed, with its Kentucky comestibles, it was the center of much of Washington's official social life.

The Lamonts, "honest and clever but a bit common," lived in a lovely yellow Colonial house next the Bryce home on Farragut Square. They entertained expertly, but it was the Olneys who knew how to entertain—they brought Boston to Washington. They had a splendid home, the counterpart of those on Beacon Street, and there one had a feeling of reserved good taste—"books, flowers, and a black silk gown." The Attorney-General's tennis court saved the disposition of many an overworked official in the four trying years which came.

In an old-fashioned residence below Pennsylvania Avenue lived the Herberts, and there one found as hostess the golden-haired, blue-eyed daughter of the Secretary of the Navy, who had studied French in Paris and German in Munich. She was a typical "white muslin and blue sash" daughter of the South, but as secretary to her father during his Congressional days she

---

[1] Cleveland-Carlisle MSS.

had handled his correspondence with dispatch. Mrs. Hoke Smith, the other truly Southern hostess, lived on Sixteenth Street, two blocks from the Carlisle home. She had brought to Washington from her Georgia home many of the old family servants and part of the furniture and family plate. Miss Morton, sister of the Secretary of Agriculture, was official hostess to the only real Westerner in the Cabinet.

In addition to the members of the Cabinet circle there were, of course, other notable people. Sir Julian Pauncefote, "a perfect old dear" with a kind but uninteresting wife and six assorted daughters, shared with Lord Bryce, who gave the most beautiful parties in all Washington, leadership of the diplomatic society. The Fullers, the McLeans, the Lodges, the Hays, and numerous others contributed their part to the society of the gay 'nineties.

Cleveland and Carlisle had little time for social engagements, for the summer of 1893 was full of political perplexities and problems for those in power. The President and his Secretary of the Treasury spent many anxious hours in consultation, but they could find no royal road to relief. The tariff bill which Carlisle hoped to write was laid aside for better days, but better days were not in store. The West was demanding free silver, while the East was urging the repeal of the Sherman silver law. Farmers and laborers were vehemently calling for the expenditure of silver money which the Treasury did not possess, and the business interests and financiers were pleading for a bond issue in order to replenish the Treasury reserve lest the gold standard completely collapse. To attempt repeal would overturn the ark of party harmony and might even destroy the party itself; to increase the public debt in time of peace by issuing bonds to maintain a standard of value which Westerners and Southerners believed to be responsible for their ills would certainly add to the ever-growing silver army.

That "middle-of-the-road" position which politicians always prefer was no longer possible; a decision either for gold or for silver must be made. But economic society was so thoroughly disrupted that there was, in fact, only the gold alternative. Cleveland gathered about him his few warriors and doggedly began the battle. The records show that Carlisle, Olney, and Lamont shared the brunt of the executive fight, but the heaviest burdens fell upon Cleveland and Carlisle. The Secretary was cheered, perhaps, by the encouraging words of John Sherman when that gentleman called at the Treasury Department as a financier to discuss the problems with him. He at once took steps to make his influence felt in the House, where the administration promptly demanded a repeal of the silver-purchase law. "Secretary Carlisle's service in the cause of sound money has been recognized on all hands as particularly effective," said the *Nation* in August, 1893. "What he has practically done is to assume the right of a Cabinet officer to a seat and voice on the floor of Congress." Godkin regretted that Carlisle could not openly cope with the Congressional conflict, for, he said, "Face to face with an opponent, and with equal right to free speech, he could not only smite the enemy through the midriff, but could twist the spear in the wound until there was an end of the business."[1]

Not only was the Secretary faced with political handicaps; he was bound down by the rules governing the Treasury Department itself. In his December report he pointed out the fact that "while the laws have imposed upon the Treasury Department all the duties and responsibilities of a bank of issue, and to a certain extent the functions of a bank of deposit, they have not conferred upon the Secretary any part of the discretionary powers usually possessed by the executive heads of institutions engaged in conducting this character of financial business.... He can neither negotiate temporary loans to meet casual deficiencies nor retire and cancel the notes of the Government without substituting other currency for them when the revenues are redundant or the circulation excessive, nor can he resort, except to a very limited extent, to any of the ex-

[1] Vol. 57, p. 127.

pedients which in his judgment may be absolutely necessary to prevent injurious disturbances of the financial situation." [1]

Cleveland and Carlisle trusted each other because of the struggles through which they had gone. Side by side they had fought the tariff battle of 1888 and the campaign of that year; together they had tried to prevent the McKinley tariff of 1890, and had worked to win the election of 1892—and side by side they rode into the valley of political death in 1893. When they emerged four years later, their followers were scarcely more numerous than the poetic six hundred.

[1] P. lxxiii.

CHAPTER XI   THE FINANCIAL HERITAGE AND
                        THE PANIC OF 1893

THERE are few periods in American history in which the administration of national finances has been attended with greater difficulties than in the year 1893; perhaps never since the time of Alexander Hamilton had such perplexing problems presented themselves to the Secretary of the Treasury. A contemporary said in April, 1894, that "Whoever undertakes to write up the business experiences of the people of this country for the calendar year 1893 will have a most difficult task on his hands. To arrive at even approximately accurate conclusions, many factors outside the year's operations and outside of the country must be considered, compared, analyzed and thoroughly digested. The business troubles of 1893 were not the outcome of trivial causes. The seeds were sown in other years. Last year was simply the reaping time." President Cleveland might well write his old friend, Richard Watson Gilder, editor of the *Century*, "I wonder if a *true* history of the last fourteen months will ever be written. It is crammed full of instructive things."

The problems which presented themselves to Secretary Carlisle were not of his making; they were the results of unsound financial legislation since the Civil War. Space forbids the tracing in this biography of the developments of the preceding quarter century, but a résumé of the legislation and practices of the Harrison administration will suffice to show the problems which were pressing for a solution.

When the Republicans came into power in 1889, the West was seething with discontent. The dissatisfaction which declining silver prices brought to the mine owners was real, but it was small in comparison with the bitterness which arose in the heart of the unhappy farmer on the plains beyond the Missouri who found himself crushed between ten-cent corn and ten per cent

THE PANIC OF 1893

mortgages. Everywhere the unrest found expression in a demand for more and cheaper money.

The lure of the great trans-Mississippi West which in the first half of the 'eighties had led farmers to attack the arid plains with hopeful vigor had lost its appeal, and the losing battle of the second half of the decade had turned into retreat by the beginning of the 'nineties. The hot, dry winds which year after year had seared the farmer's grain had finally burned the hope in his heart to ashes; the mantles of snow which had frozen his emaciated cattle to death had destroyed his faith in the honesty of those whose misfortunes had not been so great. In 1890 the dilapidated covered wagons were leaving western Kansas by every road; thousands of discouraged farmers drove their creaky prairie schooners over the Missouri bridge at Omaha, bringing with them their families and the few possessions which their creditors had left them. Not all, however, could move, for many did not even possess the necessary railroad fare; some still hoped to pay off the chattel mortgages which prevented them from taking their horses and wagons out of the State. Only seventeen counties in Kansas maintained their original population, while many in Missouri, Nebraska, and South Dakota declined scarcely less. The suffering of the farmer was indeed severe; with his farm mortgaged at less than one-third of its worth, he often found himself still in debt after the foreclosure sale had been made. The Topeka *Journal* not inappropriately said in 1891 that there were two kinds of farming in Kansas: "wet farming and dry farming. Wet farming is by irrigation and dry farming is raising a crop one year and accepting aid from the county commissioners for the next three."

The towns were no less unhappy; all were overbuilt and heavily in debt. The long lists of farms offered for sale for delinquent taxes were matched by equally long lists of city lots. In 1891 and 1892 the legislature of Kansas passed sixty-seven laws to vacate town sites. A few years later a Western paper said of this retreat from the West: "In the boom period rival towns fought with weapons over the location of county seats. To-day hillocks on the prairies mark their sites. Railroads paralleled each other. And then the buffalo grass grew between the ties. It seemed as if the homesteads were to relapse into the original desert." Miss Hallie Farmer writes of the population of the Far West at this time: "Those who left and those who stayed were alike heartsick and discouraged. The desert had exacted a heavy toll. It had taken years of life and of exhausting toil. It had devoured the little farms which had been so hopefully tilled and it had killed hope itself. In return it had given only failure, debt and despair." The great American desert had claimed its own. Decaying houses marked the sites of deserted towns, while the plains revealed little more than the ruins of sod houses and dug outs.

When the Englishman had attacked the American frontier on the Atlantic seaboard, the wilderness put moccasins upon his feet, a leathern shirt upon his body, and an Indian knife in his belt, and he had emerged eventually an American; the American's attack upon the great arid West left him a cynic, disillusioned and perhaps suffering from an overdose of sympathy administered by self-styled economists and politicians seeking to pull themselves upward through the vote of the discouraged farmer. The deserted region did not by any means include the entire West, but low prices and years full of economic want were common to all. The States of the great Mississippi valley were restless; 81 counties of the 119 in Kentucky in the year 1891 could not raise enough money to pay the expenses of their own local governments. The farmer and the cotton planter, not without justice, began to blame the wealth of the East for their situation, and they were joined in their beliefs by the small business man who year after year found it harder and harder to keep his business on a profitable basis. Rumors that the burdens were due to the activities of stock speculators, harvester twine combines, railroad corporations and goldbug conspiracies gave way to certainty in the hearts of many. State legislatures began to vie with one another in the introduction of bills which would prevent corruption. Congressmen were urged, and properly, to attack the predatory trusts. Special efforts were made to prevent the Eastern banker from buying stocks or bonds or lending his money except at low rates of interest.

Politics flourished in this fertile soil. All over inland America political cults had sprung up in the 'eighties, and along the Atlantic seaboard labor organizations had carried forward the same ideals. The Alliance, the Patrons of Husbandry, the Populists, and other groups decimated the ranks of the Democrats and the Republicans. John Sherman, man of principles which he never followed, probably did not understand the full significance of a letter which he received from one of his constituents in Ohio in June, 1890, which said: "There is an ugly outlook, the soldiers are mad and swear vengeance. The 'Farmers Alliance' wants to cut a day in two, and the free silver coinage men are ripe for revolt. And there is a movement on foot to combine the three factions and make common cause against the two old partys."[1] And indeed the day of the mushroom cult was over, for a panacea had been found in the free coinage of silver; the Alliance, the Patrons of Husbandry, and the Populists waned as millions united in one great voice for "the money of the common man."

The situation within the Republican ranks was not a pleasant one. The President and his Secretary of the Treasury, William Windom, were in full accord in earnestly desiring to promote the coinage of silver, but they were convinced that safety and soundness must be two essential principles in any course which they might take. We have seen that in December, 1889, Secretary Windom presented to Congress a silver proposal which President Harrison, although he had given it only a hasty consideration, approved. Congress, however, was not pleased, and the silver men began an immediate protest. On January 20, 1890, Senator Teller of Nevada called on the President to oppose the "Windom" silver bill; a "safe and sound" meas-

[1] A. Dewey to John Sherman, June 8, 1890. Sherman MSS. Vol. 50, #43618.

ure could mean to him only free coinage. Harrison insisted on a Republican law which would "unify the party and satisfy the country," but the financial uneasiness, the revolt among the silver men in Congress, and the increased hoarding of money were certain evidence that such an aspiration was hopeless.

Throughout the first six months of the year the doors of the Executive Mansion swung open to many and divers persons. The President, anxious to secure a compromise which would insure Republican supremacy and party harmony, admitted silver Senators and Congressmen along with those members of Congress who were urging new revenue legislation; Wall Street emissaries and industrial representatives called as well. Cabinet meetings were long and often animated. The possibility of a panic which loomed always on the horizon brought much discussion of the "disturbance" in Wall Street. James G. Blaine, the "Plumed Knight," now Secretary of State because he was less dangerous in Washington, grew excited at one session and broke up the meeting by blurting out, "To hell with Wall Street!" The President's dinner hour often found many Congressmen gathered at his table to talk over the political situation, and, although the General and Mrs. Harrison served no wines, much was accomplished by these "silver dinners." Senator Aldrich announced on April 23 that an agreement had been reached, but Senators Teller and Jones proposed to continue the fight for silver regardless of the tariff hopes of the party. Finally, as has already been recorded, Congress passed an unsatisfactory and highly unfortunate compromise measure, named after the man who had done most to smooth its path—the Sherman Act.

The Bland-Allison Act had provided that the government should purchase from 2,000,000 to 4,000,000 ounces of silver per month. The Sherman silver bill, signed on July 14, 1890, specifically stated that 4,500,000 ounces should be purchased each month. The suggestion that $4,500,000 per month be bought was defeated in conference by some of the more hope ful followers of silver because they feared that when the price of that metal went up, the purchases would be too small! With the passage of the Sherman law the net silver balance began to turn against the United States. The flow of silver from San Francisco to the Orient ceased altogether after May 1. Other countries cared no longer to hold United States bonds, but they did wish to share in the silver feast. Invitations were extended to silver venders to meet at the Treasury steps at one o'clock on Monday, Wednesday, and Friday of each week. With the largest money vault in the world rapidly being filled with silver dollars, it was certainly a bad time to set up a market at the Treasury doors! [1]

The provision for the additional purchase of silver aggravated the fears of the financial community. The great hoard which had been piled up in the Treasury under the previous silver law had done much to undermine the faith of the people in the ability of the government to maintain the gold standard. With the appearance of the Treasury notes which were now issued on the bullion purchased under the Sherman legislation, what confidence was left rapidly disappeared. Had it not been for a fortunate agricultural situation, a panic would certainly have followed immediately. The Treasury notes did not take their place along with the silver certificates as indirect obligations upon the gold reserve; they more nearly resembled the gold certificates. This was for the simple reason that, while the law which created them said that they were redeemable "in coin" at the discretion of the Secretary of the Treasury, it put upon him the duty of maintaining the two metals "at a parity." Thus the Sherman law succeeded only in increasing the gold obligations of the Treasury; it did not create the expected increase in trade or commodity prices. Quotations for the metal rose temporarily, but later fell to new low records.

[1] In 1888 the Treasury completed a vault 89 feet long, 51 feet wide and 11 feet, nine inches high, interior measurements. The first silver was stored on August 29, 1888, and it was estimated that its capacity of $100,000,000 would be sufficient for three years, but the increased purchases by the Sherman silver law made this estimate much too optimistic.

The financial crisis which had been threatening for some time appeared to be imminent in the first days of September. After the Baring failure in London the banks of New York were in a trying situation, and the smallest incident might precipitate a panic. Appeals for help from Wall Street filled the mail bags for the Executive Mansion. Harrison was at Cresson Springs in Maryland, while Secretary Windom was in Massachusetts, out of reach of the telegraph. The President took charge of the situation, and for several days following the twelfth, telegrams passed almost hourly between him and his Assistant Secretary of the Treasury at Washington. When Windom was located, he hurried home by way of New York, where he stopped to consult with the financiers. When again in his office in the Treasury Building, he ordered the purchase of bonds for the relief of the situation. The idle dollars in the Treasury were to be used as a stimulant to revive the staggering financial system.[1]

The McKinley tariff bill, following so closely on the Sherman Act, is often held responsible for the almost magical disappearance of the surplus, but it was not so greatly to blame as many other factors. Executive disbursements drew most heavily from the government coffers. The passing of the European crisis did not relieve the situation in the United States; the fear for the standard of value grew more acute as Treasury notes displaced other kinds of money in the pockets of Uncle Sam. The customs receipts showed little other currency, and the bankers' vaults were all too full of this new paper. Gold was flowing outward to Europe at an alarming rate. Certainly the prediction of the President in his message to Congress in December, 1890, that the Sherman law would bring a "quickening and enlargement" of the manufacturing industry, better markets for breadstuffs and provisions, more constant employment and better wages, and "an increased supply of a safe

[1] The author is indebted to Professor A. T. Volwiler for kindly assistance on this period.

currency for the transaction of business" was far from warranted, and equally unjustified was the statement of his Secretary of the Treasury that "it [Sherman law] has been the means of providing a healthy and much-needed addition to the circulating medium of the United States."

During the fiscal years 1890 and 1891 more than $230,000,000 of bonds were redeemed in an effort to ward off the financial crisis which the Sherman law threatened to bring. These redemptions, however, did nothing toward relieving the fear which was oppressing the industrial and business life of the nation; indeed, they did little more than to relieve the Treasury of its gold supply. More than $72,000,000 of gold disappeared from the Treasury in the twelve months following July 1, 1890; and the cash balance was reduced in the same period from $245,512,464 to $153,893,809, despite the facts that the surplus during the year was $37,000,000 and that $54,000,000 was transferred from the bank-note redemption fund to the available cash account.

With every bond purchase the silver advocates were further strengthened in their determination to fight the "bloated bond-holders." They were not content with the fact that "nearly two thousand cart loads of silver must be stowed away each year in the Government vaults." [1] Practically the entire output of the silver mines in America was represented in the 1,851 tons of silver the purchase of which the Sherman law had made compulsory, and yet the political demands for free silver were still unsatisfied. Scarcely had Congress convened in December before the representatives from the Western States were urging a financial course in conformity with the wishes of the people of their States. Under the leadership of Richard Parks Bland they pushed forward a free-silver bill in the early months of 1891. Bland, born in the flats of Muddy Creek in western Kentucky, "wanderer in the West" and pioneer in the silver cause, had able supporters. Even Mc-

[1] Report of the Treasurer, in *Report of the Finances,* 1891, p. 20.

Kinley, five years later the leader of the Republican forces against cheap money, was outspoken in the cause of silver.[1] On January 14, just six months after the passage of the Sherman silver bill, a free-silver measure was forced through the Senate —the silverites had helped Ingalls of Kansas carry out his threat to smite his enemies "under the butt end of their left ears"! The threatened legislation created great excitement in the financial centers, and some anticipation of easily gotten gains. "I quite understand that the average Congressman invariably disregards opinions from New York upon this subject, because New Yorkers are all united in a conspiracy to promote the value of gold!" wrote a financier of that city to John Sherman, but, he added, "you know very well that, whilst we are averse on commercial and moral grounds to any such foolishness as is now proposed to be enacted, on the other hand, it is our business to take advantage of monetary disturbances and Wall Street people would make no end of profit out of the inflations and fluctuations which would follow in the value of commodities, before the final and inevitable reaction. That is what we are here for!"[2]

The discussion of the silver question was particularly unfortunate at just this time. Already alarmed by the Sherman law, those who had contracts to make began to insert gold clauses in them. Such a stipulation protected the person who was to receive the money, but it placed a greater obligation upon the payer. Every man who owed debts payable in gold was forced to think of the question where that metal could be obtained should silver become the chief medium of exchange; anyone who possessed gold hesitated to pay it out except in the cancellation of those debts which could not be discharged in any other money. This applied to corporations and to the government no less than to individuals. The financiers were fearful lest the burdens upon the gold reserve should prove too heavy. They believed that the 382,245,265

[1] See Toledo, Ohio, speech, January 17, 1891.
[2] Sherman MSS. Vol. 535, #47089 Jan. 14, 1891.

THE POLITICAL SAFE-BREAKERS FOILED
(Puck, 1893)

Bland-Allison dollars, and the monthly $4,000,000 of Treasury notes as provided by the Sherman law, all took their value directly from this gold fund. The disappearance of that reserve meant to them a scaling down in value of all their possessions. The portent of the silver standard was certainly increasing, and its ability to create fear and alarm when invoked by Western political voices in the halls of Congress was prodigious. William Henry Smith of the Associated Press expressed something of the fear and pity in the hearts of the Easterners in closing a letter to John Sherman: "And poor Ingalls! proclaiming the superior wisdom of the uneducated masses in formulating a financial policy!" [1]

Meanwhile, Congressional expenditures added their part toward making a bad situation worse. Many members of the Fifty-first Congress objected to the enrichment of Eastern bondholders by Windom's purchase of their securities at far above par. They became insistent that the surplus be distributed among the common people—the common people who held the ballot! Moreover, some wanted all the surplus expended in order to force the government to print more money. Pension appropriations were increased, doles for the improvement of rivers and harbors grew, and no department was content with its usual amount; every committee made its estimates as though there were no other method of reducing the store of unused money in the Treasury. There was not, however, the "orgy" of extravagance which many have pictured, although the title of "the billion dollar Congress" was accurate. Had bond redemptions been withheld, the Treasury, despite its lessening revenues, could have sustained the Congressional extravagance without embarrassment; indeed, had such a course been followed, the balance in the Treasury at the end of the administration would have amounted to almost $275,000,000.

The excessive redemptions, in addition to depleting the assets of the Treasury, entirely changed the relations of that institution to commerce and business. By holding the redundant

[1] Jan. 16, 1891, Sherman MSS. Vol. 535, #47160.

currency in its vaults, the Department had served as practically a part of the banking machinery of the country; the high tariff had kept a constant stream of money flowing out of the channels of circulation into the Treasury. The money was returned to the people on the orders of the Secretary or upon the expressed will of Congress. This accidental and capricious system of elasticity may have been of some benefit. But when the vaults were emptied, the government lost its dominating position and became dependent upon business for its existence.

While Congress and the Executive Department were foolishly spending the money of the government, the fear in the country for the gold standard continued to grow in intensity. The Sherman notes, which were constantly increasing at the rate of over $50,000,000 per year, came month by month to make up a larger percentage of the money received by the Treasury. With an increasing mortgage upon its gold reserve, the government needed gold more and more; yet with every decline in the reserve people were less and less disposed to pay gold into the Treasury. They paid bills of a less desirable kind. When the Treasury notes increased to a sufficient amount, they might become the sole money of the government. The impending danger caused the associated banks of New York to refuse their gold for export, and the Treasury was compelled to furnish all of that metal required for shipment to Europe. This demand attracted the attention of the whole world. The United States Treasurer said of the situation, "To the Treasury this outflow was particularly significant, since the Treasury was obliged to furnish all the material . . . this gold was drawn almost altogether from the sub-treasury in exchange for other kinds of money." The exporter, he said, could not be blamed if his clients had been willing to pay his premiums, or because his operations "in the short space of six months had drained the country of the tenth part of its entire stock of gold."

The threatened crisis of 1891 was postponed only by the fortunate event of a large crop. Throughout the early summer the Department of Agriculture had been issuing encouraging reports in regard to crop prospects, and the harvest proved indeed a bountiful one. Such a harvest had come at so favorable a time once before—in 1879, when the yield was large and the European demand was pressing. Now the European demand was again abnormally large because of the failure of the Russian wheat crop and greatly decreased yields in other countries. France had not had so small a return from her farms in thirteen years.

The demand for money with which to rush the crops to market relieved the East of its gorge of Treasury notes and gave the Treasury a breathing spell. Farmers found money in their pockets again, and inland transportation systems profited. In October $16,000,000 of gold came from Europe in payment for the agricultural products. This encouraging situation, however, lasted no longer than it took to market the bumper crop. When that task was over, the money which a few months before had gone out to the interior from Eastern financial centers returned in enormous quantities, but nobody wanted it, and the government could not call it into its vaults again. The existence of great quantities of the Treasury notes was more obvious than ever, and the fear in regard to the gold reserve increased in proportion.

The goal toward which political financiering had been pointing for many years was reached by July 1, 1892; at that time began the test of whether the government could redeem its ever-accumulating promises to pay in gold. On that day $3,000,000 in gold was taken from the Treasury for export, but only $500,000 was in exchange for gold certificates. The remainder was in exchange for greenbacks and Treasury notes. By the end of the month $10,000,000 in gold had been taken from the vaults, and the account books of the government showed that only $1,500,000 in gold certificates had been received. The redemptions in July exceeded those of any previous year. Few could be in doubt as to the ultimate result. The law compelled the Secretary to re-issue the greenbacks when they were redeemed; hence, if the practice of redeeming them in gold became fixed, only the speed with which they circulated would determine the length of time which they required to withdraw all that metal from the Treasury. Because of its lack of cash the Treasury was also compelled to pay out the Treasury notes as fast as they were received, and they too became buckets on the endless chain which relentlessly dipped the gold out of the government coffers.

The behavior of the gold flow at this time demonstrated the fact that the financial relations of the United States with the rest of the world were thoroughly disrupted. Gold usually flowed out the first six months of the year and returned the last six months, but in December, 1892, the Treasurer pointed out in his annual report that the gold exports which normally stopped in July had continued to September, and that the return shipments which generally commenced early in the autumn had not begun at all. Moreover, silver as a medium of circulation was rapidly overtaking gold; on July 1, 1882, gold exceeded silver by $384,000,000, but by July 1, 1892, the difference had been reduced to $174,000,000.

In an effort to stem the inflationist movement which had been made so alarmingly plain by the course of Congressional legislation, President Harrison took steps to secure an international agreement in regard to the use of silver. A conference was practically forced upon Europe,[1] but the results were negligible. Apparently nothing could be done to avoid the long-threatened disaster. Secretary Foster plainly told Congress in December that his Department might not be able to maintain redemptions. Despite the facts that the Treasury Department had inherited $266,000,000—$196,000,000 of which was gold—from the preceding administration, that more than $75,000,000 of the bank-note redemption fund had been made available for expenditure, and that there had been a small surplus each year, the vaults of the government were, except for the $100,000,000 reserve, practically empty.

[1] See correspondence in Department of State with various European countries.

THE PANIC OF 1893

Most of the blame for the empty purse must be laid upon Harrison and Windom, for the Treasury had spent almost $275,000,000 in bond redemptions during this period. Charles Foster, who had succeeded to the position of Secretary of the Treasury upon the death of Windom in New York on January 29, 1891,[1] expressed his disapproval of this fair-weather policy by recommending the unconditional repeal of the law which permitted but in no way compelled the redemption of bonds of the government with any cash in the Treasury not otherwise appropriated. His recommendation could be of no value now because his money was gone—those desiring extravagant expenditures had gained a vantage ground, the fear of the ability of the government to maintain the gold standard had become fixed, and the gold reserve was being rapidly depleted.

By February 1, 1893, the gold in the Treasury had dropped within $8,000,000 of the established minimum reserve. Secretary Foster hurried off to New York for a conference with the bankers; a Cabinet meeting was held when he returned to Washington, and it was decided that bonds were to be issued only in case of extreme emergency.[2] The editor of the London *Economist* wrote on February 18 that the "bomb" of the week was the decision of the President not to sell bonds. The banks came to the rescue of the Secretary by exchanging some of their gold for legal-tenders, but this could be only a temporary expedient. The metal left the Treasury faster than it could be obtained. By the midde of the month Congress, under the pressure of the administration, was being urged to grant au-

---

[1] Secretary Windom gave the principal address—and as it happened, the only one—at the annual dinner of the New York Board of Trade and Transportation. He said, among other things: "As poison in the blood permeates arteries, veins, nerves, brain, and heart, and speedily brings paralysis or death, so does a debased or fluctuating currency permeate all the arteries of trade, paralyze all kinds of business, and brings disaster to all classes of people." He closed his speech at ten with the quotation, "He that loveth silver shall not be satisfied with silver"; a few seconds later he suffered a heart attack and slumped from his chair onto the knees of Secretary Tracy. Eleven minutes later he was dead.

[2] *C. F. C.*, Feb. 18, 1893, p. 262.

thority for the issue of three per cent bonds. The Senate attached a proviso of this nature to the Sundry Civil bill then pending in that body. On February 20, in anticipation of its passage, Secretary Foster ordered the Bureau of Engraving and Printing to prepare plates for the contemplated bond issue; "You are directed to hasten the preparation of the designs and plates in every possible manner," he wrote the Chief of that Department. The President and his Secretary of the Treasury were watching the gold reserve with unconcealed anxiety, hoping against hope that March 4 might come without an actual crash. Foster openly stated that his greatest wish was to pass on the office to his successor before the little gold which he possessed had been exhausted.

* * *

Thus when Carlisle took the oath of office as Secretary of the Treasury, the task which confronted him was staggering. Gold redemptions in the preceding three months had exceeded $34,000,000; the free gold in the Treasury in excess of the reserve was $982,410, and all other available money amounted to slightly more than $24,000,000, nearly half of which was in small coin.[1] The Republican administration had barely escaped the results of its practices, but the margin was sufficient to enable it to blame its successors for the financial evils of the next four years.

By March, 1893, the anxiety of many people had reached as definite a climax as had the actual monetary situation. Their apprehension expressed itself in an eager grasp for gold; advocates of silver sought it no less than defenders of the gold standard. Gold payments for customs and internal revenue dues practically ceased. The Treasury found itself in a hopeless situation, while the business of the country was severely

---

[1] See *Report of the Secretary of the Treasury*, 1893; Second reply of Carlisle to the Bond Investigation Committee in Bond Sales Investigation, *Senate Documents*, Vol. 5, 54 Congress, 2d Session. Hereafter cited as Bond Investigation.

declining. Europe felt that America was on the verge of a financial disaster.[1] A dozen men were counting silver dollars in the basement of the Treasury, and they drew several monthly checks before the labor was finished.

In order to increase his gold reserve Secretary Carlisle made use of the method which Secretary Foster had employed—that of exchanging legal-tenders for gold with the banks. These institutions were willing to aid, but their gold supply was limited. It was perfectly evident that some other method of replenishing the Treasury's stock of gold must be found. Secretary Carlisle, because he was uncertain as to his authority to act without the sanction of Congress, and because the political program made it advisable to avoid party dissensions, hesitated at first to take any positive action.

President Cleveland let it be known that suggestions from men versed in finance would be welcomed, and his invitation met with a prompt response. Many gave the subject serious consideration, among them being Henry Lee Higginson, William Endicott, Jr., Charles Paine, Dwight Braman, C. C. Jackson, J. Pierpont Morgan, and other important figures in the financial world. There also came a flood of volunteer suggestions that were by no means as sound as those given by the leading bankers who were trying to aid the country. Hundreds of letters offering solutions are preserved in the papers of the President and the members of his Cabinet; laborers, farmers, speculators, silver men, gold men, bimetallists, and every other group of currency theorists had their pet panaceas. From one ingenious mind came the idea of paying everything in

---

[1] See the files of the London *Economist;* Andrew D. White reported in a despatch of May 12, to the State Department, that the Financial Minister of Russia had spoken to him of the gloomy financial situation, "especially, as to the present and future effects of the silver bill in the United States." White asserted that the United States would maintain its credit. "To this he made answer by reading me a letter just received from his special financial agent at Paris, which . . . took a gloomy view of the general situation, and, among other causes of alarm, referred to the American Silver policy. . . ." Department of State, Despatch No. 94, Russia, Vol. 44, May 12, 1893.

silver, thus choking the advocates of that money with their own metal; another helpful soul suggested that all sales of postage stamps in lots of five dollars or over should be paid for in gold, asserting that this would bring out the hoarded coins.

While all this advice was being showered upon him, the Secretary of the Treasury was still faced with the grim facts that silver was piling up in the Treasury vaults, that the value of the metal in the silver dollar was each day growing less, and that his gold reserve was being rapidly depleted. Gold demands increased at an alarming rate in March and April, and yet the Treasury could not do otherwise than pay in gold, because the Sherman law provided that the two metals were to be maintained at a parity. Of this President Cleveland said in his *Presidential Problems* several years later: "The parity between the two metals could not be maintained, but, on the contrary, would be distinctly denied, if the Secretary of the Treasury persisted in redeeming these notes, against the will of the holders, in dollars of silver instead of gold. . . . Therefore it came to pass that the Treasury notes issued for the purchase of silver under the law of 1890 took their place by the side of the United States notes, commonly called greenbacks, as demands against our very moderate and shifting gold reserve." Secretary Carlisle found that with each successive day a smaller amount of real value could call from his precarious balance one hundred cents in gold. There was a demand in some quarters for recoining the silver dollars in order to make them worth their face value, but this was impracticable.

Secretary Carlisle was not long to watch over the $100,000,000 gold reserve; it was soon to shrink toward extinction. The bankers and other financial men had long before begun to sort out the gold from their money and pass on their paper, but in spite of these efforts the paper continued to pile up in the various bank vaults. Gold was too inconvenient a medium with which to transact business, and paper was necessary; but every day the financial community grew more fearful lest the crash might come and leave it with a large amount of depreciated currency on its hands. The actions of Secretary Carlisle were not such as to allay this uneasiness. Rumors had spread that there might be a change in the policy of redemption. Carlisle had been at one time, by repute at least, an advocate of free silver, and the public mind was not at all certain that he would adhere to the policy of redeeming all moneys in gold. This fear was increased by the fact that there was nothing in the law which made the silver certificates definitely redeemable in gold.

On April 15 the Secretary suspended the further issue of gold certificates in accordance with the law of July 12, 1882, which gave him authority to do so when the reserve fell below $100,000,000. The reason for this was obvious. A man presenting certificates to the Treasury window could not carry away a very large amount of gold; he must take his money in something more wieldy. The reserve had not at the time dropped below the minimum limit, but Secretary Carlisle was convinced that it could not be maintained at the required level. The President was of the same opinion.

As the gold reserve hovered just above the $100,000,000 mark, speculation as to what would happen when it dropped below that amount became rife. Many problems would present themselves if the Secretary failed to maintain the fund at or above this minimum. The sum had been set aside on the books of the Treasury to insure the gold value of the greenbacks. The question whether it could be used for any other purpose now became serious not only to individuals, but to the government as well. In the first place, those who possessed Treasury notes were hopeful but by no means certain that they could continue to look for gold in exchange. The Sherman law established no gold reserve to maintain the value of these notes, for they were based upon silver bullion stored in the Treasury. It could not be, then, that they represented any claim on the gold reserve; yet the law which created them declared that they were to be redeemed in gold or silver "coin" at the "discretion of the Secretary." However, if the Secretary had no gold with which to redeem these Treasury notes, he could only pay out the silver which they represented. Rumor asserted that Carlisle had talked to Senator Vest on the streets of Washington and had intimated that he might be constrained to pay them in silver. The use, then, to which the gold in the Treasury could be put after it fell below $100,000,000 was of vital interest to those who were holding this particular currency.

In the second place, there were certain obligations, such as interest on the public debt and the principal of maturing bonds, which the government was required by honor, according to all its statesmen, to meet in gold. The question whether the greenback fund could be used for any other purpose was no less interesting to the holders of these obligations than to the holders of the Treasury notes. Europeans were vitally concerned in this phase of the whole problem. In the third place, those who held greenbacks were eager to know what decision would be made, because the answer might determine whether the money which they held was worth one hundred cents in gold. Everybody knew that there were more than three dollars of greenbacks outstanding to every dollar of gold in the reserve for their redemption; if the fund was compelled to assume also the burden of the constantly increasing Sherman notes, in addition to the Treasury obligations, the reserve was of too small a ratio to be of any value. Last, but not least, was the question of what the Treasury itself would do for money with which to pay its ordinary expenses in this emergency if $100,000,000 of gold must be maintained for no other purpose than for redeeming greenbacks.

The business world was thoroughly alarmed by April, and expected to be precipitately thrown at any time upon a silver standard. "There is a feeling of disappointment and uneasiness, which is steadily growing, over the manner in which the Government has apparently allowed the business of providing to maintain the hundred million gold reserve intact, to drift along. It extends to England I know, and probably to the continent," wrote James Stillman from New York on April 16; two days later C. E. Perkins, president of the Chicago, Burlington, and Quincy Railroad, wrote Colonel Lamont: "We are all getting a little anxious about gold. If some policy could be announced it would make people feel better— To drop to a silver basis with two millions in bank would not be pleasant for the C. B. & Q." The next day Henry Lee Higginson of Boston wrote to Richard Olney: "I sit and wonder if you gentlemen in Washington know how very uneasy the legitimate property holders and merchants of the country are about the state of the currency. . . . We have perhaps gold enough, if we know that the United States Treasury is to be depleted no farther than it already is, and if we know that our paper is to be held at par; but this we do not know. People are in a state to be thrown into a panic at any minute, and, if it comes, and gold is withdrawn, it will be a panic that will wake the dead, . . . I believe it to be a very great mistake, if the gold reserve is allowed to fall below $100,000,000, for that point has been held sacred and had better be kept so. Do not forget how much imagination has to do with all business operations. People as old as we are dread panics very much, because there is no reason left and because there are terrible sacrifices for most excellent people."

Many of the New York financiers were disgruntled because the Secretary of the Treasury neither asked their advice nor told them what he intended to do. Henry Clews, author of *Twenty-eight Years in Wall Street* and defender of William K. Vanderbilt in his unfortunate remark concerning the public, wrote on April 19: "There is no disguising the fact that a feeling of distrust reigns supreme here in all business circles. Everybody is at sea like a ship without either compass or rudder, simply drifting from day to day because of ignorance as to what the Secretary of the Treasury will or will not do. During all similar trying periods within my long recollection it has been the practice of the Secretary of the Treasury to make a flying trip to New York to confer with such people as he and his sub-Treasurer would designate and innumerable panics have been averted simply by the Secretary putting in an appearance at the N.Y. Sub-Treasury. I beg to suggest therefore that it would be an extremely good thing for Secretary Carlisle to run over to New York for one day at least. It would certainly have a most cheering influence at this time of gloom. It would be a pity to have a financial crash occur in this country just at the time of the opening of the World's Fair, which everybody has been looking forward to as a means of making good times everywhere. Not being acquainted with Mr. Carlisle will account for my addressing this letter to you on a matter connected with his department." [1]

It was plain that some decision must be made by the Executive Department. On the evening of April 20 the Secretary and the President had an anxious conference at the White House. Carlisle had with him extracts from all the laws concerning the redemptions. "And then it was that, after considering the matter as carefully as we could, we determined that under the provisions of the Sherman law the Secretary had the right to use the gold in redemption of the Treasury notes." [2] The Secretary, with the approval of the President,[3] prepared a statement which appeared in the press on the morning of the twenty-first, the intent of which was to quiet the public mind and to allay the rumors concerning the redemptions of Treasury notes. The result, however, was far from satisfactory. The announcement was definite enough, but it contained the unfortunate expression that these notes would be redeemed "so long as he has gold lawfully available for that purpose." For weeks the financial community had been frantically discussing the question as to whether the $100,-

---

[1] Cleveland MSS.

[2] Bond Investigation, p. 239; no announcement was ever made as to whether the government would use gold from the reserve fund for interest payments and for ordinary expenditures. When it became necessary, however, the reserve was used freely for these purposes.

[3] Unpublished Diary of Charles S. Hamlin.

000,000 gold reserve could be lawfully used for the redemption of the Treasury notes. The Secretary had not answered the question, and the excited public, ignoring what else was said in the dispatch, persisted in interpreting "lawfully available" as meaning only that gold which was not included in the reserve fund. Holders of Treasury notes, their fears fed by the rumors that filled the streets, were convinced that the money which they held in their pockets was worth scarcely half the price which they had paid for it.

The Secretary, although he had not made his intentions clear, was not uncertain as to what he expected to do. Scarcely had the troublesome interview been cried on the streets by the newsboys before Secretary Carlisle was instructing his officials in the Treasury Department as to what should be done to uphold the gold standard. Soon J. F. Meline, assistant treasurer at Washington, was coding a telegram for the assistant treasurer at New York. At ten o'clock the wires were carrying the message: "Go ahead as usual. Receive Treasury notes of 1890 if presented for gold coin for export or other withdrawals. Do not make any change in methods until advised by the Secretary of the Treasury. Answer." There was no reply, and at eleven-thirty went the command: "Treasury notes of 1890 must be accepted. The Secretary of the Treasury wants no change; in other words, go ahead as usual. Treasury notes of 1890, if presented, must be redeemed in gold coin. Do you understand? Wire me quick."

Nothing, however, served to check the alarm which had been created. Official Washington was excited; the President, through Secretary Lamont, sent out a call to the bankers of New York City for aid in maintaining the gold in the Treasury, and Secretary Carlisle hurried Assistant-Secretary Hamlin off to Boston to urge the members of the Clearing House there to give one-half of their $10,000,000 of gold to the government in exchange for legal-tenders. James Stillman, president of the National City Bank of New York, replied: "I can hardly sufficiently express my disappointment at not being able to, at least, try and render the President some slight assistance at this juncture in the finances of the country, and I trust that you will convey to him my great disappointment in not being able to respond to his call."[1] The response from Boston was more favorable, and when the Clearing House opened on Monday —the twenty-third—the members voted unanimously to give one-half of their gold to the government in exchange for greenbacks.[2]

The financial community at New York was no less alarmed than the official family at Washington. Andrew Carnegie, canny Scotsman whose advice—as well as his Scotch whiskey, taken from the vat reserved for Queen Victoria—occasionally found its way to the Executive Mansion, felt impelled on the twenty-first to go down to his office for the first time in many months. On the following day he wrote the President: "Let me assure you that in my opinion, the decision to pay notes in gold saved this country from panic, and the entire confusion of its industrial interests. From my own experience I can tell you that foreigners had taken alarm and had begun to withdraw their capital in gold. Unless all doubt is put to rest, there is still great danger of the country being drained of its gold. Had Secretary Carlisle's statement been unequivocal, this trouble would not have arisen. All excitement can be allayed and the crisis safely passed by a simple declaration from you. If I might suggest, somewhat like the following: 'As long as I am President of the United States, the workingman is going to be paid in as good a dollar as the foreign banker is.' I think this would also be good politics. Wherever finances are concerned, there must be no room left for doubt, or everybody wants his money. Just as soon as you dispel all doubt nobody will want it."[3]

President Cleveland yielded to the advice of the financiers, and issued a second statement in regard to the policy of the

[1] Lamont MSS. April 22, 1893.
[2] Hamlin Diary.
[3] Cleveland MSS; see McElroy, II, p. 24.

government in the emergency. This was not for the purpose of calling Carlisle back into line and bolstering up his financial ideas as has been asserted—the President had been consulted in regard to the first announcement. It was to dispel the still widespread misunderstanding of the government's policy. The inclination of the public to accept rumors concerning the intention of those in charge of public finance, said Cleveland in his interview, "seems to justify my emphatic contradiction to the statement that the redemption of any kind of Treasury notes, except in gold, has at any time been determined upon or contemplated by the Secretary of the Treasury or any other member of the present administration." "The President and his Cabinet," he continued, "are absolutely harmonious in the determination to exercise every power conferred upon them to maintain the public credit, to keep the public faith and to preserve the parity between the gold and silver and between all financial obligations of the Government." But the correspondents who had spread the report that the President and his "Bluegrass Secretary of the Treasury" were not in accord were still unconvinced that all was well in the official household.

The President's announcement was given to the press on the evening of April 23, but the long-feared event had already come. On April 22, "notwithstanding the most strenuous efforts by the Department," the gold reserve dropped below $100,000,000.[1] Everybody now knew that the reserve was no longer regarded as a fund solely for the redemption of the greenbacks, but that it must also be used for redemption of the Treasury notes and for paying the obligations of the government. The attitude of the public had already reached the stage of panic. There was really nothing in the mere fact that the reserve had dropped below the $100,000,000 to cause such a calamity, but the psychological effect of the drop was overwhelming. It was overwhelming because business had been watching that index for some years, and by its status determining the probability of the maintenance of the gold standard.

[1] *Report of the Secretary of the Treasury,* p. lxxiii.

Every man hoarded his gold; no one would trust his neighbor, and the general distrust had made the crash inevitable. People were not willing to put their money into any new enterprises, industry and trade declined, and profits diminished. The old family hiding places were sought again, and millions of dollars disappeared from circulation. Because the encroachment upon the reserve did not bring instantaneous disaster, business rallied for a time, but it could not overcome its inherent fears. The event was the beginning of a long series of financial depressions and elevations marked vividly by the jagged graph of the gold reserve. Moreover, it signalized the beginning of one of America's severest panics.

On April 26 Secretary Carlisle, after having made it clear to his corps of assistants that gold must be paid for all notes, "Treasury as well as greenbacks," when requested, joined the President in a hurried visit to New York for consultation with the bankers concerning the financial situation.[1] A fifty-million-dollar loan was discussed, but no agreement was reached, and the two officials returned to Washington to do what they could to prevent the impending panic.[2]

On May 1 the World Columbian Exposition opened in Chicago amid great éclat, but a threatening cloud was present. "It came up from the Atlantic where the two rivers empty into the sea down by the Battery. Notice of its appearance was flashed over the wires of the country on the 3rd day of May, or within forty-eight hours of the opening of the World's Fair." Tension in the commercial community was widespread. Trouble soon came. On May 4 the National Cordage Company collapsed, and with it the general stock market. The day of reckoning was at hand. A few months before, a Populist leader in Kansas had told his hearers, "If all the money that is in the banks were in the pockets of the people, the country would be better off." Apparently all America was now endeavoring to follow this advice. In practically every city long lines of wait-

[1] Hamlin Diary.
[2] *C. F. C.*, April 29, 1893, LVI, 690.

HENRY WATTERSON    JOHN G. CARLISLE

Kentucky's tariff-reform leaders

ing individuals stood before the bank windows demanding their money, and they were perfectly willing to take whatever might be paid to them over the counter rather than risk receiving nothing at all. On May 25 the citizens of Denver, Col., joined by slugs, robbers, and cutthroats, started a run upon the banks which forced them to close their doors; in Helena, Mont., the bankers locked up their vaults before excited individuals could demand their deposits. From May 4 to July 12 more than $194,000,000 was withdrawn from National Banks alone, and proportionate amounts were taken from private banks. Bankers in the West and South found their cash exhausted and loans hard to collect; they called in their reserves and other deposits which they had in the East. "We are becoming alarmed about the financial situation. Banks are contracting their loans, depositors are withdrawing their money and I fear that the result will be the failure of many houses that are now doing a good business and consider themselves in good condition," wrote David R. Francis of St. Louis on June 5.[1]

Each day millions of dollars left New York to be shipped to the stricken interior. "Currency shipments from New York to the interior this week have been on nearly as large a scale as the extraordinary shipments of last week," wrote the *Commercial and Financial Chronicle* on June 17. "The gross shipments of this week have been $10,667,000, and last week were $12,847,000, making $23,514,000 for the two weeks." In the first week of June the call rate in New York rose to seventy-four per cent, and money, when it could be found, was selling on the street at a premium. Banks refused to cash the checks of their own customers unless the latter could prove that it was absolutely necessary to have the money. On June 17 the first issue of $2,500,000 of Clearing House certificates appeared in New York; before the panic had ended, the total reached $41,000,000. The West was not at all displeased with the uncomfortable situation in which the Eastern banker—synonym

[1] Cleveland MSS.

for "goldbug" and "bloated bondholder"—found himself.

The "insane effort of wildly-excited depositors to turn the entire assets of a few financial institutions into cash on a single day" led to the suspension of a large number of banks, although in many cases they really possessed ample assets to meet their liabilities. Many of those in the interior succumbed under the pressure when cash was on the way to them. One hundred and fifty-eight National Banks suspended, and sixty-five went into the hands of the receivers.[1] A large majority of these institutions were in the South, the West, and the Pacific coast region. The aggregate resources of the National Banks decreased more than $400,000,000 between September 30, 1892, and October 3, 1893; of this, $314,000,000 was in individual deposits. Sound as well as unsound financial houses suffered on account of the panic, but an overwhelming majority of all those which failed had been founded within the past few years. Europeans, by returning their securities, joined in the rush to secure cash for their holdings before the gold standard had disappeared. The Eastern bankers were no longer in a position to make loans to the West and South, and citizens of those sections were certain that the refusal was made for the purpose of forcing their representatives to vote for the repeal of the Sherman law. Moreover, with the failure of every financial institution, Western editors reminded their readers that another "goldbug"—with the blessings of "Grover"—had swallowed more millions of the people's money!

John Hay wrote a friend on July 3: "A Blue Funk is in the air, and silver gets all the blame—when it is only a drop in the bucket."[2] The situation was indeed discouraging. Shops were forced to close, the wages of labor fell, and unemployment rapidly increased. Thirty-three stocks shrank more than $400,000,000 between November, 1892, and August, 1893. The number of failures mounted month by month. The liabilities

---

[1] *Report of the Comptroller,* 1893, Vol. I, pp. 10–13.
[2] *Letters and Diaries,* II, 258. (Printed but not published, Washington, D. C., 1908.)

of these failed institutions for April amounted to $8,500,000; for May, $17,500,000; for June, $33,500,000; and for July, the high peak of $73,000,000.[1] In Denver, for the first time in the history of the city, bread money was collected at church on Sunday, July 23. In the wheat-growing region of the Northwest the grain dealers issued elevator scrip which circulated among the people as money. At Minneapolis Charles A. Pillsbury, the St. Anthony and Dakota Elevator Company, Brooks, Griffith & Co., and F. H. Peavey & Co. were able to buy the hard-pressed farmer's grain by this method, and they saw no justice in the government's effort to collect the ten per cent tax to which State currency was subject. Regardless of the need of a larger circulating medium, whoever had a few dollars on deposit was not content until he had it securely in his pocket. The banks of the East were discouraged. "They no longer believe, as affairs are at present that the Treasury can avoid going to a silver basis, and therefore desire to realize the premium on their gold," wrote Jordan to Curtis on July 24.

The story of the panic has been too fully written to be described at length here. It moved from East to West in successive waves which, before it had finished, destroyed many of the soundest of the financial and commercial institutions. The losses in the interior were severe indeed. The West was left, in fact, almost in a state of economic anarchy, which for the next few years expressed itself in the political demand for more money and condemnation of "dear money." Secretary Carlisle suffered in consequence.

There was little that the Secretary of the Treasury could do but wait until the people had come to their senses and the fury of the panic was over. As has already been seen, the dissipation of the surplus prevented the release of money by bond redemptions. The Treasury was no longer a dominating factor in the financial disturbance, but was largely dependent upon the banks for support. The aid which these institutions had given to Secretary Carlisle in his first month of office was no longer possible

[1] *Dunn's Review*, October 7, 1893.

after the panic developed. Carlisle found the problem of securing gold for redemption purposes more and more critical as the demands increased. In the three months immediately preceding June 30 more than $40,000,000 of legal-tenders was redeemed in gold; during the fiscal year the amount totaled $102,000,000. This sum was almost three times as much as had been redeemed since specie resumption began.

A Treasury deficit made the situation worse. Not a single month from July, 1893, to June, 1894, showed a surplus. Because of the premium which was put upon currency, including the silver dollar, the panic soon stopped a drain upon the Treasury by redemptions, but the lack of sufficient revenues caused gold expenditures in meeting the ordinary obligations of the government. The greatest pressure fell upon the New York sub-treasury, and it appeared at times that the Treasury branches in that city and Philadelphia might have to suspend gold payments.[1] In New York City Assistant-Treasurer Jordan used every means in his power to prevent the banks from securing an undue share of his little surplus, and he was forced to guard his legal-tenders almost as carefully as his gold.[2] On August 11 he had $7,000,000 in legal-tenders, and the next week promised to leave him with no money except gold. "I have run to the end of my tether," he wrote Assistant-Secretary Curtis on that day.[3]

With its legal-tenders practically exhausted and its gold reserve below the minimum amount, the Treasury was forced to consider the necessary means of moving the crops to market. For this purpose interior correspondents had vainly sought to secure loans from New York banks.[4] It was apparent that if money was to be obtained to meet this demand, the Treasury would have to supply it; even then there was no assurance that it would not disappear as other millions had done in the pre-

---

[1] C. N. Jordan to W. E. Curtis, Aug. 14, 1893. Curtis MSS.
[2] Curtis MSS. August 11, 1893.
[3] Curtis MSS.
[4] C. N. Jordan to W. E. Curtis, August 15, 1893. Curtis MSS.

ceding months.[1] But money from some source was necessary. Jordan wrote Curtis at Washington on August 15: "I also inclose a letter . . . of the cashier of the Southern National Bank, who says that his Southern Correspondents all want to borrow to 'move the crops,' and he can't afford to lend them in the present state of affairs. If you have any callers from that section you can show this and ask them for the answer. Currency selling at 2 per cent premium." On the following day he again wrote: "Mr. Brown, of Brown Bros. & Co., told me that he did not know how on earth these demands [for moving the cotton crop] could be met, but that he believed that it would be by the same process as in the grain market,—that is, when the price of cotton had fallen below the cost of production, the English buyers would furnish the gold and get the cotton."

Congressman J. L. McLaurin of South Carolina, in pleading for an issue of $125,000,000 of paper money, told the members of the Committee on Banking and Currency of the situation in the South. "There were witnessed every day in nearly all the towns of the cotton belt the sight of wagons, loaded with cotton, being brought into the market and then driven back home, not because there was no demand for that cotton, but because there was no money with which to buy. . . . It got so bad, during September in South Carolina, that it was impossible to get meat in some localities, and I have a letter from my own town, a wealthy town for the South . . . where it is stated that there has not been a pound of meat in the town for a week." [2]

The situation in the larger cities of the South was somewhat relieved by the use of clearing house certificates, but the plight

[1] The Comptroller of the Currency said in his December *Report* that it was not a lack of currency in circulation which had brought the troubles; no amount of money would have aided, he believed. "As long as confidence is destroyed and credit wanting, money hoarding will go on and additional issues but add to the hoardings and give but little, if any, actual relief." In *Report of the Finances,* 1893, p. 361.

[2] Unpublished *Hearings,* House Committee on Banking and Currency, 53 Congress 1st Session.

of the farmer was sad indeed. For years he had blindly worshiped at the throne of King Cotton as his land grew poorer and his debts greater; each year the economic organization of his section bound him more closely to this irresistible master.[1] Populism and free silver were the forces that sprang up from the dragon's teeth that were being sown. The cities, after having been "brightened" by the "crude currency" of the clearing houses, began an insistent demand for an issue of greenbacks.

The Secretary of the Treasury possessed only one satisfactory way of increasing the amount of money in circulation, and that was to supply National Bank notes. For the first time in many years the amount of these notes showed a real increase; the inadequate and overcrowded Bureau of Printing and Engraving was set to work supplying this currency to the banks which had been able to buy in bonds as a basis for circulation. The time for preparing and printing a note was reduced from twenty to fourteen days. "The large room on the third floor [Bureau of Engraving and Printing] revealed the proverbial bee-hive," wrote a correspondent of the Washington *Post* on August 12; tired and worn-out employees poured out of cellar and attic long after regular working hours were over. The increase between March 30 and November 30 was more than $34,000,000; of this, $27,000,000 was issued between July 12 and October 3.[2]

The additional currency aided little, however, because it went immediately into hiding. Nothing, in fact, seemed to help, though many elements were actually contributing to the relief of the situation. Security prices fell to tempting levels, and Europe began to buy back stocks and bonds which she had sold at much higher prices a short time before; the rising price of gold made importations of that metal profitable. In the last days of July gold had begun to flow in from Europe, and in

[1] See Hallie Farmer, "The Economic Background to Southern Populism," *South Atlantic Quarterly*, XXIX, 77–91.
[2] Report of the Comptroller in the *Report of the Finances*, 1893, pp. 342, 379.

August $41,572,031 reached our shores. Soon government revenues began to show an increasing amount of the yellow metal, and by September it made up 58.1 per cent of the receipts from customs. Gold came to be practically the only money used in payments at the New York Clearing House, and it constituted the major portion of the circulating medium of the Atlantic seaboard. People who before this time had seen little of the metal found themselves carrying eagles and double eagles in their pockets.

But the interior still possessed no money. It had suffered grievously, and the seeds of the coming silver crusade had been sown. Many Western towns whose recently installed electric lights had twinkled in the evening of the spring were darkened by fall because the electric companies had failed. Firms which had placarded America with glowing slogans such as "Sioux Falls, The Lowell of the West," "Investment in Kansas Farm Lands will pay better than anything in sight," and "The Red River Valley raised farm products in 1891, the value of which was greater than that of the lands upon which such crops were produced," had now closed up and gone out of business. There were no tenants for many Western farms; 100,000 of the discontented sought new land in the recently opened Cherokee Strip. Merchants in both the West and the South were lending or exchanging with one another small lots of goods in order to avoid ordering new stock. The financiers were no less unfortunate, although they, along with the administration at Washington, were blamed for all the evils which had come. Some of this hostility can be seen in the statement that "persons arrested under this act shall receive no other nor better treatment or greater privileges while in custody before conviction or after conviction than is accorded to persons in custody for violation of other laws of the United States," which Congressman William Jennings Bryan inserted in his bill to punish bank officials for embezzling or misusing funds of their institutions. Had the situation been a matter for jest, many an individual could have quoted the little ditty that was going the rounds:

> Columbus stood an egg on end
> And with a smile and sigh,
> Remarked to those who stood around,
> "It's broke, and so am I."

During these trying months the Secretary of the Treasury was severely criticized for not rendering more effective aid to the country. There was nothing which he could do, for he had no money to distribute; he refused to purchase the 4,500,000 ounces of silver required by law on the ground that the price asked was not the market price.[1] His task of maintaining the gold standard was a trying one, and appeared at times absolutely impossible. Financial men accused him of lacking vision and determination because he did not sell them bonds, while the people of the South and West heaped billingsgate upon him because he did not issue more greenbacks.[2] As a matter of fact, he had no authority to issue greenbacks; a bond sale certainly could not have been floated while the panic was in progress, and later it would have interfered with the repeal of the silver law. The Secretary justly felt that the issue should be sanctioned by Congress. Furthermore, he had no desire to fall into the hands of the Wall Street bankers. Russia offered to lend the United States gold during the stringency, but the proposed rates of interest were so high and the period of the loan so short that such an arrangement could not well be made.[3]

The President and his Secretary of the Treasury felt that the difficulties through which they were passing were caused by a fundamental defect in the financial laws of the country. The

[1] The Sherman law had provided that the Secretary of the Treasury might refuse to purchase silver bullion if the quotation was above the market price. Senator Hiscock, however, had given expression to the common belief when he said that impeachment would be the part of the Secretary who suspended the purchase.

[2] W. J. Talbert of South Carolina told the Committee of the House on Banking and Currency on October 12, 1893, "The President of the United States stands, . . . scepter in hand, daring Congress to give the people what they ask for." Unpublished *Hearings*, p. 182.

[3] See files of the Department of State, Russia, Instructions and Despatches, April to August, 1893.

defect could be remedied, they believed, only by a repeal of the obnoxious silver law. This conviction had been growing for many months, and we must now go back to the inaugural and see the hopes and plans of the party on that day, for repeal and the panic were concurrent problems.

CHAPTER XII   MIDSUMMER MADNESS: THE REPEAL OF THE SHERMAN ACT

When daybreak came to Washington on March 4, 1893, it found the city already astir; eager Democrats were preparing for the restoration of their chief who four years before had surrendered the Executive Mansion to Benjamin Harrison. The day was not so bright as the hopes of the party members. Snow was falling in fitful spurts and melting into slush, inky water poured along the curbs and into the gutters, and a northwest wind promised ice before the day was over. In the Arlington Hotel the President-elect awaited the hour for assuming the burdens of the Presidency, while diagonally across Lafayette Square the retiring Executive prepared for his journey to Cincinnati. A few hours later the two gentlemen rode down Pennsylvania Avenue toward the Capitol, while thousands of spectators shivered in the increasing cold; hucksters shoved indifferent vehicles fitted with coal-oil stoves along the fringe of the crowd and reaped a happy harvest from the sale of hot coffee and fried oysters. The wind tore the bunting from its hangings and whipped the flags into shreds; whirling snow stung the faces of the onlookers.

Grover Cleveland elected to give his inaugural address before taking the oath of office. Wearing an overcoat scarcely thick enough to protect him from the biting wind and holding his high silk hat in his left hand, without notes or manuscript the incoming President faced the great sea of upturned faces and began where he had left off four years before—at the tariff. "The verdict of our voters which condemns the injustice of maintaining protection for protection's sake," he declared, "enjoins upon the people's servants the duty of exposing and destroying the brood of kindred evils which are the unwholesome progeny of paternalism."

It was clear that the Democracy intended to take up again

the problem of tariff reform. "The immediate program of the administration had already been settled between the President and, as I understand Messrs. Gresham, Carlisle, and Lamont, without consultation with other gentlemen who afterwards entered the cabinet," wrote Richard Olney in his unfinished *Autobiography*.[1] "The burning question was of the immediate convocation of Congress. The campaign had been fought and won by the Democrats on the question of tariff reform. The elections had been overwhelmingly in favor of the new administration on that issue and the immediate enactment of a new tariff bill was expected by the country and would have been simply carrying out the pledges given by the Democratic party."

But the election promises of the Democrats were to go unfulfilled, for the financial situation that rapidly came to a crisis after March 4 turned the energies of the President to the repeal of the Sherman silver law and brought into Congress a long and bitter fight. Democratic hopes of tariff reform which had so often gone awry were again deferred, not because of the protectionists in the party, but on account of the financial condition which had been brought on by the silver demands. Regardless of their blustering tariff-reform plans before the inaugural, the Democrats realized that something must first be done in regard to the silver question. Under the leadership of Carlisle, the party had, in fact, begun efforts at repeal as early as January, 1893. Senator Carlisle led the fight not alone in the Senate, but in the House as well; on January 7 he wrote Congressman W. C. P. Breckinridge of Kentucky:

> I am quite anxious that Kendall should vote in the Committee on Banking and Currency for the bill to repeal the Sherman silver act. The proceedings today showed that the bill can be reported even if he votes against it, but it is important to have as many Democratic votes as possible for it. Kendall voted today for the free coinage amendment offered by Town-

[1] Preserved in the Olney papers.

send, but it was defeated by a large majority. Having expressed his views by that vote, he ought now to vote with all the other Democrats, *except Cox, of Tenn,* to report the bill—The Cate amendment can do no harm, and its adoption will help the bill with the free coinage members. If Kendall will vote to adopt that amendment and then vote to report the bill, he will be in accord with all his Democratic associates on the Committee, except Cox, and his course will be consistent all through, for I think the very best way—in fact the only way—to secure ultimately the full remonetization of silver is to repeal the Sherman act and thus compel other nations to agree with us upon an international ratio.

If you agree with me as to the policy of repealing the Sherman law, I hope you will see Kendall on the subject before the Committee meets on Monday.

The report that Mr. Cleveland wants the Sherman act repealed and the Bland act restored, is not true. He is very anxious to have the S. act repealed and if it can be done *only* by restoring the Bland act, he would of course take that as better than no relief—but even then only as a temporary measure.[1]

Cleveland lent his aid to the movement; he and Carlisle had nurtured the future hopes of the party in many an intimate conference during the Harrison administration. The state of the finances had gradually taken the place of the tariff topic after the election of 1892, and the President-elect was not hopeful. On January 22 he wrote the Senator:

Though I was very glad to read your reassuring words, I confess I am not as hopeful as I would like to be. My belief is most confident that if the question could be presented to both houses for a vote, that much would be favorable.

I have been thinking lately what a shame it is that you and I must worry so much over a thing that ought to be a subject of the lesser importance to any man who loves his country as with any democrat who loves his party.

I am beginning to ask myself why at this time we should

[1] Breckinridge MSS.

REPEAL OF THE SHERMAN ACT

be called upon to bear the indifference and opposition of those in our party, who, on any ground, ought to be laboring for the suspension of the purchase of silver. Its continuance, without even the promise of cessation, undoubtedly endangers the prosperity of the country; and it certainly threatens with disaster the Democratic party and the incoming administration.

I don't like to think that there are alleged democrats in Congress who do not desire the success of our administration; but it is hard to keep such thoughts out of my head.

I have made up my mind not to submit to this without at least giving some sign that I understand the situation.

If this silver business is not in some way adjusted before the 4th of March, the question will present itself whether a Special session ought not to be immediately called after that date, for the consideration of the subject; and whether in the meantime the distribution of the patronage ought not to be entirely and absolutely postponed.

One thing may as well be distinctly understood by democrats in Congress, who are heedless of the burdens and responsibilities of the incoming administration and of the duty our party owes to the people. They must not expect us to "turn the other cheek" by rewarding their conduct with patronage.[1]

The repeal effort of the Democrats in the House came to a climax in the middle of February. President-elect Cleveland was an interested observer at Lakewood. On the seventeenth Horace Kenney wired him from the Shoreham Hotel in Washington: "I saw Mr. Carlisle before he left this morning. Silver matter is ready for prompt action and the bill can be passed. Crisp, McMillin, Bacon, Andrew, Tracy, Warner, Breckinridge (Ky.), and Livingston are favorable and many others. My position is very trying and all will be lost unless yourself or Mr. Carlisle will at once wire Tracy, Warner, and Breckinridge for word to go ahead and hold caucus. They are waiting to hear and are anxious to act I beg of you to at once have these gentlemen communicated with and we can win the

[1] Cleveland-Carlisle MSS.

fight." The next day Josiah Quincy wired Cleveland from Boston: "Kenney wires me prospects of silver compromise excellent. Livingston and others standing to agreement, everything depends on action of Carlisle. I have confidence in reliability of Kenney's report." A conference was held at the home of Senator Carlisle at 1426 K Street on the evening of February 19; when it was over, Kenney hurried out to wire Cleveland: "Six pin conference over. Bill will be presented suspending operation of the Sherman act until the excess of silver in the treasury is coined at the rate of three millions a month. This gives us sixteen months to work in. The bill will positively pass." [1]

A few days later Breckinridge of Arkansas introduced in the House a bill embodying the ideas of the repeal Democrats, but its only result was to reveal clearly the division in the party. The rapidly increasing silver army had at last become a real power. The day of compromise and bargain was over; the old parties must reckon with a new force—a force, moreover, which had behind it the pent-up powers of a people who had suffered a generation of economic discontent, a movement which was beginning to revolve around a remarkable group of leaders. Such communications as "Your friends here were very glad to read the record of your four-minute round with Wall Street—which we gave in full in last week's *Signal*," indicate but the beginning of a publicity which before the great silver crusade had ended made William Jennings Bryan, already aspiring to the Senate, the idol of the West.[2]

The determination to tear down the Golden Calf which the unholy East had set up to worship was already fixed in the minds of the Westerners when Cleveland took his second inaugural oath. Governor Lewelling of Kansas had told his hearers at his induction into office in January: "Two great forces are forming in battle line: the same under different form

[1] Telegrams in Cleveland MSS.
[2] A. E. Sheldon, editor of the Chadron (Neb.) *Signal*, to Bryan, February 21, 1893. Bryan MSS.

and guise that have long been in deadly antagonism, represented in master and slave, lord and vassal, king and peasant, despots and serf, landlord and tenant, lender and borrower, organized avarice and the necessities of the divided and helpless poor. I appeal to the people of this great commonwealth to array themselves on the side of humanity and justice." He added to the growing army of the discontented with his plea to the "farmer who wearily drags himself from dawn till dark to meet the stern necessities of the mortgage on the farm, the business man, early grown gray, broken in health and spirit by the successive failures, anxiety, like a boding owl, his constant companion by day and the disturber of his dreams by night." The West was goaded to action by the sight of its own gaping economic wounds, laid bare by the hands of clever politicians.

The financial and political heritage of the Democrats on March 4, 1893, had already made the future of the party precarious. When he took the oath of office, Grover Cleveland was fully conscious of that fact. John G. Carlisle, having accepted the Secretaryship of the Treasury only because he realized that the party situation demanded that no Easterner should hold the office, knew that his official life would not be pleasant. These two leaders thoroughly understood that the political fight for the repeal of the existing silver legislation would be bitter; yet it was growing more obvious each day that the effort must be made. The financial developments after March 4 were making it clearly impossible to avoid the issue.

Cleveland and Carlisle knew that the attempt would be fraught with danger to the party, for they had seen the Democracy grow alarmingly weak in the West in the past few years. Populist doctrines had undermined the party, and free silver was devouring those who retained the name. When the Sherman bill became law in 1890, not a single Democrat had voted for the measure, but 1893 found many objecting to its repeal unless a free-silver bill or, failing that, the maximum provision of the Bland-Allison Act, was substituted. The silver advocates, regardless of party, were now ready to do battle for a piece of legislation which had pleased no one at the time of its passage.

Secretary Carlisle urged immediate action, for he had daily evidence of the ill effects of the silver act. The Treasury notes issued under its provisions had been returning to the Department at a very rapid rate. In March they made up slightly less than fifty per cent of the government receipts at New York. Redemptions in gold of Sherman notes and greenbacks also daily increased. At a Cabinet meeting held early in the administration the Secretary told his associates that "during the eleven months beginning May 31st, 1892, and ending May 1st, 1893, the coin Treasury notes issued for the purchase of silver bullion under the Act of July 14, 1890, amounted to $45,961,184, and that during the same period the amount of such notes paid in gold was $47,745,175. It thus appears that all the silver bullion purchased during the time, except $2,216,011 worth, was paid for in gold, while the bullion itself is stored in the vaults of the Treasury and can neither be sold or used for the payment of any kind of obligations. How long the Government shall thus be compelled to purchase silver bullion and increase the public debt by issuing coin obligations in payment for it, is a question which Congress alone can answer. It is evident that if this policy is continued and the Secretary of the Treasury shall be compelled to issue bonds or otherwise increase the interest-bearing debt, it will be done for the purpose of procuring gold with which to pay for silver bullion purchased under the Act referred to." [1]

The country suffered further evils in the return of securities from Europe. This back flow of foreign-held American obligations was certainly stimulated by the silver legislation. While the farming and laboring classes of all Europe were undoubtedly in favor of bimetallism, the business men felt that silver money was a dangerous experiment, and believed that the United States was rapidly becoming a prey to unsound financial policies. The Duc de Noailles said of the Sherman bill:

[1] Draft preserved in the Curtis MSS.

THE GOLDEN CALF
(*Rocky Mountain News*, 1893)

JOHN BULL GRINDS OUT HIS TUNES TO HIS AMERICAN MONKEYS
(*Rocky Mountain News*, 1893)

"It is far beyond any dream of the alchemists of the Middle Ages in their search for the transmutation of metals. It was done openly without expense or risk, by a sort of official alchemy, with the help of legal tender paper as a solvent."[1] Shortly after the panic of 1893, President Koch of the Imperial Bank of Germany wrote of the silver movement: "I am safe in regarding it as perfectly clear that quick relief is not to be expected from a change in the money standard. Of all subjects this one is the least fitted to be experimented with, for every fruitless attempt causes the ruin of hundreds and thousands of people. America's example should be a warning to us. It is known that a colossal crisis has recently prevailed there. . . . I stand with President Cleveland who has declared that a stable currency is the state's best treasure."[2]

Senator Vilas urged an early session of Congress for the purpose of repealing the Sherman law, pointing out that to wait until the regular session would mean that both the currency question and tariff revision must be presented at the same time. This, the Senator believed, might give the silver followers another opportunity for bargaining and vote trading. On May 1 he wrote Cleveland: "If you should convene Congress . . . under the imminence of financial disaster, and present the sole question not as of less magnitude or consequence, but as less instant because of the impending peril, resulting from our insane financial legislation, and then lend to the demand for the repeal of the Sherman law all the weight which can be justly thrown into the scale, gathering everything to this focus, is it not reasonable to hope for more definite, earlier, better results than if this question is handed over to Congress at the beginning of a Session commonly understood to be in advance of the regular one only that we may execute

---

[1] *Annals of Am. Acad. of Pol. and Soc. Science,* Vol. 5, p. 562.

[2] Quoted in the manuscript of the *Annual Report of the Secretary of the Treasury,* 1893, House of Representatives copy. Other valuable material on the European attitude toward the question of silver is included in these manuscripts, which are stored in the basement of the House Office Building.

the tariff policy with more political advantage?"[1] Four days later Witten McDonald, president of the Midland National Bank of Kansas City, wrote: "The operation of the Sherman law is being severely felt throughout this section and is reacting disastrously to many. . . . Public opinion is changing rapidly. . . . If you will immediately call an extra session and will bring the matter to the attention of the Western and Southern people, in your plain forcible manner, they will 'build a fire' under Senators and Congressmen such as has never been heard of before."

In addition to urging early Congressional action upon the President, the business men of the country were bringing pressure to bear upon Congressmen. M. E. Ingalls, president of the Cleveland, Cincinnati, Chicago & St. Louis Railroad Company, wrote Cleveland: "After leaving you two weeks ago I went to work at once to see what I could do with reference to some of the leading Senators who have been obstacles in the way of the repeal of the Sherman law. I put certain forces at work along our Chesapeake & Ohio Ry. which I hope will have some influence with Senator Daniels. I also took steps to let Senator Voorhees know that his constituents were being injured by the present situation and that they demanded the Chicago platform should be carried out to the letter. I enclose you a letter to this end from the most prominent banker in Indiana, which you can read and throw away. I was in St. Louis on Saturday and took occasion to see some of the intimate friends of Senator Vest. They tell me that the sentiment is changing in Missouri and that the Senator is rapidly getting information that his constituents want a change."[2]

By the middle of June the panic had come; and with gold gone into hiding, and the Treasury Department never certain from day to day that it would have enough to fill the export orders or to meet the demands for redemption, it seemed impossible to delay action much longer. Secretary Carlisle was

[1] Cleveland MSS.
[2] Ingalls to Cleveland, May 8, 1893. Cleveland MSS.

buying only a part of the silver bullion required by law. Silver Senators sought to impeach him for this failure to comply with the statutes, while at the same time many people were urging him to discontinue entirely the purchase of that metal. One citizen of Indiana wanted to enjoin the Secretary from such action. "Its [silver] purchase and storage," he wrote the President, "and the issue of certificates thereon is in no legal sense 'coining money,' and no more authority is vested in Congress to require the Secretary to purchase and store silver bullion in large quantities than there is for requiring the Secretary to purchase large quantities of any other merchantable commodity."

The business interests became insistent that repeal be attempted. Daily the mails brought petitions from the Chambers of Commerce of important cities. On May 20 the Commercial Club of St. Louis declared that the Sherman Act was "only productive of evil in our monetary system and disturbance to the national credit, and that the prosperity of the whole country, agricultural, manufacturing and commercial will be in a great degree promoted by its early and unconditional repeal." On June 30 Harvey Fisk and Sons issued from their New York office a circular which expressed the feelings of many of the financial institutions of the East:

> The demon distrust is stalking about the land, from the Atlantic to the Pacific, leaving in his trail the countless wrecks of the work of thousands of its honorable citizens. The standard of value by which the money of the poor man and the rich man is measured, is being trodden in the dust. Instead of twelve inches to the foot, we are forced to accept six or a little over. The actual intrinsic value of our present dollar is but 53 cents, and growing less daily. Still this great American nation is obliged to calmly face inevitable ruin . . . simply because its Representatives are not called together in accordance with the authority vested in its Chief Executive, and forced to remove from the Statute Books the law which is eating away the vitals of American honesty, of American credit, and casting into a great abyss a century of financial honor.

REPEAL THE SILVER ACT OF 1890. Every day's delay means untold ruin and heartrending distress. Our great United States is fast becoming a financial outcast among the nations of the world. The people of the United States are honest, yet our honesty is impinged.

Requests came by wire, by messenger, and by delegations, but still the President delayed. The party had been elected on the promise of tariff reform, and as Samuel J. Randall and his "handful of half-Democrats" were now out of Congress, there was hope that the Democracy might at last secure a low tariff. To attempt to repeal the Sherman law would certainly disrupt the party, and no one was certain that success would crown the effort. J. Pierpont Morgan, through his attorney, Francis Lynde Stetson, advised President Cleveland to accept a compromise, and then when the finances were in a better condition to repeal the Sherman bill entirely.

Secretary Carlisle was not at all sure that some concessions might not have to be made. Assistant-Secretary Curtis wrote his mother: "I have just had a long conference with Secretary Lamont and Frank Stetson on the financial situation. There will probably be an extra session and a compromise arranged to repeal the Sherman Act and reduce the National Bank tax on money." Whatever the outcome, tariff revision was bound to suffer.

It was only the evident inability of the government to continue gold payments unless something was done that finally led to Cleveland's decision to call Congress in special session on August 7. The proclamation was issued on June 30, and immediately afterward, with every precaution for secrecy, the President joined his surgeons on the yacht of Commodore Benedict in New York harbor, and while moving slowly up the Hudson had "the entire left upper jaw . . . from the first bicuspid tooth to just beyond the last molar, and nearly up to the middle line," with a part of the soft palate, removed because of the discovery of a virulent growth. Secrecy was necessary because Vice-President Adlai E. Stevenson was a silver man, and with the possibility of a free-silver President the announcement of Cleveland's real condition would undoubtedly have caused a new crisis in the financial world. Stevenson had already gathered a group about him who had come to be known among the President and his Cabinet as "the Vice-President's cabinet."

With the country—and even official Washington—ignorant of the state of the President's health, the two opposing groups began a campaign to bolster up their strength before the convocation of Congress. In order to focus the attention of the silverites upon the danger which threatened them, the officials of the mining and smelting companies of Colorado decided in consultation on the day the call for a special session was issued, to order every mine and smelter in the State to close. Colorado would rouse the West and the South to action with an "EARTHQUAKE," said the *Rocky Mountain News* on July 2. The West was ready to meet the issue if the East was determined to force it!

The West was, indeed, not greatly impressed with the reasons given for urging the repeal of the silver purchase act. To that section the idea appeared to be dictated solely by the greedy aristocracy of Wall and Lombard Streets for the purpose of forcing the people of the interior to accept a standard of value which would steal from them their sustenance while it increased the wealth of the "gold barons." The Westerners believed that the circular of Harvey Fisk and Sons and similar appeals represented another selfish plot by the "goldbugs." It seemed to them that the panic was a punitive measure instituted by the capitalists because the West had not supinely accepted the Rothschilds' death-decree to silver; that it was a deliberate, cold-blooded "squeeze" of the people of the United States in order to bring them under the domination of England! Some of the more radical demanded a new revolution of 1776!

The great West was in earnest. A host of speakers were

spread over the country to warn the people of the contemplated action at Washington. As early as May 20 the editor of the Denver *Daily News* called on all organizations to put their forces into fighting trim because "the time between now and the next meeting of Congress is of momentous importance." Charles S. Thomas, silver leader and later governor of Colorado, wrote Secretary Carlisle an open letter in which he charged him with having deserted the cause of the people, and demanded that the government pay its expenses in any kind of lawful money, thus forcing silver dollars into circulation. The Secretary, however, had few dollars other than those covered by outstanding certificates. Badly as he needed gold, he did not possess the necessary available silver dollars to accept the generous offer of individuals who were willing to exchange their gold for silver. He was, indeed, a pauper.

The trans-Mississippi region did not intend to have its financial policy dictated by the East. Governor Davis H. Waite of Colorado announced that his State would coin silver dollars at the old ratio and make them legal-tender. Declaiming to his hearers at a silver convention which met in Denver on July 12, "It is better, infinitely better, that blood should flow to the horses' bridles rather than our national liberties should be destroyed," he won for himself the name of "Bloody-Bridles Waite." Moreover, the "brawny and brainy sons" of Colorado declared that they would not submit to the destiny of poverty without a struggle. "We shall seek to open up new markets and build up our silver industry along new lines and with new and more sympathetic neighbors," they asserted!

These men looked for aid to the South. Past political favors and old alliances, the West believed, would turn that section to their cause. But the South was not, and indeed never became, a united section on the question of silver. Only the small farmer was ever thoroughly converted, and his plight was ample excuse for grasping at anything which promised relief from the virtual economic servitude into which he had been

REPEAL OF THE SHERMAN ACT

forced.[1] The merchant to whom the farmer owed his crop long before it was harvested joined with the conservative leaders of the Democracy to resist the advance of "financial heresy." "The sleep of Southern editors is broken every night by the shrieks of silver under the torture of the 'gold-maniacs' and other devils," declared the *Nation* on June 20. But a broadside issued by the Denver silver convention appealed to the South for a return of the bread which Westerners had cast upon Southern political waters in 1890:

> To the South, Colorado appeals with more soul-felt words. Two years ago you feared with sinking hearts and paling lips, the enactment of the law that threatened to deprive you of self-government and to turn your election booths over to the tender mercies of the federal bayonets on election day. To save you from the outrages of the federal force bill, Colorado's two senators—Republicans—defied the edicts of their party caucus and defeated what was to you the certain humiliation and the horrors of subjection to the electoral will of your former slaves. We saved you then. You can save us now. With us now it is more of a death's struggle than it was then with you. If the schemes of the gold kings are accomplished—if the present silver law shall be unconditionally repealed—the great bulk of us will be made paupers and our beautiful and wonderful state will be set back in its march of progress more than a quarter of a century.

A larger silver convention was called to meet at Chicago in the early days of August. According to the editor of the *Rocky Mountain News*, this was to be a great "gathering of the hosts of bimetallism by the lake shore," and much was expected from the "four days and nights of oratory."[2] Indeed, it was

---

[1] See Chapter on "The Rise of the Silver Democrats" for discussion of the economic situation in the South. The petitions which were sent to Congress at this time throw some light on this question. The merchant and business man and the "planter" were for repeal; the small farmer was against it, and labor was divided.

[2] July 30, 1893.

a great occasion for the mine owners, the Populists, officials of the Knights of Labor, and the members of the two old parties in both the South and the West who had swallowed the promises of free silver. Mayor Carter Harrison welcomed this inharmonious group, and soothed the radicals by reminding them that "while you have been called lunatics so, too, have some of the great men of history been called madmen." Weaver, Waite, Donnelly, Stewart, and others were compared to Caesar, Luther, and Columbus, with Napoleon Bonaparte thrown in for good measure! The convention resounded with scathing denunciations of the "conspiracy of the moneyed aristocracy" and the "crime of 1873" and with declarations of war against England. Joseph Medill, editor of the Chicago *Tribune*, was not moved by the flowing oratory, however. He severely condemned Harrison's welcome and depicted the convention's denunciation of the "crime of 1873" as but "trying to kill over again a horse long since dead." "The next time they want a convention it will be a long way from Chicago," he wrote. "That bloviating old humbug, Governor Waite, could not get blood enough [here] to cover a mouse's tail." The silver advocates in the West promptly boycotted the *Tribune*, as well as every industrial house in the East which did not support free silver.[1]

Meanwhile, the sound-money interests of the country had not been idle. The New York Board of Trade and similar organizations in other cities had been working for repeal. Five days after the call for a special session a fellow-member of the Cabinet wrote Secretary Carlisle: "The bankers, merchants, and others in Boston, interested in the repeal of the Sherman law, are willing to put in some work and to expend some money in accomplishing the object. They would like to know just what should be done and in what direction their energies may be employed to the best advantage. Can't you send me by return mail a list of senators whom you know to be doubtful upon the matter of repeal and who ought to be persuaded to

[1] Chicago *Tribune*, Aug. 1, 2, 3, 4, 5, 1893.

see the thing in the right light?" Secretary Carlisle sent posthaste a copy of the *Congressional Record* marked to indicate the Senators and Representatives "who ought" to be informed upon the silver question. "I do not think much can be accomplished with the gentlemen by direct communications from the East," wrote the Secretary. "The most effective way to reach them is through their personal and political friends in the States and localities where they reside. All our friends in the East have acquaintances and correspondents in the South and West, and the best way is to work through them."[1] Thousands of circulars were distributed. Congressmen of the West complained when they reached Washington that the old soldiers in their districts had been informed that if the Sherman law was not repealed, their pension checks would be payable in fifty-cent dollars.

The Treasury Department was busy during these trying months. The Secretary worked on the question of repeal, but the immediate needs of the Treasury were so pressing that it was difficult to accomplish anything. In July he began to prepare material for the President's special message. On the twenty-fifth Assistant-Secretary Curtis wrote his mother: "Almost everyone is away except the Secretary and me. He is at work on the silver question and I have been 'acting' for two days." At Gray Gables the President wrote as best he could the draft of his sober argument. Secretary Carlisle furnished the financial information, and Richard Olney aided in constructing the paper. The task was barely completed when the President returned to Washington two days before the opening of Congress. "He was accompanied by Secretary of the Treasury Carlisle, Secretary of War Lamont, Attorney General Olney and Mr. O'Brien, the assistant private secretary. . . . He walked with a firm, elastic step and looked altogether as though he had acquired a stock of energy and strength fully to carry him through the long and trying ordeal which awaits him," said the Washington *Evening News*. President Cleve-

[1] Olney MSS.

land certainly faced a trying ordeal, but he was far from energetic and healthy.

The "great battle of the standards" began with the receipt in Congress of the special message of the Chief Executive, who called attention to the fact that despite plenteous crops, abundant promises for manufacturing, and unusual invitation to safe investments, "suddenly financial distrust and fear have sprung up on every side." People who should lend their money were keeping it, he added, and values which were supposed to be fixed were rapidly becoming conjectural. The statement, "I believe these things are principally chargeable to Congressional legislation touching the purchase and coinage of silver by the General Government," seemed to the silver men evidence that the President was allied with the goldbugs. For the Chief Executive to say that "given over to the exclusive use of a currency greatly depreciated according to the standard of the commercial world, we could no longer claim place among nations of the first class" appeared to be proof of the conspiracy which the silver advocates were certain existed. Few people at this time who were not actually interested in international commerce saw any reason why the United States should in any way be concerned with the rest of the world. Cleveland's admonition, "He gives twice who gives quickly," hurried Congressmen not a whit.

The political situation in Congress was intensely sectional, and was complicated by factional jealousies. William A. Peffer, Populist Senator from Kansas, declared that the President's message was "the first attack of money kings in their final struggle for supremacy," and Senator Wolcott, Republican of Colorado, asserted that the silver question had nothing to do with the panic. Richard Bland, Democratic Congressman from Missouri, was sure that the President had made "a plea for a single gold standard because England maintains it. . . . We seem to have lost the spirit of 1776." "Weak as dish water does not express it," was "Sockless Jerry" Simpson's laconic comment in the House. "Honest Old Joe" Cannon told his colleagues in that body that the panic had come because of the fear of a Democratic tariff.[1] On August 9 the cartoonist of the *Rocky Mountain News* added the pictures of Grover Cleveland and John Sherman to "Columbia's Gallery of Execrated Celebrities," which already contained those of Benedict Arnold and Aaron Burr.

The Eastern Democrats and Republicans stood together in favor of repeal—yet the Democrats were somewhat suspicious of the Republicans, who, in turn, saw no particular reason why they should "pull the chestnuts out of the fire for the Democrats." John Sherman had said as early as January: "It is as well known as anything can be that a large majority of the Republican Senators, including myself, are decidedly in favor of the repeal of suspension of the purchase of silver bullion. They are ready to-day or to-morrow or at any moment to vote for such repeal." [2] Sherman's assistance in the repeal fight won for him the title of "assistant Democratic leader" from the silverites, and none too generous comment from the members of his own party. George S. Boutwell, one-time Republican Senator from Massachusetts, had written Senator Morrill of Vermont several weeks before the meeting of Congress: "I cannot congratulate you upon the prospect of engaging next month in a sort of aftermath politics under the leadership of Cleveland, Carlisle and Voorhees with Sherman to propose or to accept some new compromise. If in these thirty years Sherman has had any guiding principles in finance he has so concealed it that I am ignorant of its form and features." [3] But regardless of political animosities, financial fear drove the two parties together.

The gold reserve was some $4,000,000 below the established minimum amount when Congress met on August 7; rates on call loans in New York had reached seventy per cent the previous week; and the interest charged for loans on the

[1] Baltimore *Sun*, August 8, 1893.
[2] Sherman MSS.
[3] Boutwell to Morrill, July 7, 1893. Morrill MSS.

best commercial paper was hovering around fifteen per cent. There was, however, no money to be obtained at any rate. It seemed that confidence in the financial world had completely collapsed. The country was strewn with the wrecks of commercial and industrial houses, and many banks had crumpled under the strain. On August 9 James J. Hill wired President Cleveland from St. Paul, Minnesota: "Entire situation between Chicago and Pacific coast very critical. No grain or farm produce can move for want of money; another week will restrict transactions to necessaries of life. If a test vote on some question can show majority in favor of repeal would help situation." Secretary Carlisle was making frantic efforts to meet the crisis; the mints and the Bureau of Engraving and Printing were working overtime in an endeavor to supply a circulating medium.

Silver Congressmen had moved on to Washington with plenty of material to maintain their fight for an interminable period. They cared little about theories. Congressman Edward Lane of Illinois expressed the current attitude well when he said in the House: "Mr. Speaker, my people do not have to consult Chevalier, John Stuart Mill, Ricardo, or any other writer on finance in order to understand their conditions. They know from personal knowledge that they occupy the garden spot of this whole rich country; that their crops for the last decade have been reasonably abundant, yet their pocketbooks are empty. They have no bank accounts as do the people in the sterile East; and at the end of the year they can scarcely make the tongue and buckle meet." Richard Bland told his associates in Congress that the Easterners had asked the legislators of the West "to lay the blighting hand of confiscation upon the millions of people inhabiting that country, to turn them out as tramps upon the land, merely to satisfy the greed of English gold. . . . I speak for the great masses of the Mississippi Valley, and those west of it, when I say you shall not do it!" [1]

[1] *Congressional Record,* 53rd Cong., 1st Sess., p. 252, Aug. 11, 1893.

The sufferings of the East were a figment in the minds of the Eastern politicians, said the men from the West. The "soul-harrowing and tear-compelling picture of the long-suffering and patriotic New York bankers standing in the breach after the manner of Leonidas at Thermopylae and 'holding up the financial system of the country by the neck'" did not appeal to the emotions of young Champ Clark of Missouri, while "Honest Old Joe" Cannon of Illinois said that the President "for eight long years in office and out of office [had] followed the silver currency of the country with as great ferocity as Herod followed the infant Savior when he commanded that all children under two years of age should be put to death in order to make sure of the destruction of the Infant King."[1] Moreover, the silver advocates in Congress were sure that the Treasury notes had in no way disturbed financial conditions; they were certain that $146,000,000 of this currency could not create a panic or produce a stringency. Congressman Jones said in the House that "the Sherman law . . . had nothing more to do with [the then] present conditions than the laws of the Medes and Persians."

The silver Congressmen set forth many reasons why silver should not be demonetized. The two metals, they said, had been placed by Providence in the same mountains, often so intermixed as to prevent the mining of one without taking the other; more than one Senator declared that when the Lord created the two metals he meant that they should be used for the purposes for which they were created! Another argument was that the West did not have enough money. The general stock of currency in the country was sufficient, but little of it ever got across the Mississippi River. The grievance of long-falling prices which compelled the people of the West to pay more to cancel a debt than they had borrowed at the beginning was intimately tied up with this argument of money scarcity, though there is little evidence that the amount of money affected the price curve during these years.

[1] *Ibid.*, p. 717.

A universal belief on the part of the silver party, and the one which probably inspired the most bitterness, was that a great conspiracy existed among the wealthy of the world to enslave the common man. It seemed to the West that whoever suffered as a debtor was only bearing a burden which the rich had been forcing upon the common people for twenty years. The *Rocky Mountain News* had said editorially on July 24 that "under the plea of the speedy and unconditional repeal of the purchasing law, the real contest will be . . . between the adherents of an English-Rothschild's monetary system, with its scanty volume of currency resting wholly upon a gold basis, and what is still known as the American system, under which for more than eighty prosperous years silver had equal right with gold at the mints and both metals possessed the legal tender quality and were alike money of redemption." As early as May a clothing firm of Denver had inserted the following advertisement in the *Rocky Mountain News:*

A Conspiracy Against Silver Exists in the goldbug houses of Wall Street. The prayer of the people is that their strangling hand may soon be palsied, in which event the silver State will soar to the top notch of prosperity.

But until then Appel & Co. will aim to make it as easy for the people as possible by cutting clothing to the lowest margin.

At the outbreak of the panic the West had unwisely begun to call its funds from the East in preparation for the siege—"fortifying itself against loss," as explained by one editor. There can be little doubt that the West had enjoyed the discomfiture of the East and had been pleased when the bankers "grew angry." By the middle of June the demands upon the Eastern banks had become so heavy that they could not be filled by bankers who had lost their resources and whose reserves had fallen below the legal requirements. This refusal had seemed premeditated, and the great West rose up to do battle against the "CONSPIRACY" by which "Wall Street Money Sharks" were attempting "to force a panic on the country." Such statements as "They [the Eastern bankers] Absolutely Refuse to Loan a Dollar on Good Security" found lodgment in the hearts of many.

Regardless of the fact that the financiers of the East were suffering as much as anyone, the West maintained that the panic had been deliberately planned. Teller declared in Congress that the bankers would call it off when they were satisfied. Mitchell of Oregon gave a typical reply when he said: "The howl started in perfect unison—inspired across the seas —and finally the thing got away from them, proved a boomerang, and the banks suffered along with the rest." Despite the difficulties which Carlisle was having, the silver followers felt that the government itself was intimately and maliciously connected with the conspiracy. Senator Stewart said of the President, "He calls Congress together now that he has a panic on hand which he helped to make, to see if they will be more obedient to his imperial will." Congressman Call was certain as to the course he would pursue in the crisis. "I say repeal here and now every charter of every national bank unless it opens its vaults and continues its business," he proclaimed. The trouble with this suggestion was that the money was not in the banks, but in the pockets of the people, many of whom were applauding the Congressman.

In spite of the fact that the Treasury Department had spent much of its time for the past fifteen years in trying to create a plan whereby silver could be taken out of the government vaults, Senator Stewart told his associates: "I deny that the Secretary of the Treasury has attempted to put silver in circulation. . . . I deny that any national banks, the agents of the Government, have encouraged silver. On the contrary, they have done all they could to depreciate and destroy it and keep it out of circulation." [1] Gold, it seemed to the Westerners,

[1] *Congressional Record,* 53d Cong., 1st Sess., Appendix, p. 380.

was a cowardly money which fled at any appearance of real need— "It produces a wreck when it leaves the country, and it goes back to devour the carcass."

The very nature of the panic strengthened the belief that a conspiracy was afoot. Instead of being a short, decisive collapse, it was made up of a series of collapses which before they had finished left the country prostrate. Every succeeding wave, according to the belief of the silver men, came at the joint commands of John Bull and the "bloated aristocracy" of the United States, and the intent was to pinch the common man in order to force his representatives in Washington to vote for the repeal bill. The West was determined to ward off the attack. "Hunger and cold," warned one Congressman, "know no philosophy and respect no laws; and when these twin devils are let loose and you force them out upon the world:

> Then woe to the robbers who gather
>   In fields where they never have sown
> Who have stolen the jewels from labor,
>   And builded to Mammon a throne.
>
> For the throne of their god shall be crumbled,
>   And the scepter be swept from his hand,
> And the heart of the haughty be humbled,
>   And a servant be chief in the land.

Last but not least among the arguments and motives of the Westerners and Southerners in defense of the silver standard was that defeat would be in itself bitter regardless of the causes. Thomas R. Stockdale said in the House that "This is simply the home stretch in a great race. It is the last charge of the twenty years' battle. It is managed with skill. Napoleon, nor Grant, nor Hood, never drove their columns upon opposing lines with more reckless disregard of human life than do these gentlemen trample upon the slaughtered prosperity of this country—not for the purpose of rehabilitating it, but for the purpose of accomplishing what they started out to do twenty years ago."

The painful fact was evident to all that prices had been falling for a generation. Now it needed but these fiery arguments to convince the West that its very existence depended upon maintaining the silver coinage. The people certainly needed more money. The large increase in the circulating medium had apparently not added a penny to the purse of a single Westerner. When he borrowed money, the only evidence he could show for the transaction was a receipt for a debt liquidation, perhaps, and most assuredly a new statement of indebtedness. The section was a debtor always far behind in its obligations, and, in addition, it was continually enlarging its demands for the products of the East. The increasing dictates of society as to what constituted the minimum requirements of a well-regulated community added to its financial burdens. No longer were the iron pot and the covered skillet sufficient household equipment; the printing press, the school, the church, and even the clothes and manners of Eastern society had accompanied the expansion of America into the great West.

The West paid tribute to all the East—every railroad, telegraph line, and manufacturing or other industry drew from it its scanty dollars or evidence of an increasing indebtedness; the farmer sent his wheat and his corn or his cattle to the East and exchanged them for farm implements, organs, "fresh oysters from Baltimore," and other products for which he gave too much in the bargain and on which he paid to the railroads far too much in transportation charges. It is no wonder that such slogans as "1873, silver $1.29, wheat $1.17. Fattening the Farmer and Feeding the World—1893, silver 71 cents, wheat 54 cents. Fattening Wall Street and Feeding the Hogs" found ready response in the hearts of the farmers and caused the people to heed the admonition of their leaders: "Forget all past differences, ignore party and party platform, and follow the free coinage flag to victory." "One party, one platform, one line; Free Coinage of Silver!"

The repeal fight in the House was not a long struggle. The thinly populated States of the West were not able to hold their own in the conflict. The silverites were, however, given opportunity to discuss the subject, and young William Jennings Bryan of Nebraska did not neglect this chance to defend the cause to which he had recently been converted. With implicit faith in his divine guidance, he attacked the problem with the tireless energy which was to make him in a few short years the leader of the West's crusade. Indeed, the presence in the party of this handsome youth with the golden voice was scarcely less disastrous to the Cleveland Democracy than the financial heritage to which it had fallen heir.

Spurred on, perhaps, by his friends who twitted him with being a "one-poem poet" and who openly declared that he could not equal his tariff effort of a year before, Bryan spent many days upon his address. The speech was ready on August 16, and before Congress convened at noon he wrote his wife:

My Darling Girl:
 I am prepared for my speech of today. It is already in print and will only be changed to suit questions. I feel the importance of this effort. Enquiries are made constantly—"when do you speak" and the chances are I will have a good many out. I never felt more deeply the gravity of a question. I believe our prosperity depends upon its right solution and I pray that I may be the instrument in the hands of Providence of doing some good for my country and now until the ordeal is over good by. Will mail you a copy of the *Record* as soon as it appears—which I think will be tomorrow morning. With love and kiss. I am with great regret that you are not here.
Your Aff. husband
Will.[1]

It was just twelve-thirty when Speaker Crisp recognized "the gentleman from Nebraska." The orator of the day wore "a plain, loose-fitting suit of black, with a thin sack coat, a low-

[1] Bryan MSS.

cut vest and a little white tie under his turn-down collar." Every seat on the floor was full. "Big 'Tom' Reed sat in his chair on the Republican side surrounded by his little band of faithful followers, including Henderson, of Iowa; Cannon of Illinois; Payne, of New York; Burrows, of Michigan, and Dolliver, of Iowa." On the Democratic side every chair was turned toward the speaker, but not all the members of his party were in agreement with him. Bland, "gray-haired champion of the white metal," was most attentive, and when Bryan was questioned sharply by Harter of Ohio, he sent half a dozen pages scurrying off to the library to get books with which to support the statements which the orator had made. The speech was a good one, but it could not save the Sherman silver law.

On August 28, after efforts to substitute free-coinage measures with ratios of 16 to 1, 17 to 1, 18 to 1, 19 to 1, and 20 to 1 had failed, the bill passed the House by a majority of 130 votes. The event brought encouragement to the Treasury personnel and some hope to the Secretary that his troubles might soon be diminished, if not removed. Assistant-Secretary Curtis wrote his sister: "I wired you as soon as the repeal bill passed the House and we are all jubilant tonight. . . . The Senate will be greatly impressed by our majority which was eighty more than our wildest expectations contemplated. The first canvass when Congress met showed an apparent majority of five against repeal. I may get two weeks off immediately, if Congress decides not to adjourn. Mr. Carlisle is delighted, as may be expected. New York was solid, the leading State. Besides all this, we had a majority of the Democrats and therefore the Republicans cannot claim that *they* carried the measure!" [1]

The fight in the Senate, however, was not so easily nor so quickly won. The free-silver forces were confident of a majority of at least six or eight, and they expected to fight the issue until the "snows of December" came. But the gold advo-

[1] W. E. Curtis to Elizabeth Curtis. Curtis MSS.

cates were stubborn. On August 14 D. W. Voorhees, Democratic leader of the Senate, wrote the President: "I beg to assure you that I shall not hesitate a moment to vote for the immediate and unconditional repeal of the act in question whenever our friends can harmonize on that line so as to make such a vote successful. . . . I am doing all in my power to ensure success in the Senate, and to bring about as speedily as possible the result so ably and patriotically advocated and urged in your recent message. For my own part I do not regard a vote for the repeal of the Sherman Act as any test at all of a man's position on the question of the proper coinage and use of silver money. In fact that act ought to be repealed if for no other reason, because it is a hindrance to a fair, honest, and safe settlement of the Silver question." [1] Three days later Senator George G. Vest of Missouri, Democrat, native Kentuckian and enemy of the administration, wrote his old friend, James R. Doolittle of Wisconsin: "The outlook here is very dark and there seems to be little hope of a speedy compromise. The gold men are determined to have an unconditional repeal of the purchasing clause of the Sherman Act, and the friends of silver are equally determined to secure some legislation for that metal." [2]

The admission of the "omnibus" States had done much toward giving the Senate over to the control of the Senators from the West. As early as July 25 John Sherman had remarked of the representatives of silver that "most of them will want to talk." They did, indeed, talk; one correspondent in describing Teller said of him that "he talks, and talks, and talks." They talked, said Allen of Nebraska, because they were not there "with a brass collar around [their] necks, as some other Senators are in this Chamber." Senator Jones, after making a speech which filled a sizable book, ended with the quotation, "And this is all that the watcher said." "Having been one day longer about it than the heavens and the earth

[1] Cleveland MSS.
[2] Vest to Doolittle, August 17, 1893. Doolittle MSS.

were in creating, its bulk is correspondingly large," wrote the editor of the *Nation*. The talking was at first for the purpose of discussing the subject, but it soon became only a means used by the silver advocates to retard legislation. The dilatory tactics, relay-speaking, and other methods of delay found various responses in the country.

The East and the West were clearly divided; a scoundrel to one section was a hero to the other. On September 11 the New York *Times* said editorially: "Traitors in times of insurrection and war are always odious, but public enemies even in times of peace may be scarcely less dangerous and detestable. Stewart, Jones, Teller and Wolcott are the four controlling leaders in this bandit group." Four days later the Denver *Daily News* told the people of the West that "the fight the silver Senators are making is a grand one . . . they meet in daily session and pile facts, logic and rhetoric, like Pelion upon Ossa, in defense of the people's rights and the American home. All honor to such Senators as Stewart, Teller, Peffer, Wolcott, and Jones."

For those members who were urging repeal the struggle was not enjoyable. They were never sure of what the new day might bring forth, and there was little but discouragement and vexation. The stagnation in the country increased as the wearisome discussion continued. "If Nero fiddled while Rome was burning, some of our own legislators seem little better," declared the *Commercial and Financial Chronicle* on August 19. In the Treasury Department Secretary Carlisle severely felt the effects of the Congressional anarchy; at the Executive Mansion the President was restless, but confident of a successful issue.

The next four weeks, however, brought many uncertainties and clearly revealed the widening rift in the party. The first days of October came and found repeal apparently no closer than it had been in the early part of August. The repeal forces eventually decided to force a vote by continual session; a plan which greatly pleased the Westerners, who were certain that they could put the old men of the "effete East" to rout.

"One by one such old men as Morrill of Vermont, Hoar of Massachusetts, Voorhees of Indiana, and McPherson of New Jersey will go to their beds," predicted one silverite editor.

Great was the preparation for this battle which began on the eleventh. "All day long," wrote a correspondent, "there were preparations for a fight. Few Senators were in the chamber, but a glance into the cloakroom and a peep into the committee rooms showed many of them sleeping on the couches and sofas husbanding their strength for the siege. Forces on both sides of the battle were divided so as to be able to give each other relief by taking up the defense of their position in turn." The Sergeant-at-Arms had every man of his force within call; four were ready at a moment's notice to hunt any Senator who was absent. In the committee rooms and in convenient corridors couches and blankets had been made available for those who might be able to steal away for a little sleep. Throughout the night the light in the Capitol dome burned on, and when the gray dawn broke over Washington on the morning of the twelfth, it found the Senate in roll call. Assistant-Secretary Curtis wrote his mother: "I was at the Senate Chamber in the Reporters Gallery until about 12.30 last night. A stupid proceeding!"[1] All through the day the performance continued, with the repeal forces growing perceptibly weaker; the silver men had the advantage at every turn because they had only to talk, while the gold followers were compelled to maintain a quorum at any cost.

On the evening of the twelfth Secretary Carlisle went up to Capitol Hill to "feel the pulse of the Senate," and found it far from encouraging. The gold advocates were tired, but the silverites were apparently ready to talk forever. Because of an old rule in the Senate that one could talk only once on a subject, the latter never closed their speeches. Senator Allen after talking for fifteen hours said that he "might embrace the opportunity to say a few more words on the subject"! On into the night the silverites poured out their arguments in order to pre-

[1] Curtis MSS.

vent the repeal question from coming to vote; when Teller grew tired, Wolcott called for a quorum, thus giving the former an opportunity to refresh himself by drinking bouillon while the clerk of the Senate wearily read the roll.

A quorum was maintained until eleven o'clock on the night of the twelfth, although many of those present were reading novels. After that hour, however, only the guards remained while the other Senators slept in the cloakrooms. Voorhees, "the tall sycamore from the Wabash," napped under the very nose of Senator Stewart until one-thirty on the morning of the thirteenth and then moved an adjournment. Nothing was gained. The incident served only to encourage the West and to arouse the East. Witnesses of the scene probably recalled the words of a Washington *Evening Star* correspondent of a few days before: "The Samsons of the Senate are slaying the Philistines of gold and silver with their own jawbones."

The country was far from unmoved by the Congressional procedure at Washington. The "Midsummer Madness," as Eastern correspondents dubbed the wearisome proceedings, had its counterpart among the people of the nation. Throughout the East the bankers and business men were circulating petitions footed by flowing signatures requesting that Congress repeal the silver legislation immediately. In these same cities the secretaries of the Knights of Labor and other labor organizations were going through the factories and the workshops seeking the signatures of the workingmen in opposition to repeal. The Knights of Labor and the Central Labor Union of Marlboro, Massachusetts, passed typical resolutions condemning the conspiracy which was endeavoring to destroy silver as a money, declaring: "The daily press of the East wrongfully assumes to voice the sentiments of the working class on this subject." [1] In the rural districts of the East the farmers, through the Grange or Farmers' Alliance, flooded Congress with their petitions for silver.

In the South and the middle region between the East and

[1] Senate MSS.

the West the dividing line between those who favored the gold standard and those who favored free silver was similar, but farmers could often be found endorsing either petition. Some laborers in the lower South advocated "sound money." In the West, however, the mass of the people knew what they wanted —the free coinage of silver. While the banker, merchant, and shopkeeper of the East were putting down their trimly-written signatures in opposition, the citizens of the great West were clumsily and painfully scratching out in pencil their names. On the rough five-cent tablet paper of a generation ago thousands sent their names to their Representatives, valiantly fighting to prevent the "insidious goldbugs" from accomplishing their "hellish purposes." The petitions came in various languages, and in divers forms; some had been clipped from newspapers, some had been supplied by politicians, and some had been laboriously written out.

One needs but to look at the petitions and letters from the farmers and laborers to know that the process of preparing them was a painful one. Only the importance of the crisis could have prompted such labor. Spelling was not the least of their difficulties, as the following typical letter will show:

> Montgomerys [Montgomery, Indiana]
> Sep. the 13.93
>
> Harmeny a sembley No. 422 [Order of Knights of Labor] Mr Turpie Senator from Indiana Dare Sir i am requested By my a semble to rite to you and Bage of you not to vote for to repeal the Sherman Act and to votes for free and unlemeted coineg of silver and git the secport of all true nights of labor Now wey ask you to stand firme to our Call as ever yours fraturnely
>
> EDWARD DANT. R[ecording] S[ecretary]

One hundred and twenty-nine farmers signed their names to a petition in which the name of Lincoln, friend of the common man, was spelled "Lincollen." But whatever their limitations in handling the English language, there was no question as to what the people of the interior wanted. Their feelings were well expressed in the resolutions passed by the Clinton (Iowa) Local Assembly of the Knights of Labor: ". . . we air opposed to the unconditional repeal of the purching claus of the sherman act without a satisfactory substitute such for instance as the free Coinage of silver at the ratio of 16 to 1." And all the while Congress continued to argue the case.[1]

By the middle of October the Treasury Department had become hopeful of defeating compromise and of carrying unconditional repeal. Secretary Carlisle spent much of his time in the Senate. The *Nation* said of him at this time that he occupied much the same position as that of an English Cabinet member. The President, too, had been at work. In reply to a note from the Executive, Senator Voorhees wrote on October 16: "No surrender of the right of the majority to govern can be tolerated. We have the Senate by nearly, if not quite, two to one, and I will stay here and fight it out if it takes to the next 4th of July before I will surrender to the dictation of the minority. . . . I shall aim to have 12 hour sessions each day and night from this time forward, with not the slightest intention to quit anywhere, or at any time, short of a complete victory." The financiers were also interested. James Stillman of the National City Bank of New York wrote Colonel Lamont on October 23: "I have heard from our Boston connections to-day that the President assured Gov. Russell and also Mr. Josiah Quincy last Saturday evening that there would be *no compromise* and that he would not consent to any." [2]

Forces which had been quiescent came to the fore. The disruption of the economic life of the country began to tell in the opposition to the silver demands, and the President found it easier to apply force in pushing forward his policy. On

[1] The petitions are still preserved in the attic of the Capitol Building. They are particularly valuable in some instances because the age and occupation of the signer is given. In addition to laborers and farmers, the silver group included also Senators and Congressmen and a few bank presidents and university professors.

[2] Lamont MSS.

October 15, 1893, J. Sterling Morton wrote Richard Olney from Chicago: "During the last week I have talked with many merchants and businessmen, prominent in the affairs of Chicago and the Northwest. Among them were Marshall Field, Franklin MacVeagh, N. K. Fairbank, P. D. Armour, Nelson Morris, and many others, and, without a single exception, each one endorsed the President and his financial policies. Each one declared in favor of being beaten, or of carrying unconditional repeal. The Stewart-Harris-Vest combination is wrong, and Right ought to triumph over Wrong, without asking permission from anybody, or agreeing to any compromise." Senator Hill, enemy of the administration, appeared on the side of Voorhees. "Isn't it a joke that Hill should turn up in the Senate as the champion of the Administration?" wrote Assistant-Secretary Curtis on October 20. "He and McPherson are the only repeal democrats who have any nerve! . . . We expect developments daily and the silver men are willing to take almost anything they can get in the way of compromise." [1]

On October 25 many Democratic Senators who had been supporting the Western men gave notice that they would no longer aid them in their dilatory tactics. The Treasury Department began to feel that a vote might be in the offing, and it would be none too soon, for the situation in the sub-treasuries was critical, especially in New York. Jordan wrote Curtis, "We are still 'sledding on thin ice,' which I suppose must last until Congress acts 'How long! O Lord! how long!'" Richard Olney wrote on October 27:

> On the repeal question, it now looks as though we were out of the woods though I refuse to count on anything till it has become a fact accomplished. Still there seems to be no reasonable doubt that the vote will be taken and possibly this week —one strong inducement thereto being the senatorial desire to adjourn and take a rest from its protracted indulgence in senatorial courtesy. Repeal accomplished, however, you will read-

[1] W. E. Curtis to his mother. Curtis MSS.

ily understand that it is but one and not a very long step on the road that ought to be traveled. The path of this administration, indeed, however you look at it, and whether foreign or domestic affairs are considered, seems to me to be all the way up hill and very rocky at that.

October 30 found everyone confident that a vote would be taken on that day; Assistant-Secretary Curtis was in the galleries to hear the welcome "ayes." Sometime in the early evening he went home and wrote his mother: "I spent three hours in the Senate Chamber waiting for the repeal vote, but Jones started in and I gave it up. He may wander on all night."[1] But the Senator did not continue all night. It was evident to all that the great battle was over—there remained only the valedictories of the silver Senators. They prophesied another fight. Jones closed his address by repeating in tones "deep and tragic" Dundee's famous defiance of Gordon:

> There be hills beyond Pentland,
>   And firths beyond Forth,
> If there be Lords on the lowlands,
>   There be chiefs in the North.

Senator Peffer—Peffer of the "hickory-nut" head and the long flowing beard, who had sat in the Senate picking his teeth with a penknife—warned the gold idolators that "his horizon is narrow indeed who does not see a mighty people rising." "If our trade is of no consequence to our Eastern neighbors, we have good easement to the South of us," said the Senator. "We can shorten the distance to foreign markets and cheapen the cost of transportation by shipping our surplus products through ports on the Gulf of Mexico. We now have vast areas of fertile lands under cultivation, with a rapidly increasing population; and year by year we are increasing the amount of our contributions to the commerce of the world. An interstate railway from North Dakota to Galveston Bay would drain a great

[1] Curtis MSS.

region that now sends its trade across the Mississippi River eastward on its way to Liverpool and London. We shall soon be able to reclaim the semiarid lands west of us and populate them with small farmers whose labor will add to our output." [1]

Senator Wolcott of Colorado, once a student at Yale and a graduate of the Harvard Law School, said of the West: "Our people came from all the States in the Union; they found a desert; they have made it a garden. They were encouraged to search for the precious metals, and they poured millions of gold and silver into your Treasury. They built cities, founded schools and colleges, erected churches, and established happy and peaceful and contented homes. The action you contemplate is as if you should take a vast and fertile area of Eastern lands, destroy the structures upon it, and sow the ground with salt, that it might never again yield to the hand of the husbandman. . . . Your action drives our miners from their homes in the mountains, and compels the abandonment of hamlets and of towns that but yesterday were prosperous and populous. We shall turn our hands to new pursuits and seek other means of livelihood. We shall not eat the bread of idleness, and under the shadow of our eternal hills we breed only good citizens. The wrong, however, which you are inflicting upon us is cruel and unworthy, and the memory of it will return to vex you. Out of the misery of it all, her representatives in this Senate will always be glad to remember that they did their duty as God gave them the vision to see it." The President of the Senate threatened to clear the galleries because of the applause.

Senator Stewart gave the swan song of the silver forces. "Mr. President," said the Senator, "the die is cast. The surreptitious and fraudulent act of 1873 demonetizing silver is ratified and confirmed. . . . The repeal of an act already nullified by Executive usurpation is decreed to exonerate the Secretary of the Treasury from the consequences of an open violation of law in refusing to purchase the four and one-half

[1] *Congressional Record*, 53d Cong., 1st Sess., pp. 2956, 2957.

million ounces of silver per month commanded by the act of 1890." But Stewart did not overlook the opportunity to condemn the "great conspiracy." "The Trojan horse of the gold kings," he said, "bedecked with flaming banners upon which were inscribed, 'Democracy,' 'Bimetallism,' 'Local Self-Government,' 'Reduction of Taxation,' and 'Civil Service Reform,' to conceal the monometallic guns of concentrated money and bonds, made a triumphal entrance into the nation's capitol. The people opened wide the gates, and millions sang hosanna to 'Greeks bearing gifts' "—Greeks who "blocked every avenue of approach to all who bore true allegiance to the people's cause."

When the white-bearded Nevadian, "looking like an ancient patriach," sank back into his seat, the call for amendments was made for the last time. The roll call began with "Mr. Allen." Sherman and Voorhees and Hill and Butler sat in the front row talking while the clerk read the names. By a vote of forty-three to thirty-two—twenty-three Republicans voting yea—the Sherman silver bill, which had caused so much commotion in the country, was repealed.

The Congress which rescinded the law died without ever having legally adjourned because a quorum could not be again assembled. "The extra session has ignominiously melted away leaving its odorous record behind," said a Western editor.

The repeal was first of all a personal victory for the President; there can be no doubt that he was one of the main driving forces behind the legislation. But he was backed by a group of earnest and sympathetic workers. Of these the Secretary of the Treasury, John G. Carlisle, was not the least; he had had to bear silently excessive strain on his own Department, and he had given much time to the support of the political program. The assertion that money and political pressure were used to secure the repeal of the Sherman Act of 1890 cannot be successfully disputed, but that the same methods were used by the opposition is equally certain. In view of its necessity, however, any action was justified in the eyes of the administration.

Contrary to expectations, the repeal of the Sherman Act did little to lessen the burdens of Secretary Carlisle. It stopped the injection of silver into the money medium of the country, but it neither relieved the Treasury of any of its obligations nor restored confidence in the ability of the government to maintain the gold standard. The political results, however, were legion. The discontent in the hearts of the Westerners was turned to glowing hope as the silver politicians exerted their forensic abilities in describing the glories of silver. "Free coinage of silver," according to one address which was widely circulated, "will stop the fall of prices and establish them upon a much higher plane; . . . it will make the burdens of life easier in the homes of the masses; it will lighten the sky of industry; it will make music among the spindles; it will put thanksgiving in the hearts and songs on the lips of millions; it will overturn the bondholders' conspiracy and take the yoke of hopeless poverty from the necks of those who have been ground into the dust beneath the wheels of this juggernaut of gold."

Opposition and a specific cause for which to fight gave to the inarticulate groups who were sponsoring free coinage a unity which had previously been lacking. The discord which had been particularly noticeable at the silver convention in Chicago in August had nearly disappeared by November; the glowing words of silver orators brought a kindred feeling to all those who found it difficult to obtain the necessities of life. From this time forward the citizens of Kansas, Nebraska, Colorado, South Dakota, and neighboring States found it difficult to forget that it was the Easterner who was responsible for their plight, for from every side, as new orators sprang up among them, they heard this doctrine reiterated day after day.

CHAPTER XIII THE FIRST BOND ISSUE UNDER CLEVELAND

THE repeal of the Sherman silver law was not the only problem which endangered the tariff program of the incoming Democrats in 1893; concurrently with their efforts at repeal the President and his Secretary of the Treasury were compelled to consider the status of the Treasury Department in regard to the maintenance of gold payments. When Carlisle took office, it will be remembered, the national purse was empty, and the nation had come to doubt the ability of the Treasury to maintain the gold standard. There was scarcely more than twelve million dollars of available money in the Treasury vaults above the minimum $100,000,000 reserve, and less than a million of gold above that reserve.[1] President Cleveland has pointed out in his *Presidential Problems* that many people had come to feel a sort of superstitious sanctity about the gold reserve, and felt that dire calamity would befall the country if it should be encroached upon.

In the months preceding the inauguration Cleveland and Carlisle had discussed the financial situation; they had hoped that the Treasury would not reach such a state as to necessitate relief measures until their legislative program had been at least partially carried out. But at a conference at Lakewood, N. J., in January, 1893, President-elect Cleveland, Carlisle, and Walter Q. Gresham had decided that the existing financial status should be maintained at all costs. In his inaugural address Cleveland did not mention the gold reserve. His only intimation of any determination to uphold the credit of the country was his statement that "so far as the executive branch of the Government can intervene, none of the powers with which it is invested will be withheld when their exercise is

[1] There was exactly $982,410 of gold above the reserve, and $25,000,000 of other money, half of which was in subsidiary coins and thus unavailable.

deemed necessary to maintain our national credit or avert financial disaster."

Financial disaster, as has already been seen, was indeed imminent; the preceding administration had escaped calamity by the narrowest squeak, and Secretary Foster had been able to avoid drastic action in maintaining gold payments only through the aid of the banks in giving him gold in exchange for his legal-tenders. The Treasury was faced with the absolute necessity of securing sufficient gold with which to meet its redemption requests. Moreover, the strength of the silverites had increased to such an extent that no one knew at what moment a free-silver bill might be forced upon the nation. This sword of Damocles, which had hung over the heads of financial men for almost a generation, had engendered fears of a result far greater, perhaps, than would ever have really accompanied a change in the standard of value.

The fears, however, had very real consequences—hundreds of failed banks and corporations, thousands of people out of employment, closed factories and workshops in alarming number, money selling on the streets at a premium, depositors unable to withdraw their deposits from old established institutions, certified checks circulating as money, and bread lines in all the important cities from New York to Denver. Regardless of the effect upon their tariff-reform hopes, the Democrats were forced to acknowledge the situation.

President Cleveland was convinced that the economic ills of society could be cured only by the repeal of the Sherman silver law, and hoped that the gold reserve might hold out until that was accomplished. Secretary Carlisle knew that gold payments must be maintained, and yet he was conscious also that to take the necessary steps to secure gold might prevent the repeal of the Sherman silver law, which, if maintained, would probably result in ultimate ruin. He was in much the same situation as the physician whose patient is suffering from a bad blood stream and a weak heart: if no treatment is given, premature death is inevitable, but if curative serums are injected, it may occur immediately. In these cases hesitation is often wisdom, but fond relatives always heap bitter criticisms upon the "vacillating" doctor. Secretary Carlisle hesitated, and he has since borne many criticisms from economic theorists.

Carlisle delayed action because he had no satisfactory way of increasing his gold fund. There was a demand that he pay his balances in silver; but had such a course been possible, it would have immediately brought the country to a silver basis. He could not follow this procedure, even had he been so inclined, because there were no silver dollars with which to make payments except those dollars upon which there were outstanding certificates. He could not even redeem the Treasury notes of 1890 in silver unless he used Bland-Allison dollars, of which only seven millions were available. Had the Secretary followed the demands of the silverites and used silver in his payments, he would have set afloat a large amount of paper money similar to the greenbacks, with the exception that the partial security would have been depreciated silver instead of gold.[1]

The only apparent means of relief for the Treasury Department was a bond sale, but even this would irritate the already frayed nerves of business and might destroy what little confidence the business world still had in money values. This method had been used to establish resumption, and the gold reserve which had then been created was maintained through the receipts from customs and the internal revenue taxes; but the increasing amount of silver in the money medium had gradually crowded the gold out. To demand that all payments to the government be made in gold would have been as disastrous as the Specie Circular of Jackson's day, and would have stripped the Treasury immediately of the little precious metal

[1] There was only a limited amount of silver dollars coined under the Sherman law; he could have used these, of course, until they were exhausted. It would have required two years to coin the Sherman silver bullion upon which there were outstanding certificates. The silverites were aware of the nature of their demand in asking that the Secretary use the three or four hundred million dollars of silver in payment of his debts.

which it held. Gold had to be obtained, if at all, through an issue of bonds under authority of the Resumption Act of January 14, 1875.

The famous Resumption Act had been passed in order "to prepare and provide for the redemption" of the greenbacks; it gave the Secretary of the Treasury power "to the extent necessary to carry this act into full effect." There was a division of opinion, however, as to whether this law was still effective in 1893. Secretary Carlisle was doubtful of his power to act under its provisions, and, being a strict constructionist, hoped to avoid any doubtful recourse. He had, as Senator, sought to bring the matter to the attention of Congress. "I see in the *Post* that Carlisle is desirous of additional authority for the sale of bonds to maintain resumption," wrote a friend to John Sherman on February 13, 1893. "I believe the law of '75 is sufficient and the real idea of Carlisle is to put his party on record as endorsing that policy. I feel that a Republican ought not to propose such a measure because it is tantamount to an implication that the law of '75 was simply to establish resumption and not to maintain it." Secretary Foster had given much thought to the question in the last days of his office. He is said to have rushed into the room of the Senate Finance Committee with the exclamation, "For God's sake give me authority to issue bonds!" He had even ordered the preparation of plates for a bond issue, but on the assumption that the request for such authority, then pending in Congress, would be approved.

Attorney-General Olney, even before he took over his office, was called upon by Carlisle to make a decision on the question. He decided in the affirmative. It had not been contemplated by the Act of January 14, 1875, wrote Olney, "that the resumption should take place on January 1, 1879; on the contrary the process was to be a continuous one—in other words, it was intended that using the words of the act, 'on and after' the day named the legal tender notes then outstanding should be redeemable 'in coin' upon the terms named. . . . The continuing duty of resumption implies and requires a

THE FIRST BOND ISSUE

continuing power on the part of the Secretary of the Treasury. This is indicated by the language used. He is to 'prepare and provide for' such resumption—to 'use any surplus revenues from time to time in the Treasury'; he was not authorized to resume prior to Jan. 1, 1879, hence the use of the surplus revenues thus authorized was after that date; the phrase 'from time to time' applies equally to the use of surplus revenues and to the power conferred 'to issue, sell and dispose of, at not less than par in coin either of the description of the bonds of the United States described.'"

Olney further decided that while the Secretary could sell bonds for the purpose of redeeming the legal-tenders created in 1862–1863, he could not sell them for the purpose of maintaining the two metals, gold and silver, on a parity. Moreover, he declared that the bonds sold could not be made payable in gold, but could be paid at maturity in either gold or silver.[1]

Logically, the resumption law must have been meant to operate so long as the greenbacks remained fiat money, and yet there is doubt as to whether Congress had contemplated more than the one issue of bonds under discussion at the time of the passage of the law. A perpetual power to increase the public debt whenever the Secretary of the Treasury believed the redemption machinery to be in danger had assuredly not been in the minds of many legislators who voted for resumption. No stretch of the imagination could make the grant of 1875 include the power to sell bonds for the purpose of redeeming the Treasury notes of 1890 in gold. Secretary Carlisle, however, disregarding the opinions of the Attorney-General with respect to the Treasury notes, eventually elected to redeem them from his gold reserve, and if necessary to sell bonds to maintain the parity.

The silverites were certain that there was no authority for

---

[1] MSS. in Olney papers. He ruled that the Secretary could use the gold after the reserve fell below $100,000,000 because there was no law definitely establishing that reserve.

selling bonds. They demanded that the Secretary of the Treasury meet his obligations in silver dollars. The Secretary waited.

Carlisle's reluctance to sell bonds brought vigorous protests from financial men, who feared that the Treasury Department meant to take no active steps for the preservation of the standard of value. A New York financier wired the President that "Friends of the administration are growing weary of Secretary Carlisle's temporizing policy. He appears to lack depth, breadth, and vigor necessary to the proper administration of that great office." Some, however, understood the difficulties which he faced. Edmund D. Randolph, president of the Continental National Bank of New York, wrote Colonel Lamont on March 14: "The new Administration embarked on a stormy sea indeed! I suppose the repeal of the Sherman bill has been found to be hopeless just now;—and as to issuing bonds, the anticipated relief from that step seemed to be so problematical that I fancy the President is glad to escape the dilemma. Tight money—unpleasant medicine though it is—seems therefore to be the only corrective in sight. It has arrested gold exports and will tend to dislodge and send forward some of the exportable products which should have gone abroad long ago, but in default of which have been tying up sound money and have necessitated the shipment of so much gold instead. With this and with the gold the banks may continue to pay into the Treasury to procure currency, I am hopeful that the chasm may be bridged over,—and the public confidence which the change of administration has inspired in thinking men here and abroad will then do the rest;—and needful legislation must inevitably follow later on." [1]

Business men insisted that the only safe plan was for the government to prove that it could and would take care of itself. On April 19 Henry Lee Higginson wrote from Boston: "All the world is pulling for gold. That all people see, and it seems to me that if I were managing the Treasury, I should

[1] Lamont MSS.

at once say publicly what I was going to do; that I had made preparations to get gold to such and such an amount, and that I was not going to allow the reserve to go below $100,000,000. This once done, I believe that a great deal of gold which is now hoarded in vaults, (and in speaking of this I mean literally what I say, for I have seen it) would come out to be put in the banks and be of use and reassure people; but, at the present time, it does not much matter what a man brings to us, we do not want to do it." [1] On the following day Secretary Carlisle and the President held a long consultation, and on the twenty-first Carlisle's unfortunate announcement that he would redeem the Treasury notes so long as he had gold "lawfully available" for that purpose appeared in the press.

The country seethed with rumor. The gold advocates bewailed the fact that there was no one in the Treasury Department who had a true understanding of the situation, while the silver men grieved that after twenty years of patriotic service Carlisle had at last been swallowed up by the gold octopus. Eastern editors sorrowfully pictured the ruin which the ignorance of the West had forced upon the country, and Western writers condemned the "traitors" of the East. Bankers still insisted that the Secretary follow their advice. "Only some overt act, like the selling of some bonds, will do any good," wrote one financier. "If the Secretary were to offer to sell even $5,000,000 bonds, and thereby show that he had the means for getting gold and meant to use it, the business public would be reassured. . . . I have been talking the matter over with Mr. Perkins and a dozen other people here and in New York (by telephone) and this is the consensus of opinion. Only an overt act, like a sale of bonds, is likely to still the apprehensions of the business public." Two leading Boston bankers wired: "True policy is to sell at least twenty-five millions bonds abroad. If this is done confidence abroad will be largely restored, leading Europe to buy our securities and the balance against us will be favorably affected."

[1] Higginson to Olney. Olney MSS.

Meanwhile, the gold reserve dropped below one hundred million dollars. There fell upon the country a panic which, before it ended, brought disaster and hardships to the entire nation. It is doubtful that an issue of bonds could have prevented the panic; certainly the catastrophe made a bond sale needless and perhaps impossible. Redemptions which had reached twenty million in April dwindled until in midsummer even the despised silver dollar was bringing a premium on the streets of New York, the home of the gold banker. Cleveland and Carlisle turned their thoughts to the repeal of the Sherman silver law.

Early in July Henry Lee Higginson of Boston wrote Richard Olney that "nobody is doing any business, and your possible order of eleven bonds is most attractive." A few days later he wrote: "This is the worst day in a long time. People who are rich and *sound* when asked to pay up their account cannot do it, and we cannot sell their stocks. The best investment shares have declined heavily—both here and in New York. The banks are drained dry. . . . I don't know just what can be done, and see no remedy except in a sale of United States bonds to strengthen the United States Treasury and restore confidence."[1] The Treasury's gold income reflected the situation in the business world. The banks were suspected of secreting their gold in this emergency. "They no longer believe, as affairs are at present, that the Treasury can avoid going to a silver basis," wrote Jordan of the New York sub-treasury on July 24, "and therefore desire to realize the premium on their gold."[2]

August was a dismal month. "Not for years have so many men, so many furnaces, and so many mills been idle during the summer months as at this time," wrote a correspondent of the London *Economist*.[3] The panic reached its most desolate

---

[1] Olney MSS.

[2] Jordan to Curtis. Curtis MSS.

[3] Dated August 26; appeared in the Monthly Trade Supplement of September 9, 1893, p. 5.

stage. Congress met on the seventh and began the long, tiresome battle over the repeal of the Sherman silver law; and the South and West began preparation for harvesting their crops, for the purchase of which there was no money in the hands of the merchants. In a few weeks a traveler in the South could have seen many a disconsolate farmer plodding homeward along the dusty roads with his load of cotton because the merchant could secure no credit from the Eastern bankers, who had no money. Although Secretary Carlisle did what he could at Washington to increase the circulating medium, he was able to help the situation but little, for at least $210,000,000 was required to move the cotton crop alone.

On August 10 Jordan wrote Curtis from New York that a calamity was impending there—"a general suspension by the New York banks first, to be followed by the banks of the country at large." Three days later William Endicott, Jr., of Boston, wrote Attorney-General Olney:

DEAR MR. OLNEY:

I dislike to occupy your time with my letters, but the gravity of the situation must be my excuse. Mr. Perkins received a letter on Friday from Mr. Peaslee, Treasurer C. B. & Q. R. R., advising that in Chicago exchange upon New York was at four per cent discount, and that this would practically put a stop to grain shipments into Chicago, and I see that the receipts there show a large falling off for last week. The men who handled the grain do not get four per cent (probably not half of it) for doing the business, and any loss upon the N. Y. exchange made by forwarding the grain to shipboard must come out of the former, giving him about two cents a bushel less than the present very low price.

The difficulty arises from the very extensive hoarding of currency that has taken place, owing to the existing distrust. It is an unreasoning panic, for the currency that has been taken out of circulation will only be payable in silver if we come to a silver basis, which is the ground of alarm. It exists, nevertheless, and the hoarding is so extensive as to put it out of the power of the Eastern banks to send currency or gold to the

West to satisfy the demand for money to pay for the grain which is to bring back from Europe the gold that we so much need. . . .

Hitching along from week to week only tends to make matters worse by making those having dealings with foreign Countries, whether as bankers, merchants, or what not, feel that they had better get their funds out of this country and into a safer place while they can do so without loss, and those who are making purchases for future delivery will, so far as they have capital or credit here, protect themselves against a premium on gold by remitting in advance of immediate needs. . . .

It is not expedient for the country, in my opinion, that the banks should give up, or seriously weaken, their gold reserve. The whole fabric of Commercial credit of the country rests very largely upon the conservative management and sound condition of the banks of New York City. These banks hold about 65 millions of gold. If it should become known that they had parted with half this reserve it would be very likely to start a run upon the Treasury that would be very troublesome.

To prevent any such scare I would have the Government show that it means to be master of the situation, and act promptly and decisively.

The sale of 25 millions of bonds in London would furnish exchange, diminish the demand for it by quieting alarm, and probably lead to some investments here of foreign Capital, and would be taken to mean that more would be forthcoming if required. If an understanding can be quietly had that the bonds will be withheld from the market for six months or a year it will be very desirable, as the bonds will probably float back to this country sometime to be paid for in gold.

I do not regard this as a cure. That is possible only by the repeal of the Sherman bill and the stoppage of the issue of paper currency. An issue of bonds will serve to tide over the next eight or ten months and give time for Congress to act. If the repeal is not carried next winter I believe that we shall have a monkey and parrot time before the close of Mr. Cleveland's administration.[1]

[1] Olney MSS.

The eager search for gold put a premium upon that metal, and it began to flow inward from Europe; more than $41,000,000 reached our shores in this oppressive month of August. The influx broke the back of the panic, but it brought little relief to the Secretary of the Treasury. His gold reserve continued to decline, as he was forced by the scarcity of money in his vaults to use that metal in paying his ordinary expenses. The last week of August found the sub-treasury at New York hard pressed to meet its demands. Jordan sent frantic telegrams to Washington for aid. On the twenty-eighth the New York *Journal of Commerce and Commercial Bulletin* said that "the Secretary is not oblivious to the rapid shrinkage of the revenue, and has had several consultations on the subject with Assistant-Secretary Curtis, Treasurer Morgan and other Departmental officials. He feels, however, that it is better to draw somewhat upon the gold rather than precipitate a new cause of controversy into Congress while the silver question is pending."

On the day the silver-purchase repeal bill passed the Senate, October 30, 1893, the gold reserve stood at just $84,000,000, although the redemptions of that month had been scarcely more than half a million dollars. The legislative success of the administration did little to relieve the perplexities of the Treasury Department and nothing toward making maintenance of the gold standard easier. Money had come out of hiding, and the banks now found their vaults filled with an excess of silver certificates; people were fearful lest these should come to make up the money in the Treasury. Moreover, gold exports began again, and in the following weeks they rapidly increased. Every effort was made to force the New York bankers to supply the necessary gold for exportation; even the moral cudgel was applied. Each banking transaction was carefully watched, and if it did not agree with the best interests of the government, the Secretary of the Treasury immediately appealed for a more patriotic attitude. "The City Bank, which was largely debtor, settled in U. S. notes or certificates for such notes," wrote M. L. Muhleman of the New York sub-treasury, "so that it would be well to see Mr. Stillman early."[1]

The silver certificates became more and more embarrassing as they came to make up a greater percentage of the circulating medium. On November 24 Muhleman wrote Assistant-Secretary Curtis from New York in regard to the difficulties there:

Dear Mr. Secretary:

I, too, am anxious to relieve banks in other parts of the country of the burden of surplus silver certificates; ... my aim was to arrange to have New York banks lead off by taking them at their clearing-house; (if it were done here other cities would follow;) but the banks cannot fairly be asked to use 5^s, 10^s and 20^s there; the bulk would seriously delay business and the object would be defeated; so that the issue of larger denominations, to absorb the local surplus of small certificates, for this purpose, would make it possible. This issue need be only temporary and to a limited amount, (for the demand for small denominations later will bring them back;) and it is not desirable to issue them until it is known that the banks will use them, except perhaps some 100^s. . . .

As to strict redemption in kind: even admitting that the law of 1878 contemplates the redemption in silver dollars only, or in certificates, the present proposition that all forms of money should, in the near future, be freely interchangeable, is a logical deduction from the "parity clause" of the act of 1890; not only, therefore, warranted as a question of policy, but as well by legal declaration. So long as the Treasury itself rather impresses upon the public the idea that the silver money is the cheaper, the less desirable, the public will feel and act upon it. I confess that I feel a sense of chagrin at the apparent necessity that the Treasury in this silver problem should have to be so cautious and, for example, not be in a position to pay these certificates at the clearing-house without a word; but as you will have gathered, the banks are in a position to convert

[1] Curtis MSS.

all the receipts of the Treasury into silver; moreover the flood of money continues in this direction in such volume, that if more small silver certificates are added to the stock here, the banks may refuse to receive them from their correspondents; thus blocking the way much more and aggravating the situation.[1]

As the opening of the Fifty-third Congress approached, business and financial men grew restive. They were conscious of the temper of many Congressmen who only a few weeks before had left the national capital with oaths of vengeance on their lips.[2] They berated Secretary Carlisle for not issuing bonds, and bewailed the fact that Alexander Hamilton could not rise from his grave to take charge of the finances for the moment. In his work for the repeal of the Sherman silver law Secretary Carlisle had certainly given evidence of his attitude toward the standard of value, but anxious financiers yearned for a definite statement. The New York Chamber of Commerce invited him to be the speaker at their annual banquet held in late November. All the "goldbugs," great and small, of the metropolis gathered to hear what the Secretary would say. Whatever trepidations filled the hearts of these "heartless gold barons," they must have been dispelled by Carlisle's opening words:

Mr. President and Gentlemen: The subject presented by the sentiment just read is so large, and involves so many considerations, not only of public policy, but of public and private honor and good faith, that I scarcely know how to respond to it on such an occasion as this, where brevity of statement will be more appropriate than elaborate argument. I am somewhat embarrassed, also, by the fact that I am to talk to an assemblage of gentlemen who by reason of their personal experience in commercial and financial affairs are at least

[1] Curtis MSS.
[2] The special session of Congress which had met to repeal the Sherman silver law adjourned on November 3.

in as good a position as I am to understand and appreciate the value of a sound and stable currency and to foresee the injurious effects of a departure from correct financial methods.

These opening words merged into a long address in which the Secretary set forth his ideas in regard to financial principles and the monetary policy of the nation:

Money and its representatives constitute the tools with which the merchant and the banker perform their parts in the numerous and complicated transactions necessarily occurring in the growth and development of our trade at home and abroad. It is not possible to do perfect work with imperfect instruments, and if it is attempted the consequences will not fall upon you alone, but must be felt sooner or later in every part of the land. Confidence would be destroyed, trade would be interrupted, the obligations of contracts would be violated, and all the evils which have invariably attended the use of a base or fluctuating currency would afflict not the commercial and financial classes only, but the country at large. But our commercial interests are not confined to our own country; they extend to every quarter of the globe, and our people buy and sell in nearly every market of the civilized world. A very large part of our farmers, mechanics and other laboring people find constant and profitable employment in the production and transportation of commodities for sale and consumption in other countries, and the prices of many of our products are fixed in foreign markets. Without exception these prices are fixed in the markets of countries having a gold standard or measure of value either by express provision of law or by a public policy which keeps their silver coins equal in exchangeable value to the gold coins at the legally established ratio. The value of our trade with the people of other countries during the last fiscal year was more than $1,700,000,000, and more than $1,100,000,000 of this was with the people of Europe, while with the whole of Asia it amounted to a little over $100,000,000, and with all the countries of South America, excluding Brazil, which has a single gold standard, it was only $46,000,000. While it would be unfair to attribute this unequal distribution of our trade with the outside world to the character of their fiscal legislation, I think it may be safely asserted that this country could not long maintain its present position as one of the most conspicuous and important members of the great community of commercial nations which now controls the trade of the world, unless we preserve a monetary system substantially, at least, in accord with the monetary systems of the other principal nations. . . .

Gold is the only international money, and all trade balances are settled in gold, or, which is the same thing, on a gold basis, all other forms of currency being adjusted to that standard. It is useless for the advocates of a different system of currency to insist that this ought not to be so; it is so, and we can not change the fact. But the gold eagle and double eagle are not accepted at a particular valuation in these settlements simply because the United States of America have declared by law that they shall be legal tender at their nominal value, but solely because the bullion contained in them, if uncoined, would be worth everywhere the same amount. This is a great and powerful government, but there is one thing it cannot do —it cannot create money. There are some things, however, which the government can do for the establishment and preservation of a sound and stable currency. In the exercise of its constitutional authority to "coin money and regulate the value thereof," it can suspend or limit the coinage of either metal whenever it is ascertained that the coins of the two metals, of the same denomination, are of unequal value; or it can change their legal ratio so as to make them as nearly equal in value as possible; or it can maintain the parity of its coins by receiving them and their paper representatives in payment of all public ones and discharge all of its own obligations in whatever kind of money its creditors may demand.

The principle or rule of law that the option as to the kind of legal tender with which an obligation shall be discharged belongs to the debtor and not to the creditor has no just application in a case where the government issues its notes to circulate as a currency among the people, and, by making them legal tender, compels the people to receive them. The private citizen may very properly avail himself of the lawful right to discharge his private obligations, held by voluntary creditors, in any kind of legal-tender money, because he has only his own personal interest to protect and owes no public duty in the premises. But when the government of the United States has undertaken to supply the country with a currency, and has issued its obligations in the form of notes to circulate among the people in the transaction of their private business, and has received for every dollar represented by such notes a dollar's worth of the people's service or a dollar's worth of the people's property, its honor, as well as sound public policy, demands that they shall be redeemed upon presentation in money current in all the markets of the world. . . .

The country has recently heard a great deal about bimetallism and a double standard, and it is possible that these subjects will continue to be discussed to some extent in the future. For my part, I have never been able to understand what is meant by a double standard, or double measure of value, and I have never found any one who could tell me. To my mind it seems as absurd to contend that there should be two different standards of measures of value as it would be to insist upon having two yardsticks of different lengths or two gallons of different dimensions. If there were two standards, or measures, not equal in value, it is evident that one of them must be a false measure; and if they were of equal value, it is evident that, no matter what the law might declare, there would be in fact but one measure, although composed of two different kinds of material. If, for instance, the silver dollar and the gold dollar were precisely the same value, and could be so kept at all times, there would be, in fact, but one standard, one unit for the measurement of value. Whatever that actual standard may be as established by the laws of trade and finance, whether it be so many grains of fine gold or so many grains of fine silver, it is the duty of the government to conform to it in the payment of its obligations and in all its dealings with the people. . . .

Gentlemen, the question whether the obligations of the United States will be paid in coin current in all the markets in the world has already been settled, and it has, in my opinion, been settled for all time to come. It has been settled, not by

THE FIRST BOND ISSUE

any specific act of Congress prescribing the exact mode of payment, but by the spirit and obvious purpose of the whole body of existing legislation upon the subject, and by the deliberate judgment of the American people and the declared purpose of those who have been intrusted with the execution of the laws. The disposition and ability of the government to maintain its own credit at the highest possible standard, and to preserve the integrity of all the forms of currency in circulation among the people, cannot be reasonably doubted, and ought not to be subjects of serious controversy hereafter.

This does not imply that silver is to have no place in our monetary system. What is to be the ultimate fate of that metal is one of the problems which time and events alone can solve; but for many years, notwithstanding all our legislation in its support, the fluctuations in its value have been so rapid and so great as to demonstrate the fact that it cannot be safely coined without limitations into money of final redemption at the existing ratio, or at any other ratio that might be established. . . .

It is enough to say at present that we have already on hand a stock of silver, coined and uncoined, sufficient to meet all the probable requirements of the country for many years to come. The mints of the United States have coined 419,332,550 standard silver dollars, and we now have 140,699,760 fine ounces of silver bullion, which at the ratio of 16 to 1 would make $181,914,841, or $601,247,391 in the aggregate. Besides this, we have $76,977,002 in subsidiary silver coin, which is legal tender to the amount of ten dollars, and is by law redeemable in full legal-tender money on presentation. Our total stock of gold coin and good bullion is $659,167,949. . . .

The bankers went home rejoicing, and those who had maliciously whispered about the golden castles of Wall Street that Carlisle had once been an advocate of free silver were silenced—but the next day they were assailing one another with vehement questions as to why the Secretary did not make a sale of bonds for gold. Carlisle, however, properly awaited the advice of Congress.

The Fifty-third Congress met on December 4, 1893; the bitterness which the silverites had carried with them on leaving Washington a few weeks before had been deepened by the suffering which they had found among their constituents. To many of them free silver had come to be both a fetish and a weapon, an idol to be worshiped with unalterable devotion and a sword with which to destroy the "hellish" money power. The gold men were equally intolerant; they denounced the "ignorance" of the Westerners. Secretary Carlisle was not in an enviable position, for whatever he said in his report, upon which he had been working for some time, was certain to be severely condemned.

One can guess that the hopes of the Secretary were not great when he bundled up the long, bulky hand-written manuscript of the *Report of the Finances* for 1893 and sent it off to Capitol Hill. "It may be safely assured," he wrote Congress, "that the worst effects of the recent financial disturbance, and consequent business depression, have been realized, and the conditions will be much more favorable hereafter for the collection of an adequate revenue for the support of the Government; but it can scarcely be expected that the receipts during the remainder of the fiscal year will exceed the expenditures for the same time to such an extent as to prevent a very considerable deficiency. I have, therefore, estimated a probable deficiency of $28,000,000 at the close of the year. . . . On account of the difficulty of securing such a sum within time it will be required by the imposition and collection of additional taxes, I recommend that the third section of the act to provide for the resumption of specie payments, approved January 14, 1875, which confers authority upon the Secretary of the Treasury to issue and sell certain descriptions of United States bonds, be so amended as to authorize him to issue and sell, at not less than par in coin, bonds to an amount not exceeding $200,000,000, bearing a lower rate of interest and having a shorter time to run than those now provided for."

"Two-hundred millions is a lot of money," wrote the editor

of the *Banker's Magazine;* but Secretary Carlisle had no desire to sell that amount at any one time. His chief interest was in securing the power to issue bonds of a more favorable nature than the three classes (4%, 4½%, and 5%) permitted under the existing law. Carlisle explained to Congress that on the first class the interest at maturity would amount to one-half the principal, on the second to more than two-thirds the principal, and on the third to twenty per cent more than the principal. He sagaciously observed that "nothing less than the existence of a great and pressing financial emergency would . . . justify the issue and sale of any of these classes of bonds." The request and the explanation, however, were wasted, for Congress paid not the slightest attention to his remarks. The silverites saw no reason why bonds should be sold for gold, for they believed that the Treasury was piled full of perfectly usable silver. They perceived in a bond sale no aid to the common people, but only profit to the wealthy.

Secretary Carlisle, anticipating the cry on the part of Congressmen that the rich were seeking to force a bond issue for their personal gain, suavely said to Congress: "If the authority now existing should be so modified as to empower the Secretary of the Treasury to issue the bonds in denominations or sums of twenty-five dollars and multiples thereof, they could be readily disposed of through the sub-treasuries and post-offices without the agency or intervention of banks or other financial institutions and without the payment of commissions. Such bonds would afford to the people at large an opportunity to convert their surplus earnings into a form of security which, while it would be perfectly safe, would not only increase in value by reason of accumulating interest, but would be at all times available as a means of procuring money when needed."

In answer to those who opposed resumption he said: "Whatever objections may be urged against the maintenance of a large coin reserve, procured by the sale of interest-bearing bonds, it must be evident that this course can not be safely avoided unless the Government abandons the policy of issuing its own notes for circulation and limits the functions of the Treasury Department to the collection and disbursement of the public revenues for purely public purposes, and to the performance of such other administrative duties as may be appropriate to the character of its organization as a branch of the executive authority. To the extent that it is required by law to receive money on deposit, and repay it, or to issue notes and redeem them on demand it is engaged in a business which can not be conducted without having at all times the ability to comply promptly with its obligations. Its operations necessarily affect, beneficially or otherwise, the private financial affairs of all the people, and they have a right to be assured by appropriate legislation that their confidence in the integrity and power of the Government has not been misplaced."

But Congress was beyond the reach of pleas or entreaties, and Carlisle would have profited more had he frankly admitted it. That he doubted the willingness of Congress to vote an issue of bonds is attested by the fact that he proposed an alternative which could in no way become involved with the question of the gold standard. His plan, modeled on the English system of exchequer bills, was that "he be empowered to execute from time to time, as may be necessary, the obligations of the Government, not exceeding in the aggregate fifty million dollars, bearing a rate of interest not greater than 3 per cent and payable after one year from date, and that he be permitted to sell them at not less than par, or use them at not less than par, in the payment of public expenses to such creditors as may be willing to receive them." The recommendation was worthy of consideration.

Secretary Carlisle was seeking relief from two embarrassments: that of having no gold with which to meet his redemption demands, and that of having no cash with which to pay his current obligations. Both were enhanced by the large exportations of gold which were in progress, the heavy payments which had to be met at the end of the year, and the declining revenues of the government. He had no desire to postpone obligations when it was possible to pay them. "Deficiencies are not savings," he said, "but as a general rule result in larger expenditures than those that would have been made had adequate appropriations been granted in the first instance."

The Treasury Department was indeed a strange financial institution, peculiarly unfit to be the center of a financial controversy; the Secretary could neither "negotiate temporary loans to meet casual deficiencies" nor "retire and cancel" the obligations of the government without issuing new ones. This situation demanded, said Carlisle, "such legislation as will make the Department more independent of speculative interests and operations and enable it to maintain the credit of the Government upon a sound and secure basis." Like every Secretary for the past twenty years, he expressed doubt as to the ability of his Department to maintain resumption under the existing conditions. He closed his *Report* with the honest but perhaps unwise statement: "Congress alone has the power to adopt such measures as will relieve the present situation and enable the Treasury to continue the punctual payment of all legitimate demands upon it, and I respectfully but earnestly urge that immediate attention be given the subject."

The Secretary probably said too much in his first *Report*, because those of whom he asked aid threw his very words into his teeth in their Congressional arguments. Silence in the succeeding years, however, brought no reward.

While the administration waited on Congress for authority to issue bonds for gold and for providing money to meet ordinary expenses, the Treasury was compelled to turn to other sources. The government of the United States became a miser, carefully hoarding every dollar of gold. Only by using United States notes at the clearing house was the New York subtreasury able to save its small supply of the yellow metal. Heavy exportations at the end of the year brought the financial situation to a crisis. The banks again came to the aid of the Treasury and agreed to supply gold for export to the amount of $25,000,000, but they did so reluctantly; they had been aiding the nation for a year. It was evident that the government must soon find its own method of relief. Moreover, the Democratic Committee on Ways and Means made no effort to bring the new tariff bill forward, and the result was that any aid which merchants or financiers had been inclined to give was checked.

Secretary Carlisle dispatched Assistant-Secretary Curtis to New York to talk over the situation with the financiers there. Ostensibly on a visit to attend to private matters, the Assistant Secretary consulted bank officials and sought to ascertain the extent to which they would supply exporters with gold from their own vaults. Curtis was a capable man, and he was more familiar with business men in New York than his chief; but it was possibly a blunder on the part of the Secretary to send a subordinate at this juncture, for, despite the fact that the silver men believed him to be viciously allied with the moneyed interests, the feeling of the New York bankers toward Carlisle was not cordial. "It would have been in far better taste if our Blue Grass Secretary of the Treasury, Mr. Carlisle, had himself come here to consult the bankers; . . . he should have long since taken advantage of the ease in money to market a block of bonds and thus increased his working balance to a comfortable figure," said the New York *Mail and Express*.

The opening days of 1894 brought Carlisle no expectations of a happy or prosperous year. In spite of the fact that Mrs. Carlisle's reception on New Year's day "carried off all the honors not excepting the White House,"[1] there was no joy for the Secretary. The old year had ended in gloom; the country was suffering a sentimental despondency, based upon fear rather than upon judgment. During November and December the government had been running a deficit of $7,000,000 a month, which continued on into the new year; gold was flowing out of the New York sub-treasury to Europe. On December 30 the gold reserve had fallen to slightly more than $80,000,000. The gold certificates in circulation exceeded the total

[1] O. O. Stealey to Mrs. Carlisle. Mrs. William K. Carlisle MSS.

gold coin possessed by the government by more than seven million dollars, and, while the certificates were located largely in the East, the coin was scattered over the entire country. The Treasury now possessed less than $20,000,000 in other kinds of money, and there was no way to increase the amount. The holders of gold certificates alone could easily have forced the government to admit its inability to pay gold, and yet the reserve had also to be used to meet current obligations. In New York the bank vaults, because of the growing financial uncertainty, were gorged with idle money which nobody desired. If the country hoped to avoid bankruptcy, it was certainly time to make a bond sale. "Mr. Carlisle has set out in his report the authority desired," said the *Commercial and Financial Chronicle*. "Congress cannot bestir itself too quickly in conferring this authority. To leave affairs to drift is to invite trouble, while to put 50 millions of borrowed money into the Treasury would be more effectual than any other single act in restoring confidence in financial circles at home and abroad." [1]

Indeed, the situation was so critical that the daily reports were not always to be relied upon. "Don't trust my statement absolutely—I made that up for outside effect and have used the deficit twice but my excuse is that I did not use the possible redemptions—which I think will be much larger than 28 millions, but of course, we get back silver certificates for the gold paid out," wrote Jordan to Curtis on January 9. "As I have said before increase in the former means decrease in the latter. I am afraid from the rapidity with which the silver certificates are accumulating with us and the banks that we will soon receive from 75 to 85 per cent of our income in that kind of money. 'Beware of the Ides of March,' I confess to a feeling of actual alarm at the present situation. . . . Help from the banks, even if I could get it, only prolongs our agony. . . . Seriously, we are in a bad box, and I again restate my advice, that the Secretary should notify the Finance Committee that if they don't give him relief by February 1st he will sell

[1] Jan. 6, 1894.

25 millions of bonds (by that time it may be 50 millions) in order to replenish the 'Reserve Fund.' If we permit a disturbance to take place before the bonds are offered the Secretary will be lucky if he gets par for his 4's."[1]

It seemed impossible longer to avoid an issue of bonds, but Carlisle still waited on Congress. On January 6 Representative Harter of Ohio, at his request, introduced a measure seeking authority for an issue of bonds, and two days later Representative O'Neil of Massachusetts brought in a similar bill. Others were presented also, but none could catch the ear of Congress. By January 10 silver certificates made up fifty-nine per cent of the New York customs receipts. On the 14th the New York *Recorder* appeared with the headlines: "Carlisle must raise $30,000,000 in 15 days. Unless Congress provides some other means of getting money the Treasury will be broke." In a report to the Senate on the following day Secretary Carlisle pointed out that the gold coin in the Treasury had been reduced $99,000,000 in the twelve months preceding November 1, 1893. In the first seventeen days of January $11,000,000 in gold was lost to the Treasury, and the reserve stood at $69,000,000.

Richard Watson Gilder tells the story of having attended about this time a Cabinet meeting at which the President became exasperated and exclaimed, "This don't help us. I believe in taking the bull by the horns and coming out with an issue of bonds." The patience of even the Secretary was finally exhausted. He clearly saw that there was no longer any hope of receiving aid from Congress, and accordingly decided to make a bond sale under the existing authority.[2] On January 17, 1894, the first circular announcing the sale of United States bonds issued by Secretary Carlisle appeared. By virtue of the act of January 14, 1875, he announced for disposition on behalf of the Treasury Department four per cent bonds to the

---

[1] Curtis MSS.
[2] See Secretary Carlisle's statement before the Judiciary Committee, Jan. 25, 1894, p. 11.

amount of $50,000,000, in denominations of fifty dollars and multiples thereof, to run ten years, redeemable "in coin" at the pleasure of the government after that time. He stipulated that no bids would be accepted at less than 117.223, which would put the bonds on a 3 per cent basis. Payment was to be made in gold or gold certificates.

The commercial and industrial centers were greatly pleased with the announcement. "The proposed issue of Government bonds by Secretary Carlisle is almost universally approved of here," wrote the editor of the *Commercial and Financial Chronicle* on January 20. "We can only say that under the circumstances which have existed the bond proposal, in our opinion, could hardly have been issued much earlier. It was only proper that the Administration should, if possible, wait and give Congress the opportunity to provide a new security for the relief of the Treasury. Without doubt such a law was desirable. . . . The actual sale of the bonds and replenishing of the gold in the Treasury will undoubtedly have a good effect in restoring confidence everywhere."

The silver followers, however, were not so generous in their comments. A conglomeration of sense and nonsense again reigned supreme in the council halls of the nation. "It's an infernal outrage," said "Sockless Jerry" Simpson, who wanted to issue greenbacks because they bore no interest. "Silver Dick" Bland declared that there was no authority for disposing of bonds, and that the millions of silver dollars in the Treasury were all that was needed. "There is a great interest in this country that is demanding the issue of these bonds," said Senator Allen of Nebraska, "and humiliating as it is to make the statement our Government is in practical partnership with that interest. I refer to the banking interests, the brokers and the speculators, and the men who gamble on the people's credit. . . . the rest of the country may go to the dogs. And this in the face of a clamoring multitude, in the face of men and women with poverty drawing dark lines over their pale faces." He demanded that the government be divorced from the wealthy interests. "The Presidents of the United States and their secretaries of finance," continued Allen, "have been and are now fastened by golden cords to a combination of the worst men in the world. . . . In the face of idleness, destitution, hunger, and desperation in every State and in every city of the Union, and with $250,000,000 in the public Treasury, the President is compelled to sell the people's credit to appease the clamor of these misers of Wall Street." And then in the type of oratory which a few years later was to blow into flames the smouldering embers of discontent in the West, he declared that "there is a day of retribution ahead, a day of reckoning nigh at hand. The people will one day smite their enemies. . . . Standing as I do, in the night of the nineteenth century, looking towards the dawn of the twentieth, I see coming a wave of fire and blood. . . . Behind me . . . is Rome; before me—God alone in his infinite wisdom knows." [1]

Some Republicans thoroughly approved. "Senator Quay," said the *Nation* on January 25, "ranges himself alongside the legal luminaries of the Populists, and warns the 'takers of the loan' that the 'securities go out under a cloud, and their redemption will be an important political issue in the future.'"

One of the most vulnerable points on which the opponents of a bond issue attacked the administration was the fact that a part of the money obtained must of necessity be used for the running expenses of the government. Congress, as well as Secretary Carlisle, was fully conscious of that fact. "The power to issue bonds conferred upon the Secretary of the Treasury by existing laws, it is admitted on all sides, is," said Senator Dolph, "for the purpose only of the redemption of legal tender notes." The bond sale, observed Senator Stewart, was only a subterfuge to obtain money for expenses. In this criticism the silverites were joined by the Republicans. There were other objections also. Congressmen were certain that the purse strings of the nation had been handed over to the Executive Department, which, moreover, had taken unto itself the power to

[1] *Congressional Record,* 53d Cong., 2d Sess., p. 1176.

THE FIRST BOND ISSUE

make laws without the consent of the people. The Secretary of the Treasury, they asserted, had put himself into such a position as to increase the public debt at his own caprice; more than that, said the Chicago *Times*, "he abandons the plan of inviting small investors and issues the bonds so that they can only be taken by banks and big financial institutions." Senator Stewart declared that the "iron hand of contraction" was being wielded by Secretary Carlisle at the dictation of England, and that the head of the Treasury Department had announced a sale of bonds in order to provide the rich with a safe place to invest their money.

The country at large joined in the fray. The South and West heaped criticism upon Carlisle's head in countless letters. Many demands were made for the impeachment of the Kentuckian who had "turned overnight" into a "Judas," in league with the "bloated barons of wealth." Definite action, however, was taken only by the Knights of Labor. On the day following the call for bids John W. Hayes, general secretary and treasurer of that organization, wired J. R. Sovereign, Grand Master Workman, as follows: "Secure counsel and go before the United States Supreme Court immediately. Enter injunction proceedings against Carlisle restraining him from issuing $50,000,000 of bonds. The interest of the people, upon whom the burden of all taxation to pay the interest and principal of these bonds fall, require that you should immediately take this step against the Secretary of the Treasury enjoining him from incurring any further debt while the resources of the Government, if properly applied, are sufficient to meet all lawful demands."[1] Sovereign announced: "We base our appeal for the injunction on the ground that there is now no operating provision in the law demanding a reserve of $100,000,000. We claim that the Secretary of the Treasury has no specific authority conferred upon him to issue bonds for any purpose. We allege that he is not issuing the bonds for the purpose of the resumption act, for he is issuing more than double the deficit in the so-

[1] New York *World*, January 20, 1894.

called legal reserve." On arriving from New York early one morning in January, Secretary Carlisle found in his office a representative of the Knights of Labor waiting to serve him with a subpoena. The Secretary took the paper to the Cabinet meeting which assembled a few minutes later.

The labor organization meant to begin its legal proceedings in Des Moines, Iowa, the home of the Grand Master Workman, but the three law firms which had been employed discovered that the courts of that city had no jurisdiction over the Secretary of the Treasury. The case eventually came up in the Supreme Court of the District of Columbia, where Judge Cox promptly threw it out, declaring that the Secretary had an undoubted right to issue bonds for redemption purposes and that he might elect that they be paid in gold if he so chose. The East in general regarded the actions of the silver Congressmen and the Knights of Labor as a joke, but to the Secretary of the Treasury they seemed of serious import.

Contrary to what the silver men believed would happen, the financial leaders did not rush forward to obtain the bonds which the Secretary offered for sale. The interest was far less than had been expected, and many bankers who had subscribed when the announcement was made grew alarmed by the voluble opposition in Congress and withdrew their bids.[1] Congress undoubtedly possessed the power to prevent a sale and to cause unlimited embarrassment to any purchaser if a sale were made. Moreover, the hostile press sought to widen the chasm between the Secretary and the bankers. Secretary Carlisle, said many editors, had "scouted" and "sneered" at the financiers. In December the Chicago *Record* had remarked: "It has been one of the chief articles in the financial creed of Secretary Carlisle to abjure the New York banker and all his works, and he has never in any manner before consulted them concerning the financial plans or policy of the government. On one of his visits to New York, soon after the inauguration, Mr. Conrad N. Jordan, the assistant treasurer of the United States, issued

[1] See New York *Sun*, January 29, 1893, and *Bond Investigation Report*.

invitations to about twenty of the most influential bank presidents and moneyed men to meet the secretary of the treasury at Delmonico's. Mr. Carlisle accepted the invitation, supposing that it was a gathering of democratic politicians; but when he got to New York and found that he was to meet the goldbugs of Wall Street, he shied and refused to attend the dinner. He was afraid his association with the mammon of unrighteousness, as represented by the New York financial leaders, might be misunderstood by the simple-minded democrats in Kentucky and the west."[1] Carlisle had of course "sneered" at no one. He had hoped to avoid dependence upon the New York bankers, but the situation had become so acute that he was compelled to take action.

Assistant-Secretary Curtis was hurried off to New York on January 22 to discuss the bond sale with the financiers; on the twenty-seventh he wired Secretary Carlisle, "Friends advise your coming here for conference. Advices continue unfavorable."[2] The Secretary of the Treasury swallowed his prejudices against the bankers and followed his assistant to the financial Sodom. The Montreal *Star* said of the incident: "Never before has Mr. Carlisle, had a formal visit with the bankers of the metropolis. . . . Fortunately for his dignity the clamor against the validity of the bonds furnished an adequate excuse." The situation was trying. Something had to be done, and with a word of cheer from "Marse Henry" Watterson the Secretary left his hotel at ten o'clock on January 29 to make his way to Wall Street. He closeted himself for half an hour in the sub-treasury office with Assistant-Treasurer Jordan, and at noon the New York bankers whom he had invited to discuss the bond issue with him began to arrive.[3] There

---

[1] December 16, 1893.

[2] Curtis MSS.

[3] Years later Cleveland wrote of this critical situation that "bids for bonds under the offer of the Secretary came in so slowly that a few days before the first of February, when the bids were to be opened, there were plain indications that the contemplated sale would fail unless prompt and energetic measures were taken to avoid such a perilous result. Thereupon the Secretary of the Treasury

were many things to be discussed, but the two main questions were: first, on the part of the bankers, whether the Secretary of the Treasury had authority to issue bonds; and, second, on the part of the Secretary, whether the banks were trying to discredit the loan so that they could buy it all and then sell at a profit. The questions were soon cleared up. Secretary Carlisle offered almost conclusive proof that the issue was legal, and the bankers offered equally good proof that they were not trying to beat the government.

When the conference was over, Secretary Carlisle went to lunch with James Stillman, president of the National City Bank, and apparently enjoyed it. That evening the banker wrote Colonel Lamont concerning the conference: "He [Secretary Carlisle] made a very favorable impression and I think explained to the satisfaction of every one present that he had full authority to make this issue. . . . I shall devote tomorrow and the day following in trying to influence subscriptions, and while I have grave doubts of the entire amount being subscribed for I sincerely trust that a considerable portion of it may be."[1] The meeting, however, was not entirely a success. In his letter to Lamont, Stillman said of Secretary Carlisle: "I suppose that he will return to Washington with the impression that the fifty millions will not be fully subscribed for." There was, indeed, some friction created because many of the financial men felt that the Secretary appeared indifferent as to whether New York took the loan or not. Some irritation was bound to appear, for the meeting was an unnatural alliance between a statesman who honestly opposed the men of Wall Street, and the men of Wall Street themselves, who believed that they were rendering a patriotic service to the government.

The financiers eventually overcame their fears and came to

invited to a conference, in the city of New York a number of bankers and presidents of moneyed institutions, which resulted in so arousing their patriotism, as well as their solicitude for the protection of the interests that they represented, that they effectively exerted themselves, barely in time to prevent a disastrous failure of the sale." *Presidential Problems*, p. 140.

[1] Stillman to Lamont, Jan. 29, 1894. Lamont MSS.

the aid of the government. The chief credit for making the loan a success belongs to John A. Stewart, president of the United States Trust Company, who, impressed with the absolute necessity for action, took in hand the work of procuring subscriptions. He was ably assisted by Edward King of the Union Trust Company, James T. Woodward of the Hanover National Bank, and James Stillman of the City National Bank, the group becoming known as the "big four." Less than forty-eight hours before the expiration of the time set for receiving bids, no more than $6,000,000 could be counted on, and yet the untiring efforts of these bankers made the sale a success. Stewart alone raised $30,000,000 in a little over two hours. Notices of the new bids began to come in about two o'clock on January 30, but still the public was skeptical. "It did not seem possible, in view of the doleful accounts given in the morning papers of Secretary Carlisle's meeting with the bankers the day before, that such a change of front could be brought about among the moneyed men in such a short space of time. . . . Pique and pecuniary advantages had a good deal to do with many holding back until the last moment," said the New York *Times*.

The Secretary breathed a sigh of relief when the success of the bond sale was definitely assured on January 31. "The Administration has been saved from the consequences of the attitude of its own party in Congress, and what threatened to be a misfortune to the country has been changed into a benefit," said the New York *Tribune*. Every possible effort, both in and out of Congress, had been made by the silver men to discredit Secretary Carlisle's loan. Their attempts called forth the indignant and earnest protest of Senator Sherman, who stated that the authority was so plain that it had never been denied in the Senate during the fifteen years since the resumption of specie payments. Sherman said of the public credit on the floor of the Senate: "I regard it as sacred in the hands of Grover Cleveland and John G. Carlisle as if it were in the hands of Republicans. I will vote any measure of relief that is desired

"... which is consistent with the existing laws." The *Commercial and Financial Chronicle* declared that "this strange effort to wreck the Treasury Department and to leave it without funds has failed to do more than to slightly increase the burdens of the people by depreciating the price at which the bonds were marketed."

On February 2 Secretary Carlisle sent his thanks to President Stewart of the Union Trust Company and to those who had worked with him. Congress heard much concerning the bond sale on that day. Peffer forced a resolution through the Senate demanding that the Secretary submit a list of the names of all the people who had bid for these evidences of governmental corruption. Senator Sherman's protest accomplished nothing, and Senator Platt's statement that the silverites were acting as though it were a crime for men to offer—at three per cent—money to the government when it was seriously in need fell upon unhearing ears. When on the following day the Secretary announced the allotment of the bonds, a great majority of which went to New York bankers, the remark, "I told you so," echoed through every corridor of the nation's Capitol and, growing as it went, traveled on out over the snow-covered cornfields of the great valley and across the arid plains of the West, ending at last in the silver mines of the rugged Rockies. Every denial of selfish motives on the part of the bankers only increased in the hearts of the silverites the certainty of their guilt. They shook their heads in stolid disbelief when a few months later President Williams of the Chemical National Bank of New York swore in regard to the bonds: "I took $1,000,000. I did not want them; I took them to make the thing go." [1]

Thus in spite of all discouragements the first bond issue was successfully carried through. It was an event of no great importance in the constructive history of the administration. Only its failure would have been a notable occurrence. It did, how-

[1] Unpublished *Hearings* before House Committee on Banking and Currency, 53d Cong., 3d Sess., Dec. 11, 1894, p. 321.

THE FIRST BOND ISSUE

ever, have certain results of importance in the course of the Treasury Department. With the first sale of bonds Carlisle had been driven to ally himself definitely with a group of men whom he had formerly avoided and with whom he was never thoroughly at home. He was forced to admit that his power over Congress, the members of which had for so many years listened respectfully to his advice, was past history, and he could not help seeing that the laboring man, to whose service he had dedicated his life, had turned from him. From this time forward Carlisle's life was unhappy. Those for whom he believed himself to be laboring had lost all appreciation of his efforts. The rift in the party was nearing an open breach; the administration was narrowed to the President, the members of his Cabinet, and their loyal and trusted subordinates. At a later date President Cleveland expressed the situation in a letter to Ambassador Bayard: "I have at my side a Cabinet composed of pure-minded, patriotic and thoroughly loyal men. I sometimes feel guilty when I recall the troubles I have induced them to share with me." [1]

[1] McElroy, II, p. 90.

CHAPTER XIV THE YEAR OF CALAMITIES AND THE SECOND BOND ISSUE

The year 1894 is one to be long remembered in American History. In it those elements of dynamic discontent which had long been gathering strength, half unperceived, now loomed upon the political horizon with the black and sullen menace of a swelling thunder-cloud, within whose womb are pent the forces of destruction. For years, by bargain and by compromise, the day of reckoning had been postponed; but now both compromise and bargain were impossible, and the nation had to face, however fearful, the issues which would no longer down.
—Harry Thurston Peck.

TRULY the year was a trying one for the administration, and before it came to an end Secretary Carlisle resorted to two bond issues in an effort to maintain his failing gold reserve. At the end of January, 1894, the reserve stood at $65,000,000, and one year later, in spite of the fact that the two sales had netted $117,000,000 in gold, it was $21,000,000 less. Because of its lack of funds the Treasury could not hold the greenbacks and the Treasury notes in its vaults, but was forced to pay them out in meeting its ordinary obligations; these paper claims formed an endless chain by which the gold was rapidly and incessantly dipped from the government coffers. Moreover, the receipts, despite the fact that expenses were being reduced every month, fell far short of the expenditures; in the fiscal year the government received almost $70,000,000 less than it spent. The old adage that "misery loves company" was demonstrated as political complexities came to vex the already heavily burdened Secretary of the Treasury.

The year 1894 did not open with a favorable outlook for the Treasury Department. The first bond issue nearly failed, and only by appealing to the New York bankers did Secretary

Carlisle save the situation. Unfortunately the method of procedure had not been carefully thought out, and the bankers were in some instances forced to pay a higher rate than they had expected. "They say, with some show of justice that they ought not to be compelled to lose interest because of error at Washington," wrote Jordan from New York to Curtis, "and don't say very complimentary things about clerks who can't handle thirty or forty subscriptions without errors grave enough to cost the subscribers two days' interest." [1] The situation did not tend to improve the feeling between the bankers and the Secretary.

The bond sale was not an efficient business transaction; people who did not possess gold were forced to carry their legal-tenders to the Treasury or its branches and there exchange them for government gold with which to buy government bonds. In this process the citizen came out with his money—regardless of the kind—changed into United States bonds commonly believed to be payable in gold, while the government itself profited not at all by the transaction. The coin had merely been carried from the redemption window to the receiving window and returned to the account from which it had been taken. The Treasury gained only when the gold paid in was obtained from the vaults of the banks or from private hoards. On February 3 Jordan wrote Curtis, "I don't like the amount of Treasury notes we have been compelled to redeem." [2] But he had seen just the beginning, for before the month was over $19,000,000 was spent in redemptions.

Secretary Carlisle did what he could to prevent the indirect use of legal-tenders with which to buy bonds. Jordan objected, however, to any intimidation. "That a man, much as I dislike the fact of presentation, cannot present greenbacks, claim gold, and make a payment is a statement that I could think very seriously over before making," he wrote Curtis. "We are borrowing to sustain the credit of the greenback—don't we dis-

[1] Jordan to Curtis, Feb. 3, 1894. Curtis MSS.
[2] Curtis MSS.

credit it if we refuse it? Molasses is better than vinegar to catch financial flies—and you may need money again." Carlisle never appreciated the shrewdness of this last bit of advice; he never felt at ease with the bankers, and they never forgot that he should be taught a lesson in deference to big business.

In spite of the difficulties the first bond sale was not without temporary beneficial results. By the end of February the gold reserve reached $106,000,000, and it stood near that sum throughout the following month. Many were hopeful that it might never again fall below $100,000,000. "Mr. Carlisle should now study to have on hand an ample balance," wrote the *Commercial and Financial Chronicle*. "That policy is an imperative requirement of the situation until Congress has passed a satisfactory law authorizing a 3 per cent bond or Treasury note which can be used at any time to meet current wants." Congress, however, was busy with other matters and gave little attention to the financial condition of the government or to Secretary Carlisle's requests for aid in his discouraging task of maintaining the gold standard.

Reform of the laws concerning the form of bonds which could be sold by the Treasury Department was not the only task to which Congress could have applied itself. The revenue system needed revision, and the party in power was under distinct obligation to give the country a reduction in the existing tariff rates. A more elastic currency was demanded by the business interests of the nation, while because of the repeal of the Sherman silver law a safe and stable means of adding to the general circulating medium was especially important. But the forces of discontent which had been growing for many years prevented effective action. For twenty years the South and the West had been listening to Democratic promises of an easier life that would come when tariff reform became a reality. As the glowing hope which had been born in their hearts dimmed, free silver became their guiding star. They now had little faith in their party, for the leaders who had promised them relief from their oppressions had apparently joined the "goldbugs." The silver forces, united by the repeal of the Sherman silver law and the first bond issue, were more interested in the coinage of the seigniorage than in the tariff.

Regardless of all the disturbing elements, the reform advocates had begun work upon a new tariff measure soon after the opening of Congress in December. The plans of the party had not been carried out, however, for Secretary Carlisle had not spent the summer months of '93 in writing a tariff bill. William L. Wilson, chairman of the Ways and Means, did service in his stead, and on December 19 he introduced the administration tariff bill. It was a better tariff proposal than many had expected from the former schoolmaster, but there were heated objections. It was, said Mills, "only a Sabbath Day's journey on the way to reform," while Henry Watterson declared the measure "merely better than the McKinley Bill in degree, not in kind, and if Protectionism is ever to be dislodged, I doubt the Trojan-horse stratagem to which it seems to incline. We live in the age of Carnegies and Goulds, not in that of Priam and Aeneas."

The Wilson bill was forced to run a severe gauntlet before agreement could be reached. The Ways and Means Committee in particular and the House personnel in general tore it to pieces bit by bit and then endeavored to reconstruct it into a symmetrical whole which would include the desires of each individual. Indeed, the fate of any tariff measure in the Congressional arena of this generation was scarcely less cruel than that which befell the gladiators in the days of ancient Rome. There was some justification for the belief that it was the great "interests" who sat nearby and gave the signal of death or mercy. Whatever its fate—an unmourned grave or a properly recorded law—no tariff bill ever emerged from one of these conflicts in a recognizable form. Of the treatment which the Wilson bill received *Harper's Weekly* said, "There has been nothing more grotesque and contemptible in our political annals."

When the Democratic tariff bill was presented to the House,

it contained an income tax provision which had been obtained, says Benton McMillin, its author, through the connivance of Thomas B. Reed of Maine. The story is that whenever the income tax subject was broached in the committee by Mr. McMillin, the other Democratic members promptly walked out; Reed, believing that condemnation would befall any political party which sponsored such an experiment and having no particular aversion to allowing the Democracy to hang itself if it so desired, agreed to hold his Republican associates in the committee room for the purpose of completing a quorum. A quorum was duly obtained, and the income tax provisions were forced into the tariff bill.[1] The measure was distinctly democratic and perhaps Democratic as well, but it brought new complications to a situation which was already sufficiently embarrassing.

The income tax proposal brought immediate opposition from the wealthy classes, who made their objections known in an emphatic manner. "It is an unjust discrimination and will array the honest thrifty people of the whole country against those who are responsible for it," wrote James Stillman to Colonel Lamont.[2] Secretary Carlisle did not believe the tax to be politically expedient, for he realized the difficulties which it would bring to his Department if he were compelled again to seek gold; he knew that the concession to the representatives of the debtor group was not sufficient to win a vote should bond authority be asked another time. The chief difficulty in levying an income tax at this time lay in the fact that the men upon whom the burden would fall were offering aid to the government. Financiers saw no reason why they should furnish their gold for the purpose of upholding the single standard and pay the revenues in addition.

The press of the East generally condemned the proposal as a vicious product of Populism in the South and the West, the

---

[1] This story was obtained from Mr. McMillin at Nashville, Tennessee, in September, 1930. No other proof has been found.
[2] Lamont MSS.

Nation characterizing it as a "dangerous experiment." Western papers, however, earnestly defended the measure. Almost a year before, C. H. Jones, editor of the St. Louis *Republic*, had written William Jennings Bryan urging him to become the standard bearer of those advocating a tax upon the abnormal incomes of the wealthy:

> I want to suggest to you that by far the most effective weapon for use against the Plutocratic policy is the graded income tax or an income tax of 5 per cent or 10 per cent on all incomes in excess of $10,000 per annum. There is nothing which those Eastern Plutocrats dread so much as that, and it is a weapon which the Democrats should have used long ago to stop the piling up of pensions. At the present juncture I am quite sure there is nothing which could be so effectually used to put a cog in the wheels of the Plutocratic program. About three weeks ago the *Republic* threw out the suggestion that plenty of gold, even for the payment of silver certificates in gold, could be placed in the Treasury by an income tax levied in gold on abnormal incomes. It made a sensation at once, as I knew it would, and I think I see signs already that the Plutocrats and their newspapers are not nearly so anxious to force the issue as they were a little while back.
>
> The income tax is one that ought to be levied at the next session of Congress. Some way of increasing the revenues must be found, especially if we are to redeem our pledges of tariff reform, and an income tax on abnormal incomes is far preferable to a replacing of the duty on sugar or even to an increase on the internal revenue tax on whiskey, though the latter may have to be resorted to also.
>
> I suggest that you equip yourself for taking the lead in urging a tax on incomes. I do not believe there is any way in which a member of the House could impress himself on legislation and on the country more effectively than by fighting such a measure through. I think you could do it, and if you will undertake it I will be in Washington to back you up.[1]

[1] Jones to Bryan, May 8, 1893. Bryan MSS.

The tariff measure reached a vote in the House on February 1. The closing day of any debate is always interesting, and this one was no exception. The House was crowded to suffocation. Cardinal Gibbons sat in the Speaker's Gallery; many Senators, including the venerable Senator Morrill, were present; a squad of city police stood about to assist the Sergeant-at-Arms in preserving order. Thomas B. Reed, holding a prepared speech, impatiently awaited the hour for declaiming the blessings of protection to the worker. John G. Carlisle was not there to answer the leader of the Republican forces as he had done when the Mills bill came to vote in 1888, but William L. Wilson was not less effective in stating the Democratic principles. Both addresses were admirable.

Immediately after passing the House, the tariff bill went to the committee of three appointed by the Democrats to revise it before presentation to the Senate. After three weeks of labor and many consultations with Carlisle, these three Senators—Jones of Arkansas, Vest of Missouri, and Mills of Texas—reported the revised measure. It at once fell into the "talons" of Arthur P. Gorman of Maryland and Calvin S. Brice of Ohio, both Democrats, and Nelson W. Aldrich, Republican, of Rhode Island. Gorman, said the *Nation*, wanted a "free lunch" tariff, and the editor asserted that his talk about "concessions" was "only the polite and parliamentary way of saying that Messrs. Gorman and Brice and Murphy and Smith and Faulkner and Caffery took the Finance Committee by the throat and frightened it into an abandonment of all pretense of a rational or honest tariff reform." For months wearisome discussion and intrigue continued; secret political councils and surreptitious manipulations of the lobbyists flourished.

Meanwhile, the Secretary of the Treasury watched his declining balance. The tariff troubles and delay were not the only sources of annoyance. Congressmen of the South and West were at every opportunity still demanding free coinage; they had not forgotten the humiliation of the repeal of the Sherman silver law, and they championed the cause of their people with persistent vigor. They demanded the coinage of the silver seigniorage in order to overcome "the great lack of money" which they believed to exist. But there was no seigniorage to coin, for the silver bullion was worth far less than the dollars which could be minted from it. Abram S. Hewitt of New York aptly described this effort to coin dollars from the value which the government seal lent to silver as "coining a vacuum." Nevertheless, the silverites pushed forward their bill.

Whatever the outcome of the seigniorage struggle, Carlisle was bound to suffer. A request for bond authority was pending in Congress, the Treasury needed money, and the fear as to the ability of the government to maintain the gold standard had not abated. If the bill passed and was vetoed by the President, the pleadings of the Secretary would fall on even more barren ground than before; if it became a law the inclination of the financial interests to support the Treasury would be dampened. Indeed, the bankers seemed to think that Carlisle should have rushed to Capitol Hill and plucked out this financial thistle, root and branch. The Secretary had promised the bankers at the time of the bond sale, said one editor, that "he would let this business [of seigniorage] severely alone; yet as soon as the Treasury was supplied with more gold, loaned on the belief that his promise would be faithfully regarded, he began to seriously consider the desirability of coining it." The business interests were disgruntled, although they realized the critical situation in which Carlisle found himself. "Mr. Carlisle's views of finance are sound enough," said the editor of the *Banker's Magazine,* "and the temptation to resort to this miserable subterfuge [of coining the seigniorage] sprang from the necessity to obtain more money from some source to pay the bills of the Government. Doubtless, if the Government had possessed ample revenues, he would not have thought of resorting to such an expedient to replenish the national exchequer." But it was Congress and not Secretary Carlisle that was urging the coinage of the seigniorage.

"The financial question is of much more importance than

the tariff question," advised William Endicott, Jr., of Boston. "We can get on fairly well with a bad tariff, but with bad money prosperity is not possible. The immediate effect of the promised issue of fiat currency will be the renewal of gold exports, and this will come from the Treasury, already very weak in gold."[1] Jordan of the New York sub-treasury knew well what the result would be. "The passage of this bill and its presentation to the President will put him in a bad position politically, as refusing money which will on its face, cost nothing—but which may cost millions," he wrote Assistant-Secretary Curtis on March 8, and on the twentieth he added, "The movement I wrote of to the Secretary has already begun—today we shall lose $370,000 exchanged for U. S. The banks are hoarding their greenbacks and paying at the Clearing House in Treasury notes alone, and unfortunately we are adding fuel to the fire by paying our debt balances in the same vehicle. I think we are going to the devil at much faster speed than before if this 'abomination of desolation' is signed—because we are now wholly in the power of the banks."

The President was perplexed. He held many consultations with Secretary Carlisle, but the discussions have passed into the realms of the unknown. Secretary Gresham, David R. Francis, and other sound-money men urged Cleveland to sign the bill because of the inevitable political results of a veto. Others, however, urged a veto, and they were supported by the financiers. The President heard them all, even inviting the banker James A. Stewart to come to Washington for conference. The silverites also came, and the President lost his temper when they threatened him and his party with extinction—though it was not an empty threat which they made.

On March 18 Cleveland wrote Don M. Dickinson of Michigan: "These are days of especial perplexity and depression and the path of public duty is unusually rugged."[2] But his mind was apparently running in the same trend as was that of

[1] Olney MSS.
[2] Cleveland MSS.

his shrewd friend, A. B. Farquar of York, Pa. "Only a Jesuit ever undertakes to defend the policy of doing wrong that good may come of it," Farquar wrote him on March 21. "What," he asked, "is to be gained by trying to propitiate the knaves and fools who have brought this trouble upon you?"

Three days later Cleveland's veto message went to Congress. The President clearly stated the reasons for his action, but he informed Congress that had the Treasury been granted power to sell bonds, he would have signed the bill regardless of his objections. The silver forces could not muster enough strength to defeat the veto, and they spent their anger on the succeeding requests of the administration.

Meanwhile, labor troubles also complicated the situation. Despite President Cleveland's statement that "confidence in our absolute solvency is to such an extent reinstated and faith in our disposition to adhere to sound financial methods is so far restored as to procure the most encouraging results both at home and abroad," the economic situation was still acute. The Secretary's prediction of December that "conditions will be much more favorable hereafter for the collection of an adequate revenue" was not fulfilled, for the government deficit continued month after month. The industries of the country were paralyzed; seldom if ever had unemployment been so widespread in the United States. Workers were plentiful, but jobs were few. The temper of the laboring man was sorely tried, and economic unrest began to manifest itself in various ways. Events of little importance in themselves were so exaggerated by the excited people that they took on the appearance of vital issues; many individuals frequently turned to violence in defense of their rights, whether imaginary or just.

Soon after the first bond issue the citizens of inland America, incensed by what they believed to be the illegal and corrupt actions of the administration at Washington, began aggressive steps against the "gold idolators" of the East. It seems that the entire working class had an idea that if only they could get to Washington to present their case, the whole difficulty would soon be settled. In the West many citizens gathered into little "armies" and began their march eastward; they seized trains, deprived the crews (often with their permission) of their positions, and started for the national capital, usually to get no farther than Chicago, where they came within the grasp of the law and were deprived of their new-found means of transportation. It was, in fact, a "tramping West"—"a petition in boots"—which America saw in the first half of the year 1894. Countless numbers of men and mere boys wandered about looking for work and money. From as far west as California they came, and each succeeding city eagerly helped them on in order to be rid of the "undesirables." From Dakota those wishing to go to Washington floated in rafts or boats down the Missouri to Sioux City, Iowa, where they joined other groups on their way East. Those so unfortunate as to find neither rail nor river available were compelled to walk.

The most dramatic movement to the seat of government was the march which started from Massillon, Ohio, under the leadership of Jacob S. Coxey, on March 24, 1894—the day on which President Cleveland sent his veto of the seigniorage bill to Congress. His army was not a violent organization, and, although many members were indeed "gentlemen of the great outdoors," they were not in themselves a threat to American institutions. But the lawmakers of the nation and the East in general viewed their approach with much perturbation.

Coxey's army eventually encamped in Washington and came to an end when the leaders were arrested because they "did then and there step upon certain plants, shrubs, and turf then and there being and growing" on the grounds of the Capitol. The judge, dominated by "powerful interests," said the counsel for the defense, fixed a sentence of twenty days and five dollars —demanded, said the counsel, "by those who are in favor of the gold standard." Coxey's army was at an end. "As an organized movement," wrote Richard Olney, "it was remarkable principally for its entire collapse without any serious con-

THE YEAR OF CALAMITIES 331

sequences either to the commonwealers themselves or to the communities visited by them." [1]

The *Nation* chronicled the disappearance of the industrial armies on May 10, but the troubles of the country were far from over. On the following day the workers in the shops of the Pullman Palace Car Company went on strike. They were joined in late June by the American Railway Union. Again those people who had hurled bitter epithets at the industrial armies demonstrated their lack of understanding by condemning the strikers as "the party of lawlessness, of murder, of incendiarism, and of defiance of authority." They pointed with pride to the fact that the Pullman company "provided houses for its employees, kept up open stretches of lawn, flower beds and lakes," and later refused to believe the actual facts when investigation proved that the "model village" was little more than a convenient method of extraction and coercion. The *Nation* characterized Eugene V. Debs as a dipsomaniac whose excessive drinking had beclouded his mind, while others regarded him as an idiot leading the idiotic.

The opinions of the East were confirmed when, against the wishes of the leaders, lawlessness and violence were introduced into the strikes. Millions of dollars' worth of property was destroyed, and President Cleveland was eventually constrained to send United States troops to Illinois. Governor Altgeld protested vigorously against this assumption of power on the part of the national Executive, but "the party of loyalty to the United States" thoroughly approved. "Altgeld is probably as unconscious of his own bad manners as he is of the bad odor of his own principles," wrote the *Nation*, "but boorish, impudent, and ignorant as he is, he can scarcely fail to wince under the treatment which he receives from the President." The President sent his troops and issued proclamations not because he desired to protect "the idle holders of idle capital," but because he believed that he was obligated to pre-

[1] In his "unfinished *Autobiography*." Olney MSS.

serve established society. He probably regretted the necessity for action, but many rejoiced because Grover Cleveland had at last out-Jacksoned Andrew Jackson himself. Cleveland understood, however, as Jackson had not, that disturbances in society have underlying causes, and he accordingly appointed a commission to study the labor situation. But the division between the debtor and creditor, those who had and those who had not, continued to grow.

The financial situation grew critical as the nation-wide disturbance hampered the work of the Treasury. The apprehensions in the East added to the difficulties. No place was more excited than the national capital, where, said Curtis, "lots of officers have been ordered to join their regiments, leaves of absence are cancelled, and the War Department is in a ferment." On July 7 Secretary Carlisle, although ill, drove to the White House for a conference with the President. On that day Curtis again wrote his mother: "We are all very much bothered about the strikes at Chicago and elsewhere ... I think Altgeld ought to be whipped. I had a long talk with the President yesterday at the Secretary's request. He proposes to stand up and stamp this out if it takes the whole army and militia to do it." [1]

The Treasury was alarmed for the safety of its branches; the total cash holdings of the Department were so small that any loss would be a calamity. Consultations were held with Secretary Lamont of the War Department in regard to protecting the sub-treasury at Chicago, and special guards were rushed to that point. Jordan of the New York sub-treasury made application for a change "especially as to efficiency in the character of the arms given this office for its defence. It must rely on the pluck of those inside for a while in case of attack, and I think we should be provided—amply—for such an event." [2] Moreover, the uncertainty and dangers of transportation were such that the Treasury Department refused to send

[1] Curtis MSS.
[2] Jordan to Curtis, July 9, 1894. Curtis MSS.

currency South or West except at the risk of the consignee.[1] The end of the strikes brought a great deal of relief to Secretary Carlisle, but the use of the troops had increased the doubt that his request for aid in solving his gold problem would be granted.

Thus the seigniorage question, the "industrial armies," and the strikes made Carlisle's position more and more precarious as the financial situation both at home and abroad grew worse. "The unsettling of confidence in all things American, which never seem to be settled to stay, has scared European capitalists who had money loaned since the panic," said the *Banker's Magazine*. The disturbances caused the return of American securities held abroad and started an increase in the outflow of gold. "This fright of foreign capital has been shared by home capital as well," wrote one correspondent, "and all contemplated enterprises, to be begun after the settlement of the tariff fiasco, are now held in abeyance awaiting the end of the strikes. What more will happen to break Uncle Sam's back when the strikes are ended Heaven only knows in this land as prolific in new isms and political fads as is her soil." The situation was made even more trying for the Secretary by the busy work of the scandalmongers. Rumor had it that "the slimy trail of the trust" in connection with sugar rates in the new tariff had not ended in the Senate Chamber, but had been "traced suspiciously near the executive departments of the national Government." Carlisle was accused of being involved in the corruption; and a great chorus of denunciation arose from the silverites, who had become convinced that he was in league with the "bloated plutocrats" and cared nothing for the welfare of the common man.

In order to understand the charges of graft and bribery which wrapped the Secretary of the Treasury in their filthy embrace and brought great embarrassments to him in his efforts to maintain the gold standard, we must now go back to the early days of May and follow the devious course of the Democratic tariff

[1] Curtis MSS.

bill. The appointment of Jones, Vest, and Mills as a committee to revise the tariff before its presentation to the Senate has already been noted. Whatever may be said about the wisdom of the changes which they made, it must be admitted that they labored earnestly. They often consulted Carlisle regarding their proposed amendments, frequently calling upon him to put their schedules into legal phraseology.

On the morning of May 5 Senator Jones arose early—he may have had a sleepless night over the sugar schedule—and Secretary Carlisle found him in his parlor when he came down to breakfast that morning. The Senator held in his hand a slip on which was sketched the sugar rate the committee wished substituted for the House provisions; an increase in duty was suggested because Mills in particular feared that the Wilson bill as then written would not provide sufficient revenue to wipe out the existing government deficit. Carlisle had always favored "a moderate duty on sugar as a revenue article," and in the minority report on the McKinley tariff bill in 1890 had objected to placing sugar on the free list. He readily agreed to help the committee, and immediately on arriving at his office dictated the proposed schedule to his stenographer. At two-thirty, in accordance with Senator Jones' invitation, he was at the Senate with the typed draft; unable to find the Senator, he walked over to the rooms of the Appropriations Committee of the House and there found Senators Jones, Vest, and McPherson, Congressman Clifton R. Breckinridge, and the Clerk of the House Committee on Appropriations all busy over the Democratic tariff. Carlisle waited in the outer room and was soon joined by Jones and Vest, to whom he presented the schedule. The trio became four when Senator Gorman appeared, and there soon began a discussion of the Democratic tariff and its possibilities of passing the Senate which, if known, might lend brilliance to these pages. During the conversation someone suggested that the rates on sugar be made entirely ad valorem instead of half ad valorem and half specific. Carlisle was asked to write the schedule again; he took the typed draft which he had brought and made the changes directly upon it—and thereby hangs a political tale.

That night when Secretary Carlisle was again alone in his study, it occurred to him that the tariff schedule was not consistent; as now written, it left a period of six months in which there would be neither a bonus nor a duty. He made a new draft in which the dates were not at variance; early the next morning he drove to the home of Senator Jones, but, not finding him in, sought him at the Senate. As the Secretary drove down Pennsylvania Avenue toward the Capitol that Sabbath morning, he wove, all unknown to himself, a web of rumor which was soon to receive a generous share of printer's ink. At the Senate he found the same individuals whom he had seen the day before, with the exception of Senator Gorman. A few minutes later Senator Jones accompanied him to the door and informed him that the committee had abandoned the amendment which they had discussed on the preceding day. "All right," said the Secretary, and the only visit he ever made to the Senate without invitation was ended.

A few days later Carlisle left the city and did not return until May 24. In the interim rumors concerning the sugar scandal grew to such an extent that the Senate demanded an investigation. According to the "talk of the street" the slimy trail of the trust crossed the path of every man; indeed, on the morning after the Secretary's departure there appeared in the Philadelphia *Press* a long article, signed "Holland," which purported to show his connection with the scandal. The events which have just been related were presented to the nation in such a distorted form as to be unrecognizable. "Upon one occasion," wrote the zealous "Holland" (E. J. Edwards), "some time in February when the Finance Committee, or the Democratic members of it, were in perhaps informal session, there came into the room unexpectedly to all those present, excepting two members, none other than the Secretary of the Treasury, Mr. Carlisle. His going there at that time has never been reported until this writing of it. He went secretly and came away secretly. His visit was supposed to be a confidential one. It was a confidence not imposed upon one member of that Committee, and, therefore, it is possible now to make report of what Mr. Carlisle said. They looked upon him as speaking, not so much for Mr. Carlisle as for the administration."

In an emphatic "and for him, excited manner" Carlisle was supposed to have said:

> Gentlemen, there is one thing that I am bound to say to you as earnestly and impressively as I can do it, and I speak to you as a Democrat to Democrats. No party, or the representative of no party, can afford to ignore honorable obligations. I want to say to you that there seems to be danger that this is going to be done. Gentlemen associated with the sugar refining interests (I may tell you what, perhaps, you do not know) subscribed to the campaign fund of the Democratic party in 1892, a very large sum of money. They contributed several hundred thousand dollars, and at a time when money was urgently needed. I tell you that it would be wrong, it would be infamous, after accepting that important contribution, given at a time when it was imperatively needed, for the Democratic party now to turn around and strike down the men who gave it. It must not be done. I trust you will prepare an amendment to the bill which will be reasonable and in some measure satisfactory to these interests.

"It was a plea powerfully put," said the correspondent. "Mr. Carlisle said but little more; he had said enough. . . . The chairman of the Finance Committee received and showed to certain favored friends the draft of an amendment in Secretary Carlisle's own handwriting to the sugar schedule, and that draft is in Mr. Voorhees's possession to this day, unless he has destroyed it."

On May 30 President Cleveland and Secretaries Gresham, Carlisle, Smith, and Morton drove to Arlington to participate in the Decoration Day exercises. What did they talk about on that solemn journey? With the finances in a serious condition, strikes disturbing the land, their party hopelessly divided even now, and open charges of graft and corruption on every hand, they probably reflected that peace as well as war has its burdens. On the following day Secretary Carlisle drove to Capitol Hill to defend himself against the charges brought by a newswriter whose information had come "from the street" and from an individual whose name he would not reveal—thin whisperings of the air.

The Secretary of the Treasury had given some assistance in making up the tariff, as every one of his predecessors had done since the beginning of the tariff question. "From the time it started, as would naturally be supposed," he declared, "everybody seemed to think that the Secretary of the Treasury would have some agency in the preparation of the bill, and they came to me and talked with me about a great number of things, about iron, steel, woolen goods, cotton goods, guns, percussion caps, screws, cigarettes, condensed milk, window shades, machinery, bagging, and there are perhaps forty or fifty other things that people have been to see me about." His usual answer had been, he stated, "You have come to the wrong place; you should go and talk to members of the committee." He plainly admitted that on two occasions he had seen Havemeyer for fifteen minutes and had given him a three-line letter of introduction to Senator Mills. He had not, he said, made a voluntary or independent statement concerning the sugar schedule and had no knowledge of any contribution ever having been made by the sugar trust; "I want to say that so far as my having made a secret visit to the Committee on Finance of the Senate, or the Ways and Means Committee of the House, or to any subcommittee of either of them, or any member of either of them, it is absolutely false." His Department had put many paragraphs into shape, and the Secretary told his inquisitors, "I want to say further, if I am asked hereafter by the committee to assist them in the preparation of the bill, I intend to do it."

The investigation revealed the political tale which hung on the incidents of May 5 and 6 already noted. But all the oaths or printer's ink in America could not have convinced many that the events had not occurred in February and that corruption had not been present. "Humbug" Carlisle, "Racoon" Vest, Voorhees, and Jones should not "talk too trippingly" of innocence, said the Chicago *Times*, or a life-size photograph of the Carlisle schedule, with Carlisle's "foolish handwriting" all mixed up with the typewriting, might appear "in a New York paper any morning at all." The *Nation*, however, gave expression to the attitude of thoughtful men; "He [Carlisle] swore," said the editor, "that he made no such statement, and he is a man whose word is to be believed. Moreover, it came out that, while he did present a draft of a proposed schedule in response to a suggestion from the Democratic members of the Committee, this draft was not accepted. Instead of the schedule which is now in the bill being dictated by the Sugar Trust through the Secretary of the Treasury, as was charged, Mr. Carlisle presented no demand of the Trust, and his own recommendations were not adopted without change by the Committee. There is thus nothing left of the original charge." [1]

The general results of the investigation, however, were not very cheerful. It was found that H. O. Havemeyer had been in Washington with his samples and arguments, that speculation in sugar stock had been indulged in by some members of Congress, and that bribery, although "not proved," had perhaps been present. In February the *Banker's Magazine* had said that one exception in the dull market was an active demand for sugar trust securities. Congressmen were partly responsible, but the investigation committee could do nothing in the face of Senator Quay's defiant query, What are you going to do about it? The smoke was greater than the fire, but the embers cooled slowly.

On account of these difficulties the tariff bill dragged slowly in the "cowardly Congress." Republican Senators, encouraged by the revolt of Gorman and Brice, joined in the good old

[1] June 7, 1894, Vol. 58, p. 419; see Senate *Reports*, 2d Session, 53d Cong., Vol. 10, Doc. 606, for investigation. Serial number 3188.

game of "grab." Senator Quay declared that he would talk the bill to death if his desires were not granted, and he began a speech which outdid even that of Senator Jones on the repeal bill in the previous session. Jones had talked "one day longer than the Heavens and the earth in forming," but Quay spoke nearly twice as long. The weeks passed by, and eventually the Senate became weary of politics and profligacy and on July 3 passed the tariff measure by a vote of thirty-nine to thirty-four, with twelve Senators not voting.

On July 7 the House refused to concur in the 634 amendments which the Senate had attached to the Wilson bill. Democratic Representatives fought strenuously for their measure, smothering the Republicans whenever possible. Thomas B. Reed, the outstanding leader of his party, objected to curtailment of debate, declaring that the whole principle of the Wilson bill had been changed. But the Democrats did not intend to have the results of their labors destroyed by the work of a conference, and they stubbornly stuck to their guns.

The administration was sorely vexed, and the President, disgusted with the changes which had been made, eventually wrote Representative Wilson a letter in which he denounced the Senate bill as involving "party perfidy and party dishonor." On July 19 Wilson reported that the conferees were unable to agree, and took the opportunity to read the President's letter into the *Record*. "I happened to be in the House when Wilson presented the conference report, and heard his speech, the reading of Cleveland's letter, and Reed's reply," wrote Redfield Proctor to Senator Morrill on July 23. "It was the most dramatic scene I have ever witnessed in that dramatic body, or any other. At one time, when Wilson proposed to stay in session until the House policy prevailed, at least in part, the Democracy shouted, and filled the air with their books and bills. The Republicans jeered at some points in Cleveland's letter . . . The Senate Friday was not so demonstrative of course, but there was much excitement and intense feeling on the Democratic side. Hill was in his element, his countenance wreathed in smiles, and busy conferring with Republicans and his few friends on that side of the Chamber. Gorman is silent as ever but has every appearance of being determined." [1]

Cleveland's letter to Wilson electrified the nation as had his famous message of 1887, but the complicated political situation was not improved. "The President's letter to Wilson is the absorbing topic of the day and has created the most intense political excitement," wrote Assistant-Secretary Curtis to his mother on July 21. "Many Senators feel like Mr. Vest but many agree with the President. The House and the outside Democrats are with Mr. Cleveland on all points. I agree with the President's views. I think further that it would have been wiser not to have used the letter in that way and to have taken his own friends in the Senate into confidence in regard to it. I also think that it was unnecessary to characterize the action of the Senate. It only creates bad feeling and avails nothing. The facts are enough in regard to the bill without attacking presumed motives. These are my private views. Publicly, I am in entire accord with everything. I think it would have been better to have tried further compromise. I doubt now whether any bill can pass the Senate." [2]

Seldom in our history have politics been more exciting than in the hot days succeeding July 19, 1894. As the conflict continued in Congress, the rift in the party widened perceptibly. On July 23 Senator Gorman publicly attacked the President and the administration. "It is to be hoped," remarked the *Nation*, "that he feels better for it." On the following day Curtis wrote his mother: "I hope you read Mr. Gorman's speech. It was a very powerful one and not by any means as rancorous as expected. Senator Hill, however, is very angry and intends to attack Gorman to-day, so we are in a pretty kettle of fish. . . . I presume if they get through fighting to-day that something will be done to-morrow. We are waiting with the greatest interest!" On the twenty-fifth he again

[1] Morrill MSS.
[2] Curtis MSS.

wrote: "I suppose you have seen Mr. Hill's defense of Cleveland. He was really in earnest and people are flabbergasted. As for his former Southern supporters in the Senate they cannot abuse him too much. It is very exciting and feeling is running high. Harris [1] and the Secretary are in the next room holding a conference and I am aching to know what is up! The general opinion this morning is that there will be an agreement in some form." [2]

It was indeed a "pretty kettle of fish" into which the Democrats had fallen. Not only had the President become a man without a party, but internecine war was obliterating all the forces of unity in the Democracy. Three days after Gorman's speech one William Wilkinson wrote Cleveland: "I have no doubt but what our party is dead for a great many years to come, and it has been brought about by the dily daly of the U.S. Senate, Mr. Gorman is the man who caused all this dily daly, at least he is more to blame than any other living individual. I wrote him a letter just prior to the speech he made day before yesterday, and I assure you I scored him as heavily as I knew how." [3] But the Marylander did not lack defenders; several years later Matthew C. Butler of South Carolina wrote a letter to Henry Watterson in which he defended Gorman as no more responsible than a majority of the Democratic Senators:

No doubt Mr. Gorman felt, what many of us felt, that the Wilson Bill, as it came from the House, was not a wise revision of the Tariff, appropriate to the industrial conditions then prevailing, but that it meant destruction to many industries in all parts of the country. It was the work of doctrinaires, unmindful, as it seemed to many of us, of the consequences of so radical a revision of our Tariff laws. . . .

But neither he nor his democratic colleagues were, or are protectionists, as that impeachment is intended by his unrea-

[1] Isam G. Harris, member of the Senate Finance Committee.
[2] Curtis MSS.
[3] Cleveland MSS.

sonable critics. He and they simply dealt with conditions as they found them—did the best they could to carry out the pledges of the party, compromising, if you please, to get the best results attainable under the circumstances. The industrial enterprises in all parts of the country has been developed—bloated—by the active stimulant of high protection—in many instances a prohibitive Tariff; to have suddenly and abruptly withdrawn that stimulant would have been as unwise and fatal as to take away from a dipsomaniac, at once, the stimulant on which he had become bloated and besotted by excessive use; collapse and prostration would inevitably follow in either, or both cases.

I have, therefore, never been able to understand how the President, informed as he was of the exact condition of the Senate, could get his consent to say that the democrats of the Senate, his party associates, had been guilty of "perfidy and dishonor." [1]

During the remaining days of July and far into August the tariff arguments continued. The days were excessively hot, and progress was exceedingly slow. The Democratic majority had still not learned how to marshal its forces into effective array, and the powers of protection found the divided party an easy conquest. Some of the Republicans were not certain as to the course which they should pursue, and on August 4 Justin S. Morrill wrote a friend: "In reply to your favor of the 31st ult. I have to say that if we could postpone a Democratic tariff until March 4, 1897, it ought to be done, but if only to give the President a chance to call Congress together again at an early day, it would be a very doubtful policy. We cannot afford to set an example of filibustering by the minority, as if we soon obtain a majority of either House, it must be by a slender majority, and our example would excuse them in doing what they have shown little reluctance in doing heretofore. So that any important measures of ours would always be defeated. We must abide by the principles of our government—

[1] Butler to Watterson, October 14, 1903. Watterson MSS.

that the majority shall rule. No Republican will vote for the measure or help it along—that cannot be expected. But if it should fail through Democratic incompetency or failure of Democratic wings to flap together, we should cheerfully acquiesce, and not be among the chief mourners." [1]

Wilson at last gave up hope and joined the rapidly growing group of Democratic tariff reformers who had become convinced that the will of the people could not find effective expression in Congress. Cleveland and Carlisle had long before known the disappointments of that conviction. The President wrote the West Virginian a letter of appreciation, to which Wilson replied on August 15: "I called to see you last night to express my warmest thanks for your timely and much prized letter, which I carry out of this contest with a feeling of comfort and gratitude I cannot well exaggerate." He had little else for consolation, for the tariff-reform bill which he had sponsored was sent a few days later to the Executive Mansion with an open label of defeat—the "Wilson-Gorman" tariff bill. It became a law on August 28 without the President's signature.

The Wilson-Gorman tariff brought no relief to the Treasury Department. Secretary Carlisle was still faced with a deficiency of revenue, and the decision of the Supreme Court early the following year that the income clause was illegal destroyed what little hope there was of bringing the expenditures and the revenues into agreement. Gold receipts were small, and exports heavy. From January 1 to the last day of October the Treasury redeemed $105,000,000 of legal-tenders in gold. The reports from the New York sub-treasury were a catalog of these losses. "Today we shall lose $370,000," wrote Jordan on March 20, and on the following day he reported to the Department, "Amount presented today $400,000. I don't think the movement is general yet, tho' you can see signs of a disturbed feeling." [2] The silver certificates were a constant worry; the condition of business left no demand for them in

[1] Morrill to Wilbur F. Wakeman. Morrill MSS.
[2] Curtis MSS.

any form. "I am doing everything in my power to divert the stream of silver certificates from New York and don't pay out a dollar but for redemptions," wrote Jordan on April 25. They had become such a stumbling block by the fall months that Secretary Carlisle sought to call them under cover by making them required reserves for the National Banks. The continual outflow of gold to Europe brought a severe strain to the New York sub-treasury. "As you see the work of depleting the Treasury goes 'gaily on,'" wrote Jordan to Curtis on May 23. "We are down to $4,225,000 XX, 250,000 X, 500,000 ½X [1]. . . . So far there has not been any symptoms of fright at the continued shipment, but if the gentlemen at the other end of the Avenue don't give you relief before long the devil will be to pay. . . . If it were only the Republicans we could put the blame upon it would be all right but that is not so. Why not try for a temporary loan?" [2]

The New York bankers were also urging that the Secretary sell more bonds while the money market was easy. James Stillman wrote Secretary Lamont on May 9: "With the extreme ease in the money market at present I believe a block of bonds could be negotiated if the matter was handled judiciously and presented in such a way that it would be looked upon as a privilege to get them rather than being a favor to the Government to take them." [3] Secretary Carlisle was not ready, however, to try another loan; he still had hopes that Congress would give him authority to issue a more favorable bond. In addition, he was aware of the many serious objections to the procedure suggested, and realized that an overwhelming majority of the people of the country opposed such action. Criticisms of the first issue had been indeed severe. The midlands had seethed with resentment, and hundreds of thousands had fled the party fold. Many of the invectives are too bitter to be honored by preservation, but two examples—one of the

---

[1] Twenties, tens, and fives.
[2] Curtis MSS.
[3] Lamont MSS.

extremely radical type and the other of the more conservative —will serve to illustrate the trends of criticism. On May 5 there appeared in an inland paper the following comparatively conservative article:

Talk about Cleveland fishing at Buzzard's Bay! You should see him fish in the house and senate. But so far as bonds are concerned they would not bite. Yet, according to the conspiracy between Cleveland, Wall Street, and the national banks, bonds must be issued. The spectacle of a country borrowing money, running in debt and issuing bonds in a period of peace does not strike the Cleveland intelligence as unusual at all. A spring bonnet doesn't strike a hound pup as unusual as he chews it up. Indeed the hound pup, as he flies curling and ki-yi-ing from the wrath which follows in the wake of a chewed spring bonnet no doubt marvels mightily at the displeasure his act excited. . . .
And Friday Humbug Carlisle then went to work behind the public back and at the New York subtreasury sold almost half the gold to bond buyers to buy these very bonds withal. . . . He deals with the public as if it were an infant in arms, gives it a dose of soothing syrup, of the 'must-pay-gold-for-these-bonds' variety, croons it to sleep with a lullaby about rebuilding the gold reserve, lays it down into a crib and virtually sells bonds for any sort of money at all—paper, silver, or gold—just as the old Treasury Fagin under his orders from Cleveland and the ring intended all of the time. . . .
Oh, Cleveland and the ring and Humbug Carlisle and all these other public leeches who in the aggregate of their bloodsucking make up the real business of this Cleveland administration, know mighty well how to stop the gold from going to Europe. They don't want to. They want bonds, just as wolves want flesh, and their method is to reduce the gold reserve. Mark this, within two months, and probably just as Congress adjourns, the administration window will be lifted and another flock of bonds will flutter forth like pigeons. They will be homing pigeons, too, and make straight for their home coop in Wall Street.[1]

[1] The Chicago *Times*.

A few weeks later there came to Attorney-General Olney's desk a typical letter; the language was so vile that Olney tore half the sheet away and filed only the top, on the back of which was the last paragraph of the letter:

Love to Grover, the course [sic] brute who does his thinking with his guts; the the swinish dipsomaniac who stopped begetting illegitimates to mary [sic] and beget Idiots.
Invoking God's curse upon you I am
Most humbly, Dickey
Homer Heywood.[1]

Secretary Carlisle turned to the New York banks for aid, but the arrangements which were made were not satisfactory to either party. The banks were not anxious to part with their gold in this period of depression; furthermore, neither they nor the government had satisfactory machinery for weighing the metal, and no one was sure of the method by which it should be done. But the situation was critical. "I wish you could impress upon Congress the gravity of the situation here," wrote Jordan on June 22. "The Banks (or a part of them) have an unhappy way of making their contribution, and it looks as if the scheme were a failure. We ought to look at the thing straight in the face if anything in the way of a temporary loan is devised—it must be done quickly and forced upon Congress. A few days and a remedy that costs little will be impossible— and we will be in for an endless chain of an issue of bonds— that should be a three per cent, but nothing should be conceded as to the power already granted the 4^s $4\frac{1}{2}^s$ & 5^s. There is alarm abroad, which has its repercussion here and people are getting nervous. Between the —— papers and the Bank fiasco (fill in the blank with the longest cuss word you ever make use of) we are in a bad state, and the way out is hard to find."

Various methods were used, especially at the sub-treasury in New York, to prevent the true state of the finances from being revealed. Jordan was making strenuous efforts to prevent a

---

[1] Olney MSS.

note "jam" there, and at times his reports did not state the actual conditions. "Truth has had clothes put on her from time to time," he wrote the Department. "But as long as we pay cash to all comers, is it material that we should tell the press the kind of cash we pay, or that we haven't got any of the kind to pay in?"

In the late days of June several New York bankers began a concerted effort to replace the gold in the sub-treasury lost by exportation. "Since last writing you Mr. Williams and I have been trying to induce our associates to supply the Sub-Treasury with gold coin in order to counteract the bad effect of the heavy withdrawals for export," wrote Stillman to Colonel Lamont on the twenty-third. "We at first thought, as I wrote you, that this could be done quietly by a few of us and so avoid newspaper comment. We found, however, that what we were led to expect would be done was not done, and that the whole matter was soon public property, and one of the principal criticisms was that all the Clearing House banks should be asked to participate. We have therefore, after a number of conferences, in which this matter, and many others were thoroughly discussed issued a call requesting each bank to contribute in proportion to its holdings of gold its pro rata share to make up the seven millions that have been withdrawn from the Treasury this week. They should do so, but I doubt very much if all will." [1]

In return for the aid which they so generously gave, the bankers expected Secretary Carlisle to follow without question their suggestions regarding finances. That official, however, realized that there were other considerations involved beyond those immediately concerning the financiers. No other evidence is needed to prove that he was not in alliance with the bankers than the discontent which they freely expressed. Stillman wrote to Lamont: "I was surprised to ascertain the extent of the ill feeling against Secretary Carlisle, and the almost universal distrust of his ability to administer safely and success-

[1] Lamont MSS.

fully the Government's finances ... it is reported that the Secretary feels no concern; does not see any necessity for issuing bonds to increase his gold reserve, and was reported as saying ... that the New York banks were obliged to take the action they were taking for their own and not the Treasury's protection.... The opinion is that the Government's finances are getting into a very weak and dangerous condition, and that the time will come when the reserves of the New York banks will be the only bulwark to prevent disaster to the financial interests of the country, and that unless the Secretary of the Treasury in a prompt, straightforward and unequivocal manner assures the banks that if they part with their gold reserves the Government will stand behind them and protect them by issuing bonds for gold, it would be very unwise and dangerous for them to further deplete themselves." [1]

The Treasury Department was truly "skating on very thin ice" during the months of June and July, and Secretary Carlisle grew alarmed. On July 30 Assistant-Secretary Curtis, probably at the direction of his chief, began to send out feelers in regard to the financial status. "What do you think of the gold situation now?" he wrote James Stillman. "Would you advise the Secretary to go to New York? Some people are anxious to have him do so. I myself do not see the advantage in it unless some practical direction is pointed out for an effort—'Bonds' is a loud cry, but there are so many objections to that panacea, of a practical character, that I doubt its efficiency if attempted. If the Banks feel that they would prefer the gold reserve to be depleted rather than that their unaccustomed hoard be encroached upon, they are the people to determine their policy; but they should not criticise the Treasury for not attempting impossibilities. Please let me hear from you by return mail." [2]

On the following day Stillman answered: "It seems to me that the most popular step to take with Congress and the coun-

[1] Cleveland MSS.
[2] Curtis MSS.

try would be for the Treasury to ask for subscriptions throughout the country for three per cent bonds to be paid in gold. Of course the great bulk of them would be taken here in New York, but offering them throughout the whole country would disarm the criticisms which have been made by politicians in Congress. I believe that an issue of bonds can be placed now on a three per cent basis, but the feeling of distrust is growing so rapidly that any day such a change may take place that the gold could not be obtained except on higher terms." [1]

The depleted gold reserve and the approach of the season for heavy exports of that metal brought up the question of another issue of bonds, but there was also the problem of the fall elections. The announcement in State after State of a determination on the part of the Democracy to fight for free silver made the situation alarming. Secretary Carlisle, hampered as he was by the lack of a satisfactory way of increasing his holdings, preferred the dangers of a small gold reserve to the possibility of a thoroughly free-silver Congress. In August he had written Secretary Hoke Smith: "The condition of the Treasury was such last February that the issue of bonds was the only manner by which the credit of the Government could be preserved and the parity of the two metals maintained. At that time the gold balance in the Treasury was $65,650,175, and the other kinds of money belonging to the Treasury amounted to $18,431,924, making in all $84,082,099. At the same time the monthly expenditures were largely in excess of the monthly receipts, and consequently this balance was constantly decreasing. At the present time, however, although the gold is only $52,499,788, the other available money in the Treasury is $64,411,725, making in all $117,975,710, as against $84,082,099 in February last, and the monthly receipts are now about equal to the monthly expenditures." [2]

---

[1] Stillman to Curtis, July 31, 1894. Cleveland MSS. Carlisle and Curtis had been having consultations with President Cleveland all through June and July. Evidently this letter was carried to the President in one of these consultations.
[2] Carlisle to Smith, August 11, 1894, Cleveland MSS.

At best the party hopes were certainly not bright, and the joke which Secretary Morton spread about the Departments probably brought reflection along with the chuckles. The story went as follows:

A modern fable relates that one of the most zealous and mellifluent of the wild-eyed advocates of the free coinage of silver recently died, and there was great mourning among the Nevada and Colorado mine and bullion owners because of his untimely taking off. In the midst of their grief, while their sympathy was yet bubbling warm from their hearts, and tears bedewed their cheeks, they contributed a princely sum for the erection of a monument. On the marble tablet they inscribed the following line:

"Here lies the friend of the people, who advocated the free and unlimited coinage of silver at the ratio of 16 to 1; and an honest man."

An Irishman, standing before this commemorative rock, said to a bystander:

"Oi am in a great quan-*da*-ry."

"What about?" said the party addressed.

"Because," said Pat, "Divil take me if Oi can see why they bury *the two of them in wan grave.*"

"What two?"

"The 'advocate of free coinage' *and the* 'honest man,' to be sure."

Whether they were regarded as honest or not, the silver forces were growing with remarkable rapidity. In the West they were dissolving the Republican party as well as the Democratic. On June 21 George L. Miller had written from Omaha: "A great gathering of democrats of the State marks the hour and day upon which I write—it means Free Silver and Bryan. It is intended to influence the character and actions of the coming regular state convention which will meet not later than the early days of September. No man can foretell the result. The object is a double one, viz: to repudiate the President's financial policy, to declare for Free and Unlimited Silver, and to send Mr. Bryan to the Senate by a formal nomination of him before the electors for that place, and perhaps for Governor, or both. We shall do what we can to stem this sudden uprising of Democratic discontent which is far from being wholly Democratic discontent. It is invading the Republican ranks and pervading the Republican masses, and in the event of Mr. Bryan's success, threatens to disrupt party fealty to a greater or less extent on all sides." [1]

In spite of the discouraging outlook the Democrats did what they could to stem the silver tide. Secretary Carlisle supplied Cabinet members and Congressmen with gold-standard arguments. On August 14 he wrote Secretary Hoke Smith one of the longest letters, perhaps, of his entire political career:

My Dear Sir:

I am in receipt of your letter, enclosing certain questions, hereto appended, and take the earliest opportunity to make brief replies to them.

Your first and second questions can be considered together, because the free coinage of silver at the ratio of 16 to 1 would undoubtedly place the country on a silver basis. But before proceeding to answer any of the questions propounded by you, it would be well, perhaps, to state as briefly as possible exactly what is meant by the free coinage of silver at the ratio of 16 to 1, as now proposed by the advocates of that policy.

The intrinsic or commercial value of the bullion contained in the United States standard silver dollar is today 48.8 cents, while the gold bullion contained in the United States gold dollar is worth 100 cents, or the equivalent of 100 cents, all over the world. The free coinage of silver at the ratio of 16 to 1 means, therefore, that the Government shall receive from private individuals and corporations—principally wealthy corporations—48.8 cents worth of silver bullion, coin it at the expense of the people, stamp it as a dollar and compel the people by law to receive it as a dollar in the payment of debts due them. In this way the mine-owners and speculators in bullion are to receive for their property nearly twice its actual

[1] Miller to Lamont. Lamont MSS.

value and at the same time have it coined by the Government without any expense to themselves.

The bullion contained in a gold dollar is worth as much before it is coined as it is afterwards, and for some purposes it is worth more. Nothing whatever is added to its value by coinage, but its weight and fineness are by this process correctly ascertained and authenticated by the stamp of the Government and it is thus put into a convenient form for use as money by the people.

Assuming that the free coinage of silver at the ratio of 16 to 1 would place the Government upon a silver basis—a proposition which, I believe, is not seriously disputed by any one—you desire to know what, in my opinion, would be its effect upon the country. Whenever the country reaches a silver basis, gold will of course cease to constitute any part of our circulating medium. It will at once command a premium, and will be hoarded or held for speculative purposes or be exported to pay the obligations of our people held by foreign countries, for these obligations cannot be paid with either paper or silver. The first effect of such a policy, therefore, would be to contract the volume of our own currency to the extent of about $600,000,000. The value of silver is constantly fluctuating and consequently no country on a silver basis can have a stable currency. Without a stable currency business cannot be conducted with safety, especially business which involves credit. Our surplus cotton, wheat, pork and other products are all sold in foreign markets, while the articles which our people need and do not themselves produce are purchased in foreign markets. If this country were upon a silver basis, those who purchase our products would pay us in silver, that being our standard of value, but those from whom we purchase would demand payment in gold, that being their standard of value. The man who purchases from us would have to make two transactions in order to get our products and pay for them, and he would charge the risk of both transactions to our producer. For instance, if he purchases cotton he must take into consideration the risk he runs of having the price of that article fall in the market before he can transport it and sell it, and if he is to pay us for it with silver he must purchase the silver

THE YEAR OF CALAMITIES 353

and in doing that he must take into consideration the fluctuations which may occur in the value of that metal before the transaction can be completed. In order, therefore, to guarantee himself against loss he must pay a lower price for the cotton than he would otherwise pay.

Suppose, on the other hand, one of our citizens has made a purchase abroad. He must pay for it in gold, or its equivalent, because gold is the only international currency. In order to procure the gold he must either buy it here at a premium equal to the difference between the intrinsic value of a gold dollar and a silver dollar, and then ship the gold abroad, or he must purchase foreign exchange, which is payable in gold, at a premium equal to the difference between the intrinsic value of a gold dollar and a silver dollar. If, for instance, his purchase abroad amounts to a thousand dollars he would, at the present price of silver, have to pay more than two thousand dollars in order to procure the gold or the exchange necessary to discharge his obligation.

In my opinion, it was not only wise, but under the circumstances absolutely necessary, to pay in gold the obligations of the Government which, under the law, could have been paid either in silver or gold.[1]

The Congressional election came at last, and the Democrats were overwhelmingly defeated. Thomas B. Reed's prediction of early 1894 that "The Democratic mortality will be so great next fall that their dead will be buried in trenches and marked 'unknown'"[2] was amply fulfilled. William L. Wilson and even many who had fought against repeal were left at home. Champ Clark characterized the results as "the greatest slaughter of the innocents since the days of Herod."[3]

On election day the available cash in the Treasury amounted to scarcely more than one hundred million dollars, some sixty million of which was in gold. A few days later Secretary Carlisle regretfully began negotiations looking toward a new is-

[1] Cleveland MSS.
[2] William A. Robinson, *Thomas B. Reed, Parliamentarian* p. 321.
[3] *My Quarter Century*, 1, 325.

sue of bonds. He had learned the painful lesson that it was not safe to attempt a loan without the full coöperation of the New York bankers. In the papers of Assistant-Secretary Curtis is a memorandum in Carlisle's own handwriting setting forth in six paragraphs his proposals for the second issue. He submitted this plan to John A. Stewart of the United States Trust Company of New York, who in turn consulted other New York bankers.[1] A comparison of the Secretary's original plan and the official notice of the issue shows that many of the suggestions of those consulted were accepted.

On November 9 Stewart wrote the Secretary: "I have received your favor of yesterday and have conferred with Mr. Stillman, Mr. King, and a few other financial men regarding the terms of the proposed loan. As a result you and the President may rest assured that it will all be taken *at not less than a 3 per cent basis.*" That evening the New York *Press* carried the rumor that fifty million of bonds would be sold immediately. This the Secretary instantly denied. He admitted that if it were necessary to issue bonds to maintain the public credit he would do so unhesitatingly, but added that "no action of this kind is in immediate contemplation."

On the same day Assistant-Treasurer Jordan arrived from New York and went into secret consultation with Secretary Carlisle and Assistant-Secretary Curtis. The conference over, Secretary Carlisle made off for Woodley and had a long talk with the President. He gave no statement to the press. On the following day the Secretary, closely followed by Comptroller Eckles, again visited Cleveland. The press could no longer refrain from an excited surmise—a hitch between the President and his Secretary of the Treasury! The papers fairly bulged with the news of this supposed quarrel. The New York *Tribune* pointed out that it had given notice some time before that an agent of the President was in New York consulting with the bankers; others reminded the public that E. C. Benedict, the broker, had discussed with a downtown banker the question

[1] Curtis MSS.

of a bond issue, and one story had it that the sale had been put into his hands; still others said that the President was handling the situation through Assistant-Secretary Curtis; and across the East River in Brooklyn the rumor was that the President himself was acting as Secretary of the Treasury.

The New York *Herald* investigated and came to the conclusion that there was no radical disagreement between the Secretary of the Treasury and the President. "The only point of difference between them is whether the bonds should be issued before Congress assembles or afterwards," said the report. This statement did little, however, to quiet the public mind, and the rumor that Carlisle would resign gained ground. It was felt generally that he was opposed to an issue of bonds, especially when the condition of the Treasury was no worse than it had been and there was no immediate prospect that it would grow any worse. New York, at least, believed that President Cleveland had taken all power out of the hands of Secretary Carlisle and meant to put the bond sale through on his own personal responsibility. Citizens of that city were sure that news of the Secretary's resignation would not have created much surprise in Washington.

On November 12 the Associated Press gave out a definite statement that there were no negotiations in progress looking toward an issue of bonds. The denials, however, were not considered seriously, for conditions were such as to make a loan almost unavoidable. The gold reserve was depleted, renewed exports to Europe were certain, and the decline of income under the Wilson-Gorman tariff was ominous. On the same day there arrived from New York a letter from Stewart:

The Hon. John G. Carlisle
   Secy of the Treasury.
Dr. Sir:
   Yours of the 10 inst. just received. My letter of last Friday was written in haste and under great pressure. It was stupid on my part, if I did so, to say "at not less than 3 per cent, for I meant not less than a 3 per cent *basis*. In other words I wished

you to understand that it would all be subscribed for at such a premium that it would cost the Government no more than 3 per cent interest, if so much, and this I now confirm. I mentioned in my last letter that a leading banker with whom I conferred with your permission suggested leaving out the words "in whole or in part." I did not think it material one way or the other, being of the opinion that if left out the discretion would still rest with you to decide your amounts when a bid was made at different rates if you thought proper. This suggestion came from Mr. J. Pierpont Morgan, who thought it possible to make up a bid for the entire amount and wished you to be in a position to decline all other bids, if such a bid would net you the most money. I felt it desirable that the form of advertisement should have the approval of leading bankers with foreign connections and wrote you accordingly. Of course you are quite at liberty to exercise your best judgment in the matter and I shall be quite satisfied whatever that may be. I am quite confident that *it will all be subscribed for* and at as good if not better rates for the Government than was obtained for the last issue.

It is important, however, that the advertisement appear without further delay.[1]

On November 15 President Cleveland issued, as was his wont in these years of rumors, a statement to quiet the public mind. "Never since our association together has there been the slightest unpleasantness or difference concerning the affairs of the Treasury Department or any other matter," he said concerning his relations with Secretary Carlisle. "I have every reason to believe that his attachment to me is as sincere and great as mine is for him. I should be much afflicted if anything should cause him to entertain the thought of giving up his position when he is doing so much for his country. We have agreed exactly as to the issue of bonds, and there has been no backwardness on his part on that subject." The trouble seemed to be, explained the President, "that those charged with the

[1] Curtis MSS.

executive duties of the Government do not appear willing at all times to take the counsels of the newspapers and make public all they intend to do."

The press, a little dampened by the President's release, poked some good-natured fun at the episode. "Not on your life, Says Grover," and "Everything is lovely in the President's Official Family," ran the headlines in the Columbus (Ohio) *Journal*. "He Fairly dotes on Carlisle and Loves Him as David did Jonathan."

But the uncertainty regarding a sale of bonds was soon over. On November 14, 1894, the Secretary of the Treasury issued a circular calling for bids on $50,000,000 of bonds. The gold reserve on that day stood at $61,000,000. The difficulties now facing Secretary Carlisle were not so numerous nor so complicated as with the first issue, but he did not mean to be caught again with no subscriptions forty-eight hours before the expiration of the period set for receiving them.

Bids were to close at twelve, noon, on November 24. On the nineteenth the Secretary dispatched a letter to all the important bankers of the East, and especially of New York, asking their opinions as to the success of the loan. "The new loan, as you know, is bound to be a success," wrote Edward King of the Union Trust Company of New York a few hours later. In the same mail John A. Stewart of the United States Trust Company replied cheerfully: "The matter of the bond subscriptions progresses satisfactorily and I have no reason to change the view heretofore expressed to you that the loan will all be bid for at a figure which will make it cost the Government not over 3 per cent per annum." Two days later a letter came from G. G. Williams of the Chemical National Bank saying that "the universal opinion in financial circles here is that the bonds will be over-subscribed." On the following day James Stillman of the National City Bank wrote that he knew "of subscriptions to the new Government Loan amounting to over thirty million dollars, and that there is not the slightest doubt but that it will be largely over-subscribed for."[1] Secretary Carlisle could well congratulate himself.

Carlisle had learned by experience that an issue of bonds drove bidders in streams to the sub-treasuries to secure gold with which to pay their bids. This time he decided to reduce the presentation of legal-tenders by moral intimidation. The idea was not a new one, for the Department had been compelled to take such measures in the early months of the financial difficulties; whenever a banking house or brokers' concern made itself too prominent around the gold coffers of the Treasury, pressure had been brought to bear upon its agents through personal conference or public appeal. The plan proposed at this time was to avoid all sales which would eventually require the individual to secure his gold from the Treasury. The banks agreed to coöperate by refusing to aid their customers in such deals, and the Treasury undertook to publish the names of those presenting legal-tenders for gold. Such a plan was excusable under the circumstances, but it was not desirable and did much toward defeating itself despite the support of the banks.

The creation of a sentiment that it was unpatriotic to go to the sub-treasury for gold with which to pay for bonds led to the withdrawal of many bids. "They have not the gold, and are not at all sure that they can get it anywhere except from the Treasury; and so much has been said to create the impression that it is wrong to do this, and that the perpetrators are guilty of some want of patriotism that I find a good many people hesitating about making any subscriptions at all," wrote Charles S. Fairchild, former Secretary of the Treasury. "I had thought of making a subscription for this company; but as I do not know where to get the gold, with certainty, except at the sub-treasury, I have about made up my mind not to subscribe."[2] Regardless of such difficulties, the bankers did what they could toward securing bids.

[1] Curtis MSS.
[2] Curtis MSS.

THE YEAR OF CALAMITIES 359

At noon on November 24 the Assistant Secretaries of the Treasury, New York financiers, newspaper men, and others gathered at the Secretary's office in the Treasury Building for the opening of the bids. At 12:15 Secretary Carlisle arrived with the offers in a black box under his arm. The bids would be opened in secret, he said; but Assistant-Secretary Curtis protested, and after much argument in the Secretary's private room, in which Curtis, Morgan, Fiske, and others took part, it was finally agreed that they should be opened in public. Only two of the thirty reporters present, however, were admitted. The results were satisfactory, there being 486 bids, totaling $178,836,050. One bid from a New York syndicate proposed "to purchase United States 5 per cent ten-year bonds, described in said circular, of the face value of $50,000,000, and we agree to pay therefor at the rate of 117.077, and accrued interest, per $100. This bid is for the whole $50,000,000, but not for any lesser amount." It was found that the proceeds from the syndicate offer would amount to $49,517.62 more than the aggregate of the other highest bids, and the Secretary awarded the entire $50,000,000 to this group of financiers. Secretary Carlisle pointed out that "a very important advantage to the Government in accepting this bid is the fact that all the gold will be furnished outside and none drawn from the Treasury. It is also more convenient and less expensive to the Department to deal with one party rather than with many." The financiers who had made the bid expected to keep half the issue as an investment and to sell the remaining half, but because of later financial developments the sale did not go well, and the syndicate actually lost money on the deal—a fact of which the public was never thoroughly convinced.

The efforts to prevent the presentation of legal-tenders at the Treasury for gold were fairly successful; scarcely $10,000,000 of gold was paid out for redemptions during the period of payments which began on November 26 and ended on December 4. Most of the withdrawals had come shortly after the announcement of the sale. Early in December the gold reserve reached $111,000,000.

While the last payments on the second bond issue were being made, the third session of the Fifty-third Congress was assembling at Washington. On December 3 President Cleveland sent his annual message to that body. In regard to the gold reserve he declared: "We have an endless chain in operation constantly depleting the Treasury's gold and never near a final rest." The only way the stock of gold could be replenished was by an issue of bonds; "and yet Congress has not only thus far declined to authorize the issue of bonds best suited to such a purpose, but there seems a disposition in some quarters to deny both the necessity and power for the issue of bonds at all." And in his curt, determined language he added that "as long as no better authority for bond issues is allowed than at present exists, such authority will be utilized whenever and as often as it becomes necessary to maintain a sufficient gold reserve, and in abundant time to save the credit of our country and make good the financial declarations of the Government." He had come quite a distance since his first message, in which he had suggested that the statutes might be revised in regard to the issuance of bonds, but had expressed no policy of the government toward the question.

The President was belligerent and almost defiant, but Secretary Carlisle was still ready to plead with Congress for relief. "I repeat the recommendation made in my last annual report," wrote the Secretary, "that in the interest of the Government and people power be conferred upon the Secretary of the Treasury to negotiate loans at a lower rate of interest and for a shorter period of time." The laws regarding bonds then in existence, he went on to say, had been passed nearly a quarter of a century before and were not suited to the changed conditions of credit and the improved resources of the country. "The law should be so amended as to conform to the conditions and requirements of the public credit and service at the present time, and I earnestly hope that Congress will take early and favorable action upon the subject." To Carlisle the government's policy of redeeming its own notes in coin and reissuing them seemed a great evil.

Secretary Carlisle attached to his annual report a currency reform plan on which he had been working for several months. It presented two main ideas: a greater elasticity in the volume of circulation, and the retirement of the legal-tenders. The New York *Commercial Bulletin* commented that "If the Secretary of the Treasury needed to atone for any imputed lack of executive force by an exhibition of the higher qualities of constructive or reconstructive ability, he has certainly made the atonement. Mr. Carlisle's annual report will command the respect of the country for the thoroughness with which it exposes the radical faults of our currency system and the ability with which it provides a sound and consistent reconstruction of our monetary arrangements. His conceptions are clear and his proposals are courageous. He respects nothing for mere prestige of usage; he accepts for his purpose whatever has real economic and practical merit." The soundness of the report received recognition several years later when students of finance began work upon the present Federal Reserve System.

The year 1894 was truly a year of misfortunes, misunderstandings, misjudgments, and misrepresentations. Almost every possible evil had come to plague the administration. Strikes had disturbed the functioning of the government; industrial unrest had limited its actions; financial uneasiness had congealed the normal flow of business; and political forces had acted as an abettor to all. The small group of men around the President seemingly stood alone, and the press did its part in trying to break it down. Carlisle bore the brunt of the criticism, and it is possible that his reticence encouraged the attack. It is doubtful whether the President and the Secretary of the Treasury ever thought of breaking their relations over the second bond issue, and yet that they disagreed appears certain. President Cleveland, never so much a theoretical democrat as was his Secretary of the Treasury, early gave up dependence on Congress. Secretary Carlisle had too long been a member of the legislative body to do likewise, and he held such views of democracy as to make that course practically impossible. Although he was forced to ally himself with the banking interests, there is overwhelming proof that the alliance was patriotic. The New York bankers who came to the aid of the government in November, 1894, have received much undeserved criticism.

President Cleveland, his Cabinet members, their subordinates, and a few intimate friends were a loyal group, fighting under difficulties what they felt to be a sacrificial battle in the defense of a nation which appeared unappreciative. Whether they were right or wrong in their methods, they were certainly sincere. The President, as head of this little group, felt the responsibility keenly. Toward the end of the long year, in a letter to his old friend, Richard Watson Gilder, Cleveland said of the misfortunes that had come:

I know too there is a God but I do not know his purposes, nor when their results will appear. I know the clouds will roll away, but I do not know who, before that time, will be drowned in their floods.

CHAPTER XV   THE MORGAN-BELMONT SYNDI-
                CATE BOND ISSUE

IN so far as ultimate preservation of the gold reserve was concerned, the two bond issues of 1894 were failures; indeed, the task to which Secretary Carlisle had set himself was scarcely less hopeless than that of Sisyphus. Professor J. Lawrence Laughlin well said at the time that "To push the reserve slightly above the $100,000,000 by a small issue of bonds, inevitably followed by its disappearance below the line, impresses no one very forcibly." [1] The relief was only temporary, and each sale of bonds for gold brought from the silver advocates additional criticism and a better organized opposition.

The problem which faced Secretary Carlisle in the early days of 1895 was somewhat different from those of the previous months. There had been two decidedly impressive reasons for the bond sales of February and November, 1894: the protection of the gold standard, and the preservation of the actual solvency of the government. By the beginning of the year 1895 the necessity of securing money for the conduct of the nation's business had disappeared, but the need of gold was no less pressing. The month of January was indeed discouraging for the Secretary. Never before had so much gold gone out of his coffers within so short a time; the reserve had begun to show signs of uneasiness, in fact, soon after the completion of the bond sale in November of the previous year. On December 4 it had stood at $111,000,000, but by the fifteenth a dispatch from Washington stated that the gold vaults were again being invaded and that another bond issue might soon become necessary. The situation was made worse by the facts that foreign balances fell due in that month, and that the Treasury had to meet heavy domestic obligations also. From $1,000,000

[1] "Our Monetary Programme," *Forum*, XX, pp. 652–666.

to $4,000,000 in gold was leaving the vaults of the government daily. Secretary Carlisle had hoped that the new revenues from wool, to be received on January 1 when that commodity would be removed from bond, might give relief. They proved, however, an ineffectual remedy. Redemptions rapidly depleted the gold reserve and lessened the possibility of avoiding another recourse to bonds; during the month of December $31,000,000 in legal-tenders were presented and the gold carried away. Nine millions were exported, and the remainder went into banks or private hoards.

In the first days of 1895 the Secretary of the Treasury was again forced to turn to Congress for relief. He found friends who would introduce his measures, but in the face of the silver opposition their passage seemed impossible. As the days passed, the stream of outflowing gold continually increased. "If golden manna could only be rained upon us, or our receipts equal our expenditures, we might get out of this mess, but short of a miracle neither will come to pass while we are on this 'uncertain sea,' " wrote Jordan to Curtis on January 16. "If you could only coax or bully Congress into giving us the right to make temporary loans we could put an end to all this. Bond issues are only repetitions."[1] The withdrawals of gold from the Treasury reached an alarming amount, and during January $45,000,000 was taken from the vaults of the government.

On January 3 Edmund Randolph, New York financier, wrote Colonel Lamont: "I heartily wish I could discern some hopeful signs in the financial outlook or could offer some suggestions, as you pay me the compliment to suppose I might do; —but it must be admitted that the circumstances and the conditions are not propitious, or such as to make it a happy lot just now I fancy to be at the head of the Government. Edward Atkinson's recent characterization of the 'inescapable mob calling themselves the Democratic party in Congress' depicts graphically the kind of backing (or rather thwarting) the President has had of all the measures he has proposed for the

[1] Curtis MSS.

public welfare,—and I for one prefer to have had the party defeated with such a camp-following, that it may be reorganized on the basis of sounder doctrines more in unison with those of its Chief." Two days later he again wrote: "Foreign bankers here say that the tide of investment would be turned to this country and an influx of gold would begin if the issuing of a 2½% gold bond were merely authorized for the distinct purpose of retiring our paper currency and the Secretary was authorized to sell some when he deemed it necessary or advantageous to do so. . . . If our Government should try to sell another block of 50 or 100 million coin 5s [5% bonds] under present conditions their price would indicate a sad decline in the national credit due to the growing appreciation of our serious currency situation, and the belief that Congress cannot be made to move in time to avoid trouble. The new coin 5s are now offered on about a 3% basis (116¾) and there is little or no demand. The market is congested and lower than the Syndicate price and as the big dealers and bankers have not sold, they are not in a position to buy again, besides being antagonized and alarmed; our banks are certainly not disposed to part with any gold and our weak financial policy discredits our bonds abroad." [1]

By January 17 the daily reports clearly indicated that private hoarding had begun; on that day over $1,500,000 disappeared from the Treasury, followed the next day by more than $3,500,000. Jordan wrote Curtis: "If we don't have prompt action, we will be ashamed of the results of a new loan—the Banks will not part with their gold—the Scare is on—'if ever delay is dangerous' it is now." On the twenty-third he again wrote Curtis, "I can only at the risk of being tiresome say hasten up action as to a loan—whether temporary or a long one —try the 4%—at 12½ years time you pay just as much for a ten year 5%. . . . We will ship 6 to 8 million this week— as much next and it seems to me we are inviting a renewal of a run upon us." Two days later he reported, "We have lost

[1] Lamont MSS.

this week beyond shipments over 6 million, and it has gone into the banks in large part for other corporations and persons." In the past nine days the Treasury had lost almost twenty millions in gold.

"The feeling is growing quite disturbed here and I regret to say a good deal of gold is being quietly tucked away by those who ought to be ashamed to do it," wrote Edmund Randolph on the twenty-third. "Just now I have been exercising my eloquence to dissuade one of our own large depositors (a corporation) from a panicky withdrawal of that kind that was in contemplation."[1] Business at New York was at a standstill, and no merchant dared to make time contracts. "The Administration," wrote one editor on the twenty-sixth, "sits in sullen stupor while Congress plays politics." But Cleveland and Carlisle had spent many hours in vain efforts to formulate a solution to the problem which was facing them. They knew full well the failures of the two preceding domestic bond issues, and realized that unless Congress came to the rescue they must find some method of securing gold from abroad. Every day's delay only increased the difficulties, the opposition in Congress growing while the financiers became more impatient. "The feeling here is that the President will not get the desired relief, and that if he adheres to his idea as to the non-issue of existing 5s bonds the end is at hand," wrote Jordan on the twenty-eighth.

As the demands upon the reserve increased, indications of a panic began to appear. "The banks are beginning a general run —I mean those who have heretofore abstained," wrote Jordan. "We must have more gold from nearby points. San Francisco is too risky. Our coin gold is reduced to 13,639m [$13,639,000] which we shall lose this week. . . . Women as well as men, are now on the 'gold path.' Try the temporary certificates. . . . This thing may degenerate or rise into a panic as you prefer."[2] It was perfectly apparent that the Treasury

[1] Lamont MSS.
[2] Curtis MSS.

would soon be reduced to gold bars, and it was not at all certain that the government might not have to sell them to meet its obligations. On January 29 at the close of business the gold coin on hand at the New York sub-treasury was $13,000,000, a very close margin for a place with so many heavy demands to meet. The office requested from the Secretary of the Treasury written authority to sell gold bars, the letter to be filed and opened only when the available gold coin had been reduced to $3,000,000. Secretary Carlisle had ordered all the gold that could be spared at the other sub-treasuries to be sent to New York. A small amount remained at San Francisco, but that was too far away to be available for any immediate demand.[1]

In spite of its inaction and the rabid utterances of some of its members, Carlisle had never turned from Congress; he still continued to urge his friends there that something be done in order to allow the Treasury Department to extricate itself from the financial mire in which it was floundering. The outlook, however, was not hopeful. On January 26 the *Commercial and Financial Chronicle* said, "Perhaps the greatest blessing to the country since 1892 will follow from the circumstance that a short session of Congress was the fixed order of things in 1895." Before the session ended, however, the silver men in the legislature found another incident—the syndicate bond sale—over which they might harangue the Secretary of the Treasury and the President, and some of them were delighted with the occasion. "They can't exhaust the gold reserve too quickly to suit me," said Cockrell of Missouri. "We can go to a silver basis without so much as a ripple in our financial system." To all appeals for aid the only reply of the silver advocates was, "Gold is a badge of oppression." Senator Stewart, in the forefront of the silver attack, formed a guard by which his group kept someone always in the Senate to see

---

[1] The figures for the sub-treasury are taken largely from the department manuscript forms from which the daily consolidated reports were made up. They are preserved in the Curtis collection. The files of the sub-treasuries were destroyed when the Federal Reserve System was established.

that nothing was slipped in by the gold advocates. Appropriation bills were threatened with defeat if they contained anything inimical to silver. "The Committee [on Finance] is equally divided upon the question," said Senator Sherman. "A measure which all can approve can not be reported unless there is attached to it a proposition to make the free coinage of silver at once the law of the land." Indeed, the committee shortly answered Cleveland and Carlisle's request for a bond issue by recommending a free-coinage measure. "This may not be the first time that bread has been asked for that a stone has been presented," said Senator Vilas, "but it is the first time that a committee of the Senate seems to have perpetuated a practical joke almost good enough for the clown of Barnum's menagerie."

The situation became so critical that President Cleveland sent a special message to Congress on January 28 in which he clearly set forth the difficulties under which Secretary Carlisle was laboring. A new currency system which would obviate the dangers of the past two years had been presented to Congress, said the President, but it had not been acted on; under the old system the situation had again become acute, and gold was necessary if the national credit was to be preserved. There was only one way to obtain gold—the sale of bonds; but the only bonds for which authority of sale existed, Cleveland pointed out, were those which had been authorized twenty-five years before during a period of great stress, and these were not now satisfactory. "The most dangerous and irritating feature of the situation, however, remains to be mentioned," he added. "It is found in the means by which the Treasury is despoiled of the gold thus obtained without canceling a single Government obligation and solely for the benefit of those who find profit in shipping it abroad or whose fears induce them to hoard it at home." [1]

The press of the East was pleased with the President's statement of the case, but that of the West was not convinced. "The

[1] Richardson, IX, 556–565.

WILLIAM E. CURTIS

message is the production of an accomplished hypocrite," said the *Rocky Mountain News*. "In the name of averting calamity he would intensify ten-fold the financial distress of the country. . . . The scheme is a damnable one. If carried out it will entail nothing but misery—misery the depth of which has never been reached. Like the car of juggernaut, it will not only crush the life out of its own worshippers, but it will also destroy those who protest against its enormities. . . . Professing friendship for silver, like Brutus, snake-like in the Roman forum stabbing Caesar, he would do bimetallism to death and bury it beyond all hope of resurrection." [1]

The agitation increased the inrush of legal-tender notes and forced upon Cleveland and Carlisle the fact that the evils of the silver legislation had not died with the repeal of the silver law. There was now another essential to obtain relief, and that was the retirement of the greenbacks and the Treasury notes, which pumped the gold out of the Treasury faster than it could be placed therein. In the last days of January Carlisle had Representative Springer introduce a bill which would permit the sale of gold bonds in denominations of twenty and fifty dollars and multiples thereof, redeemable in ten years and payable in fifty, on which the interest was to be not more than three per cent per annum. The gold thus obtained could be used, if desired, to redeem greenbacks and Treasury notes for the purpose of retiring them. If the bonds were paid for in this form of currency, the notes could then be destroyed.[2]

The silver men were impressed with neither the President's message nor the Springer bill. They saw in the proposal to retire the greenbacks only a scheme to aid the National Banks, which they hated with Jacksonian fervor. Senator Vest asserted that the President had declared war on silver and swore that "never, never, in a time of profound peace, will I vote to issue one bond by this Government for the purpose of securing gold in order that the country shall remain upon a single gold

[1] Editorial, January 29, 1895.
[2] H. R. 8705, introduced by Springer on January 28, 1895. Curtis MSS.

standard." "Besides," said Senator Stewart, "if there is an emergency and more coin is wanted, there are three hundred and thirty or three hundred and forty millions of silver dollars in the Treasury. It is true they are pledged for the redemption of a like amount of silver certificates, but they are not needed to that extent for that purpose. No one pretends that it is necessary that the redemption fund should be as large as the paper issues."

In the House William Jennings Bryan, orator laureate of the silver men, marshaled his Democratic followers, and despite Republican efforts to aid the administration the proposed bill was defeated.

The Republicans were scarcely less divided than the Democrats, but some members of the party gave unselfish assistance to the administration's non-partisan problem of maintaining the gold standard. Of the first two bond issues Nelson Dingley, Jr., of Maine, said: "There was no other course open to the Secretary unless he proposed to have this Government go to protest, and I would not vote today to condemn him for taking the course he did take. The Government must be preserved. But I do condemn this House and Congress for not giving him plain, clear authority to issue bonds bearing not more than 3 per cent interest, for the double purpose of meeting any deficiency in the Treasury and of maintaining the gold redemption fund, in consequence of which failure he has been obliged to issue 5 per cent ten-year bonds at great disadvantage and loss to the country, when he might have made a loan at 2½ per cent if we had given him authority to do so." The party as a whole, however, could not resist the opportunity to condemn the "political imbecility" of the opposition in passing the Wilson-Gorman tariff bill; the troubles had come, many declared, because of a lack of money. Little more is necessary to refute this argument than the statement that even though the redemptions were greater than ever before, the available balance in the Treasury at this time was nearly $150,000,000.

Happily, many Republicans agreed with Thomas B. Reed

when he said that "we are face to face with the situation, and while as a party man I may not be melancholy about the condition of the Democratic party, as a citizen of the United States I am ready at all times to assist the country in which I live."

The Secretary of the Treasury could only sit helpless, hoping that by some miracle the demands on his reserve would be checked. On January 31, in spite of the fact that scarcely more than two months earlier $50,000,000 of bonds had been sold for gold, the reserve reached its lowest point, standing at $45,000,000. It was evident to Carlisle that if some measure of relief did not soon appear, the government would be in immediate danger of defaulting on its gold payments. To the President, his Cabinet, and the financial interests of the country this would have meant immediate and irreparable ruin. What would have happened no one can say, but it is certain that there would have been a serious panic in the financial world. The administration was alarmed; Cabinet meetings ran far into the night, and the President and Secretaries Carlisle, Lamont, and Olney often remained in anxious discussion in the White House until the morning sun had begun to drive away the stars.

It was not difficult to see that no aid was to be expected from Congress. In the face of these conditions there began the intricate and complicated negotiations which finally resulted in the sale of bonds to a New York syndicate. The details of this transaction have never been clearly set forth; it is doubtful whether they can be fully told, for the contemporary evidence is so complicated that a clear and lucid statement is difficult to make.

The New York financial world was keenly alive to the situation in government finances—too keenly alive, according to the silver men. It was from that city that the gold was flowing to Europe, and it was there that the bankers saw their gold go over their counters for private hoarding. London was aware of the crisis, and on January 24 a syndicate of British bankers offered to buy £20,000,000 worth of bonds. On this same date one of the night trains from New York to Washington carried August Belmont, who called the next morning on Secretary Carlisle. In somber colors the financier painted the situation in New York to the Secretary, who had obviously not decided just how the crisis should be met. As a private citizen Belmont urged the absolute necessity of an immediate bond issue. Upon his return to New York he began to cable European financial houses as to the possibility of floating United States bonds there.

In the meantime, contrary to what many believed, Secretary Carlisle was learning all he could as to possible sources of aid; he consulted "not only bankers, but merchants and everybody else disposed to talk about it [the financial situation and bond issue]." It was clear to him that relief could be obtained only through a gold loan from abroad, but the replies to the cablegrams sent by Belmont decisively showed that Europe felt "a general indisposition to have anything to do with United States securities at that time." To be effective the remedy had to reëstablish public confidence and secure gold which the government did not already possess. Previous issues had not done either. At this time the bonds which were sold in November were quoted at several points lower than the price which had been paid for them, and the gold in the Treasury could last only a few days at most.

Secretary Carlisle was thoroughly alarmed. He hurried Assistant-Secretary Curtis off to New York to talk over the situation there. Again and again in the past year Curtis had caught a train for that city to go directly to the offices of various bank presidents to confer with them regarding money matters or to urge fuller coöperation with the Treasury. This time, however, his mission was more serious; he went with the direct instructions of the Secretary to see "whether the gold could be got from abroad." Curtis found the situation critical and Belmont discouraged. He called his chief for further instructions, but Carlisle could only suggest another consultation with Belmont. The day had been a perplexing one for Curtis, and at night he wrote the following letter:

University Club
Madison Square
30 January 1895
10 P. M.

Dear Mr. Secretary:

I have been with B. since 7.15 and just left him. He has cabled to learn whether foreigners would do anything with the 5s. at all and expects an answer in the morning. He does not think it will be favorable. He says that the selling of American Securities must be stopped by inspiring foreigners with confidence and until that is done the *gold* must go to them. He says he tried to see Stillman today and failed, but saw Baker. They decided that $100,000,000 was necessary with an option for $100,000,000 more if desired. Syndicate to be arranged to take ⅓ here and ⅔ abroad. They think this figure only would help situation and loan of $50,000,000 must be *immediate* in his opinion. Jordan was here to meet me. He lost over $3,000,000 today. Thinks he can hold on until Saturday night and tomorrow may decide. Urges immediate action as necessary. Look at Meline's gold statement of tomorrow morning showing transfers made and to come. People seem scared and panicky in the Club. I have seen no one on this business except B. and Jordan. Reporters were on the train, at the ferry and elsewhere. Impossible to elude them or do anything but hold one's tongue. If you will call me up at the Club here at *half past nine* tomorrow from the long distance telephone in my office I would like instructions. First— To whom shall I talk? (B. evidently would like to try to arrange the Syndicate if you decide to go ahead, but shall we not make some advances elsewhere through him or personally?). Second— What representations can I make, if any, as to the intentions of the Government? I think it should be decided at once whether a bond issue should be made or not. If the former and to a syndicate the amount, terms, method &c. to be suggested by B. and such others as you may name and to be approved by you. If there is to be no issue, it should be so stated at once. B. thinks we have overstayed our time. The question also as to the probable effect of suspension with a bond issue pending, or advertised for, must be well thought out. If we decide upon an issue *by advertise-*

ment, they should be printed tomorrow, proposals to be handed in and opened at the Treasury next Monday. *This time* have provisions made for allotment, if necessary, and take the highest; no "all or none." I think the country might respond to this. Instalments after first round amount to be easy and in gold. This is a personal opinion merely. I feel the responsibility here and would like to divide it. I sent a note to F. but got no answer and think he may be away. You of course know the Congressional outlook. I do not and my views are simply based on what I see here. I send this by special delivery.

Yrs. truly
W. E. Curtis.

On the morning of January 31 August Belmont, J. Pierpont Morgan, and Assistant-Secretary Curtis met in the office of Assistant-Treasurer Jordan in the sub-treasury building. Morgan had come on the invitation of both Curtis and Belmont, and from that time he took the active lead in the syndicate negotiations. Belmont felt that the crisis was so acute and the public mind in such anxiety that it would be absolutely impossible to secure gold by public advertisement. He plainly told Curtis that it was doubtful that a loan could be sold in Europe for gold, but he urged that such negotiations be attempted. During the day Morgan, Belmont, and Curtis discussed the tentative provisions of a contract with the government. They agreed that if the banking houses could secure the necessary gold from Europe, a private contract should be made for a bond sale of $100,000,000. That night Curtis carried tentative propositions to Washington, having agreed to call Belmont if they were satisfactory. On the following day Morgan telephoned Curtis to bring over any counter-proposals which the Secretary might desire to suggest.

Whatever the value of Curtis' consultations in New York, the relief to the Treasury Department was immediate; the press soon began to publish rumors of a pending bond issue. Reporters had followed Curtis to Belmont's home, where they were left to use their imagination as to what was being discussed between the agent of the Treasury and the banker. Although the reports in the press on January 31 were not correct, they were definite enough to cause the requests for redemptions to lessen materially; the demands for gold fell off more than $1,000,000 on that day and still more on the following. Nine millions in gold which had been placed aboard ship for export was returned to the sub-treasury during the night. Many believed that the proposed issue would be a large one. President Cleveland, "grown weary of making two bites of a cherry," would sell $100,000,000 of bonds, said the Chicago *Times*.

Regardless of the advice of financiers that a public loan could not be made at the time, Carlisle was still hesitant as to a private sale. On February 2 he again sent Curtis to New York to consult with Belmont and Morgan. This time the Assistant Secretary was to talk over the matter at length with the bankers and see upon what basis, if any, a negotiation might be entered into. The New York financiers had now received authority from their correspondents in Europe to make a contract for $50,000,000 of bonds to be paid for in gold, not more than half of which was to be obtained in Europe. With an option in hand, however, every effort would be made to obtain an additional $50,000,000 if necessary. The European houses demanded a bond which would pay $3\frac{1}{2}$ per cent to the investor, and Morgan and Belmont were accordingly compelled to ask $3\frac{3}{4}$ per cent from the government. Apparently all the difficulties were settled on this second visit, and Assistant-Secretary Curtis, promising to telephone Morgan and Belmont the next day, made his way back to Washington with the provisions of the proposed contract.

The Secretary of the Treasury found himself in a difficult situation. He knew that the credit of the government must be maintained; and yet he was by nature and by political training opposed to secret dealings by the government. The press had already begun to talk about "dark lantern financiering," and the charge of dealing with the "goldbugs" was still ringing in the ears of the administration leaders. Carlisle desired to make a popular loan rather than a private one, and he hoped that even yet Congress might be induced to come to his rescue by authorizing a sale. The scraps of messages written in his own hand, now preserved in the Curtis collection, are indisputable evidence as to the agitated state of his mind. On the other hand, Morgan and Belmont felt that the agreement was already made. "Neither Mr. Belmont nor myself doubted for a moment that the terms would be satisfactory and that the business was practically settled," said J. Pierpont Morgan later. The Secretary, however, decided not to take the step. At three o'clock on Sunday, February 3, Curtis telephoned the New York bankers that the decision had been withheld in the Treasury Department. That night his private secretary left for New York with a letter from Secretary Carlisle saying that the offer was not acceptable as the rate was too high.

If any kind of sale, public or otherwise, was to be attempted, the assistance of Morgan and Belmont was highly desirable; to reject their offer of services now and yet leave them in such a humor as to be willing to serve him again required no little amount of diplomacy on the part of Secretary Carlisle. There are several drafts of the message he wrote to the bankers, and the numberless changes and interlineal corrections show the difficulty with which the decision was carried out. One, recorded on a sheet of foolscap paper, so poorly written and so much corrected as to be almost illegible, begins:

Having fully considered the information communicated by you in pursuance of the suggestions of Mr. Belmont touching the negotiations of a foreign loan to replenish our gold reserve we are satisfied that the terms upon which it could be accomplished as indicated by your advice are so different from what was hoped, and the probable results fall so far short of what is desired, that the plan for a sale through a syndicate arrangement made in advance is inexpedient.[1]

The decision involved more than simply retaining the coöp-

[1] Preserved in the Curtis MSS.

MORGAN-BELMONT BOND ISSUE

eration of the bankers. It might mean the failure of the United States government to maintain the gold standard of value. All the available evidence was against a successful public issue of bonds. That the Secretary was determined to try the experiment, however, is shown by another letter, written more legibly and dated February 3, 1895:

Messrs J. P. Morgan & August Belmont.
GENTLEMEN:

Regretting that for the reasons stated in the communication which accompanies this note, and others which will occur to you we are constrained to dispose of the four per cent bonds thirty year bonds [sic], to the amount of $100,000,000, in the manner heretofore adopted in the sale of the five per cents. In this attempt to re-establish the reserve and maintain the public credit, we hope to have your co-operation and the co-operation and support of all others interested in the financial affairs of the country.

The Secretary was following his desires in making the loan a public one, but his better judgment told him that this was far from the wisest course. As eventually made, the bond issue was for little more than $50,000,000, but it is clear that Carlisle wished to make it $100,000,000. Curtis had discussed the latter sum with the bankers in New York, and a memorandum in the handwriting of Secretary Carlisle, found among the Curtis papers, stipulates:

1. Want $100,000,000 in gold to be delivered at New York.
2. The bonds to be four per cent 30 year bonds, payable in coin, interest payable quarterly in coin. Bonds to be dated Feby. 1, 1895.
3. Cannot stipulate for secrecy as to the terms if information called for by Congress.
4. Will co-operate with syndicate in effecting [?] and sale to full extent authorized by law and not involving a loss by the Government.

The actual letter which Morgan and Belmont received from Carlisle has not been revealed, but if necessary it could easily be reconstructed from the evidence. The letter reached New York on Monday morning, February 4. It was a distinct surprise to the bankers, and Morgan was sure that a popular call for gold at this time would react disastrously upon the Treasury and upon business. "Knowing, as I did know, the inevitable results of a public announcement of the abandonment of the negotiations," said Morgan at the investigation which was held in 1896, "I urged Mr. Belmont to leave at once for Washington, and stated that I would communicate with the Department by telephone or telegraph as soon as possible after reaching the office. Upon so communicating I learned that it was proposed to issue a public advertisement that afternoon, and I urged the Secretary in the strongest terms not to do this, and at least to delay its issue until Mr. Belmont and myself should have an interview with the President and himself, stating at the same time that in view of the negotiations which we had undertaken and in view of what we had accomplished we felt entitled at least to that consideration."

Belmont left immediately for Washington. That afternoon Morgan ordered his private coach attached to the Washington train, and in the evening he started for the capital with his counsel, Francis Lynde Stetson, and his junior partner, Robert Bacon. "There may be papers to be drawn, and I want you," he had said to his legal adviser. Their personal interest, if nothing else, would have prompted Morgan and Belmont to take the action they did.

When August Belmont arrived in Washington, he first called at the office of the Secretary of War; finding that Colonel Lamont had gone home for the evening, however, he walked over to the Treasury Department. Carlisle also was absent, and after a short talk with Assistant-Secretary Curtis the financier went in search of the Secretary, whom he found at dinner. Thirty-six years have not sufficed to dispel the belief that the banker was walking the streets of Washington on this midwinter night with premeditated greed in his heart, seeking to buy the honor of the national government.

Early on the morning of February 5, according to a tentative arrangement of the preceding day, the two leaders of New York finance called at the White House to impress upon the President the gravity of the situation. Representing the financial interests of the country at this meeting were J. Pierpont Morgan, Francis Lynde Stetson, Robert Bacon, and August Belmont; and acting for the administration were the President, Secretary Carlisle, and Attorney-General Olney.[1] Assistant-Secretary Curtis, who had borne the brunt of the financial negotiations, was not present. "I will be in my office and you can send for me if wanted," he had written Secretary Carlisle just before the conference.

The meeting was long, and the discussion was earnest on both sides. Secretary Carlisle explained the situation from the viewpoint of the government; J. Pierpont Morgan stated it from the side of the financier. An immediate supply of gold coin from Europe, declared Morgan, was the only means of averting panic and widespread disaster. He explained that such a purchase of gold need not interfere with a public issue of bonds later, if desired. For four hours the group sat in consultation, the President leaving the room for an hour while Secretary Carlisle continued the discussion. The case was clear; the Secretary and the President realized the strength of the points made by Morgan, but they were not convinced that public action should be abandoned. It is doubtful whether they still had faith in Congress, but they at least felt that it would be wisest to give that body a little more time. "We had asked for legislation, and we thought it was hardly respectful to Congress to undertake to negotiate a sale of bonds pending the very legislation which the President in his message had asked for," said Secretary Carlisle in his testimony in 1896.

[1] Olney MSS; Curtis MSS; Bond Investigation.

Although Carlisle was in favor of a popular loan, he realized that an effort to float one would be dangerous. On the morning of the conference Curtis, on whom he greatly depended in these matters, had written him:

Tuesday

Dear Mr. Secretary:

. . . .

I am terribly anxious about the popular loan offer *without preliminary arrangements*. I cannot see how we can help the situation without foreign gold in some way. Nothing can apparently be done in New York on the lines we mentioned—*i. e.* temporary borrowings. The difference in price between quotations for foreign bids and our views is nothing compared with panic and suspension. Do get all the information about the business side of the situation from Morgan, who thinks the situation the most critical since the war, and I must say I agree. . . . I think a private conversation between you and M. would be advantageous. . . .

Yrs. hastily
W. E. C.

Secretary Carlisle was fully cognizant of all these dangers, and yet he had not forgotten that all his efforts to keep the country on a sound financial basis had called forth every conceivable criticism. He would wait! Because of this determination, the conference with Morgan and Belmont came to an end with no definite decision, but it was tentatively agreed that 3,500,000 ounces of gold would be bought on the terms of the contract if it became apparent that Congress would grant no better means of securing gold. The ounces of gold were to be exchanged for bonds under the law of 1862, Revised Statutes, Section 3700. The powers under this section were discussed while the President was absent from the conference. The Secretary was fully familiar with the provisions and his powers under it. Contemporary and family evidence shows that Assistant-

Secretary Curtis first discovered this clause and that he brought it to the attention of Carlisle and Morgan.[1]

Yet to wait further on Congress was a course pregnant with danger. Its perils are indicated by the Secretary's accounts as set forth in reports sent to his office. Between December 1, 1894, and February 13, 1895, although the gold exports had amounted to only a little more than $36,000,000, the total amount of gold withdrawals had been well over $80,000,000, showing that about $43,000,000 had been withdrawn for hoarding purposes during that period. The banks had not taken the metal; on December 1, 1894, the total amount of gold held by these institutions in New York was $96,000,000, and on the first of February they had $13,000,000 less than they had held on the former date. New York and Boston were the principal centers of export and, naturally, of redemptions. Early in January every available gold coin had been gathered at those two centers. Yet despite these efforts the assistant treasurer at New York had reported on January 30 (Wednesday) that while he hoped to hold out until Saturday, the next day might decide the question.[2]

The financial situation, indeed, was not merely critical—it was desperate. On February 2 the gold coin in the sub-treasury at New York amounted to less than $9,000,000, and there was no possible way to relieve the condition.[3] The amount of gold coin owned by the United States was exceeded by the demand certificates outstanding against it. The government was practically borrowing gold coin from the owners of these certificates and substituting gold bullion in its place in order to carry on specie payments in gold.[4] Every sub-treasury and mint in the

---

[1] The evidence on this point is conclusive. In a letter in the New York *Evening Post* of July 8, 1908, Horace White said of Mr. Curtis and his discovery of Section 3700 that "if a laurel crown is due to anybody for calling attention to it in that crisis, he is entitled to wear it."

[2] Curtis MSS., and departmental forms; *Commercial and Financial Chronicle*.

[3] Sub-treasury memorandum, Curtis MSS.

[4] Secretary Carlisle's testimony at bond investigation; Curtis MSS; *Treasury Report*, 1895.

South and West was now ordered to send all its gold to New York, where Jordan was instructed to fill the gold requests in chronological order. A trifle could have precipitated an immediate run on the sub-treasury, and in that case any bank of importance in New York could have compelled the United States Treasury to admit its inability to meet its obligations on *gold certificates*. There might be some doubt about paying legal-tenders in gold, but there could be no question as to *gold certificates,* and their refusal would plainly have indicated the Treasury's incapacity to maintain the gold standard. The officials of the Treasury Department were at their wits' end. On the morning of February 5 Assistant-Secretary Curtis wrote his chief, "Pardon all these suggestions, but the matter has kept me awake all night and the slightest hesitance in the public view will precipitate trouble." There can be no doubt that the country was facing a new standard of value. What the results would have been had the change come about is problematical. It is certain that they could not have been of a trivial nature. European bankers had already begun to advise financiers in South America not to deal in American securities except on a gold basis.

Of these alarming days Secretary Carlisle said in his annual *Report* in December: "The large withdrawals . . . increased in intensity from day to day until [they] nearly reached the proportions of a panic, and it was evident to all who were familiar with the situation that, unless effectual steps were promptly taken to check the growing distrust, the Government would be compelled within a few days to suspend gold payments and drop to a depreciated silver and paper standard."

In Congress the silverites were delighted with the situation. Cheered by the bright outlook for victory, they rushed to the fight with great vigor. Their oratory filled the halls of Congress, and the press broadcasted their speeches over America. "It would seem that again we must meet the insidious and persistent efforts of the money power in the form of another bond and currency bill," said Coffeen regarding the bill which Secretary Carlisle had had introduced in the House. The fight very nearly ended in victory for the silver attackers. "The republic was within a hair's breadth of bankruptcy. Only the promptest help could ward off the catastrophe," wrote Carl Schurz in later years.[1] The mercury in the gold barometer had again been rapidly falling: it had stood at $83,000,000 on January 5, $79,000,000 on the twelfth, $74,000,000 a week later, $63,000,000 on the twenty-sixth, and $42,000,000 on the second day of February. But the Springer bill, to grant the Treasury Department authority for the sale of gold bonds, was doomed. At six o'clock on the evening of February 7 it was defeated in the House, and the last hope of the Secretary was gone. "When it failed it became evident, at least to me, that something had to be done, or that the comparatively small amount of gold then in the Treasury would be taken out immediately," said Secretary Carlisle. The New York *World* observed editorially: "The only thing left for the Administration to do is to make a loan on the best terms obtainable. That these terms will be harsh and discrediting is due as much to the wilfulness and imbecility of Congress as to the incapacity of the Administration."

There could now be only one question, and that was the method by which the bonds were to be sold. They might be advertised to the public, or they might be sold privately to any who wished the task of underwriting gold at a time when America held such a low rank in the financial world. The President and the Secretary of the Treasury favored a public issue; but it appears certain that such a procedure was not feasible, for the gold or a large part of it must necessarily come from the Treasury Department, and with the first presentations the government would have defaulted. A public announcement must have been followed by a second announcement of the suspension of specie payments. Secretary Carlisle somewhat unwillingly turned to the New York bankers, Morgan and Belmont, for further consultation.

[1] *McClure's Magazine,* IX, 638.

One has only to read the discordant statements of those who were interested in making the Morgan-Belmont contract of February 8, 1895, to understand how critical the situation was and how excited the participants became. In later years President Cleveland endeavored to record the facts of the syndicate deal. "I propose to give the details of that interview as gathered from a recollection which I do not believe can be at fault," he wrote, and at the beginning says, "Therefore, on the evening of the seventh day of February, 1895, an interview was held at the White House with Mr. J. P. Morgan of New York."[1] Richard Olney wrote to Colonel Lamont at the same time, "My recollection is not the same as Mr. Cleveland's. As I recall what took place, you were present at all the important conferences between the President and the bankers. Do you remember coming, with Messrs. Morgan, Belmont, and Bacon, to my house in the evening—when Morgan stated that they despaired of accomplishing anything in Washington and were going to return to New York that night and let things take their course?"[2] Neither the President nor his Attorney-General remembered the incidents correctly. The interview did not take place on the evening of the seventh as stated by the former, and Belmont had nothing to do with the making of the contract as stated by the latter.[3]

From the conflicting evidence, none of which is fundamentally important, one is able to gather a fairly accurate account of how the gold deal was made. Just why J. Pierpont Morgan chose to go to Washington on the evening of Thursday, February 7, is not clear. Carl Hovey relates that when the markets closed and the withdrawals from the Treasury were reported on the news sheets of the afternoon, Morgan, who had been watching the returns from the tickers, put on his hat and coat and, calling Bacon, left his office. He passed through the knot of reporters gathered outside without speaking, entered a cab

---

[1] *Presidential Problems*, 148–50.
[2] Olney MSS.
[3] Cleveland read his manuscript to Carlisle before publication.

THE LONE WORSHIPER OF THE SILVER GOD
(*Judge*, 1893)

TO THE PAWNSHOP AT LAST
(*Judge*, 1895)

for the Cortland Street Ferry, and took the Congressional Limited for Washington. He might easily have done this, but it is certain that he took with him also his counsel, Francis Lynde Stetson. The records of the Pennsylvania Railroad show that Morgan and a party of four others left Jersey City for Washington on February 7 in the banker's private car attached to train number 59 (the Congressional Limited), which departed at 3.20 in the afternoon.[1] A few days before (on February 4) Morgan had gathered these men into his coach and hastened to Washington to talk over the situation, and it is clear that at that time the President had told him he might return Thursday or Friday.

When Morgan reached the station in Washington with his two associates—some two and a half hours after the failure of the Springer bond bill—he was surprised to find Secretary Lamont waiting for him, and more surprised and probably chagrined to learn that the President would not see him. "The President's objection was, I know, not personal to Mr. Morgan," says Richard Olney, "but arose from the well-founded feeling that his presence at the White House would not facilitate any financial legislation the President might find it imperative to ask of Congress." [2]

Had the great "Pierpontifex Maximus" come to buy the government? Or was the meeting, as suggested by Max Lerner, a contest for power between the huge, bull-necked, large-nosed man who personified Wall Street and the huge, bull-necked man who ruled over the White House? The facts do not support either contention. The banker, disgruntled, prepared to return to New York, but was induced by members of the Cabinet to remain in the city. In 1904 Olney wrote Colonel Lamont, "I think you and I persuaded them [Morgan and his associates] to hold on and try the results of an interview with Mr. Cleveland the next morning which we felt certain we could bring

[1] W. E. Blachley, General Passenger Agent, Pennsylvania Railroad, to the writer, June 23, 1930.
[2] Olney MSS.

about." The financiers went to the Arlington Hotel, where, it is said, Morgan sat over a game of solitaire until far after midnight.

The night was a dramatic one. The nation was held in the icy grip of a blizzard which struck the capital at midnight; the gold standard hung in the balance; in the Executive Mansion sat a man without a party; and on K Street a statesman who had led the battle for tariff reform for almost twenty years saw his hopes fade away as the financial situation drew him into an alliance with the representatives of a group who supported protection. The capital was a miniature of the nation that cold night. The streets were deserted and barren; opulence and poverty flourished side by side. With the exception of Mrs. Carlisle, the wives of the Cabinet members were holding brilliant receptions, and luxurious Washington was indulging in its "social season." But poverty stalked near by. All day long wagonloads of provisions had been going out from the buildings of the *Post* and the *Evening Star* to the squalid alleys of the city; at the central relief station on Louisiana Avenue busy workers did what they could to aid the poor. The Central Union Mission was full, and in the past twenty-four hours nineteen hundred had filed by the soup kitchen. The frosty ring of steel tires broke the silence of South Washington down by the frozen swamps of the Potomac as loads of coal were sent to relieve the suffering there. Hundreds were hungry and cold as the great banker played solitaire in the Arlington.

Out in the nation there was no one to bring relief to the Southern farmers who had a few months before sold their cotton for six cents per pound; nor was there anyone to bring succor to the Westerners whose farm products would not pay the cost of marketing them. Many a citizen of the midlands believed that Cleveland was dreaming that night of ill-gotten gold.

When morning came, the banker received word that the President would see him. The day was cold and dark, and snow filled the air as Morgan and his junior partner made their way across Lafayette Square to the White House, where they found the President and Secretaries Carlisle, Olney, and Lamont. The day was perhaps in keeping with the spirit of the administration. These events of February 8 "were preceded, and had been for a week or more, by many anxious consultations of the Cabinet . . . suspension of specie payments by the United States Treasury was imminent." [1]

In the conference Morgan was inclined to complain of Secretary Carlisle's previous policy toward the bankers. He had presented a bill for currency reform, said the financier, in contradiction to his promises to the buyers of the second issue of bonds, thereby causing them to lose money on the deal. Morgan did not want to make any pledge without a clear understanding as to the course of the government. Carlisle and Cleveland were still in favor of a public issue. Morgan did not think this advisable, but admitted that bonds could probably be sold at some price by that method; he agreed to keep up the gold reserve during the pendency of the loan, provided that the gold could be kept from going abroad. Obviously such a guarantee could be given by neither the President nor his Secretary of the Treasury, who had been fighting that problem for two years and had been plainly defeated.

The factors which convinced Cleveland and Carlisle that a public issue could not be made are obscure, but they eventually agreed to buy gold with bonds by a private contract under section 3700, Revised Statutes. "This was a proposition entirely new to me," wrote President Cleveland in his *Presidential Problems*. The section, however, had been mentioned in the consultation with Morgan and Belmont on February 4; Secretary Carlisle was already familiar with it at that time, for Assistant-Secretary Curtis had discussed its possibilities with him. The conference that morning was one of great tension, and the story is related that J. Pierpont Morgan unconsciously ground his unlighted cigar into ashes.[2]

[1] Olney to Satterlee, Apr. 15, 1914. Olney MSS.
[2] Carl Hovey, *Life of J. Pierpont Morgan*.

Whatever the difficulties, the outcome was predetermined before the little gathering met in the President's room. It was reasonably certain that there was no alternative to getting gold from Europe, and only some strong banking concern like the Morgans, Belmonts, or Rothschilds could undertake such a transaction. The mode of procedure finally settled, the financiers, the Secretary of the Treasury, Assistant-Secretary Curtis, and Attorney-General Olney gathered in the Treasury Building sometime during the morning to write the contract. "When you need money you have to get it on the best practical terms," Carlisle later said. "I think we did the best we could. At one time we almost came to the conclusion that we could make no transaction at all, as we were afraid we could not make acceptable terms. I recognize the fact that the terms were hard for the Government." But if the terms were hard for the government, the difficulties facing the syndicate were formidable also.

The actual writing of the contract was left largely to Francis Lynde Stetson, counsel for J. Pierpont Morgan, and Assistant-Secretary Curtis, Secretary Carlisle's adviser on the loan deals. In form it closely followed the contract made by John Sherman with Morgan and Belmont in 1878. The syndicate agreed to furnish the Treasury Department in exchange for bonds 3,500,000 ounces of gold, at least one-half of which was to be obtained in Europe. It moreover solemnly agreed to protect the Treasury from withdrawals during the period of the loan in so far as lay within its power. If any other bonds were issued before the first day of October, they were to be first offered to the syndicate. The bonds were to bear interest at the rate of four per cent; but if Congress would within ten days substitute the words "gold bonds" for "coin bonds," the interest rate would be reduced to three per cent.

President Cleveland was not present when the terms of the contract were drawn up, but he was afterwards consulted on some of the points in question. In a letter written to an old friend that evening he did not mention the incident; he did say in regard to the finances, however, that he hoped "to see a little blue sky bye and bye."[1] Neither was Belmont present; he had left New York on a morning train, but had become snow-bound and did not reach Washington until about two in the afternoon. As soon as the provisions of the contract were determined, Secretary Carlisle hurried to the Executive Mansion to give them to the President.

The special message which the President sent to Congress immediately after the agreement was signed was the curt announcement of a fact. Gold had been bought at a price, and it was expressly reserved to Congress to modify that price if it so desired; but, regardless of the action of Congress, gold had been bought.[2] Congress had failed to pass timely legislation to uphold the efforts of the Executive to maintain a gold reserve, said President Cleveland, and independent action had been taken accordingly.

The message was a distinct surprise to Congress, and it created a great deal of commotion in that body. The majority of the Ways and Means Committee succeeded in introducing a resolution granting authority to the Secretary of the Treasury to issue not more than $65,116,275 in bonds, bearing interest at three per cent and payable in gold. Secretary Carlisle was called before that committee, and his influence is clearly shown in the majority report: "As it is not believed by the committee that the issue of bonds specifically payable in gold will impose

[1] Cleveland to Benedict, February 8, 1895. Cleveland MSS.

[2] The story of the syndicate negotiations as told by Davis Rich Dewey (volume 24 in the *American Nation Series*), Harry Thurston Peck (*Twenty Years of the Republic*), Henry Jones Ford (The Cleveland Era in *The Chronicles of America Series*), and others is based on Cleveland's *Presidential Problems* and is subject to the inaccuracies and false interpretations of a single uncertain source. Professor Dewey says: "Mr. Morgan then suddenly asked the President why the treasury did not buy $100,000,000 in gold at a fixed price, and pay for it in bonds. This was a new proposition, but it was agreed that the law authorized such a transaction. On the next day it was announced that an agreement with bankers for the purchase of gold would be executed unless Congress would authorize the issue of gold interest-bearing bonds. As Congress did not act, a contract was entered into, February 8, 1895." The plan of exchanging bonds for gold was not a happy thought of the moment, and no message except the announcement of the sale was sent to Congress.

any additional burden or liability upon the Government than if they are made payable in coin, under its pledge and policy to preserve the parity of the coins in the two metals, the saving of this large amount [$16,000,000] becomes a matter of substantial moment and advantage to the Government; and as the parties to take the bonds are under contract to furnish gold coin for them it seems no hardship on the Government to contract to pay them back in the same coin that they furnish to it."

But the arguments presented did not appeal to all the members of the committee.[1] William Jennings Bryan was determined to have none of the "insidious bankers"; he would keep the government standing on its old foundations, free from the domination of "foreign financiers" who could have no good motive in coming to the relief of the Secretary of the Treasury! The question was, he said, whether the contract made by the Executive should be ratified. Regardless of what the party owed its leader, he himself was decidedly opposed to the action. "I want to suggest to my Democratic friends that the party owes no great debt of gratitude to its President. What gratitude should we feel? The gratitude which a confiding ward feels toward his guardian without bond who has squandered a rich estate. . . . The gratitude which a passenger feels toward the trainman who has opened a switch and precipitated a wreck. What has he done for the party? He has attempted to inoculate it with Republican virus, and blood poisoning has set in.

"What is the duty of the Democratic party? If it still loves its President it is its duty, as I understand it, to prove that it has at least one attribute of divinity left by chastening him whom it loveth."

Bryan was sure that an insult had been offered the government by a foreign syndicate which was seeking to change the financial policy of the United States. "We cannot afford to put ourselves in the hands of the Rothschilds, who hold mortgages on most of the thrones of Europe," he asserted. "The

[1] Only two Democrats, Wilson of West Virginia and Bynum of Indiana, signed the report.

President may be persuaded that this country has reached the point where it cannot control its own course . . . but he mistakes the sentiment of the American people if he thinks that they share with him in this alarm." Few other speakers had the appeal of this young Demosthenes from the West, but many Congressmen joined Bryan in condemning the government. The passage of the three per cent gold bond bill would have saved the country $16,000,000, and the administration made strenuous efforts to force it through. Secretary Carlisle pleaded and explained until he grew tired and gave up in disgust.

"I feel like opening my heart to you this afternoon, or rather pouring out vials of wrath in your sympathetic ear," wrote A. B. Farquar of York, Pennsylvania, to Congressman Michael D. Harter. "Is Congress going to rob us of sixteen million dollars rather than permit the President to substitute the word 'gold' for 'coin' in a bond that will unquestionably be paid in gold, anyhow? Is it going to add direct robbery of the people to its attempt to debauch and disgrace them with a bankruptcy law, and crush them under the dead weight of inertia?" Two days later the Congressman replied, "Congress is an ass and the worldly-minded is fully justified in saying a d—d ass." [1] Nothing could prevent the defeat of the pending measure. "It seems almost incredible," says Carl Schurz, "but the House deliberately threw away that saving because a large majority of the members were too much afraid of the word 'gold' to accept it."

The silverites and the gold men battled with each other during February, halting occasionally to complain of the foul air which filled the House and the Senate. Many Congressmen probably did not believe an investigating committee's report that the offensive odor came from either the tons of molding documents in the basement or the hot steam from the Capitol's turkish bath, but concluded instead that the opposition had become noticeably rotten. The silver forces called the Secretary of the Treasury to Capitol Hill for questioning, and they dis-

[1] Cleveland MSS.

covered at the same time a new scheme for defeating the goldbugs. A law of 1856 required the acceptance at a stated price of Mexican silver coins, which were then to be converted into American dollars. The silverites planned to send silver into Mexico, have it coined, and then present it to the Treasury of the United States. The one difficulty was that Mexico had no machinery with which to carry out its part in this fantastic scheme.

The syndicate had promised to make every effort to prevent the withdrawal of gold during the pendency of the contract; and indeed, no gold was taken from the Treasury with which to pay for bonds, nor was any withdrawn for shipment to Europe until after the delivery had been completed under the contract. A week after the making of the agreement Belmont wrote the President: "Our syndicate transactions are progressing very favorably, and it is my sincere hope and belief that we will reward the firm stand which you have taken for the benefit of the country at large, in the face of hostile criticism, by accomplishing what we have undertaken to your entire satisfaction and most fully."[1] Small difficulties, however, were bound to appear. The contract had been made under such pressure that it could be scarcely more than a working hypothesis, its details later to be worked out. But, being bankers, Morgan and Belmont were certain to interpret the points in question in their favor. "Mr. Morgan 'paddles his own canoe' in his own way," wrote Assistant-Treasurer Jordan. "I've known him a long time, and never known him to do anything else."[2]

It was necessary that the syndicate take drastic measures in order to make the bond deal successful. Morgan and Belmont gathered around them the officials of a few strong banking houses, with whose aid they were able to dominate the exchange market. They also controlled the amount of gold in the Treasury reserve in order that it might not interfere with their exchange operations. This supervision of the nation's purse was

[1] Cleveland MSS.
[2] Curtis MSS.

irritating to the Treasury, and many were the heated arguments between Jordan and the bankers. Throughout March, April, and May, Morgan refused to allow the gold reserve to rise above ninety millions, and he held in his possession at all times sufficient claims against the gold to reduce it to the desired amount.[1] He used these claims, however, only occasionally, and the Treasury aided in preventing other withdrawals by exerting moral pressure. "The firm of James Walsh & Sons have been withdrawing gold bars daily for a week or ten days," Jordan wrote with resentment on February 19, "and I have now the best evidence that they are offering them at a premium in the street. Members of the syndicate have been approached with offers to sell them, but they of course declined to purchase. It seems to me that the Department might take some action to check this." In so far as possible legal-tenders were held in the vaults of the Treasury. The fact that half of the bonds were sold in Europe aided also in preventing withdrawals from the small store of gold.

The delivery of $31,157,700 of the gold bonds in Europe by Assistant-Secretary Curtis and Chief Clerk Logan Carlisle marked the completion of the sale. The syndicate contract was faithfully carried out with one exception. Morgan and Belmont found in May that they had exhausted their stock of gold in Europe. If any more drafts were drawn there, they would have to send over the gold to meet them; the syndicate, however, had gold in its own vaults with which to make the last $10,-000,000 payment due to the United States Treasury. This gold had been secured from Canada, and permission was asked to pay it into the Treasury. Secretary Carlisle granted the request, and the bankers were accordingly not compelled to send gold to Europe only to bring it immediately back again.

The storm which the bond sale raised in the country and in Congress eventually blew over. After all, there was nothing that could be done; Congress could only make more expensive and uncertain what might have been easily accomplished had

[1] The Jordan letters in the Curtis manuscripts clearly reveal these difficulties.

there been harmony among all branches of the government. With the consummation of the bond deal, however, the following of the administration in the West rapidly melted away, while the silverites and Populists as rapidly increased. The Westerners believed that they had been betrayed by a Democrat whom they had trusted.

There can be no doubt that a great majority of the people believed with Senator Morgan of Alabama that J. Pierpont Morgan and August Belmont had waited until they found the government in a serious condition, and had then "choked it." It is certain that the government had been in a serious condition—so serious, indeed, that it is probable that no other course could have been taken. Anything which would tend to create excitement or to start the legal-tenders to the sub-treasuries would have brought the government immediately to a suspension of specie payments. The country could be saved only by a desperate effort, and the fewer people who knew the real state of the Treasury, the greater the margin of safety. Public knowledge of the situation would have resulted only in the presentation of both legal-tenders and gold certificates. The conclusion is logical, therefore, that a popular loan could not have been made at the time without exposing the government to great financial loss. Criticism of Cleveland and Carlisle for having allowed the situation to become so complicated has been founded on the theory of what should have been done and not what could have been done.

Were the terms of the contract harsh? Secretary Carlisle openly expressed the opinion that they were, but declared that nothing better could be done. The evidence today indicates that the Secretary may have been pessimistic. It is not at all certain that the terms, although severe, were not favorable for the government. The two financiers would not have undertaken such a contract in their private business, and it is doubtful that any other combination of financial houses could have accomplished the task. Morgan and Belmont in America and the Morgans and Rothschilds in Europe were a powerful alliance, with unlimited resources at their command. The conditions which existed when the bond contract was made were such as to require the assistance of a financial concern of unrestricted monetary possibilities both at home and abroad. The government bonds which had been sold to a syndicate in November at 117 were now selling on the market at 111; the country was on the verge of bankruptcy; the hoarding of gold was greatly on the increase; and the practice of using the Treasury as a source of gold supply was firmly established. In the face of these facts, Morgan and Belmont undertook to do what the government had signally failed to do: keep gold in the Treasury and thereby protect the gold standard.

Morgan and Belmont both asserted that they had entered upon the task of supplying gold for the government merely to save the standard of value. "I had but one aim in the whole matter," declared J. Pierpont Morgan later, "to secure the gold that the Government needed and to save the panic and widespread disaster that was sure to follow if the gold was not got." The wealth of America was at stake, many believed; no one owned more of that wealth than Morgan and Belmont, and few could do as much as they toward saving it. Their own private fortunes stood to dwindle under the attack of the silver hosts. To say what the change to a silver standard would have brought is difficult; it would take the mind of a keen economist to calculate the resulting depreciation of value. A panic could not have been avoided, and the profits which the bankers made were insignificant in comparison to the losses incident to such a catastrophe.

The profit made by the syndicate will probably never be known. It is doubtful that it can be ascertained, but no one would say that it was not large. The bankers never denied, but expressly asserted, that they desired a proper margin of gain in addition to payment of expenses. At the bond investigation a year later Senator Platt asked Morgan: "And so your sole purpose . . . in this transaction was not the idea that you could take this bond issue and make money out of it, but that you could prevent a panic and distress in the country?" The financier indignantly replied: "I will answer the question, though I do not think it is necessary in view of all that I have done . . . I had no object except . . . to save the disaster that would result in case that foreign gold had not been obtained." The inconsistent answer did not convince even Joseph Pulitzer, who had himself recently pocketed fifty thousand dollars in profits from the patriotic public bond issue which he had sponsored!

The value of the syndicate deal is proved by the success of the venture. Gold immediately stopped flowing to Europe, and by selling bills at a loss in New York, Morgan and Belmont were able to keep the rates of exchange at such a point as to prevent further export until after the syndicate had fulfilled the stipulations of its contract with the government. They supplied, in fact, $16,000,000 in excess of the requirement, for which they received paper money. Every house which took any of the securities from the syndicate was first required to swear that none of the gold had come from the vaults of the government. The syndicate was in no way responsible for the fact that the gold reserve ultimately began to fall again, necessitating a further issue of bonds; that was due to conditions beyond the control of the bankers.

Had Congress and the press not educated the public in untruth during the life of the syndicate, history might have recorded a far different impression of the facts. The acts of the administration were condemned with no measure of restraint. Congress was sure that Cleveland and Carlisle had sold themselves for a mess of pottage. These two men, it was charged, had carried the fair name of the country to the sign of the three balls to barter it away, and had received in return a part of the spoils. If only the fair maiden silver could creep into the councils of the government, she would dispel the corruption through the radiance of her innocence! Sincerity and asininity together filled page after page of the *Congressional Record,* while printer's ink flowed freely in stamping on the front pages of Western newspapers the likenesses of the men who had robbed the country.

Every conceivable point of attack was used. The syndicate, said the *World*, was made up of Jews and non-Americans who cared nothing for the country and who desired only profit. Representative Haugen of Wisconsin tried to buy $100,000 of bonds for the Northwestern National Bank of Superior City, and after learning that the bonds had been sold to a syndicate, wired his bank: "In the matter of bonds, no American need apply." This was malicious slander, and yet he who writes the history of America on such evidence may be recording the truth as the people knew it. Much of the bitterness was undoubtedly due to the fact that the men involved were bankers—immense bankers—and such men were disliked then as today. It is significant, however, that Arthur Brisbane decided after lunching with Belmont that the financiers had not "choked the government."

There were some unfortunate acts on the part of the administration which increased the criticisms. On February 12 the public discovered that the contract had been withheld, and that by mutual agreement its provisions were not to be divulged until the following day. A greater feeling of indignation arose, however, when on February 20 Morgan and Belmont advertised the bonds of the government for public sale at $112\frac{1}{4}$. Every person opposed to the syndicate deal immediately pictured the government as having lost the difference. It was entirely forgotten that government bonds were selling as much below what had been paid for them when the syndicate made its contract as they were now selling above the purchase price. The public was certain that Morgan and Belmont knew they could sell the bonds for such a profit; and yet the two financiers themselves must have been surprised, and they clearly lost six or seven per cent by underestimating their own prestige, as the bonds readily resold for 119 before the allotments were made. "They saved the Government from going to default on its gold payments, and took large risks upon themselves to do it," said the *Bankers' Magazine* of the syndicate members, "and because a quick and large profit was the result of their own business ability and high standing, the unfair or unthinking multitude heap criticism upon the syndicate in no measured terms."

The fact that all the vituperation made no impression upon J. Pierpont Morgan irritated the press; he went silently about his business as though no storm were blowing about him; he read the billingsgate heaped upon him by numerous editors, and never once threw down his paper to rush out and shout his denial to some straggling reporter. Apparently the writers had the idea that he sat and gloated over his fat profits as he read. It was equally futile to criticize the head of the Treasury Department, for he, too, made no reply; and, the editors growing weary of the attack, the bond issue after February 27 occupied the front page of the papers only intermittently. Whatever criticisms may be made of the method used, the credit of the government had been sustained in spite of Congress, the press, and the public.

While no justification of a policy of selling bonds to private syndicates can be made, it is clearly evident that under the circumstances in February, 1895, no other course could have been followed. Certainly Cleveland and Carlisle would have refused such personally distasteful and nationally humiliating action had it been at all possible. The bankers rendered a great service to the country, albeit they were well paid for that aid. History must give Carlisle and Cleveland credit for the heroic step they took when as individuals they had nothing to gain and everything to lose. It was, however, an act necessary at the moment, and not the expression of a policy. In 1904 President Cleveland wrote of the incident:

> Without shame and without repentance, I confess my share of the guilt; and I refuse to shield my accomplices in this crime who, with me, held high places in that administration.

CHAPTER XVI PULITZER'S ATTACK AND THE LAST BONDS

THE success of the syndicate loan and the faithfulness with which Morgan and Belmont performed their part of the contract bargain are protrayed in the graph of the gold reserve after February 8, 1895. At the end of January the reserve stood at $44,000,000, while the redemptions in that month amounted to $45,000,000. Beginning with February the reserve steadily increased toward $100,000,000. In the meantime the withdrawals rapidly decreased; after the month of February they did not far exceed $1,000,000. The effectiveness of the loan is readily seen by computing the total loss or gain of gold from the announcement of the call until the final payment. On counting up his total receipts of gold for the first issue the Secretary found that he had lost over $21,000,000 in the deal; in the second issue the loss was slightly in excess of $9,000,000; but for the syndicate bids there was a gain of more than $1,500,000, not counting the gold turned in for paper money by the syndicate.[1]

It appeared that the difficulties of the Treasury Department in regard to the matter of the gold reserve might be at an end; but, however hopeful they might be, the officials were to go through several severe trials before March 4, 1897. Some threats of renewed gold exports appeared in the early summer, but through much cabling and some pressure exerted by the great financial houses the danger was avoided, and the gold reserve continued to increase steadily. The incident, however, was enough to show that the financial condition of America

[1]
Date of announcement	Reserve at announcement	Proceeds	Reserve at final payment
January 17, 1894	$69,757,824.00	$58,633,295.71	$107,211,727.00
November 13, 1894	62,001,106.00	58,538,500.00	111,142,020.00
February 8, 1895	41,340,181.00	65,116,244.62	107,553,773.00

Memorandum, Office of the Treasurer of the United States, dated March 31, 1896. Curtis MSS.

was still unstable, only a trifle being necessary to turn it again into an embarrassing problem. From New York there came at intervals little messages from the sub-treasurer which boded ill for the continuation of the peaceful days that had settled down over the gold reserve. The syndicate, although the provision was not in the contract as written, had agreed to keep up the gold reserve until some time in the late summer months; Assistant-Treasurer Jordan in his testimony before the Bond Investigation Committee placed the time at September 5. The last payment of the syndicate was made, however, on September 11. No one appeared to be certain just when the guardianship was to end; some said in September, others in October. The uncertainty soon began to tell, and by the first days of August the situation in the Treasury Department again began to appear alarming.

The Secretary set out on a tour of the Great Lakes to inspect the government lighthouses and other property under the supervision of the Treasury Department, but he did not leave his cares behind him. On August 3 he wrote Assistant-Secretary Curtis: "The withdrawals of gold reported in the papers this morning are somewhat discouraging, but I hope they will not continue to any great extent. If necessary you might telegraph me at Marquette, care of Commander Meade, Light House Steamer *Amarath*." The situation did not improve, and the syndicate came to the rescue. After August 13 the reserve, which had been steadily declining toward the hundred-million mark, required constant care. In an effort to keep up the gold fund the syndicate paid in a total of $81,243,677.56.[1]

The danger to the gold reserve brought renewed objections to the bankers' domination of government finances. On September 13 Charles Tracy wrote from Albany:

The complications arising from the withdrawal of gold are so serious that some way should be found by the administra-

[1] Curtis MSS.

THE LAST BONDS

tion to keep the gold reserve intact without putting itself at the mercy of the bank syndicate. Would it not be possible to have arrangements made with the Bank of France or the Bank of England, or the Bank of Spain, or all of them, so that from time to time gold could be secured and shipped from abroad by paying these institutions a commission? Mr. Hendricks, the president of the bank in New York, who was in Congress with me, first suggested this idea, especially in connection with the Bank of France. It does not seem wise to have the Treasury Department so absolutely in the power of New York banking interests.[1]

The suggestion was not new, for many people had been urging such a course since 1893.

As August wore on, the presentations of legal-tenders for gold became more and more insistent; the Treasury could only redeem them and hope that the fall balances would turn toward the United States. Still on his tour of the Great Lakes, the Secretary was watching the papers carefully and receiving from Curtis telegraphic reports. "Your telegrams were received yesterday, and I was glad to learn that the syndicate had made the deposits," the Secretary wrote Curtis. "The situation must certainly change within a short time unless our securities begin to return in large amounts. The cotton and wheat bills cannot be much longer delayed, and unless other causes intervene, they must turn the tide our way, or at least stop it from running against us." The flow of gold to and from Europe had acted so contrary to the normal law of things, however, that Secretary Carlisle was not certain that he could hope for relief on that score. Curtis, who was now Acting Secretary, was also alarmed and fearful that another bond issue might be necessary. He expressed his fears in his telegrams to the Secretary, who replied, "At what point it would be necessary to resort to another loan must be determined by the conditions existing at the time, and consequently I have reached no conclusion

---

[1] Tracy to Eugene T. Chamberlain; Chamberlain forwarded the letter to Lamont. Lamont MSS.

upon the subject," except, he added significantly, "the general one that the reserve must not be so reduced as to impair public confidence. It is very important in my opinion to preserve the feeling of security that has prevailed during the last few months, and when that begins to weaken, a remedy ought to be applied."[1]

The House of Morgan was not unmindful of the danger to the gold reserve. On August 21, after having on the previous day deposited $2,000,000 in gold in exchange for paper currency, Robert Bacon, J. Pierpont Morgan's junior partner, wrote the Treasury Department at Washington: "He [Morgan] is apparently not ready to-day to say to you that it is necessary to act immediately. Personally I can tell you, however, that the Reserve will fall below $100,000,000 this week or early in next and I can see no way to prevent it, as our stock of gold is practically exhausted. The exchange situation, however, is somewhat easier but not enough to put the price down to the shipping point and as long as it remains *above* gold will go in small quantities as it has been going lately."[2] Two days later the Secretary began his return trip to Washington. He was soon to find himself faced with the old problem of trying to keep the declining gold reserve from reaching the danger mark. On September 5 Assistant-Secretary Curtis was ready to pack his bag for another hurried trip to New York. "I am going over in 11 o'clock train tomorrow morning and will go directly to the Sub-Treasury on arrival," he wrote his mother on that date. "The gold reserve still keeps bothering us." Four days later it was doubtful, on account of the pressing situation in the Department, that Curtis could get away on his leave. "Make your visit," wrote Carlisle on the ninth. "I will go to G[ray] G[ables] next week if necessary." The Assistant Secretary did not find the condition in New York at all encouraging; the sub-treasury there had little available money. Jordan had $26,000,000 in silver dollars which could be used

[1] Curtis MSS.
[2] Curtis MSS.

and which were really his only available assets. He had in his vaults $40,000,000 in Treasury notes which, as he explained, were "literally without value, or rather a positive injury, if used in our daily payments, because of the ensuing loss of coin [gold] produced by their use in currency payments."

Curtis and Jordan felt that the situation was so serious as to require a new issue of bonds, and both recommended that the bids be thrown open to the public. Curtis urged Secretary Carlisle to take immediate action. "I would go to see the President this week," replied Carlisle, "except for the fact that I have fixed next Monday and Tuesday to hear arguments in two matters pending in the Department. . . . I think, however, nothing will be lost by a postponement of the visit until next week." The Secretary wrote the President: "Our New York friends are getting uneasy again, and are beginning to agitate for an additional issue. I do not think it advisable to take such a step at this time, and would like very much to see you and talk over the whole situation." [1]

September was an uneasy month in the gold market, and $17,000,000 went abroad in that brief period. Curtis was in New York a great deal of the time, but all efforts to stop the flow were unsuccessful. Gold was coming from Europe, but it found its way into the banks rather than into the government vaults. The redemptions at the Treasury Department were chiefly for export; from September until December $48,000,000 was sent abroad, while the withdrawals from the Treasury were $55,000,000. The last day of September saw the gold reserve again below $100,000,000, but the following month brought only $2,000,000 in redemptions. This was increased to $16,000,000 in November.

Congress, now overwhelmingly Republican, but no more hostile toward the administration than the previous session had been, met on December 2, 1895. Throughout the year the industrial situation of the country had been slowly but surely improving, but the fear for the standard of value had not di-

[1] Carlisle to Cleveland, Sept. 10, 1895. Cleveland MSS.

minished. In spite of the fact that the available balance in the Treasury amounted to more than $175,000,000, redemptions had continued. The government of the United States was still financially dependent upon the pleasure of individual bankers. In an address before the Chamber of Commerce of the State of New York on November 19 Secretary Carlisle said of the financial perplexities:

> Two years ago I had the honor to attend your annual banquet, and to make some remarks, in the course of which I said that the disposition and ability of the government to maintain its own credit at the highest standard, and to preserve the integrity of all the forms of currency in circulation among the people, could not be reasonably doubted, and ought not to be the subject of further controversy. While scarcely any one now seriously doubts either the disposition or the ability of the executive branch of the government to accomplish these objects, all who have given any attention to the subject must realize that, in the existing state of our legislation, the task is both difficult and expensive. Since that declaration was made here, interest-bearing bonds to the amount of $162,315,400 have been issued to procure gold for the redemption of United States notes and Treasury notes, and the obligations of the government on account of the notes remain the same as at the beginning. The notes are redeemed, but they are not paid, and if our legislation is not changed, no matter how often they may be presented and redeemed hereafter, they will still remain unpaid. If this policy of redemption and re-issue is continued, the interest-bearing debt will be greatly increased, while the non-interest-bearing debt will not be in the least diminished. . . . The government has undertaken to keep an unlimited amount of circulation notes equal in value to gold coin, and at the same time it has no legal authority to compel anybody to give it gold in exchange for the notes, or to pay gold on any demand due to it. The obligation is all on one side and the power is all on the other. . . . So long as these notes are outstanding, the slightest diminution of the coin reserve authorized by law for their redemption at once excites

a feeling of apprehension and distrust in the public mind, affects the values of all our securities, curtails investments, and more or less seriously embarrasses all the business affairs of the people. . . . With an almost constant drain upon it, with frequent and sudden demands for very large sums for hoarding or for export, and with no certain means of replenishing it, except by sales of bonds, it is absolutely impossible to maintain the reserve at any fixed amount, and, therefore, impossible to keep the public constantly assured of financial stability and safety.

Little could be expected of Congress; in his annual message, however, the President again presented the state of the Treasury Department, and, though he did not ask for authority to issue bonds, he reminded that body that he had proposed a remedy. If Congress, said the President, was not willing to act on his suggestion, he was ready to join it in any measure of relief which it might offer. But the legislators, already preparing for the campaign of the following year, made no effective efforts to aid the administration. The situation grew critical. On December 20 the President sent a special message urging some action before the holiday recess. "I ask at the hands of the Congress," he wrote, "such prompt aid as it alone has the power to give to prevent, in a time of fear and apprehension, any sacrifice of the people's interests and the public funds or the impairment of our public credit in an effort by Executive action to relieve the dangers of the present emergency."

On the same day came a communication from Jordan in New York: " 'The Philistines are upon us'—in other words private hoarding has begun—and we must stand both foreign and interior drains. We lose $4,069,000 practically today—the $100,000 is in our hands in greenbacks, but I refused to pay or count them today on the ground that our ordinary business would fill all our time—which was true. Whatever is to be done to be well done should be done quickly. If I were the Secretary, a temporary loan would be asked for immediately—that is, the power to obtain them to the extent of $100,000,000 with the promise that the loan certificates with the accrued interest would be received in payment of any future time loan. Whatever action is had should be pursued quickly—because we can't stand both drains."

Three days later the New York sub-treasury was contemplating withdrawing from the Clearing House. The banks were coöperating with the Treasury, and promised to refuse legal-tenders to those who wished to draw out gold. Jordan was not sure that it would be wise to withdraw. "The Clearing House took the action I suggested in our talk of today," he wrote to Curtis, "but I did not send in notice of withdrawal for the following reasons. It seemed to me that our withdrawal might add fuel to the fire, and that is needless. . . . I was further restrained from action, because of the idea which occurred to me that the Secretary in the near future in his endeavors to keep up the United States on a gold basis might need to use the Banks in the making of payments either to the Treasury or vice versa." An effort was made to suspend specie payments silently through the aid of the banks without allowing the country to realize that the action was being sponsored by the government. "I ask instruction from him [the Secretary of the Treasury] as to what action I shall take as to the Clearing House," continued the sub-treasurer to Curtis, "because of the serious state of things here and will put before you the consequences, as I see it, of its action in suspending specie payments, for that is the real purpose. First, in the joint action of the banks the government is involved, as putting itself in a state of suspension,—though not a party to the action except by silent consent, it must suffer from the consequences. Those consequences will fall in the first instance upon the Treasury—there has been a quasi-run upon our office today, and I am afraid that this will continue from day to day."

If only the legal-tenders could be kept out of the hands of the people, it might be possible to stop the bucket which had dipped again and again into the Treasury's gold. The banks in New York were as anxious as was the Treasury to check this withdrawal, because the gold was flowing to Europe. If any attempts were made to prevent the legal-tenders from falling into the hands of the public, however, the results would be a greater demand and a consequent increase in effort to secure them. "Mr. Tappan (of the Clearing House) informs me that it is the purpose of the Banks to refuse legal-tenders to those persons who desire to draw gold," continued the sub-treasurer in his long letter of December 23. He was doubtful of the benefits. "If this is done gold will go to a premium—legal-tenders and treasury notes will follow. This means trouble for the Treasury here and elsewhere."[1] Many feared that the same results would follow as in the panic of 1893—that New York might again be called upon to supply the needed money throughout the country and thereby be emptied of its resources.

The Christmas holidays came, and Congress recessed, leaving the Treasury Department in its critical condition. In the market the price of stocks had increased; but, because of efforts on the part of the banks and the government to keep the legal-tenders from the hands of those who desired to use them as a ladle on the gold reserve, there was talk of a premium on greenbacks. On Christmas Eve Jordan sent a message of cheer to the Washington office: "Order reigns in Warsaw. Stocks are booming and everything is for the best,—but there is another side to the shield caused by the refusal of greenbacks today to the shippers of gold—talk is loud . . . of a loan by the Government before the 1st which I hope will prove to be true, as I believe, if successful, that will settle the question for a year at least—provided the loan is large enough—75 or a 100 million, the larger the better sum. If the loan is not made we will be run upon from all points of the country, and lose gold rapidly—legal-tenders and treasury notes go to a premium, which will give us plenty to do until by the 'income' into the Treasury of legal-tenders, etc., the rate of money will put a stop to the drain."

In addition to helping keep the legal-tenders out of the hands of exporters, the banks came to the aid of the Treasury by offering to exchange gold for greenbacks. But, despite the

[1] Curtis MSS.

efforts of the banks and the Treasury Department to prevent redemptions, $20,000,000 in gold was dipped out of the stock during the month of December, $15,000,000 of that amount going abroad. On the last day of the month the reserve stood at $63,000,000.

It had long been felt that the Secretary would not again let the credit of the government fall to as low a point as it had reached in February, 1895. As early as September the Washington *Star* had said that "it is not believed that Mr. Carlisle will let the gold reserve be rapidly depleted . . . without taking some steps to check it." There appeared to be no way of avoiding the remedy which time had proved never to be a permanent cure, and over the country a cry for bonds was set up. Again the mail bag of the administration rapidly increased as the business men urged upon the President and his Secretary of the Treasury the necessity for prompt action.

Prominent industrialists traveling over the country studied the financial situation and reported to the administration. On December 28 James J. Hill wrote from St. Paul: "On my way home from New York I stopped in Chicago to learn as far as I could how much gold could be depended on from their Banks and others who would be at all likely to do anything to help to protect the Treasury and in that way to support all the business interests of the Country. I found the feeling among the best men that everybody should help, but when it came to naming what could be depended upon, there was nothing more than good wishes. I do not think Chicago would take over $5,000,000 bonds and pay gold for them. I am forced to the conclusion that New York will have to bear full three quarters of the entire burden and I am also reasonably certain that they will go to the full extent of their ability in any movement to protect the credit of the Govt and at the same time save the business of the Country." [1]

Had the office which Secretary Carlisle held been divorced

[1] Cleveland MSS.

from all occurrences outside his own Department, he might have had less difficulty in controlling the affairs directly under his command. This was not the case, however, and during the four years of his tenure of office every event, important or trivial, had its influence on his work. The year 1894 had been full of distractions, and 1895 was not entirely devoid of them. A boycott of the National Bank notes by labor in September was strong enough to ruffle the workings of the financial scheme; and just at the time when the problems were greatest and the Secretary was trying to readjust himself after the syndicate deal, foreign troubles nearly ruined his plans.

On December 17 President Cleveland sent to Congress one of the belligerent messages which he knew so well how to write. It concerned Venezuela and to the world seemed verily to bristle with threats of war. Carlisle had opposed the issuance of the message for the very good reason that it would affect the finances disastrously; he immediately felt its results.[1] Call rates, ranging generally between four and ten per cent, rose to eighty; in the flurry some $20,000,000 of deposits disappeared from the New York banks, and several stock exchange firms, both in New York and in Philadelphia, were forced to suspend. The New York Clearing-House Association held a meeting on December 23 and decided to issue certificates to any banks which might require assistance. The clearing houses of Boston and Philadelphia took similar action. What was most injurious of all to the Treasury, the tendency to hoard gold was greatly increased.

There occurred at this time one of those trifling incidents which often have serious consequences in times of international irritation. Lady Pauncefote and Miss Maude, wife and daughter of Lord Pauncefote, British Ambassador, were by some unfortunate error compelled on entering New York to go through the regular routine of travelers coming to the country, and were evidently not treated with any great degree of courtesy. Secretaries Carlisle and Olney handled the matter very well indeed,

[1] Hamlin Diary.

and their task was facilitated by the fine forbearance of Lord Pauncefote. The incident never became the property of the press, and no embarrassing consequences resulted.[1]

Whatever the actual danger of war with England, the administration was hit from two sides. In America many thoughtless people, especially in the West, felt that it did not matter if the two nations came to blows. The wealth of the world, they felt, had been gathered into the hands of the few, and there was no relief for the many. The Portland *Oregonian* expressed this feeling in the statement, "We are at the mercy of England, as far as our finances go, and this [war] is our only way out." On the other hand, England had become scornful of the American nation; her response to the agitation of the silver men was shown in her constant return of United States securities. While the feeling did not find open expression, Morley Roberts must have portrayed the general attitude of England toward America when he wrote, "Who can be proud of a politically corrupt and financially rotten country, with no more than a poor minority vainly striving after health?"

Although a bond issue could possibly not have been long avoided anyway, the Venezuela message was the event which precipitated the fourth issue in the Cleveland administration. There was a great deal of discussion over the type of sale to be used, and it was almost unanimously felt, as it still is, that Carlisle and Cleveland were anticipating another syndicate loan. There is, however, no positive evidence. It is true that after gathering statistics the officers of the Treasury Department reached the conclusion that, whether the sale was made through public bids or through a syndicate, the idea of widespread buying was delusive; the records clearly showed that the loans had inevitably been taken by the banks and bankers of the larger financial circles. It is true also that a few Democratic financiers did urge a syndicate loan upon the administration; on January 3 W. C. Whitney wrote Colonel Lamont: "Personally I think it very fortunate there is such an alliance to be had by the gov-

[1] Carlisle-Olney correspondence. Olney MSS.

ernment as Morgan and his great power. . . . I think the only thing hanging over the country really is the fear of the government's financial condition. I believe we should have a year of great prosperity but for that. The amount of business doing has been swelling through all the avenues of trade for the last two years—there is no better test than iron ore and pig. With almost no new railroads building the general demand for iron and its products has shown such an increase that the output of ore is getting to be the largest we have ever had. There is no question in my mind but what general business is swelling slowly throughout the country. If I were the President whatever I did I should do with Morgan. It will fail of effect otherwise and the President will not be credited with good judgment in the matter. I should make him take a lot of obligations, as he did before—as to outflow of gold . . . especially I should act quickly." [1]

Neither President Cleveland nor Secretary Carlisle, however, agreed with Whitney. In a letter to Senator Caffery written on January 5 Cleveland vigorously denied any negotiations looking toward a private sale; "No banker or financier nor any other human being," he declared, "has been invited to Washington for the purpose of arranging in any way or manner for the disposition of bonds to meet the present or future needs of the gold reserve." The Secretary later swore on oath that a syndicate deal had not been contemplated, and his statement was supported by J. Pierpont Morgan's testimony. "All our sales of bonds," Carlisle told the investigating committee which met in June, "have been made by public proposals except one. That was the exception; not the rule. . . . We departed from that rule in the case of the syndicate transaction simply on account of the exigency, which, as I have said, we supposed existed at that time; and when no such exigency existed, we pursued the course which had been pursued before." [2] Nevertheless, the rumors of another syndicate continued.

[1] Lamont MSS.
[2] Bond Investigation, p. 227.

No one was more offended by these rumors of private negotiations than Joseph Pulitzer. From his retreat at Lakewood, N. J., he began a campaign against the money power of Wall Street. Throughout the United States went telegrams asking if gold bonds would be bought on public offer, and covering the front page of the *World* were reproductions of affirmative answers. The recent demise of the *World* (1931) has revived the story of how the "editor defeated the House of Morgan in the 1896 gold crisis." Pulitzer defeated no one, but he did furnish valuable publicity among those people who, although unable to buy bonds, were a determining factor in the conduct of the nation's business. Incidentally, he deeply offended the group from whom aid must come. On January 3 James Stillman wrote: "The situation is very grave and discouraging. To have one's motives misinterpreted and reviled in the manner in which it is being done is very trying, and I think that the disposition exists among some of those prominently interested to withdraw from their efforts to coöperate to place a large amount of gold in the Treasury and save the Government from suspension of gold payments and the nation from bankruptcy. I am amazed at the ignorance, and if not ignorance the conduct of the *World* and of the leaders in Congress. It seems as if they were running riot. . . . I sincerely trust that my efforts to be of some service and relief have not produced a contrary effect and of all things I should hate to be misunderstood by . . . the President." [1]

Practically every banker in New York shared Stillman's views. Nevertheless, the next day Morgan sent to the White House an offer to purchase an issue of $200,000,000 of bonds on substantially the same terms as those at which he had bought almost exactly a year before. "I do not hesitate to affirm," wrote Morgan, "in fact to urge that such a contract would in every way be for the best interests of the Government and the people, and would be followed by less derangement of the money market, of trade, in fact of all interests including foreign exchanges,

[1] Stillman to Lamont. Cleveland MSS.

which until recently were in such an increasingly prosperous condition and I urge your serious consideration of such a contract. At the same time I recognize the effect of legislation which has been proposed and the discussions thereupon in both houses of Congress all of which might lead you to hesitate to make a private contract, and consequently, in view of the gravity of the situation, I feel bound to say, that if after a conference, in which I can more fully lay the matter before you, and without expressing any confidence in such a mode of procedure in face of previous failures of similar attempts but recognizing as I do that the responsibility of decision lies with you I pledge to you every influence and effort in my power to assist the Government in its endeavor to make successful a negotiation by public advertisement which shall result in the sale to the Treasury of 11,500,000 ounces United States gold coin, and further, I will so far as I possibly can, take such steps as will enable the Syndicate, which I represent, to join in making the negotiation successful to the full amount."

Morgan made his suggestion with the advice and consent of the other leading bankers of New York,[1] and he had arranged through the Deutsche Bank of Berlin and Messrs. Morgan, Harjes and Company of Paris for public sales in Germany, France, Holland, Belgium, and Switzerland.[2] No plans were made for sales in England, for the Rothschilds refused to consider any further purchases.

It is evident that the syndicate had not been formed with the intention of forcing the Secretary of the Treasury to sell bonds to its members; but if patriotism was the only motive which stirred the bankers to action, it would have been in better taste had they waited until the financial situation more definitely de-

[1] James Stillman wrote Lamont on January 9: "I sincerely trust the President will very shortly reply to Mr. Morgan's letter of last Saturday, which was written partly at my request, and thank him for his offer to cooperate with him etc etc. He certainly is entitled to something more than a telegram, and he can and will do much if merely appreciation is shown." Cleveland MSS.

[2] See circular issued by Morgan on January 14, at the dissolution of the syndicate.

manded their services. Moreover, while the low price paid the previous year by Morgan and Belmont had been justified by the seriousness of the situation, that excuse no longer existed, and the low bids which they contemplated were unwarranted and deserved severe criticism. Joseph Pulitzer rendered a real service to his country in issuing his appeals, through which public sentiment, already stirred by Cleveland's Venezuelan message, became so aroused as to force the price of the bonds upward. The editor offered to buy $1,000,000 of bonds at the top price, whatever that happened to be.

The rumors that the government was about to make another deal with a syndicate and that J. Pierpont Morgan had cornered the gold in order to force the President into an agreement were not only carried in the press, but heard in the halls of Congress as well. Midnight, January 5, 1896, however, found Secretary Carlisle writing out the announcement of the fourth bond issue of the Cleveland administration. The sale was to be public, and the amount $100,000,000. Pulitzer wired James Creelman, his representative at Washington: "Tell Mr. Cleveland that the *World* is as sincere in its congratulations as it was in its criticism and that he can depend upon it for its million and for anything else within its power that will assist in the success of the loan." [1]

"The Secretary of the Treasury had a right to offer bonds to the public and I do not see why the public should not be able to obtain the gold with which to pay for them," said Morgan in a press interview the following day. "The bond syndicate has no corner in gold and the notion that it has is absurd." [2] Even before the Secretary's announcement many bankers had begun work in the interest of a public loan. James T. Woodward had written the President: "I want to repeat somewhat that which I said to you last Friday morning. I believe, should the Government issue bonds, that you have friends throughout the

[1] Cleveland MSS.
[2] New York *Tribune,* January 6, 1896.

country that would take them, and you would be greatly relieved. It would seem to me that the Secretary could get up a scheme, and through well selected national banks in the different large cities could place them at a more satisfactory price, as they know just where the gold is located." C. C. Baldwin of Boston had written: "If you intend having the bonds issued they will be taken outside of the syndicate if the proper scheme is arranged to give them to the public. The present syndicate would not throw *cold* water on any issue made by the government. If they were so disposed public opinion would prevent you from it. Your friends are ready to aid you and I believe take the bonds at 110. If you wish to consult anyone of them you can intimate it to me."

The banks did indeed perform valuable service during the next few weeks. On January 9 James Stillman wrote President Cleveland: "As I wrote you day before yesterday, your efforts to save the country from financial calamity are not only fully appreciated, but will meet with the most hearty coöperation on the part of financial institutions in this City. This has been the universal expression on the part of every one I have come in contact with. . . . The position that this bank has taken from the start has been that the larger part of its gold reserve was at the service of the Government and that the bonds that the Government gave in return for it could be had by any dealer whose account with the bank entitled him to such consideration, upon the same terms as the bank obtained them, without its making any profit whatever upon the transaction. . . . I mention this to show you the spirit in which we are meeting the situation and I have no doubt but that many other institutions, according to their ability, are doing the same. If there was as much patriotism and appreciation of the needs of the Country elsewhere as there is among the business men and financial institutions in this City our present financial troubles and many others would be speedily and permanently solved. With this consciousness it is most painful to hear of its leaders in finance spoken of in Congress as robbers and must be very discouraging to them in their efforts to co-operate with you in maintaining the nation's financial honor." [1]

Five days later J. Pierpont Morgan sent word to the President that "my services are in every way at your disposal and that of the Secretary of the Treasury, and, if I can be of any assistance at any time, I shall be glad even to go to Washington, and I suppose, now that the matter is practically 'res judicata,' my doing so would not excite undue comment or curiosity." [2]

In an effort to secure bids for the new loan the New York bankers communicated with their correspondents throughout the entire country. The results were satisfactory, and some bids came even from Canada. On January 17 Woodward wrote that "the atmosphere is gradually clearing up, and the people will get through their heads that this bond is a desirable one for them to own, and if the volume could be run up into two or three times the amount offered it would do that which I spoke of before, and go far toward reestablishing credit;—that in itself would greatly protect the Treasury; foreign loans would be made, and merchants and others would not be in such haste to anticipate their debts." [3] Through correspondence with political friends and financiers both President Cleveland and Secretary Carlisle kept closely in touch with the sentiment in every part of the country.[4] The bonds were advertised in banks and post offices as well as in the press; in order that no new charges of dealing with the big moneyed interests might be hurled at Carlisle, every effort was made to acquaint the entire public with the issue.

Regardless of the assistance given by the banks, there arose in every bond issue the question whether the government could stand the drain on its gold reserve from the time bids were announced until the first payments for the bonds. In this fourth sale there was in addition the danger that the great amount of

---
[1] Cleveland MSS.
[2] Cleveland MSS.
[3] Cleveland MSS.
[4] The Cleveland, Lamont, Olney, and Curtis MSS. are all valuable in a study of the fourth bond issue.

CONRAD N. JORDAN

RICHARD OLNEY

the issue would so contract the currency in circulation as to injure business materially and place money at a premium. By January 9 it appeared that the sub-treasury in New York was again in need of gold. "The fact of my being in want leaked out," wrote Jordan on that day. But James T. Woodward and others came to the rescue by depositing gold and taking for it receipts which were to be credited on any bonds allotted them. The bankers were alarmed at the dangers attending the contraction of the currency. The speculators could not be barred from rigging the market, and they soon ran money to a premium. Zimmerman and Forshay, New York bankers, announced in a public circular:

> We are paying a premium on American Gold (full weight), U. S. Legal Tenders and Coin Notes.
> For the last few days we have paid the premium of one half of one per cent, and this rate seems likely to hold good for some time.
> Should you wish either to buy or to sell, we should be pleased to hear from you.
> Should you make us a shipment, we require the Coin notes separate from the Legal Tenders. The $5 bills in packages. . . .
> We have done an extensive business in this line within the past month.
> A number of our Customers having authorized us to bid for the new 4% POPULAR LOAN in their behalf, (some at prices fixed by them, others leaving the price to OUR judgment). We beg to call attention to the fact that we are prepared to make such bids for you and to furnish the necessary Gold on the dates when the respective instalments become due.

During January this firm withdrew from the Treasury nearly $1,000,000 in gold; the first week of February it carried away almost twice that sum, and during the next three weeks more than $7,000,000. This sort of speculation, which gathered in all the legal-tenders and gold that it could in order to pay the instalments of its patrons, was a cruel drain upon the Treasury; had the loan been popularly taken, it might have resulted in paying the same gold into the Treasury over and over with no increase to the reserve. Speculators were guided by the statements of the Treasury Department, through which they could determine when to present legal-tenders. Many financiers felt that the quantity of gold held in the vaults should not be published. "Is it not possible for you to keep the amount of the gold reserve from the knowledge of those persons who are gambling on the credit of our country?" wrote James Foster Milliken to the President on January 16, 1896.

It was not practicable to suppress the public statement of the Treasury, but efforts were made otherwise to check speculative practices. On January 16 the sub-treasurer at New York refused $170,000 of gold for counting from Zimmerman and Forshay. "These people Z & F made the rather cheeky proposition," wrote Jordan, "that I should examine their gold—purchased I believe from the Merchants Bank Canada and save them the labor—giving them a receipt, which they could sell in that shape. I very naturally declined to facilitate the 'pumping' dry of the Treasury of its coin. This firm—though I should refuse any firm the same privilege—has been . . . every day, and frequently two or three times a day, presenting small legal-tenders in lots from $10,000 to $40,000 at our counter—demanding and getting gold. They buy these legal-tenders from city firms and nearby banks, as well as some city banks who want to get rid of their small bills in this manner. They—Z & F—want to do as much of the business as possible, because they are making from $⅛$ to $½$ per cent—and as they have only a small force of clerks, desire us to count and inspect this gold for their benefit. . . . I don't think I should do anything to aid anybody in draining the U. S. Treasury. We shall lose enough gold between this and Feb 5th without aiding in the operation."

Before the bond sales were completed, Jordan needed someone to chase the money-changers out of his temple. "You will see in the papers about a 'row' in which I disturbed 'Jones Family Vault,'" he wrote to the Department on February 10. "Messrs Zimmerman and Forshay undertook to sell gold and deliver it on the floor of the Treasury. To this I objected and refused to receive about say $900,000 gold which fell in this category. Mr Zimmerman was very indignant at this behavior of mine. Said that I did partial things—permitted others to do things he couldn't do etc. I told him that I did not intend to permit the Treasury to be made a broker's office—that could and should not be done—and that he must take his gold away —which finally he did. I think I am right and when I agree with myself I follow Luther's example." [1]

Fear of contraction in the currency led the New York bankers to suggest that the time of payments of the instalments be extended in order to avoid any more pressure on the specie circulation than necessary. Secretary Carlisle, however, while determined to make the loan a success without disturbing the money situation, did not agree. He probably had in mind printing more money, the machinery for which had been greatly improved during the panic days of 1893. On January 16 he wrote to John A. Stewart:

All the suggestions made by you and other gentlemen at New York and elsewhere have been carefully considered, and the conclusion reached is embodied in the additional circular which appears in the public press of this morning, extending the time for the payment of instalments.

For many reasons, which I think you would fully appreciate if presented to you, it is not considered advisable to take any further action at this time in anticipation of an emergency which may not arise, especially in view of the fact that the Treasury Department will always have the power to make adequate provisions to prevent disturbance in the financial situation by the too rapid withdrawal of money needed in the circulation. What has been done heretofore to meet such a condition can be done hereafter, whenever and wherever necessary, in conducting the transactions connected with the pending

[1] Curtis MSS.

loan, and you can safely assure all who express any doubt upon this subject that there is no real ground for apprehension. The success of the proposed loan seems now to be assured, and it would be very unwise, to say the least, for the Treasury Department to do, or omit to do anything that might have a tendency to destroy or diminish the benefits expected to result from it.

The natural effect of such a large sale as $100,000,000 was to put gold at a premium. There can be little doubt that the demand, together with the activities of speculators, so tightened the money market as to crowd out many who desired to purchase bonds. The results were felt not only in New York but also in the cities of the West. James J. Hill, writing to Colonel Lamont from St. Paul, reported: "I have been watching the 'bond issue' with much interest since my return to the West, and as matters now stand I think the whole amount of $100,000,000 will be subscribed. If the public had the gold or could get gold from the banks they would subscribe quite largely, . . . the public can only get it by paying a premium of from 1% to 1½%. I think our banks here will send in bids for one million or possibly more, if in the meantime the premium on gold does not go much higher. However should the premium advance I think the effect will be to materially reduce the country subscriptions. . . . I will do all I can to increase the amount from our cities and from Chicago." [1]

As the time for closing the bids approached, the fear of the New York banks as to their ability to meet the demands and at the same time keep their required reserve increased. On February 1 Jordan wrote the Treasury Department that "the Banks here are very uneasy as to the effect of the loss of so much 'legal tender money' including their gold, etc., as available for reserve and I think would be very glad to know that some provision is to be made for deposits in the banks as heretofore. If there is any scheme will you be so kind as to telegraph me."

[1] January 14, 1896. Cleveland MSS.

February 1 found the gold reserve reduced to $49,000,000. Five days later the bids for the bond issue were opened. In the Secretary's large office, near a window overlooking the Potomac and the Washington monument, a table had been placed. There, in a black box, were the bids, each carefully dated. Exactly at noon the Secretary arrived and was received with cheers. Besides Assistant-Secretary Curtis and other officials, many were there who had come to present their bids in person; most of these were from New York, a few from Boston, and some from as far west as Cincinnati and Chicago. The efforts at popularization had been successful; 4,641 bidders had asked for bonds at varying prices, which amounted in the aggregate to $688,000,000. The vigorous publicity campaign made by the Treasury had undoubtedly helped, but the predominant reason for the unusual number of bids was the fact that in the previous deal a group of financiers had made a handsome profit.

As was to be expected, many of the bids were bogus, and many had been made with no thought of how the gold could be secured. The New York *Tribune* carried the story that a Michigan physician had bid for the entire $100,000,000. "I hope you will use a 'short shrift' with the 'dead beats,' " wrote Jordan on February 8, "and you have more of them this time than ever before. . . . I saw hesitation today in paying in on the part of the banks with the idea that they could get longer deposits. I don't like this because we want the vaults filled up in the Treasury with the greatest possible speed or it will leave a bad impression." As an afterthought he added, "Our friend Mr. M[organ] I think is very much disgruntled at the smallness of his amount and thinks there is something mysterious about it."

With the publication of the results of the bids, business, which had been at a standstill, again began to revive; call rates fell, and stocks commenced to increase in price. The loan had apparently been a success. The general impression is that the financial difficulties of the government came to an end after this issue of bonds, but the statement is far from correct. The loan stimulated business, it put the gold reserve above the $100,000,-

000 line, and it was soon forgotten by the public in the interest of the coming presidential campaign. For several reasons, not the least of which was the action of the New York syndicate, the gold assets had been held within the limit of tolerance during the pendency of the loan; and the reserve, which had been only $49,845,508 on January 31, stood on February 29 at $123,-962,980. The country in general was well pleased with the sale. It had little basis, however, on which to claim plaudits, for it was New York which had again come to the rescue of the Treasury Department. Of the $111,166,232.65 realized on the sale more than $97,000,000 had come from that city, and most of that amount had been subscribed by the men who from the beginning had been supplying gold for the Treasury.

The payments on the loan began on February 10 with the reserve at $44,000,000. On the day of the announcement of bids the reserve had stood at $61,251,710. The last payments were made on June 15, at which time the reserve was approximately $105,000,000, showing a gain in gold of about $44,000,000. The proceeds of the loan were slightly over $111,-000,000, which, after deducting the exports of about $28,000,-000, left a loss of some $40,000,000. In percentage of efficiency the last bond issue was obviously the least successful of all the issues made by the government during Cleveland's second administration. Considering the ultimate results, the loan was no more successful than the first two popular loans and not nearly so successful as the syndicate deal. By the first of May the exports had again started toward Europe at a rapid rate; $19,-000,000 was shipped during the month, and along with the export there continued a certain amount of hoarding. After reaching the high point of $128,000,000 on March 30, the gold rapidly faded away. When the Democratic National Convention met at Chicago on July 7, the reserve stood at $100,989,-867.81. The West had decided to appeal the case to the highest tribunal of the land—the people.

The public bond sale of 1896 was the last under the Cleveland administration. The four sales had brought to the Treasury almost three hundred million dollars in gold, but much of the metal had been furnished by the government itself in exchange for greenbacks and Treasury notes to those who desired to buy bonds. Never before had the public debt been so increased in time of peace, and the criticism evoked was unmeasured. One of the points upon which the opponents of the bond issues attacked the administration was that the receipts of the government were less than the expenses. Throughout Cleveland's second administration the President and the Secretary maintained that they were selling bonds only for the purpose of upholding the gold standard, but it is clear that during the first two years much of the money was used for meeting current expenses. The receipts were far less than the expenditures, and the only outside source of income was the sale of bonds. It helps but little to explain that the gold thus obtained was used only for redemption purposes, the legal-tenders being then utilized for paying the debts of the government. The money had come indirectly from bond issues, even though the sales had served the purpose for which bond authority was granted when they provided gold for those who desired it instead of their greenbacks.

No definite decision has been rendered by history upon the wisdom of issuing bonds in these years; the facts have been too little known to warrant impartial judgment. "The sales of United States bonds in the years 1894, 1895, and 1896 for the purpose of replenishing the stock of gold in the public Treasury have been greatly misunderstood by many honest people, and often deliberately misrepresented," wrote Grover Cleveland eight years after his retirement from the White House, but his explanation of the reasons for the actions taken in regard to the finances of the country was not accepted by the nation even at that time. Records have since shown that the public was grossly ignorant of the real conditions, and yet the bond sales can be justified only on the basis of what might have happened had they not been sold. The story is that of a fight against a calamity that never came, the results of which one cannot measure. It is perfectly obvious, however, that the struggle was one of heroic character. The administration fought devotedly under irksome circumstances. The manuscripts which are now available prove that the responsibility for the preservation of the standard of value fell especially upon four men—Grover Cleveland, John G. Carlisle, Richard Olney, and Colonel Lamont. Assistant-Secretary Curtis also deserves praise for his outstanding services during the bond negotiations. Gresham, Morton, and others rendered valuable assistance, but they do not appear to have been among the small group of men who were actually carrying forward the fight. The criticism of the public was limited largely to President Cleveland and Secretary Carlisle, and it was these two men who most often found themselves pictured as heartless enemies of the common man. But posterity will honor them as men who upheld the credit of the country at the time of its most trying attack and in the face of overwhelming difficulties.

CHAPTER XVII THE SILVER HERESY AND THE DEMOCRATIC SCHISM, 1893-97

By 1896 the Democracy was hopelessly divided on the question of free coinage, and the bitterness which had arisen grew in intensity as the spring wore on. Carlisle was no longer regarded as one of America's unimpeachably honest statesmen. In nominating him for Congress in the 'eighties Judge Hallam had said that his "little hands have been stained with walnuts in the Sixth District, but they have never become stained in Congressional representation. His bare feet have often got stuck in the clay mud of the Sixth District, but in official life they have always trod the road of righteousness." Everyone knew that the Kentucky leader was poor in worldly goods, but many now believed that he had at last come under the domination of the moneyed aristocracy. There had been no fundamental change in Carlisle's attitude toward free coinage, but that fact did not lessen the criticism. "When he became a single Gold Standard advocate," wrote Champ Clark in later years, "it nearly broke the hearts of his friends, who had followed his fortunes with unshaken fidelity and who had dreamed for twenty years of placing him in the White House."[1]

It was not an accident that the year 1896 saw two Democratic parties in the United States bitterly fighting each other. Some of the factors which led to this conflict had been growing for more than thirty years, but the division in the Democratic ranks had for the most part developed since 1890. Let us turn back to the beginning of the decade and follow the fortunes of the party to the dramatic crusade of 1896.

Carlisle, as Senator, had seen as early as 1889 that the tariff question was in danger of being entirely obliterated by the demands for free silver; he saw, moreover, the dangers to the

[1] Champ Clark, *My Quarter Century of American Politics,* I, p. 236.

party. Indeed, in the West and the South, Democrats and Republicans alike were leaving the two old parties as rats flee from a burning barn. Throughout 1890, 1891, and 1892 countless numbers of farmers, as well as the discontented of every other walk in life, joined the Alliance, the Populists, and other cults of a similar nature and began a persistent fight for local control. State leaders, both Democratic and Republican, were compelled to bargain in order to preserve the party vote for national elections. A letter of 1890 tells the story in Kansas: "We few Democrats in Kansas feel good. While we did not elect a member of Congress on a strict party fight we united with the People's party, and instead of two Congressmen as I wrote you sixty days ago we have five." [1]

Year after year, as the burdens of his debts, often unwisely contracted, grew heavier, the honest farmer became more convinced that he was being robbed of his heritage. Slowly the things which he had hitherto perceived but dimly became perfectly clear: he saw gold-bugs devouring his neighbor; he saw bankers in New York signaling the mortgage-holder to squeeze out the livelihood of his friends; he saw Shylocks and Rothschilds sitting over the bones of upright citizens; he saw conspiracies without limit and corruption without end. Democracy had come to a new crossroad, and the inhabitants of the trans-Mississippi region turned out in force to save it from complete destruction. "The campaign of 1890," wrote Frank Basil Tracey, "was the most thrilling ever known in the West. The country school-houses were packed with excited throngs. County, district and State conventions were attended by great crowds of eager, earnest and indignant farmers. The excitement and enthusiasm were contagious. . . . In vain the reports of the meetings were suppressed by the partisan press. In vain the Republican and Democratic leaders sneered at and ridiculed this gospel, while they talked tariff and War issues to small audiences. . . . All the ridicule, abuse and evasion aided wonderfully the Alliance cause. Its members shouted that they were being persecuted

[1] A. L. Taylor to W. C. P. Breckinridge. Breckinridge MSS.

THE SILVER HERESY

in their 'battle for human rights,' and converts came more rapidly."[1]

It was not alone in the West that new political doctrines were disrupting the old order; throughout the cotton kingdom the farmers were beginning to stir. During the 'eighties the small planter found each year that his cotton crop brought him less money and that his mortgage was harder to meet. Half the cotton growers mortgaged their crops and before harvest forfeited them on charge accounts at the stores of the merchants who had taken the mortgages. They, as well as the Westerners, saw conspiracies and corruption on every side and turned in great number from the teachings of the party which had dominated the South for a generation. Throughout the section in the elections of 1890 "the old guard of the Democratic party was put to shame—completely routed, as in Georgia, South Carolina, and Tennessee, or thoroughly frightened, as in Alabama, North Carolina, and Missouri."[2]

The great army which was disturbing the equilibrium of conservatism in America in 1890 had no single leader and no particular cause. Peffer, Simpson, Weaver, Mrs. Lease, and other Westerners wanted government ownership of railroads, subtreasuries for the storage of perishable and non-perishable products, and similar much-feared paternalistic measures; Western suffragists demanded votes for women; many clamored for prohibition; and the Southerners, fearful of negro domination should they weaken their party, would probably have been satisfied for the time with lower rates of interest. The political divergencies were nowhere more evident than in the various conventions which were held over inland America in an effort to form a national party. In May, 1891, fourteen hundred men gathered at Cincinnati in inharmonious assemblage; they were, said a Republican paper of Iowa, "a medley of malcontents,

---

[1] "Rise and Doom of the Populist Party" in the *Forum*, Vol. XVI, pp. 243–244.
[2] John Donald Hicks, "The Birth of the Populist Party," in *Minnesota History*, Vol. 9, pp. 219–247; Hallie Farmer, "The Economic Background of Southern Populism," in *The South Atlantic Quarterly*, Vol. XXIX, pp. 77–91.

one-idea hobby-ists, unreasoning fiatists, steadily unfortunates, 'born-tired' theorists, and blatant demagogues."[1] Out of the confusion was born the uncertain Populist party.

Before the convention adjourned, a delegation was sent across the Ohio River to interview Senator Carlisle. They talked railroad ownership, but the Kentucky leader was not interested. "Would you confiscate the railroads?" he asked, and even the most radical denied such an intention. But, said the Senator, it will cost fourteen billion dollars to buy the roads. "Are you willing to raise the taxes to pay for them?" Furthermore, he said, it would add 1,200,000 people to the number already appointed by the government. "How will you turn out an Administration with this hold upon the nation?" He severely condemned their sub-treasury plans. The delegation returned to Cincinnati with no hope of winning the leader of the Kentucky Democracy to their cause.

The excited Populist party had no one weapon wherewith to slay "the enemy," but there was a group just coming into prominence which possessed a keen sword in the demand for the free coinage of silver. The idea which the silverites were propounding was an old one, but it gained new life and new recruits from the ranks of the discontented. The officers of this silver army hoped to gain control of one of the old parties. If straws show the way the wind is blowing, then the Democracy should have been early alarmed. In the spring of 1890 there came to the desk of Representative W. C. P. Breckinridge from a wealthy and traveled but illiterate farmer of the borderland a letter full of significance and poor spelling:

Jericho Ky Ap 16/19

Hon W C P Breckinridge
 Dear Sir:
I hardly expected any reply to my communication but I was agreeably dissapointed the answer and contense of your letter indicates to me that you ar thinking of what has brought

[1] Quoted in Hayes, *Third Party Movements*, pp. 248-249.

our country to its preasent phynantial condition   you still I find
think the tariff is the greatest trouble   pardon me for the pre-
sumpsion in Stating to you that while the tariff neads reamid-
ing in many thing it is of utter insignificance to some other
matters that should be remidid first   the supply of money per
cappity is hurting the farmer and laborer worse than any thing
else   Senator Plumb said A few days ago that it was about 10
per capity in circulation   the next worst thing for the agricultural interest is the way Armoure & Co manage our cattle
interest. . . . in this great free American country men come
to me in my neighborhood and offer to work for 75 cts per day
and bord themselves and family if I will give them work and
A house to live in   at present prices I cannot employ them and
come out eaven   my tenants raise tobacco and corn on the
Shares and dont average 50 cts per day for their labor and
their families suffer for the necessarys of life and many times I
give them supplies with A full Knowledge that I will never be
paid   it is A terrible thing to sea little children suffer thus in
A country like this on Account of A few million Airs contracting the money in use to be able to buy too dollars worth of
property with one dollar   this is no longer A free country. . . . I have bin A Democrat always but I would not now
voat for Cleaveland Again for President to save him from the
hangman   our state will organise A farmers and laborers
union in many counties soon   Kansas and some Others or or-
ganised and Senators and representatives from Kansas or scared
already when this organization gets in pour it may Abuse the
pour but they have had the example set them and Mr bond-
holders and money loaner will have to hunt other ocupations
and then the starving children of this country may be able to
buey something to eat. . . .

                                                                 I M Smith [1]

During the campaign year of 1892 the silver issue grew apace. On May 2 J. B. Crouch, editor of the Hutchinson (Kan.) *Times*, wrote Grover Cleveland: "I trust I am not intruding too much upon your valuable time, by asking your advice in a matter

---

[1] Breckinridge MSS. Extra spaces have been left between the sentences in order to make the letter more intelligible.

that is perplexing to me in the extreme. Two years ago, I was chairman of the Democratic Congressional Committee in the 4th Kansas district, which includes Topeka. Contrary to my own judgment I yielded to a bare majority in the convention and turned the machinery and influence of the Democratic party in that district toward the defeat of Harrison Kelly the Republican candidate, and in favor of Mr. Otis, the alliance man. . . . Now, this year, it is proposed by a faction only of Democrats in the State to repeat the experiment of two years ago by having the Democrats join the alliance in five of our seven districts. Do you think Democrats can afford to do that as a matter of either principle or expediency? Would we not suffer grievously at the hands of the thinking people for uniting our forces with a party that advocates the wildest doctrines of finances? Is there, in your judgment a national emergency that would justify this sacrifice of principle?" [1]

Six weeks later a citizen of the midlands wrote: "I believe we are going to have a remarkable canvass and that the People's party are going to cut a wide swath in the West. My experience in the West inclines me to think that Kansas, Nebraska, the Dakotas, Colorado and the other silver states will go with that party. The Alliance people are bent on the silver issue and I don't think any thing can turn them with Cleveland on the one side and Harrison on the other." [2] Late in August Representative Joseph Wheeler wrote Cleveland from Alabama: "I have been among the people of North Alabama since Congress adjourned and regret to say, there is not that harmony of feeling which has usually prevailed, and I fear that an extraordinary effort will be made to carry the State for either Weaver or Harrison. On Wednesday last the disappointed Kolb [3] element and the Weaver faction fused, and agreed to support the Weaver electoral ticket, and efforts are being made to induce the Repub-

---

[1] Cleveland MSS.

[2] Emmett Orr to W. C. P. Breckinridge. Breckinridge MSS.

[3] Kolb was the gubernatorial candidate in opposition to Governor Thomas G. Jones, the regular Democratic nominee.

licans to support the Weaver ticket, in the hope that they can thus carry the State and take Alabama from the Democratic column. If that plan cannot be carried out, they will join as many disaffected Democrats as possible to the People's Party in the hope of taking off sufficient Democrats to carry the State for the Republican ticket. . . . The People's Party speakers made the most possible of your views upon silver." [1]

Before the close of the campaign of 1892 Professor Taussig wrote that "the same ancient fallacies which were advanced in the years from 1867 to 1879 to show that plenty of greenbacks were the one saving thing for the republic, re-appear now to show that plenty of silver will save us from ruin." [2] There was little in this development of silver sentiment, however, which would indicate that the conflict over the question would come in the Democratic party. That it did was largely the result of the appearance of two irreconcilable leaders—Grover Cleveland and William Jennings Bryan—and the succession of the Democracy to control of the government in 1893. There was also the widespread feeling that the party represented that citizen who had made his entrance into American political life in the decade after 1830—the common man. In 1891 Bryan wrote to an Eastern Democrat: "The Democratic party has always claimed to represent the mass of the people. The Republican party has long since ceased to do so. It stands nearer to the corporations and to the special interests than the Democratic party could ever get if it wished to, and when we desert the cause of the people we have nowhere to go but to the grave." [3]

The origins of the schism in the Democratic party may be seen in the entrance of William Jennings Bryan into national politics in 1890. It is true that there was then no particular significance in that event, but the years were to lend it importance. When he first entered Congress, Bryan had no definite princi-

---

[1] August 22, 1891. Cleveland MSS.
[2] "The Silver Situation in the United States," Vol. VII, Publications of the American Economic Association, 1892, p. 85.
[3] Bryan to A. B. Farquar, October 3, 1891. Bryan MSS.

ples in regard to finances. He admitted that gold was the best medium of exchange, but he opposed its single use because of its limited quantity.[1] The demands which were taking possession of the entire West, however, soon led him to become an ardent advocate of the free and unlimited coinage of silver. He wrote a friend on July 20, 1891: "The more I have studied the silver question the better satisfied I have become that the free and unlimited coinage of silver at the present ratio is the necessary settlement of the question." [2]

Many party friends regretted to see the youthful Nebraska politician turn to the cause of free silver, for he understood as few Westerners did the question of the tariff. Thomas Kilpatrick wrote him: "Though I do not mingle much in the world, still I know from many personal expressions which I have had myself that many of your friends whose opinion and friendship you would value are very sorry and disappointed to find you advocating what seems to them a theory that is fraught with mischief. . . . I will say to you frankly that I believe you are at present with the majority, and what troubles me is the belief that free coinage will win the day, and that its results must be learned by experience. In learning this lesson, I am greatly afraid that the farmer and the laboring man will get the worst of it." [3] But Bryan was not convinced, and a few weeks before the Fifty-second Congress opened he wrote A. B. Farquar of Pennsylvania: "I think the country has suffered enough by the fact that Democratic representatives from protected states insist on the policy of robbery simply because their people got the benefit of it and I am sorry if the same thing is going to be attempted on the money question. I cannot tell what the result of this Congress will be but if the Democratic party allows itself to be frightened away from the support of free coinage, I have little hope of our immediate success." [4]

---

[1] Bryan to Thomas Kilpatrick, Lincoln, Nebraska, July 20, 1891. Bryan MSS.
[2] Bryan to Kilpatrick. Bryan MSS.
[3] Kilpatrick to Bryan, July 13, 1891. Bryan MSS.
[4] October 3, 1891. Bryan MSS.

RICHARD P. BLAND

WILLIAM JENNINGS BRYAN

THE SILVER HERESY

Bryan knew that the future of his faction lay in the great number of discontented who were filling the West with their lamentations. "I believe," he wrote a silver friend, "that our gain is to be made from the independent party, and my hope is that when the sub-treasury idea and the loaning of money are dropped, as they will be before many years, that the independents will say then that they are Democratic in principle and come into our party and that the way for us to succeed is to show by our actions that we are better friends to the people than the independents and thus win them." [1] Later events were to prove the wisdom of his choice.

The definite conversion of Bryan to the silver standard was significant. To the Democracy it foretold a trouble not then apparent, and to the silver cause it gave a real political leader yet to be fully appreciated. He was able to give the silver movement a crusading and humanitarian element which it had previously lacked, and, in addition, he was able to fuse the various unrelated groups into a unity and to inspire them with a consciousness of power and a hope of victory. His success in amalgamating the Populists, the Independents, the Silver Democrats, and the Silver Republicans did much toward enabling him later to carry his own party, in spite of the opposition of Cleveland, Carlisle, and others, to a position which few felt it could reach.

One of the first of Bryan's ambitions in national politics was to make the cause of the West the dominant concern of the Democratic party. This is clearly expressed in a letter of 1891, in which he said, "I hope that the two wings of the Democratic party may flap together, but I believe the time has come when the western wing shall have some say so in regard to the flapping." [2] The next year in the minority report at the State convention of the Nebraska Democracy he began to put this belief into action with the definite announcement, "We declare our-

---

[1] Bryan to Edgar Howard, newspaper man, secretary to Bryan at the Chicago convention, and later member of Congress from Nebraska. Bryan MSS.

[2] Bryan to Farquar, October 31, 1891. Bryan MSS.

selves in favor of the free-coinage of silver."[1] The statement might have been more significant to the Democratic presidential candidate of 1892 had he used the singular pronouns.

A fight between the eastern and western Democracy was inevitable. The forces of battle were already arrayed when Cleveland took the oath of office as President on March 4, 1893. The President called Carlisle to assist him in the impending contest, and the four years which they shared were filled to overflowing with condemnation and abuse. As Senator, Carlisle might have lived his span of life with a great majority of his followers still believing in him. Every indication had pointed toward his wearing his toga for the remaining years of his life. The acceptance of the Secretaryship of the Treasury, however, made it impossible for him to avoid alienating many of his admirers—he must lose either his gold-standard or his silver-standard friends.

The silverite speeches made in the special session of 1893 unified the South and West and drew no small following from the East. "Talk about wages in this country!" exclaimed Senator Stewart. "The farmers have worked for twenty years for less than nothing. If a farmer has kept out of debt and supported his family by the most extreme exertions he is fortunate, but his farm is not worth more than half as much as it was then, and his entire labor is gone." Representative Hutton said that "no czar or kaiser would desolate any insurrectionary province as we are desolating the silver States of the West. You have struck down in those States everything that makes life dear. You have impoverished men in those States, men who were yesterday millionaires, and you have shut out the sunlight from the homes and hearts of all our people." Senator Morgan, physically ill, climbed laboriously up the Capitol steps that the South might hear his protest against the "calamity" which was about to befall the country in the repeal of the silver legislation.

Congressman Newton C. Blanchard of Louisiana told the members of the House Committee on Banking and Currency that "As matters now stand in the South, and equally so in the

[1] William J. Bryan, *The First Battle*, p. 72.

THE SILVER HERESY

States of the West, so far as our money affairs are concerned, we have been going from bad to worse. Things have been getting a little worse from year to year. Money has been getting scarcer each year among the people." [1] A few weeks later Governor Thomas G. Jones of Alabama wrote the President: "It is not so often what things *really* are, but what they *seem* to be, which controls votes in declaring for or against governmental policy. Whether right or wrong, the people generally throughout the South desire a larger circulating medium. They think that the volume of our circulation has much to do with the prices that of late years have obtained for their products. They believe that it is essential to their prosperity that there should be a gradual increase of the circulating medium, to keep pace with the increase of population and business of the country. Something on this line the people have determined to insist on, be the consequences what they may." [2] In the West a vigorous silverite wrote: "The people of Idaho don't desire to secede or fight but we would like to have John Sherman's head in an ore sack." [3]

While misfortunes were bringing discouragement to "Cleveland and his cuckoos," the great silver crusade was beginning to take definite form in the West and South. The Western congresses of silver followers did much to unite the leaders of the cause, and local meetings stirred the imagination of the discontented farmers. The movement did not lack leaders, each with his own peculiar appeal. None was more striking than Benjamin R. Tillman with his "wool hat" clubs and his pitchfork to stick in Cleveland's ribs, or Mrs. Lease with her advice to "stop raising corn and start raising hell," or Governor Altgeld of Illinois, friend "of the mocked and the scorned and the wounded, the lame and the poor." But greatest of all was William Jennings Bryan, for he combined a knowledge of political organization with his superb oratorical power. Writers, too, were busy, and

---

[1] Unpublished "Hearings," 53rd Cong., 1st Sess., p. 205.
[2] November 14, 1893. Cleveland MSS.
[3] Quoted in pamphlet, "Review of Financial Message of President," by George Wilson of Missouri.

out of Chicago came in June, 1894, W. H. Harvey's "Coin's Financial School" with its simple woodcuts, which taught that the goldbugs were destroying the money of the world and bringing suffering to the common man.

The last event which set the silver men against the gold advocates was the "syndicate" bond sale of February, 1895, to Morgan and Belmont, "princes of the aristocracy." Bryan declared in the House: "On these financial questions we find that the Democrats of the East and the Republicans of the East lock arms and proceed to carry out their policies, regardless of the interests and the wishes of the rest of the country. If they form this union, offensive and defensive, they must expect that the rest of the people of the country will drop party lines, if necessary, and unite to preserve their homes and their welfare. If this is sectionalism, the East has set the example." The rift in the Democracy was rapidly becoming impassable.

On February 22, 1895, "a number of leading bimetallists" met in Washington and began plans for the formation of a third party. A few weeks later the Silver Democrats in Congress, under the leadership of Bryan, issued an announcement challenging the efforts of Cleveland and Carlisle to hold the Democracy to the gold standard. But the silverites hesitated to begin the open pre-convention battle. They were relieved of this embarrassment, however, by definite action on the part of the gold Democracy. On April 13 President Cleveland wrote Henry S. Robbins of Chicago a public letter which marked the beginning of the fight in the Democratic party for control of the convention in 1896. "Disguise it as we may," said the President, "the line of battle is drawn between the forces of safe currency and those of monometallism." The words were a bugle call to both factions—the break had come!

The Silver Democrats gallantly picked up the gauntlet thrown down by the President. Bryan answered Cleveland's letter with a vigorous challenge. But the gold advocates, though small in number, were determined. Secretary Carlisle turned bravely to the task of destroying the monetary heresy within the

THE SILVER HERESY

party. On April 27 he wrote a friend: "It is, in my opinion, the first duty of every patriotic citizen to contribute all in his power to the promotion of a healthy public sentiment upon this subject, and while I may not be able to participate in this work to the same extent that I did in the contest for tariff reform, my services will be as cheerfully rendered now as they were then." [1]

Carlisle was particularly grieved to see the South turn toward free silver. Indeed, the Gold Democrats in that section were thoroughly alarmed. They began early in March, 1895, to lay plans for educating the rebelling Southern farmers, but cheap cotton and appealing promises of freedom from the merchant class were relentless enemies. Moreover, the press was hostile, and there was no money with which to establish gold-standard papers. Ben Carter, R. H. Clarke, and other Alabamans applied to New York for funds. On March 25 Clarke wrote Colonel Lamont: "I am going to New York tonight and wish to consult freely with Mr. Fairchild, Mr. Orr, and Mr. Gustave Schwab as to the organization and prosecution of a sound money campaign in the ranks of the Democratic party in Alabama." [2] In Tennessee Colonel Patterson was endeavoring to arrange for a sound-money convention, but Gustave H. Schwab objected to the proposal "for the reason that, especially in the country districts of Alabama and other Southern States, a campaign of education should be undertaken before such a convention could be profitably called and before it could be successfully held." [3]

Congressman J. C. Catchings of Mississippi frantically hurried off to New York to see what could be done to buy a paper "to bolster up our people." His efforts met with little success; on April 2 Murray F. Smith wrote Colonel Lamont: "I am free to say that I had not anticipated such a chilly reception to Mr. Catchings in New York. We, in Mississippi, are poor, and have no large investments in public securities which will be affected by this free and unlimited coinage of silver, and we are making

---

[1] E. P. Wheeler, *Sixty Years of American Life*, 216, 217.
[2] Lamont MSS.
[3] Schwab to Lamont, March 29, 1895. Lamont MSS.

a fight upon principle and for honest sound money, therefore the capitalists in the East have a much larger pecuniary stake than we have, and it is rather discouraging to us down here to feel that a proposition, which is manifestly to the interest of sound money, should have been so curtly received. If the Republicans in Alabama (as is currently reported) could afford to spend $40,000.00 or $50,000.00 to aid Kolb in his efforts to defeat Governor Oates, it seems to me that sound money men, both Democrats and Republicans, could, and would, take hold of this matter." [1]

A few days later Catchings wrote Lamont: "A little free silver book called 'Coin's Financial School' is being sold on every railroad train by the newsboys and at every cigar store." And, more significant to the sound-money followers, he added, "it is being read by almost everybody." "The low price of cotton," said the Congressman in closing, "is the strongest foe we have." [2] On April 8 he again wrote: "Everything is wild in this State, though we hope to make an impression at least. Unless we can check it, I am gone next year, though of course my fortunes are as nothing compared with the principles involved." Eight days later he commented, "We are about to begin our canvass, but the tide is running strong against us now."

Perceiving the urgency of the situation, Carlisle turned the administration of the Treasury Department over to Assistant-Secretary Curtis and began a tour of the borderland and upper South. On May 20 he spoke for two and one-half hours in his home city of Covington, Kentucky, concluding:

You have been detained too long already, but in view of the determination exhibited in some quarters to criticize my personal record upon this question rather than answer my arguments, I think my old friends here at my own home have a right to expect at least a brief reference to that subject. It is proper, in the first place, to say that my opposition to free coinage is not dictated by any prejudice against the use of silver as

[1] Lamont MSS.
[2] Catchings to Lamont, April 6, 1895. Lamont MSS.

the standard of value merely because it is silver, nor by any preference for the use of gold as the standard merely because it is gold; for if the conditions now existing were reversed, if silver was our standard of value and gold was depreciated in value as silver now is, I would be as much opposed to a change from silver to gold as I am now to a change from gold to silver. The preservation of the existing monetary unit and measure of value upon which the contracts of the people have been made and the wages of labor have been adjusted is the vital thing involved in this controversy; for if the standard is preserved everybody is willing to use and will use every available form of currency that can be kept equal to it in value. As long as there appeared to be reasonable ground for the hope that silver could be raised to a parity of value with gold at the ratio of 16 to 1 by the separate action of the United States, I was willing to make the experiment, but I was never willing to make it by legislation providing for the free and unlimited coinage of silver at that or any other ratio. The only speech I ever made in Congress on this subject was delivered in the House of Representatives more than seventeen years ago, at a time when the value of the bullion contained in a silver dollar was only about seven cents less than the value of the bullion contained in a gold dollar, and I, together with many other opponents of free coinage, believing that a restoration of silver to our mints would bring it to a parity with gold, supported a measure providing for the limited coinage of silver dollars on Government account—not on account of private individuals and corporations as is now proposed. Fifteen years' experience, however, demonstrated that those of us who believed in 1878 that a larger use of silver by the United States would enhance its price or value were mistaken. Instead of increasing the price of silver, it continued to fall with greater rapidity than before, notwithstanding all the efforts made by the Government to uphold it, until now the bullion contained in a silver dollar is worth only about half as much as the bullion contained in a gold dollar. The conditions have entirely changed since 1878, and I do not understand that even our free-coinage friends in Kentucky or elsewhere now contend that any legislation by this country alone could place silver on a parity with gold at the ratio of 16 to 1. On the contrary, they insist that the free and unlimited coinage of silver at that ratio would give the people cheap money, and I agree with them that it would have that effect, but it would not be cheap money if it were equal in value to gold.

Two days later Carlisle opened the official Southern campaign with his speech before the Sound Money Convention at Nashville, Tenn. Here he met the business men of the section and asked for their approval of the gold standard:

> I do not think that the importance of the questions you are called to consider can be overestimated, or that the gravity of the situation can be overstated. The proposition to revolutionize our monetary system and thus destroy the credit of the government and the people at home and abroad, violate the obligations of all contracts, unsettle all exchangeable values, reduce the wages of labor, expel capital from our country, and seriously obstruct the wages of labor, and seriously obstruct the trade of our people among themselves and with the peoples of other countries, is one which challenges the intelligence, patriotism and commercial honor of every man to whom it is addressed. No matter what may be the real purposes and motives of those who make the proposition to legalize the free and unlimited coinage of silver at a ratio of 16 to 1, these are the consequences involved in their scheme, and, in my opinion, they cannot be avoided if it should be adopted. In no part of the country will the consequences of such a policy prove more injurious to the material interests of the people than in the undeveloped and progressive South. . . . Your . . . coal and iron, your fertile soil, adapted to the growth of cotton, sugar and many other products which no other part of the country will yield, your unrivaled facilities for the manufacture of iron and steel, cotton goods, lumber, oil, furniture, and almost innumerable other articles which can be cheaply produced from the raw materials within your limits, constitute the elements of a marvelous growth and prosperity which nothing can prevent if the people of the South will continue to exhibit in the

future the same spirit of conservatism and the same devotion to principle that has characterized them in the past. The world has never witnessed a grander exhibition of courage and fortitude than was presented here when a defeated and impoverished people, without money or credit, and almost destitute of the tools and implements necessary to the performance of manual labor, went uncomplainingly to work to re-establish their social order, renew their commercial relations, and reconstruct their industrial system; and I am unwilling to believe that the same people can now be so discouraged by a temporary business depression, or so moved by appeals to their prejudices, that they will hastily resort to new and hazardous experiments with the currency in which all their transactions must be conducted.

"It is not necessary," he said of the silverites, "to impeach their motives in order to answer their arguments, nor would it be wise or proper to underestimate the intellectual and material forces behind this great popular movement in the South and West—a movement which now seriously threatens to disrupt existing political organizations and reform party lines; but, no matter what may be the motives or the present numerical strength of our opponents in this controversy, the merits of the policy they propose to inaugurate must be subject to the tests of reason and experience, and if it is shown to be impracticable, or fundamentally wrong in principle, we may be confident that it will not finally command the support of a majority of our people."

On May 25 Carlisle resolutely faced a group of hostile farmers at Bowling Green, Kentucky; he spoke to them in their own language.[1] "Suppose, my farmer friends," he said, "that a bushel of wheat was worth more in the markets before it was converted into flour than it was afterwards, you would sell it in the form of the wheat because by having it ground you would lose money.

[1] There was some opposition to the speech. In opening he said: "I came here first in 1871, and again at a later date . . . as a Democrat to discuss the public questions which were then engaging the attention of the people and nobody then questioned my right to do so."

So, if one ounce of gold bullion is worth more in the markets of the world in the form of bullion than it would be in the United States under the law after it was coined, no man would have it coined, but would send it out of the country." It was the same, he stated, as if Congress were to undertake to say by law that one bushel of oats should be worth a bushel and a half of wheat, and if one found that this was not true, "that you could sell your bushel and a half of wheat for more than your bushel of oats, or if you found you could procure in the market, in the way of exchange for other commodities, more with your bushel and a half of wheat than with your bushel of oats, you would never use your bushel and a half of wheat in payment of your debts, but would sell it and use your bushel of oats." The value of the silver dollars at that time, Carlisle told his audience, was due to the fact that the government coined them in a limited amount and gave them equal value with gold by statute provision and by every consideration of good faith. This could not be done if they were coined for and returned to individuals. The poor man deserved as good money as the rich man, he said; and if silver was the money of the poor man, it was his purpose to keep it as good as the money of the millionaire.

Finally, said Carlisle in closing, he wished to state five propositions which he held himself ready to maintain anywhere:

First—That there is not a free-coinage country in the world to-day that is not on a silver basis.
Second—That there is not a gold standard country in the world to-day that does not use silver as money along with gold.
Third—That there is not a silver-standard country in the world to-day that uses gold as money along with silver.
Fourth—That there is not a silver-standard country in the world to-day that has more than one-third as much money in circulation per capita as the United States have; and
Fifth—That there is not a silver-standard country in the world to-day where the laboring man receives fair pay for his day's work.

THE SILVER HERESY 443

Before his return to Washington, Carlisle made other speeches; the tour was plainly an effort to hold the South in line. As a loyal Democratic section for thirty years, it owed allegiance to Grover Cleveland, for he still represented the genuine Democracy. The South was, in fact, one of the chief battle-fields of this pre-convention conflict. Whichever faction of the party won this region would have a decided advantage in the coming convention. On May 25 John P. Irish wrote the President: "The Memphis convention and Mr. Carlisle's speeches have made it apparent that the business forces which control the South stand with you. Immediately the politicians pause. Their noise lessens. They fear that after all the South may not favor discredit and disorder, and they are waiting for their second wind to shoot on the other side. The campaign for sense and sound money was wisely planned when the South was selected for its field."[1]

Meanwhile, the silverites also were busy in the South. A committee in Jackson, Tenn., had written Bryan on April 22: "In the great financial battle to be fought for gold monometallism, it is apparent that an organized movement is on foot to throw the South into the gold column. We want to start a movement for the organization of friends of silver in Tennessee and all over the South."[2] The Nebraskan needed no further prompting—he spoke in Nashville on the evening following Carlisle's address. Throughout the next few weeks the opposition was feverishly preparing "to demolish the gold men." A great non-partisan meeting was planned for Nashville in June, and out over the blue-grass section of Tennessee and into the foothills of the Appalachians was sent a legion of posters. Josephus Daniels wrote Bryan from Raleigh, North Carolina, "I hope to be present at the *real* Sound Money Convention and meet you."[3]

[1] Cleveland MSS.
[2] Bryan MSS.
[3] Daniels to Bryan, June 1, 1895. Bryan MSS.

When the convention met, Bryan was present, busy writing its resolutions. It was here that a definite organization was begun with the intent of capturing the Democratic convention in the following year.[1] The plan adopted was that which had been used in Nebraska in 1894.

Throughout the year 1895 the party battle raged, and the advantage was decidedly with the silver followers. As early as March 23 Cleveland had written Richard Watson Gilder of the *Century* that "If occasional words of encouragement did not reach me like a breath of fresh air in this dreadful atmosphere, I would be in danger of sinking into a condition of mere anxiety for my release from the things that surround me here." All over the midlands, the West, the South, and even the East the Populists were uniting in "unholy" matrimony with the Democrats, and a legion of "Popocrats" was springing up. The doctrine of free silver was consuming the land, and everywhere was Bryan, turning the tide ever in his favor with a vigorous speech or letter.

"Matters are certainly looking better for the Silver cause—and what is still better—within the Democratic party," wrote P. A. Regan of Boise City, Idaho, to Bryan on April 24. "I thank you very much for your note and clippings. I used them with good effect," said Josephus Daniels in a letter of June 1. A few weeks later C. O. Baldwin wrote from Duluth, Minnesota, "I have been watching with considerable interest your progress in political matters and I believe you are on the right track and that you and your free silver idea are going to win." [2]

By the middle of June, Indiana and Illinois had been organized, and effective work had been done in Ohio. John R. Commons, then a young professor in Indiana University, wrote: "So far as I have been able to observe, Easterners are not well posted regarding the strength which the movement has accumulated. They have some idea of it, but there is far from a

---

[1] The idea had been present since early in the year, but no definite plan of action had been adopted.
[2] Bryan MSS.

general understanding of the almost unanimous Western feeling in favor of the free coinage of silver. . . . At the last election, Indiana elected a solid Republican delegation in favor of free silver. One of the delegates informed me that three fourths of the Republicans of Indiana are for free coinage. It is freely asserted among Democrats that three fourths to four fifths of them throughout the State are in the same boat on this issue." [1]

On June 5 the Illinois Democrats held a silver convention at Springfield. On the previous day the trains had disgorged a motley crowd upon the city. "Buck" Hinrichsen was there in his shirt sleeves. "Gov. Altgeld's officeholders, together with the employes of the Secretary of State, a few hundred disappointed applicants for Federal patronage, aided and abetted by a faction of Democrats who want to get out of the party a lot of the old leaders, are here howling for free silver in anticipation of tomorrow's convention," wrote the Chicago *Tribune* on June 4. On the following day the delegates declared for the free coinage of silver in no uncertain terms. "A puny baby was born here today," wrote the *Tribune* on the sixth. "It is a weakling. A five months' young one, and it will of necessity be fed on a bottle. 'Buck' Hinrichsen stands godfather to it and John P. Altgeld is godmother. 'Billy' Bryan gave it his benediction and blessing."

The editor was soon to learn the enormity of his error, and the gold advocates the strength of their opponents. The gold followers were certainly not hopeful. Early in May, A. B. Farquar wrote Henry Thurber, secretary to the President: "Have been pretty well over the country since we last met, traveling through twenty-four States, more than ten thousand miles, South and West. The people in that section are simply crazy upon the money question; they cannot discuss it rationally." [2] On July 12 David R. Francis of St. Louis reported that "the free silver craze is still predominant in Missouri." A month later a citizen of Mississippi compared the excitement and pas-

[1] *American Investments,* July, 1895, p. 350.
[2] Farquar to Thurber, May 2, 1895. Cleveland MSS.

sion in his State with those of the secession days.[1] "If there was a penitentiary devoted to the incarceration of those who commit crimes against the Democratic party," Cleveland wrote Dickinson, "how easily it could be filled just at this time." [2]

As the fall elections approached, the conflict in the party grew more intense. In August the free-coinage Democrats held a conference at Washington for the purpose of perfecting their campaign machinery. A few days afterwards John W. Tomlinson of Alabama wrote Bryan: "I have just returned from the conference of the free coinage Democrats at Washington, having stopped by the Tennessee summer resorts on my return, and I want to say that I talked with a great many of those present, and nearly every one I talked with was in favor of nominating you for President, which I hope will be done." [3] Almost two months previously Josephus Daniels had written: "We are going to send a solid 16 to 1 delegation to the next Democratic National Convention and nominate nobody whose record and position are not in accordance with the platform. Personally I should rather see you head the ticket than anyone else." [4] On October 16 the first issue of the *National Bimetallist* appeared, and its work in the cause of free silver was exceedingly important. The paper carried at its head extracts from Carlisle's and Sherman's silver speeches of 1878.

Secretary Carlisle, still worrying over the gold reserve, found time to address the Reform Club of Boston on October 12 and the New York Chamber of Commerce on November 19. He pleaded for a sound system of currency and at the New York meeting declared that the theory that the government could create money by the mere process of stamping a value upon it was a vagary. "The proposition that a promise of the government to pay money is money," he said, "is just as absurd as the proposition that a promise to deliver a horse is a horse."

---

[1] Francis to Henry F. Thurber, July 12, 1895. Cleveland MSS; Thomas C. Catchings to Lamont, August 14, 1895. Lamont MSS.
[2] Cleveland to Dickinson, July 31, 1895. Cleveland MSS.
[3] Tomlinson to Bryan, August 26, 1895. Bryan MSS.
[4] Daniels to Bryan, June 1, 1895. Bryan MSS.

The banker, the merchant, the farmer, and the mechanic must all prosper together, he told the dinner guests; "there must be perfect freedom of production and exchange and to secure these there must be sound and stable money and a free instrument of credit." He characterized the idea that America could punish England or enrich herself by destroying the value of her own money as "one of the most remarkable delusions of the age."

A few days later there appeared in the Washington *Star* a cartoon depicting Carlisle in wilderness garb, with the caption: "In Those Days Came John, Preaching in the Wilderness." And, indeed, in those days the midlands did not comprehend that there were such peoples as "Yurrupeans." "The world was shut out from us," Thomas Beer tells his readers, "and to a degree you people cannot get, even from the best descriptions in Willa Cather and *The Grandmothers*."[1] But if inland America was not cosmopolitan, it was patriotic; and patriotism meant the free coinage of silver. Over the unfortunate land the *National Bimetallist* spread its soothing doctrine:

ORGANIZE! Now is the time—your city, town or neighborhood the place. The National Bimetallic Union is in the field to stay, and has raised the righteous standard of "16 to 1," under which may freely gather in full confidence and security, and without partisan feeling or prejudice, all classes and conditions of people, devoted to the support of a common purpose, and the speedy, certain accomplishment of a national necessity.

The restoration of silver to its constitutional right as money of the people and equal companionship with gold at 16 to 1 is the only issue before us, and the zealous, determined, well united action of American patriotism will in '96 finally successfully overthrow the despotism of the gold syndicate and give us an administration free from the disloyalty, avarice and cruel disregard for our sacred institutions, which in their wanton operation are destroying our common comfort and painfully distressing all departments of life outside the conscienceless pathways of the Golden Empire of Wall Street.

[1] Thomas Beer, *Hanna*, p. 118.

Our printed instructions are simple, explicit, easily followed and involve little expense. They point the short route to certain victory. . . . The "Silver Craze" is not dead! It will not die!

Free silver was everywhere; it went with the farmer on his icy chores in the winter of '95, and it followed his plow in the springtime. Thousands sent their dimes and quarters to the *National Bimetallist* for tie-pins, lapel-buttons, and cuff-links that they might show their allegiance. Western swains talked boastfully to their inland ladies of what they would accomplish when the "bloated money-holders" were destroyed; dusty farmers condemned the "furrin conspirators" as they swapped "chaws" of tobacco over neighboring fences; and old ladies mixed 16 to 1 with their gossip. The great crusade was shoutingly in progress by the spring of 1896.

On January 16 Edwin B. Light, Secretary of the National Bimetallic Union, wrote Bryan: "Our plan is to work on the lines you are working on. Have each person stay with his party until the Conventions meet. Then if they refuse to adopt such a platform as you can approve, then notify them that you have come to the parting in the road." On January 20, 1896, many friends of silver gathered at the Baltimore and Ohio station in Chicago to begin their journey to Washington—at a fare and one-third—to talk over the silver hopes.

Meanwhile, Cleveland and Carlisle were discouraged; the gold reserve was again nearly exhausted, and the nation, spurred on by Joseph Pulitzer, was sure that the government was contemplating another bond sale to the capitalists. "I have never been so depressed as now in my view of the affairs of my country and my party. I have never felt so keenly as now the unjust accusations of political antagonists and the hatred and vindictiveness of ingrates and traitors who wear the stolen livery of Democracy," wrote the President. Cleveland's only hope of saving the party was that the South might see the error of its ways before July, but the hope was slender.

Indeed, the "goldbugs" were meeting defeat everywhere.

THE SILVER HERESY 449

The situation in Illinois, wrote Calvin Tomkins on March 24, was "exceedingly complicated," but, he added, "everything is being done there for Sound Money . . . that can be done." A month later, in spite of the donations of "John R. Walsh and other well-to-do friends of Sound Money in Chicago," he was complaining of a lack of funds. W. D. Bynum was greatly discouraged with the outlook in Indiana. "In all my long experience in politics, I have never seen so dark a day as the present —for our party and the country at large," wrote Samuel M. Shaw of Cooperstown, N. Y., editor of *The Freedman's Journal*. "It all grows out of the silver craze. It, even to a greater extent than you might deem possible, prevails among the Farmers of this State—who are seeing very hard times. It looks as though the silver men will have control at Chicago—and that means party disruption. N. Y. Democrats will 'none of that.' "[1] From a rural editor in Kentucky came the wail: "Politics down here has gone mad. Every crank in the country is loose and nothing less than a stone wall will stop them. Four men out of seven are to be made wealthy by a simple twist of the wrist and paupers are to become princes when silver assumes the position it occupied previous to 73 so they say."[2]

Late in March a determined effort was begun in the Middle West to stem the rising tide of silver. Activities were centered in Chicago with the idea of winning, if possible, the States of Illinois, Indiana, Ohio, and perhaps Missouri.[3] Secretary Carlisle packed his bag and hurried off to Chicago, where, on April 15, he gave before the workingmen a sound-money address which Champ Clark has called "the best single gold-standard speech ever delivered since the world began."[4] With blue-clad policemen scattered liberally throughout the crowd and boisterous silverites watching for an opportunity to scotch his argu-

---

[1] Shaw to Lamont, April 18, 1896. Lamont MSS.
[2] Emmett Orr to W. C. P. Breckinridge, Owenton, Ky., April 20, 1896. Breckinridge MSS.
[3] Bynum, Cleveland, and Lamont MSS.
[4] *My Quarter Century of American Politics*, I, 236.

ments, the Secretary wasted no time in preliminaries, but came directly to the point:

Whether the general business of the people shall be transacted with good money or bad money, whether the wages of labor shall be paid in a sound and stable currency, with full purchasing power in the markets where they are exchanged for the necessaries of life, or in a depreciated and fluctuating currency, having no fixed value and therefore bearing no permanent relation to the currency prices of commodities, are questions which affect the comfort and happiness of every home and the peace and prosperity of every community. While all are deeply interested in the settlement of these questions, it is unfortunately the case that all will not be equally affected by an erroneous decision upon them. The wealthy man, the man who has accumulated property or hoarded money, is always exempt from many of the most serious consequences of a financial or industrial disturbance. He has both means and credit, and while he may be subjected to much loss and inconvenience, neither he nor his family will be pinched by hunger, or compelled to go without raiment or shelter.

It is the poor man and the man of moderate means—the man who has not been fortunate enough to accumulate property or money, but who depends upon his wages or upon the products of his own labor for the means of supporting himself and his family—that always feels the first and most disastrous effects of a business or industrial depression, no matter whether it results from a depreciated and fluctuating currency or from other causes. Such a man has nothing to dispose of but his labor, and nothing with which to support himself or his family but his wages or the proceeds of his own labor, and any policy that even temporarily suspends or obstructs the industrial progress of the country by diminishing the demand for the products of labor, or by impairing the capacity or disposition of capital to employ labor, must be injurious to his interests and inflict more or less suffering upon all who are dependent upon him. Labor cannot be hoarded; the idle day is gone forever; lost wages are never reimbursed; and therefore, steady employment and good pay in good money are essential to the comfort and happiness of the American laborer and his wife and children, and he will be unfaithful to himself and to them if he does not insist upon the adoption and maintenance of such a policy as will most certainly preserve the value and stability of all our currency and promote the regular and profitable conduct of all our industrial enterprises. He cannot prosper when the country is in distress, when its industries are prostrated, its commerce paralyzed, its credit broken down, or its social order disturbed; nor can he prosper when the fluctuations of the currency are such that he cannot certainly know the value of the dollar in which his wages are paid, or estimate in advance the cost of the necessaries of life.

The gold advocates were pleased, and Senator Vilas read the speech into the *Congressional Record.* "Whatever may have been the previous sentiments of those workingmen who were fortunate enough to hear Mr. Carlisle, when they left the Auditorium they were convinced that 50-cent dollars were not the dollars for them," said the *Tribune.* "His speech is a plain, straightforward, business-like talk, which will sweep away the falsehoods with which Altgeld, Hinrichsen, and some of the labor demagogues have been deceiving Illinois workers." But the silverites were not moved. "The boxes and a considerable portion of the parquet were well filled with federal office holders, bankers, and other horny-handed sons of toil whose flashing diamonds, spotless linen and fine broadcloth lent éclat to the occasion, and gave a somewhat patrician tinge to an assemblage that might otherwise have been too severely plebeian in character," wrote a correspondent of the *National Bimetallist.*[1] The Chicago *Record* spoke of Carlisle as coming "fresh from the banquet table of Wall Street goldbugs to tell the idle and starving workingmen of Chicago" to submit to robbery.

The address undoubtedly had a great deal of influence in the city, but its arguments did not appeal to the farmers down-State. Kenesaw M. Landis wrote of this class in Indiana and Illinois at the time: "Some people may tell you this silver

[1] April 29, 1896, p. 441.

matter out here is not serious business when the God's truth is the Democratic party in Indiana and Illinois is wildly insane on this subject. Every fellow who has had a hard time of late has allied himself with the rapscallion element which makes a specialty of taking up with every off color financial and economic proposition that comes along. . . . The farmers are especially unruly. They are carrying their wheat and corn and renewing their notes and, I might add, are going 'hell bent for silver.' Judge Grosscup of the Federal court told me last night that more than half of the thirty men from the county who served in his jury at the last term of court were for free silver. And those men were average Northern Illinois men. And in addition to this cheap-debt-paying argument let it be remembered that the Western farmer can outass anything on earth. The lightning rod man and the green goods gentleman are still doing business in this neighborhood. I've got a lot of farmer uncles down in Indiana—good honest and intelligent men as honesty and intelligence go at this day—but utterly wild on the money question. You can't do anything with them—just got to let them go." [1]

On May 2 Tillman arose in the Senate and in a voice which "rasped like a file on a piece of chilled iron" swore bitter oaths against the gold followers and predicted rapine and bloodshed. "They are linked together," he said. "Grover Cleveland, John Sherman, and John Carlisle are affinities. The question is, will the people be so damnably foolish as to trust them again?" He turned his wrath upon John Sherman, and the Ohioan probably agreed with him when he observed that "the fools are not all dead yet, but they are getting mighty restless"! A week later Bryan, bold with the ardor of youth and the confidence of a golden tongue, bearded Secretary Carlisle. "Your record challenges you to joint debate, will you accept?" wrote the Westerner. "Are you willing to take up your speech of 1878 and answer it, one proposition at a time? If you are, you will silence those who doubt your sincerity and question your motives. If

[1] Landis to Lamont, May 23, 1896. Lamont MSS.

you are not willing to face your own arguments and overcome them, you cannot complain if your opponents adopt the philosophy of Shakespeare and attribute your cowardice to a guilty conscience." But Carlisle had answered his critics on that point almost a year before, and he had at the same time nailed his five theses on the door of his commonwealth.

The Democracy was rapidly being consumed by free silver. W. H. Hinrichsen, secretary of state of Illinois, wrote Bryan on April 16: "I think at least 90 of the 102 counties will declare for 16 to 1. We held our Convention in Sangamon County yesterday. This was regarded as a gold stronghold, but the convention passed 16 to 1 resolutions by a vote of 125 to 25." [1] On May 25 Judge Lambert Tree wrote Don M. Dickinson from Chicago: "The movement to obtain control of the primaries by the honest money men has failed in this county. . . . There is not the shadow of a doubt that the free silver men will control the delegation." Three days later Dickinson replied: "There is a great danger . . . that the cohorts of populism and the champions of national dishonor and repudiation, will capture the organization of the party to which you and I belong." [2] Indeed, the specter of free silver stalked into every county and State convention. One by one the States in the South and the West instructed their delegates to Chicago to vote for the white metal; often not a single gold advocate appeared, and the names of Cleveland and Carlisle were but a hissing and a byword. Many gold men bolted their local organizations, but they could find few followers.

Notwithstanding the difficulties, the Gold Democrats were not ready to surrender to the forces of "national dishonor." They had little expectation of writing the platform, but they hoped through the two-thirds rule to prevent a silver nomination. Throughout the spring months Carlisle, Russell, Olney, Whitney, and others were being urged as candidates for the "genuine" Democracy. Carlisle had a strong following in the East and

[1] Bryan MSS.
[2] Cleveland MSS.

many friends in the South; numerous devotees in Kentucky urged him to announce his candidacy. On April 4 he wrote the chairman of the Kentucky State Central Committee: "I have not been able to reach the conclusion that the existing conditions require me to comply with their requests. . . . While I feel a profound interest in the welfare of my party, I am much more concerned about its declaration of principles than in its selection of candidates, because, in my opinion, its failure or success at the election, as well as its capacity for useful service in the country in the future, depends upon the position it takes or omits to take upon the public questions now engaging the attention of the people, and especially the questions affecting the monetary system of the country and the character and amount of taxation to be imposed upon our citizens . . . In order that its deliberations may be embarrassed as little as possible by the contentions of rival aspirants and their friends, I think my duty to the party will be best performed by declining to participate in a contest for the nomination." He would, he said, regard the indorsement of his public course as an ample reward.[1]

In spite of the Secretary's refusal, "Carlisle Clubs" began a campaign to secure a million letters to take to the Chicago convention, and more than 640,000 were obtained in a short time. On May 10 W. A. Bryant of Riverton, Alabama, wrote the editor of the *Arkansas Gazette:* "If you are in favor of Hon. John G. Carlisle for the next President of the United States, write a letter to the Kentucky Carlisle Club, Owensboro, Ky., and add your endorsement. . . . Then write two letters, exact copies of this letter, to two good Democrats, and help to nominate and elect the 'Greatest American.'" The editor curtly replied: "We are not in favor of Mr. Carlisle, Mr. Bryant; nor shall we write to the Carlisle Democratic Club, nor to any other club or person endorsing him. The truth is, Mr. Bryant, the *Gazette* is opposed to Mr. Carlisle, and inasmuch as that gentleman announced more than a year ago that he would not support

[1] Letter published in Louisville *Courier-Journal,* April 6, 1896.

a free silver man for President if one were nominated, we do not see under what obligations any Democrat would be to support him should he receive the nomination. In this section of the country Mr. Carlisle is regarded with less admiration than Judas Iscariot, for the latter had the decency to hang himself after betraying the Saviour." [1]

Evidence seems to prove that during the hectic month of April someone quietly slipped into Newark, N. J., with a photograph of Carlisle in his pocket and placed an order for campaign buttons. They were delivered in due time and were stored in some secret place to await the proper moment for their appearance. The moment, much to the disgust of Mrs. Carlisle, never came. Today the family attic yields up these mementos, which bear an unfaded likeness of the Kentuckian and the legend, "For President J. G. Carlisle"—evidence of an unrealized dream of the Gold Democrats.

The little army of gold workers was courageous, but hope rapidly waned. Carlisle reluctantly admitted that his native State was thoroughly silver; he saw the futility of further argument and refused to enter the State campaign. When the silver men, smiling and happy, met at Louisville on June 3, there was not a single gold advocate present from the western end of the State and few from the eastern. The name of Cleveland was hissed, and when the chairman declared that Carlisle "stands before the American people as one of the purest and ablest statesmen to-day," his words were lost in angry cries.

"The Democratic State Convention of Kentucky drowns the name of Secretary Carlisle in hisses, cat-calls, and hooting," wrote an editor. "Yet Mr. Carlisle's character, career, and reputation are such that to be opposed to him is not a matter for self-congratulation." But the delegates believed that they had been saved from the evils of a wicked politician. "I have lived a long time, but I never thought I would live long enough to be as happy as I am today," declared Senator Joe C. S. Blackburn in the presence of 4,000 enthusiastic Silver Democrats "as he

[1] Quoted in *National Bimetallist*, May 27, 1896.

stood on the ruined hopes of Secretary Carlisle and the blasted love the Kentuckians formerly had for President Cleveland."[1] State after State held similar conventions. On June 10 President Cleveland wrote Dickinson: "I believe I am by nature an undismayed and persistent fighter and I do not believe in giving an inch until we are obliged to; and yet it is hard to call on friends to maintain a struggle which seems so hopeless." There was no longer any hope of victory, but the President resolutely declared: "There is but one chance for future Democratic success—a perfectly and unequivocal sound money platform at Chicago. If this means the loss of votes, present defeat, or even a party division, the seed will be saved from which I believe Democratic success will grow in the future."[2]

The silver forces were jubilant. They had been very successful in their organization, and they evidently had more money, time, and energy than the gold men. While "Silver Dick" Bland and Horace Boies were distributing lithographs and lapel buttons, Bryan and his wife were laboriously writing countless letters, the returns from which, though not apparent on the surface, were great. The pre-convention machine which Bryan had created was highly effective. It is doubtful that it has ever been surpassed in national politics. A study of his papers reveals the fact that before each State convention he wrote the chairman and afterwards requested the name and address of every delegate to the national convention.[3] To these State chairmen he sent a copy of the platform of the Nebraska Democracy, asking that it be adopted in their conventions.[4] Every silver delegate knew

---

[1] Chicago *Record*, June 5, 1896.

[2] Cleveland MSS.; McElroy, II, 221 ff.

[3] Such letters as: "Your favor of the 25th received and I hasten to reply. The names and post office addresses of the delegates from this State to Chicago are as follows:" are numerous in the Bryan papers.

[4] Three letters must suffice as illustrations: C. S. Thomas of Denver, Colorado, wrote on April 13, "I have only time to acknowledge the receipt of yours of the 11th, with enclosures, and to say that in the preparation of our platform we will endeavor to use the identical language expressed in the slip which you enclosed"; on April 30 Josephus Daniels of Raleigh, North Carolina, wrote, "I will endeavor to get the North Carolina platform in the same shape as adopted by the Democracy

before he started to Chicago exactly on what ground he stood; his mind was bent on only one thing—the free coinage of silver "without waiting for the aid or consent of any other nation on earth." Moreover, the delegates were supplied with briefs of the cases where contests were likely to appear. Bryan, with many others, was reasonably certain several months before the convention that silver would win.[1] With the increased hopes of the silver followers came also a greater demand for Bryan as the leader of the party; his immense correspondence and incessant labor had undoubtedly done a great deal to effect this result.

On May 23 J. Burrows of Filley, Neb., wrote the Populist leader, J. B. Weaver: "Mr. Bryan has the courage of his convictions. He is brave to a degree—the very man we want for president in the present crisis. He can carry the solid South. No Populist can do that and we *must have* the solid South. At the outset in the convention I think he will have the delegation of several Western States. It looks now as though he might also have that of Illinois. He will have the delegations of his own State, and, more than that, he can carry it in November, and probably also carry in the State the whole Populist ticket. If the Democrats will nominate Mr. Bryan it will be an easy thing for the Populists to endorse him. . . . We want a union of all free silver forces. And we want to win. . . . If you concur in my view, let me add that it is not a moment too soon to take action to secure Mr. Bryan's nomination at Chicago and St. Louis." Six days later Weaver wrote Bryan: "As we are nearing the time of our National Conventions I think it important that I shall make the following suggestion to you. We all understand that a union of all the silver forces is absolutely essential to victory. Should the silver men be able to control the Chicago

of Nebraska"; on May 4 E. W. Carmack wrote from Columbia, Tennessee, "I am not a delegate in the State convention but will try to have the money plank you enclosed put in the platform. It is admirable." Bryan MSS.

[1] The Bryan papers show the growth of the silver sentiment as State after State instructed for free coinage. He was constantly informed on the situation.

convention both as to platform and nominations be careful to have the platform cover the entire money question: second, let your nominations be advisory simply and not final. This will afford opportunity to confer with our conventions at St. Louis and open the way for union. Should your forces be in control, the gold men will doubtless bolt and this will afford ample reason for making your nominations advisory. I regard these suggestions as important. I am at the head of the Iowa delegation to St. Louis and will do all in my power to bring about a consolidation of forces." [1]

Over Illinois were spread copies of a letter declaring that "in the person of Hon. W. J. Bryan of Nebraska, we can offer a native-born Illinoisan, who possesses all the attributes to be desired in a Democratic President, and is with the people and for the people in their struggle for the restoration of their stolen right." Letters came to Bryan from all over the South and West, hailing his leadership.

In late May a tornado struck St. Louis, leaving in its path death and destruction. A few days later, when the Republican National Convention assembled in the city, the McKinley forces struck the city with almost equal force, leaving in their wake many a favorite son. Bryan was on the scene urging his friends to bolt if the expected gold plank was inserted in the platform.[2] With a feeling of joy he watched Senator Teller—"the absconding Teller"—followed by his silver associates, march forever out of the councils of the Republican party. The Omaha *World-Herald*, Bryan's paper, immediately struck what was to be the keynote of the Democratic platform: "We are unalterably opposed to the single gold standard and demand the free and unlimited coinage of gold and silver at the present legal ratio of 16 to 1, without waiting for the aid or consent of any other nation on earth."

[1] Bryan MSS.
[2] See *The Memoirs of William Jennings Bryan,* by himself and his wife, Mary Baird Bryan, 99-100.

THE SILVER HERESY

The break in the Republican party increased the hopes of the Silver Democrats.[1] And so, three days after the 4th of July, the silver forces, jubilant and expectant, moved on to Chicago to do battle for "the money of the common man."

It is needless to recount the events of the Democratic National Convention. The perspiring crowd was called to order with a gavel (carried to Chicago in the pocket of Senator Tillman) made of wood from Fort Hill, Calhoun's old home. After some brief—and to the gold men disastrous—preliminaries, the convention got under way with Senator Daniel's tribute to the far-flung silver army: "It begins with the sunrise in Maine and spreads into a sunburst in Louisiana and Texas. It stretches in unbroken line across the continent from Virginia and Georgia to California. It sends forth its pioneers from Plymouth Rock and waves the palmetto in South Carolina. It has its strongholds in Alabama and Mississippi and its outposts in Delaware and Minnesota, Florida and Oregon. It sticks like a tar heel in the old north State and writes 16 to 1 on the saddle bags of the Arkansas traveler. It pours down its rivulets from the mountains of New Hampshire and West Virginia and makes a great lake in New Mexico, Arizona, Wyoming and Idaho, Montana and Colorado. It stands guard around the National Capitol in the District of Columbia and taps at the door in far-off Washington. It sweeps like a prairie fire over Iowa and Kansas and lights up the horizon in Nebraska. It marshals its massive battalions in Ohio, Indiana, Illinois and Missouri."

The results of the convention are familiar to all. The well-regulated silver machine, the existence of which was unknown to many, rolled relentlessly over the opposition. One gold member recorded in his diary at the time, "The delegates were monomaniacs," and a few days later he again confided to that little book: "Left Chicago. The platform had been announced

---

[1] Bryan records in his *Memoirs*, p. 100: "The convention turned out as I expected and the looked-for bolt took place. I felt sure that the action of this convention would have a large influence at Chicago."

and there was nothing more to be done—no respectable man could afford to remain." [1]

The split in the party and the nomination of Bryan constitute one of the most skilfully prepared and carefully executed "accidents" in American politics. The glowing oratory at Chicago was most important, perhaps, in distracting attention while the Nebraskan pulled the cloak of respectability over a babel of political faiths and gave the name Democracy to what was essentially a third party. With the selection of Bryan the direst fears of the Gold Democrats were realized. "The platform and the nominees are both worse than ever my fears conjectured," wrote Josiah Patterson to the President, and the Democratic chief, now off at his summer home at Buzzard's Bay, refused to see one of his returning officials with the query, "Haven't we heard enough from the convention?"

[1] Hamlin Diary.

CHAPTER XVIII   BRYAN'S CRUSADE AND DEFEAT, 1896

An excited barber in Chicago did his best to keep the lather out of the ears of his patron and to avoid nicking the massive jaw upon which he was wielding his razor; William Jennings Bryan was getting a shave when the news came that he had been nominated on the fifth ballot as the Democratic candidate for the Presidency. Bryan was not greatly surprised, for the hopes which he had held when he came to the convention had become a certainty as he saw the great crowd in the hall completely dominated by the brilliance of his oratory.

The nation, however, was thrilled, for a new Demosthenes, a William the Conqueror, a Cromwell, a Lincoln, had come at last to lead the common man into the fields of honest government. Over the wires from the home of the new leader came the words: "All Lincoln rejoicing Whistles Blowing Bells ringing and Bonfires Burning in pride of your genius which rises with the mantle of Jefferson in a Blaze of oratory unsurpassed in all the ages and moves toward the chair once occupied by him for whom the City was named." [1] This youth from the Platte had brought a fountain of joy into the drab lives of the farmers and laborers of the land; his appeal to the great mass of his party excelled that of the indomitable Andrew Jackson of Tennessee. The fight on the National Bank was but a skirmish in comparison with the attack on the great bankers of Wall and Lombard Streets.

But discontented Democrats were not the only forces which rallied under the banner of the people in these dramatic days. On July 15 William M. Teller, leader of the insurgent Republicans, wrote Bryan: "I need not assure you that your nomination was more than satisfactory to me. I think we shall be able to consolidate all the friends of free coinage in your support, and

[1] J. H. Broody to Bryan, July 10, 1896. Bryan MSS.

if we do this I believe you will be elected, although I do not overlook the tremendous power that will be arrayed against us in this campaign. All the power of money and organized wealth, corporations and monopolies of all kinds will be against us. The ignorance that prevails among the people on the financial question in some parts of the country will be a great obstacle to success. However, justice is on our side and this is the cause of the people. It is a contest for industrial independence and for freedom from the domination of foreign capital, and it does not seem possible that in such a contest before the American people justice should fail and wrong prevail. I do not believe we shall fail. I think I can promise you the cordial support of the Western silver men who have heretofore acted with the Republican party, and if you get that I think all of the Western coast and Inter-mountain States will be for you. . . . It will afford me pleasure to place myself at the disposition of the National Committee to make such speeches in your behalf as my health will permit, where and when they may think I will do good." [1]

A few days later Edward C. Little of Kansas stood on the convention floor of the Silver party in St. Louis and defied Wall Street and the challenge which the Republican party had issued in that city in mid-June. He was presenting the name of Bryan not as a Democrat, but as the man to defend the rights of an awakened people. He quoted:

> Pleasant it is for the Little Tin Gods,
> When the Great Jove nods.
> But the Little Tin Gods make their mistakes,
> That they miss the hour when the Great Jove wakes.

Speaking of the grievances of the people, Little declared that "The sophistical logic of 'business' argument cannot avoid, the enticing glitter of Lombard gold cannot disguise, the sonorous periods of rounded eloquence cannot disprove the simple proposition that for a long term of years our property has

[1] Bryan MSS.

diminished in value, while our liabilities make greater demands than are named in the stipulation. The honest dollar is the dollar of the contract. We stand ready to endure the due and forfeit of our bond—no more, no less. 'If you deny it fie upon your law.'" "I present to you," he continued, "no Moses to lead the people forty years in the wilderness, but a gifted young Joshua who shall bid the golden sun and the silver moon stand still while he fights the battle of human freedom.

"The nation cried out in her hour of peril and the West gave her Abraham Lincoln:

> The land that loves him guards his rest,
> The West, the West, the Rowdy West.

Again the nation calls and the West gives her a man sprung from the same soil, inspired by the same motives, loved by the same neighbors, and blessed we fondly believe by the same God."

While the members of the Silver party were declaring that "The hour has come, the man appeared, the hero has been found, worthy to stand by Demosthenes and Brutus and Hampden and Mirabeau and Henry and Brown," John B. Weaver was admonishing the Populists, in convention in the same city, that "assailed as is this gallant knight by the sleuth hounds of the money power of the world, you may deliberate here as long as you please, but you cannot prevent the people from rushing to the support of their recognized defender and leader. If you will not say the word, they will break over all restraints and go themselves, leaders or no leaders, and may God bless them for so doing."

On July 27 a young labor official sat writing in the office of the American Railway Union and Railway Times in Terre Haute, Indiana, and into the mails to join the thousands of others went this letter to the youthful candidate:

My Dear Mr. Bryan:
With millions of others of your countrymen I congratulate you most heartily upon being the People's standard bearer in

the great uprising of the masses against the classes. You are at this hour the hope of the Republic, the central figure of the civilized world. In the arduous campaign before you the millions will rally to your standard and you will lead them to glorious victory. The people love and trust you—they believe in you as you believe in them, and under your administration the rule of the money power will be broken and the gold barons of Europe will no longer run the American government.

With all good wishes believe me always

Yours faithfully

EUGENE V. DEBS.[1]

In addition to these regularly constituted groups, Bryan led into the conflict a multitude of camp followers who, before November came, probably detracted from his success. Indeed, his following was legion; and day by day, as the glamour of his great oration spread with consuming rapidity over the land, he reaped a harvest of new recruits. The army of discontented, whatever its grievances, had at last found a leader. The crusade against the money powers had moved into its final stage. The attackers had little in common, for they included Democrats, Republicans, Populists, Woman Suffragists, Prohibitionists, Knights of Labor, and cults without name; but they were united in their determination to lift mankind from the cross of gold and to remove the crown of thorns.

Yet the Nebraskan, though he possessed the machinery of the Democracy, could not hold all its members; many refused to follow their old party in a futile journey after false gods. The fulfillment of the prediction of the midlands that the major issue of 1896 would be silver or gold presented a serious problem to both Democrats and Republicans. To bolt the party of their preference was no panacea, for gold with high tariff or silver with free trade made a bitter concoction to the fastidious palates of many old-line politicians; some preferred to wander in lonely political woods rather than deny their traditional views on the tariff. Nevertheless, many former enemies were united.

[1] Bryan MSS.

THANKSGIVING, 1896
(*Puck*)

THE GRAND REVIVAL MEETING IN 1900
"All who have seen the true financial light stand up"

BRYAN'S CRUSADE AND DEFEAT

The statement, "This is a time when patriotism should be placed above party, and national honor above sectional necessity; there is no politics in honesty," found itself doing duty for both the silver followers and the gold advocates.[1]

The Gold Democrats were particularly embarrassed. On the day following Bryan's nomination Roswell Miller, president of the Chicago, Milwaukee and St. Paul Railway, wrote a friend in the East: "What an unfortunate condition we are in as to national Politics! It will need a vigorous effort and a combination of all who don't want the country ruined to prevent it. I fear you Eastern people don't appreciate the popular strength of the Free Silver craze— I don't like to believe it will win, but I am scared. It is pretty tough to ask a Democrat to vote for McKinley (I don't like to do it myself) but it is a choice of two evils, and an Independent Sound Money Democratic ticket at this time will simply give the election to the Populistic element. If the Free Silver theory could have a trial and be easily abandoned when demonstrated a failure, without permanent disaster, it would not be so bad—but if we get into that bog I don't see how we can get out." [2]

Members of the administration were sorely perplexed. Party honor demanded that they support their political organization, and the only escape was to deny that Bryan and his followers represented the Democracy. Such a denial, however, would involve supporting the Republican party, which they had been fighting for so many years, and it would mean, in addition, the severing of long-standing friendships. President Cleveland wrote Secretary Lamont shortly after the convention: "I have an idea, quite fixed and definite, that for the present at least we should none of us say anything. I have heard from Herbert to-day. He says he has declared he will not support the ticket. I am sorry he has done so. We have a right to be quiet—indeed I feel that I have been invited to

---

[1] Louis F. Golding, editor of the *Commercial Advertiser* of New York, to Lamont, July 21, 1896. Lamont MSS.
[2] Miller to Secretary Lamont. Lamont MSS.

that course. I am not fretting except about the future of the country and party, and the danger that the latter is to be compromised as an organization." [1] A few days later Postmaster-General William L. Wilson wrote W. C. P. Breckinridge of Kentucky:

I am as yet saying nothing except to friends and keeping in the "middle of the road," resolved that I shall not fall into the mire of protectionism, and not less so not to leap into the foul pit of repudiation, socialism, anarchy, *et cetera.* temporarily called or miscalled by the grand old name Democracy. Much as I love my party, I put duty to my country higher, and with my conviction as to the effect of free silver, and its moral stain on the country to say nothing of the other heresies of the platform, I cannot see how I can vote with it under any circumstances. Yet this will cut for the present, and, possibly, for all my future, ties as close and precious as public man was ever called on to sever. As to your course I can offer no helpful suggestion, ordinarily I should say that you could do nothing more patriotic or honorable to yourself than to assume the leadership of true Democracy in Ky at this time, and to canvass the state on that somewhat heroic plane.[2]

Secretary Carlisle, still worrying over the gold reserve, was vitally interested in the campaign which was just beginning. Success for the party in which he had labored for a lifetime would mean the complete failure of the task which he had fought so hard to accomplish. If November found Bryan victorious, the energy which the Secretary had expended to maintain the gold standard would have gone for naught, and his break with a great mass of the Democracy of America would have had no recompense. He sincerely believed that the nation had reached such a point financially that any change in the existing standard of value would only increase the hardships of

[1] McElroy's *Cleveland,* II, 226.
[2] Breckinridge MSS.

the poor. "For the time being," he declared, "ordinary party obligations sink into utter insignificance," and he resolutely set himself to the task of refuting the heresy which had at last captured his party. It was no credit to Bryan to say that "The highest compliment he can pay me is to oppose me." Carlisle opposed free silver because of an intellectual conviction based on a knowledge of world financial conditions not then exceeded by any statesman.

Many Democrats, regardless of their regret over the course which the party had taken, preferred to remain in the organization and suffer its ills. "I am still a Democrat, very still," said David B. Hill when asked regarding his position. "I do not see my way to change with you and other friends in the course which you have marked out for yourselves," he wrote Secretary Lamont. "There are many reasons why it is desirable to control, or at least keep in touch with the regular organization of our State, which of course represents three-fifths or four-fifths of the party's voters. If I withdraw the organization will go into the hands of adventurers and the blatherskites. Will I not be serving the country better to remain passive and at the same time virtually control the organization?" He refused to go to the State convention at Buffalo, but predicted that both a gold and a silver candidate would be nominated, "and h—— will be let loose all around." "The times are out of joint," concluded the leader of the New York Democracy.[1]

From Josiah Patterson of Tennessee came the wail, "What are we to do?" "My inclination is to advise a democratic convention and a democratic nomination," wrote the ex-governor. "However, this might endanger McKinley. Perhaps the more patriotic course would be to call a convention, adopt a platform of principles, and then after advising all sound money democrats to vote for McKinley, adjourn. . . . The democracy must not die forever." James Stillman, representative of the New York bankers, wrote Lamont: "I trust the sound money

[1] Hill to Lamont, Sept. 14, 1896. Lamont MSS.

Democrats will not put up candidates, but will unite to elect McKinley."[1]

But the old-line Democracy could not follow the lead of the "Grand Old Party," whose policy of high tariff it suspected of being responsible for the ills that had come. "I still hope that those of us who are opposed to McKinleyism, but still desire a sound monetary system may have a ticket for which we can conscientiously vote," wrote a citizen of Binghamton, New York. There was only one means of relief, and that was to bolt the party. This decision had not been made after the convention. For weeks before the Chicago meeting the Gold Democrats had been preparing for the appearance there of non-delegates, "not so much with the hope of influencing the action of the convention as for the purpose of protesting against the course which will likely be taken and of consulting together as to the best course for sound money men to pursue subsequently."[2] President Cleveland and Secretary Carlisle had given their approval of this plan, and the latter had urged that headquarters be opened where speeches might be made.[3]

The gold advocates did not delay long; seven days after the regular convention a committee assembled in Chicago for the purpose of making some decision. Unabashed by their unofficial status, the members issued a call for a meeting of national Gold-Democrat committeemen to be held at Indianapolis in early August. Much time and energy had to be spent before these committeemen could be secured. At the conference, which was held on August 7, every Southern State with the exception of Mississippi was represented, but the delegates had not been secured with ease. W. B. Haldeman of the Louisville *Courier-Journal*, who had been assigned the duty of obtaining men, wrote Watterson that "It was by no means an easy task, for the free silver heresy had thoroughly permeated the South."

The committee decided to hold the nominating convention

[1] Lamont MSS.
[2] Bynum MSS.
[3] Cleveland, Bynum, and Lamont MSS.

at Indianapolis on September 2, and Louisville was designated as the place of notification. Both selections were wise, because these cities lay in the two borderlands—that between the East and the West, and that between the North and the South. On August 22 Haldeman wrote Watterson: "We have done much hard, and, I am glad to say, effective work, and the promise now is for a great convention of first class men, the delegates representing every State and Territory in the American Union, excepting possibly three of the rotten boroughs of the West." [1]

The difficulties facing the Gold Democrats in forming a new party were monumental. They could certainly not carry the South, for there Democracy was traditional, and that section now owed allegiance to Bryan; the united party had only a few times won the North; and all knew that to look to the West for any support was a hopeless aspiration. There were signs of weakness even in the little group which had so valiantly fought for sound money against ever-increasing odds. To the President's desk came a letter of resignation from Hoke Smith, who, as Secretary of the Interior, had been speaking in the South in the interest of the gold standard, but who, as editor of the Atlanta *Journal*, felt impelled because of "Democratic regularity" to support the regular nominee of the party. Cleveland was annoyed and perplexed, and turned to other members of his Cabinet for advice. Secretary Carlisle and Postmaster-General Wilson spent many hours over the problem, and the latter wrote the Chief Executive that because of the facts "that the Administration is without organized party support at present; has but a few months to continue, and that Mr. Smith's retirement for these reasons, just now, would make some stir in the country, and give him somewhat the position of a 'persecuted' man, for party's sake, and throwing into the medley a hearty liking for a brother official, I conclude that it is better to preserve the status, than to have him leave the Cabinet." [2]

[1] Watterson MSS.
[2] Wilson to Cleveland. Cleveland MSS.

There were only two factors which held the Gold Democrats to their course—the desire to preserve the seeds of Democracy for the future, and the ambition to defeat "Bryanism," their hatred of which was intense. The call for the Indianapolis convention had declared that "The Democratic party will therefore cease to exist, unless it be preserved by the voluntary action of such of its members as still adhere to its fundamental principles," and General Palmer had told the delegates: "It is left to us to create the nucleus around which the true Democrats . . . can rally once more, and to preserve a place for our erring brothers, if the time comes when they repent, and God forgives them for their transgressions; we will be ready to receive them with open arms! Come back to the party of your fathers." [1]

The question of who should lead the Gold Democrats was serious. Carlisle was perhaps the logical man, but because of Cleveland's hesitancy he was somewhat handicapped now, as he had been before the regular convention. The President was still uncertain as to his moral obligation to his party and to the country; he felt that duty might impose on him the onus of again being a candidate.[2] He opposed any connection with a third ticket by any member of the Cabinet. Candidates, however, were plentiful. William F. Vilas of Wisconsin was among those suggested, as was General Bragg of that State; and for a time it seemed as though Henry Watterson might have to rush home from his European trip to take up the banner. Availability prevailed at last, however, and General John M. Palmer of Illinois and General Simon Bolivar Buckner of Kentucky, respectively Unionist and Confederate, Western and Southern border-State representatives, were chosen. As early as July 30 William M. Wilson had written Breckinridge: "The personnel of [the] ticket, though as yet a matter to be

---

[1] Typed "Proceedings" in the Bynum MSS.

[2] This conclusion is substantiated by entries in the unpublished diary of Hamlin, letters in the Bynum collection, letters from Otto Gresham in the Watterson collection, and other sources.

kept in the background, is very important. It ought to be headed by some such man as Palmer, with a Southern Confederate V.P. . . . While it is the impression of Eastern politicians that Bryan's chances are somewhat past the zenith and will further wane, they have been so steadily mistaken and so blind to the strength and volume of the silver movement, that one does not know what faith to put in their judgment. Be this as it may, it does not relieve the situation of its distress to Democrats like you and me who look at principles and not at names or 'regularity.'" [1]

The followers of sound money were pleased, for they had launched a party to fight the heresy which had arisen in the ranks of the Democracy. Cleveland wrote Vilas: "I feel grateful to those who have relieved the political atmosphere with such a delicious infusion of fresh air. Every Democrat after reading the platform ought to thank God that the glorious principles of our party have found defenders who will not permit them to be polluted by impious hands." Secretary Carlisle wired the chairman of the notification meeting at Louisville: "I am proud to take my stand with the old-fashioned Democrats who have refused to abandon their honest convictions in order to form unnatural alliances with political and social organizations whose purposes are dangerous to the country and wholly inconsistent with the fundamental principles of our party." The "real" Democracy had unfurled its banner under which it would fight the "black flag of piracy" which the hosts of Nebraska had raised at Chicago. Sound-money Democrats were glad to hear the group gathered at Louisville say, "We are the Democrats and they are the bolters." Welcome, too, were the words, "Our Democracy was not breathed first across the plains of Nebraska. It speaks tonight from the tomb at Monticello, and the grave at the Hermitage."

The political situation at the beginning of the campaign of 1896 was peculiar. Each contending group found embarrass-

[1] Breckinridge MSS.

ment in its own status. Regardless of the outcome, the Silver Democrats could scarcely hope to conduct more than one campaign; the composition of the party was too diverse and its binding forces too volatile. The Gold Democrats had offended too many people in following the Biblical admonition, "If thy right hand offend thee, cut it off"; they had no greater future than to stand puritanically by their principles and wait for the wounds of this year to heal. The Republicans, leaderless and unfitted for the only issue which the people would hear, were compelled to put away their theory of the protective tariff and take up the fight for sound money; Mark Hanna's "prosperity" was certainly to be desired, but few felt that the tariff was involved in that question now. The standard of value was the only issue in the fight, and the gold-standard dress suited "the Majah" far less satisfactorily than the high-tariff clothes of the "advance agent of prosperity."

These difficulties, however, did not prevent a vigorous campaign. After a short visit to the recently widowed Mrs. Lyman Trumbull of Chicago, Bryan began one of the most remarkable canvasses in American history. That of 1840 was somewhat similar in the emotions played upon, but Harrison sat at home in his country mansion while his advocates proclaimed his "log cabin" doctrine. Bryan, on the contrary, was the preeminent leader of his party's fight. His speeches, filled with phrases taken from all the patriotic addresses in American history which he had learned in countless declamations as a youth, caught the fancy of the people, and they would hear no others. Long familiar with every word that he spoke, they felt that he knew their problems; they looked to him for the miracle which would bring relief from long-borne burdens.

On Friday, August 8, with a rabbit's foot in his pocket and a great hope in his heart, the Democratic candidate began his journey into the "enemy's country" to receive official notification of his nomination. Through the midlands thousands of shouting and perspiring citizens sought to shake his hand or to touch the hem of his garment; at every station the train stopped so that Bryan might address the gathering. At Newton, Ia., named for the great thinker, he told his hearers that if a stone were thrown into the air it would come down, and deftly reached the conclusion that "If we have a gold standard, prices are as certain to fall as the stone which is thrown into the air." At Princeton, Ill., John Howard Bryant, brother of the great poet, sent a cheering message to "the people's man." At Chicago he was introduced to the more than 15,000 people "who filled Monroe Street from east of Wabash Avenue to west of State Street" with the words: "Among the many thousands who greet you to-night are the hewers of wood and the drawers of water. These are they who produce all the honest wealth of the country. Among them are hundreds of noble, courageous men, who have felt their little children tugging at their coattails for bread that they could not give them because they could not find work. None of those drones of society who produce nothing but laws and panics are here to honor you. Not one of that class who arrogate to themselves the holy name of leading citizens, and who form trusts to control the necessaries of life, will be found in this vast assembly. None of those toadies who think it is stylish to be called gold bugs is here to-night."

Bryan, on his way East to plead, Lazarus-like, at the rich man's table, appreciated these words all the more, he said, because the chairman "though a Republican heretofore is a patriot to-day." Bryant Webb, the fifteen-year-old "Boy Orator of Illinois," who bore a striking resemblance to "Coin" Harvey, "then sang a silver song to the tune of 'Marching Through Georgia.'" On across the continent the idol of the West, thirty-six years old—"the age of Napoleon at Austerlitz"—traveled. As he neared New York, the financiers grew alarmed, for his power was indisputably portrayed in the falling prices on the stock market. The New York address, however, was not a success; Bryan did not rely upon his oratory, but read a carefully prepared manuscript, thereby losing the advantage of his greatest gift without any compensating gain. "Now that the dramatic undertaking is an event of the past, the general verdict would seem to be that the whole affair has been a dismal failure—a real disappointment to his party friends and evidently somewhat of a relief in financial circles," stated the *Commercial and Financial Chronicle* on August 15, and two days later Edwin F. Uhl wrote from the United States Embassy in Berlin: "The situation (political) to a true Democrat and patriot is indeed disheartening. It would appear at this distance that Bryan's march 'to the sea'-board fell quite flat. I am not surprised, in fact have expected this, since hearing that his Chicago effort, launched as an impromptu fomentation, was really an old speech, warmed over, and made to fit the occasion." [1]

The trip to New York was but the beginning of Bryan's campaign tours; his admirers were thrilled by his "crossing and recrossing a continent fulfilling with such vigor his mission to the masses of heterogeneous humanity." He did not, however, cross and recross the continent; he planned his journeys with a great deal of political acumen. The conflict was actually won in the Ohio and upper-Mississippi valleys. Here the Gold Democrats and the Republicans united in a desperate effort to overcome the silver following. Bryan, too, recognized the strategic importance of this section. Of the 249 major stops which he made in the campaign 160 were in the eight States of Illinois, Indiana, Ohio, Iowa, Wisconsin, Michigan, Kentucky, and West Virginia; two-thirds of these 160 were in Illinois, Indiana, Ohio, and Michigan.

The National Democrats, as the gold advocates chose to call themselves—and the courts sustained them in their contention—were late in getting their candidate forward, but that fact had little to do with the active campaign. The individual efforts which had characterized the pre-convention fight for the gold standard continued with redoubled vigor after the nomination of Bryan. Sound-money organizations in the larger cities carried forward the movement without regard to political

[1] Uhl to Lamont. Lamont MSS.

affiliations. Banking houses and financial institutions published articles written by the advocates of the gold standard, enclosed them in advertising jackets, and distributed them over the various States to whoever would take and read them. Emory McClintock of the Mutual Life Insurance Company of New York wrote to Secretary Lamont: "I enclose with some hesitation, the ten thousandth paper lately written on the money question. Every one has been at it, openly or secretly." Press material was furnished in lavish quantities to newspapers all over the country.

Secretary Carlisle, with an abiding faith in the ability of the people to choose the safest course if the facts were logically and calmly presented, set the clerks of the Treasury Department to work gathering information on the relative merits of the gold and the silver standard as exhibited in the various countries of the world.[1] He himself, when he could get away from his office, made campaign speeches, as did also the assistant secretaries. He wrote to Colonel Lamont: "It is perfectly evident that we cannot be silent during this fierce campaign, and there is no reason why we should not speak out plainly at once. Delay has the appearance of indecision and indecision hurts the cause." [2]

The Secretary, however, had little time to spend speaking for the gold standard; few have yet realized the difficulties which faced the Treasury Department in the summer and fall months of 1896. Even before spring the vexatious gold reserve had again begun to cause trouble; sub-Treasurer Jordan had induced the banks of New York to furnish gold to the shippers on the promise that if they got into difficulties he would come to their rescue. On April 6 he had written Assistant-Secretary Curtis: "If this loss of gold goes on much longer, we shall gradually drift into a repetition of '93, and financial quiet is the only thing that will be of use to the country. I have little hope of this, and can only say that the Banks, if this movement con-

[1] The State Department also assisted in this work.
[2] Carlisle to Lamont, September 11, 1896, Lamont MSS.

tinues, will soon be drained of their legal-tenders, and be compelled to resort to Clearing House certificates. If so, the opposition to the distribution of the excessive balances of a few of the Banks will cease perforce because these Banks cannot go into a Bank suspension with their tills full of legal tenders held for government account. There is but one 'if' in this conclusion—shipments may soon stop, because of the 'cost' of legal tenders—gold is now at a premium, legal-tenders will be if the Banks actually suspend. It is time that the demand for shipment may cease suddenly, but we are within one month of the normal shipping period. Again, going abroad may not be fashionable this year. I hope this will be so, but don't believe it. I am sorry to say that we had a million 'legals' paid into us to-day—as you will see by the bank reports they would do more good in their tills." The run on the Treasury was increasing, gold was at a premium, and it was feared that a price might even be set upon the greenbacks. On May 28 Curtis had written Secretary Carlisle from New York: "We have used up all our gold and think it would be well enough to reduce our bars to 1/10 again, or whatever it was, and let $10,000,000 of them go. It is expected that the exports of gold will continue through the next two months about 2,000,000 per week. Everything is stagnant here."

The Democratic nomination at Chicago had further depressed the financial situation; government bonds had dropped several points. By the time the campaign got under way, the situation was critical. Unless preventive measures were taken, the gold reserve would certainly be exhausted long before election day, but a bond sale would give the silver followers a great advantage and might even turn the tide of victory in their favor. Secretary Carlisle was fully aware of the political dangers which were impending. Six days after the nomination of Bryan he wrote President Cleveland:

Mr. Curtis left for New York last evening to attend to some quarantine business and look after some private affairs but I told him that if he met any of the financial people he ought to impress upon them the great importance of preventing a condition that would necessitate a bond issue or even cause an agitation of that subject. I think this is of the greatest importance in the political situation—and our friends ought to help us, if necessary, to the full extent of their means. What the syndicate did to prevent withdrawals in the summer of 1895, can certainly be done by the associated banks at New York at this time. The little losses they might sustain in helping us now would be nothing in comparison to the ruin that would follow the election of the Chicago ticket, and I hope they can be induced to take this view of the subject. I write in great haste, as I am just leaving for the boat to go down the river for a few days. Upon my return if the situation seems to require immediate consultation, I will try to run over and see you.[1]

Stillman of the National City Bank of New York commented on July 20, "I do not think a bond issue wise except in the very greatest emergency on the eve of such a political contest as we are entering upon." Three days later John P. Branch of the Merchants National Bank of Richmond, Virginia, wrote President Cleveland: "The financial situation is worse than I have ever known it, and the clouds are becoming thicker and thicker. The present condition of affairs is unparalleled in my experience of nearly fifty years as merchant and banker; and I see nothing to prevent a panic between now and the 1st of November next, far surpassing anything of the kind in the past fifty years. . . . If a panic comes before the Presidential election, I think it will be a guarantee of the election of the Chicago Democratic ticket, which would be deplorable."[2]

Secretary Carlisle, knowing that only through individual effort could silent and effective aid be secured, appealed to the bankers over the country. The response was prompt. Offers of assistance came from as far west as Chicago, but real help was

[1] Cleveland MSS.
[2] Cleveland MSS.

limited largely to New York City, and the bankers there dominated the situation in this emergency. "The New York people have come up well," wrote Assistant-Secretary Curtis to his mother on July 23, "and we see the curious spectacle of the U.S. finances being controlled by a committee, of which J. P. Morgan is Chairman, and the majority of whom are Hebrews, while the Secretary of the Treasury sits practically powerless in his office. The only enlivening feature just at present is to get lonely appeals from Republicans for information who have bitterly opposed the administration's policy and attacked the bond issues." [1]

The gold reserve stood at eighty-nine million dollars on July 23, and the demands from the interior for money with which to move the crops threatened to bring a situation comparable to that of 1893. Secretary Carlisle hoped, however, that fall balances—and the cotton crop was three weeks earlier than usual—might turn the gold balance in favor of the United States. With the assistance of the banks he was able to increase the reserve to $110,000,000 by August 4. But the financial troubles were still acute. "We are on the high road to a panic," wrote Jordan. On August 8 the Chicago Stock Exchange closed after the failure of Moore Brothers of that city with liabilities of $20,000,000. At San Francisco it was not certain that the government could coin gold fast enough to meet the demands for redemption. Had the situation been known, it would have brought much additional criticism from the silver followers. The gold reserve was maintained only by the most strenuous efforts on the part of the financiers of the East.

Regardless of the difficulties which they faced, the Gold Democrats continued to fight for what they believed to be sound finances. The two old generals who were leading the party charged with all their might, but with little effect. Kenesaw M. Landis wrote Colonel Lamont on September 22, "You would laugh yourself sick could you see old Palmer. He has

[1] Curtis MSS.

actually gotten it into his head he is running for office."[1] The greatest hope of the dissident Democrats was to draw sufficient ballots from Bryan in the border States to throw the electoral vote to McKinley. On August 10 Josiah Patterson wrote from Memphis: "I believe Bryan could be beaten in Tennessee. This remark will probably lead you to believe that while voting for Bryan I am praying for his defeat. That is true."[2] On the twenty-second Haldeman wrote from Louisville: "The third ticket will poll 40,000 Democratic votes in Kentucky, which will give the electoral vote of this State to McKinley." Palmer is said to have told a Missouri audience: "I promise you, my fellow Democrats, I will not consider it any very great fault if you decide . . . to cast your ballots for William McKinley, although you may, if you desire, vote for Palmer and Buckner." A citizen of New York wrote Bryan: "We have a few Gold Democrats in this county I am sorry to say it, they had a meeting the other night their speaker did not amount to anything at the wind up he advised every one to 'vote for McKinley.'"[3]

As the conflict progressed, the danger of a silver victory forced the Gold Democrats and the Republicans closer together. Never before, perhaps, had so fine an opportunity to criticize the opposing administration been compelled to go unnoticed; four years crammed full of good campaign material was of little use. The Republicans could not attack the Gold Democrats, for they themselves were but proposing to take up the financial fight which Cleveland and Carlisle had been carrying on for four years. Certainly Bryan and his followers were not responsible for anything which the administration had done! The sonorous voice of Tom Reed which had for three years been telling of the evils of the "Democratic panic" was stilled; few Republicans, whose party had barely escaped the

[1] Lamont MSS.
[2] Lamont MSS.
[3] Bryan MSS.

ills that had come, dared criticize. As early as July, Senator Redfield Proctor, Republican of Vermont, wrote Secretary Lamont: "Was in Washington to get literature on silver sent to our State as our election is the first day of September, the first of the Northern States, and we want to show that the heresy has taken no serious hold here. It has somewhat, but I do not think to much extent. I wish we were in shape to join with you and make the main issue to preserve and protect the credit and honor of the country, but suppose our platform goes so far on points of difference that we cannot expect the mass of sound money Democrats to join with us. All I can say is, God save the Commonwealth." [1]

But the Gold Democrats fretted because necessity had forced upon them such a distasteful alliance. James W. Bradley expressed the feelings of many when he wrote the President on October 29: "In what an unfortunate position the Chicago Convention has placed honest, constitutional Democrats. To save the country from *ruin* we are compelled to give aid and support to the party that sowed the seeds of, and made that ruin possible!" From the United States Embassy in London came the lament that "it is humiliating to see Bryan and his following masquerading as Democrats. . . . McKinley I imagine will be elected and I hope by a large majority; nothing else will finally put a stop to this crazy and insensate silver notion amongst our people. But it is certainly a bitter pill for us to swallow!" [2]

In spite of the hostility between them, however, the two gold parties fought vigorously for the single standard. Their efforts were not without results. By the middle of September it was clear to all that the silver cause was losing its strength. "The silver people seem badly puzzled, there is much less cheerfulness apparent than a week or two since," wrote a citizen of Kentucky on August 3. "Kavanaugh was down from Harpers Ferry, says that everything there seems for free sil-

[1] Proctor to Lamont, July 27, 1896. Lamont MSS.
[2] L. J. Roosevelt to Lamont. Lamont MSS.

THE REPUBLICAN NATIONAL CONVENTION IN 1896—A WESTERN VIEW (*National Bimetallist*)

BRYAN AND HIS CABINET—AN EASTERN VIEW

ver, but that a word from you will work a 'wonderous' change, but that it must come *very* soon; could you open the campaign there the day after the Louisville Convention gives us a platform to stand on?"[1] On September 2 Roswell Miller wrote from Chicago: "The free silver sentiment in these states began to wane the latter part of July, and is still waning. I think the sound money cause will have the support of practically all the business element and the larger part of the labor element. The free silver strength is strongest among the farmers, but not so strong as it was."[2]

On September 22 Kenesaw M. Landis wrote from Lauderdale, Wis.: "While this silver business has been terribly serious throughout this whole section of the United States (due to the great scarcity of men who have not been pinched in some way by the hard times) in my view of conditions now there is not the element of doubt in the situation. At about the time of the Chicago Convention there was a strong disposition to clutch at most anything that promised a change, the general feeling appearing to be that anything would be better and nothing could be worse. But Bryan was stronger on the ninth of July than he has been at any time since and with each succeeding day he undoubtedly grows weaker."[3] James J. Hill wrote from St. Paul that "Sound money is making progress here every day, and I think the Northwest may be safely placed in the sound money column." Tom Taggart, mayor of Indianapolis, on September 28 expressed the opinion that the Populists, the Prohibitionists, and many former Republicans in the rural districts would vote for free silver, but added: "My belief is that if at this time there was an election in Indiana the Democrats would carry the state by 10,000 to 15,000, but it is a question in my mind if they will be able to hold their own for the next five weeks, which you well know will be the test of loyalty in our party. I do not think that the Palmer and Buckner ticket will

[1] G. D. Ripley of Eminence, Ky., to W. C. P. Breckinridge. Breckinridge MSS.
[2] Lamont MSS.
[3] Lamont MSS.

have a very large vote. As I said before, the majority will vote directly for McKinley." [1]

"The political situation changes in a small way like a kaleidoscope and on the whole sound money is making a steady improvement all along the line," wrote James J. Hill on October 1. "I think Minnesota will give sound money a majority of 20 to 25,000. . . . Both North and South Dakota are reasonably safe . . ., but more work will have to be done. My friends write from Oregon and Washington that they are hopeful, and lately a feeling has arisen in Montana that it would not be difficult to bring the Miners' Union, which really controls 30% of the state vote, into line for sound money. The 'old Democracy' is covering itself with honor." [2] From Watertown, N. Y., word came on October 15: "We are going to get a pretty good vote for our State ticket and the chances of a good vote for Palmer and Buckner improve of course as Bryan's chances disappear. . . . Dismissing all fears, I see no reason to believe that Bryan will not be well beaten." [3] James Ford Rhodes, the historian, wrote on October 25: "I presume there is no longer a doubt that the sound money cause will win." [4]

As the tide turned against them in the last few weeks of the

[1] Taggart to Lamont. Lamont MSS.
[2] Hill to Lamont. Lamont MSS.
[3] D. L. Griffin to Secretary Lamont. Lamont MSS.
[4] Rhodes to Julian, Julian-Giddings MSS.; the Cook County Democratic Central Committee broadcast over Chicago in October a circular admonishing the Gold Democrats that "To vote for Bryan is not only to throw away your vote, but to give your approval to the platform on which he stands. It will not elect him. It will encourage the leaders of factions who betrayed democracy to continue their organization and to make new assaults upon the integrity of the democratic faith and upon the honor of the republic.

". . . Palmer and Buckner, standing squarely on the Indianapolis platform, represent the democratic ideas which must ultimately prevail over the errors of McKinleyism and the kindred errors of Bryanism—all of them ephemeral.

"Although there is no possibility of their election, no democratic vote that may be cast for Palmer and Buckner will be thrown away. Every vote so cast will be a vote for the perpetuity and the honor of the democratic party—a party whose principles are eternal.

"So far as democrats are concerned in this campaign, all else is already lost. All else was surrendered at Chicago in July."

campaign, the silver followers daily grew more excited; their aroused emotions found expression in violence at gold-standard meetings. The most grievous insult was suffered by John G. Carlisle, whom no political opponent had ever accused of narrow partisanship and who had never in any speech during the campaign attacked the opposition. He had sought only to convince the silverites that the ideal they were chasing was a bubble which would burst and leave them poorer and possibly wiser. The climax came on the night of October 22, 1896, at his home city of Covington, where he had been invited by the sound-money advocates to speak. Scarcely had he finished his admonition: "This is not a time for the exhibition of passion and prejudice; it is not a time for personal abuse and misrepresentation; it is not a time for emotional oratory or dramatic display; but it is a time for calm and earnest deliberation and for courageous and patriotic action," when some of the silver group began to interrupt him with cries and jeers. Rotten eggs, pieces of bricks, cigar stubs, and other missiles were thrown at him in the town in which, scarcely ten years before, his carriage had been drawn through the streets by hand.

The incident received justly deserved criticism. A group of the foremost citizens of Louisville, inviting Carlisle to speak in their city, wired: "You will have such complete protection against insult and so grand an ovation . . . as will wipe out forever the attempt of last night to dishonor the fair name of Kentucky and to discredit her foremost citizen." [1] George C. Tichenor wrote President Cleveland: "When . . . a statesman distinguished alike for his purity of character and eminent abilities, is publicly insulted and threatened, . . . by a mob of the partisans of a candidate for the Presidency of the United States, the need for the admirable advice and admonitions given in your Princeton address, appears singularly urgent." [2] From New York came a letter: "A deep feeling of anxiety prevails among the people who appreciate the consequences of the success of Bryan and

[1] Telegram in Mrs. William K. Carlisle collection.
[2] Cleveland MSS.

every one will be glad when this anxiety is relieved. The outrage upon Mr. Carlisle is so infamous that the blood of any one who knows him must boil with indignation. He is one of the most lovable men I ever knew. I hope the people of Kentucky will rebuke this infamy as it deserves." [1]

Champ Clark, friend of Bryan and young silver advocate, has said of the event: "What Mr. Carlisle thought on that sad and unfortunate occasion can only be imagined. Being a well-read man, he may have had the poor consolation of recalling certain historical facts—that Hannibal was banished by the Carthaginians and died by suicide in a foreign land; that John DeWitt was torn limb from limb in front of his own Senate House by an infuriated mob; that Socrates was compelled to drink the fatal hemlock; that the windows in the home and carriage of the Duke of Wellington were broken fifteen years after Waterloo by his enraged countrymen; that the doors of Faneuil Hall were shut in the face of Daniel Webster; that the Legislature of Massachusetts passed resolutions of censure upon Charles Sumner in his old age, and other like instances." [2] Whatever Carlisle thought, he left no record; but it is certain that he was weary with politics and that his now declining years were not happy. Politically, the silverites had committed a grave error, for there was then only one other man in political life upon whom an attack would have brought greater censure —and that was the President of the United States.

Political disturbances were widespread. Assistant-Secretary Hamlin, who was then speaking in Massachusetts, noted in his diary on October 24, "Silver men tried to break up meeting," and again a week later, "Some trouble with the silverites." On October 31 Palmer and Buckner were met by a crowd in Paris, Mo., which hooted, jeered, and shouted, "Look at the McKinley Aid Society!" In Arkansas the hard-pressed farmers made the life of the gold advocates miserable. These demonstrations of passion were unfortunate, and they were probably

---

[1] C. S. Cary of Olean, N. Y., to Lamont, Oct. 24, 1896. Lamont MSS.
[2] *My Quarter Century*, II, pp. 235-236.

greatly regretted by Bryan. The attack on Carlisle most assuredly lost the silver party votes in Kentucky, easily accounting for the 281 ballots by which Bryan was defeated, and many voters in other States who had heretofore been undecided thereupon swallowed their prejudices and voted for McKinley.

The monetary situation grew more critical on the eve of the election. In New York alone over a million dollars of the Treasury's gold was drawn out on October 30 in exchange for legal-tenders. On that day Jordan of the New York subtreasury wrote Curtis at Washington, "The banks are hard up for currency and may need more to-morrow and Monday, but I think aid will come from Morgan." Interest rates on call money rose as high as 127 per cent; many people rushed to the Treasury to get gold for their legal-tenders, or to brokers to buy foreign securities. Large quantities of gold were hidden away to provide against the threatened danger of Bryan's election and to recoup in a measure the losses which would be incident to such a catastrophe.[1]

The vote on election day had two striking results: scarcely had the ballots been counted before the people who had carried the gold away from the treasury were back wanting to change it into legal-tenders; and at the same time numberless small groups over America were nominating William Jennings Bryan for the Presidency in 1900.

The emotions which were provoked by the outcome of the election were varied. No greater relief or keener disappointment, perhaps, has ever marked the termination of a campaign. The failure of the silver cause was certainly a grievous blow to its followers. They ascribed their defeat to two factors—corrupt practices on the part of the gold advocates, and the ignorance which had prevented the common people from understanding the opportunity which was within their grasp. "I take off my hat to Mr. Hanna and the 'campaign of education,' and at the same time I divest myself of every vestige of respect I may hitherto have entertained for 'the masses,'" wrote one of

[1] See *Commercial and Financial Chronicle,* November 7, 1896.

Bryan's followers. "Laboring men are, it seems, as purchasable as street walkers."[1] Women and children shared in the grief which fell upon the midlands; they had no idea of the economic principles involved, but they had felt the emotional call of the Bryan campaign. The letters which made up Bryan's mail in the weeks succeeding election day graphically reveal the hopes of both youth and age and the tragedies common in American life.

"You will no doubt be surprised to receive a letter from me," wrote Edna C. Norton of Cassapolis, Mich., "but we are all feeling so *blue* in southern Michigan that I wanted to tell you. We did try with all our *might* to have Free Silver win. I felt *sure* you would be elected, and it seemed as if you were truly a friend of the poor. at first I felt so sory for you, it must have been a great trial to be defeated then I began to feel sorry for myself for we are farmers and. we are in debt. have a little village property of my own, but have had to mortgage it. in order to save the farm. and if we have another four years of hard times, I am afraid we will lose every thing. these hard times. made a Christien of me, but it has worked differently with my Husband, he is proud, and it is very humilieting to be so reduced in our means & I fear for him. your election seemed the only hope we had. of better times. but we can think of thousands who are worse off than we are. I prayed every night that God would guide, direct, and keep you for it seemed as if you would go beyond your strength in the campaign. . . . I hope the time will come when we shall see you our President. and if you ever are. *pleas pension the Farmers,* for they never have had a friend in Washington yet. . . . it seems as if Free Silver, is the only thing that will help the farmers."[2]

On the same day came a letter from Carlisle, Ind.: "You will pardon me for addressing you when I tell you that I am an old farmer woman, who wants to congratulate you on the splendid canvass you have made. If you had won, I should

---
[1] Frank O. Howe to Bryan, November 4, 1896. Bryan MSS.
[2] Bryan MSS.

never have thought of writing to you, because in the triumph of success, you would not have needed the sympathy nor assurances of those for whom you fought so valiantly. But I want to tell you, that here in my country home, in the intervals of butter making, and poultry raising, and the work incident to life in this condition, I put on my spectacles and read *every one* of your speeches, and I want to tell you that your utterances had in them the gospel of righteousness, and that your cause was above criticism. You have risen as nobly to the rescue as ever Washington or Lincoln did in times of the country's need, and your work is not lost though temporarily defeated."

An old man sat down in his home in St. Louis and wrote: "My dear Boy. I have been looking for a Leader of Men for ten years— Now I have found him. . . . God has sent you to bless the American People. The Education and Reform will go on, & 4 years will soon pass. . . . The chain of Industrial Slavery will wear to the bone, the poor ignorant workers may vote right next time. . . . I am 'Pa' Chase, Reformer, 77 years old, a 'damned abolitionist' in 1836." J. E. Wick wrote from Murray, Ia.: "I was an American reformer before you were born. I voted for Frémont in 56. and for Lincoln in 60 & 64 I voted for Grant in 68—but not in 72. I was and am A Peter Cooper Greenbacker I write this to express my pledge anew to support you in 1900 if I am alive." "I am but one of millions made sad by your defeat in the cause of Bi Metalism," wrote a citizen of Waco, Texas, and a Kentuckian sent the message, "I am heartily ashamed that this the good old State of Kentucky should have gone astray, although the power of the enemy was against us." The old soldiers in Sioux Falls, S. D., passed resolutions declaring: "Although we have not accomplished all we attempted, yet, Ours is a victory. Not a defeat. We have made a gallant fight for freedom, and have not been vanquished, in this the Great Battle for Humanity. Our cause is eternal, and will yet prevail."

Daniel N. Crowley, an attorney of Salem, Mass., wrote the defeated candidate: "The fight is over. The field is lost. But the vanquished need not despair." The Reverend James H. Lathrop of Cortland, New York, sent a message of hope: "Dear Friend of the *great common people*. Your defeat is only temporary. God has chosen you as the greatest deliverer of an oppressed people. . . . The mighty battle you have fought has made you the greatest leader of our time. The Lord gird you with strength." T. C. Dodson, Jr., wrote in behalf of the citizens of Hermitage, Tenn.: " 'Truth crushed to Earth will rise again' and when this silver wave rises again the Devil himself cannot stop it. You remember 'Old Hickory' did not get it in his first race for Presidency but the next time there was nothing that he did not get. The same thing will be true of you."

J. E. Rickards, governor of Montana, wrote from the executive office on November 5: "I write to express to you my deep regret that the magnificent campaign made by you for humanity and the welfare of men in every honorable vocation, has not been crowned with the success it so richly merited. Your defeat falls upon your friends and admirers in this State as a personal affliction. . . . Here and now I place you in nomination for the presidency in 1900, and believe it will be seconded by a chorus of millions who feel that your elevation to the White House is the manifest destiny of national affairs and consistent with the best interests of the republic." Four days later John P. Altgeld, governor of Illinois, wrote from Springfield: "You have done a work for humanity which time will not efface and while we were not able to batter down all the fortified strongholds of plutocracy and corruption in our fight I am convinced that another assault will drive them from the land."

Children, too, were saddened; there is no reason to disbelieve the hundreds of letters which say that the youthful writers had sat down and cried. They had imbibed the hatred of "the bloated aristocracy" which possessed their elders. One little girl refused to wear gold-rimmed glasses, and another wrote from Greensboro, N. C.: "We are all so sorry here in

Greensboro that you are not elected. We little children have been shouting hurrah for Bryan, 16 to 1 and hoping that you would be the next president. We all love you and we don't like McKinley and we hate old Hanna." Elvira D. Cuffe of Mount Solon, Va., confided to the Democratic leader: "I am very sory that you was not elected for I wanted lots of money but I now [know] I will get plenty of it in four years from now. Papa is a stong Bryan man and I cryed when I heard that you was bet [beat]. I am a little girl eight years old."

The campaign was certainly thorough; perhaps at no time has a greater percentage of the population of the country been so completely interested. Bryan has said of it, "The campaign of 1896 was a remarkable one whether we measure it by the magnitude of the issues involved or by the depth of interest aroused." The two groups were intensely concerned over the outcome. The gold men were fighting against an event which they feared, the dangers of which could not be exactly known. They sincerely believed that the success of the silver forces would mean calamity and complete destruction of the only sound standard of value. They desired to protect not only their own property, but also the property of the deluded brother from himself. On the other hand, the silver men were battling with equal sincerity in a great crusade against the "gold barons" of Europe and America. "We enlist in a cause," said Joseph C. Sibley, leader of the silver movement in Pennsylvania, "the triumph of which shall bless not less the vanquished than the victors."

In some ways, however, the contest was not a satisfactory one. Many of the silver votes were cast, especially in the East, not because the voters understood the principles of free silver, but because they held to the theory that "things could be no worse." Over the land the people were constantly reminded that "the interests of the man who has a large amount of money and those of one who has none, are generally directly opposed to each other with reference to this [money] question." It is true also that many gold votes were cast not because the voters perceived what gains could be secured from a gold standard of value, but because they had been led to believe that the silver demands were dishonest. Railroad officials are said to have forbidden their employees to distribute silver literature in the West. Large amounts of money were spent by the gold advocates. The Republican campaign chest was swollen by donations from life insurance companies, bankers, and others of the Wall Street group. Even the Gold Democrats were able to share in these lavish gifts. They could not draw such generous sums as did the Republicans, however, and they were often in need of funds. This lack was made up in part by donations from the Republicans. Indeed, the two parties united their energies and their money in a desperate effort to cover the midlands with a multitude of pamphlets and to assail the voters with a legion of speakers. Mark Hanna himself supplied some of the cash which carried on the Palmer-Buckner ticket.[1]

It is not strange that the silver strength began to wane in the last weeks of the campaign. Whatever sympathies one has with the unfortunate farmers and laborers, he must admit that their cause was not well expounded by their political leaders. The orators who filled the land with pleas for free silver overlooked the sound arguments at hand and appealed to the emotions of an excited people. They deepened the faith of those who were already convinced, but won few new converts. The student of today must look elsewhere for his knowledge of the actual conditions of the followers after free silver. William Jennings Bryan put forth little actual argument. He appeared before a crowd, the band played "Hail to the Chief," and he walked upon the stage. He raised one hand and then the other, and a smile overspread his great mouth; he spoke to the hearts of the people, but when the occasion was over, there was little residue for thought. John G. Carlisle was not met by enormous crowds, and no band played "Hail to the

---

[1] See James A. Barnes, "The Gold-Standard Democrats and the Party Conflict," in *The Mississippi Valley Historical Review*, December, 1930, pp. 422–450. See also Beer's *Hanna*, Croly's *Marcus Alonzo Hanna*, and Olcott's *McKinley*.

Chief"; he raised no hand, and neither did a smile spread over his face. He looked much like a college professor who, although giving a good course, was somewhat bored with his students; and yet, when he had ended, his listeners had heard principles stated so clearly that they were compelled, regardless of their agreement or disagreement, to think upon the questions discussed.

It is not necessary to defend the gold advocates or to deny the fact that immense sums were spent in the campaign in order to prove that economic coercion or purchase was not a determining factor in the election. The South had few factories, and therefore the threat of no work if Bryan was elected could not have any effect; furthermore, no political leader would have sent purchase-money into these States. Yet Bryan failed to equal the Cleveland vote of 1892 in Alabama, Georgia, Louisiana, and Virginia—and, if the Populist vote is counted as silverite, in Florida and North Carolina in addition. His increase over Cleveland's vote was only 84,000, while McKinley polled some 285,000 more ballots than had Harrison. It is perfectly evident that in the South many people believed in free coinage, but the factor which in the main guided the hand of the Southerner in marking his ballot on November 3 was "Democratic regularity"—and even this was considerably shaken. Success came to the gold forces because doubt arose in the minds of the voters of America as to the value of the free-silver experiment. It does not lessen one's sympathy with the farmer and laborer in his grievous lot to say that the followers of Bryan were on the whole incapable of comprehending the principles involved.

The victory of the gold advocates did not quiet their fears. R. H. Clarke of Alabama revealed his lack of understanding of the forces behind the silver crusade when he wrote on November 5: ". . . the Bible says, I believe, that you may bray a fool in the mortar and yet not beat his folly out of him."[1] The cartoonist who depicted the defeat of Bryan in the words, "It

---
[1] Clarke to Breckinridge. Breckinridge MSS.

may be Fo(u)r Years and it may be Forever," caught what was in the minds of the victors. This fear led to a continuation of the fawning tolerance which the Gold Democrats and the Republicans had shown each other in the campaign. Richard Watson Gilder is authority for the statement that when Cleveland and McKinley parted at the latter's inauguration, the former said to the new President: "I beg you to remember that the time may come again when it will be necessary for another union of the forces which supported honest money; and for this reason I ask you to use your influence against any such executive action as would prevent such a union." McKinley replied that he had remembered that in the make-up of his Cabinet; and, indeed, Lyman J. Gage, a gold-standard Democrat of Chicago, was appointed Secretary of the Treasury. Had McKinley only been sound on the tariff question, the thoughts of Grover Cleveland on his way to Princeton might have been as pleasant as those of Andrew Jackson as he rode over the Allegheny Mountains toward the Hermitage after seeing his beloved Martin Van Buren safely lodged in the White House.

As it was, however, he knew that protection would again become paramount when Thomas B. Reed took up the Speaker's gavel in the Fifty-fifth Congress, and he knew, too, that he carried with him the hatred of millions of America's citizens—citizens, moreover, who implicitly believed that they would be able further to condemn the Cleveland-Carlisle policies in 1900. But the great crusade was over, for the free-silver cause evaporated before the century could count off its few remaining years. The millions who had enlisted in the dramatic conflict had reasons enough, and their labors were not without results. The six and one-half million people who voted for Bryan were not fools, and neither were the seven million who cast their ballots for McKinley thieves and robbers. It seems now a rational statement to say that the condition of the Westerner in these years was worse than is commonly believed, and that the actions of the Easterner were prompted by far less selfish motives than those with which he is credited.

The citizens of the midlands still look back with pleasure upon this well-fought battle, and today, when hard-pressed farmers haul eight times as many bushels of wheat to market to pay the interest on their notes as it required in the halcyon days after the war, and when forty bushels of oats are necessary to purchase a pair of slippers for "the lady," and when tires and gas are needed for the car and tubes for the radio, they are asking with Vachel Lindsay:

> Where is that boy, that Heaven-born Bryan,
> That Homer Bryan, who sang from the West?

Let us hope that their burdens may never become so real as those of the 'eighties and 'nineties; but should the silver question, under a new leader from the West, rise from its thirty-year grave and shake off the winding sheet which financiers, politicians, and business men felt was so securely tied, may the bitterness of the Great Crusade be absent, and may the records of honest and brilliant statesmen who may oppose it be not buried under an avalanche of misdirected hatreds.

Peace did not come to the Treasury Department even with the decision of the people concerning the gold standard; sub-Treasurer Jordan of New York, always fearful, yet always annoyingly correct in his foresight, wrote Assistant-Secretary Curtis in the last days of the administration:

> I think I am at the end of my tether. There is but say 2 millions of legal tenders in the office, and no more in sight. Sixty per cent of our receipts are in silver—rather more than less, and we are running behind about $650,000 per day. I had hoped that at least 10 million would come in from the U.P. sale, but that hope is knocked out, so that on the 1st Feb. if not before, I must pay in gold at the C[learing] H[ouse]—the Treasury notes are too small to use there (without Meline can send me large) I have been paying in ½ Ty notes ½ legal tender and have shinned until I can shin no more. If you can send large Treasury notes—all right, if not, an authority from Congress

to use Treasury notes in the same manner as legal tenders (that is for C.H. certificates) would carry us through in triumph and permit us to deliver to the incoming Adm say $140,000,000 Gold. If we pay *that* out we will never get a dollar back. My fear is that when we get to losing gold—it will go with great rapidity. You had better come over to Macedonia and help us.[1]

[1] Jordan to Curtis, January 26, 1897. Curtis MSS.

CHAPTER XIX CARLISLE'S LAST YEARS

"WHEN the conductor 'rolled him off at Princeton' on March 18, 1897, his sixtieth birthday as it chanced, Mr. Cleveland believed himself the most unpopular man in America, and there was some justification for the belief." [1] With his retirement, there went also John G. Carlisle. For four years the two statesmen had struggled against heavy odds, and though they lost the friendship of a great number of those who had followed them, they had the satisfaction of knowing that they had maintained the existing standard of value, and had lived to see the free-silver heresy defeated. Carlisle had lost more, if possible, than Cleveland, because he had been longer in the service of the people, had depended more on them, and had been more closely connected with all the movements for the relief of the common man which had come up in national politics for twenty years. It is difficult to know what were Carlisle's thoughts on his withdrawal from public office, because he left no record.

Carlisle could not retire to some secluded spot to reflect on the ingratitude of the American people; he was nearly twenty thousand dollars in debt, and it is doubtful that there was any gift within the power of the people with which they would have entrusted him. He had only two interests in life—politics and law—and he must now turn to the latter. He considered practising in Washington or Louisville, but eventually decided to go to New York, the city from which he had received the least abuse during his Treasury years. There he joined the firm of Curtis, Mallet-Provost & Colt as counselor, maintaining branch offices in Washington and Louisville.

In New York, Carlisle is described as a great lawyer with few clients, and yet it appears that he was kept busy by his profession. The few letters written by him show that he was

[1] McElroy, *Grover Cleveland*, II, p. 256.

unable to leave his practice. On September 30, 1897, he declined an invitation from Henry Watterson to visit Kentucky. "Most of my law cases are coming in a *bunch*," he said, "and I have been as busy as a sailor preparing briefs which are not yet finished. Four of my cases are set for oral argument in the Supreme Court in October. . . . Besides, I have an important case set for trial in the U. S. Circuit Court at New York, in October, and I am troubled to see how I will be able to get away from here to attend to it. Choate and Evarts are on the other side and my clients will never forgive me if I fail to be on hand, especially if . . . absent on a political expedition."[1] On June 6, 1906, he again wrote Watterson: "It does not seem at the present time that I will be able to attend the Home-Coming at Louisville, as our courts here do not take their annual recess until the last week in June, and my affairs are in such a condition that it would be almost impossible to leave them."[2] On July 1, 1907, he wrote his brother from Washington: "I have been [here] for more than a month, engaged on a railroad arbitration."[3] A year before his death he could not accept an invitation from Henry Watterson to join him on a trip to Europe; "I would be delighted to go across with you and Mrs. Watterson," he wrote, "and hope I may be able to do so—I need the rest, the air and the 25 cents, but my business is in such a condition that I cannot say at this time whether I can go or not. That Virginia case [West Virginia vs. Virginia] and one or two others may keep me at home all summer. I have had no vacation since 1905 and had hoped to get a little rest before autumn, but the prospect is not very encouraging."[4] It is not at all certain that he had a large practice, but he was considered a great lawyer, and the professional journals spoke highly of him.[5] He may have been too old, as

[1] Carlisle to Watterson, September 30, 1897. Watterson MSS.
[2] *Ibid.,* June 6, 1906.
[3] Letter presented to the writer by Napoleon H. Carlisle.
[4] Carlisle to Watterson, June 4, 1909. Watterson MSS.
[5] See the *Green Bag* and the *Bench and Bar* (New York) at the time of his death.

CARLISLE'S LAST YEARS

some thought, to succeed in a new field, and he may never have been able, as others said, to grasp the movement of big business and charge sufficient fees for his services.[1] Neither of these opinions is borne out, however, by the little evidence available..

Carlisle was an attorney in prominent cases, and he was associated with the leading lawyers of the Supreme Court. He acted in a Texas tax case involving more than a million dollars, for which he received a fee of $30,000. In the case of Knolton vs. Moore [2] he was retained with Wheeler H. Peckham and Charles H. Otis for the plaintiff in error, with Thomas B. Reed among his opponents. The action involved an estate of more than two and one-half million dollars on which taxes had been improperly levied. The court upheld Carlisle's contentions. His most important cases were, perhaps, those of a constitutional nature which arose from our Spanish-American War acquisitions. He had actively opposed the imperialistic policy of the United States, but once the possessions had been acquired, he saw no way of withholding any part of the Constitution from them. The question was complicated by the fact that there were three different periods in the acquisition: first, from the beginning of the war to the signing of peace; second, from the signing of peace to the Foraker Act; and third, after the Foraker Act. Carlisle was retained by the plaintiffs in all three periods. The decision that the Constitution might be applied in part must have grated harshly on his ears.[3]

---

[1] Urey Woodson, Democratic National Committeeman from Kentucky, wrote the author on January 1, 1926: "I remember to have asked Mr. Thomas Fortune Ryan once if he thought Carlisle would be a success in New York. He very emphatically told me 'No,' explaining that he, himself, had employed Mr. Carlisle in one case; that Mr. Carlisle had practiced it perfectly and successfully but that when he asked him to send him his bill, Carlisle only asked him for $2,000. He said 'I would have paid him $50,000 without hesitation, and any man who has no more sense than that about charging a fee can not succeed in New York.'"

[2] 178 U. S. 41.

[3] Downes V. Bidwell, 182 U. S. 244. The decision was in part that "the Island of Porto Rico is a territory appurtenant and belonging to the United States, but not a part of the United States within the revenue clauses of the Constitution";

Carlisle was retained in the famous Virginia vs. West Virginia controversy, and was prepared to make the leading speech when death overtook him.[1] As a Supreme Court lawyer the former Secretary retained the same logic and preciseness which had marked his political career. "There never was a man who practiced at the Supreme Court bar who was such a miser for words as John G. Carlisle," wrote a lifelong associate. "He saw the weakness of his adversary and the strength of his own side. The latter he made manifest, and the former he took by the throat and throttled."[2] Charles S. Hamlin has written: "I remember that Mr. Justice Gray of the United States Supreme Court told me one day, I think in 1898 or 1899, that Mr. Carlisle had argued an important case before the Court that morning, and that he never heard as brilliant and cogent an argument as that given by Mr. Carlisle. President Cleveland once told me he considered him one of the most brilliant intellects of the day. He had a rare faculty, in arguing, of stating the case of his opponent most fairly, often better than the opponent could do himself."[3]

But Carlisle's career as a lawyer brought him few pleasures; his life lay behind him, and his mind was wrapped up in the services he had given to the host of people who had followed him in his early political years, but who had turned away from him and practically forgotten his existence. Many friends, it is true, called at his home at 2 Gramercy Park, and New York officially paid him high honor, but he was lost in the great city. "I like New York well enough," he told a friend; yet there is much in his further comment: "One does miss the knowing of every one you meet, the buoying up with smiles around you."

"New York swallows statesmen and great politicians as

---

he was also attorney in the cases of Dooley v. United States (182 U. S. 222 and 183 U. S. 151—one before and one after the Foraker Act) and he made at least one trip to Cuba and Porto Rico in preparation of his arguments.

[1] See *Courier-Journal*, August 2, 1910; *Bench and Bar*, XXII, No. 2, August, 1910.

[2] O. O. Stealey in the *Courier-Journal*, Aug. 1, 1910.

[3] Charles S. Hamlin to the writer, March 3, 1931.

calmly as it digests a millionaire from Kalamazoo or a copper king from Montana," wrote a correspondent of a Manhattan paper. "South of St. Paul's they move daily among the half million of the busy bees and their buzz does not rise above the crowd. . . . One sees a tall man of clean shaven, thoughtful face, crossing Broad street. He wears a tall hat and a long frock coat that makes him look taller still. He is steering in and out among the 'curbstone' brokers, who dispute the middle of the roadway with cabs, wagons and itinerant lunch stands. A young clerk, eager for quotations, jostles him; a trader with a big book walks into him. He keeps his course. One can follow his top hat above the derbys of the crowd. He walks dreamily under a great stone entrance, and without looking for or getting a salute, he is presently whisking upward among a cageful of nonentities packed as tight as sardines. At the eighth floor he struggles out, and on a glass door you may learn that John G. Carlisle is there engaged in the practice of law with several experts." There was, continued the newswriter, a slightly pathetic touch about the lonely figure "that the tall and courteous Kentuckian, dignified without effort and commanding without pose, would be the last to desire to impart." Throughout the land countless former friends believed that this once great statesman now lived in affluence on the bounties of the gold barons whom he had assisted in robbing the government; instead, he toiled diligently day after day in order to obtain the necessaries of life.

Loss of political friends was not the only misfortune which Carlisle suffered. Scarcely had he established himself in his new life when death stalked into his household and took his two sons—his only children to reach manhood. In February, 1898, Logan Carlisle dropped dead in his bath, and a few months later William K. Carlisle died of pneumonia. The letters which came from all over the world proved that there were still many who cared, but they could not fill the aching void. Henry Nelson Loomis of *Harper's*, the editor of the *Nation*, and thousands of others sent their condolences, but no one was more grieved than Cleveland. A few months before, he had written Richard Olney: "Carlisle spent a day or two with me last week and I enjoyed his visit very much. What an able good man he is!" [1] On February 16 he wrote his former Cabinet member: "My dear Mr. Carlisle. Since I heard the shocking news of Logan's death you have been much in my mind and I have daily wanted to write to you. I have failed to do this only because I did not know what to say that could possibly be of any comfort to you. I heard something of the sad details from Col. Lamont. . . . I only hope that time and the sincere sympathy of devoted friends will turn the edge of grief." [2]

Even more letters came at the death of his second and last son. Mrs. Walter Q. Gresham wrote Mrs. Carlisle: "You and your dear husband were such a comfort to me when I went back to Washington on my sad mission.[3] You are connected with my dear one's last days. Now your hearts ache as mine has done. May the good Lord help you and give you strength to bear it." Alonzo H. Stewart wrote from Washington: "My dear 'Senator': Permit me to offer you my most sincere sympathy for the great loss you have just entertained. You see I still think of you as I knew you, a Senator who was always so kind to Yours most truly." Wagner Swayne wrote that "One could hardly be acquainted with you and not realize that such a nature must suffer more than is usual even in a calamity such as yours." From Princeton came a simple but earnest letter: "Such afflictions must be borne unaided by mortal help, except as they may be mitigated by the sympathy of true friends. How I wish I could take you by the hand and assure you how fully you have mine. Your sincere friend, Grover Cleveland." [4]

But the most touching of all the letters was one written by

[1] April 14, 1897. Olney MSS.
[2] Mrs. William K. Carlisle MSS.
[3] Walter Q. Gresham died on May 28, 1895, while Secretary of State.
[4] Mrs. William K. Carlisle MSS.

the father himself; it reveals the patient fortitude of a man who, regardless of the political or personal afflictions which came, toiled uncomplainingly on:

July 13, 1898

J. W. Posinfrey Esq.
Covington, Ky.,

DEAR SIR: Mrs. Carlisle and I thank you most sincerely for the beautiful tribute to the memory of our late son, Will, contained in the last issue of your paper. We hear also in grateful remembrance the kindly and appreciative memorial to Logan published by you soon after he left us; less than six months ago. Both of our boys are gone and we feel that there cannot be many more troubles in store for us, but whether they be few or many we will meet them without complaint and bear them with all the courage and forbearance at our command.

Yours truly
J. G. CARLISLE

Although sorrow had weighted his already stooping form, Carlisle still loved the old Democracy. He and Cleveland were both out of politics, but they could not forget the party which had given them so many gifts along with so much abuse, and their ideal was to steer it back into the channels it had followed before it had turned aside to follow after the false gods of Bryan. As the Republicans revived the protective tariff, Carlisle grieved that the party was incapable of combating it. He wrote Desha Breckinridge of Lexington, Kentucky: "Your favor inclosing the editorial on Mr. Bailey's recent speech is received, for which please accept my thanks. The free silver party is hopelessly divided on the tariff question, and can be of no service to us in the coming contest for free trade. Free raw material lies at the very foundation of the policy, for if the materials used in our industries are taxed, of course the finished products must be taxed also. Whatever Mr. Bailey, or those who agree with him, may say to the contrary, they are protectionists. They admit the correctness of the principle of protection and quarrel with the Republicans only in regard to its application." [1]

The Democracy was, indeed, little interested in tariff reform, for the two groups were still quarreling over the financial question. In anticipation of future conflicts, the Gold Democrats pushed forward their educational program after 1896 with greater energy than ever. William D. Bynum, chairman of the executive committee, remained at his office in Indianapolis and made every possible effort to extend his political organization into all States. On November 18 he wrote to George M. Davey of Louisville: "I fully agree with you that the impression should not be allowed to prevail that our work is completed and that we are ready to lay down our arms and surrender the leadership of the Democratic party to the hands of those who controlled the Chicago Convention." [2] Headquarters were eventually moved to New York City, but the work became less and less important as dissension arose, and as the issue dwindled in the face of new developments which dwarfed this once great rallying point.

The Democratic organization under Bryan was not without its difficulties in the years immediately succeeding the election of 1896. Internal discord appeared, and it taxed the energies of the great campaigner to hold the dissimilar groups together.[3] With economic changes the cry of "free silver" lost its power as a political talisman, and many people deserted the party. The reason for this desertion was truthfully though not

[1] Quoted in Lexington *Morning Herald*, August 11, 1897.

[2] Bynum Letter Books; letters of this nature were sent to the leaders in practically every State. See also the Breckinridge MSS.

[3] On April 26, 1900, James K. Jones wrote Bryan: "I don't think it is possible to get a vote in the Senate on the amendment to elect Senators by the people, and if we could, there would be a very formidable division amongst ourselves. Daniel, who has got in the habit of being wrong on many questions, is very strongly opposed to this proposition. . . . I am afraid a vote would develop such differences amongst us as to deprive us of any advantage from it. . . . There does not seem to be a feeling of cordial confidence between the Democrats and the Populists [in Kansas] that I would like to see, and both are to blame." Similar difficulties were experienced in many States. Bryan MSS.

delicately put by W. M. Disher when he wrote Bryan that "the average workingman cannot, or will not, think beyond a full belly." These losses were in part made up by the enlistment of Gold Democrats, even though Bryan aggressively objected to their return. Senator Jones, however, opposed this ostracism, and he wrote the Nebraskan on April 26, 1900: "If men who opposed you in '96 [want] to stand up in the front row now, and throw their hats around and yell, and do things of that kind, I for one [am] willing that they should do it."

The difficulty was that each of the Democratic groups expected the members of the other to see the error of their ways and return to the fold. Indomitable Grover Cleveland was sure that if the party was ever to accomplish anything again, "it must cease to wander and return to the old faith, diligently seeking the old landmarks,"[1] while ponderous Ollie M. James of Kentucky believed that "Judas Iscariot would have had as much right to have been clambering over the hill of Calvary after his Master's Crucifixion attempting to reorganize the believers in christianity as Grover Cleveland, John Carlisle or Don Dickinson have to rush forth to reorganize the party they betrayed."[2]

Had opposing leaders been willing to forget the financial controversy, the Democracy could have united upon the issue provided by the Spanish-American War. The question whether the United States should enter into the enticing fields of imperialism called for thorough debate. In an article on "Our Future Policy" Carlisle presented in his singularly lucid and brilliant manner the arguments of a particular school of defenders of the Monroe Doctrine. "Whether we shall enter upon a career of conquest and annexation in the islands of the seas adjacent to our shores and in distant parts of the world, or adhere to the peaceful continental system which has heretofore characterised our national course," he wrote, "is by far the most important question yet presented for the considera-

[1] Cleveland to W. J. Curtis, September 1, 1897. Cleveland MSS.
[2] James to Bryan, January 30, 1901. Bryan MSS.

tion of our people in connection with the existing war with Spain." The purpose for which the war was begun had been forgotten, he asserted, and results were appearing which might "make this struggle with a feeble monarchy in Europe the commencement of a new era in the history of the great American republic." He saw the beginning of a revolution in the opinions and aspirations of the people "which may ultimately prove fatal to the simple republican institutions under which we now live."

The nation, he argued, had professed to enter the war for moral reasons, and hence should indulge in no spoliation of the enemy's property; to exact territory to cover the costs of the war would be to place the United States in the humiliating attitude "of demanding compensation for our humanity and love of liberty." Moreover, the nation was pledged by its previous policy not "to make acquisitions of territory or establish governments in other quarters of the world" and was likewise bound not to interfere in European affairs. James Monroe could not have said in 1823 that the United States would expand when and where it demanded; the doctrine was binding on the government that promulgated it as much as upon those against whom it was issued. Nations live long, asserted Carlisle, and if the United States assumed the right to expand where she liked, Europe would at some time assume the same privilege. Moreover, our polity was not designed for the government of colonies and provinces. The Union was a republic of self-governing States, and there was no provision for holding a territory except in preparation for admission into the Union upon a footing of perfect equality.

The races which America was about to absorb, continued Carlisle, knew nothing of her liberties and ideals; their civilization and their concepts of right and wrong were entirely different from those of the American people. Unless she violated her organic law and held and governed the territories perpetually, they must some day be taken into the Union as States and send their Senators and Representatives into the

American Congress. Once started, where would this stop? It must continue until it had fastened upon the government "a black and yellow horde of conscript citizens to debauch the suffrage and sap the foundations of our free institutions." The new policy was leading America to neglect grave domestic questions in order to pursue "dreams of wealth, of commercial supremacy abroad, martial glory, and autocratic dictation in great international councils of the world." Such a policy would throw a great burden of taxation upon the nation for the support of a large army and navy. The glory would go to a military class, and "the people at large will simply enjoy the privilege of paying the cost." It seemed better by far to Carlisle "that monarchial Spain should continue to rule a people against their will than that the United States should usurp her place and hold them in subjection in the name of liberty and humanity." Expansion, it appeared to him, could have but one result: the throwing of America into the European vortex and into European diplomacy. An alliance of the Anglo-Saxon nations, with a settlement of difficulties by arbitration if diplomacy failed, was his ideal.[1]

An admirer compared the article to the best papers in the *Federalist,* and Cleveland wrote from Princeton:

I cannot tell you how much I was gratified with your "expansion" article. I can't for the life of me see how such a thing can be insisted on in the face of such a plain exposure of its dangers and the political inconsistency it entails. It often seems to me that the ears of our people are closed to reason.

The campaign of 1900 supplied the first real test of the attitude which the two Democratic wings were to take toward each other. Early in the year William Randolph Hearst, a staunch supporter in '96, wired Bryan: "My people everywhere from the Atlantic to the Pacific tell me there is no free silver senti-

[1] John G. Carlisle, "Our Future Policy," in *Harpers,* Vol. 97, (1898) pp. 720–728.

ment. I have become convinced that the people don't want free silver and that we can't make them want free silver and that if we try we will lose the opportunity to do great good in other directions." Ex-Governor Stone of Missouri also objected to restating the 16 to 1 policy, but Bryan was adamant. In spite of its declining popularity, he forced the silver issue into the platform. "If it were not for the fight that has been made against the silver plank for the last four years, it would not now be so necessary to restate it," he declared. "The Republicans have come out boldly for the gold standard. It is the only positive plank in their platform. If we do anything that can be construed as a surrender or as cowardice they will make their fight upon that question and assert that after making silver the paramount issue in '96 we are willing now to accept the gold standard and that in 1904 we will be willing to accept trusts and imperialism." [1]

The election brought another and even more emphatic defeat to the party. The Bryan papers show that the Nebraskan had lost much of his hold upon the common people. Late in November Watterson, perhaps hopeful that he might serve as peacemaker, wrote the twice-defeated candidate:

My Dear Mr. Bryan:
On returning from New York, where I have been spending the past two weeks, I find your letter of the 16th. Allow me to thank you for it and to say that I appreciate most highly the kind sentiments it embraces. I want you to know that I am your friend, and that throughout the campaign of 1896 I wrote no word and countenanced no word which was not wholly courteous and considerate. Our differences have related to one single issue and perhaps to some matters of expediency and method. I am twenty years older than you and during the years from my thirty-fifth to my fifty-fifth year, I traversed much of the ground you have been traversing the last ten years. I am not hopeless, but in the nature of the case I cannot be as buoyant at sixty as a man of forty. I enclose you a proof slip

[1] Bryan MSS.

embracing some reflections which will appear in tomorrow's issue of the Courier-Journal. I throw them out by way of suggestion merely. It may happen during the next two or three months that we shall be within reach of one another. I should greatly like to sit down quietly somewhere and have an unrestrained talk with you. It may be that you may be able to extract something from my experiences. I have nothing before me except my newspaper work and am, as far as the concrete things of politics go, as unselfish and disinterested as it is possible for man to be. As matters stand, it seems to me the least said the soonest mended.

Your friend
HENRY WATTERSON.[1]

Carlisle, maintaining that the South had isolated herself in the deadening coils of a hopeless issue, pleaded for reorganization and new ambitions. A few weeks after the election he wrote of the Democracy:

Whether there shall or shall not be a reorganization of the Democratic party and a return to its old principles and traditional policies depends, in my opinion, almost entirely upon the action of the Democrats in the South. Of the 155 electoral votes secured at the recent election for the candidates nominated by the three allied political parties only thirteen were chosen outside of the Southern States, and these thirteen were chosen in only four States by popular majorities aggregating less than 50,000.

The Southern people have thus separated themselves from the great body of their friends in the North and West and attached themselves to the mining States of Colorado, Idaho, Montana and Nevada, four comparatively small States, which have, or think they have a special interest in the free coinage of silver and the other Populistic policies promulgated for the first time in a national convention at Chicago in 1896.

On all these questions the true interests of the South are identical with the interests of the great industrial and com-

[1] Bryan MSS.

mercial States, whose votes have been cast on the other side, and which will continue to be cast the same way as long as the same questions are agitated.

Surely, the two overwhelming defeats sustained by the party since its new departure at Chicago in 1896 ought to be sufficient to convince the most obstinate mind that further efforts in that direction will be useless, and that the party must either retrace its steps or cease to be considered a formidable power in national politics.[1]

Cleveland, too, was fretting over the misfortunes of the party which he believed thieves had stolen. He wrote on December 14:

My Dear Mr Carlisle:

Mrs. Cleveland and I have lately discussed with painful uncertainty, the proposition whether or not we have either of us acknowledged with proper appreciation, the receipt of the fine mackerel you sent us a long time ago. Whether we are in default or not I want to say to you that we are grateful to you for the fish, which was the best I have ever tasted—which is saying a good deal as I consider myself an expert.

It's very queer that so long a time has elapsed since we have met or communicated— I have heard about you sometimes. I was pleased very much by your interview given out just after the election. Though I thought at the time it was about right, I have been more and more convinced that it hit the nail on the head. I was very much encouraged at first by the tone of some of the Southern papers, but I am not now feeling so well, since I see that many others of them are still inclined to play the fool and ass.

I am actually ashamed to read some of their outgivings indicating that the South is not getting its share in the *control of the Democratic party:*—and this at a time when so many good Northern Democrats are attempting to repair the damage which has been visited on the party largely through the solidity

[1] In *The Review of the Republic,* December, 1900; see also the New York *World,* Dec. 17.

and preponderating influence of the Southern contingent in the present organization.

It appears to be a question whether sense will prevail in that quarter. It may be that the weight of sentiment will settle on the right side. If it does I can see a bright prospect for rehabilitated Democracy—otherwise a longer flounder in the mire of wilful defeat. . . .

Just at this moment a representative of the Atlanta *Journal* called and I have been giving him and his paper a "piece of my mind." [1]

The two staunch old Democrats and firm friends—still unconvinced that American politics had changed in its nature—sorrowfully went their ways. While Cleveland was suffering much of the time from his "old enemy" the gout, Carlisle puzzled over the technicalities of "big business" law. During the next two years they saw much of each other, for Cleveland was writing his *Presidential Problems,* and Carlisle was searching for documents to support the statements of his former chief.

In 1904 Carlisle was present at the Parker notification meeting in New York—an old man, quite stooped, showing something of his disappointments, but undoubtedly heartened for the moment. "I had heard so much about him that I looked upon him with wonder not unmixed with sadness, remembering past greatnesses," Mrs. Champ Clark has written.[2] Cleveland wrote him on August 3: "I am exceedingly interested in the Parker campaign and I note with pleasure what you say concerning the new hope that has aroused the old sound democratic spirit. The deflection of Oscar Straus and John A. McCall amazes and disappoints me. I cannot conceive how any Democrat professing to desire the redemption of the party from the low state to which the folly of the last long sad eight years has brought it, can now turn his back on the promise of better days."

[1] Cleveland-Carlisle MSS.
[2] Mrs. Genevieve Bennett Clark, Bowling Green, Mo., in a letter to the writer, December 2, 1925.

But better days were not in store, for Parker was hopelessly beaten, and four years more brought Bryan again. Cleveland did not live to witness the defeat of 1908; he died on June 24 of that year, leaving Carlisle, after a friendship of nearly a quarter of a century between the greatest leaders of the Northern and the Southern Democracy which the party produced in their generation, to mourn his death.

Carlisle was little interested in the campaign, for patient perseverance had ended with the death of his wife on August 4, 1905. The telegram, "Mrs. Carlisle died this morning, funeral here Sunday at one o'clock," which he sent his faithful friends, "Marse Henry" and Mrs. Watterson, had filled his cup of life. The remaining years were lonely, and in spite of hard work his income scarcely sufficed to maintain his home. Even then no bitterness entered his heart, but as the end drew near with nothing of hope, with nothing to leave to those few who would grieve for him, and with little evidence of any appreciation of his laborious years in the interest of his country, he turned again, after a long abstinence, to some of the habits of his youth. Not often, but occasionally, he shuffled around the corner to a saloon near by to swallow a drink and come home to his granddaughters to say that he had been "out for a little walk."[1] It is no credit to him or discredit to anyone else to say that many American statesmen probably drank more in their last years than did Carlisle; surely forgiveness is his, for after suffering the most grievous insults which a republic can give its servants, he died with the same love for his nation as when a vast throng paid him devotion. But his defamers have even yet not had their fill.

Carlisle's last long years came to an end on July 31, 1910, in his apartments at the Hotel Wolcott in New York City[2] as he was preparing his arguments for one of his greatest law cases.

---

[1] His daughter-in-law, Mrs. William K. Carlisle, and her two daughters, Laura and Jane, lived with him after the death of Mrs. Carlisle.

[2] After Mrs. Carlisle's death Carlisle lived in Washington much of the time. He had gone to New York on a law case when his last illness overtook him.

CARLISLE'S LAST YEARS

Of worldly goods he left only a house in Washington, mortgaged for $10,000, and a medley of beautiful gifts which friends of happier days had presented him. His law associate and Assistant Secretary in the Treasury years, William E. Curtis of New York, was in charge of the funeral services, which were held in the capital, and the body, borne by Curtis, W. J. Kehoe, Isidor Straus, Dr. Joseph D. Bryant, and Charles S. Hamlin,[1] was buried in Washington. His remains were later taken to Kentucky to rest by those of his wife under an unpretentious marker in the city cemetery of Covington, his early home. No bronze plaque or marble shaft honors his statesmanship; he came into the world with nothing and went out leaving little more than the tribute from friend and foe that he was one of the greatest intellects of his age. No better conclusion for his biography is needed, perhaps, than the comment of one of his bitterest critics, the New York *World:*

It is pathetic to think that John G. Carlisle should have been so poor at the time of his death that he could not provide for his burial at his old home in Kentucky. But it is sadder still that he should have been the victim of the most cruel injustice a public man can suffer.

Carlisle was Secretary of the Treasury during the greatest financial crisis this country has experienced. With his conduct of affairs The World was in aggressive disagreement. It differed with him both as to his policy and his methods.

But in the state of popular excitement then prevailing, Carlisle was recklessly accused by political enemies in his own state of selling out to Wall street for millions. Not an atom of evidence was ever adduced reflecting on his personal integrity. The overheated imagination of partisan fanatics produced the charges of corruption and irresponsible agitators gave the slander circulation throughout the country during the free-silver campaign. Even later, when Carlisle had left the Government service and public life for all time and practised his profession, his political enemies continued to denounce him as

[1] Mr. Hamlin also was one of his Assistant Secretaries of the Treasury.

a corporation lawyer who was getting his pay for betraying his official trust.

If any proof of Carlisle's honesty was ever needed, the circumstances of his death should fill even his blindest defamer with confusion and shame. But they can never make amends to him.[1]

[1] New York *World,* Nov. 28, 1910.

CHAPTER XX   THE MAN AND HIS WORK

To measure a man who has passed out of American life leaving behind him a bare mention in history is not easy, and it is no less difficult to say why John G. Carlisle has such a small share in the written record of the country which he served so conscientiously. No statesman of the latter half of the nineteenth century excelled him in ability to state clearly and logically the arguments for tariff reform and sound money, and yet few who played a part in those years have received less space in the chronicles of the time. It seems certain that as the history of the period comes to be more fully written, his name will be given a prominent place on its pages.

Other men of the time were more greatly loved than Carlisle, but it is doubtful that many had more personal admirers than he. No man in Congress ever won greater respect from his political opponents, and, says Champ Clark, he was the most popular man in America among the rank and file of Democrats.[1] From his early years in Congress, when Frye of Maine called him "the jewel of the Democratic party," he retained the esteem of everyone until the bitter division of America by the silver question. Even then those who knew him best but opposed his stand had no harsh words for him. "I have never abused him," wrote Champ Clark. "I could not find it in my heart so to do."

The tributes of his associates adequately express the estimation in which the Kentuckian was held. He was not a man to call forth insincere approbation, because he cared little for praise. Hoar, Hiscock, Sherman, Cannon, and a host of others tell, each in a few brief lines, of an admiration which was real. One of his lifelong associates, his confidential secretary, has said of him: "John G. Carlisle was an extraordinary man, a

---

[1] Champ Clark, *My Quarter Century*, I, p. 273.

genius, a great figure in affairs of an important epoch of our political history, covering a period of more than a double decade. His mind was gigantic in strength and his thoughts were as clear as crystal. Nor is that all. The man was so transparently honest that it was impossible for him to greet error with cordiality. Few men were simpler in their walk and talk among intimates. I never saw him that his heart was not on his sleeve for all to read. He was never secretive but always open. He was never violent, but always gentle. Cruel abuse was hurled at him but he gave no sign, and John G. Carlisle was the one man incapable of recrimination. That was an attitude of greatness, and pity it was that it was so rare in our land. I knew him patiently to bear the malice and detraction of little men not worthy to untie his shoes or black his boots." [1]

Even Grover Cleveland, staunch as he was, could not bear the sting of the malice and criticism of his second administration without hurling back something of the same tenor; Carlisle never uttered a word of contempt or rancor. "He was," says Watterson, "a sure but a broad-minded and liberal partisan, deeply learned in the lore of his own school of political philosophy, clear-headed and upright." [2] His private secretary wrote of him: "I never knew him ever to speak unkindly to any of his subordinates or to any member of the House. . . . He was so kind to everybody that he would rather be imposed upon himself than to impose upon others. To my personal knowledge he has on two or three occasions made as much effort to get a poor man or woman a little place in the government printing office as he has to get a personal friend a position as foreign minister." [3] The pages in the House usually asked him to see that they got their pay. He never, so far as the records reveal, had a personal enemy.

In person Carlisle was striking only in facial characteristics;

---

[1] O. O. Stealey in the *Courier-Journal*, August 1, 1910.

[2] *Courier-Journal*, editorial, August 2, 1910.

[3] James M. Kehoe, Carlisle's private secretary, quoted in the Washington *Evening Star*, August 1, 1910.

he was of average size, not robust, and in mature years he had a slight stoop—the stoop which characterized the scholar of his day. His dress was neither especially good nor noticeably bad, but distinctive in its simplicity. His trousers were not filled with rolls and horizontal creases as were those of Thomas B. Reed, and he did not, like "Uncle Joe" Cannon, attach his suspenders with nails if buttons were missing; but he certainly had none of the fastidiousness of the aristocratic Henry Cabot Lodge or the politic "Chet" Arthur, in whose administration Mrs. Carlisle acted as first lady of the land. He looked, say his friends, like a Roman Senator; "His face was of classic mould, his eyes were deep-set and austere; his jaw hard and unyielding." The strong lines of his face appeared to best advantage at a distance. Even the magnetic Clay made no more powerful an impression in the Speaker's Chair than the fellow-Kentuckian who took up the gavel sixty years later.

No one would have feared Carlisle in physical combat, but his appearance warned the most unwary that he was a dangerous antagonist in intellectual battle. Indeed, Carlisle the man is remembered less clearly by his friends than Carlisle the intellect; his acquaintances differ widely in their descriptions of his person and his habits, but there is no disagreement concerning his outstanding mentality and his ability to marshal his thoughts. His bitterest critics could quarrel only with his premises. William McKinley once said of him, "That man never had a clouded thought," and R. H. Nelson commented in the Boston *Post:* "Mr. Carlisle's mind is never overloaded. No matter how many facts he may cram into it, they are all thoroughly digested, turned into neat and compact deductions, and laid away carefully and in such order that their maker and proprietor can lay hold of any one of them at any given moment." The editor of *Harper's Weekly* said at the time of his death: "In all the notices of Mr. Carlisle one thing that has been dwelt on is the luminosity of his mind. It lighted up whatever it dwelt upon. Intellectually he was a very wonderful person. One reads of Joe Blackburn, his neighbor, grumbling that Carlisle was entitled to little credit for what he was because he was born so. 'He knows,' said Blackburn, 'about four times as much as I do, and it has all come to him without an effort, whereas the little I know I have worked hard for.' Carlisle worked hard too, but it came easy to him because he was by nature a student."[1] His was "one of the most remarkable memories I have ever encountered," says Isaac F. Marcosson. "I once had a small part in an amazing demonstration of it. He came to Kentucky to make a series of 'Sound Money' speeches at the tide of the silver craze. He had only one copy of his speech which bristled with figures. He asked me to 'hold copy' on it while he spoke. He had written the speech the day before and had not made the slightest effort to memorize it. Yet he did not vary one word or a single figure in an address that consumed two hours and a half for delivery . . . the moment that he put pen to paper the written word was almost photographically fixed in his memory."[2]

Carlisle could depend only upon his mental ability to win him a place among statesmen; his leadership was entirely intellectual. He had no oratorical tricks; "He went straight to his subject and followed straight to the end, tying the parts together so that they made a symmetrical and convincing whole. His voice was clear, his words distinct and his conclusions strong without any serious show of effort."[3] At no time did he use a superfluous word; report has it that a friend once said to him, "You must have been born where the roads were winding,—because you always take the shortest cut across fields." He never told a single story in any public address, but in his home he showed a quiet humor. A citizen of Pendleton County once asked him if he favored the improvement of the Licking River, and his calm reply was, "Yes, by macadamizing it."

The land of his birth was no asset to Carlisle in his public career. In Kentucky politics accomplishment has always been

[1] Vol. 54, p. 5.
[2] Isaac F. Marcosson, *Adventures in Interviewing*, pp. 21–32.
[3] George G. Perkins to the writer, February 28, 1931.

founded upon the uncertain grounds of pleasing oratory and polished manner. The Clay-Breckinridge tradition in the State still gives the laurel crown to the facile speaker and sends orators to sit in the Congress. "Mr. Carlisle's success in politics was extraordinary for more than the height he attained," wrote the editor of the Washington *Evening Star*. "In a state where oratory has always exercised charm and power, and where the gift has always been rewarded far beyond its intrinsic value in practical affairs; where personal address in men aspiring to high political office has been fashioned on heartiness, this man, without a single oratorical device, and reserved at times almost to the point of austerity, topped all the orators, and put the storytellers and the handshakers into the background."[1]

Although the plaudits may even yet be given grudgingly, Carlisle must be ranked as the outstanding statesman of the South in that long stretch of years between the end of the Civil War and the turn of the century. In his party Grover Cleveland alone surpassed him, and that only because of his greater courage and aggressiveness. Beginning with his Internal Revenue bill in the Forty-fifth Congress, Carlisle's leadership of the tariff-reform forces is not open to serious question. Silently, without any thought of personal triumph, he fought day after day the battle for low tariff which he believed would relieve the masses of the country of their burdens.

The House of Representatives has had few greater Speakers than Carlisle, and none who exceeded him in parliamentary knowledge. "When he became Speaker," said the *Nation*, "he added to it [knowledge of parliamentary law] a fine judicial quality which made his decisions unusually respected. He was popular even with his opponents, not for genial personal traits, but for their belief in his absolute fairness as Speaker. . . . It has often been said that a more judicial-minded man never occupied the Speaker's Chair."[2] He directed legislation through his policy of recognition, and exercised severe disci-

---
[1] Washington *Evening Star*, August 1, 1910.
[2] Vol. 91, pp. 93–94.

pline. His constitutional views on the rights of members of the House made him, however, a defensive rather than an aggressive Speaker. He could prevent legislation which he regarded as evil from coming to vote, but he could not force through the House the laws which he believed necessary. His intellectual concepts led him to hold the theory that man is a rational being, and his disappointments on that score were many.

Carlisle led his party in the Committee of the Whole as Clay had done, but he did not possess the magnetism of his predecessor. He was not so apt in party politics as Randall, and he lacked the diplomatic touch of Blaine and the autocracy of Reed; but, although his legislative accomplishments were probably fewer than those of any of the three, he excelled them all in clarity of thought and in fairness. His name must be included in the short roll of great Speakers.

In the Senate Carlisle served no apprenticeship; he moved immediately into the front rank and continued his leadership in the fight for tariff reform. He carried forward the argument which he had begun against the Sherman bill in the House, and found himself at no disadvantage in conflict with the strongest figures which the Senate presented. He suffered nothing in comparison with Morgan, Vance, Gray, or Gorman of his own party, and he needed no assistance in combat with Hoar, Evarts, Edmunds, Morrill, or Aldrich. Had he remained a Senator, his place in history might be more secure than it is. "Possibly if he had stayed in the Senate, where he would have always been a great figure," declared *Harper's Weekly* in 1910, "he might have kept his hold on his constituents, and have done something to prevent the Democratic party from wandering off into the free-silver wilderness with the Nebraskan Moses. If anyone could have held back the party from that fatuity, he might have done it, but it is not probable that it could have been done. It would have been something though, to have spared Kentucky the memory that she cast out such a man because he saw clearer than his constituents, and refused either to lead them into the ditch or to fall into it with them under the leadership of another." [1]

His acceptance of a seat in the Cabinet less than three years after becoming a Senator marked the beginning of the end of Carlisle's political career. "He lost everything," wrote the editor of the Washington *Evening Star*, "his seat in the Senate, his hold on his home people, and the ear of the country completely. And the loss was as great for the country at large as for him and his party." [2] No Secretary of the Treasury in time of peace has ever faced a more difficult task than he, and none has ever tried harder or more successfully to master the current knowledge upon the subject of finance. The Kentuckian has been called a theoretical financier, but his theories were based upon sound research. He set the machinery of the government to work in the far reaches of the world to determine the successes and failures of the gold and the silver standard; his manuscript *Reports* to the House of Representatives contain information on the status of the money question in every nation. The President, although long fixed in his attitude toward "sound" money, depended on Carlisle for his financial facts.

Carlisle's ideas on finance could not in the very nature of things be definitive, but they were sound. He was mistaken in his belief that if natural laws were allowed to function, money would adjust itself according to the demand; he did not realize that the free flow of currency is not rapid enough to be of value in a nation of divergent economic interests. In his opinion the gold reserve was one of the great evils of the currency situation; to him the logical solution seemed adherence to the old Democratic theory of bullion: both silver and gold. He did not object to paper money if its issue was properly supervised, but he believed that it should not be such as to keep the government continually fearful regarding its redemption.

[1] Vol. 54, p. 5.
[2] August 1, 1910.

"The issue and redemption of circulating notes is not a proper function of the Treasury Department, or of any other department of the Government," he told Congress. "Such a policy, even if sanctioned by the Constitution, instead of imparting strength and stability to our currency system, seriously endangers it by the introduction of political and partisan considerations into the management of a subject which ought to be regulated entirely by the business interests of the people and by the laws of trade and the principles which control honest commercial intercourse."

If the second Cleveland administration deserves credit for preserving the standard of value, Carlisle must share equally with the President the honor of that accomplishment. He aggressively fought for the gold standard; he wished to retire the legal-tenders which made a constant demand on the government; he saw the need for increased elasticity; he urged enlargement of the banking system; he wanted to take the government out of the banking business or else give it power of protection; and he was certain that the finances of the country could never be sound until they were removed from politics. The reforms which were made under McKinley he had repeatedly recommended to Congress.

Through all the vilification which fell upon him in his Treasury years Carlisle held strictly to the gold standard, and as counselor at law, despite his "honorable exile," he carried on his fight for the principles which he and his former chief had tried so hard as officials to uphold. With the death of Grover Cleveland and—almost exactly two years later—of John G. Carlisle, a peculiar and distinctive part of the Democratic party passed out of existence. Because of his personal vigor Cleveland was the more commanding figure of the two, but Carlisle's was the greater intellect. "He died politically in the shade of a man whom he . . . could have taught the very rudiments of government," wrote the editor of the Washington *Evening Star*, but Carlisle would have been first to deny his greater statesmanship. The two were thoroughly suited to each other—one a scholar in the fundamentals of government, the other a fearless executive. Had Carlisle been willing to accept it, Cleveland would have given him the appointment as Secretary of the Treasury at the death of Daniel Manning in 1887; he did not, however, as is commonly believed, offer him a position on the Supreme Court bench in 1888.[1] The universal opinion is that he would have made an admirable Justice, for he was by nature a law interpreter rather than a law enforcer.

Carlisle's personal characteristics contributed to the unfortunate neglect of his name. He was lacking in that romantic element which statesmen must of necessity have to secure recognition. He was ambitious, but he paid too little attention to personal accomplishments—he left them to take care of themselves. He was a prominent presidential possibility in four national conventions, but he never really approached the nomination. He was handicapped, too, by the fact that in his youth he had drunk a great deal; by sheer force of character he overcame the habit when he entered national politics, but rumors of his excesses, nurtured by the multitude of scandalmongers of the day, would have raised their ugly heads to strike him had he ever become a candidate. Rumor still whispers in the ears of those who are easily shocked that he was always a drunkard and that his political power was based on the noxious lottery of his State; and yet the legislature of his commonwealth voted him public thanks for destroying the lottery system, and his friends bear testimony to his abstinence.

Like Henry Clay, Carlisle suffered much from the lack of mental discipline incident to a college education. He was not a good judge of men, and his scrupulous honesty may have made him too trusting of apparent friends. Although his brilliant mind immediately penetrated the complexities of opposing

[1] Affirmative evidence on this question is strong, but the writer has in his possession a letter written by Carlisle saying that he would appreciate any recommendations which might be sent to the President in his behalf; he has also the letters which were sent from Kentucky. In the Cleveland-Carlisle MSS. is a letter written by Cleveland to Carlisle in which the former could not have avoided mentioning the matter had he offered the latter the position.

propositions, he was often slow in choosing the one which he would follow. He held tenaciously to his conclusions, but at no time refused to be convinced and converted. He never became accustomed to the clamor and shouting of twentieth-century politics, however, and without bitterness called himself "old-fashioned" in his last days. With his death an old politician in a new setting, a man who Henry Watterson said "might have been mistaken for a Yale or Harvard professor," passed from the stage of American politics.

So ends the story of a Kentucky statesman—the poor Scotch farm boy whose brilliant mind was the open sesame which, without any other qualifications, gained him admittance to the seat of the Clays and the Breckinridges to dominate the politics of his State for twenty years, and which led him into the council rooms of the nation to sit with her great. His hard-conquered fortune failed at last, and he died a political exile far from the land of his birth. Today while his commonwealth pays tribute to mere orators, the ashes of one of her greatest men rest unhonored on the south bank of the Ohio.

BIBLIOGRAPHY

Manuscript Material

Jeremiah S. Black MSS. Contains many letters of value concerning the protectionist element in the Democratic party, especially those from Samuel J. Randall. Library of Congress.

W. C. P. Breckinridge MSS. A valuable collection for a study of the Democratic party in its fight for low tariff and sound money. It contains many personal letters from Carlisle. Library of Congress.

William Jennings Bryan MSS. An exceedingly valuable source of informaation on the West in the nineties; indispensable in following the split in the Democratic party over the question of silver and gold. Library of Congress.

Napoleon H. Carlisle MSS. Contains a few letters of John G. Carlisle, and some clippings of lesser importance. In the possession of the author.

Mrs. William K. Carlisle MSS. Mrs. Carlisle is the daughter-in-law of John G. Carlisle and is in possession of his paintings, furniture, gifts from political friends, and many other interesting personal possessions. The collection contains also several volumes of clippings, many photographs, and two books of letters written to Mr. and Mrs. Carlisle at the deaths of their sons. In the custody of Mrs. William K. Carlisle, Frederick, Maryland.

Grover Cleveland MSS. An enormous collection which cannot be omitted in any study which concerns the Democratic party between the years 1884–1908. See McElroy's *Cleveland* for complete description. Library of Congress.

Cleveland-Carlisle MSS. Some twenty letters written by Cleveland to Carlisle in the years after their retirement from politics. The letters show clearly the work of the two former leaders in an effort to rehabilitate the party. Library of Congress.

William E. Curtis MSS. A most valuable collection for a study of the difficulties of the United States Treasury in the years 1893–1897. It is made up of letters of Mr. Curtis to his mother which give an intimate picture of the troubles; of a series of almost daily letters from sub-treasurer Jordan of New York, the point of greatest pressure during the period; of a large amount of the working papers of the Treasury in relation to the gold reserve, income and expenditures; of many letters from bank officials and others regarding the problems of the administration of the Treasury; and also of especial value, many letters to Secretary Carlisle and many of his memoranda in dealing with the bond issues. Recently presented to the Library of Congress by Miss Elizabeth Curtis, New York.

James R. Doolittle MSS. Contains some letters of value on the tariff in the eighties. Library of Congress.

Department of State MSS. The files of this department contain much valuable information on the monetary developments in other countries. Indispensable for a study of various monetary conferences.

Governors of Kentucky MSS. Contains election returns for Kentucky and much other information of value in studying Carlisle's career in Kentucky politics. In custody of the Kentucky Historical Society. See Catalogue of Records, Documents, Papers, etc. of Kentucky Governors, 1792–1926. Edited by Mrs. Emma Guy Cromwell.

Walter Q. Gresham MSS. A small collection which contains valuable letters on the party troubles of the Cleveland administration during its first two years.

Charles S. Hamlin MSS. A collection of 196 volumes of clippings, manuscripts, working papers of the Treasury, a diary, and some letters. All are valuable. Mr. Hamlin is now a member of the Federal Reserve Board.

House MSS. The original handwritten reports of the Secretary of the Treasury contain much valuable information which is not included in the printed reports.

BIBLIOGRAPHY

George W. Julian and Joshua R. Giddings MSS. Contains a few letters of interest in this period. Library of Congress.

Conrad N. Jordan MSS. Jordan was connected with the Treasury Department in both Cleveland administrations, and his letters offer much valuable information on the finances. In the custody of Archibald N. Jordan, New York.

Daniel S. Lamont MSS. A very large collection of letters concerning the problems of the party in the second Cleveland administration. Especially valuable on financial affairs and on the financial division in the party. Library of Congress.

Harry B. Mackoy MSS. A small collection of personal material concerning Carlisle. In the custody of Mr. Mackoy, Cincinnati, Ohio.

Mrs. Martha Metcalf MSS. A small collection containing some clippings and other material, among which is the family Bible. In the custody of Mrs. Metcalf, Lake Worth, Florida.

William R. Morrison MSS. A small collection of much value; contains letters of David A. Wells and J. S. Moore on the fight for tariff reform in the years immediately succeeding the Civil War. In the custody of Carlisle B. Morrison, Waterloo, Illinois.

Justin S. Morrill MSS. Contains some letters of value regarding the Republican attitude toward the administration in its political and financial difficulties in the years 1893–1897. Library of Congress.

John T. Morgan MSS. A large collection, but contains little information on the tariff and silver question. Library of Congress.

Richard Olney MSS. A large collection of letters covering every phase of the administration in the second Cleveland presidency. Contains much information on the attitude of Boston toward the financial question, and also some letters written by Secretary Carlisle. Library of Congress.

George G. Perkins MSS. A small collection of letters, among which are the recommendations which were sent in behalf of Carlisle's appointment to the Supreme Court bench in 1888. In possession of the author.

Roger Sherman Pitkins MSS. Made up largely of clippings. In the custody of Mr. Pitkin of Hartford, Connecticut.

Shelly D. Rouse MSS. A half dozen letters written by Carlisle to Judge James O'Hara, Jr.; they concern themselves largely with Carlisle's preparation for the Speakership. In custody of Mr. Rouse, Covington, Kentucky.

Senate MSS. In various boxes and bundles in the attic of the Capitol are to be found the petitions which were sent to the Senate in the nineties concerning silver and gold. They are exceedingly valuable in indicating the regions of gold and silver following. Many petitions contain the age and occupation of the signers.

John Sherman MSS. An exceedingly large collection of letters and papers concerning Sherman personally and politically. Valuable on the question of the Republican attitude toward Democratic problems of tariff and money. Library of Congress.

Treasury Department MSS. The files of the Treasury Department are less valuable than one would expect, but they show the efforts which Carlisle made in his Treasury years to keep down expenses.

Henry Villard MSS. Contains some good letters on international monetary questions and on Western railroads. Harvard University Library.

William S. Vilas MSS. The collection is not open to use, but some Carlisle letters have been extracted. In the custody of the Wisconsin Historical Society.

Henry Watterson MSS. Watterson, like many Southerners, threw a great majority of his letters away when he had read them. The collection is valuable, however, and contains some Carlisle letters.

Printed Material

Alexander, De Alva Stanwood. History and procedure of the House of Representatives. Boston, 1916.

BIBLIOGRAPHY

Altgeld, John P. Live questions. Chicago. 1890.

Andrews, E. Benjamin. The history of the last quarter century in the United States. 2 vols. New York. 1896.

Angell, James W. The theory of international prices. Cambridge. 1926.

Arnett, Alex Mathews. The Populist movement in Georgia. New York. 1922.

Barry, David S. Forty years in Washington. Boston. 1924.

Banker's Magazine. New York.

Banker's Magazine. London.

Barnes, James A. Illinois and the gold-silver controversy, 1890-1896. *Transactions,* Illinois Historical Society, 1931.

Barnes, James A. The gold-standard Democrats and the party conflict. *Mississippi Valley Historical Review.* vol. 17, pp. 422-450.

Beer, Thomas. Hanna. New York. 1929. A popular biography which contains some interesting letters on the silver-gold question.

Bond sales investigation. Senate Doc. vol. 5, 54 Cong. 2d sess.

Boston *Commercial Record.*

Bryan, William Jennings. The first battle. Chicago. 1896. The most usable compilation of facts concerning the Chicago convention and the Bryan campaign.

Bryan, William Jennings. The memoirs of William Jennings Bryan, by himself and his wife, Mary Baird Bryan. Chicago. 1925.

Busbey, L. White. Uncle Joe Cannon: The story of a pioneer American. New York. 1927.

Canfield, J. H. Is the West discontented? A local study of facts. Forum. vol. 18. pp. 449-461. An interesting account of a college official's investigation into the life of his community.

Carlisle, John G. Dangers of our electoral system, and Dangers of our electoral system: a remedy. *Forum.* vol. 24. pp. 257-266, 651-659.

Carlisle, John G. Our future policy. *Harper's Magazine.* vol. 97. pp. 720-728.

Carlisle, John G. The limitations of the Speakership. *North American Review.* vol. 150. p. 399 ff.

Carothers, Thomas P. Some great lawyers of Kentucky. *Proceedings,* Kentucky Bar Association. 1923.

Chicago *Record, Times,* and *Tribune.*

Cincinnati *Daily Commercial,* and *Gazette.*

Clark, Champ. My quarter century of American politics. 2 vols. New York. 1910. Contains much interesting personal material.

Cleveland, Frederick A. The bank and the Treasury. New York. 1908.

Cleveland, Grover. Presidential problems. New York. 1904. Cleveland's recollections of the important events of his second administration.

Coleman, McAlister. Eugene V. Debs, a man unafraid. New York. 1930.

Collins, Louis and Richard. History of Kentucky. 2 vols. Covington. 1874.

Commerical and Financial Chronicle, The. (With annual supplement) 1873-1897. An indispensable account of the finances during this period.

Congressional Record, 1877-1900.

Coulter, E. Merton. The civil war and readjustment in Kentucky. Chapel Hill. 1925. The best account of post-war Kentucky.

Croly, Herbert. Marcus Alonzo Hanna: his life and work. New York. 1919.

Cullom, Shelby M. Fifty years of public service. Chicago. 1911.

Dewey, Davis Rich. National problems, 1857-1897. New York. 1907.

Dunn, Arthur Wallace. From Harrison to Harding. 2 vols. New York. 1922.

Eckenrode, H. J. Rutherford B. Hayes: a statesman of reunion. New York. 1930.

Farmer, Hallie. The economic background of southern Populism. *South Atlantic Quarterly.* vol. 29. pp. 77-91. A careful study of the economic life of the South in the eighties and nineties.

Follett, Mary P. The Speaker of the House of Representatives. New York. 1896.

Ford, Henry Jones. The Cleveland era. New Haven. 1921. A brief, critical account of the Cleveland administration with little appreciation of the problems faced.

Forum, The. Contains many valuable articles by leading statesmen.

Frankfort (Kentucky) *Commonwealth,* and *Yoeman.*

Fuller, H. B. Speakers of the House. Boston. 1909.

Gilder, Richard Watson. A record of friendship. New York. 1920.

Gleed, J. W. The true significance of the Western unrest. Forum. vol. 16. pp. 251-260.

Gresham, Matilda. Life of Walter Quentin Gresham. 2 vols. Chicago. 1919.

Harper's Weekly. A valuable source of information concerning the attitude of the East toward the financial and political questions of the day.

Harvard Review of Economic Statistics, The. Contains many interesting charts and graphs.

Hayes, Rutherford B. Diary and Letters. Edited by C. R. Williams. 4 vols. New York. 1924.

Haynes, Fred Emory. James Baird Weaver. Iowa City. 1919.

Haynes, Fred Emory. Third party movements since the civil war. Iowa City. 1916. An able discussion of Western politics.

Hearings, unpublished, of the House Committee on Banking and Currency. 1893-1896.

Hepburn, A. Barton. A history of currency in the United States. New York. 1915.

Hibben, Paxton. The peerless leader, William Jennings Bryan. New York. 1929.

Hicks, John Donald. Birth of the Populist party. *Minnesota History.* vol. 9. pp. 233 ff.

Hinds, Asher C. Parliamentary precedents of the House of Representatives. 8 vols. Washington, D. C. 1907-1908.

Hoar, George F. Autobiography of seventy years. 2 vols. New York. 1903.

Hovey, Carl. The life of J. Pierpont Morgan. New York. 1911. Contains an interesting, although undocumented, chapter on the syndicate bond sale.

James, Henry. Richard Olney. New York. 1923.

Kentucky Senate *Journal*, 1860-1874; House *Journal*, 1859-1867.

Kentucky *Documents*, 1861, 1865-66, 1866-67.

Kinley, David. The Independent Treasury of the United States and its relations to the banks of the country. Washington, D. C. 1910.

La Follette, Robert M. Autobiography: a personal narrative of political experiences. Madison. 1913.

Lauck, William Jett. The causes of the panic of 1893. New York. 1907. The best brief account of the causes of the panic.

Laughlin, J. Lawrence. The history of bimetallism in the United States. New York. 1896. 3d edition.

Laws of the United States concerning money, banking and loans, 1878-1909. Compiled by A. T. Huntington and Robert J. Mawhinney. Washington, D. C. 1910.

Lingley, Charles R. Since the civil war. New York. 1926.

Louisville *Courier-Journal, Evening Post, Times,* and *Ledger*.

McCall, Samuel W. The life of Thomas Brackett Reed. Boston. 1914.

McElroy, Robert. Grover Cleveland, the man and the statesman. 2 vols. New York. 1923.

McMurray, Donald L. Coxey's army. Boston. 1929. A carefully prepared account of the incidents connected with the march of the various armies of the unemployed.

Marcosson, Isaac F. Adventures in interviewing. New York. 1920.

Mitchell, Wesley Clair. Gold, prices, and wages. Berkely. 1908.

Mitchell, Wesley Clair. A history of the greenbacks. Chicago. 1903.

Nation, The. Indispensable.

National Bimetallist, The. The leading organ of the silverites in 1895 and 1896.

New York *Financial News, Herald, Journal of Commerce and Commercial Bulletin, Mail and Express, Post, Press, Times, Tribune,* and *World.*

North American Review, The. Contains many interesting articles on tariff and the monetary question.

Noyes, Alexander Dana. Forty years of American finances. New York. 1907. The best history of post-war finances.

Olcott, Charles S. The life of William McKinley. 2 vols. New York. 1916.

Paxson, Frederic L. The new nation. New York. 1927.

Peck, Harry Thurston. Twenty years of the Republic, 1885-1905. New York. 1906.

Perkins, George Gilpin. A Kentucky judge. Washington, D. C. 1931. The recollections of a lifelong friend of Carlisle.

Philadelphia *Public Ledger.*

Pittsburgh *Commercial Gazette.*

Rhodes, James Ford. History of the United States. 8 vols. New York. 1920.

Richardson, James D. Messages and papers of the Presidents. 1897 and 1909.

Robinson, William A. Thomas B. Reed, parliamentarian. New York. 1930.

Rocky Mountain News, The. One of the leading Western advocates of silver.

Saint Louis *Republic.*

San Francisco *Chronicle.*

Schurz, Carl. Second administration of Grover Cleveland.

McClure's Magazine. vol. 9, pp. 638 ff. A defense of the President and the gold standard.

Scott, William A. Money and banking. New York. 1903.

Seitz, Don. Joseph Pulitzer, his life and letters. New York. 1924.

Smith, Edward Conrad. The borderland in the civil war. New York. 1927.

Sound Currency. Articles concerning sound money. Pamphlets on this subject are too numerous to catalog. The Vilas collection in the Wisconsin Historical Society, the collection in the Library of Congress, and the private collection of George Shibléy of Washington, D. C., are very valuable. Pamphlets on free silver are equally numerous.

Sprague, O. M. W. History of crises under the National Banking System. Washington, D. C. 1910.

Stanwood, Edward. American tariff controversies in the nineteenth century. Boston. 1903.

Statistics for the United States, 1867-1909. Compiled by A. Piatt Andrew. Washington, D. C. 1910.

Stealey, O. O. Twenty years in the press gallery. New York. 1906. The recollections of Henry Watterson's leading correspondent in Washington for more than twenty-five years.

Stephenson, Nathaniel Wright. Nelson W. Aldrich, a leader in American politics. New York. 1930. A scholarly biography of Carlisle's leading opponent in the Senate.

Stoddard, Henry Luther. As I knew them; presidents and politics from Grant to Coolidge. New York. 1927.

Sullivan, Mark. Our times: the turn of the century, 1900-1904. New York. 1926.

Tarbell, Ida M. Tariff in our times. New York. 1911.

Taussig, F. W. The tariff history of the United States. New York. 1914.

Thomas, Harrison Cook. The return of the Democratic party to power in 1884. New York. 1919.

Thompson, Charles Willis. Presidents I've known and two near presidents.

Tracy, Frank Basil. The rise and doom of the Populist party. *Forum*. vol. 16. pp. 241 ff. A vivid account of the Western unrest in the nineties.

Treasury of the United States. *Annual Report of the Finances*, 1865-1900.

Washington *Evening Star, Post*.

Watterson, Henry. Marse Henry, an autobiography. New York. 1919. The personal recollections of Carlisle's closest tariff-reform friend.

Wellborn, Fred. The influence of the silver-Republicans, 1889-1891. *Mississippi Valley Historical Review*. vol. 14. pp. 462-480.

Wilson, Woodrow. Congressional government; a study in American politics. Boston. 1885.

Wilson, Woodrow. Mr. Cleveland's Cabinet. *Review of Reviews*. vol. 8. pp. 286 ff. Contains an estimate of Carlisle as a statesman.

INDEX

Addams, Jane, 149
Agricultural discontent, *see* farmers
Aldrich, Nelson W., 102, 165, 189, 326
Alliance, The, 219, 426, 430
Altgeld, John P., 331, 435, 451, 488
American frontier, gradual closing of, 101
American Iron and Steel Association, 79, 119
American Protective League of Philadelphia, 119
American Protective Tariff League, 127
American Railway Union Strike, 331
American Tobacco Company, 47
Americus Club, 100
Anderson, E. Ellery, 194
Anthony, Susan B., 157
Appropriation bills, 89, 110, 175
Appropriations Committee, curtailment of power of, 96
"Armies" of the unemployed, 330
Armour, P. D., 282
"Army of the discontented," 101, 107, 464
Arthur, Chester A., 51, 53, 57, 91, 515
Atkinson, Edward, 46, 193, 364
Avot, Joe, 5

Bacon, Robert, 378, 384, 402
Baker, Jehu, 123
Baldwin, C. C., 415, 444
Bancroft, George, 147
Bank deposits, decline in, 87
Bank of England, Bank of France, Bank of Spain, 401
Bankers' attitude toward Carlisle, 308, 316, 322, 347
Bankers, consulted by Treasury, under Harrison, 204, 229; under Cleveland, 231, 240, 308, 372; dominate Treasury, 393, 400, 401, 404, 478; help in bond issues, *see* Bond issues; urge purchase of bonds by Treasury, 50
Bankruptcy bill, 81, 86

Banks, exchange gold for greenbacks, 407; short of currency, 485; supply gold to Treasury, 237, 288, 307, 347; suspension of, 242, 295
Banks, Nathaniel P., 156
Baring failure, 222
Barnum, William Henry, 70
Bate, William B., 120
Bayard, Thomas F., 65, 84
Beck, James B., 103, 180
Beer, Thomas, 447
Bellamy, Edward, 149
Belmont, August, calls on Secretary Carlisle, 371; discouraged about possibilities of third bond issue, 372; surprised at delay in negotiations, 376; goes to Washington, 378; power of, 388, 394; not present at writing of Morgan-Belmont Contract, 389. *See also* Morgan-Belmont Syndicate
Belmont, Perry, 75
Benedict, E. C., 354
Benton, M. M., 23
Bessemer Steel, 58
Big business, growth of, 62
"Billion dollar Congress," 225
Bimetallism, 103, 302, 369, 436, 447, 487
Bissell, Wilson S., 210
Blackburn, J. S. C., 59, 75, 455, 515
Blaine, James G. ("The Plumed Knight"), attitude toward South, 40; nominated by Republicans, 83; decries efforts of Democrats for tariff reform, 127; statement on trusts, 144; one of the great Speakers of the House, 156; emotionalism of, 161; burden to Republican party, 165; proposition of reciprocity made by, 191; Secretary of State under Harrison, 220; diplomatic gifts of, 518
Blair Education bill, 85, 112, 137, 152
Blair, Frank P., 139

535

INDEX

Blanchard, Newton C., 434
Bland-Allison Act, requirements of, 202, 220; relation to gold reserve, 225, Cleveland's attitude toward, 252; demand for maximum provision of, 255
Bland free-silver bill, supported by Carlisle, 34
Bland, Richard Parks ("Silver Dick"), high priest of free silver, 152; leads fight for free silver, 223; criticizes Cleveland's message, 266; attacks motives of Easterners, 268; opposes first bond issue, 311; helps Bryan's campaign, 456
"Bloated bond holders," 103, 223, 242
Blodgett, Rufus, 121
"Bloody shirt," 40
Blount, James H., 120
Boies, Horace, 197, 456
Bond investigation, 381, 395, 411
Bond issues, authorized by Congress, 37; bogus bids in, 421; criticized by silverites, 363; drain on gold reserve, 358, 416; justification for, 423; relation to ultimate preservation of gold reserve, 363
Bond issues of U. S. Treasury, under Carlisle:
First, preliminaries, 287, 304-310; distribution, 310-318; no rush for bonds, 314; success secured by help of bankers, 317; criticized in Congress, 318; results, 319; criticism on methods of handling, 321
Second, preliminaries, 348-357; distribution, 357-358; entire issue awarded to one group of financiers, 359
Third (Morgan-Belmont Syndicate), Preliminaries, 371-388; distribution, see Morgan-Belmont Syndicate; storm in Congress over, 393; justification for private sale, 394, 398
Fourth, preliminaries, 401-413; distribution, 414-421; public approval of, 415, 422; effects of, 417-420; results compared with previous issues, 422

Bond legislation struggle (for the issue of 3% bonds), 229, 305, 310, 327, 360, 364, 368-370, 382, 389, 405
Bond purchases by Treasury, as means of reducing surplus, 49; as means of relief to bankers, 50
Bond redemptions, resumed, 105, 115; abolishment of, results in increase of surplus, 115; deplete Treasury, 223, 225, 229
Bonds, bought by Treasury to relieve bankers, 50, 222; Civil War, 37; consent of Congress required to buy in open market, 105; decline in value of, 365, 372, 395
Boston Clearing House, 237, 238
"Bourbon Democracy," 44, 46
Boutwell, George S., 267
Bowker, R. R., 127
"Boy Orator of Illinois," 473
Bradley, James W., 480
Bragg, Edward S., 54, 470
Braman, Dwight, 231
Branch, John P., 477
Breckinridge, bill to repeal Sherman law, 254
Breckinridge, Clifton R., 120, 127
Breckinridge, Desha, 501
Breckinridge, John C., 2, 8
Breckinridge, W. C. P., letter from J. Q. Ward, 103; urges unified effort of Democrats, 115; wire from Harry Weissinger, 146; letters from William L. Wilson, 149, 466; letter from E. W. Sawyer, 188; letter from A. L. Taylor, 198; letter to Carlisle, 251; letter from Kentucky farmer, 428
Brice, Calvin S., 326
Brice, Lloyd, 213
Bright, Jesse D., 120
Brisbane, Arthur, 210
Bristow, Benjamin H., 32
Brown Bros. & Co., 245
Bryan, William Jennings:
The young legislator, combats "McKinleyism," 195; introduces bill to punish bank officials, 247; aspires to Senate, 254; opposes repeal of Sherman law, 274;

INDEX 537

emerges as leader of silver forces, 350; secures defeat of Springer bond bill, 370; attacks Cleveland, 390; refuses to cooperate with "insidious bankers," 390; opposes bond issues, 390; opinions of, on gold and silver, 432

Leader of the silver forces, conversion to silver standard, 433; powers of, 435; makes tour of South, 443; emerges as presidential candidate, 446; challenges Carlisle to debate, 452; at Republican National Convention, 458

Presidential candidate, learns of nomination, 461; enthusiasm created by nomination of, 461-465; remarkable campaign of, 463-465, 472-474, 489; nominated by groups for presidency in 1900, 485; widespread disappointment at defeat, 485-489

Declining influence, faces dissention among followers, 502; opposes return of gold Democrats to party, 503; insists upon continuing free silver issue, 506; losing hold on common people, 506; defeated in 1908, 510

Reasons for success and failure, 481, 491; personal hold on followers, 486-489; emotional element in campaign, 486, 490; as campaigner, compared with Carlisle, 490

"Bryanism," hatred of Gold Democrats for, 470
Bryant, John Howard, 473
Bryant, Dr. Joseph, 511
Bryant, W. A., 454
Buchanan, James, 132
Buckner, General Simon Bolivar, 470
Bullion silver, coinage of, 34; purchase and coining of, required by law, 50, 202, 220; value of, in dollars, 351
Burrows, J., 457
Business, increase in 1895, 411; revival of, as result of fourth bond issue, 421

Butler, Benjamin F., 28, 82, 341
Bynum, W. D., 449, 502

Caffery, Senator, 411
Call rates, 241, 267, 421, 485
Canada, bids for bonds from, 416
Cannon, Joseph G., 73; nominates Reed as Speaker, 94, 123; ascribes panic to fear of Democratic tariff, 266; compares Cleveland with Herod, 269; admires Carlisle, 513; careless in dress, 515
Canville and Copiah riots, 76
Carlisle, Lilbon Hardin, 4
Carlisle, Logan, 393, 499
Carlisle, John Griffin:
Ancestry and childhood, 1-4, 44
Education and early associations, 4-6, 45, 122
Marriage, 7
Teacher, 5-7
Lawyer, in Covington, 12; in New York, 495-498; standing as a lawyer, 7, 9, 29, 496-498
Member of Kentucky State Legislature, 25-26
In Congress:
House of Representatives, elected Speaker pro tempore, 29; urges international agreement on silver and gold, 35; demands funding of national debt, 37; labors for change in postal rates, 38; an important figure in House, 42; appointed to Committee on Ways and Means, 46; leading member of the Democratic party, 51; forces votes on tariff, 57-58; nominated to Speakership in Democratic caucus, 71; opinions of press on nomination, 72; begins duties as Speaker of 48th Congress, 73; efforts for party harmony, 76; gives notice that tariff reform fight will continue, 80; postpones tariff reform activities until after inauguration of Cleveland, 84-85; elected Speaker of 49th Congress, 94; pushes tariff reform, 102; election contested, 107; meets op-

position in own party, 107; urged to remove Randall from Appropriations Committee, 116; elected Speaker of 50th Congress, 123; faces contest for seat in House, 128-130; driving force behind tariff reform, 137; tries to push Mills bill through, 139; methods as Speaker, 109-110, 140, 146, 151-156; contribution toward reform of House procedure, 147; in 51st Congress, opposes Reed's arbitrary rulings, 155-156, 169-171, 175; minority leader, 163; fights McKinley bill, 179

In the Senate, enters, 182; opposes Force bill, 187; opposes McKinley bill, 182, 189, 190; leader of tariff reform, 195; leadership in Senate, 518

Secretary of the Treasury: invited by Cleveland to enter cabinet, 205; qualifications for office, 206-208; faces problems and limitations of the office, 208, 213, 214, 230, 307; suspends issue of gold certificates, 233; consults Cleveland about authority under Sherman law, 236; instructs assistants to uphold gold standard, 237; acts under Resumption act of 1875, 290-291; issues unfortunate announcement on redemption of Treasury notes, 293; asks Congress to authorize issue of 3% bonds, *see* Bond legislation struggle; issues bonds, *see* Bond Issues of U. S. Treasury; presents currency reform proposal, 361; learns of power to buy gold under law of 1862, 380; appears before bond investigation, 391, 411; makes tour of Great Lakes, 400; given credit for share in preservation of standard of value, 424; makes tour of borderland in campaign for sound money, 438-442; speaks for sound currency, 446; challenged by Bryan to debate, 452; fears result of Bryan's election on finances, 466; heckled by silverites, 483-485; sacrifices made in becoming Cabinet officer, 434, 519

Last days, retires from political life, 495; death of sons, 499-500; asks reorganization of Democratic party, 507; at Parker notification meeting, 509; death of wife, 510; death, 510

Rank as statesman, compared with other leaders, 8, 202, 490-491, 517-522

Beliefs and convictions:

Financial; opposes resumption of gold payments, 33; believes silver should hold equal place with gold, 34; warns of danger of large surplus, 138; votes reluctantly for silver proposal, 186; advocates repeal of Sherman law, 265, 278, 281; declares for sound currency, 299-303, 352, 437, 520; joins Gold Democrats, 471

Political and Economic; Democrat, increasingly Jacksonian, 10; views of democracy, 362; devotion to Democratic party, 501; sympathies in Civil War, 19-22, 38-39, 44; upholds constitutional rights of individual, 24, 28, 78, 154, 518; advocates moderation in tariff reform, 29, 45, 67, 69, 74, 125; opposes protective tariff, 60, 114, 196; opposes secrecy in government negotiations, 375, 380, 383, 387; opposes executive domination, 38, 39, 40; dislikes financiers, 37, 316, 347, 362, 387; upholds freedom at polls, 41; faith in Congress, 52, 367, 376; interested in common man, 45, 51-52, 56, 61, 160, 207, 450-451, 475; upholds freedom of debate, 59, 155-156, 169-171, 175; opposes government ownership of railroads, 428; opposes imperialistic policy of U. S., 497

Religious, 9

INDEX

Friendship with Cleveland, called into conference by Cleveland, 86, 98, 116, 146; receives Cleveland's congratulations on election to Senate, 181; visits Buzzards Bay, 198; selected for Cabinet position, 199; trusted by Cleveland, 215; rumors of disagreements, 239, 355, 361; friendly association, 509

Personal characteristics, amusements, 159, 205; appearance and dress, 9, 61, 75, 123, 160, 209-210, 499, 515; clear mindedness, 5, 24, 27, 513, 515, 518; intemperance, 7, 510, 521; power as orator, 9, 63; social charm, 156, 161, 484; studiousness, 3-4; tolerance, 27, 29, 82, 107, 183, 514, 517, 518; financial difficulties due to honesty and inability to charge large fees, 495, 497, 510-512

Home and Social Life, 156-158, 182-183, 212, 498-499

Seen by friends and opponents: approbation, 5, 74, 81, 146, 163, 513, 515, 516; adverse criticism, 262, 271, 312-314, 333, 345, 347, 396, 423, 425, 455, 503

Writings and speeches, statement of willingness to change opinion, 29; speech in Tammany Hall, 42; speeches and letters on tariff, 54-55, 61-62, 67, 69, 191; speeches before New York Chamber of Commerce, 299 *et seq*, 404 *et seq;* letter on sixteen-to-one theory, 351-352; speech on sound money, 450-451; letter on death of sons, 501; article on Monroe Doctrine, 503-504

As a Presidential possibility, 83-84, 196-197, 425, 453-455, 470

Carlisle, Mrs. John G. (Mary Jane Goodson), 7, 68, 122, 156, 211, 308

Carlisle, William K., 499
Carnegie, Andrew, 238
Carter, Ben, 437
Castor oil, 57, 135
Catchings, J. C., 437
Cather, Willa, 447
Chamber of Commerce of the State of New York, 299, 404, 446
Chandler, William E., 120
Charn, James, 117
Chase, "Pa," 487
Cherokee Strip, 247
Chicago Stock Exchange, 478
Children, letters from, to Bryan, 488-489
Chinese issue, 56
Churchill, Randolph, 210
Clark, Champ, 269, 425, 449, 484
Clark, Mrs. Champ, 509, 513
Clarke, John B., 94, 122
Clarke, R. H., 437, 491
Class groups developing in America, 101
Clay, Henry, 2, 4, 8, 156, 518
Clearing House Certificates, 241, 245, 476
Clemens, Samuel L., 64
Clews, Henry, 235
Coal, 80, 119, 133
Coast defense, 119
Cobb, "Gigantic," 123
Cobden Club, 134
Cockran, Bourke, 124
Cleveland, Grover:

First administration, elected, 84; letter recommending suspension of silver coinage, 89; inauguration, 90-92; sends for Carlisle, 92; urged to consult Randall on tariff, 99; refuses to continue bond redemptions, 104; faced by silver question, 102-103; advocates moderation in tariff reform and tax reform, 108; compelled to resume bond redemptions, 115; fully converted to tariff reform, 115; "it is a condition which confronts us . . ." 126; message to 49th Congress, 108, to 50th Congress, 126; effects of message on tariff reform, 126-128; defeated for reelection, 145

Second administration: bond issues, *see* Bond issues, U. S. Treasury; cabinet, 209 *et seq*, 319, 361; ladies of cabinet, 210 *et seq*, 386; inaugural, 250; problems, 201, 213; program, 251; calls special session of Congress, 260; vetoes seigniorage bill, 328; sends troops to Illinois, 331; writes letter on safe currency, 436; messages to Congress, 266, 360, 368, 389, 405, 509; Republican help, 370

Unpopularity and abuse: 140, 141; attacked by Gorman, 340; "man without a party," 341, 386; belligerent toward Congress, 360; thwarted by Congress, 364; attacked by Bryan, 390; loses adherents in West, 394; criticized for Morgan-Belmont Contract, 396; name hissed, 455; believes himself most unpopular man in America, 495; called betrayer of party, 503

Retirement from politics, 492-510

Cleveland, Mrs. Grover, 118, 182, 210

"Cleveland poles," 144

"Coin," controversy about meaning, 36, 203, 221, 234

"Coining a vacuum," 327

Colfax, Schuyler, 156

College settlements, 149

Colored men in Congress, 95

Committees become dominating factor in House, 65

Commons, John R., 444

Congress, bond issues in, *see* Bond legislation struggle *and* Bond issues; committees in, 65; extravagance in, 225; filibustering in, 76; House of Representatives, *see* House of Representatives; 45th Congress, 28; 47th Congress, 60; 48th Congress, 72-82, 84-90, 94, 152; 49th Congress, 93-113, 152; 50th Congress, 120-147; 51st Congress, 163-195; 52nd Congress, 195; 53rd Congress, 266-295, 299-318, 323-327, 333-340, 360-367; tariff reform efforts in, *see* Tariff reform

Congressional Library, 112

Contraction of currency, *see* Currency

Conventions, National, *see* Presidential campaigns

Converse, George L., 81, 82

Cooper Union, 58

Cotton, low prices on, 245, 386, 427, 438

Cotton goods, tariff on, 178

"Counting a quorum," *see* Quorum controversy

Cox, Judge, 314

Cox, Samuel S. ("Sunset"), 57, 67, 68, 71, 75, 123, 124, 130

Coxey, Jacob S., 330

Creelman, James, 414

"Crime of 1873," 264

Crisp, Charles S., 75, 129, 168, 195

Crittenden Compromise, 17

Crops, funds needed for, 30, 49, 227, 244, 245, 295, 478

"Cross of gold," 464

Crouch, J. B., 429

Crowley, Daniel N., 487

Crutchfield, Nat, 156

Cuffe, Elvira D., 489

Cummings, Amos J., 124

Currency, power of banks to contract, 37; demand for more and cheaper, 51, 217, 435; elasticity needed, 31, 322, 520; issued by individuals, 243; premium on, 244; shipments from New York to interior, 241; stringency, 30, 37, 38, 115, 245, 247, 268, 273, 417, 419

Currency reform plan, 361, 368

Curtis, George Ticknor, 85

Curtis, William E., Assistant Secretary of the Treasury, 208; discusses finance with New York bankers, 308, 315, 372; calls Carlisle's attention to law of 1862, 381, 387; helps write Morgan-Belmont contract, 388; delivers gold bonds in Europe, 393; Acting Secretary of the Treasury, 401; recommends fourth bond issue, 403; at Carlisle's funeral, 511

Daniel, John W., 121

Daniels, Josephus, 443, 444, 446

"Dark lantern financiering," 375

Davey, George M., 502

Davis, Cushman K., 121

Davis, Jefferson, 4, 121

INDEX 541

Davis, L. H., 88
Debs, Eugene V., 331, 464
Debtor class, difficulties of, 31, 32
Decentralization in House, Democratic efforts to achieve, 96
Delano, Columbus, 58, 119
Democratic Party, after 1896, 502-510, 520; conventions, see Presidential campaigns; Gold Democrats, see Gold Democrats; majority in House, 74, 193; minority in House, 163, 353; protectionist element in, 80; representative of common man, 134, 431; rift in, chronic lack of harmony, 46-47, 97, 112, 131, 173; divided on tariff, 63, 79, 81, 82, 99; divided on internal revenue taxes, 133; divided on free silver, 88, 193, 254, 349, 350; schism begun by entrance of Bryan into national politics, 431; conflict growing, 444, 446; rift complete, 460; split between East and West, 434; diverse elements in party, 472
Depression, business and financial, 31, 79, 87, 288, 329
Desha, Lucius, 25
Deutsche Bank of Berlin, 413
Dickinson, Don M., 328, 453, 503
Dilatory motions, 167, 172
Dingley, Nelson, Jr., 190, 370
Disher, W. M., 503
Dodson, T. C., Jr., 488
Doolittle, James R., 83, 276
Dorsheimer, William, 75
Dred Scott Decision, 11
Duke Foundation, 47
Duke Washington, 47

East and West, growing division between, 103, 148, 163, 277, 436
Eckels, Comptroller, 209, 354
Economic anarchy in West, 243
Economic conditions at beginning of Cleveland's second administration, 216 et seq
Economic depression, 87
Economic situation, improvement in, 116
Economic stagnation, 294-295

Economic unrest, 329
Economics, central interest of the 'eighties, 148
Egypt, British expedition into, 50
Elasticity in currency, see currency
Election laws, Federal, 38-39
Elections, use of troops at, 38
Eliot, President, 194
Elliott, F. B., 134
Endicott, William, Jr., 231, 295, 328
England, fear of, in West, 272, 313, 410
Epsom salts, 135
Europe, interested in gold payments, 234; indisposed to invest in American securities, 372; bonds sold in, 393; increase in immigration from, 101
European bankers advise South American investors, 382
Extradition treaty, Carlisle's interpretation of, 8
Extravagance during Harrison's administration, 193, 225

Failures, increase in, 242
Fairbank, N. K., 282
Fairchild, Charles S., 358, 437
Farmer, Carlisle's interest in the, 45
"Farmer Goodman," 135
Farmer, Miss Hallie, 218
Farmers' Alliance, 101
Farmers, growing discontent among, 31, 46, 51, 101, 216, 217, 426, 434, 449, 452; prosperity for, 227; relation of tariff to, 191
Farquar, A. B., 329, 391, 432, 445
Faulkner, Charles J., 120
Federal Election bill, 187
Federal Election laws, demand for repeal of, 38, 39
Federal Reserve System, 361
Federalism fostered by Republicans, 149
Fiat money, 291, 328
Field, Marshall, 282
Filibustering in Congress, 59, 77-78, 86, 172-173
Financial condition of America, instability of, 400
Financial crisis under Harrison, 192, 200, 222

INDEX

Financial laws of U. S., fundamental defect in, 248
Financial legislation unsound, 216 *et seq*
Financial machinery of U. S., inadequacy of, 30
Financial practices, unsound, 203
"Financial rebellion," 37
Financial troubles in U. S., development of, 203, 234, 332, 361, 381, 476, 477, 485; responsibility for, 230
Financiering, Congressional, 38
Financiers, *see* Bankers
Finley, High F., 122
Fisk, Harvey, and Sons, 259
Flax, 178
Floral offerings in Congress, 73, 122
Foraker Act, 497
Force bill, 165, 187, 188, 193
Ford, Worthington C., 134
Foster, Charles, Secretary of the Treasury under Harrison, 204, 228, 229, 288
Foster, Stephen Collins, 2
Francis, David R., 241, 445
Free coinage of silver, *see* Bland-Allison bill; Bryan, William Jennings; Sherman bill, Silver; Silverites; Free silver fight
Free silver fight, in Congress, 304, 367-368, 382, 434; in the Democratic party, *see* Democratic party, Bryan, Presidential campaigns, Bland-Allison bill, Sherman bill
Free traders, 119
Fuller, Melvin W., 127

Gage, Lyman J., 492
G. A. R., pension bill, 119; hostile to Cleveland, 144
Garfield, James A., 40, 42, 50
Gary, Judge Joseph E., 102
Geddes, George W., 71, 73
General Orders No. 51, 22
George, Henry, 127
German opposition to McKinley bill, 199
Gibbons, Cardinal, 326
Gilder, Richard Watson, 310, 362, 444
Godkin, E. L., 46, 74

Gold bars, permission asked to sell, 367
Gold basis demanded by foreign buyers of American securities, 382
Gold-bugs, 218, 242, 261, 376, 426, 436, 448
Gold certificates, exceed gold coin, 308-309; issue suspended by Carlisle, 233
Gold clauses inserted into contracts, 224
Gold corner by Morgan, 414
Gold crowded out of Government coffers by silver, 50
Gold, decrease of, 106
Gold Democrats, preconvention activities, 453; nominate candidates, 470; platform of, approved by Cleveland, 471; weakness of, 472; adopt name "National Democrats," 474; campaign of, 474-475, 478-480, 483-485; find alliance with Republicans distasteful, 480; educational program of, after 1896, 502
Gold exports, 183, 222, 227, 228, 297, 306, 328, 333, 343, 344, 347, 349, 381, 396, 403, 406, 422
Gold, hoarding of, *see* Hoarding
Gold imports, 228, 246, 297, 366, 403
Gold in banks, 381
Gold payments, establishment of, 31; fear of suspension of, 88; resumption of, *see* Resumption
Gold, premium on, 30, 297, 393, 407, 420, 476
Gold, purchasable under law of 1862, 380
Gold redemptions, 203, 230
Gold reserve, in banks, 420
Gold reserve, U. S. Treasury; bankers help to keep up, 237, 387, 400; below $100,000,000, 239, 244, 267, 294, 297; depleted, by Bond issues, 358, 359, 363, 416; by retirement of greenbacks and Treasury notes, 369; fluctuations—falling, 86, 88, 104, 223, 226, 229, 232, 256, 297, 320, 349, 353, 355, 363, 383, 396, 402, 408, 421, 448, 475, 478—rising, 104, 322, 360, 375, 399, 422, 478;

INDEX 543

lowest point, 371; Morgan controls rise of, 393; question as to lawful use of, 236, 237; sanctity of, 287
Gold, returned to Treasury after McKinley election, 485
Gold and silver coinage, ratios, 49
Gold-silver standard controversy, 213
Gold standard, fears for, 226; upheld by Carlisle, 237; hangs in the balance, 386
Gold supplied to Treasury by banks, 288, 307
Gold withdrawals from Treasury, 381
Goodson, Major, 7
Goodson, Mary Jane, 7
Gorman, Senator Arthur P., 140, 197, 326, 340, 518
Government ownership of railroads, demand for, 427; Carlisle's opinion of, 428
Government ownership of telegraph lines, 81, 119
Government revenues, decline in, 306
Grain shipments endangered by panic, 295
Grant and Ward, 87
Grant, Jesse, 7
Grant, U. S., 89
"Great battle of the standards," 266
"Great objector," 75
Greenbackers, 36, 487
Greenbacks, banks hoarding, 328; demand for issue of, 246; drain on gold reserve, 227, 320, 369; issue of, 31; decrease in one-dollar denomination, 105; redemption of, 37; retirement of, 33
Gresham, Walter Q., 209
Gresham, Mrs. Walter Q., 211, 500
Grosscup, Judge, 452
"Gulliver-snail of politics," 97

Halderman, W. B., 468, 479
Hallam, Judge, 425
Hamlin, Charles S., 208, 484, 498, 511
Hancock, General, 48
Hanna, Mark, 472, 490
Harper's Ferry, 12
Harpster, David, 58
Harrison administration, 138, 229

Harrison, Benjamin, nominated, 141; first message to Congress, 165-166; signs McKinley bill, 192; approves silver proposal, 219; works for compromise on silver question, 220; forces international agreement on silver, 228
Harrison, Carter, 264
Harter, Michael D., 391
Harvester twine combines, 218
Harvey, W. H. ("Coin"), 473
Haskell, Dudley C., 57, 59, 167
Haugen, Representative, 397
Havemeyer, W. O., 131, 337, 338
Hay, John, 242
Hayes, John L., 53
Hayes, Rutherford B., 30, 41
Haymarket riots, 102, 107
Hearst, William Randolph, 505
Hemp, 178, 189
Henderson, John S., 153
Hendricks, Thomas A., 84, 86, 93
Herbert, Hilary A., 29, 210, 212, 465
Hewitt, Abram S., 27, 63, 75, 82, 88, 100, 103, 327
Higginson, Henry Lee, 231, 235, 292, 294
Hill, David B., 197, 467
Hill, James J., 268, 408, 420, 482
Hinrichsen, W. H. ("Buck"), 445, 451, 453
Hiscock, Senator, 80, 183, 513
Hoar, George F., 111, 513, 518
Hoarding, of gold, 240, 365, 366, 371, 381, 385, 395, 422; of money, 220, 246, 295, 405
Hoffman, Charles Fenno, 2
"Hog swindle," 20
Holman, William S., 75
Home Market Club, 153
Horizontal reduction in tariff, 78
House of Representatives, Democratic efforts to achieve decentralization in, 96; development of unworthy political practices in, 155; doors locked before opening of session, 164; fist fights in, 120; first session of, 156; floral offerings in, 73, 122; great speakers of, 156; growing autocracy in, 96; increased powers of committees, 173; minority

power decreased in, 173; quorum, *see* Quorum controversy; rules, reform of, 66, 90, 97, 147, 163, 166, 167, 171, 172, 174, 195; tumultuous times in, 63, 64, 65, 89, 90, 110, 111, 174, 190
Hovey, Carl, 384
Hull House, 149
Hurd, Frank, 75

Illinois, Cleveland sends troops into, 331
Imports exceed exports, 49
Income tax, 324
Independents, 433
Indian appropriation bill, 186
Industrial conditions, 79, 80, 361, 403
"Infant industries," 136
Inflation, 30, 31, 32, 228
Inland transportation systems, 227
Internal revenue taxes, 109, 117, 133, 146, 153, 191
International complications, 409-410
Interstate commerce regulation, 70, 85, 102
Irish, John P., 443
Iron, 79, 178, 411
"Iron-clad oath," 76, 95
Irredeemable paper currency, 32

Jackson, Andrew, 492
Jackson, C. C., 231
Jackson inaugural, 91
James, Jesse, 64
James, Ollie M., 503
Johnson, Richard Malcolm, 4
Jones, Thomas G., 435
Jones, William F., 139
Jordan, Conrad M., in third bond issue negotiations, 374; on conditions of New York Sub-treasury, 244, 245, 282, 493; on J. P. Morgan, 392; on threatened suspension of banks, 295; plans meeting between Carlisle and New York financiers, 314; recommends fourth bond issue, 403; refuses to count gold for Zimmerman and Forshay, 418; urges temporary loans, 364, 365, 405
Juror's test oath, 39

Kansas-Nebraska bill, 11
Kasson, John A., 75
Kehoe, James M., 514, 515
Kehoe, W. J., 511
Keifer, J. Warren, 60, 73, 75
Kelley, Judge (Father of the House), 94
Kelley, William D. ("Pig Iron"), 28, 54, 59, 60, 63, 121
Kelly, Harrison, 430
Kelly, Mrs. Sarah A., 98
Kenney, Horace, 253
Kentucky, birthplace of Carlisle, 1; famous men born in, 4; in Civil War and Reconstruction, 15-24; influence of, in Carlisle's home, 157
Kilgore, C. Buckley ("Kicking Buck"), 190
Kilpatrick, Thomas, 432
King, Edward, 317, 357
Knights of Labor, 101; contest Carlisle's election, 107, 128; work against repeal of Sherman law, 279; serve sub poena on Carlisle in bond issue, 314; support Bryan, 464
Knott, J. Proctor, 29
Know-nothing party, 10
Ku Klux, 25

Labor, boycotts National Bank notes, 409; Carlisle's interest in, 45, 450; difficulties faced by, 30, 32, 242; growing dissatisfaction of, 101; resorts to violence, 102, 106, 148, 331
La Follette, Robert M., 155, 167
Lamar, L. Q. C., 135
Lamont, Daniel S., Secretary of War, 210; home and social life, 212; sends Cleveland's call to bankers, 237; in third bond issue, 387; share in credit for preservation of standard of value, 424
Landis, Kenesaw M., 451, 478, 481
Lathrop, Rev. James H., 488
Laughlin, Professor J. Lawrence, 363
Law of 1862, Revised Statutes, Section 3700, 380
Lawrence, William, 58
Lease, Mrs., 427, 435

INDEX

Lee, Fitzhugh, 124
Legal tenders, exhausted at New York Sub-treasury, 244; redemption of, 343; efforts to prevent presentation of, 358, 359; inrush of, 369; drain on gold reserve, 394, 401; attempts to keep from hands of exporters, 406-407; speculation in, 417; shortage of, 476; Carlisle favors retirement of, 520
Lerner, Max, 385
Leslie, Preston H., 25
Light, Edwin B., 448
Lincoln, Abraham, 4, 13
Lincoln-Douglas debates, 12
"Lincoln guns," 18, 19
Lindsay, Vachel, 493
Little, Edward C., 462
Lodge, Henry Cabot, shows solicitude for labor, 130; advocates bayonets at polls, 165; introduces Federal Election bill, 187; fastidiousness of, 515
"Lodgeism," 193
"Lombard" gold, 462
Lottery system, Carlisle credited with destruction of, 521
Lowell, James Russell, 122
Lumber, 80
Lyman, Arthur T., 139

MacMaster, John Bach, 148
MacVeagh, Franklin, 282
Magoffin, Beriah, 13, 14
Majority, growing power of, in House of Representatives, 167
Manning, Daniel, 106, 113, 207, 521
Marble, Manton, 89
Marcosson, Isaac F., 516
Marine Band, 158
Martin, William H., 122
Matthews, Stanley, 35
McCall, John A., 509
McClintock, Emory, 475
McClure, A. K., 99
McCulloch, Secretary of the Treasury, 30, 88
McDonald, Joseph E., 84
McDonald, Witten, 258
"McKinley Aid Society," 484
McKinley bill, in Congress, 165, 177, 182, 183, 185; opposed by Carlisle, 179, 182, 189; passed, 192; results of, 192, 201, 222
McKinley, William, in House with Carlisle, 29; opposes Morrison bill, 81; speech in Mills bill debate, 134; brings ten-dollar suit to House, 136; head of Ways and Means Committee, 167; in quorum controversy, 171; condemns filibustering, 172; begins preparation of tariff bill, 176; champions silver, 224; election as President, 485; appoints Democrat to Cabinet, 492; comment on Carlisle, 515
"McKinleyism," 193
McKinzie, James A., 65, 84
McLaurin, J. L., 245
McMillin, Benton, 171, 324
Medill, Joseph, 110, 126, 264
Meline, J. F., 237
Mexican War pension bill, 76
Mexico, plan to coin silver in, 392
Mica, 189
Miller, George L., 350
Miller, Roswell, 465, 481
Milliken, James Foster, 418
Mills, Roger Q., in tariff-reform fight, 53, 57, 119, 132; advocates coinage of silver, 88; "a free poker and a taxed Bible," 123; refuses to meet W. O. Havemeyer, 131; spoils McKinley's ten-dollar suit coup, 136
Mills tariff-reform bill, shortcomings of, 132-133; debate on, 134; Carlisle tries to push through House, 139; passed by House, 142; not passed by Senate at adjournment of Congress, 144; revival of, 176
Minority, lessening power of, in House of Representatives, 167
Monroe Doctrine, Carlisle's article on, 503
Moonlight, Thomas R., 150
Moore Brothers, 478
Moore, J. S. ("The Parsee Merchant"), 46, 47, 99
Morgan-Belmont contract of 1878, 388
Morgan-Belmont Syndicate in third

bond issue under Cleveland, conditions under which contract was made, 384; authorized by Section 3700, 387; mode of procedure determined, 388; difficulties in carrying through, 392; terms of contract, 394; accomplishments of, 395, 396; attitude of Congress, the press and the public toward, 396-398; effectiveness of, 399

Morgan, Harjes and Company, 413

Morgan, J. Pierpont, advises Cleveland to accept compromise on Sherman law repeal, 260; takes active part in syndicate negotiations, 374; goes to Washington, 378; at the White House, 384, 387; plays solitaire, 386; complains about Carlisle, 387; power of, 388, 394, 411; "paddles his own canoe," 392; testifies at bond investigation, 395, 411; effect of criticism on, 398; offers to buy $200,000,000 of bonds, 412; rumor of gold corner by, 414; offers services in fourth bond issue, 416; disgruntled at share in fourth bond issue, 421; chairman of committee of financiers in 1896, 478. *See also* Morgan-Belmont Syndicate

Morgan, Senator, 71, 394, 434, 518

Morrill, Senator, 109, 518

Morrill tariff of 1861, 78

Morris, Clara, 107

Morris, Nelson, 282

Morrison bill for reform of House rules, 97

Morrison bill for tariff reform, 81, 83, 100, 109

Morrison, William R., leading advocate of tariff revision, 46; introduces bill to reduce import duties and war-tariff taxes, 78; unavailable as presidential candidate, 83; presents amendments on House rules, 95; prepares tariff bill, 98; strained relations with Randall, 107, 109

Morton, J. Sterling, 210, 282, 350

Motions, dilatory, 167, 172

Muhleman, M. L., 298
Muhlenberg, Frederick A. C., 156
Mulligan, Senator, 180

National Bank notes, contraction of, 105; increase in issue of, 246; boycotted by labor, 409
National Bimetallic Union, 447, 448
National Cordage Company, 240
National Debt, funding of, demanded by Carlisle, 37
National Democrats, *see* Gold Democrats
National Peace Convention, 17
Nebraska's platform, 456
Negro domination, fear of, 427
Negroes fear effect of Cleveland's election, 118, 144
Negroes, Force bill for equality of, 187
Nelson, Knute, 119
Nelson, R. H., 515
Newcomb, Simon, 134
New York Chamber of Commerce, 299, 404, 446
New York Clearing House, 104, 406
New York Sub-treasury, resumption at, 37; strain on, 244, 282, 307, 343, 346, 402, 406, 417, 475
Noailles, Duc de, 256
North and South, division between lessening, 148, 163
Norton, Edna C., 486

Oates, Governor, 438
O'Ferrall, Representative, 189
"Ohio Platform," 83, 84
Oleomargarine, 111
Olney, Richard, Attorney General, 210; on tariff reform, 251; helps Cleveland with message, 265; on repeal of Sherman law, 282; gives opinion on Carlisle's powers as Secretary of the Treasury, 290; on Coxey's army, 330; in third bond issue, 379, 384-387; given credit for share in preservation of standard of value, 424
"Omnibus states," 276
Otis, Charles H., 497

Page, Walter Hines, 45, 53
Page, William Tyler, 111

INDEX

Paine, Charles, 231
Palmer, Major-General, General Orders No. 51, 22
Palmer-Buchner ticket, 470, 478, 479, 484
Panic, of 1873, 31; near, in 1881, 50; ascribed to Carlisle's refunding bill, 70; of 1884, 87; of 1893, 240, 258, 268, 272, 295; threatening in 1895, 366, 395
Paregoric, 135
Parity of gold and silver, 221, 232
"Parity clause," 298
Parker campaign, 509
Party lines, growing looseness of, 112
Pasco, Samuel, 121
Paternalistic measures, demand for, 427
Patrons of Husbandry, 219
Patterson, Colonel, 437
Patterson, Josiah, 460, 467, 479
Pauncefote, Sir Julian, 213; "incident," 409
Payne, Henry B., 83
Peace party, during Civil War, 21
Peckham, Wheeler H., 497
Peffer, William A., 266, 283, 427
Pension appropriations, increase in, 225
Pension bills, for Mexican War veterans, 76, 98; for Indian fighters, 77; prepared by G. A. R., 119; for increases, 166
People's party, 426, 430
Perkins, C. E., 235
Perkins, George G., 3, 9, 158
Perry, Professor A. L., 67
Phillips, U. B., 3
"Pienpontifex Maximus," 385
Platt, Senator, 184
Political cults, growth of, 83, 149, 163, 219, 426, 429
Political divergences shown in multiplicity of conventions, 427
Popocrats, 444
Populism, 246, 255
Populist convention, 463
Populist leader advises Bryan, 457
Populist party, birth of, 428
Populist vote counted as silverite, 491
Populists, increase of, 394; support Bryan, 464, 481

"Pork-barrel" delights, 137
Posinfrey, J. W., 501
Postal rates, reduction of, 38
Powderly, Terrence V., 101, 107, 119
Presidential campaigns, 1860, 13; 1864, 21; 1884, 82-83; 1888, 140-141; 1892, 196-200, 431; 1896, 459-492; 1900, 506
Presidential succession, 111
Proctor, Redfield, 480
Prohibition bills, 89
Prohibition question interests midlands, 56
Prohibitionists support Bryan, 464, 481
Prosperity, at end of 'seventies, 48; threatened by silver question, 49
Prosperity slogan in 1896, 472
Protection, Republican belief in, 49, 165; attacked by Carlisle, 53; Republican fight for, 57, 60, 62. *See also* McKinley bill
Protectionists, in Democratic party, 46, 70, 72; Carlisle discusses problem of, 116
Protective system, benefits of, prize offered for essay on, 119
Public buildings, 119
Public debt, record increase in peace time, 423
Pugh, George E., 11
Pulitzer, Joseph, 396, 412, 414
Pullman strike, 331

Quay, Matthew Stanley, 121, 142, 143, 312, 338, 339
Quincy, Josiah, 254, 281
Quinine, 48, 80
Quorum controversy, in House of Representatives, 77, 89, 131, 146, 151, 168, 169-174, 189
Quorum, disappearing, 167

"Rag babies," 33, 50
Railroad wars, 50, 87
Railroads, corruption of, in West, 165; encourage migration to West, 147; government ownership of, urged, 427; influence of, 26; oppose legislation for regulation of interstate commerce, 70; pro-

moters of national unity, 82; receive lands and bond loans from Government, 33; tyranny of, 102

Randall, Samuel J. ("half-Democrat"), protectionist, 46, 81, 96, 100, 117, 119; head of Appropriations Committee, 76, 95, 96, 116, 152; favors repeal of internal revenue taxes on tobacco and whiskey, 82, 85, 109, 114, 153; strained relations with Morrison, 107, 109; personal relations with Carlisle, 175

Randolph, Edmund, 364
Reagan, John H., 39, 121
Reciprocity, Blaine's proposition of, 191
Reconstruction, Carlisle's attitude toward, 44
Redemptions, increase in, 227; fears for maintenance of, 228; drain on gold reserve, 364
Reed, Silas, 103
Reed, Thomas B., present for first time in House, 29; presents a "monstrous proposition," 59-60; attacks Mills bill, 132, 134, 139; moves resolution of thanks to Carlisle, 146; elected Speaker, 164; arbitrary methods, 155, 156, 164, 167, 170-171, 175, 187, 189, 190, 201; untidy dress of, 515; compared with Carlisle, 518
"Reedism," 193
Reform Club of Boston, 446
Reform in House procedure, *see* Rules
Regan, P. A., 444
Republican party, beginnings, 13; fixed belief in protection, 49; pushes protective tariff legislation, 53, 60, 62, *see also* McKinley bill; invaded by corruption, 51; solidarity of, 112; spending the surplus, 119, 225, 229; victorious in 1888, 145; fosters Federalism, 149; in silver craze, *see* Bland-Allison bill, Bryan, Free Silver, Sherman law; gives aid to Cleveland, 370; forced into alliance with Gold Democrats, 479-480; National convention at St. Louis, 458; campaign funds, 490

Resumption Act of 1875, 33, 290; attempts to repeal, 34; becomes effective, 36
Revenue, increase in Government, 48
Revenue system in need of revision, 322
Rhodes, James Ford, 482
Richards, J. E., 488
Riis, Jacob, 149
River and harbor appropriations, 89, 119, 166, 225
Robbins, Henry S., 436
Roberts, Morley, 410
Robinson, George D., 73
Roosevelt, Theodore, 161
Rothschilds, 261, 388, 390, 394, 413
Russell, William E., 188, 197
Russian gold, 248
Ryan, Thomas Fortune, 497

Salt, 80
Savings banks protest efforts of silver advocates, 104
Sawyer, E. W., 188
Schurz, Carl, 383, 391
Schwab, Gustave, 437
Section 3700, Revised Statutes, 387
Sectionalism in Congress, 266
Securities returned from Europe, 256, 333
Security prices fall, 246
Seigniorage, 34, 323, 327, 333
Senators, direct election of, 180
Seward, William H., 13
Shaw, Samuel M., 449
Sherman law, struggle to pass, 149, 165, 185, 187; consequences of, 192; condemned by silverites, 193; adds to danger of silver question, 201; uncertainty about meaning of word "coin" in, 202; requirements of, 220; fight for repeal of, 204, 213, 249, 252, 255-260, 264, 274-285, 281, 285; Carlisle uncertain of authority under, 236; effects of repeal, 286; Carlisle's opposition to, 518
Sherman, John, Secretary of the Treasury, 35; expresses regret

INDEX

for part in tariff bill of 47th Congress, 63; letter to George F. Hoar, 111; urges two-plank platform, 119; speech before Home Market Club, 153; "assistant Democratic leader," 267; upholds Carlisle's authority, 317; makes contract with Morgan and Belmont, 388; linked with Cleveland and Carlisle, 452; admiration for Carlisle, 513

Shipping fleet, 119

Sibley, Joseph C., 489

Silver bills, *see* Bland-Allison bill *and* Sherman law

Silver bullion, purchase required by law, 50, 86

Silver certificates, for one dollar, issued, 105; status of, 221; burden of, 298, 343

Silver congressmen, arguments of, 269-272

Silver conventions, 263-264, 445

Silver crusade, *see* Bland-Allison bill; Bryan; Free Silver; Sherman law

Silver deposits in U. S. Treasury, efforts to reduce, 104, 221; increasing in amount, decreasing in value, 232

Silver, discovery of rich deposits in West, 34; increase in coinage of, 88; suspension of coinage recommended by Cleveland, 89; falling prices of, 103, 216; forced into circulation, 105; increase in volume of, 184; purchase required by law, 202, 220, 223; international agreement on, forced by Harrison, 228; fluctuations of, 352

Silver dollars, coinage and circulation of, 50; plethora of, 86; monthly coinage of, 87; no demand for, 88; at a premium, 294; in Treasury, 370, 402

Silver exports, 221

Silver gavel presented by Colorado delegation, 141

Silver party, belief in conspiracy of wealthy to enslave common man, 270; convention in St. Louis, 462

Silver question, *see* Bland-Allison bill; Bryan; Free Silver; Sherman law

Silver Republicans, 186, 266, 433, 458, 461

Silver Senators, arguments of, 276 *et seq*

Silver standard, fear of, 88, 234

Silver vault of Treasury, 221

Silver and gold coinage, ratios of, 49, 50

Silverites, attack resumption, 36; condemn Sherman law, 193; increase in strength of, 288; oppose bond issues, 292, 311, 317, 363; oppose Springer bill, 369; activities in South, 443; instigate violence against Gold Democrats, 483; sincerity of, 489

Simpson, "Sockless Jerry," 266, 311, 427

Sixteen-to-one theory clarified by Carlisle, 351

Slocum, Henry W., 75

Smalls, Robert, 95

Smith, Hoke, 210, 349, 351, 469

Smith, Mrs. Hoke, 157, 213

Smith, I. M., 429

Smith, Murray F., 437

Smith, William Henry, 225

Snuff, 191

Social life in Washington, 210 *et seq*

Social order, growing upheaval in, 101

Sound money, Carlisle's fight for, 446, 520

Sound money advocates, activities of, 264, 436, 437, 449, 455; beliefs of, 489; fear Bryan, 492

Sound money convention at Nashville, 440

Sound money organizations in 1896, 474. *See also* Gold Democrats

Sound money platform, Cleveland's hope for, 456

South and North, lessening of division between, 148, 163

South, economic distress in, 44, 245, 386, 427, 434; turns to free silver, 322, 443, 491; fear of negro domination in, 427;

growth of political cults in, 426; faith of, in "Democratic regularity," 491; influence of, in Democratic party, 507
Southern Power Company, 47
Spanish War issue presents opportunity to Democratic party, 503
Specie Circular, 289
Specie payments, resumption of, 31; danger of suspension of, 383, 387, 394; efforts made to suspend quietly, 406
Speculation in legal-tenders and gold, 417; efforts to check, 418
Springer bill for 3% bond issues, 369, 370, 383
Springer, William M., 61
Springer's "pop-gun" bills, 195
Stalwart-Half-Breed schism, 56
Standard of value, credit for preservation of, 424
Standard Oil, 70
Standards, great battle of, 266
Star, Ellen Gates, 149
States admitted to the Union, 184
Stealey, O. O., 26
Steel, 178
Stephens, Alexander H., 28
Stetson, Francis Lynde, 260, 378, 379, 385, 388
Stevens, Thaddeus, 28
Stevenson, Adlai E., nominated for vice president, 198; free silver advocate, 211, 261
Stevenson, John W., 7, 11
Stevenson, Mrs. Letitia Greene, 211
Stewart, Alonzo H., 500
Stewart, John A., 317, 328, 354, 357, 419
Stewart, Senator, 367, 369, 434
Stillman, James, 235; unable to help maintain gold reserve, 237; to Lamont, 281, 347; Carlisle lunches with, 316; urges bond issue, 344, 349; offended by Pulitzer, 412; promises cooperation in fourth bond issue, 415; urges Democrats to support McKinley, 467-468; does not advocate bond issue on eve of presidential campaign, 477
Stock laws, 121

Stock market, rise in, 49; stagnation created by assassination of Garfield, 50
Stock speculators, 218
Stockbridge, Francis B., 121
Stockdale, Thomas R., 272
Stocks, shrinkage of, 242; increase in price, 407, 421
Straus, Isador, 511
Straus, Oscar, 509
Strikes, 30, 79, 101, 181, 331, 361
Sub-treasuries for storage of products, suggested, 427; Carlisle's attitude toward, 428
Suffragists, 427
Sugar interests oppose tariff reform, 47, 79
Sugar scandal, 333-338
Sumner, William Graham, 46
Surplus in Treasury, leads to demands of bankers for assistance, 31; adds force to tariff reform movement, 46; problem of returning to circulation, 48; possible methods of reducing, 49; derivation of, 106; danger of continuing increase in, 108, 114, 138, 148, 165; efforts to reduce, 118, 119; guarded from reckless spending by Carlisle, 137; Harrison's message on, 165; disappearance of, under Harrison, 201, 203, 222, 225, 228; responsibility for disappearance of, 229
Suspension of gold payments, fear of, 88
Swank, James M., 79, 119
Swayne, Wagner, 500
Syndicate selling of bonds, *see* Morgan-Belmont Syndicate

Taggart, Tom, 481
Talmadge, T. Dewitt, 64
Tammany Hall, 42, 90
Tariff, controversy between protectionists and moderate revisionists, 98; low, supported by Minnesota Republicans, 112; lack of interest in, 114
Tariff commission, appointed by President Arthur, 51, 53, 57, 59

INDEX

Tariff, protective, fight for, 165, 176-179, 182, 189, 196 *et seq*
Tariff reform, Carlisle's leadership in, 45, 102, 501, 517
Tariff reform, division in Democratic party on, 79, 82; opposed by manufacturing interests, 99; Cleveland's message on, 126; Democrats carry on campaign of education on, 195-196; leading policy in Democratic plans, 251
Tariff reform movement, early efforts in, 46, 51; fight for, in Congress, 57-62, 76-79, 81-87, 107-110, 115-118, 124-128, 132-137, 142-146, 323-326, 342-343, 379
Tariff revision, Carlisle declares against sudden and radical changes, 74
Taussig, Professor, 431
Tax, indirect, not comprehended by laborer, 114
Taxation, Cleveland's belief regarding, 108
Taxes, war-time, Democratic efforts to reduce, 148
Taylor, A. L., 198
Teller, William M., 219, 458, 461
Temporary loans, 364, 366, 380, 405
Tenure-of-Office Act, repealed, 111
Thobe, George H., 128, 130
Thomas, Charles S., 262
Thurber, Henry, 445
Tichenor, George C., 483
Tilden-Hayes dispute, 26
Tilden, Samuel J., 47, 84
Tillman, Benjamin R., 435, 452, 459
Tin plate, 182, 192
Tobacco, efforts for repeal of taxes on, 82, 85, 109, 114, 119, 127, 146, 153, 191
Tomkins, Calvin, 449
Tomlinson, John W., 446
Tracey, Frank Basil, 426
Tracy, Charles, 400
Trade balance of the United States, 183
Trade dollars, 81
Trade regulations during the Civil War, 20
Transylvania University, 2

Treasury, U. S., and crops, 244; as agency of relief in periods of stringency, 106; as source of gold, 395; difficulties of, 475, 493 (*see also* Bond issues); dominating position occupied by, 116; effects on, of repeal of Sherman law, 286, of Wilson-Gorman bill, 343, of McKinley's election, 485; helped by banks, 307, 407; legislation for relief of, urged by Cleveland, 405; loses position of dominance, 243; rules governing, 214
Treasury balance, *see* Gold reserve
Treasury deficit, 244
Treasury notes, issued under Sherman law, 221; drain on gold reserve, 225-228, 232, 237, 256, 320, 328, 369; fears for value of, 237; in New York Sub-treasury, 403
Treasury, Secretary of the, powers and restrictions of, 202, 246, 248, 307
Tree, Judge Lambert, 453
Trumbull, Mrs. Lyman, 472
Trusts, Blaine's statement about, 144; Senator Mulligan on, 181; predatory, 219
Tucker, John R., 75, 94
Turnbull, S. M., 79
Turner, Frederick Jackson, 148
Turner, Thomas, 29
Turpie, David, 120

Uhl, Edwin F., 474
Unemployment, 242
United States, debt of, to Europe, 183; securities returned to, 410
United States finances, controlled by committee, 478
United States notes, "the favorite money of the people," 49; no issue of one- and two-dollar denominations, 105

Van Buren, Martin, 492
Vance, Robert B., 88
Vance, Zebulon B., 121
Venezuela message, 409, 410, 414
Vest, George G., 276, 369
Vilas, William F., 194, 257, 368, 451, 470
Voorhees, D. W., 276

INDEX

Waite, Davis H. ("Bloody Bridles"), 262
Walsh, James, and Sons, 393
Walsh, John R., 449
Wanamaker, John, 143, 192
Ward, Judge J. Q., 103
Warner, A. J., 89
Watterson, Henry, works for reduction of postal rates on manuscripts, 38; on Republicans, 64, 76; on Congress, 67; on Mrs. Kelly and Pennsylvania, 99; on the people of the South, 162; on Carlisle, 96, 110, 204, 514; on Wilson tariff bill, 323; urges Carlisle for president, 197; writes to Bryan, 506
Weaver, John B., 427, 457, 463
Webb, Bryant, 473
Weissinger, Henry, 146
Wells, David A., 45, 46, 47, 48, 79, 99
West, becomes favorite field of investment, 49; draws funds from East, 49, 270; growth of interest in silver question in, 184, 213, 254, 322, 445; expansion of, 106; migration to, 147; growth of political power in, 148, 167; recession from, 149, 217; economic discontent in, 192, 216, 243, 247, 273, 435, 492; growth of political cults in, 426
West and East, growing division between, 103, 148, 163, 277, 436
West and South, alliance between, 188, 262
Wheeler, Joseph, 430
Whiskey, demand for repeal of internal revenue taxes on, 82, 85, 109, 114

White, Horace, 46
White, William Allen, 161
Whitney, William C., 91, 410
Wick, J. E., 487
Wike, Scott, 208
Wilkinson, William, 341
Williams, G. G., 357
Wilson bill, in House, 333-336, 339; in Senate, 336; Gorman's opinion on, 341; becomes law without President's signature, 343
Wilson-Gorman bill, 343, 355, 370
Wilson, James J., Jr., 139
Wilson, William L., letter to W. C. P. Breckinridge, 149; writes tariff bill, 323; reads Cleveland's letter into *Record,* 339; consents to compromise, 343; defeated for Congress, 353; in silver craze, 466, 470
Wilson, Woodrow, 66, 75, 161, 206
Windom, William, 184, 219, 222, 229
Winthrop, Robert C., 156
Wise, George D., 153
Wolcott, Senator, 266, 284
Woman suffrage, 427, 464
Wood, Fernando, 28
Woodward, James T., 317, 414, 417
Wool Growers' Association, 119
Wool interests oppose tariff reform, 79
Wool Manufacturers Association, 53
Wool, tariff on, 133, 364
"Wool trinity," 58
Woolen goods, 54, 178
World's Fair at Chicago, 236, 240

Yancey, William L., 11
Year of Calamities, 320

Zimmerman and Forshay, 417, 418, 419